WORD
of the LORD

ENLARGED TYPE

NAB EDITION

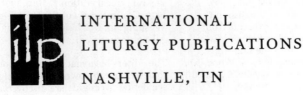
INTERNATIONAL
LITURGY PUBLICATIONS
NASHVILLE, TN

Product no. PB201820

Published by International Liturgy Publications
PO Box 50476
Nashville, TN 37205
www.ilpmusic.org   888-898-SONG

Printed in the United States of America.

25 24 23 22 21 19 18   1 2 3 4 5

ISBN 978-1-941542-14-9

Published with ecclesiastical approval.
NIHIL OBSTAT Very Rev. John J. H. Hammond, JCL, *Censor librorum*
IMPRIMATUR   + Most Rev. J. Mark Spalding, JCL, *Bishop of Nashville*
             July 19, 2018

CONTENTS

5   Guidelines for the Reception of Holy Communion

ORDER OF MASS

7   Introductory Rites
15   Liturgy of the Word
19   Liturgy of the Eucharist
49   Communion Rite
54   The Concluding Rites
55   Rite for the Blessing and Sprinkling of Water

RITES AND ORDERS

61   Rite of Eucharistic Exposition and Benediction

LECTIONARY, YEAR A

65   Advent
77   Christmas Time
100 Lent
141 Easter Time
173 Solemnities of the Lord During Ordinary Time
183 Ordinary Time

LECTIONARY, YEAR B

269 Advent
280 Christmas Time
310 Lent
345 Easter Time
369 Solemnities of the Lord During Ordinary Time
381 Ordinary Time

LECTIONARY, YEAR C

466 Advent
477 Christmas Time
506 Lent
542 Easter Time
567 Solemnities of the Lord During Ordinary Time
578 Ordinary Time

THE SACRED PASCHAL TRIDUUM

669 Holy Thursday
677 Friday of the Passion of the Lord
699 Easter Vigil in the Holy Night
740 Easter Sunday of the Resurrection of the Lord

744 Solemnities, Feasts, and Various Occasions

805 Prayers

809 Acknowledgments
819 Calendar of Readings
827 Index of Psalm Refrains

GUIDELINES FOR THE RECEPTION

OF HOLY COMMUNION

As Catholics, we fully participate in the celebration of the
Eucharist when we receive Holy Communion. We are encouraged
to receive Communion devoutly and frequently. In order to be
properly disposed to receive Communion, participants should not
be conscious of grave sin and normally should have fasted for one
hour. A person who is conscious of grave sin is not to receive the
Body and Blood of the Lord without prior sacramental confession
except for a grave reason where there is no opportunity for
confession. In this case, the person is to be mindful of the
obligation to make an act of perfect contrition, including the
intention of confessing as soon as possible (canon 916). A frequent
reception of the Sacrament of Penance is encouraged for all.

FOR OTHER CHRISTIANS

We welcome our fellow Christians to this celebration of the
Eucharist as our brothers and sisters. We pray that our common
baptism and the action of the Holy Spirit in this Eucharist
will draw us closer to one another and begin to dispel the sad
divisions which separate us. We pray that these will lessen and
finally disappear, in keeping with Christ's prayer for us "that
they may all be one" (Jn 17: 21).

Because Catholics believe that the celebration of the Eucharist
is a sign of the reality of the oneness of faith, life, and worship,
members of those churches with whom we are not yet fully
united are ordinarily not admitted to Holy Communion.
Eucharistic sharing in exceptional circumstances by other
Christians requires permission according to the directives of the
diocesan bishop and the provisions of canon law (canon 844 § 4).
Members of the Orthodox Churches, the Assyrian Church of
the East, and the Polish National Catholic Church are urged

to respect the discipline of their own Churches. According to Roman Catholic discipline, the Code of Canon Law does not object to the reception of communion by Christians of these Churches (canon 844 § 3).

FOR THOSE NOT RECEIVING COMMUNION

All who are not receiving Holy Communion are encouraged to express in their hearts a prayerful desire for unity with the Lord Jesus and with one another.

FOR NON-CHRISTIANS

We also welcome to this celebration those who do not share our faith in Jesus Christ. While we cannot admit them to Holy Communion, we ask them to offer their prayers for the peace and the unity of the human family.

The Order of Mass

INTRODUCTORY RITES

Greeting   All stand.

When the people are gathered, the Priest approaches the altar with the ministers while the Entrance Chant is sung.

When the Entrance Chant is concluded, the Priest and the faithful, standing, sign themselves with the Sign of the Cross, while the Priest, facing the people, says:

> In the name of the Father,
> and of the Son, and of the Holy Spirit.

The People respond: **Amen.**

A - men.

Then the Priest greets the people saying:

> The grace of our Lord Jesus Christ,
> and the love of God,
> and the communion of the Holy Spirit
> be with you all.

Or:

> Grace to you and peace from God our Father
> and the Lord Jesus Christ.

Or: The Lord be with you.

The people reply: **And with your spirit.**

And with your spi - rit.

In this first greeting a Bishop, instead of **The Lord be with you,** says: **Peace be with you.**

Rite of Blessing and Sprinkling of Water

On Sundays, especially in Easter Time, instead of the customary Penitential Act, the blessing and sprinkling of water may take place as a reminder of Baptism (see page 55).

Penitential Act

The Priest invites the faithful to the Penitential Act, saying:
Brethren (brothers and sisters), let us acknowledge our sins, and so prepare ourselves to celebrate the sacred mysteries.

A brief pause for silence follows.

Form 1:

Then all recite the general confession:
**I confess to almighty God
and to you, my brothers and sisters,
that I have greatly sinned,
in my thoughts and in my words,
in what I have done and in what I have failed to do,**

And, striking their breast, they say:
**through my fault, through my fault,
through my most grievous fault;**

Then they continue:
**therefore I ask blessed Mary ever-Virgin,
all the Angels and Saints,
and you, my brothers and sisters,
to pray for me to the Lord our God.**

Form 2:

The Priest says: Have mercy on us, O Lord.
The people reply: **For we have sinned against you.**

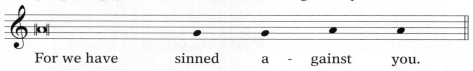

For we have   sinned   a - gainst   you.

The Priest: Show us, O Lord, your mercy.
The people: **And grant us your salvation.**

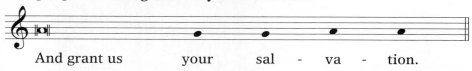

And grant us   your   sal - va - tion.

Form 3:

The Priest, or a Deacon or another minister, says the following
or other invocations with Kyrie eleison (Lord, have mercy):
   You were sent to heal the contrite of heart:
   Lord, have mercy.   Or: Kyrie, eleison.

The people reply:
   Lord, have mercy.   Or: Kyrie, eleison.

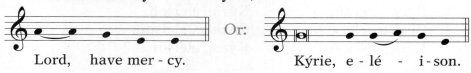

Lord,   have mer - cy.   Or: Kýrie, e - lé - i - son.

The Priest:
   You came to call sinners:
   Christ, have mercy.   Or: Christe, eleison.

The people:
   Christ, have mercy.   Or: Christe, eleison.

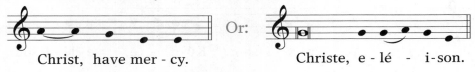

Christ, have mer - cy.   Or: Christe, e - lé - i - son.

The Priest:
>You are seated at the right hand of the Father to intercede
>for us:
>Lord, have mercy.   Or: Kyrie, eleison.

The people:
>**Lord, have mercy.**   Or: **Kyrie, eleison.**

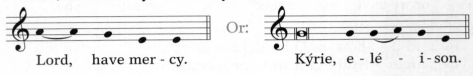

The absolution by the Priest follows:
>May almighty God have mercy on us,
>forgive us our sins,
>and bring us to everlasting life.

The people reply: **Amen.**

Kyrie

The Kyrie, eleison (Lord, have mercy) invocations follow, unless
they have just occured in a formula of the Penitential Act.

℣	Kýrie, eléison.	℟	**Kýrie, eléison.**
℣	Christe, eléison.	℟	**Christe, eléison.**
℣	Kýrie, eléison.	℟	**Kýrie, eléison.**

Or:

Ký - ri - e,   e - lé - i - son.

Or:

℣ Lord, have mercy.   ℟ **Lord, have mercy.**
℣ Christ, have mercy.   ℟ **Christ, have mercy.**
℣ Lord, have mercy.   ℟ **Lord, have mercy.**

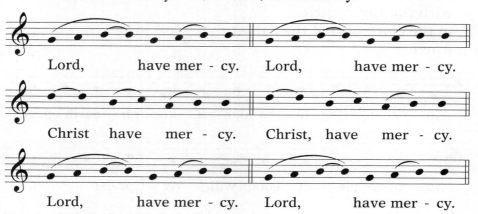

Lord,   have mer - cy.   Lord,   have mer - cy.

Christ   have   mer - cy.   Christ, have   mer - cy.

Lord,   have mer - cy.   Lord,   have mer - cy.

Gloria

Then, when it is prescribed, this hymn is either sung or said:

Glory to God in the highest,
and on earth peace to people of good will.

We praise you,
we bless you,
we adore you,
we glorify you,
we give you thanks for your great glory,
Lord God, heavenly King,
O God, almighty Father.

Lord Jesus Christ, Only Begotten Son,
Lord God, Lamb of God, Son of the Father,
you take away the sins of the world,

have mercy on us;
you take away the sins of the world,
receive our prayer;
you are seated at the right hand of the Father,
have mercy on us.

For you alone are the Holy One,
you alone are the Lord,
you alone are the Most High,
Jesus Christ,
with the Holy Spirit,
in the glory of God the Father.
Amen.

Glo - ry   to God   in   the high-est,   and   on   earth   peace

to   peo - ple   of   good   will.   We   praise   you,

we   bless   you,   we   a - dore   you,   we   glo - ri -

fy   you,   we   give   you thanks for   your great   glo - ry,

Lord   God,   heav - en - ly   King,   O   God,   al - might - y

Fa - ther.   Lord   Je - sus Christ, On - ly   Be - got - ten   Son,

Lord God, Lamb of God, Son of the Fa - ther,

you take a - way the sins of the world, have mer - cy

on us; you take a - way the sins of the world,

re - ceive our prayer; you are seat - ed

at the right hand of the Fa - ther, have mer - cy

on us. For you a - lone are the Ho - ly One,

you a - lone are the Lord, you a - lone are the

Most High, Je - sus Christ, with the Ho -

ly Spi - rit, in the glo - ry of God the

Fa - ther. A - men.

Collect

When this hymn is concluded, the Priest says: **Let us pray.**

And all pray in silence with the Priest for awhile.

The Priest says the Collect prayer, at the end of which the people acclaim: **Amen.**

LITURGY OF THE WORD

First Reading

The people sit.

The reading goes to the ambo and reads the First Reading, while all sit and listen.

To indicate the end of the reading, the reader
acclaims: **The word of the Lord.**
All reply: **Thanks be to God.**

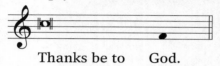

Thanks be to   God.

Responsorial Psalm

The psalmist or cantor sings or says the Psalm, with the people making the response.

Second Reading

On Sundays and Solemnities, a reader reads the Second Reading from the ambo, as above. To indicate the end of the reading, the reader acclaims: **The word of the Lord.**
All reply: **Thanks be to God.**

Thanks be to   God.

Gospel Acclamation   All stand.

Then follows the **Alleluia** or another chant laid down by the rubrics, as the liturgical time requires.

Gospel

The Deacon, or the Priest, then proceeds to the ambo, accompanied, if appropriate, by ministers with incense and candles. There he says: **The Lord be with you.**
The people reply: **And with your spirit.**

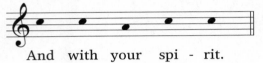

And with your spi - rit.

The Deacon, or the Priest: **A reading from the holy Gospel according to N.**
The people acclaim: **Glory to you, O Lord.**

Glory to you,   O   Lord.

The the Deacon, or the Priest, incenses the book, if incense is used, and proclaims the Gospel.

At the end of the Gospel, the Deacon, or the Priest, acclaims: **The Gospel of the Lord.**
All reply: **Praise to you, Lord Jesus Christ.**

Praise to you, Lord Je - sus Christ.

Homily   The people sit.

Profession of Faith   All stand.

At the end of the Homily, the Symbol or Profession of Faith or
Creed, when prescribed, is either sung or said:
  I believe in one God,
  the Father almighty,
  maker of heaven and earth,
  of all things visible and invisible.

  I believe in one Lord Jesus Christ,
  the Only Begotten Son of God,
  born of the Father before all ages.
  God from God, Light from Light,
  true God from true God,
  begotten, not made, consubstantial with the Father;
  through him all things were made.
  For us men and for our salvation
  he came down from heaven,

At the words that follow, up to and including and became man,
all bow.
  and by the Holy Spirit was incarnate of the Virgin Mary,
  and became man.

  For our sake he was crucified under Pontius Pilate,
  he suffered death and was buried,
  and rose again on the third day
  in accordance with the Scriptures.
  He ascended into heaven
  and is seated at the right hand of the Father.
  He will come again in glory
  to judge the living and the dead
  and his kingdom will have no end.

  I believe in the Holy Spirit, the Lord, the giver of life,
  who proceeds from the Father and the Son,
  who with the Father and the Son is adored and glorified,
  who has spoken through the prophets.

I believe in one, holy, catholic and apostolic Church.
I confess one Baptism for the forgiveness of sins
and I look forward to the resurrection of the dead
and the life of the world to come. Amen.

Instead of the Niceno–Constantinopolitan Creed, especially
during Lent and Easter Time, the baptismal Symbol of the
Roman Church, known as the Apostles' Creed, may be used.

I believe in God,
the Father almighty,
Creator of heaven and earth,
and in Jesus Christ, his only Son, our Lord,

At the words that follow, up to and including the Virgin Mary,
all bow.

who was conceived by the Holy Spirit,
born of the Virgin Mary,
suffered under Pontius Pilate,
was crucified, died and was buried;
he descended into hell;
on the third day he rose again from the dead;
he ascended into heaven,
and is seated at the right hand of God the Father almighty;
from there he will come to judge the living and the dead.
I believe in the Holy Spirit,
the holy catholic Church,
the communion of saints,
the forgiveness of sins,
the resurrection of the body,
and life everlasting. Amen.

Universal Prayer (Prayer of the Faithful)

The Deacon or other minister offers the petitions, and
then says: We pray to the Lord.
All respond: **Lord, hear our prayer.**   Or: **Lord, have mercy.**

LITURGY OF THE EUCHARIST

Preparation of the Gifts   The people sit.

When all this has been done, the Offertory Chant begins.

The offerings are then brought forward, as well as other gifts to relieve the needs of the Church and of the poor.

If, however, the Offertory Chant is not sung, the Priest may say the following two prayers aloud, with the people saying the acclamation.

The Priest takes the paten with the bread, saying:
  Blessed are you, Lord God of all creation,
  for through your goodness we have received
  the bread that we offer you:
  fruit of the earth and work of human hands,
  it will become for us the bread of life.
The people acclaim: **Blessed be God for ever.**

The Priest then takes the chalice, saying:
  Blessed are you, Lord God of all creation,
  for through your goodness we have received
  the wine we offer you:
  fruit of the vine and work of human hands,
  it will become our spiritual drink.
The people acclaim: **Blessed be God for ever.**

If appropriate, he also incenses the offerings, the cross, and the altar. A Deacon or other minister then incenses the Priest and the people.

Then the Priest says:
  Pray, brethren (brothers and sisters),
  that my sacrifice and yours

may be acceptable to God,
the almighty Father.

The people rise and reply:
May the Lord accept the sacrifice at your hands
for the praise and glory of his name,
for our good
and the good of all his holy Church.

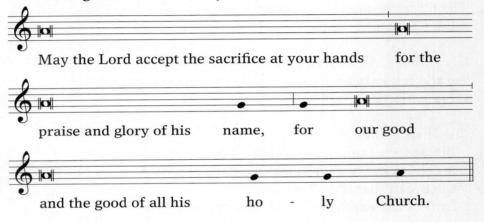

May the Lord accept the sacrifice at your hands   for the

praise and glory of his   name,   for   our good

and the good of all his   ho - ly   Church.

Then the Priest prays the Prayer over the Offerings, at the end of which the people acclaim: **Amen.**

THE EUCHARISTIC PRAYER

Then the Priest begins the Eucharistic Prayer,
saying: The Lord be with you.
The people reply: **And with your spirit.**

The Priest continues: Lift up your hearts.
The people: **We lift them up to the Lord.**

The Priest adds: Let us give thanks to the Lord our God.
The people: **It is right and just.**

℣ The Lord be with you. ℟ And with your spi - rit.

℣ Lift up your hearts. ℟ We lift them

up to the Lord. ℣ Let us give thanks to the

Lord our God. ℟ It is right and just.

The Priest continues the Preface.

At the end of the Preface, he joins his hands and concludes the
Preface with the people, singing or saying aloud:
  Holy, Holy, Holy Lord God of hosts.
  Heaven and earth are full of your glory.
  Hosanna in the highest.
  Blessed is he who comes in the name of the Lord.
  Hosanna in the highest.

Ho - ly,   Ho - ly,   Ho - ly Lord God of hosts.

Heav - en and earth are full of your glo - ry.

Ho - san - na in the high - est. Bless - ed is

he   who comes in the name of the Lord.

Ho - san - na in the high - est.

Or:

Sanc - tus,   Sanc - tus,   Sanc-tus Do - mi - nus De - us

Sa - ba - oth. Ple - ni sunt cae - li et ter - ra

glo - ri - a tu - a. Ho - san - na in ex - cel - sis.

Be - ne - dic - tus qui ve - nit in no - mi - ne

Do - mi - ni. Ho - san - na in ex - cel - sis.

The Priest continues the Eucharistic prayer using one of the following forms:

Eucharistic Prayer I, page 24,
Eucharistic Prayer II, page 32,
Eucharistic Prayer III, page 37,
Eucharistic Prayer IV, page 43,

or another form from the Roman Missal.

EUCHARISTIC PRAYER I

(THE ROMAN CANON)

℣ The Lord be with you.
℟ **And with your spirit.**

℣ Lift up your hearts.
℟ **We lift them up to the Lord.**

℣ Let us give thanks to the Lord our God.
℟ **It is right and just.**

Then follows the Preface to be used in accord with the rubrics, which concludes:
Holy, Holy, Holy Lord God of hosts.
Heaven and earth are full of your glory.
Hosanna in the highest.
Blessed is he who comes in the name of the Lord.
Hosanna in the highest.

The people kneel.

The Priest says:
To you, therefore, most merciful Father,
we make humble prayer and petition
through Jesus Christ, your Son, our Lord:
that you accept
and bless ✝ these gifts, these offerings,
these holy and unblemished sacrifices,
which we offer you firstly
for your holy catholic Church.
Be pleased to grant her peace,
to guard, unite and govern her
throughout the whole world,
together with your servant N. our Pope
and N. our Bishop,

and all those who, holding to the truth,
hand on the catholic and apostolic faith.

Remember, Lord, your servants N. and N.
and all gathered here,
whose faith and devotion are known to you.
For them, we offer you this sacrifice of praise
or they offer it for themselves
and all who are dear to them:
for the redemption of their souls,
in hope of health and well-being,
and paying their homage to you,
the eternal God, living and true.

In communion with those whose memory we venerate,
especially the glorious ever-Virgin Mary,
Mother of our God and Lord, Jesus Christ,
† and blessed Joseph, her Spouse,
your blessed Apostles and Martyrs,
Peter and Paul, Andrew,
(James, John,
Thomas, James, Philip,
Bartholomew, Matthew,
Simon and Jude;
Linus, Cletus, Clement, Sixtus,
Cornelius, Cyprian,
Lawrence, Chrysogonus,
John and Paul,
Cosmas and Damian)
and all your Saints;
we ask that through their merits and prayers,
in all things we may be defended
by your protecting help.
(Through Christ our Lord. Amen.)

Proper Forms of the Communicantes

On the Nativity of the Lord and throughout the Octave:
   Celebrating the most sacred night (day)

on which blessed Mary the immaculate Virgin
brought forth the Savior for this world,
and in communion with those whose memory we venerate,
especially the glorious ever-Virgin Mary,
Mother of our God and Lord, Jesus Christ, †

On the Epiphany of the Lord:
    Celebrating the most sacred day
    on which your Only Begotten Son,
    eternal with you in your glory,
    appeared in a human body, truly sharing our flesh,
    and in communion with those whose memory we venerate,
    especially the glorious ever-Virgin Mary,
    Mother of our God and Lord, Jesus Christ, †

From the Mass of the Easter Vigil until the Second Sunday of Easter:
    Celebrating the most sacred night (day)
    of the Resurrection of our Lord Jesus Christ in the flesh,
    and in communion with those whose memory we venerate,
    especially the glorious ever-Virgin Mary,
    Mother of our God and Lord, Jesus Christ, †

On the Ascension of the Lord:
    Celebrating the most sacred day
    on which your Only Begotten Son, our Lord,
    placed at the right hand of your glory
    our weak human nature,
    which he had united to himself,
    and in communion with those whose memory we venerate,
    especially the glorious ever-Virgin Mary,
    Mother of our God and Lord, Jesus Christ, †

On Pentecost Sunday:
    Celebrating the most sacred day of Pentecost,
    on which the Holy Spirit
    appeared to the Apostles in tongues of fire,
    and in communion with those whose memory we venerate,

especially the glorious ever-Virgin Mary,
Mother of our God and Lord, Jesus Christ, †

The Priest continues:
Therefore, Lord, we pray:
graciously accept this oblation of our service,
that of your whole family;
order our days in your peace,
and command that we be delivered from eternal damnation
and counted among the flock of those you have chosen.
(Through Christ our Lord. Amen.)

Or, from the Mass of the Easter Vigil until the Second Sunday
of Easter:
Therefore, Lord, we pray:
graciously accept this oblation of our service,
that of your whole family,
which we make to you
also for those to whom you have been pleased to give
the new birth of water and the Holy Spirit,
granting them forgiveness of all their sins;
order our days in your peace,
and command that we be delivered from eternal damnation
and counted among the flock of those you have chosen.
(Through Christ our Lord. Amen.)

Be pleased, O God, we pray,
to bless, acknowledge,
and approve this offering in every respect;
make it spiritual and acceptable,
so that it may become for us
the Body and Blood of your most beloved Son,
our Lord Jesus Christ.
On the day before he was to suffer,
he took bread in his holy and venerable hands,

and with eyes raised to heaven
to you, O God, his almighty Father,
giving you thanks, he said the blessing,
broke the bread
and gave it to his disciples, saying:

TAKE THIS, ALL OF YOU, AND EAT OF IT,
FOR THIS IS MY BODY,
WHICH WILL BE GIVEN UP FOR YOU.

He shows the consecrated host to the people, places it again on the paten, and genuflects in adoration.

In a similar way, when supper was ended,
he took this precious chalice
in his holy and venerable hands,
and once more giving you thanks, he said the blessing
and gave the chalice to his disciples, saying:

TAKE THIS, ALL OF YOU, AND DRINK FROM IT,
FOR THIS IS THE CHALICE OF MY BLOOD,
THE BLOOD OF THE NEW AND ETERNAL COVENANT,
WHICH WILL BE POURED OUT FOR YOU AND FOR MANY
FOR THE FORGIVENESS OF SINS.
DO THIS IN MEMORY OF ME.

He shows the chalice to the people, places it on the corporal, and genuflects in adoration.

Then the Priest says: The mystery of faith.

And the people continue, acclaiming:
**We proclaim your Death, O Lord,
and profess your Resurrection
until you come again.**

We pro - claim your Death, O Lord, and pro - fess

your Res - ur - rec - tion un - til you come a - gain.

Or:

When we eat this Bread and drink this Cup,
we proclaim your Death, O Lord,
until you come again.

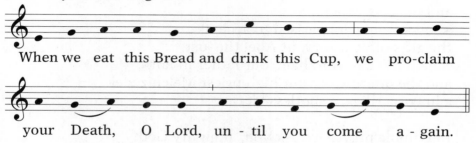

When we eat this Bread and drink this Cup, we pro-claim

your Death, O Lord, un - til you come a - gain.

Or:

Save us, Savior of the world,
for by your Cross and Resurrection
you have set us free.

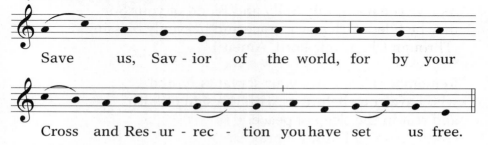

Save us, Sav - ior of the world, for by your

Cross and Res - ur - rec - tion you have set us free.

Then the Priest says:
Therefore, O Lord,
as we celebrate the memorial of the blessed Passion,
the Resurrection from the dead,

and the glorious Ascension into heaven
of Christ, your Son, our Lord,
we, your servants and your holy people,
offer to your glorious majesty
from the gifts that you have given us,
this pure victim,
this holy victim,
this spotless victim,
the holy Bread of eternal life
and the Chalice of everlasting salvation.

Be pleased to look upon these offerings
with a serene and kindly countenance,
and to accept them,
as once you were pleased to accept
the gifts of your servant Abel the just,
the sacrifice of Abraham, our father in faith,
and the offering of your high priest Melchizedek,
a holy sacrifice, a spotless victim.

In humble prayer we ask you, almighty God:
command that these gifts be borne
by the hands of your holy Angel
to your altar on high
in the sight of your divine majesty,
so that all of us, who through this participation at the altar
receive the most holy Body and Blood of your Son,
may be filled with every grace and heavenly blessing.
(Through Christ our Lord. Amen.)

Remember also, Lord, your servants N. and N.,
who have gone before us with the sign of faith
and rest in the sleep of peace.
Grant them, O Lord, we pray,
and all who sleep in Christ,
a place of refreshment, light and peace.
(Through Christ our Lord. Amen.)

To us, also, your servants,

who, though sinners,
hope in your abundant mercies,
graciously grant some share
and fellowship with your holy Apostles and Martyrs:
with John the Baptist, Stephen,
Matthias, Barnabas,
(Ignatius, Alexander,
Marcellinus, Peter,
Felicity, Perpetua,
Agatha, Lucy,
Agnes, Cecilia, Anastasia)
and all your Saints;
admit us, we beseech you,
into their company,
not weighing our merits,
but granting us your pardon,
through Christ our Lord.

Through whom
you continue to make all these good things, O Lord;
you sanctify them, fill them with life,
bless them, and bestow them upon us.

He takes the chalice and the paten with the host and, raising
both, he says:
Through him, and with him, and in him,
O God, almighty Father,
in the unity of the Holy Spirit,
all glory and honor is yours,
for ever and ever.
The people acclaim: **Amen.**

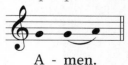

A - men.

Then follows the Communion Rite on page 49.

EUCHARISTIC PRAYER II

Although it is provided with its own Preface, the Eucharistic
Prayer may also be used with other Prefaces, especially those
that present an overall view of the mystery of salvation, such as
the Common Prefaces.

℣ The Lord be with you.
℟ **And with your spirit.**

℣ Lift up your hearts.
℟ **We lift them up to the Lord.**

℣ Let us give thanks to the Lord our God.
℟ **It is right and just.**

It is truly right and just, our duty our salvation,
always and everywhere to give you thanks, Father most holy,
through your beloved Son, Jesus Christ,
your Word through whom you made all things,
whom you sent as our Savior and Redeemer,
incarnate by the Holy Spirit and born of the Virgin.

Fulfilling your will and gaining for you a holy people,
he stretched out his hands as he endured his Passion,
so as to break the bonds of death and manifest the
resurrection.

And so, with the Angels and all the Saints
we declare your glory,
as with one voice we acclaim:

Holy, Holy, Holy Lord God of hosts.
Heaven and earth are full of your glory.
Hosanna in the highest.
Blessed is he who comes in the name of the Lord.
Hosanna in the highest.

The people kneel.

The Priest says:
 You are indeed Holy, O Lord,
 the fount of all holiness.
 Make holy, therefore, these gifts, we pray,
 by sending down your Spirit upon them like the dewfall,
 so that they may become for us
 the Body and ✝ Blood of our Lord Jesus Christ.

 At the time he was betrayed
 and entered willingly into his Passion,
 he took bread and, giving thanks, broke it,
 and gave it to his disciples, saying:

 TAKE THIS, ALL OF YOU, AND EAT OF IT,
 FOR THIS IS MY BODY,
 WHICH WILL BE GIVEN UP FOR YOU.

He shows the consecrated host to the people, places it again on
the paten, and genuflects in adoration.

 In a similar way, when supper was ended,
 he took the chalice
 and, once more giving thanks,
 he gave it to his disciples, saying:

 TAKE THIS, ALL OF YOU, AND DRINK FROM IT,
 FOR THIS IS THE CHALICE OF MY BLOOD,
 THE BLOOD OF THE NEW AND ETERNAL COVENANT,
 WHICH WILL BE POURED OUT FOR YOU AND FOR MANY
 FOR THE FORGIVENESS OF SINS.
 DO THIS IN MEMORY OF ME.

He shows the chalice to the people, places it on the corporal,
and genuflects in adoration.

Then he says: The mystery of faith.

And the people continue, acclaiming:

We proclaim your Death, O Lord,
and profess your Resurrection
until you come again.

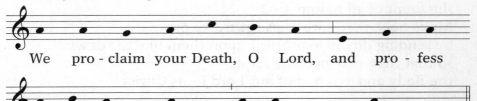

We pro - claim your Death, O Lord, and pro - fess
your Res - ur - rec - tion un - til you come a - gain.

Or:

When we eat this Bread and drink this Cup,
we proclaim your Death, O Lord,
until you come again.

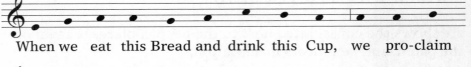

When we eat this Bread and drink this Cup, we pro-claim
your Death, O Lord, un - til you come a - gain.

Or:

Save us, Savior of the world,
for by your Cross and Resurrection
you have set us free.

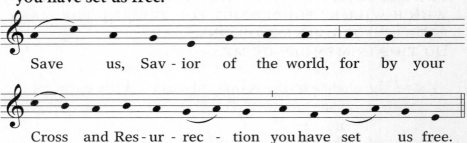

Save us, Sav - ior of the world, for by your
Cross and Res - ur - rec - tion you have set us free.

Then the Priest says:

> Therefore, as we celebrate
> the memorial of his Death and Resurrection,
> we offer you, Lord,
> the Bread of life and the Chalice of salvation,
> giving thanks that you have held us worthy
> to be in your presence and minister to you.
>
> Humbly we pray
> that, partaking of the Body and Blood of Christ,
> we may be gathered into one by the Holy Spirit.
>
> Remember, Lord, your Church,
> spread throughout the world,
> and bring her to the fullness of charity,
> together with N. our Pope and N. our Bishop
> and all the clergy.

In Masses for the Dead, the following may be added:

> Remember your servant N.,
> whom you have called (today)
> from this world to yourself.
> Grant that he (she) who was united with your Son in a death
>   like his,
> may also be one with him in his Resurrection.

> Remember also our brothers and sisters
> who have fallen asleep in the hope of the resurrection,
> and all who have died in your mercy:
> welcome them into the light of your face.
> Have mercy on us all, we pray,
> that with the Blessed Virgin Mary, Mother of God,
> with blessed Joseph, her Spouse,
> with the blessed Apostles,
> and all the Saints who have pleased you throughout the ages,

we may merit to be coheirs to eternal life,
and may praise and glorify you
through your Son, Jesus Christ.

He takes the chalice and the paten with the host and, raising
both, he says:
Through him, and with him, and in him,
O God, almighty Father,
in the unity of the Holy Spirit,
all glory and honor is yours,
for ever and ever.
The people acclaim: **Amen.**

A - men.

Then follows the Communion Rite on page 49.

EUCHARISTIC PRAYER III

℣   The Lord be with you.
℟   **And with your spirit.**

℣   Lift up your hearts.
℟   **We lift them up to the Lord.**

℣   Let us give thanks to the Lord our God.
℟   **It is right and just.**

Then follows the Preface to be used in accord with the rubrics, which concludes:

Holy, Holy, Holy Lord God of hosts.
Heaven and earth are full of your glory.
Hosanna in the highest.
Blessed is he who comes in the name of the Lord.
Hosanna in the highest.

The people kneel.

The Priest says:

You are indeed Holy, O Lord,
and all you have created
rightly gives you praise,
for through your Son our Lord Jesus Christ,
by the power and working of the Holy Spirit,
you give life to all things and make them holy,
and you never cease to gather a people to yourself,
so that from the rising of the sun to its setting
a pure sacrifice may be offered to your name.

Therefore, O Lord, we humbly implore you:
by the same Spirit graciously make holy
these gifts we have brought to you for consecration,
that they may become the Body and ✠ Blood
of your Son our Lord Jesus Christ,
at whose command we celebrate these mysteries.

For on the night he was betrayed
he himself took bread,
and, giving you thanks, he said the blessing,
broke the bread and gave it to his disciples, saying:

TAKE THIS, ALL OF YOU, AND EAT OF IT,
FOR THIS IS MY BODY,
WHICH WILL BE GIVEN UP FOR YOU.

He shows the consecrated host to the people, places it again on
the paten, and genuflects in adoration.

In a similar way, when supper was ended,
he took the chalice
and, giving you thanks, he said the blessing,
and gave the chalice to his disciples, saying:

TAKE THIS, ALL OF YOU, AND DRINK FROM IT,
FOR THIS IS THE CHALICE OF MY BLOOD,
THE BLOOD OF THE NEW AND ETERNAL COVENANT,
WHICH WILL BE POURED OUT FOR YOU AND FOR MANY
FOR THE FORGIVENESS OF SINS.
DO THIS IN MEMORY OF ME.

He shows the chalice to the people, places it on the corporal,
and genuflects in adoration.

Then the Priest says: The mystery of faith.

And the people continue, acclaiming:
**We proclaim your Death, O Lord,
and profess your Resurrection
until you come again.**

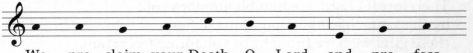

We   pro - claim your Death, O   Lord, and   pro - fess

your Res - ur - rec - tion un - til you come a - gain.

Or:

When we eat this Bread and drink this Cup,
we proclaim your Death, O Lord,
until you come again.

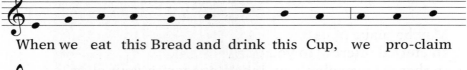

When we eat this Bread and drink this Cup, we pro-claim

your Death, O Lord, un - til you come a - gain.

Or:

Save us, Savior of the world,
for by your Cross and Resurrection
you have set us free.

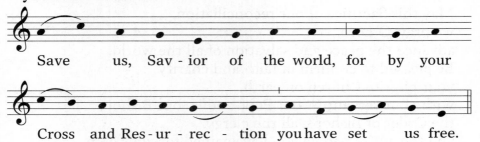

Save us, Sav - ior of the world, for by your

Cross and Res - ur - rec - tion you have set us free.

Then the Priest says:

Therefore, O Lord, as we celebrate the memorial
of the saving Passion of your Son,
his wondrous Resurrection
and Ascension into heaven,
and as we look forward to his second coming,

we offer you in thanksgiving
this holy and living sacrifice.

Look, we pray, upon the oblation of your Church
and, recognizing the sacrificial Victim by whose death
you willed to reconcile us to yourself,
grant that we, who are nourished
by the Body and Blood of your Son
and filled with his Holy Spirit,
may become one body, one spirit in Christ.

May he make of us
an eternal offering to you,
so that we may obtain an inheritance with your elect,
especially with the most Blessed Virgin Mary, Mother of God,
with blessed Joseph, her Spouse,
with your blessed Apostles and glorious Martyrs
(with Saint N.: the Saint of the day or Patron Saint)
and with all the Saints,
on whose constant intercession in your presence
we rely for unfailing help.

May this Sacrifice of our reconciliation,
we pray, O Lord,
advance the peace and salvation of all the world.
Be pleased to confirm in faith and charity
your pilgrim Church on earth,
with your servant N. our Pope and N. our Bishop,
the Order of Bishops, all the clergy,
and the entire people you have gained for your own.
Listen graciously to the prayers of this family,
whom you have summoned before you:
in your compassion, O merciful Father,
gather to yourself all your children
scattered throughout the world.

† To our departed brothers and sisters
and to all who were pleasing to you

at their passing from this life,
give kind admittance to your kingdom.
There we hope to enjoy for ever the fullness of your glory
through Christ our Lord,
through whom you bestow on the world all that is good. †

He takes the chalice and the paten with the host and, raising
both, he says:
Through him, and with him, and in him,
O God, almighty Father,
in the unity of the Holy Spirit,
all glory and honor is yours,
for ever and ever.
The people acclaim: **Amen.**

A - men.

Then follows the Communion Rite on page 49.

When this Eucharistic Prayer is used in Masses for the Dead, the
following may be said:
† Remember your servant N.
whom you have called (today)
from this world to yourself.
Grant that he (she) who was united with your Son in a death
    like his,
may also be one with him in his Resurrection,
when from the earth
he will raise up in the flesh those who have died,
and transform our lowly body
after the pattern of his own glorious body.
To our departed brothers and sisters, too,
and to all who were pleasing to you
at their passing from this life,
give kind admittance to your kingdom.
There we hope to enjoy for ever the fullness of your glory,

when you will wipe away every tear from our eyes.
For seeing you, our God, as you are,
we shall be like you for all the ages
and praise you without end,
through Christ our Lord,
through whom you bestow on the world all that is good. †

EUCHARISTIC PRAYER IV

It is not permitted to change the Preface of this Eucharistic Prayer because of the structure of the Prayer itself, which presents a summary of the history of salvation.

℣   The Lord be with you.
℟   **And with your spirit.**

℣   Lift up your hearts.
℟   **We lift them up to the Lord.**

℣   Let us give thanks to the Lord our God.
℟   **It is right and just.**

It is truly right to give you thanks,
truly just to give you glory, Father most holy,
for you are the one God living and true,
existing before all ages and abiding for all eternity,
dwelling in unapproachable light;
yet you, who alone are good, the source of life,
have made all that is,
so that you might fill your creatures with blessings
and bring joy to many of them by the glory of your light.

And so, in your presence are countless hosts of Angels,
who serve you day and night
and, gazing upon the glory of your face,
glorify you without ceasing.

With them we, too, confess your name in exultation,
giving voice to every creature under heaven,
as we acclaim:

Holy, Holy, Holy Lord God of hosts.
Heaven and earth are full of your glory.
Hosanna in the highest.

**Blessed is he who comes in the name of the Lord.
Hosanna in the highest.**

The people kneel.

The Priest says:
    We give you praise, Father most holy,
    for you are great
    and you have fashioned all your works
    in wisdom and in love.
    You formed man in your own image
    and entrusted the whole world to his care,
    so that in serving you alone, the Creator,
    he might have dominion over all creatures.
    And when through disobedience he had lost your friendship,
    you did not abandon him to the domain of death.
    For you came in mercy to the aid of all,
    so that those who seek might find you.
    Time and again you offered them covenants
    and through the prophets
    taught them to look forward to salvation.

    And you so loved the world, Father most holy,
    that in the fullness of time
    you sent your Only Begotten Son to be our Savior.
    Made incarnate by the Holy Spirit
    and born of the Virgin Mary,
    he shared our human nature
    in all things but sin.
    To the poor he proclaimed the good news of salvation,
    to prisoners, freedom,
    and to the sorrowful of heart, joy.
    To accomplish your plan,
    he gave himself up to death,
    and, rising from the dead,
    he destroyed death and restored life.

    And that we might live no longer for ourselves

but for him who died and rose again for us,
he sent the Holy Spirit from you, Father
as the first fruits of those who believe,
so that, bringing to perfection his work in the world,
he might sanctify creation to the full.

Therefore, O Lord, we pray:
may this same Holy Spirit
graciously sanctify these offerings,
that they may become
the Body and ✝ Blood of our Lord Jesus Christ,
for the celebration of this great mystery,
which he himself left us
as an eternal covenant.

For when the hour had come
for him to be glorified by you, Father most holy,
having loved his own who were in the world,
he loved them to the end:
and while they were at supper,
he took bread, blessed and broke it,
and gave it to his disciples, saying:

TAKE THIS, ALL OF YOU, AND EAT OF IT,
FOR THIS IS MY BODY,
WHICH WILL BE GIVEN UP FOR YOU.

He shows the consecrated host to the people, places it again on
the paten, and genuflects in adoration.

In a similar way,
taking the chalice filled with the fruit of the vine,
he gave thanks,
and gave the chalice to his disciples, saying:

TAKE THIS, ALL OF YOU, AND DRINK FROM IT,
FOR THIS IS THE CHALICE OF MY BLOOD,
THE BLOOD OF THE NEW AND ETERNAL COVENANT,

WHICH WILL BE POURED OUT FOR YOU AND FOR MANY
FOR THE FORGIVENESS OF SINS.
DO THIS IN MEMORY OF ME.

He shows the chalice to the people, places it on the corporal,
and genuflects in adoration.

Then the Priest says: The mystery of faith.

And the people continue, acclaiming:
**We proclaim your Death, O Lord,
and profess your Resurrection
until you come again.**

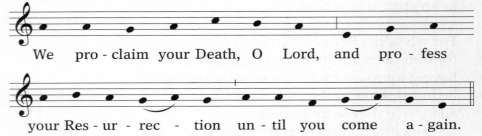

We   pro - claim your Death, O   Lord, and   pro - fess
your Res - ur - rec - tion un - til you   come   a - gain.

Or:
**When we eat this Bread and drink this Cup,
we proclaim your Death, O Lord,
until you come again.**

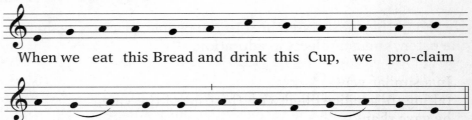

When we eat this Bread and drink this Cup, we   pro-claim
your   Death,   O Lord, un - til you   come   a - gain.

Or:
**Save us, Savior of the world,
for by your Cross and Resurrection
you have set us free.**

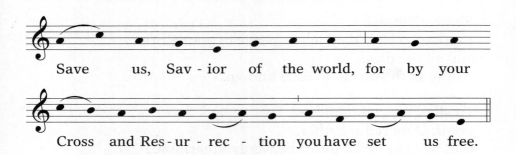

Save us, Sav-ior of the world, for by your
Cross and Res-ur-rec-tion you have set us free.

Then the Priest says:

Therefore, O Lord,
as we now celebrate the memorial of our redemption,
we remember Christ's Death
and his descent to the realm of the dead,
we proclaim his Resurrection
and his Ascension to your right hand,
and, as we await his coming in glory,
we offer you his Body and Blood,
the sacrifice acceptable to you
which brings salvation to the whole world.

Look, O Lord, upon the Sacrifice
which you yourself have provided for your Church,
and grant in your loving kindness
to all who partake of this one Bread and one Chalice
that, gathered into one body by the Holy Spirit,
they may truly become a living sacrifice in Christ
to the praise of your glory.

Therefore, Lord, remember now
all for whom we offer this sacrifice:
especially your servant N. our Pope,
N. our Bishop, and the whole Order of Bishops,
all the clergy,
those who take part in this offering,
those gathered here before you,
your entire people,
and all who seek you with a sincere heart.

Remember also
those who have died in the peace of your Christ
and all the dead,
whose faith you alone have known.

To all of us, your children,
grant, O merciful Father,
that we may enter into a heavenly inheritance
with the Blessed Virgin Mary, Mother of God,
with blessed Joseph, her Spouse,
and with your Apostles and Saints in your kingdom.
There, with the whole of creation,
freed from the corruption of sin and death,
may we glorify you through Christ our Lord,
through whom you bestow on the world all that is good.

He takes the chalice and the paten with the host and, raising
both, he says:
Through him, and with him, and in him,
O God, almighty Father,
in the unity of the Holy Spirit,
all glory and honor is yours,
for ever and ever.
The people acclaim: **Amen.**

A - men.

COMMUNION RITE

The Lord's Prayer   *All stand.*

After the chalice and paten have been set down, the Priest says:
At the Savior's command
and formed by divine teaching,
we dare to say:

All continue:
Our Father, who art in heaven,
hallowed be thy name;
thy kingdom come,
thy will be done
on earth as it is in heaven.
Give us this day our daily bread,
and forgive us our trespasses,
as we forgive those who trespass against us;
and lead us not into temptation,
but deliver us from evil.

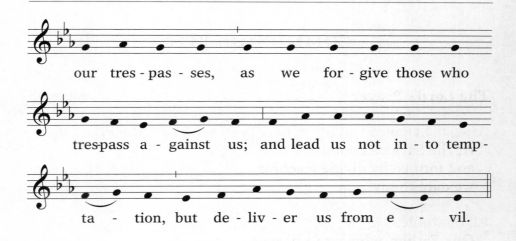

our tres-pas-ses, as we for-give those who

tres-pass a-gainst us; and lead us not in-to temp-

ta - tion, but de-liv-er us from e - vil.

The Priest continues, saying:
Deliver us, Lord, we pray, from every evil,
graciously grant peace in our days,
that, by the help of your mercy,
we may be always free from sin
and safe from all distress,
as we await the blessed hope
and the coming of our Savior, Jesus Christ.

The people conclude the prayer, acclaiming:
**For the kingdom,
the power and the glory are yours
now and for ever.**

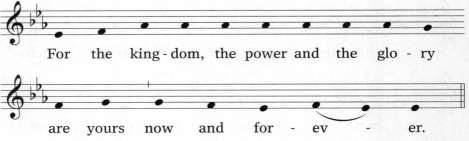

For the king-dom, the power and the glo-ry

are yours now and for-ev-er.

The Rite of Peace

Then the Priest says aloud:
Lord Jesus Christ,
who said to your Apostles:

Peace I leave you, my peace I give you,
look not on our sins,
but on the faith of your Church,
and graciously grant her peace and unity
in accordance with your will.
Who live and reign for ever and ever.
The people reply: **Amen.**

The Priest adds: The peace of the Lord be with you always.
The people reply: **And with your spirit.**

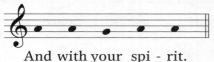

And with your spi - rit.

Then the Deacon, or the Priest, adds: **Let us offer each other the sign of peace.**

All offer one another a sign that expresses peace, communion, and charity.

The Fraction of the Bread

Then the Priest takes the host and breaks it over the paten. Meanwhile, the following is sung or said:
**Lamb of God, you take away the sins of the world,
have mercy on us.
Lamb of God, you take away the sins of the world,
have mercy on us.
Lamb of God, you take away the sins of the world,
grant us peace.**

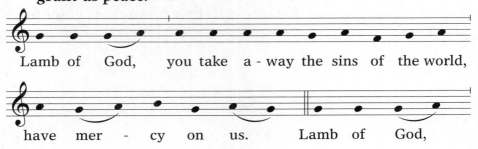

Lamb of God, you take a - way the sins of the world, have mer - cy on us. Lamb of God,

you take a - way the sins of the world, have mer -

cy on us.   Lamb of   God,   you take a - way

the sins of the world,   grant   us   peace.

Or:

A - gnus De - i, qui tol - lis pec - ca - ta mun - di: mi - se -

re - re no - bis. A - gnus De - i, qui tol - lis pec - ca -

ta mun - di: mi - se - re - re no - bis. A - gnus De - i,

qui tol - lis pec - ca - ta mun - di: do - na no - bis pa - cem.

This invocation may even be repeated several times if the
fraction is prolonged. Only the final time, however, is **grant us
peace** said.

Invitation to Communion   The people kneel.

The Priest genuflects, takes the host and, holding it slightly
raised above the paten or above the chalice, says aloud:
    Behold the Lamb of God,
    behold him who takes away the sins of the world.
    Blessed are those called to the supper of the Lamb.

All continue:
    Lord, I am not worthy
    that you should enter under my roof,
    but only say the word
    and my soul shall be healed.

Reception of Communion   All stand.

While the Priest is receiving the Body of Christ, the
Communion Chant begins. After this, he takes a paten or
ciborium and approaches the communicants. The Priest
or Deacon raises a host slightly and shows it to each of the
communicants, saying: **The Body of Christ.**

The communicant replies: **Amen.**   And receives Holy
Communion.

The Guidelines for the Reception of Holy Communion can be
found on page 5.

When the distribution of communion is over, the Priest or
a Deacon or an acolyte purifies the paten and the chalice.
A sacred silence may be observed for a while, or a psalm or
other canticle of praise or a hymn may be sung. Then the Priest
says: **Let us pray.**

Then the Priest says the Prayer after Communion, at the end of
which the people acclaim: **Amen.**

THE CONCLUDING RITES

If they are necessary, any brief announcements to the people follow here.

Blessing and Dismissal

All stand.

The Priest says: **The Lord be with you.**
The people reply: **And with your spirit.**

And with your spi - rit.

The Priest blesses the people, saying:
    May almighty God bless you,
    the Father, and the Son, + and the Holy Spirit.
The people reply: **Amen.**

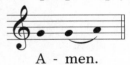

A - men.

Then the Deacon, or the Priest himself, says: **Go forth, the Mass is ended.**

Or: **Go and announce the Gospel of the Lord.**

Or: **Go in peace, glorifying the Lord by your life.**

The people reply: **Thanks be to God.**

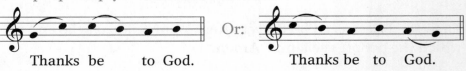

Thanks be   to God.   Or: Thanks be   to   God.

RITE FOR THE BLESSING

AND SPRINKLING OF WATER

On Sundays, especially in Easter Time, the blessing and sprinkling of water as a memorial of Baptism may take place from time to time in all churches and chapels, even in Masses anticipated on Saturday evenings.

If this rite is celebrated during Mass, it takes the place of the usual Penitential Act at the beginning of Mass.

After the greeting, the Priest stands at his chair and faces the people. With a vessel containing the water to be blessed before him, he calls upon the people to pray, saying:

Dear brethren (brothers and sisters),
let us humbly beseech the Lord our God
to bless this water he has created,
which will be sprinkled on us
as a memorial of our Baptism.
May he help us by his grace
to remain faithful to the Spirit we have received.

And after a brief pause for silence, he continues:

Almighty ever-living God,
who willed that through water,
the fountain of life and the source of purification,
even souls should be cleansed
and receive the gift of eternal life;
be pleased, we pray, to + bless this water,
by which we seek protection on this your day, O Lord.
Renew the living spring of your grace within us
and grant that by this water we may be defended
from all ills of spirit and body,
and so approach you with hearts made clean
and worthily receive your salvation.
Through Christ our Lord.   ℟ **Amen.**

Or:
Almighty Lord and God,
who are the source and origin of all life,
whether of body or soul,
we ask you to + bless this water,
which we use in confidence
to implore forgiveness for our sins
and to obtain the protection of your grace
against all illness and every snare of the enemy.
Grant, O Lord, in your mercy,
that living waters may always spring up for our salvation,
and so may we approach you with a pure heart
and avoid all danger to body and soul.
Through Christ our Lord.   ℟ **Amen.**

Or, during Easter Time:
Lord our God,
in your mercy be present to your people's prayers,
and, for us who recall the wondrous work of our creation
and the still greater work of our redemption,
graciously + bless this water.
For you created water to make the fields fruitful
and to refresh and cleanse our bodies.
You also made water the instrument of your mercy:
for through water you freed your people from slavery
and quenched their thirst in the desert;
through water the Prophets proclaimed the new covenant
you were to enter upon with the human race;
and last of all,
through water, which Christ made holy in the Jordan,
you have renewed our corrupted nature
in the bath of regeneration.
Therefore, may this water be for us
a memorial of the Baptism we have received,
and grant that we may share
in the gladness of our brothers and sisters
who at Easter have received their Baptism.
Through Christ our Lord.   ℟ **Amen.**

Where the circumstances of the place or the custom of the

people suggest that the mixing of salt be preserved in the blessing of water, the Priest may bless salt, saying:

We humbly ask you, almighty God:
be pleased in your faithful love to bless ✝ this salt
you have created,
for it was you who commanded the prophet Elisha
to cast salt into water,
that impure water might be purified.
Grant, O Lord, we pray,
that, wherever this mixture of salt and water is sprinkled,
every attack of the enemy may be repulsed
and your Holy Spirit may be present
to keep us safe at all times.
Through Christ our Lord.

℟   **Amen.**

Then he pours the salt into the water, without saying anything.

Afterward, taking the aspergillum, the Priest sprinkles himself and the ministers, then the clergy and people, moving through the church, if appropriate.

Meanwhile, one of the following chants, or another appropriate song is sung.

Outside Easter Time:

Antiphon 1 Ps 51 (50): 9 **Sprinkle me with hyssop, O Lord, and I shall be cleansed; ◆ wash me and I shall be whiter than snow.**

Or:

A - sper - ges me, ∗ Do - mi - ne,

hys - so - po, et mun-da - bor: la -

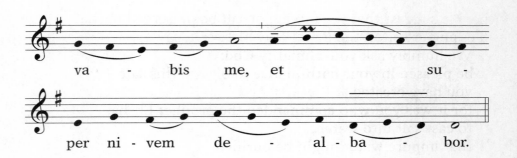

va - bis me, et su - per ni - vem de - al - ba - bor.

Antiphon 2 Ez 36: 25–26 I will pour clean water upon you, ◆ and you will be made clean of all your impurities, ◆ and I shall give you a new spirit, says the Lord.

Hymn cf. 1 Pt 1: 3–5 Blessed be the God and Father of our Lord Jesus Christ, ◆ who in his great mercy has given us new birth into a living hope ◆ through the Resurrection of Jesus Christ from the dead, ◆ into an inheritance that will not perish, ◆ preserved for us in heaven ◆ for the salvation to be revealed in the last time!

During Easter Time:

Antiphon 1 cf. Ez 47: 1–2, 9 I saw water flowing from the Temple, ◆ from its right-hand side, alleluia: ◆ and all to whom this water came ◆ were saved and shall say: Alleluia, alleluia.

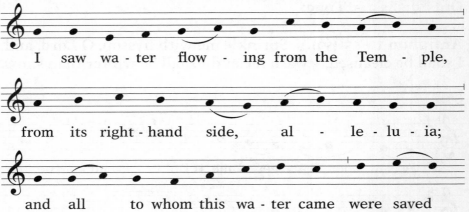

I saw wa - ter flow - ing from the Tem - ple,

from its right - hand side, al - le - lu - ia;

and all to whom this wa - ter came were saved

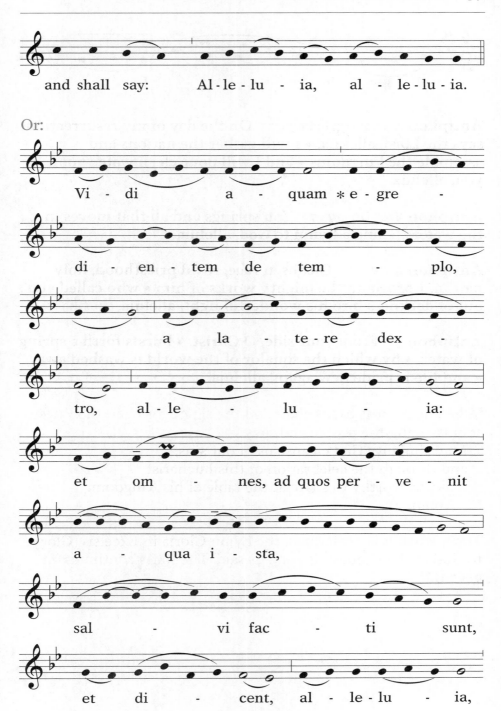

and shall say: Al - le - lu - ia,   al - le - lu - ia.

Or:

Vi - di   a - quam *e - gre -

di - en - tem de tem - plo,

a   la - te - re dex -

tro,   al - le - lu - ia:

et   om - nes, ad quos per - ve - nit

a - qua i - sta,

sal - vi fac - ti sunt,

et di - cent, al - le - lu - ia,

al - le - lu - ia.

Antiphon 2 cf. Wis 3: 8; Ez 36: 25 **On the day of my resurrection, says the Lord, alleluia, ◆ I will gather the nations and assemble the kingdoms ◆ and I will pour clean water upon you, alleluia.**

Antiphon 3 cf. Dn 3: 77, 79 **You springs and all that moves in the waters, ◆ sing a hymn to God, alleluia.**

Antiphon 4 1 Pt 2: 9 **O chosen race, royal priesthood, holy nation, ◆ proclaim the mighty works of him ◆ who called you out of darkness into his wonderful light, alleluia.**

Antiphon 5 **From your side, O Christ, ◆ bursts forth a spring of water, ◆ by which the squalor of the world is washed away ◆ and life is made new again, alleluia.**

When he returns to his chair and the singing is over, the Priest stands facing the people and says:

May almighty God cleanse us of our sins,
and through the celebration of this Eucharist
make us worthy to share at the table of his Kingdom.

℟   **Amen.**

Then, when it is prescribed, the hymn Gloria in Excelsis (Glory to God in the Highest) is sung or said. The Mass continues on page 11.

Rite of Eucharistic Exposition and Benediction

EXPOSITION

After the people have assembled, **O salutaris Hostia** or another song may be sung while the minister comes to the altar:

O Salutáris Hóstia
Quae caeli pandis óstium,
Bella premunt hostília
Da robur, fer auxílium.

Uni trinóque Dómino
Sit sempitérna glória:
Qui vitam sine término
Nobis donet in pátria.
Amen.

Or:

O Saving Victim, open wide
The gate of heaven to man below,
Our foes press on from every side;
Thine aid supply, Thy strength bestow.

To Thy great Name be endless praise
Immortal Godhead, one in three!
Oh, grant us endless length of days
In our true native land with Thee.
Amen.

After exposition, if the monstrance is used, the minister incenses the sacrament. If the adoration is to be lengthy, he may then withdraw.

ADORATION

During the exposition there should be prayers, songs, and readings to direct the attention of the faithful to the worship of Christ the Lord.

Part of the liturgy of the hours, especially the principle hours, may be celebrated before the blessed sacrament when there is a lengthy period of exposition.

BENEDICTION

Eucharistic Hymn and Incensation

Toward the end of the exposition the priest or deacon goes to the altar, genuflects, and kneels. Then **Tantum ergo Sacramentum** or another eucharistic song is sung:
>**Tantum ergo Sacraméntum**
Venerémur cérnui,
Et antíquum documéntum
Novo cedat rítui;
Praestet fides suppleméntum
sénsuum deféctui.

>**Genitóri Genitóque**
Laus et jubilátio,
Salus, honor, virtus quoque
Sit et benedíctio;
Procedénti ab utróque
Compar sit laudátio.
Amen.

Or:
>**Down in adoration falling,**
Lo! the sacred Host we hail;
Lo! o'er ancient forms departing,

Newer rites of grace prevail;
Faith, for all defects supplying,
Where the feeble senses fail.

To the Everlasting Father,
And the Son who reigns on high,
With the Holy Ghost proceeding
Forth from Each eternally,
Be salvation, honor, blessing,
Might, and endless majesty.
Amen.

Meanwhile the minister, while kneeling, incenses the sacrament if the exposition has taken place with the monstrance.

Prayer

Afterward the minister rises and sings or says: **Let us pray.**

After a brief period of silence, the minister continues:
Lord Jesus Christ,
you gave us the eucharist
as the memorial of your suffering and death.
May our worship of this sacrament of your body and blood
help us to experience the salvation you won for us
and the peace of the kingdom
where you live with the Father and the Holy Spirit,
one God, for ever and ever.
All respond: **Amen.**

Other prayers from *Eucharistic Worship Outside Mass* may be chosen.

Eucharistic Blessing

After the prayer the priest or deacon puts on the humeral veil, genuflects, and takes the monstrance or ciborium. He makes the sign of the cross over the people with the monstrance or ciborium, in silence.

REPOSITION

After the blessing the priest or deacon who gave the blessing, or another priest or deacon, replaces the blessed sacrament in the tabernacle and genuflects. Meanwhile the people may sing or say an acclamation, and the minister then leaves.

The Divine Praises
Blessed be God.
Blessed be His holy Name.
Blessed be Jesus Christ, true God and true Man.
Blessed be the Name of Jesus.
Blessed be His most Sacred Heart.
Blessed be His most Precious Blood.
Blessed be Jesus in the Most Holy Sacrament of the altar.
Blessed be the Holy Spirit, the Paraclete.
Blessed be the great Mother of God, Mary most holy.
Blessed be her holy and Immaculate Conception.
Blessed be her glorious Assumption.
Blessed be the name of Mary, Virgin and Mother.
Blessed be Saint Joseph, her most chaste spouse.
Blessed be God in His angels and in His saints.

Advent † YEAR A

FIRST SUNDAY OF ADVENT

Entrance Antiphon *cf. Ps 25 (24): 1–3* To you, I lift up my soul, O my God. ♦ In you, I have trusted; let me not be put to shame. ♦ Nor let my enemies exult over me; ♦ and let none who hope in you be put to shame.

First Reading *Is 2: 1–5* This is what Isaiah, son of Amoz, saw concerning Judah and Jerusalem.
 In days to come,
 the mountain of the LORD's house
  shall be established as the highest mountain
  and raised above the hills.
All nations shall stream toward it;
  many peoples shall come and say:
"Come, let us climb the LORD's mountain,
  to the house of the God of Jacob,
that he may instruct us in his ways,
  and we may walk in his paths."
For from Zion shall go forth instruction,
  and the word of the LORD from Jerusalem.
He shall judge between the nations,
  and impose terms on many peoples.
They shall beat their swords into plowshares
  and their spears into pruning hooks;
one nation shall not raise the sword against another,
  nor shall they train for war again.
O house of Jacob, come,
  let us walk in the light of the LORD!

Responsorial Psalm   Ps 122: 1–2, 3–4, 4–5, 6–7, 8–9   Brian J. Nelson

Let us go re - joi-cing to the house   of the Lord.

I rejoiced because they said to me,
    "We will go up to the house of the LORD."
And now we have set foot
    within your gates, O Jerusalem. ℟

Jerusalem, built as a city
    with compact unity.
To it the tribes go up,
    the tribes of the LORD. ℟

According to the decree for Israel,
    to give thanks to the name of the LORD.
In it are set up judgment seats,
    seats for the house of David. ℟

Pray for the peace of Jerusalem!
    May those who love you prosper!
May peace be within your walls,
    prosperity in your buildings. ℟

Because of my brothers and friends
    I will say, "Peace be within you!"
Because of the house of the LORD, our God,
    I will pray for your good. ℟

Second Reading Rom 13: 11–14 Brothers and sisters: You know the time; it is the hour now for you to awake from sleep. For our salvation is nearer now than when we first believed; the night is advanced, the day is at hand. Let us then throw off the works of darkness and put on the armor of light; let us conduct ourselves properly as in the day, not in orgies and drunkenness, not in promiscuity and lust, not in rivalry and jealousy. But put on the Lord Jesus Christ, and make no provision for the desires of the flesh.

Alleluia *cf. Ps 85: 8*   *Joe Higginbotham*

Al - le - lu - ia,   al - le - lu - ia,   al - le - lu - ia.

Al - le - lu - ia,   al - le - lu - ia,   al - le - lu - ia.

Show us, Lord, your love; / and grant us your salvation.
Alleluia, alleluia.

Gospel Mt 24: 37-44 Jesus said to his disciples: "As it was in the days
of Noah, so it will be at the coming of the Son of Man. In those
days before the flood, they were eating and drinking, marrying
and giving in marriage, up to the day that Noah entered the
ark. They did not know until the flood came and carried them
all away. So will it be also at the coming of the Son of Man.
Two men will be out in the field; one will be taken, and one will
be left. Two women will be grinding at the mill; one will be
taken, and one will be left. Therefore, stay awake! For you do not
know on which day your Lord will come. Be sure of this: if the
master of the house had known the hour of night when the thief
was coming, he would have stayed awake and not let his house
be broken into. So too, you also must be prepared, for at an hour
you do not expect, the Son of Man will come."

Communion Antiphon Ps 85 (84): 13 **The Lord will bestow his
bounty, ◆ and our earth shall yield its increase.**

SECOND SUNDAY OF ADVENT

Entrance Antiphon cf. Is 30: 19, 30 **O people of Sion, behold, ◆ the
Lord will come to save the nations, ◆ and the Lord will make
the glory of his voice heard ◆ in the joy of your heart.**

First Reading   *Is 11: 1–10*

On that day, a shoot shall sprout from the stump of Jesse,
  and from his roots a bud shall blossom.
The spirit of the LORD shall rest upon him:
  a spirit of wisdom and of understanding,
a spirit of counsel and of strength,
  a spirit of knowledge and of fear of the LORD,
  and his delight shall be the fear of the LORD.
Not by appearance shall he judge,
  nor by hearsay shall he decide,
but he shall judge the poor with justice,
  and decide aright for the land's afflicted.
He shall strike the ruthless with the rod of his mouth,
  and with the breath of his lips he shall slay the wicked.
Justice shall be the band around his waist,
  and faithfulness a belt upon his hips.
Then the wolf shall be a guest of the lamb,
  and the leopard shall lie down with the kid;
the calf and the young lion shall browse together,
  with a little child to guide them.
The cow and the bear shall be neighbors,
  together their young shall rest;
  the lion shall eat hay like the ox.
The baby shall play by the cobra's den,
  and the child lay his hand on the adder's lair.
There shall be no harm or ruin on all my holy mountain;
  for the earth shall be filled with knowledge of the LORD,
  as water covers the sea.
On that day, the root of Jesse,
  set up as a signal for the nations,
the Gentiles shall seek out,
  for his dwelling shall be glorious.

Responsorial Psalm   *Ps 72: 1–2, 7–8, 12–13, 17*   *Bill Svarda*

Jus - tice   shall   flour - ish   in   his   time,

and full-ness of peace for ev-er.

O God, with your judgment endow the king,
   and with your justice, the king's son;
he shall govern your people with justice
   and your afflicted ones with judgment. ℟

Justice shall flower in his days,
   and profound peace, till the moon be no more.
May he rule from sea to sea,
   and from the River to the ends of the earth. ℟

For he shall rescue the poor when he cries out,
   and the afflicted when he has no one to help him.
He shall have pity for the lowly and the poor;
   the lives of the poor he shall save. ℟

May his name be blessed forever;
   as long as the sun his name shall remain.
In him shall all the tribes of the earth be blessed;
   all the nations shall proclaim his happiness. ℟

Second Reading *Rom 15: 4–9* Brothers and sisters: Whatever was written previously was written for our instruction, that by endurance and by the encouragement of the Scriptures we might have hope. May the God of endurance and encouragement grant you to think in harmony with one another, in keeping with Christ Jesus, that with one accord you may with one voice glorify the God and Father of our Lord Jesus Christ.
   Welcome one another, then, as Christ welcomed you, for the glory of God. For I say that Christ became a minister of the circumcised to show God's truthfulness, to confirm the promises to the patriarchs, but so that the Gentiles might glorify God for his mercy. As it is written:
Therefore, I will praise you among the Gentiles
   and sing praises to your name.

Alleluia Lk 3: 4, 6

Joe Higginbotham

Al - le - lu - ia,   al - le - lu - ia,   al - le - lu - ia.

Al - le - lu - ia,   al - le - lu - ia,   al - le - lu - ia.

Prepare the way of the Lord, make straight his paths: / all flesh shall see the salvation of God. **Alleluia, alleluia.**

Gospel Mt 3: 1–12 John the Baptist appeared, preaching in the desert of Judea and saying, "Repent, for the kingdom of heaven is at hand!" It was of him that the prophet Isaiah had spoken when he said:

A voice of one crying out in the desert,
Prepare the way of the Lord,
*   make straight his paths.*

John wore clothing made of camel's hair and had a leather belt around his waist. His food was locusts and wild honey. At that time Jerusalem, all Judea, and the whole region around the Jordan were going out to him and were being baptized by him in the Jordan River as they acknowledged their sins.

When he saw many of the Pharisees and Sadducees coming to his baptism, he said to them, "You brood of vipers! Who warned you to flee from the coming wrath? Produce good fruit as evidence of your repentance. And do not presume to say to yourselves, 'We have Abraham as our father.' For I tell you, God can raise up children to Abraham from these stones. Even now the ax lies at the root of the trees. Therefore every tree that does not bear good fruit will be cut down and thrown into the fire. I am baptizing you with water, for repentance, but the one who is coming after me is mightier than I. I am not worthy to carry his sandals. He will baptize you with the Holy Spirit and fire. His winnowing fan is in his hand. He will clear his threshing floor and gather his wheat into his barn, but the chaff he will burn with unquenchable fire."

Communion Antiphon *Bar 5: 5; 4: 36* Jerusalem, arise and stand upon the heights, ◆ and behold the joy which comes to you from God.

THIRD SUNDAY OF ADVENT

Entrance Antiphon *Phil 4: 4–5* Rejoice in the Lord always; again I say, rejoice. ◆ Indeed, the Lord is near.

First Reading *Is 35: 1–6a, 10*

The desert and the parched land will exult;
    the steppe will rejoice and bloom.
They will bloom with abundant flowers,
    and rejoice with joyful song.
The glory of Lebanon will be given to them,
    the splendor of Carmel and Sharon;
they will see the glory of the LORD,
    the splendor of our God.
Strengthen the hands that are feeble,
    make firm the knees that are weak,
say to those whose hearts are frightened:
    Be strong, fear not!
Here is your God,
    he comes with vindication;
with divine recompense
    he comes to save you.
Then will the eyes of the blind be opened,
    the ears of the deaf be cleared;
then will the lame leap like a stag,
    then the tongue of the mute will sing.

Those whom the LORD has ransomed will return
    and enter Zion singing,
    crowned with everlasting joy;
they will meet with joy and gladness,
    sorrow and mourning will flee.

Responsorial Psalm   Ps 146: 6–7, 8–9, 9–10   *Bill Svarda*

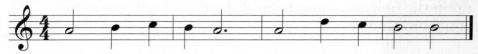

Lord, come and save us.   Lord, come and save us.

Or: ℟ **Alleluia.**

The LORD God keeps faith forever,
     secures justice for the oppressed,
     gives food to the hungry.
The LORD sets captives free. ℟

The LORD gives sight to the blind;
     the LORD raises up those who were bowed down.
The LORD loves the just;
     the LORD protects strangers. ℟

The fatherless and the widow he sustains,
     but the way of the wicked he thwarts.
The LORD shall reign forever;
     your God, O Zion, through all generations. ℟

Second Reading Jas 5: 7–10 Be patient, brothers and sisters, until
the coming of the Lord. See how the farmer waits for the
precious fruit of the earth, being patient with it until it receives
the early and the late rains. You too must be patient. Make your
hearts firm, because the coming of the Lord is at hand. Do not
complain, brothers and sisters, about one another, that you
may not be judged. Behold, the Judge is standing before the
gates. Take as an example of hardship and patience, brothers and
sisters, the prophets who spoke in the name of the Lord.

Alleluia   Is 61: 1 (cited in Lk 4: 18)   *Joe Higginbotham*

Al - le - lu - ia, al - le - lu - ia,   al - le - lu - ia.

Al - le - lu - ia, al - le - lu - ia, al - le - lu - ia.

The Spirit of the Lord is upon me, / because he has anointed me to bring glad tidings to the poor. **Alleluia, alleluia.**

Gospel Mt 11: 2–11 When John the Baptist heard in prison of the works of the Christ, he sent his disciples to Jesus with this question, "Are you the one who is to come, or should we look for another?" Jesus said to them in reply, "Go and tell John what you hear and see: the blind regain their sight, the lame walk, lepers are cleansed, the deaf hear, the dead are raised, and the poor have the good news proclaimed to them. And blessed is the one who takes no offense at me."

As they were going off, Jesus began to speak to the crowds about John, "What did you go out to the desert to see? A reed swayed by the wind? Then what did you go out to see? Someone dressed in fine clothing? Those who wear fine clothing are in royal palaces. Then why did you go out? To see a prophet? Yes, I tell you, and more than a prophet. This is the one about whom it is written:

Behold, I am sending my messenger ahead of you;
he will prepare your way before you.

Amen, I say to you, among those born of women there has been none greater than John the Baptist; yet the least in the kingdom of heaven is greater than he."

Communion Antiphon cf. Is 35: 4 **Say to the faint of heart: Be strong and do not fear. ◆ Behold, our God will come, and he will save us.**

FOURTH SUNDAY OF ADVENT

Entrance Antiphon *cf. Is 45: 8* **Drop down dew from above, you heavens, ◆ and let the clouds rain down the Just One; ◆ let the earth be opened and bring forth a Savior.**

First Reading *Is 7: 10–14* The LORD spoke to Ahaz, saying: Ask for a sign from the LORD, your God; let it be deep as the netherworld, or high as the sky! But Ahaz answered, "I will not ask! I will not tempt the LORD!" Then Isaiah said: Listen, O house of David! Is it not enough for you to weary people, must you also weary my God? Therefore the Lord himself will give you this sign: the virgin shall conceive, and bear a son, and shall name him Emmanuel.

Responsorial Psalm   *Ps 24: 1–2, 3–4, 5–6*   Joe Higginbotham

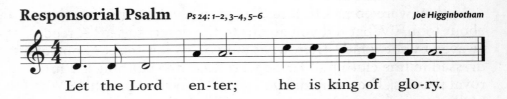

Let the Lord en-ter; he is king of glo-ry.

The LORD's are the earth and its fullness;
 the world and those who dwell in it.
For he founded it upon the seas
 and established it upon the rivers. ℟

Who can ascend the mountain of the LORD?
 or who may stand in his holy place?
One whose hands are sinless, whose heart is clean,
 who desires not what is vain. ℟

He shall receive a blessing from the LORD,
 a reward from God his savior.
Such is the race that seeks for him,
 that seeks the face of the God of Jacob. ℟

Second Reading *Rom 1: 1–7* Paul, a slave of Christ Jesus, called to be an apostle and set apart for the gospel of God, which he promised previously through his prophets in the holy Scriptures, the gospel about his Son, descended from David according to the flesh, but established as Son of God in power according to the Spirit of holiness through resurrection from the dead, Jesus Christ our Lord. Through him we have received the grace of apostleship, to bring about the obedience of faith, for the sake of his name, among all the Gentiles, among whom are you also, who are called to belong to Jesus Christ; to all the beloved of God in Rome, called to be holy. Grace to you and peace from God our Father and the Lord Jesus Christ.

Alleluia   Mt 1: 23   Joe Higginbotham

Al-le-lu-ia, al-le-lu-ia, al-le-lu - ia.

Al-le-lu-ia, al-le-lu-ia, al-le-lu - ia.

The virgin shall conceive, and bear a son, / and they shall name him Emmanuel.   **Alleluia, alleluia.**

Gospel Mt 1: 18-24 This is how the birth of Jesus Christ came about. When his mother Mary was betrothed to Joseph, but before they lived together, she was found with child through the Holy Spirit. Joseph her husband, since he was a righteous man, yet unwilling to expose her to shame, decided to divorce her quietly. Such was his intention when, behold, the angel of the Lord appeared to him in a dream and said, "Joseph, son of David, do not be afraid to take Mary your wife into your home. For it is through the Holy Spirit that this child has been conceived in her. She will bear a son and you are to name him Jesus, because he will save his people from their sins." All this took place to fulfill what the Lord had said through the prophet:
Behold, the virgin shall conceive and bear a son,
    and they shall name him Emmanuel,
which means "God is with us." When Joseph awoke, he did as

the angel of the Lord had commanded him and took his wife into his home.

Communion Antiphon *Is 7:14* **Behold, a Virgin shall conceive and bear a son; ◆ and his name will be called Emmanuel.**

Christmas Time   †   YEAR A

THE NATIVITY OF THE LORD

❖ At the Vigil Mass ❖

Entrance Antiphon   *cf. Ex 16: 6–7* **Today you will know that the Lord will come, and he will save us, ◆ and in the morning you will see his glory.**

First Reading   *Is 62: 1–5*

For Zion's sake I will not be silent,
    for Jerusalem's sake I will not be quiet,
until her vindication shines forth like the dawn
    and her victory like a burning torch.

Nations shall behold your vindication,
    and all the kings your glory;
you shall be called by a new name
    pronounced by the mouth of the LORD.
You shall be a glorious crown in the hand of the LORD,
    a royal diadem held by your God.
No more shall people call you "Forsaken,"
    or your land "Desolate,"
but you shall be called "My Delight,"
    and your land "Espoused."
For the LORD delights in you
    and makes your land his spouse.
As a young man marries a virgin,
    your Builder shall marry you;

and as a bridegroom rejoices in his bride
  so shall your God rejoice in you.

Responsorial Psalm   Ps 89: 4–5, 16–17, 27, 29   *Joe Higginbotham*

For ev-er I will sing the good-ness of the Lord.

I have made a covenant with my chosen one,
  I have sworn to David my servant:
Forever will I confirm your posterity
  and establish your throne for all generations. ℟

Blessed the people who know the joyful shout;
  in the light of your countenance, O LORD, they walk.
At your name they rejoice all the day,
  and through your justice they are exalted. ℟

He shall say of me, "You are my father,
  my God, the rock, my savior."
Forever I will maintain my kindness toward him,
  and my covenant with him stands firm. ℟

Second Reading Acts 13: 16–17, 22–25 When Paul reached Antioch in
Pisidia and entered the synagogue, he stood up, motioned with
his hand, and said, "Fellow Israelites and you others who
are God-fearing, listen. The God of this people Israel chose
our ancestors and exalted the people during their sojourn in
the land of Egypt. With uplifted arm he led them out of it.
Then he removed Saul and raised up David as king; of him
he testified, 'I have found David, son of Jesse, a man after my
own heart; he will carry out my every wish.' From this man's
descendants God, according to his promise, has brought to
Israel a savior, Jesus. John heralded his coming by proclaiming
a baptism of repentance to all the people of Israel; and as John
was completing his course, he would say, 'What do you suppose
that I am? I am not he. Behold, one is coming after me; I am
not worthy to unfasten the sandals of his feet.'"

Alleluia

Jim Hughes

Al-le-lu-ia   Al-le-lu-ia   Al - le-lu - ia.

Tomorrow the wickedness of the earth will be destroyed: /
the Savior of the world will reign over us. **Alleluia, alleluia.**

Gospel Mt 1: 1–25 or 1: 18–25 The book of the genealogy of Jesus Christ,
the son of David, the son of Abraham.

Abraham became the father of Isaac, Isaac the father of Jacob,
Jacob the father of Judah and his brothers. Judah became the
father of Perez and Zerah, whose mother was Tamar. Perez
became the father of Hezron, Hezron the father of Ram, Ram
the father of Amminadab. Amminadab became the father of
Nahshon, Nahshon the father of Salmon, Salmon the father of
Boaz, whose mother was Rahab. Boaz became the father of Obed,
whose mother was Ruth. Obed became the father of Jesse, Jesse
the father of David the king.

David became the father of Solomon, whose mother had been
the wife of Uriah. Solomon became the father of Rehoboam,
Rehoboam the father of Abijah, Abijah the father of Asaph.
Asaph became the father of Jehoshaphat, Jehoshaphat the father
of Joram, Joram the father of Uzziah. Uzziah became the father
of Jotham, Jotham the father of Ahaz, Ahaz the father of
Hezekiah. Hezekiah became the father of Manasseh, Manasseh
the father of Amos, Amos the father of Josiah. Josiah became
the father of Jechoniah and his brothers at the time of the
Babylonian exile.

After the Babylonian exile, Jechoniah became the father of
Shealtiel, Shealtiel the father of Zerubbabel, Zerubbabel the
father of Abiud. Abiud became the father of Eliakim, Eliakim
the father of Azor, Azor the father of Zadok. Zadok became the
father of Achim, Achim the father of Eliud, Eliud the father of
Eleazar. Eleazar became the father of Matthan, Matthan the
father of Jacob, Jacob the father of Joseph, the husband of Mary.
Of her was born Jesus who is called the Christ.

Thus the total number of generations from Abraham to David

is fourteen generations; from David to the Babylonian exile, fourteen generations; from the Babylonian exile to the Christ, fourteen generations.

Now [this is how the birth of Jesus Christ came about. When his mother Mary was betrothed to Joseph, but before they lived together, she was found with child through the Holy Spirit. Joseph her husband, since he was a righteous man, yet unwilling to expose her to shame, decided to divorce her quietly. Such was his intention when, behold, the angel of the Lord appeared to him in a dream and said, "Joseph, son of David, do not be afraid to take Mary your wife into your home. For it is through the Holy Spirit that this child has been conceived in her. She will bear a son and you are to name him Jesus, because he will save his people from their sins." All this took place to fulfill what the Lord had said through the prophet:

Behold, the virgin shall conceive and bear a son,
  and they shall name him Emmanuel,
which means "God is with us." When Joseph awoke, he did as the angel of the Lord had commanded him and took his wife into his home. He had no relations with her until she bore a son, and he named him Jesus.]

During the Creed, all kneel at the words and by the Holy Spirit was incarnate.

Communion Antiphon *cf. Is 40: 5* The glory of the Lord will be revealed, ◆ and all flesh will see the salvation of our God.

◈   At the Mass During the Night   ◈

Entrance Antiphon *Ps 2: 7* The Lord said to me: You are my Son. ◆ It is I who have begotten you this day.

Or:
Let us all rejoice in the Lord for our Savior has been born in the world. ◆ Today true peace has come down to us from heaven.

First Reading   *Is 9: 1–6*

The people who walked in darkness
    have seen a great light;
upon those who dwelt in the land of gloom
    a light has shone.
 You have brought them abundant joy
    and great rejoicing,
as they rejoice before you as at the harvest,
    as people make merry when dividing spoils.
For the yoke that burdened them,
    the pole on their shoulder,
and the rod of their taskmaster
    you have smashed, as on the day of Midian.
For every boot that tramped in battle,
    every cloak rolled in blood,
    will be burned as fuel for flames.
For a child is born to us, a son is given us;
    upon his shoulder dominion rests.
They name him Wonder-Counselor, God-Hero,
    Father-Forever, Prince of Peace.
His dominion is vast
    and forever peaceful,
from David's throne, and over his kingdom,
    which he confirms and sustains
by judgment and justice,
    both now and forever.
The zeal of the LORD of hosts will do this!

Responsorial Psalm   *Ps 96: 1–2, 2–3, 11–12, 13*   *Joe Higginbotham*

To - day is born our Sav - ior,

our Sav - ior, Christ the Lord.

Sing to the LORD a new song;

sing to the LORD, all you lands.
Sing to the LORD; bless his name.   ℟

Announce his salvation, day after day.
    Tell his glory among the nations;
    among all peoples, his wondrous deeds.   ℟

Let the heavens be glad and the earth rejoice;
    let the sea and what fills it resound;
    let the plains be joyful and all that is in them!
Then shall all the trees of the forest exult.   ℟

They shall exult before the LORD, for he comes;
    for he comes to rule the earth.
He shall rule the world with justice
    and the peoples with his constancy.   ℟

Second Reading   *Ti 2: 11–14*   Beloved: The grace of God has appeared,
saving all and training us to reject godless ways and worldly
desires and to live temperately, justly, and devoutly in this age,
as we await the blessed hope, the appearance of the glory of
our great God and savior Jesus Christ, who gave himself for us
to deliver us from all lawlessness and to cleanse for himself a
people as his own, eager to do what is good.

Alleluia   *Lk 2: 10–11*   *Jim Hughes*

Al-le-lu-ia   Al-le-lu-ia   Al - le-lu - ia.

I proclaim to you good news of great joy: / today a Savior is
born for us, / Christ the Lord.   **Alleluia, alleluia.**

Gospel   *Lk 2: 1–14*   In those days a decree went out from Caesar
Augustus that the whole world should be enrolled. This was the
first enrollment, when Quirinius was governor of Syria. So all
went to be enrolled, each to his own town. And Joseph too went
up from Galilee from the town of Nazareth to Judea, to the city

of David that is called Bethlehem, because he was of the house
and family of David, to be enrolled with Mary, his betrothed,
who was with child. While they were there, the time came for
her to have her child, and she gave birth to her firstborn son.
She wrapped him in swaddling clothes and laid him in a manger,
because there was no room for them in the inn.

Now there were shepherds in that region living in the fields
and keeping the night watch over their flock. The angel of the
Lord appeared to them and the glory of the Lord shone around
them, and they were struck with great fear. The angel said to
them, "Do not be afraid; for behold, I proclaim to you good news
of great joy that will be for all the people. For today in the city
of David a savior has been born for you who is Christ and Lord.
And this will be a sign for you: you will find an infant wrapped
in swaddling clothes and lying in a manger." And suddenly there
was a multitude of the heavenly host with the angel, praising
God and saying:
  "Glory to God in the highest
    and on earth peace to those on whom his favor rests."

During the Creed, all kneel at the words and by the Holy Spirit
was incarnate.

Communion Antiphon Jn 1:14 **The Word became flesh, and we
have seen his glory.**

❖ At the Mass at Dawn ❖

Entrance Antiphon cf. Is 9:1, 5; Lk 1:33 **Today a light will shine
upon us, for the Lord is born for us; ◆ and he will be
called Wondrous God, ◆ Prince of peace, Father of future ages:
◆ and his reign will be without end.**

First Reading Is 62:11–12
  See, the LORD proclaims
    to the ends of the earth:
  say to daughter Zion,
    your savior comes!

Here is his reward with him,
   his recompense before him.
They shall be called the holy people,
   the redeemed of the LORD,
and you shall be called "Frequented,"
   a city that is not forsaken.

Responsorial Psalm   Ps 97: 1, 6, 11–12   *Bill Svarda*

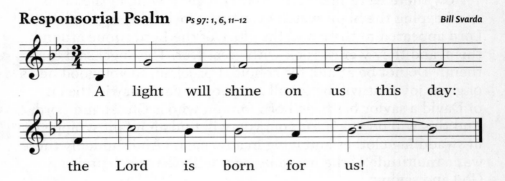

A light will shine on us this day:
the Lord is born for us!

The LORD is king; let the earth rejoice;
   let the many isles be glad.
The heavens proclaim his justice,
   and all peoples see his glory. ℟

Light dawns for the just;
   and gladness, for the upright of heart.
Be glad in the LORD, you just,
   and give thanks to his holy name. ℟

Second Reading   Ti 3: 4–7
Beloved:
   When the kindness and generous love
      of God our savior appeared,
   not because of any righteous deeds we had done
      but because of his mercy,
   he saved us through the bath of rebirth
      and renewal by the Holy Spirit,
   whom he richly poured out on us
      through Jesus Christ our savior,

so that we might be justified by his grace
and become heirs in hope of eternal life.

Alleluia Lk 2: 14   *Jim Hughes*

Al-le-lu-ia   Al-le-lu-ia   Al - le-lu - ia.

Glory to God in the highest, / and on earth peace to those /
on whom his favor rests.   **Alleluia, alleluia.**

Gospel Lk 2: 15–20 When the angels went away from them to
heaven, the shepherds said to one another, "Let us go, then, to
Bethlehem to see this thing that has taken place, which the
Lord has made known to us." So they went in haste and found
Mary and Joseph, and the infant lying in the manger. When
they saw this, they made known the message that had been told
them about this child. All who heard it were amazed by what
had been told them by the shepherds. And Mary kept all these
things, reflecting on them in her heart. Then the shepherds
returned, glorifying and praising God for all they had heard and
seen, just as it had been told to them.

During the Creed, all kneel at the words and by the Holy Spirit
was incarnate.

Communion Antiphon cf. Zec 9: 9 Rejoice, O Daughter Sion; lift
up praise, Daughter Jerusalem: ◆ Behold, your King will come,
the Holy One and Savior of the world.

❖   At the Mass During the Day   ❖

Entrance Antiphon cf. Is 9: 5 A child is born for us, and a son is
given to us; ◆ his scepter of power rests upon his shoulder, ◆
and his name will be called Messenger of great counsel.

First Reading Is 52: 7–10

How beautiful upon the mountains
    are the feet of him who brings glad tidings,
announcing peace, bearing good news,
    announcing salvation, and saying to Zion,
    "Your God is King!"

Hark! Your sentinels raise a cry,
    together they shout for joy,
for they see directly, before their eyes,
    the LORD restoring Zion.
Break out together in song,
    O ruins of Jerusalem!
For the LORD comforts his people,
    he redeems Jerusalem.
The LORD has bared his holy arm
    in the sight of all the nations;
all the ends of the earth will behold
    the salvation of our God.

Responsorial Psalm Ps 98: 1, 2–3, 3–4, 5–6   **Don Fishel**

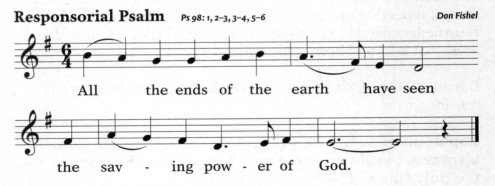

All the ends of the earth have seen the sav - ing pow - er of God.

Sing to the LORD a new song,
    for he has done wondrous deeds;
his right hand has won victory for him,
    his holy arm. ℟

The LORD has made his salvation known:
    in the sight of the nations he has revealed his justice.
He has remembered his kindness and his faithfulness
    toward the house of Israel. ℟

All the ends of the earth have seen
  the salvation by our God.
Sing joyfully to the LORD, all you lands;
  break into song; sing praise. ℟

Sing praise to the LORD with the harp,
  with the harp and melodious song.
With trumpets and the sound of the horn
  sing joyfully before the King, the LORD. ℟

Second Reading *Heb 1:1–6* Brothers and sisters: In times past, God spoke in partial and various ways to our ancestors through the prophets; in these last days, he has spoken to us through the Son, whom he made heir of all things and through whom he created the universe,
  who is the refulgence of his glory, the very imprint of his
    being,
  and who sustains all things by his mighty word.
  When he had accomplished purification from sins,
  he took his seat at the right hand of the Majesty on high,
  as far superior to the angels
  as the name he has inherited is more excellent than theirs.

For to which of the angels did God ever say:
You are my son; this day I have begotten you?
Or again:
I will be a father to him, and he shall be a son to me?
And again, when he leads the firstborn into the world, he says:
Let all the angels of God worship him.

Alleluia *Jim Hughes*

Al-le-lu-ia   Al-le-lu-ia   Al - le-lu - ia.

A holy day has dawned upon us. / Come, you nations, and adore the Lord. / For today a great light has come upon the earth. **Alleluia, alleluia.**

Gospel   Jn 1: 1–18 or 1: 1–5, 9–14

For the shorter form, read only the parts in brackets.

[In the beginning was the Word,
and the Word was with God,
and the Word was God.
He was in the beginning with God.
All things came to be through him,
and without him nothing came to be.
What came to be through him was life,
and this life was the light of the human race;
the light shines in the darkness,
and the darkness has not overcome it.]
A man named John was sent from God. He came for testimony,
to testify to the light, so that all might believe through him. He
was not the light, but came to testify to the light. [The true light,
which enlightens everyone, was coming into the world.
He was in the world,
and the world came to be through him,
but the world did not know him.
He came to what was his own,
but his own people did not accept him.
But to those who did accept him he gave power to become
children of God, to those who believe in his name, who were
born not by natural generation nor by human choice nor by a
man's decision but of God.
And the Word became flesh
and made his dwelling among us,
and we saw his glory,
the glory as of the Father's only Son,
full of grace and truth.]
John testified to him and cried out, saying, "This was he of
whom I said, 'The one who is coming after me ranks ahead of
me because he existed before me.'" From his fullness we have
all received, grace in place of grace, because while the law was
given through Moses, grace and truth came through Jesus Christ.
No one has ever seen God. The only Son, God, who is at the
Father's side, has revealed him.

During the Creed, all kneel at the words and by the Holy Spirit was incarnate.

Communion Antiphon *cf. Ps 98 (97): 3* **All the ends of the earth have seen the salvation of our God.**

THE HOLY FAMILY

OF JESUS, MARY, AND JOSEPH

When a Sunday does not occur between December 25 and January 1, this feast is celebrated on December 30 with only one reading before the Gospel.

Entrance Antiphon *Lk 2: 16* **The shepherds went in haste, ◆ and found Mary and Joseph and the Infant lying in a manger.**

First Reading   *Sir 3: 2–6, 12–14*
God sets a father in honor over his children;
    a mother's authority he confirms over her sons.
Whoever honors his father atones for sins,
    and preserves himself from them.
When he prays, he is heard;
    he stores up riches who reveres his mother.
Whoever honors his father is gladdened by children,
    and, when he prays, is heard.
Whoever reveres his father will live a long life;
    he who obeys his father brings comfort to his mother.

My son, take care of your father when he is old;
    grieve him not as long as he lives.
Even if his mind fail, be considerate of him;
    revile him not all the days of his life;
kindness to a father will not be forgotten,
    firmly planted against the debt of your sins
    —a house raised in justice to you.

Responsorial Psalm   Ps 128: 1–2, 3, 4–5   *Beverly McDevitt*

Bless - ed   are   those   who fear the   Lord   and   walk   in   his   ways.

Blessed is everyone who fears the LORD,
> who walks in his ways!
For you shall eat the fruit of your handiwork;
> blessed shall you be, and favored.   ℟

Your wife shall be like a fruitful vine
> in the recesses of your home;
your children like olive plants
> around your table.   ℟

Behold, thus is the man blessed
> who fears the LORD.
The LORD bless you from Zion:
> may you see the prosperity of Jerusalem
> all the days of your life.   ℟

Second Reading   Col 3: 12–21 or 3: 12–17
For the shorter form, read only the parts in brackets.
[Brothers and sisters: Put on, as God's chosen ones, holy and
beloved, heartfelt compassion, kindness, humility, gentleness,
and patience, bearing with one another and forgiving one
another, if one has a grievance against another; as the Lord
has forgiven you, so must you also do. And over all these put
on love, that is, the bond of perfection. And let the peace of
Christ control your hearts, the peace into which you were also
called in one body. And be thankful. Let the word of Christ
dwell in you richly, as in all wisdom you teach and admonish
one another, singing psalms, hymns, and spiritual songs with
gratitude in your hearts to God. And whatever you do, in word

or in deed, do everything in the name of the Lord Jesus, giving thanks to God the Father through him.]

Wives, be subordinate to your husbands, as is proper in the Lord. Husbands, love your wives, and avoid any bitterness toward them. Children, obey your parents in everything, for this is pleasing to the Lord. Fathers, do not provoke your children, so they may not become discouraged.

Alleluia   *Col 3: 15a, 16a*   *Joe Higginbotham*

Al - le - lu - ia,   al - le - lu - ia,   al - le - lu - ia.

Al - le - lu - ia,   al - le - lu - ia,   al - le - lu - ia.

Let the peace of Christ control your hearts; / let the word of Christ dwell in you richly. **Alleluia, alleluia.**

Gospel *Mt 2: 13–15, 19–23* When the magi had departed, behold, the angel of the Lord appeared to Joseph in a dream and said, "Rise, take the child and his mother, flee to Egypt, and stay there until I tell you. Herod is going to search for the child to destroy him." Joseph rose and took the child and his mother by night and departed for Egypt. He stayed there until the death of Herod, that what the Lord had said through the prophet might be fulfilled, *Out of Egypt I called my son.*

When Herod had died, behold, the angel of the Lord appeared in a dream to Joseph in Egypt and said, "Rise, take the child and his mother and go to the land of Israel, for those who sought the child's life are dead." He rose, took the child and his mother, and went to the land of Israel. But when he heard that Archelaus was ruling over Judea in place of his father Herod, he was afraid to go back there. And because he had been warned in a dream, he departed for the region of Galilee. He went and dwelt in a town called Nazareth, so that what had been spoken through the prophets might be fulfilled, *He shall be called a Nazorean.*

Communion Antiphon *Bar 3: 38* Our God has appeared on the earth, and lived among us.

SOLEMNITY OF MARY,
THE HOLY MOTHER OF GOD

THE OCTAVE DAY OF THE NATIVITY

Entrance Antiphon   Hail, Holy Mother, who gave birth to the King ✦ who rules heaven and earth for ever.

Or: *cf. Is 9: 1, 5; Lk 1: 33* Today a light will shine upon us, for the Lord is born for us; ✦ and he will be called Wondrous God, ✦ Prince of peace, Father of future ages: ✦ and his reign will be without end.

First Reading *Nm 6: 22–27* The LORD said to Moses: "Speak to Aaron and his sons and tell them: 'This is how you shall bless the Israelites. Say to them:
 The LORD bless you and keep you!
 The LORD let his face shine upon you, and be gracious to you!
 The LORD look upon you kindly and give you peace!'
So shall they invoke my name upon the Israelites, and I will bless them."

Responsorial Psalm   *Ps 67: 2–3, 5, 6, 8*   *Bill Svarda*

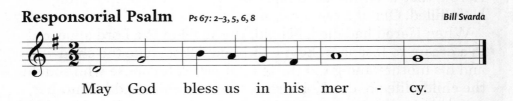

May God bless us in his mer - cy.

May God have pity on us and bless us;
   may he let his face shine upon us.
So may your way be known upon earth;
   among all nations, your salvation. ℟

May the nations be glad and exult
  because you rule the peoples in equity;
  the nations on the earth you guide. ℟

May the peoples praise you, O God;
  may all the peoples praise you!
May God bless us,
  and may all the ends of the earth fear him! ℟

Second Reading *Gal 4: 4–7* Brothers and sisters: When the fullness
of time had come, God sent his Son, born of a woman, born
under the law, to ransom those under the law, so that we might
receive adoption as sons. As proof that you are sons, God sent
the Spirit of his Son into our hearts, crying out, "Abba, Father!"
So you are no longer a slave but a son, and if a son then also an
heir, through God.

Alleluia *Heb 1: 1–2*   Brian J. Nelson

Al - le-lu - ia, al - le - lu - ia, al-le-lu - ia.

In the past God spoke to our ancestors through the
prophets; / in these last days, he has spoken to us through
the Son. **Alleluia, alleluia.**

Gospel *Lk 2: 16–21* The shepherds went in haste to Bethlehem and
found Mary and Joseph, and the infant lying in the manger.
When they saw this, they made known the message that had
been told them about this child. All who heard it were amazed
by what had been told them by the shepherds. And Mary kept
all these things, reflecting on them in her heart. Then the
shepherds returned, glorifying and praising God for all they had
heard and seen, just as it had been told to them.

When eight days were completed for his circumcision, he was
named Jesus, the name given him by the angel before he was
conceived in the womb.

Communion Antiphon   *Heb 13: 8* Jesus Christ is the same yesterday, today, and for ever.

THE EPIPHANY OF THE LORD

Where the Solemnity of the Epiphany is not to be observed as a Holy day of Obligation, it is assigned to the Sunday occurring between 2 and 8 January as its proper day.

Entrance Antiphon

At the Vigil Mass: *cf. Bar 5: 5* Arise, Jerusalem, and look to the East ✦ and see your children gathered from the rising to the setting of the sun.

At the Mass During the Day: *cf. Mal 3: 1; 1 Chr 29: 12* Behold, the Lord, the Mighty One, has come; ✦ and kingship is in his grasp, and power and dominion.

First Reading   *Is 60: 1–6*
Rise up in splendor, Jerusalem! Your light has come,
    the glory of the Lord shines upon you.
See, darkness covers the earth,
    and thick clouds cover the peoples;
but upon you the LORD shines,
    and over you appears his glory.
Nations shall walk by your light,
    and kings by your shining radiance.
Raise your eyes and look about;
    they all gather and come to you:
your sons come from afar,
    and your daughters in the arms of their nurses.

Then you shall be radiant at what you see,
    your heart shall throb and overflow,
for the riches of the sea shall be emptied out before you,
    the wealth of nations shall be brought to you.

Caravans of camels shall fill you,
  dromedaries from Midian and Ephah;
all from Sheba shall come
  bearing gold and frankincense,
and proclaiming the praises of the LORD.

Responsorial Psalm   Ps 72: 1–2, 7–8, 10–11, 12–13   Brian J. Nelson

Lord, ev - ery na - tion on earth will a - dore you.

O God, with your judgment endow the king,
  and with your justice, the king's son;
He shall govern your people with justice
  and your afflicted ones with judgment. ℟

Justice shall flower in his days,
  and profound peace, till the moon be no more.
May he rule from sea to sea,
  and from the River to the ends of the earth. ℟

The kings of Tarshish and the Isles shall offer gifts;
  the kings of Arabia and Seba shall bring tribute.
All kings shall pay him homage,
  all nations shall serve him. ℟

For he shall rescue the poor when he cries out,
  and the afflicted when he has no one to help him.
He shall have pity for the lowly and the poor;
  the lives of the poor he shall save. ℟

Second Reading Eph 3: 2–3a, 5–6 Brothers and sisters: You have
heard of the stewardship of God's grace that was given to me
for your benefit, namely, that the mystery was made known to

me by revelation. It was not made known to people in other generations as it has now been revealed to his holy apostles and prophets by the Spirit: that the Gentiles are coheirs, members of the same body, and copartners in the promise in Christ Jesus through the gospel.

Alleluia   Mt 2: 2   Joe Higginbotham

Al - le - lu - ia,   al - le - lu - ia,   al - le - lu - ia.

Al - le - lu - ia,   al - le - lu - ia,   al - le - lu - ia.

We saw his star at its rising / and have come to do him homage.   **Alleluia, alleluia.**

Gospel Mt 2: 1–12 When Jesus was born in Bethlehem of Judea, in the days of King Herod, behold, magi from the east arrived in Jerusalem, saying, "Where is the newborn king of the Jews? We saw his star at its rising and have come to do him homage." When King Herod heard this, he was greatly troubled, and all Jerusalem with him. Assembling all the chief priests and the scribes of the people, he inquired of them where the Christ was to be born. They said to him, "In Bethlehem of Judea, for thus it has been written through the prophet:

And you, Bethlehem, land of Judah,
are by no means least among the rulers of Judah;
since from you shall come a ruler,
who is to shepherd my people Israel."

Then Herod called the magi secretly and ascertained from them the time of the star's appearance. He sent them to Bethlehem and said, "Go and search diligently for the child. When you have found him, bring me word, that I too may go and do him homage." After their audience with the king they set out. And behold, the star that they had seen at its rising preceded them, until it came and stopped over the place where the child was.

They were overjoyed at seeing the star, and on entering the house they saw the child with Mary his mother. They prostrated themselves and did him homage. Then they opened their treasures and offered him gifts of gold, frankincense, and myrrh. And having been warned in a dream not to return to Herod, they departed for their country by another way.

Communion Antiphon

At the Vigil Mass: cf. Rv 21: 23 **The brightness of God illumined the holy city Jerusalem, ♦ and the nations will walk by its light.**

At the Mass During the Day: cf. Mt 2: 2 **We have seen his star in the East, ♦ and have come with gifts to adore the Lord.**

THE BAPTISM OF THE LORD

SUNDAY AFTER JANUARY 6 | FIRST SUNDAY IN ORDINARY TIME

In dioceses where the Epiphany is transferred to a Sunday that falls on January 7 or 8, the Baptism of the Lord is transferred to the Monday immediately following. Only one reading before the Gospel is used.

Entrance Antiphon cf. Mt 3: 16–17 **After the Lord was baptized, the heavens were opened, ♦ and the Spirit descended upon him like a dove, ♦ and the voice of the Father thundered: ♦ This is my beloved Son, with whom I am well pleased.**

First Reading Is 42: 1–4, 6–7
Thus says the LORD:
Here is my servant whom I uphold,
    my chosen one with whom I am pleased,
upon whom I have put my spirit;
    he shall bring forth justice to the nations,
not crying out, not shouting,
    not making his voice heard in the street.

a bruised reed he shall not break,
  and a smoldering wick he shall not quench,
until he establishes justice on the earth;
  the coastlands will wait for his teaching.

I, the LORD, have called you for the victory of justice,
  I have grasped you by the hand;
I formed you, and set you
  as a covenant of the people,
  a light for the nations,
to open the eyes of the blind,
  to bring out prisoners from confinement,
  and from the dungeon, those who live in darkness.

Responsorial Psalm Ps 29: 1–2, 3–4, 3, 9–10   *based on* EVENTIDE

The Lord will bless his peo - ple with peace.

Give to the LORD, you sons of God,
  give to the LORD glory and praise,
Give to the LORD the glory due his name;
  adore the LORD in holy attire. ℟

The voice of the LORD is over the waters,
  the LORD, over vast waters.
The voice of the LORD is mighty;
  the voice of the LORD is majestic. ℟

The God of glory thunders,
  and in his temple all say, "Glory!"
The LORD is enthroned above the flood;
  the LORD is enthroned as king forever. ℟

Second Reading Acts 10: 34–38 Peter proceeded to speak to those
gathered in the house of Cornelius, saying: "In truth, I see that
God shows no partiality. Rather, in every nation whoever fears
him and acts uprightly is acceptable to him. You know the word

that he sent to the Israelites as he proclaimed peace through Jesus Christ, who is Lord of all, what has happened all over Judea, beginning in Galilee after the baptism that John preached, how God anointed Jesus of Nazareth with the Holy Spirit and power. He went about doing good and healing all those oppressed by the devil, for God was with him."

Alleluia   *cf. Mk 9: 7*   *Laura Lea Duckworth*

Al-le - lu-ia, al-le - lu-ia, al - le - lu - ia.

The heavens were opened and the voice of the Father thundered: / This is my beloved Son, listen to him. **Alleluia, alleluia.**

Gospel *Mt 3: 13–17* Jesus came from Galilee to John at the Jordan to be baptized by him. John tried to prevent him, saying, "I need to be baptized by you, and yet you are coming to me?" Jesus said to him in reply, "Allow it now, for thus it is fitting for us to fulfill all righteousness." Then he allowed him. After Jesus was baptized, he came up from the water and behold, the heavens were opened for him, and he saw the Spirit of God descending like a dove and coming upon him. And a voice came from the heavens, saying, "This is my beloved Son, with whom I am well pleased."

Communion Antiphon *Jn 1: 32, 34* **Behold the One of whom John said:** ♦ **I have seen and testified that this is the Son of God.**

Lent † YEAR A

ASH WEDNESDAY

Entrance Antiphon Wis 11: 23, 24, 26 You are merciful to all, O Lord, ✦ and despise nothing that you have made. ✦ You overlook people's sins, to bring them to repentance, ✦ and you spare them, for you are the Lord our God.

The Penitential Act is omitted on Ash Wednesday.

First Reading Jl 2: 12–18
Even now, says the LORD,
  return to me with your whole heart,
  with fasting, and weeping, and mourning;
Rend your hearts, not your garments,
  and return to the LORD, your God.
For gracious and merciful is he,
  slow to anger, rich in kindness,
  and relenting in punishment.
Perhaps he will again relent
  and leave behind him a blessing,
Offerings and libations
  for the LORD, your God.
Blow the trumpet in Zion!
  proclaim a fast,
  call an assembly;
Gather the people,
  notify the congregation;
Assemble the elders,
  gather the children
  and the infants at the breast;
Let the bridegroom quit his room

and the bride her chamber.
Between the porch and the altar
    let the priests, the ministers of the LORD, weep,
And say, "Spare, O LORD, your people,
    and make not your heritage a reproach,
    with the nations ruling over them!
Why should they say among the peoples,
    'Where is their God?'"
Then the LORD was stirred to concern for his land and took
pity on his people.

Responsorial Psalm   Ps 51: 3–4, 5–6, 12–13, 14, 17   *Bill Svarda*

Be mer-ci-ful, O Lord,   for we have sinned.

Have mercy on me, O God, in your goodness;
    in the greatness of your compassion wipe out my offense.
Thoroughly wash me from my guilt
    and of my sin cleanse me. ℟

For I acknowledge my offense,
    and my sin is before me always:
"Against you only have I sinned,
    and done what is evil in your sight." ℟

A clean heart create for me, O God,
    and a steadfast spirit renew within me.
Cast me not out from your presence,
    and your Holy Spirit take not from me. ℟

Give me back the joy of your salvation,
    and a willing spirit sustain in me.
O Lord, open my lips,
    and my mouth shall proclaim your praise. ℟

Second Reading   *2 Cor 5: 20–6: 2*   Brothers and sisters: We are
ambassadors for Christ, as if God were appealing through us. We

implore you on behalf of Christ, be reconciled to God. For our sake he made him to be sin who did not know sin, so that we might become the righteousness of God in him.

Working together, then, we appeal to you not to receive the grace of God in vain. For he says:

In an acceptable time I heard you,
and on the day of salvation I helped you.

Behold, now is a very acceptable time; behold, now is the day of salvation.

Verse Before the Gospel   Ps 95: 8   Amy Righi

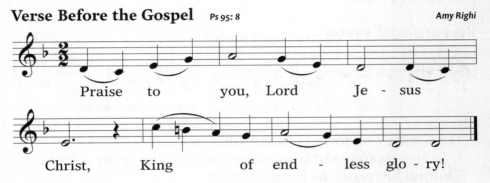

Praise to you, Lord Je - sus Christ, King of end - less glo - ry!

If today you hear his voice, / harden not your hearts.

Gospel Mt 6: 1–6, 16–18 Jesus said to his disciples: "Take care not to perform righteous deeds in order that people may see them; otherwise, you will have no recompense from your heavenly Father. When you give alms, do not blow a trumpet before you, as the hypocrites do in the synagogues and in the streets to win the praise of others. Amen, I say to you, they have received their reward. But when you give alms, do not let your left hand know what your right is doing, so that your almsgiving may be secret. And your Father who sees in secret will repay you.

"When you pray, do not be like the hypocrites, who love to stand and pray in the synagogues and on street corners so that others may see them. Amen, I say to you, they have received their reward. But when you pray, go to your inner room, close the door, and pray to your Father in secret. And your Father who sees in secret will repay you.

"When you fast, do not look gloomy like the hypocrites. They neglect their appearance, so that they may appear to others to

be fasting. Amen, I say to you, they have received their reward. But when you fast, anoint your head and wash your face, so that you may not appear to be fasting, except to your Father who is hidden. And your Father who sees what is hidden will repay you."

BLESSING AND DISTRIBUTION OF ASHES

After the Homily, the Priest, standing with hands joined, says:
  Dear brethren (brothers and sisters),
    let us humbly ask God our Father
  that he be pleased to bless with the abundance of his grace
  these ashes, which we will put on our heads in penitence.

After a brief prayer in silence, and, with hands extended, he continues:
  O God, who are moved by acts of humility
  and respond with forgiveness to works of penance,
  lend your merciful ear to our prayers
  and in your kindness pour out the grace of your + blessing
  on your servants who are marked with these ashes,
  that, as they follow the Lenten observances,
  they may be worthy to come with minds made pure
  to celebrate the Paschal Mystery of your Son.
  Through Christ our Lord ℟ **Amen.**

Or:
  O God, who desire not the death of sinners,
  but their conversion,
  mercifully hear our prayers
  and in your kindness be pleased to bless + these ashes,
  which we intend to receive upon our heads,
  that we, who acknowledge we are but ashes
  and shall return to dust,
  may, through a steadfast observance of Lent,
  gain pardon for sins and newness of life
  after the likeness of your Risen Son.
  Who lives and reigns for ever and ever. ℟ **Amen.**

He sprinkles the ashes with holy water, without saying anything.

Then the Priest places ashes on the head of all those present who come to him, and says to each one: Repent, and believe in the Gospel.

Or: Remember that you are dust, and to dust you shall return.

Meanwhile, the following are sung:

Antiphon 1 Let us change our garments to sackcloth and ashes, ✦ let us fast and weep before the Lord, ✦ that our God, rich in mercy, might forgive us our sins.

Antiphon 2 *cf. Jl 2: 17; Est 4: 17* Let the priests, the ministers of the Lord, ✦ stand between the porch and the altar and weep and cry out: ✦ Spare, O Lord, spare your people; ✦ do not close the mouths of those who sing your praise, O Lord.

Antiphon 3 *Ps 51 (50): 3* Blot out my transgressions, O Lord.

This may be repeated after each verse of Psalm 51 (50), (Have mercy on me, O God).

Responsory *cf. Bar 3: 2; Ps 79 (78): 9*
℞ Let us correct our faults which we have committed in ignorance, let us not be taken unawares by the day of our death, looking in vain for leisure to repent. Hear us, O Lord, and show us your mercy, for we have sinned against you.

℣ Help us, O God our Savior; for the sake of your name, O Lord, set us free.
℞ Hear us, O Lord, and show us your mercy, for we have sinned against you.

Another appropriate chant or hymn may also be sung.

After the distribution of ashes, the Priest washes his hands and

proceeds to the Universal Prayer, and continues the Mass in the usual way. The Creed is not said.

Communion Antiphon *cf. Ps 1: 2–3* **He who ponders the law of the Lord day and night ◆ will yield fruit in due season.**

The blessing and distribution of ashes may also take place outside Mass. In this case, the rite is preceded by a Liturgy of the Word, with the Entrance Antiphon, the Collect, and the readings with their chants as at Mass. Then there follow the Homily and the blessing and distribution of ashes. The rite is concluded with the Prayer of the Faithful (Universal Prayer), the Blessing, and the Dismissal of the Faithful.

FIRST SUNDAY OF LENT

Entrance Antiphon *cf. Ps 91 (90): 15–16* **When he calls on me, I will answer him; ◆ I will deliver him and give him glory, ◆ I will grant him length of days.**

First Reading *Gen 2: 7–9; 3: 1–7* The LORD God formed man out of the clay of the ground and blew into his nostrils the breath of life, and so man became a living being.

Then the LORD God planted a garden in Eden, in the east, and placed there the man whom he had formed. Out of the ground the LORD God made various trees grow that were delightful to look at and good for food, with the tree of life in the middle of the garden and the tree of the knowledge of good and evil.

Now the serpent was the most cunning of all the animals that the LORD God had made. The serpent asked the woman, "Did God really tell you not to eat from any of the trees in the garden?" The woman answered the serpent: "We may eat of the fruit of the trees in the garden; it is only about the fruit of the tree in the middle of the garden that God said, 'You shall not eat it or even touch it, lest you die.'" But the serpent said to the woman: "You certainly will not die! No, God knows well that the moment you eat of it your eyes will be opened and you will be like gods who know what is good and what is evil." The woman saw that the tree was good for food, pleasing to the eyes, and desirable for gaining wisdom. So she took some of its fruit and ate it; and she also gave some to her husband, who was with her, and he ate it. Then the eyes of both of them were opened, and they realized that they were naked; so they sewed fig leaves together and made loincloths for themselves.

Responsorial Psalm Ps 51: 3–4, 5–6, 12–13, 14, 17   Don Fishel

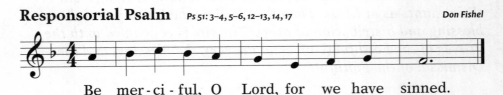

Be mer-ci-ful, O Lord, for we have sinned.

Have mercy on me, O God, in your goodness;
    in the greatness of your compassion wipe out my offense.
Thoroughly wash me from my guilt
    and of my sin cleanse me. ℟

For I acknowledge my offense,
    and my sin is before me always:
"Against you only have I sinned,
    and done what is evil in your sight." ℟

A clean heart create for me, O God,
    and a steadfast spirit renew within me.
Cast me not out from your presence,
    and your Holy Spirit take not from me. ℟

Give me back the joy of your salvation,
    and a willing spirit sustain in me.
O Lord, open my lips,
    and my mouth shall proclaim your praise. ℟

Second Reading Rom 5: 12–19 or 5: 12, 17–19
For the shorter form, read only the parts in brackets.
[Brothers and sisters: Through one man sin entered the

world, and through sin, death, and thus death came to all men, inasmuch as all sinned—] for up to the time of the law, sin was in the world, though sin is not accounted when there is no law. But death reigned from Adam to Moses, even over those who did not sin after the pattern of the trespass of Adam, who is the type of the one who was to come.

But the gift is not like the transgression. For if by the transgression of the one, the many died, how much more did the grace of God and the gracious gift of the one man Jesus Christ overflow for the many. And the gift is not like the result of the one who sinned. For after one sin there was the judgment that brought condemnation; but the gift, after many transgressions, brought acquittal. [For if, by the transgression of the one, death came to reign through that one, how much more will those who receive the abundance of grace and of the gift of justification come to reign in life through the one Jesus Christ. In conclusion, just as through one transgression condemnation came upon all, so, through one righteous act, acquittal and life came to all. For just as through the disobedience of the one man the many were made sinners, so, through the obedience of the one, the many will be made righteous.]

Verse Before the Gospel   Mt 4: 4b   Amy Righi

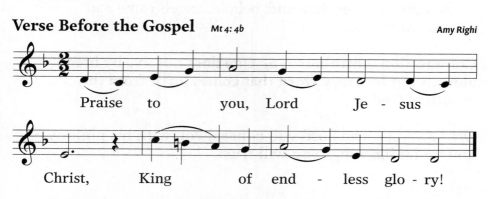

Praise to you, Lord Je - sus Christ, King of end - less glo - ry!

One does not live on bread alone, / but on every word that comes forth from the mouth of God.

Gospel Mt 4: 1-11 At that time Jesus was led by the Spirit into the desert to be tempted by the devil. He fasted for forty days and forty nights, and afterwards he was hungry. The tempter

approached and said to him, "If you are the Son of God,
command that these stones become loaves of bread." He said
in reply, "It is written:

One does not live on bread alone,
but on every word that comes forth
from the mouth of God."

Then the devil took him to the holy city, and made him stand
on the parapet of the temple, and said to him, "If you are the
Son of God, throw yourself down. For it is written:

He will command his angels concerning you
and with their hands they will support you,
lest you dash your foot against a stone."

Jesus answered him, "Again it is written,

You shall not put the Lord, your God, to the test."

Then the devil took him up to a very high mountain, and
showed him all the kingdoms of the world in their magnificence,
and he said to him, "All these I shall give to you, if you will
prostrate yourself and worship me." At this, Jesus said to him,
"Get away, Satan! It is written:

The Lord, your God, shall you worship
and him alone shall you serve."

Then the devil left him and, behold, angels came and
ministered to him.

Communion Antiphon Mt 4:4 **One does not live by bread
alone, ◆ but by every word that comes forth from the
mouth of God.**

Or: cf. Ps 91 (90):4 **The Lord will conceal you with his pinions, ◆
and under his wings you will trust.**

SECOND SUNDAY OF LENT

Entrance Antiphon cf. Ps 27 (26):8–9 **Of you my heart has spoken:
Seek his face. ◆ It is your face, O Lord, that I seek; ◆ hide not
your face from me.**

Or: cf. Ps 25 (24): 6, 2, 22 **Remember your compassion, O Lord, ◆ and your merciful love, for they are from of old. ◆ Let not our enemies exult over us. ◆ Redeem us, O God of Israel, from all our distress.**

First Reading Gen 12: 1–4a The LORD said to Abram: "Go forth from the land of your kinsfolk and from your father's house to a land that I will show you.

"I will make of you a great nation,
 and I will bless you;
I will make your name great,
 so that you will be a blessing.
I will bless those who bless you
 and curse those who curse you.
All the communities of the earth
 shall find blessing in you."

Abram went as the LORD directed him.

Responsorial Psalm Ps 33: 4–5, 18–19, 20, 22 *Beverly McDevitt*

Lord, let your mer - cy be on us, as we place our trust in you.

Upright is the word of the LORD,
 and all his works are trustworthy.
He loves justice and right;
 of the kindness of the LORD the earth is full. ℟

See, the eyes of the LORD are upon those who fear him,
 upon those who hope for his kindness,
to deliver them from death
 and preserve them in spite of famine. ℟

Our soul waits for the LORD,
    who is our help and our shield.
May your kindness, O LORD, be upon us
    who have put our hope in you. ℟

Second Reading *2 Timothy 1: 8b–10* Beloved: Bear your share of
hardship for the gospel with the strength that comes from God.
    He saved us and called us to a holy life, not according to
our works but according to his own design and the grace
bestowed on us in Christ Jesus before time began, but now made
manifest through the appearance of our savior Christ Jesus,
who destroyed death and brought life and immortality to light
through the gospel.

Verse Before the Gospel   *cf. Mt 17: 5*   *Amy Righi*

Praise   to   you,   Lord   Je - sus

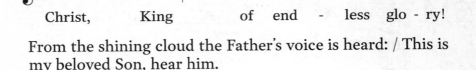

Christ,   King   of   end - less   glo - ry!

From the shining cloud the Father's voice is heard: / This is
my beloved Son, hear him.

Gospel *Mt 17: 1-9* Jesus took Peter, James, and John his brother,
and led them up a high mountain by themselves. And he was
transfigured before them; his face shone like the sun and his
clothes became white as light. And behold, Moses and Elijah
appeared to them, conversing with him. Then Peter said to Jesus
in reply, "Lord, it is good that we are here. If you wish, I will
make three tents here, one for you, one for Moses, and one for
Elijah." While he was still speaking, behold, a bright cloud cast
a shadow over them, then from the cloud came a voice that said,
"This is my beloved Son, with whom I am well pleased; listen to
him." When the disciples heard this, they fell prostrate and were

very much afraid. But Jesus came and touched them, saying, "Rise, and do not be afraid." And when the disciples raised their eyes, they saw no one else but Jesus alone.

As they were coming down from the mountain, Jesus charged them, "Do not tell the vision to anyone until the Son of Man has been raised from the dead."

Communion Antiphon Mt 17: 5 This is my beloved Son, with whom I am well pleased; ◆ listen to him.

THIRD SUNDAY OF LENT

Entrance Antiphon cf. Ps 25 (24): 15–16 My eyes are always on the Lord, ◆ for he rescues my feet from the snare. ◆ Turn to me and have mercy on me, ◆ for I am alone and poor.

Or: cf. Ez 36: 23–26 When I prove my holiness among you, ◆ I will gather you from all the foreign lands; ◆ and I will pour clean water upon you ◆ and cleanse you from all your impurities, ◆ and I will give you a new spirit, says the Lord.

First Reading Ex 17: 3–7 In those days, in their thirst for water, the people grumbled against Moses, saying, "Why did you ever make us leave Egypt? Was it just to have us die here of thirst with our children and our livestock?" So Moses cried out to the LORD, "What shall I do with this people? A little more and they will stone me!" The LORD answered Moses, "Go over there in front of the people, along with some of the elders of Israel, holding in your hand, as you go, the staff with which you struck the river. I will be standing there in front of you on the rock in Horeb. Strike the rock, and the water will flow from it for the people to drink." This Moses did, in the presence of the elders of Israel. The place was called Massah and Meribah, because the Israelites quarreled there and tested the LORD, saying, "Is the LORD in our midst or not?"

Responsorial Psalm   Ps 95: 1–2, 6–7, 8–9   *Vince Ambrosetti*

If to-day you hear his voice, hard-en not your hearts.

Come, let us sing joyfully to the LORD;
  let us acclaim the Rock of our salvation.
Let us come into his presence with thanksgiving;
  let us joyfully sing psalms to him. ℞

Come, let us bow down in worship;
  let us kneel before the LORD who made us.
For he is our God,
  and we are the people he shepherds, the flock he guides. ℞

Oh, that today you would hear his voice:
  "Harden not your hearts as at Meribah,
  as in the day of Massah in the desert,
  where your fathers tempted me;
    they tested me though they had seen my works." ℞

Second Reading *Rom 5: 1–2, 5–8* Brothers and sisters: Since we have
been justified by faith, we have peace with God through our
Lord Jesus Christ, through whom we have gained access by faith
to this grace in which we stand, and we boast in hope of the
glory of God.
  And hope does not disappoint, because the love of God has
been poured out into our hearts through the Holy Spirit who
has been given to us. For Christ, while we were still helpless,
died at the appointed time for the ungodly. Indeed, only with
difficulty does one die for a just person, though perhaps for a
good person one might even find courage to die. But God proves
his love for us in that while we were still sinners Christ died
for us.

Verse Before the Gospel   *cf. Jn 4: 42,15*   Amy Righi

Praise to you, Lord Je - sus
Christ, King of end - less glo - ry!

Lord, you are truly the Savior of the world; / give me living water, that I may never thirst again.

Gospel   *Jn 4: 5–42 or 4: 5–15, 19b–26, 39a, 40–42*

For the shorter form, read only the parts in brackets.
Jesus came to a town of Samaria called Sychar, near the plot of land that Jacob had given to his son Joseph. Jacob's well was there. Jesus, tired from his journey, sat down there at the well. It was about noon.

A woman of Samaria came to draw water. Jesus said to her, "Give me a drink." His disciples had gone into the town to buy food. The Samaritan woman said to him, "How can you, a Jew, ask me, a Samaritan woman, for a drink?"—For Jews use nothing in common with Samaritans.—Jesus answered and said to her, "If you knew the gift of God and who is saying to you, 'Give me a drink,' you would have asked him and he would have given you living water." The woman said to him, "Sir, you do not even have a bucket and the cistern is deep; where then can you get this living water? Are you greater than our father Jacob, who gave us this cistern and drank from it himself with his children and his flocks?" Jesus answered and said to her, "Everyone who drinks this water will be thirsty again; but whoever drinks the water I shall give will never thirst; the water I shall give will become in him a spring of water welling up to eternal life." The woman said to him, "Sir, give me this water, so that I may not be thirsty or have to keep coming here to draw water."]

Jesus said to her, "Go call your husband and come back." The woman answered and said to him, "I do not have a husband." Jesus answered her, "You are right in saying, 'I do not have a husband.' For you have had five husbands, and the one you have now is not your husband. What you have said is true." The woman said to him, "Sir, [I can see that you are a prophet. Our ancestors worshiped on this mountain; but you people say that the place to worship is in Jerusalem." Jesus said to her, "Believe me, woman, the hour is coming when you will worship the Father neither on this mountain nor in Jerusalem. You people worship what you do not understand; we worship what we understand, because salvation is from the Jews. But the hour is coming, and is now here, when true worshipers will worship the Father in Spirit and truth; and indeed the Father seeks such people to worship him. God is Spirit, and those who worship him must worship in Spirit and truth." The woman said to him, "I know that the Messiah is coming, the one called the Christ; when he comes, he will tell us everything." Jesus said to her, "I am he, the one speaking with you."]

At that moment his disciples returned, and were amazed that he was talking with a woman, but still no one said, "What are you looking for?" or "Why are you talking with her?" The woman left her water jar and went into the town and said to the people, "Come see a man who told me everything I have done. Could he possibly be the Christ?" They went out of the town and came to him. Meanwhile, the disciples urged him, "Rabbi, eat." But he said to them, "I have food to eat of which you do not know." So the disciples said to one another, "Could someone have brought him something to eat?" Jesus said to them, "My food is to do the will of the one who sent me and to finish his work. Do you not say, 'In four months the harvest will be here'? I tell you, look up and see the fields ripe for the harvest. The reaper is already receiving payment and gathering crops for eternal life, so that the sower and reaper can rejoice together. For here the saying is verified that 'One sows and another reaps.' I sent you to reap what you have not worked for; others have done the work, and you are sharing the fruits of their work."

[Many of the Samaritans of that town began to believe in him] because of the word of the woman who testified, "He told me everything I have done." [When the Samaritans came to him, they invited him to stay with them; and he stayed there two days. Many more began to believe in him because of his word, and they said to the woman, "We no longer believe because of your word; for we have heard for ourselves, and we know that this is truly the savior of the world."]

The First Scrutiny of the Rite of Christian Initiation of Adults may be celebrated after the homily.

Communion Antiphon Jn 4: 13–14 **For anyone who drinks it, says the Lord, ◆ the water I shall give will become in him ◆ a spring welling up to eternal life.**

FOURTH SUNDAY OF LENT

Entrance Antiphon cf. Is 66: 10–11 **Rejoice, Jerusalem, and all who love her. ◆ Be joyful, all who were in mourning; ◆ exult and be satisfied at her consoling breast.**

First Reading 1 Sm 16: 1b, 6–7, 10–13a The LORD said to Samuel: "Fill your horn with oil, and be on your way. I am sending you to Jesse of Bethlehem, for I have chosen my king from among his sons."

As Jesse and his sons came to the sacrifice, Samuel looked at Eliab and thought, "Surely the LORD's anointed is here before him." But the LORD said to Samuel: "Do not judge from his appearance or from his lofty stature, because I have rejected him. Not as man sees does God see, because man sees the appearance but the LORD looks into the heart." In the same way Jesse presented seven sons before Samuel, but Samuel said to Jesse, "The LORD has not chosen any one of these." Then Samuel asked Jesse, "Are these all the sons you have?" Jesse replied, "There is still the youngest, who is tending the sheep." Samuel said to Jesse, "Send for him; we will not begin the sacrificial banquet until he arrives here." Jesse sent and had the young man brought to them. He was ruddy, a youth handsome to behold and making a splendid appearance. The LORD said, "There—anoint him, for this is the one!" Then Samuel, with the horn of oil in hand, anointed David in the presence of his brothers; and from that day on, the spirit of the LORD rushed upon David.

Responsorial Psalm   Ps 23: 1–3a, 3b–4, 5, 6   *Joe Higginbotham*

The Lord is my shepherd; there is noth-ing I shall want.

The LORD is my shepherd; I shall not want.
    In verdant pastures he gives me repose;
beside restful waters he leads me;
    he refreshes my soul. ℟

He guides me in right paths
    for his name's sake.
Even though I walk in the dark valley
    I fear no evil; for you are at my side
with your rod and your staff
    that give me courage. ℟

You spread the table before me
    in the sight of my foes;
you anoint my head with oil;
    my cup overflows. ℟

Only goodness and kindness follow me
    all the days of my life;
and I shall dwell in the house of the LORD
    for years to come. ℟

Second Reading Eph 5: 8–14 Brothers and sisters: You were once
darkness, but now you are light in the Lord. Live as children
of light, for light produces every kind of goodness and
righteousness and truth. Try to learn what is pleasing to the
Lord. Take no part in the fruitless works of darkness; rather
expose them, for it is shameful even to mention the things done

by them in secret; but everything exposed by the light becomes visible, for everything that becomes visible is light. Therefore, it says:

"Awake, O sleeper,
 and arise from the dead,
 and Christ will give you light."

Verse Before the Gospel Jn 8: 12

Amy Righi

Praise to you, Lord Je - sus Christ, King of end - less glo - ry!

I am the light of the world, says the Lord; / whoever follows me will have the light of life.

Gospel Jn 9: 1–41 or 9: 1, 6–9, 13–17, 34–38

For the shorter form, read only the parts in brackets.
[As Jesus passed by he saw a man blind from birth.] His disciples asked him, "Rabbi, who sinned, this man or his parents, that he was born blind?" Jesus answered, "Neither he nor his parents sinned; it is so that the works of God might be made visible through him. We have to do the works of the one who sent me while it is day. Night is coming when no one can work. While I am in the world, I am the light of the world." When he had said this, [he spat on the ground and made clay with the saliva, and smeared the clay on his eyes, and said to him, "Go wash in the Pool of Siloam"—which means Sent—. So he went and washed, and came back able to see.

His neighbors and those who had seen him earlier as a beggar said, "Isn't this the one who used to sit and beg?" Some said, "It is," but others said, "No, he just looks like him." He said, "I am."] So they said to him, "How were your eyes opened?" He replied, "The man called Jesus made clay and anointed my eyes and told me, 'Go to Siloam and wash.' So I went there and washed and was able to see." And they said to him, "Where is he?" He said, "I don't know."

[They brought the one who was once blind to the Pharisees. Now Jesus had made clay and opened his eyes on a sabbath. So then the Pharisees also asked him how he was able to see. He said to them, "He put clay on my eyes, and I washed, and now I can see." So some of the Pharisees said, "This man is not from God, because he does not keep the sabbath." But others said, "How can a sinful man do such signs?" And there was a division among them. So they said to the blind man again, "What do you have to say about him, since he opened your eyes?" He said, "He is a prophet."]

Now the Jews did not believe that he had been blind and gained his sight until they summoned the parents of the one who had gained his sight. They asked them, "Is this your son, who you say was born blind? How does he now see?" His parents answered and said, "We know that this is our son and that he was born blind. We do not know how he sees now, nor do we know who opened his eyes. Ask him, he is of age; he can speak for himself." His parents said this because they were afraid of the Jews, for the Jews had already agreed that if anyone acknowledged him as the Christ, he would be expelled from the synagogue. For this reason his parents said, "He is of age; question him."

So a second time they called the man who had been blind and said to him, "Give God the praise! We know that this man is a sinner." He replied, "If he is a sinner, I do not know. One thing I do know is that I was blind and now I see." So they said to him, "What did he do to you? How did he open your eyes?" He answered them, "I told you already and you did not listen. Why do you want to hear it again? Do you want to become his disciples, too?" They ridiculed him and said, "You are that man's disciple; we are disciples of Moses! We know that God spoke to Moses, but we do not know where this one is from." The man answered and said to them, "This is what is so amazing, that you do not know where he is from, yet he opened my eyes. We know that God does not listen to sinners, but if one is devout and does his will, he listens to him. It is unheard of that anyone ever opened the eyes of a person born blind. If this man were not from God, he would not be able to do anything." [They answered and said to him, "You were born totally in sin, and are you trying to teach us?" Then they threw him out.

When Jesus heard that they had thrown him out, he found him and said, "Do you believe in the Son of Man?" He answered and said, "Who is he, sir, that I may believe in him?" Jesus said to him, "You have seen him, and the one speaking with you is he." He said, "I do believe, Lord," and he worshiped him.] Then Jesus said, "I came into this world for judgment, so that those who do not see might see, and those who do see might become blind."

Some of the Pharisees who were with him heard this and said to him, "Surely we are not also blind, are we?" Jesus said to them, "If you were blind, you would have no sin; but now you are saying, 'We see,' so your sin remains."

The Second Scrutiny of the Rite of Christian Initiation of Adults may be celebrated after the homily.

Communion Antiphon cf. Jn 9: 11, 38 **The Lord anointed my eyes: I went, I washed, ◆ I saw and I believed in God.**

FIFTH SUNDAY OF LENT

Entrance Antiphon cf. Ps 43 (42): 1-2 **Give me justice, O God, ◆ and plead my cause against a nation that is faithless. ◆ From the deceitful and cunning rescue me, ◆ for you, O God, are my strength.**

First Reading Ez 37: 12-14 Thus says the Lord God: O my people, I will open your graves and have you rise from them, and bring you back to the land of Israel. Then you shall know that I am the LORD, when I open your graves and have you rise from them, O my people! I will put my spirit in you that you may live, and I will settle you upon your land; thus you shall know that I am the LORD. I have promised, and I will do it, says the LORD.

Responsorial Psalm   Ps 130: 1–2, 3–4, 5–6, 7–8   Joe Higginbotham

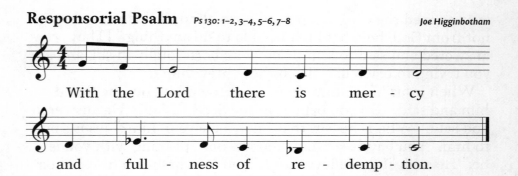

With the Lord there is mer - cy and full - ness of re - demp - tion.

Out of the depths I cry to you, O LORD;
    LORD, hear my voice!
Let your ears be attentive
    to my voice in supplication. ℟

If you, O LORD, mark iniquities,
    LORD, who can stand?
But with you is forgiveness,
    that you may be revered. ℟

I trust in the LORD;
    my soul trusts in his word.
More than sentinels wait for the dawn,
    let Israel wait for the LORD. ℟

For with the LORD is kindness
    and with him is plenteous redemption;
And he will redeem Israel
    from all their iniquities. ℟

Second Reading *Rom 8: 8–11* Brothers and sisters: Those who are
in the flesh cannot please God. But you are not in the flesh;
on the contrary, you are in the spirit, if only the Spirit of God
dwells in you. Whoever does not have the Spirit of Christ does
not belong to him. But if Christ is in you, although the body
is dead because of sin, the spirit is alive because of righteousness.
If the Spirit of the One who raised Jesus from the dead dwells
in you, the One who raised Christ from the dead will give life to
your mortal bodies also, through his Spirit dwelling in you.

Verse Before the Gospel   Jn 11: 25a, 26   Amy Righi

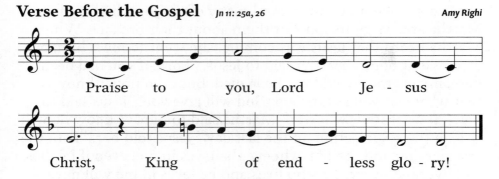

Praise to you, Lord Jesus Christ, King of endless glory!

I am the resurrection and the life, says the Lord; / whoever believes in me, even if he dies, will never die.

Gospel *Jn 11: 1–45* Now a man was ill, Lazarus from Bethany, the village of Mary and her sister Martha. Mary was the one who had anointed the Lord with perfumed oil and dried his feet with her hair; it was her brother Lazarus who was ill. So the sisters sent word to him saying, "Master, the one you love is ill." When Jesus heard this he said, "This illness is not to end in death, but is for the glory of God, that the Son of God may be glorified through it." Now Jesus loved Martha and her sister and Lazarus. So when he heard that he was ill, he remained for two days in the place where he was. Then after this he said to his disciples, "Let us go back to Judea." The disciples said to him, "Rabbi, the Jews were just trying to stone you, and you want to go back there?" Jesus answered, "Are there not twelve hours in a day? If one walks during the day, he does not stumble, because he sees the light of this world. But if one walks at night, he stumbles, because the light is not in him." He said this, and then told them, "Our friend Lazarus is asleep, but I am going to awaken him." So the disciples said to him, "Master, if he is asleep, he will be saved." But Jesus was talking about his death, while they thought that he meant ordinary sleep. So then Jesus said to them clearly, "Lazarus has died. And I am glad for you that I was not there, that you may believe. Let us go to him." So Thomas, called Didymus, said to his fellow disciples, "Let us also go to die with him."

When Jesus arrived, he found that Lazarus had already been in the tomb for four days. Now Bethany was near Jerusalem,

only about two miles away. And many of the Jews had come to
Martha and Mary to comfort them about their brother. When
Martha heard that Jesus was coming, she went to meet him; but
Mary sat at home. Martha said to Jesus, "Lord, if you had been
here, my brother would not have died. But even now I know
that whatever you ask of God, God will give you." Jesus said to
her, "Your brother will rise." Martha said to him, "I know he will
rise, in the resurrection on the last day." Jesus told her, "I am the
resurrection and the life; whoever believes in me, even if he dies,
will live, and everyone who lives and believes in me will never
die. Do you believe this?" She said to him, "Yes, Lord. I have
come to believe that you are the Christ, the Son of God, the one
who is coming into the world."

When she had said this, she went and called her sister Mary
secretly, saying, "The teacher is here and is asking for you." As
soon as she heard this, she rose quickly and went to him. For
Jesus had not yet come into the village, but was still where
Martha had met him. So when the Jews who were with her in
the house comforting her saw Mary get up quickly and go out,
they followed her, presuming that she was going to the tomb to
weep there. When Mary came to where Jesus was and saw him,
she fell at his feet and said to him, "Lord, if you had been here,
my brother would not have died." When Jesus saw her weeping
and the Jews who had come with her weeping, he became
perturbed and deeply troubled, and said, "Where have you laid
him?" They said to him, "Sir, come and see." And Jesus wept. So
the Jews said, "See how he loved him." But some of them said,
"Could not the one who opened the eyes of the blind man have
done something so that this man would not have died?"

So Jesus, perturbed again, came to the tomb. It was a cave, and
a stone lay across it. Jesus said, "Take away the stone." Martha,
the dead man's sister, said to him, "Lord, by now there will be a
stench; he has been dead for four days." Jesus said to her, "Did
I not tell you that if you believe you will see the glory of God?"
So they took away the stone. And Jesus raised his eyes and said,
"Father, I thank you for hearing me. I know that you always hear
me; but because of the crowd here I have said this, that they
may believe that you sent me." And when he had said this, he
cried out in a loud voice, "Lazarus, come out!" The dead man

came out, tied hand and foot with burial bands, and his face was wrapped in a cloth. So Jesus said to them, "Untie him and let him go."

Now many of the Jews who had come to Mary and seen what he had done began to believe in him.

Or (shorter form):   Jn 11: 3–7, 17, 20–27, 33b–45   The sisters of Lazarus sent word to him saying, "Master, the one you love is ill." When Jesus heard this he said, "This illness is not to end in death, but is for the glory of God, that the Son of God may be glorified through it." Now Jesus loved Martha and her sister and Lazarus. So when he heard that he was ill, he remained for two days in the place where he was. Then after this he said to his disciples, "Let us go back to Judea."

When Jesus arrived, he found that Lazarus had already been in the tomb for four days. When Martha heard that Jesus was coming, she went to meet him; but Mary sat at home. Martha said to Jesus, "Lord, if you had been here, my brother would not have died. But even now I know that whatever you ask of God, God will give you." Jesus said to her, "Your brother will rise." Martha said to him, "I know he will rise, in the resurrection on the last day." Jesus told her, "I am the resurrection and the life; whoever believes in me, even if he dies, will live, and everyone who lives and believes in me will never die. Do you believe this?" She said to him, "Yes, Lord. I have come to believe that you are the Christ, the Son of God, the one who is coming into the world."

He became perturbed and deeply troubled, and said, "Where have you laid him?" They said to him, "Sir, come and see." And Jesus wept. So the Jews said, "See how he loved him." But some of them said, "Could not the one who opened the eyes of the blind man have done something so that this man would not have died?"

So Jesus, perturbed again, came to the tomb. It was a cave, and a stone lay across it. Jesus said, "Take away the stone." Martha, the dead man's sister, said to him, "Lord, by now there will be a stench; he has been dead for four days." Jesus said to her, "Did I not tell you that if you believe you will see the glory of God?" So they took away the stone. And Jesus raised his eyes and said,

"Father, I thank you for hearing me. I know that you always hear me; but because of the crowd here I have said this, that they may believe that you sent me." And when he had said this, he cried out in a loud voice, "Lazarus, come out!" The dead man came out, tied hand and foot with burial bands, and his face was wrapped in a cloth. So Jesus said to them, "Untie him and let him go."

Now many of the Jews who had come to Mary and seen what he had done began to believe in him.

The Third Scrutiny of the Rite of Christian Initiation of Adults may be celebrated after the homily.

Communion Antiphon *cf. Jn 11: 26* **Everyone who lives and believes in me ✦ will not die for ever, says the Lord.**

PALM SUNDAY OF THE PASSION OF THE LORD

On this day the Church recalls the entrance of Christ the Lord into Jerusalem to accomplish his Paschal Mystery. Accordingly, the memorial of this entrance of the Lord takes place at all Masses, by means of the Procession or the Solemn Entrance before the principal Mass or the Simple Entrance before other Masses. The Solemn Entrance, but not the Procession, may be repeated before other Masses that are usually celebrated with a large gathering of people.

✧ The Commemoration of the Lord's ✧ Entrance Into Jerusalem

FIRST FORM: THE PROCESSION

At an appropriate hour, a gathering takes place at a smaller church or other suitable place other than inside the church to which the procession will go. The faithful hold branches in their hands.

Wearing the red sacred vestments as for Mass, the Priest and the Deacon, accompanied by other ministers, approach the place where

*the people are gathered. Meanwhile, the following antiphon or
another appropriate chant is sung.*

Antiphon Mt 21: 9 Hosanna to the Son of David; ◆ blessed is he
who comes in the name of the Lord, ◆ the King of Israel. ◆
Hosanna in the highest.

The Priest and people sign themselves, while the Priest says: In
the name of the Father, and of the Son, and of the Holy Spirit.
*Then he greets the people in the usual way. A brief address is
given, in which the faithful are invited to participate actively and
consciously in the celebration of this day, in these or similar words:*
Dear brethren (brothers and sisters),
since the beginning of Lent until now
we have prepared our hearts by penance and charitable works.
Today we gather together to herald with the whole Church
the beginning of the celebration
of our Lord's Paschal Mystery,
that is to say, of his Passion and Resurrection.
For it was to accomplish this mystery
that he entered his own city of Jerusalem.
Therefore, with all faith and devotion,
let us commemorate
the Lord's entry into the city for our salvation,
following in his footsteps,
so that, being made by his grace partakers of the Cross,
we may have a share also in his Resurrection and in his life.

After the address, the Priest says one of the following prayers.
Let us pray.
Almighty ever-living God,
sanctify + these branches with your blessing,
that we, who follow Christ the King in exultation,
may reach the eternal Jerusalem through him.
Who lives and reigns for ever and ever.   ℟ **Amen.**

Or:
Increase the faith of those who place their hope in you, O God,
and graciously hear the prayers of those who call on you,
that we, who today hold high these branches

to hail Christ in his triumph,
may bear fruit for you by good works accomplished in him.
Who lives and reigns for ever and ever. ℟ **Amen.**

The Priest sprinkles the branches with holy water without saying anything. Then a Deacon or, if there is no Deacon, a Priest, proclaims in the usual way the Gospel concerning the Lord's entrance according to one of the four Gospels.

Gospel Mt 21: 1–11 When Jesus and the disciples drew near Jerusalem and came to Bethphage on the Mount of Olives, Jesus sent two disciples, saying to them, "Go into the village opposite you, and immediately you will find an ass tethered, and a colt with her. Untie them and bring them here to me. And if anyone should say anything to you, reply, 'The master has need of them.' Then he will send them at once." This happened so that what had been spoken through the prophet might be fulfilled:
  Say to daughter Zion,
"Behold, your king comes to you,
    meek and riding on an ass,
    and on a colt, the foal of a beast of burden."
The disciples went and did as Jesus had ordered them. They brought the ass and the colt and laid their cloaks over them, and he sat upon them. The very large crowd spread their cloaks on the road, while others cut branches from the trees and strewed them on the road. The crowds preceding him and those following kept crying out and saying:
  "Hosanna to the Son of David;
    blessed is the he who comes in the name of the Lord;
  hosanna in the highest."
And when he entered Jerusalem the whole city was shaken and asked, "Who is this?" And the crowds replied, "This is Jesus the prophet, from Nazareth in Galilee."

After the Gospel, a brief homily may be given.

Then, to begin the procession, an invitation may be given by a Priest or a Deacon or a lay minister, in these or similar words:
  Dear brethren (brothers and sisters),
  like the crowds who acclaimed Jesus in Jerusalem,

let us go forth in peace.

Or: Let us go forth in peace.
In this latter case, all respond: **In the name of Christ. Amen.**

The procession to the church where Mass will be celebrated then sets off in the usual way. As the procession moves forward, the following or other suitable chants in honor of Christ the King are sung by the choir and people.

Antiphon 1   The children of the Hebrews, carrying olive branches, ♦ **went to meet the Lord, crying out and saying:** ♦ **Hosanna in the highest.**

If appropriate, this antiphon is repeated between the strophes of the following Psalm.

Psalm 24 (23)
The LORD's is the earth and its fullness,
the world, and those who dwell in it.
It is he who set it on the seas;
on the rivers he made it firm.   *(The antiphon is repeated.)*

Who shall climb the mountain of the LORD?
The clean of hands and pure of heart,
whose soul is not set on vain things,
who has not sworn deceitful words. *(The antiphon is repeated.)*

Blessings from the LORD shall he receive,
and right reward from the God who saves him.
Such are the people who seek him,
who seek the face of the God of Jacob.
          (The antiphon is repeated.)

O gates, lift high your heads;
grow higher, ancient doors.
Let him enter, the king of glory!
Who is this king of glory?
The LORD, the mighty, the valiant;
the LORD, the valiant in war.   *(The antiphon is repeated.)*

O gates, lift high your heads;
grow higher, ancient doors.
Let him enter, the king of glory!
Who is this king of glory?
He, the LORD of hosts,
he is the king of glory.   (*The antiphon is repeated.*)

Antiphon 2   The children of the Hebrews spread their
garments on the road, ♦ crying out and saying: Hosanna
to the Son of David; ♦ blessed is he who comes in the name
of the Lord.

*If appropriate, this antiphon is repeated between the strophes of the
following Psalm.*

Psalm 47 (46)
All peoples, clap your hands.
Cry to God with shouts of joy!
For the LORD, the Most high, is awesome,
the great king over all the earth.   (*The antiphon is repeated.*)

He humbles peoples under us
and nations under our feet.
Our heritage he chose for us,
the pride of Jacob whom he loves.
God goes up with shouts of joy.
The LORD goes up with trumpet blast.
                            (*The antiphon is repeated.*)

Sing praise for God; sing praise!
Sing praise to king; sing praise!
God is king of all earth.
Sing praise with all your skill.   (*The antiphon is repeated.*)

God reigns over the nations.
God sits upon his holy throne.
The princes of the peoples are assembled
with the people of the God of Abraham.
The rulers of the earth belong to God,
who is greatly exalted.   (*The antiphon is repeated.*)

Hymn to Christ the King

Chorus:
Glory and honor and praise be to you, Christ, King and
   Redeemer,
to whom young children cried out loving Hosannas with joy.

All repeat:
Glory and honor and praise be to you,
   Christ, King and Redeemer,
to whom young children cried out loving Hosannas
   with joy.

Chorus:
Israel's King are you, King David's magnificent offspring;
you are the ruler who come blest in the name of the Lord.
All repeat: **Glory and honor ...**

Chorus:
Heavenly hosts on high unite in singing your praises;
men and women on earth and all creation join in.
All repeat: **Glory and honor ...**

Chorus:
Bearing branches of palm, Hebrews came crowding to
   greet you;
see how with prayers and hymns we come to pay you
   our vows.
All repeat: **Glory and honor ...**

Chorus:
They offered gifts of praise to you, so near to your Passion;
see how we sing this song now to you reigning on high.
All repeat: **Glory and honor ...**

Chorus:
Those you were pleased to accept; now accept our gifts of
   devotion,
good and merciful King, lover of all that is good.
All repeat: **Glory and honor ...**

As the procession enters the church, there is sung the following responsory or another chant, which should speak of the Lord's entrance.

℟ **As the Lord entered the holy city, the children of the Hebrews proclaimed the resurrection of life. Waving their branches of palm, they cried: Hosanna in the Highest.**

℣ When the people heard that Jesus was coming to Jerusalem, they went out to meet him.
℟ **Waving their branches of palm, they cried: Hosanna in the Highest.**

When the Priest arrives at the altar, he venerates it, and if appropriate, incenses it. Omitting the other Introductory Rites of the Mass and, if appropriate, the Kyrie (Lord, have mercy), *he says the Collect of the Mass, and then continues the Mass in the usual way.*

SECOND FORM: THE SOLEMN ENTRANCE

When a procession outside the church cannot take place, the entrance of the Lord is celebrated inside the church by means of a Solemn Entrance before the principal Mass.

Holding branches in their hands, the faithful gather either outside, in front of the church door, or inside the church itself. The Priest and ministers and a representative group of the faithful go to a suitable place in the church outside the sanctuary, where at least the greater part of the faithful can see the rite.

While the Priest approaches the appointed place, the antiphon Hosanna (*page 125*) *or another appropriate chant is sung. Then the blessing of branches and the proclamation of the Gospel of the Lord's entrance into Jerusalem take place as in the First Form. After the Gospel, the Priest processes solemnly with the ministers and the representative group of the faithful through the church to the sanctuary, while the responsory,* As the Lord entered, *or another appropriate chant is sung.*

Arriving at the altar, the Priest venerates it. He then goes to the chair and, omitting the Introductory Rites of the Mass and, if appropriate, the Kyrie (Lord, have mercy), *he says the Collect of the Mass, and then continues the Mass in the usual way.*

THIRD FORM: THE SIMPLE ENTRANCE

At all other Masses of this Sunday at which the Solemn Entrance is not held, the memorial of the Lord's entrance into Jerusalem takes place by means of a Simple Entrance.

While the Priest proceeds to the altar, the Entrance Antiphon with its Psalm or another chant on the same theme is sung. Arriving at the altar, the Priest venerates it and goes to the chair. After the Sign of the Cross, he greets the people and continues the Mass in the usual way.

Entrance Antiphon *cf. Jn 12: 1, 12–13; Ps 24 (23): 9–10* Six days before the Passover, / when the Lord came into the city of Jerusalem, / the children ran to meet him; / in their hands they carried palm branches / and with a loud voice cried out: * **Hosanna in the highest! ◆ Blessed are you, who have come in your abundant mercy!**

O gates, lift high your heads; / grow higher, ancient doors. / Let him enter, the king of glory! / Who is this king of glory? / He, the Lord of hosts, he is the king of glory.   * **Hosanna in the highest! ◆ Blessed are you, who have come in your abundant mercy!**

❖ At the Mass ❖

First Reading *Is 50: 4-7*
The Lord GOD has given me
   a well-trained tongue,
that I might know how to speak to the weary
   a word that will rouse them.

Morning after morning
   he opens my ear that I may hear;
and I have not rebelled,
   have not turned back.
I gave my back to those who beat me,
   my cheeks to those who plucked my beard;
my face I did not shield
   from buffets and spitting.

The Lord GOD is my help,
   therefore I am not disgraced;
I have set my face like flint,
   knowing that I shall not be put to shame.

Responsorial Psalm   Ps 22: 8–9, 17–18, 19–20, 23–24   *Steve Harmon*

My God, my God, why have You a - ban-doned me?

All who see me scoff at me;
   they mock me with parted lips, they wag their heads:
"He relied on the LORD; let him deliver him,
   let him rescue him, if he loves him." ℞

Indeed, many dogs surround me,
   a pack of evildoers closes in upon me;
They have pierced my hands and my feet;
   I can count all my bones. ℞

They divide my garments among them,
   and for my vesture they cast lots.
But you, O LORD, be not far from me;
   O my help, hasten to aid me. ℞

I will proclaim your name to my brethren;
   in the midst of the assembly I will praise you:
"You who fear the LORD, praise him;

all you descendants of Jacob, give glory to him;
revere him, all you descendants of Israel!" ℟

Second Reading   *Phil 2: 6–11*

Christ Jesus, though he was in the form of God,
did not regard equality with God
something to be grasped.
Rather, he emptied himself,
taking the form of a slave,
coming in human likeness;
and found human in appearance,
he humbled himself,
becoming obedient to the point of death,
even death on a cross.
Because of this, God greatly exalted him
and bestowed on him the name
which is above every name,
that at the name of Jesus
every knee should bend,
of those in heaven and on earth and under the earth,
and every tongue confess that
Jesus Christ is Lord,
to the glory of God the Father.

Verse Before the Gospel   *Phil 2: 8–9*   *Amy Righi*

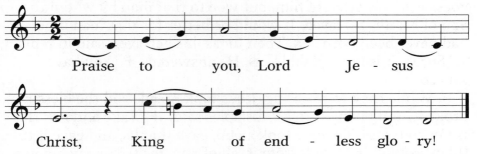

Praise to you, Lord Jesus Christ, King of endless glory!

Christ became obedient to the point of death, / even death
on a cross. / Because of this, God greatly exalted him / and
bestowed on him the name which is above every name.

Gospel Mt 26: 14–27: 66 or 27: 11–54

For the shorter form, read only the parts in brackets. The shorter form begins on page 137. The symbols of the following passion narrative represent Christ (✛), the narrator (N), the voice (V), and the crowd (C).

N. The Passion of our Lord Jesus Christ according to Matthew.

One of the Twelve, who was called Judas Iscariot, went to the chief priests and said, V. "What are you willing to give me if I hand him over to you?" N. They paid him thirty pieces of silver, and from that time on he looked for an opportunity to hand him over.

On the first day of the Feast of Unleavened Bread, the disciples approached Jesus and said, V. "Where do you want us to prepare for you to eat the Passover?" N. He said, ✛ "Go into the city to a certain man and tell him, 'The teacher says, "My appointed time draws near; in your house I shall celebrate the Passover with my disciples."'" N. The disciples then did as Jesus had ordered, and prepared the Passover.

When it was evening, he reclined at table with the Twelve. And while they were eating, he said, ✛ "Amen, I say to you, one of you will betray me." N. Deeply distressed at this, they began to say to him one after another, V. "Surely it is not I, Lord?" N. He said in reply, ✛ "He who has dipped his hand into the dish with me is the one who will betray me. The Son of Man indeed goes, as it is written of him, but woe to that man by whom the Son of Man is betrayed. It would be better for that man if he had never been born." N. Then Judas, his betrayer, said in reply, V. "Surely it is not I, Rabbi?" N. He answered, ✛ "You have said so."

N. While they were eating, Jesus took bread, said the blessing, broke it, and giving it to his disciples said, ✛ "Take and eat; this is my body." N. Then he took a cup, gave thanks, and gave it to them, saying, ✛ "Drink from it, all of you, for this is my blood of the covenant, which will be shed on behalf of many for the forgiveness of sins. I tell you, from now on I shall not drink this fruit of the vine until the day when I drink it with you new in the kingdom of my Father." N. Then, after singing a hymn, they went out to the Mount of Olives.

Then Jesus said to them, ✝ "This night all of you will have your faith in me shaken, for it is written:

I will strike the shepherd,
  and the sheep of the flock will be dispersed;
but after I have been raised up, I shall go before you to Galilee." **N.** Peter said to him in reply, **V.** "Though all may have their faith in you shaken, mine will never be." **N.** Jesus said to him, ✝ "Amen, I say to you, this very night before the cock crows, you will deny me three times." **N.** Peter said to him, **V.** "Even though I should have to die with you, I will not deny you." **N.** And all the disciples spoke likewise.

Then Jesus came with them to a place called Gethsemane, and he said to his disciples, ✝ "Sit here while I go over there and pray." **N.** He took along Peter and the two sons of Zebedee, and began to feel sorrow and distress. Then he said to them, ✝ "My soul is sorrowful even to death. Remain here and keep watch with me." **N.** He advanced a little and fell prostrate in prayer, saying, ✝ "My Father, if it is possible, let this cup pass from me; yet, not as I will, but as you will." **N.** When he returned to his disciples he found them asleep. He said to Peter, ✝ "So you could not keep watch with me for one hour? Watch and pray that you may not undergo the test. The spirit is willing, but the flesh is weak." **N.** Withdrawing a second time, he prayed again, ✝ "My Father, if it is not possible that this cup pass without my drinking it, your will be done!" **N.** Then he returned once more and found them asleep, for they could not keep their eyes open. He left them and withdrew again and prayed a third time, saying the same thing again. Then he returned to his disciples and said to them, ✝ "Are you still sleeping and taking your rest? Behold, the hour is at hand when the Son of Man is to be handed over to sinners. Get up, let us go. Look, my betrayer is at hand."

N. While he was still speaking, Judas, one of the Twelve, arrived, accompanied by a large crowd, with swords and clubs, who had come from the chief priests and the elders of the people. His betrayer had arranged a sign with them, saying, **V.** "The man I shall kiss is the one; arrest him." **N.** Immediately he went over to Jesus and said, **V.** "Hail, Rabbi!" and he kissed him. **N.** Jesus answered him, ✝ "Friend, do what you have come for." **N.** Then stepping forward they laid hands on Jesus and arrested him. And behold, one of those who accompanied Jesus put his hand to his sword, drew it, and struck the high priest's servant, cutting off his ear. Then Jesus said to him, ✛ "Put your sword back into its sheath, for all who take the sword will perish by the sword. Do you think that I cannot call upon my Father and he will not provide me at this moment with more than twelve legions of angels? But then how would the Scriptures be fulfilled which say that it must come to pass in this way?" **N.** At that hour Jesus said to the crowds, ✛ "Have you come out as against a robber, with swords and clubs to seize me? Day after day I sat teaching in the temple area, yet you did not arrest me. But all this has come to pass that the writings of the prophets may be fulfilled." **N.** Then all the disciples left him and fled.

Those who had arrested Jesus led him away to Caiaphas the high priest, where the scribes and the elders were assembled. Peter was following him at a distance as far as the high priest's courtyard, and going inside he sat down with the servants to see the outcome. The chief priests and the entire Sanhedrin kept trying to obtain false testimony against Jesus in order to put him to death, but they found none, though many false witnesses came forward. Finally two came forward who stated, **C. "This man said, 'I can destroy the temple of God and within three days rebuild it.'"** **N.** The high priest rose and addressed him, **V.** "Have you no answer? What are these men testifying against you?" **N.** But Jesus was silent. Then the high priest said to him, **V.** "I order you to tell us under oath before the living God whether you are the Christ, the Son of God." **N.** Jesus said to him in reply, ✛ "You have said so. But I tell you:

From now on you will see 'the Son of Man
　　seated at the right hand of the Power'
　　and 'coming on the clouds of heaven.'"

N. Then the high priest tore his robes and said, **V.** "He has blasphemed! What further need have we of witnesses? You have now heard the blasphemy; what is your opinion?" **N.** They said in reply, **C. "He deserves to die!"** **N.** Then they spat in his face and struck him, while some slapped him, saying, **C. "Prophesy for us, Christ: who is it that struck you?"**

N. Now Peter was sitting outside in the courtyard. One of the maids came over to him and said, **C. "You too were with Jesus the Galilean."** **N.** But he denied it in front of everyone, saying, **v.** "I do not know what you are talking about!" **N.** As he went out to the gate, another girl saw him and said to those who were there, **c.** **"This man was with Jesus the Nazorean."** **N.** Again he denied it with an oath, **v.** "I do not know the man!" **N.** A little later the bystanders came over and said to Peter, **c.** **"Surely you too are one of them; even your speech gives you away."** **N.** At that he began to curse and to swear, **v.** "I do not know the man." **N.** And immediately a cock crowed. Then Peter remembered the word that Jesus had spoken: "Before the cock crows you will deny me three times." He went out and began to weep bitterly.

When it was morning, all the chief priests and the elders of the people took counsel against Jesus to put him to death. They bound him, led him away, and handed him over to Pilate, the governor.

Then Judas, his betrayer, seeing that Jesus had been condemned, deeply regretted what he had done. He returned the thirty pieces of silver to the chief priests and elders, saying, **v.** "I have sinned in betraying innocent blood." **N.** They said, **c.** **"What is that to us? Look to it yourself."** **N.** Flinging the money into the temple, he departed and went off and hanged himself. The chief priests gathered up the money, but said, **c.** **"It is not lawful to deposit this in the temple treasury, for it is the price of blood."** **N.** After consultation, they used it to buy the potter's field as a burial place for foreigners. That is why that field even today is called the Field of Blood. Then was fulfilled what had been said through Jeremiah the prophet, *And they took the thirty pieces of silver, the value of a man with a price on his head, a price set by some of the Israelites, and they paid it out for the potter's field just as the Lord had commanded me.*

(*The shorter form begins here.*)

Now [Jesus stood before the governor, (*shorter form:* Pontius Pilate,) and he questioned him, **v.** "Are you the king of the Jews?" **N.** Jesus said, **+** "You say so." **N.** And when he was accused by the chief priests and elders, he made no answer. Then Pilate said to him, **v.** "Do you not hear how many things they are testifying against you?" **N.** But he did not answer him one word, so that the governor was greatly amazed.

Now on the occasion of the feast the governor was accustomed to release to the crowd one prisoner whom they wished. And at that time they had a notorious prisoner called Barabbas. So when they had assembled, Pilate said to them, **v.** "Which one do you want me to release to you, Barabbas, or Jesus called Christ?" **N.** For he knew that it was out of envy that they had handed him over. While he was still seated on the bench, his wife sent him a message, "Have nothing to do with that righteous man. I suffered much in a dream today because of him." The chief priests and the elders persuaded the crowds to ask for Barabbas but to destroy Jesus. The governor said to them in reply, **v.** "Which of the two do you want me to release to you?" **N.** They answered, **c. "Barabbas!"** **N.** Pilate said to them, **v.** "Then what shall I do with Jesus called Christ?" **N.** They all said, **c. "Let him be crucified!"** **N.** But he said, **v.** "Why? What evil has he done?" **N.** They only shouted the louder, **c. "Let him be crucified!"** **N.** When Pilate saw that he was not succeeding at all, but that a riot was breaking out instead, he took water and washed his hands in the sight of the crowd, saying, **v.** "I am innocent of this man's blood. Look to it yourselves." **N.** And the whole people said in reply, **c. "His blood be upon us and upon our children."** **N.** Then he released Barabbas to them, but after he had Jesus scourged, he handed him over to be crucified.

Then the soldiers of the governor took Jesus inside the praetorium and gathered the whole cohort around him. They stripped off his clothes and threw a scarlet military cloak about him. Weaving a crown out of thorns, they placed it on his head, and a reed in his right hand. And kneeling before him, they mocked him, saying, **c. "Hail, King of the Jews!"** **N.** They spat upon him and took the reed and kept striking him on the head. And when they had mocked him, they stripped him of the cloak, dressed him in his own clothes, and led him off to crucify him.

As they were going out, they met a Cyrenian named Simon; this man they pressed into service to carry his cross.

And when they came to a place called Golgotha—which means Place of the Skull—, they gave Jesus wine to drink mixed with gall. But when he had tasted it, he refused to drink. After they had crucified him, they divided his garments by casting lots; then they sat down and kept watch over him there. And they placed over his head the written charge against him: This is Jesus, the King of the Jews. Two revolutionaries were crucified with him, one on his right and the other on his left. Those passing by reviled him, shaking their heads and saying, **C.** **"You who would destroy the temple and rebuild it in three days, save yourself, if you are the Son of God, and come down from the cross!"** **N.** Likewise the chief priests with the scribes and elders mocked him and said, **C.** **"He saved others; he cannot save himself. So he is the king of Israel! Let him come down from the cross now, and we will believe in him. He trusted in God; let him deliver him now if he wants him. For he said, 'I am the Son of God.'"** **N.** The revolutionaries who were crucified with him also kept abusing him in the same way.

From noon onward, darkness came over the whole land until three in the afternoon. And about three o'clock Jesus cried out in a loud voice, ✠ *"Eli, Eli, lema sabachthani?"* **N.** which means, ✠ "My God, my God, why have you forsaken me?" **N.** Some of the bystanders who heard it said, **C.** **"This one is calling for Elijah."** **N.** Immediately one of them ran to get a sponge; he soaked it in wine, and putting it on a reed, gave it to him to drink. But the rest said, **C.** **"Wait, let us see if Elijah comes to save him."** **N.** But Jesus cried out again in a loud voice, and gave up his spirit.

Here all kneel and pause for a short time.

And behold, the veil of the sanctuary was torn in two from top to bottom. The earth quaked, rocks were split, tombs were opened, and the bodies of many saints who had fallen asleep were raised. And coming forth from their tombs after his resurrection, they entered the holy city and appeared to many. The centurion and the men with him who were keeping watch over Jesus feared greatly when they saw the earthquake and all that was happening, and they said, **C.** **"Truly, this was the Son of God!"**] **N.** There were many women there, looking on from a distance, who had followed Jesus from Galilee, ministering to him. Among them were Mary Magdalene and Mary the mother of James and Joseph, and the mother of the sons of Zebedee.

When it was evening, there came a rich man from Arimathea named Joseph, who was himself a disciple of Jesus. He went to

Pilate and asked for the body of Jesus; then Pilate ordered it to be handed over. Taking the body, Joseph wrapped it in clean linen and laid it in his new tomb that he had hewn in the rock. Then he rolled a huge stone across the entrance to the tomb and departed. But Mary Magdalene and the other Mary remained sitting there, facing the tomb.

The next day, the one following the day of preparation, the chief priests and the Pharisees gathered before Pilate and said, **c. "Sir, we remember that this impostor while still alive said, 'After three days I will be raised up.' Give orders, then, that the grave be secured until the third day, lest his disciples come and steal him and say to the people, 'He has been raised from the dead.' This last imposture would be worse than the first."** **N.** Pilate said to them, **v. "The guard is yours; go, secure it as best you can."** **N.** So they went and secured the tomb by fixing a seal to the stone and setting the guard.

Communion Antiphon Mt 26:42 **Father, if this chalice cannot pass without my drinking it, ◆ your will be done.**

The readings for the Sacred Paschal Triduum begin on page 669.

Easter Time † YEAR A

The readings for Easter Sunday can be found on page 740.

SECOND SUNDAY OF EASTER

DIVINE MERCY SUNDAY

Entrance Antiphon *1 Pt 2: 2* Like newborn infants, you must
long for the pure, spiritual milk, ✦ that in him you may grow
to salvation, alleluia.

Or: *4 Esdr 2: 36–37* Receive the joy of your glory, giving thanks to
God, ✦ who has called you into the heavenly kingdom, alleluia.

First Reading *Acts 2: 42–47* They devoted themselves to the teaching
of the apostles and to the communal life, to the breaking
of bread and to the prayers. Awe came upon everyone, and
many wonders and signs were done through the apostles. All
who believed were together and had all things in common;
they would sell their property and possessions and divide
them among all according to each one's need. Every day they
devoted themselves to meeting together in the temple area and
to breaking bread in their homes. They ate their meals with
exultation and sincerity of heart, praising God and enjoying
favor with all the people. And every day the Lord added to their
number those who were being saved.

Responsorial Psalm   Ps 118: 2–4, 13–15, 22–24   *based on* ICH WILL DICH LIEBEN

Give thanks to the Lord for he is good, his love is ev - er - last - ing.

Or: ℟ **Alleluia.**

Let the house of Israel say,
    "His mercy endures forever."
Let the house of Aaron say,
    "His mercy endures forever."
Let those who fear the LORD say,
    "His mercy endures forever."   ℟

I was hard pressed and was falling,
    but the LORD helped me.
My strength and my courage is the LORD,
    and he has been my savior.
The joyful shout of victory
    in the tents of the just.   ℟

The stone which the builders rejected
    has become the cornerstone.
By the LORD has this been done;
    it is wonderful in our eyes.
This is the day the LORD has made;
    let us be glad and rejoice in it.   ℟

Second Reading 1 Pt 1: 3–9 Blessed be the God and Father of our
Lord Jesus Christ, who in his great mercy gave us a new birth
to a living hope through the resurrection of Jesus Christ from
the dead, to an inheritance that is imperishable, undefiled, and
unfading, kept in heaven for you who by the power of God are
safeguarded through faith, to a salvation that is ready to be
revealed in the final time. In this you rejoice, although now for a

little while you may have to suffer through various trials, so that the genuineness of your faith, more precious than gold that is perishable even though tested by fire, may prove to be for praise, glory, and honor at the revelation of Jesus Christ. Although you have not seen him you love him; even though you do not see him now yet believe in him, you rejoice with an indescribable and glorious joy, as you attain the goal of your faith, the salvation of your souls.

Alleluia   *Jn 20: 29*   *Laura Lea Duckworth*

Al - le - lu - ia, al-le-lu - ia.

Al - le - lu - ia, al-le-lu - ia.

You believe in me, Thomas, because you have seen me, says the Lord; / blessed are they who have not seen me, but still believe! **Alleluia, alleluia.**

Gospel *Jn 20: 19–31* On the evening of that first day of the week, when the doors were locked, where the disciples were, for fear of the Jews, Jesus came and stood in their midst and said to them, "Peace be with you." When he had said this, he showed them his hands and his side. The disciples rejoiced when they saw the Lord. Jesus said to them again, "Peace be with you. As the Father has sent me, so I send you." And when he had said this, he breathed on them and said to them, "Receive the Holy Spirit. Whose sins you forgive are forgiven them, and whose sins you retain are retained."

Thomas, called Didymus, one of the Twelve, was not with them when Jesus came. So the other disciples said to him, "We have seen the Lord." But he said to them, "Unless I see the mark of the nails in his hands and put my finger into the nailmarks and put my hand into his side, I will not believe."

Now a week later his disciples were again inside and Thomas was with them. Jesus came, although the doors were locked, and

...their midst and said, "Peace be with you." Then he said ...omas, "Put your finger here and see my hands, and bring ...ur hand and put it into my side, and do not be unbelieving, but believe." Thomas answered and said to him, "My Lord and my God!" Jesus said to him, "Have you come to believe because you have seen me? Blessed are those who have not seen and have believed."

Now, Jesus did many other signs in the presence of his disciples that are not written in this book. But these are written that you may come to believe that Jesus is the Christ, the Son of God, and that through this belief you may have life in his name.

Communion Antiphon *cf. Jn 20: 27* **Bring your hand and feel the place of the nails, ◆ and do not be unbelieving but believing, alleluia.**

THIRD SUNDAY OF EASTER

Entrance Antiphon *cf. Ps 66 (65): 1–2* **Cry out with joy to God, all the earth; ◆ O sing to the glory of his name. ◆ O render him glorious praise, alleluia.**

First Reading *Acts 2: 14, 22-33* Then Peter stood up with the Eleven, raised his voice, and proclaimed: "You who are Jews, indeed all of you staying in Jerusalem. Let this be known to you, and listen to my words. You who are Israelites, hear these words. Jesus the Nazorean was a man commended to you by God with mighty deeds, wonders, and signs, which God worked through him in your midst, as you yourselves know. This man, delivered up by the set plan and foreknowledge of God, you killed, using lawless men to crucify him. But God raised him up, releasing him from the throes of death, because it was impossible for him to be held by it. For David says of him:
I saw the Lord ever before me,
with him at my right hand I shall not be disturbed.
Therefore my heart has been glad and my tongue has exulted;
my flesh, too, will dwell in hope,
because you will not abandon my soul to the netherworld,

nor will you suffer your holy one to see corruption.
You have made known to me the paths of life;
you will fill me with joy in your presence.

"My brothers, one can confidently say to you about the
patriarch David that he died and was buried, and his tomb is
in our midst to this day. But since he was a prophet and knew
that God had sworn an oath to him that he would set one of
his descendants upon his throne, he foresaw and spoke of the
resurrection of the Christ, that neither was he abandoned to the
netherworld nor did his flesh see corruption. God raised this
Jesus; of this we are all witnesses. Exalted at the right hand of
God, he received the promise of the Holy Spirit from the Father
and poured him forth, as you see and hear."

Responsorial Psalm Ps 16: 1–2, 5, 7–8, 9–10, 11 Joe Higginbotham

Lord, you will show us   the path of   life.

Or: ℟ **Alleluia.**

Keep me, O God, for in you I take refuge;
   I say to the LORD, "My Lord are you."
O LORD, my allotted portion and my cup,
   you it is who hold fast my lot. ℟

I bless the LORD who counsels me;
   even in the night my heart exhorts me.
I set the LORD ever before me;
   with him at my right hand I shall not be disturbed. ℟

Therefore my heart is glad and my soul rejoices,
   my body, too, abides in confidence;
because you will not abandon my soul to the netherworld,
   nor will you suffer your faithful one to undergo
      corruption. ℟

You will show me the path to life,
   abounding joy in your presence,

the delights at your right hand forever. ℟

Second Reading 1 Pt 1: 17-21 Beloved: If you invoke as Father him who judges impartially according to each one's works, conduct yourselves with reverence during the time of your sojourning, realizing that you were ransomed from your futile conduct, handed on by your ancestors, not with perishable things like silver or gold but with the precious blood of Christ as of a spotless unblemished lamb.

He was known before the foundation of the world but revealed in the final time for you, who through him believe in God who raised him from the dead and gave him glory, so that your faith and hope are in God.

Alleluia   cf. Lk 24: 32   *Laura Lea Duckworth*

Al - le - lu - ia, al-le-lu - ia.

Al - le - lu - ia, al-le-lu - ia.

Lord Jesus, open the Scriptures to us; / make our hearts burn while you speak to us. **Alleluia, alleluia.**

Gospel Lk 24: 13-35 That very day, the first day of the week, two of Jesus' disciples were going to a village seven miles from Jerusalem called Emmaus, and they were conversing about all the things that had occurred. And it happened that while they were conversing and debating, Jesus himself drew near and walked with them, but their eyes were prevented from recognizing him. He asked them, "What are you discussing as you walk along?" They stopped, looking downcast. One of them, named Cleopas, said to him in reply, "Are you the only visitor to Jerusalem who does not know of the things that have taken place there in these days?" And he replied to them, "What sort of things?" They said to him, "The things that happened to Jesus the Nazarene, who was a prophet mighty in deed and word before God and all the people, how our chief priests and rulers

both handed him over to a sentence of death and crucified him.
But we were hoping that he would be the one to redeem Israel;
and besides all this, it is now the third day since this took place.
Some women from our group, however, have astounded us: they
were at the tomb early in the morning and did not find his body;
they came back and reported that they had indeed seen a vision
of angels who announced that he was alive. Then some of those
with us went to the tomb and found things just as the women
had described, but him they did not see." And he said to them,
"Oh, how foolish you are! How slow of heart to believe all that
the prophets spoke! Was it not necessary that the Christ should
suffer these things and enter into his glory?" Then beginning
with Moses and all the prophets, he interpreted to them what
referred to him in all the Scriptures. As they approached the
village to which they were going, he gave the impression that he
was going on farther. But they urged him, "Stay with us, for it
is nearly evening and the day is almost over." So he went in to
stay with them. And it happened that, while he was with them
at table, he took bread, said the blessing, broke it, and gave it to
them. With that their eyes were opened and they recognized
him, but he vanished from their sight. Then they said to each
other, "Were not our hearts burning within us while he spoke to
us on the way and opened the Scriptures to us?" So they set out
at once and returned to Jerusalem where they found gathered
together the eleven and those with them who were saying, "The
Lord has truly been raised and has appeared to Simon!" Then the
two recounted what had taken place on the way and how he was
made known to them in the breaking of bread.

Communion Antiphon *cf. Lk 24: 35* **The disciples recognized the
Lord Jesus ✦ in the breaking of the bread, alleluia.**

FOURTH SUNDAY OF EASTER

Entrance Antiphon *cf. Ps 33 (32): 5–6* **The merciful love of the Lord
fills the earth; ✦ by the word of the Lord the heavens were
made, alleluia.**

First Reading *Acts 2: 14a, 36–41* Then Peter stood up with the Eleven, raised his voice, and proclaimed: "Let the whole house of Israel know for certain that God has made both Lord and Christ, this Jesus whom you crucified."

Now when they heard this, they were cut to the heart, and they asked Peter and the other apostles, "What are we to do, my brothers?" Peter said to them, "Repent and be baptized, every one of you, in the name of Jesus Christ for the forgiveness of your sins; and you will receive the gift of the Holy Spirit. For the promise is made to you and to your children and to all those far off, whomever the Lord our God will call." He testified with many other arguments, and was exhorting them, "Save yourselves from this corrupt generation." Those who accepted his message were baptized, and about three thousand persons were added that day.

Responsorial Psalm *Ps 23: 1–3a, 3b–4, 5, 6*   *Vince Ambrosetti*

The Lord is my shep-herd; there is noth-ing I shall want.

Or: ℟ **Alleluia.**

The LORD is my shepherd; I shall not want.
  In verdant pastures he gives me repose;
beside restful waters he leads me;
  he refreshes my soul. ℟

He guides me in right paths
  for his name's sake.
Even though I walk in the dark valley
  I fear no evil; for you are at my side
with your rod and your staff
  that give me courage. ℟

You spread the table before me
  in the sight of my foes;
you anoint my head with oil;
  my cup overflows. ℟

Only goodness and kindness follow me
  all the days of my life;
and I shall dwell in the house of the LORD
  for years to come. ℟

Second Reading 1 Pt 2: 20b–25 Beloved: If you are patient when you suffer for doing what is good, this is a grace before God. For to this you have been called, because Christ also suffered for you, leaving you an example that you should follow in his footsteps. *He committed no sin, and no deceit was found in his mouth.* When he was insulted, he returned no insult; when he suffered, he did not threaten; instead, he handed himself over to the one who judges justly. He himself bore our sins in his body upon the cross, so that, free from sin, we might live for righteousness. By his wounds you have been healed. For you had gone astray like sheep, but you have now returned to the shepherd and guardian of your souls.

Alleluia Jn 10: 14   *Laura Lea Duckworth*

I am the good shepherd, says the Lord; / I know my sheep, and mine know me. **Alleluia, alleluia.**

Gospel Jn 10: 1–10 Jesus said: "Amen, amen, I say to you, whoever does not enter a sheepfold through the gate but climbs over elsewhere is a thief and a robber. But whoever enters through the gate is the shepherd of the sheep. The gatekeeper opens it

for him, and the sheep hear his voice, as the shepherd calls his
own sheep by name and leads them out. When he has driven
out all his own, he walks ahead of them, and the sheep follow
him, because they recognize his voice. But they will not follow
a stranger; they will run away from him, because they do not
recognize the voice of strangers." Although Jesus used this figure
of speech, the Pharisees did not realize what he was trying to
tell them.

So Jesus said again, "Amen, amen, I say to you, I am the gate
for the sheep. All who came before me are thieves and robbers,
but the sheep did not listen to them. I am the gate. Whoever
enters through me will be saved, and will come in and go out
and find pasture. A thief comes only to steal and slaughter and
destroy; I came so that they might have life and have it more
abundantly."

Communion Antiphon
**The Good Shepherd has risen, ◆ who laid down his life for his
sheep ◆ and willingly died for his flock, alleluia.**

FIFTH SUNDAY OF EASTER

Entrance Antiphon cf. Ps 98 (97): 1-2 **O sing a new song to the Lord,
◆ for he has worked wonders; ◆ in the sight of the nations ◆ he
has shown his deliverance, alleluia.**

First Reading Acts 6: 1-7 As the number of disciples continued to
grow, the Hellenists complained against the Hebrews because
their widows were being neglected in the daily distribution. So
the Twelve called together the community of the disciples and
said, "It is not right for us to neglect the word of God to serve
at table. Brothers, select from among you seven reputable men,
filled with the Spirit and wisdom, whom we shall appoint to
this task, whereas we shall devote ourselves to prayer and to
the ministry of the word." The proposal was acceptable to the
whole community, so they chose Stephen, a man filled with

faith and the Holy Spirit, also Philip, Prochorus, Nicanor, Timon, Parmenas, and Nicholas of Antioch, a convert to Judaism. They presented these men to the apostles who prayed and laid hands on them. The word of God continued to spread, and the number of the disciples in Jerusalem increased greatly; even a large group of priests were becoming obedient to the faith.

Responsorial Psalm   Ps 33: 1–2, 4–5, 18–19   *Beverly McDevitt*

Lord, let your mer - cy be on us, as we place our trust in you.

Or: ℟ **Alleluia.**

Exult, you just, in the LORD;
  praise from the upright is fitting.
Give thanks to the LORD on the harp;
  with the ten-stringed lyre chant his praises. ℟

Upright is the word of the LORD,
  and all his works are trustworthy.
He loves justice and right;
  of the kindness of the LORD the earth is full. ℟

See, the eyes of the LORD are upon those who fear him,
  upon those who hope for his kindness,
To deliver them from death
  and preserve them in spite of famine. ℟

Second Reading 1 Pt 2: 4–9 Beloved: Come to him, a living stone, rejected by human beings but chosen and precious in the sight of God, and, like living stones, let yourselves be built into a spiritual house to be a holy priesthood to offer spiritual sacrifices acceptable to God through Jesus Christ. For it says in Scripture:

Behold, I am laying a stone in Zion,
a cornerstone, chosen and precious,
and whoever believes in it shall not be put to shame.

Therefore, its value is for you who have faith, but for those without faith:

The stone that the builders rejected
has become the cornerstone,

and

a stone that will make people stumble,
and a rock that will make them fall.

They stumble by disobeying the word, as is their destiny.

You are "a chosen race, a royal priesthood, a holy nation, a people of his own, so that you may announce the praises" of him who called you out of darkness into his wonderful light.

Alleluia Jn 14: 6   *Laura Lea Duckworth*

Al - le - lu - ia, al-le-lu - ia.

Al - le - lu - ia, al-le-lu - ia.

I am the way, the truth and the life, says the Lord; / no one comes to the Father, except through me. **Alleluia, alleluia.**

Gospel Jn 14: 1–12 Jesus said to his disciples: "Do not let your hearts be troubled. You have faith in God; have faith also in me. In my Father's house there are many dwelling places. If there were not, would I have told you that I am going to prepare a place for you? And if I go and prepare a place for you, I will come back again and take you to myself, so that where I am you also may be. Where I am going you know the way." Thomas said to him, "Master, we do not know where you are going; how can we know the way?" Jesus said to him, "I am the way and the truth and the life. No one comes to the Father except through me. If you know me, then you will also know my Father. From now on you do know him and have seen him." Philip said to him, "Master, show us the Father, and that will be enough for us." Jesus said to him, "Have I been with you for so long a time and you still do not know me, Philip? Whoever has seen me has seen the Father. How can you say, 'Show us the Father'? Do you not believe that I am in the Father and the Father is in me? The words that I speak to you I do not speak on my own. The Father who dwells in me is doing his works. Believe me that I am in the Father and the Father is in me, or else, believe because of the works themselves. Amen, amen, I say to you, whoever believes in me will do the works that I do, and will do greater ones than these, because I am going to the Father."

Communion Antiphon *cf. Jn 15: 1, 5* **I am the true vine and you are the branches, says the Lord. ◆ Whoever remains in me, and I in him, bears fruit in plenty, alleluia.**

SIXTH SUNDAY OF EASTER

Entrance Antiphon *cf. Is 48: 20* **Proclaim a joyful sound and let it be heard; ◆ proclaim to the ends of the earth: ◆ The Lord has freed his people, alleluia.**

When the Ascension of the Lord is celebrated the following Sunday, the second reading and Gospel from the Seventh Sunday of Easter (see page 159) may be read on the Sixth Sunday of Easter.

First Reading *Acts 8: 5-8, 14-17* Philip went down to the city of Samaria and proclaimed the Christ to them. With one accord, the crowds paid attention to what was said by Philip when they heard it and saw the signs he was doing. For unclean spirits, crying out in a loud voice, came out of many possessed people, and many paralyzed or crippled people were cured. There was great joy in that city.

Now when the apostles in Jerusalem heard that Samaria had accepted the word of God, they sent them Peter and John, who went down and prayed for them, that they might receive the Holy Spirit, for it had not yet fallen upon any of them; they had only been baptized in the name of the Lord Jesus. Then they laid hands on them and they received the Holy Spirit.

Responsorial Psalm   Ps 66: 1–3, 4–5, 6–7, 16, 20   *Bill Svarda*

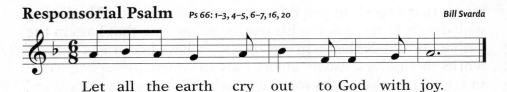

Let all the earth cry out to God with joy.

Or: ℟ **Alleluia.**

Shout joyfully to God, all the earth,
 sing praise to the glory of his name;
 proclaim his glorious praise.
Say to God, "How tremendous are your deeds!" ℟

"Let all on earth worship and sing praise to you,
 sing praise to your name!"
Come and see the works of God,
 his tremendous deeds among the children of Adam. ℟

He has changed the sea into dry land;
 through the river they passed on foot;
 therefore let us rejoice in him.
He rules by his might forever. ℟

Hear now, all you who fear God, while I declare
 what he has done for me.
Blessed be God who refused me not
 my prayer or his kindness! ℟

Second Reading 1 Pt 3: 15–18 Beloved: Sanctify Christ as Lord in your hearts. Always be ready to give an explanation to anyone who asks you for a reason for your hope, but do it with gentleness and reverence, keeping your conscience clear, so that, when you are maligned, those who defame your good conduct in Christ may themselves be put to shame. For it is better to suffer for doing good, if that be the will of God, than for doing evil. For Christ also suffered for sins once, the righteous for the sake of the unrighteous, that he might lead you to God. Put to death in the flesh, he was brought to life in the Spirit.

Alleluia   Jn 14: 23   Laura Lea Duckworth

Al - le - lu - ia, al-le-lu - ia.

Al - le - lu - ia, al-le-lu - ia.

Whoever loves me will keep my word, says the Lord, /
and my Father will love him and we will come to him.
Alleluia, alleluia.

Gospel Jn 14: 15-21 Jesus said to his disciples: "If you love me, you will keep my commandments. And I will ask the Father, and he will give you another Advocate to be with you always, the Spirit of truth, whom the world cannot accept, because it neither sees nor knows him. But you know him, because he remains with you, and will be in you. I will not leave you orphans; I will come to you. In a little while the world will no longer see me, but you will see me, because I live and you will live. On that day you will realize that I am in my Father and you are in me and I in you. Whoever has my commandments and observes them is the one who loves me. And whoever loves me will be loved by my Father, and I will love him and reveal myself to him."

Communion Antiphon Jn 14: 15-16 If you love me, keep my commandments, says the Lord, ◆ and I will ask the Father and he will send you another Paraclete, ◆ to abide with you for ever, alleluia.

THE ASCENSION OF THE LORD

Where the Solemnity of the Ascension is not to be observed as a Holyday of Obligation, it is assigned to the Seventh Sunday of Easter as its proper day.

Entrance Antiphon

At the Vigil Mass   Ps 68 (67): 33, 35   **You kingdoms of the earth, sing to God; ◆ praise the Lord, who ascends above the highest heavens; ◆ his majesty and might are in the skies, alleluia.**

At the Mass During the Day   Acts 1: 11   **Men of Galilee, why gaze in wonder at the heavens? ◆ This Jesus whom you saw ascending into heaven ◆ will return as you saw him go, alleluia.**

First Reading Acts 1: 1-11 In the first book, Theophilus, I dealt with all that Jesus did and taught until the day he was taken up, after giving instructions through the Holy Spirit to the apostles whom he had chosen. He presented himself alive to them by many proofs after he had suffered, appearing to them during forty days and speaking about the kingdom of God. While meeting with the them, he enjoined them not to depart from Jerusalem, but to wait for "the promise of the Father about which you have heard me speak; for John baptized with water, but in a few days you will be baptized with the Holy Spirit."

When they had gathered together they asked him, "Lord, are you at this time going to restore the kingdom to Israel?" He answered them, "It is not for you to know the times or seasons that the Father has established by his own authority. But you will receive power when the Holy Spirit comes upon you, and you will be my witnesses in Jerusalem, throughout Judea and Samaria, and to the ends of the earth." When he had said this, as they were looking on, he was lifted up, and a cloud took him from their sight. While they were looking intently at the sky as he was going, suddenly two men dressed in white garments stood beside them. They said, "Men of Galilee, why are you standing there looking at the sky? This Jesus who has been taken up from you into heaven will return in the same way as you have seen him going into heaven."

Responsorial Psalm Ps 47: 2–3, 6–7, 8–9   Joe Higginbotham

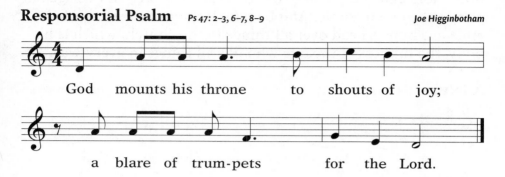

God mounts his throne to shouts of joy;
a blare of trum-pets for the Lord.

Or: ℟ **Alleluia.**

All you peoples, clap your hands,
   shout to God with cries of gladness,
For the LORD, the Most High, the awesome,
   is the great king over all the earth. ℟

God mounts his throne amid shouts of joy;
   the LORD, amid trumpet blasts.
Sing praise to God, sing praise;
   sing praise to our king, sing praise. ℟

For king of all the earth is God;
   sing hymns of praise.
God reigns over the nations,
   God sits upon his holy throne. ℟

Second Reading Eph 1: 17–23 Brothers and sisters: May the God of our Lord Jesus Christ, the Father of glory, give you a Spirit of wisdom and revelation resulting in knowledge of him. May the eyes of your hearts be enlightened, that you may know what is the hope that belongs to his call, what are the riches of glory in his inheritance among the holy ones, and what is the surpassing greatness of his power for us who believe, in accord with the exercise of his great might, which he worked in Christ, raising him from the dead and seating him at his right hand in the heavens, far above every principality, authority, power, and dominion, and every name that is named not only in this age but also in the one to come. And he put all things beneath his feet and gave him as head over all things to the church, which is his body, the fullness of the one who fills all things in every way.

Alleluia   Mt 28: 19a, 20b   *Laura Lea Duckworth*

Go and teach all nations, says the Lord; / I am with you always, until the end of the world.   **Alleluia, alleluia.**

Gospel Mt 28: 16–20 The eleven disciples went to Galilee, to the mountain to which Jesus had ordered them. When they saw him, they worshiped, but they doubted. Then Jesus approached and said to them, "All power in heaven and on earth has been given to me. Go, therefore, and make disciples of all nations, baptizing them in the name of the Father, and of the Son, and of the Holy Spirit, teaching them to observe all that I have commanded you. And behold, I am with you always, until the end of the age."

Communion Antiphon

At the Vigil Mass   cf. Heb 10: 12 **Christ, offering a single sacrifice for sins, ◆ is seated for ever at God's right hand, alleluia.**

At the Mass During the Day   Mt 28: 20 **Behold, I am with you always, ◆ even to the end of the age, alleluia.**

SEVENTH SUNDAY OF EASTER

Entrance Antiphon *cf. Ps 27 (26): 7–9* O Lord, hear my voice, for I have called to you; ◆ of you my heart has spoken: Seek his face; ◆ hide not your face from me, alleluia.

First Reading *Acts 1: 12–14* After Jesus had been taken up to heaven the apostles returned to Jerusalem from the mount called Olivet, which is near Jerusalem, a sabbath day's journey away.

When they entered the city they went to the upper room where they were staying, Peter and John and James and Andrew, Philip and Thomas, Bartholomew and Matthew, James son of Alphaeus, Simon the Zealot, and Judas son of James. All these devoted themselves with one accord to prayer, together with some women, and Mary the mother of Jesus, and his brothers.

Responsorial Psalm *Ps 27: 1, 4, 7–8*   *based on* ELLACOMBE

I be-lieve that I shall see the good things of the Lord in the land of the liv-ing.

Or: ℟ **Alleluia.**

The LORD is my light and my salvation;
  whom should I fear?
The LORD is my life's refuge;
  of whom should I be afraid? ℟

One thing I ask of the LORD;
  this I seek:
To dwell in the house of the LORD
  all the days of my life,

That I may gaze on the loveliness of the LORD
and contemplate his temple.   ℟

Hear, O LORD, the sound of my call;
have pity on me, and answer me.
Of you my heart speaks; you my glance seeks.   ℟

Second Reading 1 Pt 4: 13–16 Beloved: Rejoice to the extent that
you share in the sufferings of Christ, so that when his glory is
revealed you may also rejoice exultantly. If you are insulted for
the name of Christ, blessed are you, for the Spirit of glory and
of God rests upon you. But let no one among you be made to
suffer as a murderer, a thief, an evildoer, or as an intriguer. But
whoever is made to suffer as a Christian should not be ashamed
but glorify God because of the name.

Alleluia cf. Jn 14: 18   *Laura Lea Duckworth*

Al - le - lu - ia, al-le-lu - ia.

Al - le - lu - ia, al-le-lu - ia.

I will not leave you orphans, says the Lord. / I will come
back to you, and your heart will rejoice.   **Alleluia, alleluia.**

Gospel Jn 17: 1–11a Jesus raised his eyes to heaven and said, "Father,
the hour has come. Give glory to your son, so that your son may
glorify you, just as you gave him authority over all people, so
that your son may give eternal life to all you gave him. Now this
is eternal life, that they should know you, the only true God, and
the one whom you sent, Jesus Christ. I glorified you on earth by
accomplishing the work that you gave me to do. Now glorify me,
Father, with you, with the glory that I had with you before the
world began.

"I revealed your name to those whom you gave me out of the
world. They belonged to you, and you gave them to me, and they

have kept your word. Now they know that everything you gave me is from you, because the words you gave to me I have given to them, and they accepted them and truly understood that I came from you, and they have believed that you sent me. I pray for them. I do not pray for the world but for the ones you have given me, because they are yours, and everything of mine is yours and everything of yours is mine, and I have been glorified in them. And now I will no longer be in the world, but they are in the world, while I am coming to you."

Communion Antiphon *Jn 17: 22* **Father, I pray that they may be one ♦ as we also are one, alleluia.**

PENTECOST SUNDAY

❖ At the Vigil Mass ❖

For the simple form of the Vigil, only one of the four Old Testament readings is used, with Psalm 104 as the Responsorial Psalm.

Entrance Antiphon *Rom 5: 5; cf. 8: 11* **The love of God has been poured into our hearts ♦ through the Spirit of God dwelling within us, alleluia.**

First Reading *Gen 11: 1–9* The whole world spoke the same language, using the same words. While the people were migrating in the east, they came upon a valley in the land of Shinar and settled there. They said to one another, "Come, let us mold bricks and harden them with fire." They used bricks for stone, and bitumen for mortar. Then they said, "Come, let us build ourselves a city and a tower with its top in the sky, and so make a name for ourselves; otherwise we shall be scattered all over the earth."

The LORD came down to see the city and the tower that the people had built. Then the LORD said: "If now, while they are one people, all speaking the same language, they have started to do this, nothing will later stop them from doing whatever they presume to do. Let us then go down there and confuse their language, so that one will not understand what another says." Thus the LORD scattered them from there all over the earth, and they stopped building the city. That is why it was called Babel, because there the LORD confused the speech of all the world. It was from that place that he scattered them all over the earth.

Responsorial Psalm   Ps 33: 10–11, 12–13, 14–15   Jane Terwilliger

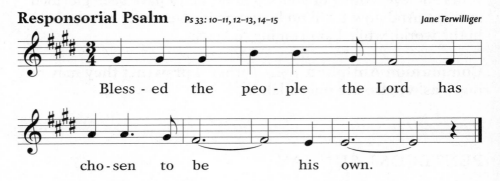

Bless - ed   the   peo - ple   the Lord   has cho - sen   to   be   his   own.

The LORD brings to nought the plans of nations;
    he foils the designs of peoples.
But the plan of the LORD stands forever;
    the design of his heart, through all generations.   ℟

Blessed the nation whose God is the LORD,
    the people he has chosen for his own inheritance.
From heaven the LORD looks down;
    he sees all mankind.   ℟

From his fixed throne he beholds
    all who dwell on the earth,
He who fashioned the heart of each,
    he who knows all their works.   ℟

Second Reading   Ex 19: 3–8a, 16–20b Moses went up the mountain to God. Then the LORD called to him and said, "Thus shall you say to the house of Jacob; tell the Israelites: You have seen for yourselves how I treated the Egyptians and how I bore you up on eagle wings and brought you here to myself. Therefore, if you hearken to my voice and keep my covenant, you shall be my special possession, dearer to me than all other people, though all the earth is mine. You shall be to me a kingdom of priests, a holy nation. That is what you must tell the Israelites." So Moses went and summoned the elders of the people. When he set before them all that the LORD had ordered him to tell them, the people all answered together, "Everything the LORD has said, we will do."

On the morning of the third day there were peals of thunder and lightning, and a heavy cloud over the mountain, and a very loud trumpet blast, so that all the people in the camp trembled. But Moses led the people out of the camp to meet God, and they stationed themselves at the foot of the mountain. Mount Sinai was all wrapped in smoke, for the LORD came down upon it in fire. The smoke rose from it as though from a furnace, and the whole mountain trembled violently. The trumpet blast grew louder and louder, while Moses was speaking, and God answering him with thunder.

When the LORD came down to the top of Mount Sinai, he summoned Moses to the top of the mountain.

Responsorial Psalm Dn 3:52, 53, 54, 55, 56 Alexander Young

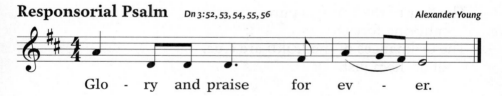

Glo - ry and praise for ev - er.

"Blessed are you, O Lord, the God of our fathers,
    praiseworthy and exalted above all forever;
And blessed is your holy and glorious name,
    praiseworthy and exalted above all for all ages." ℟

"Blessed are you in the temple of your holy glory,
    praiseworthy and glorious above all forever." ℟

"Blessed are you on the throne of your Kingdom,
    praiseworthy and exalted above all forever." ℟

"Blessed are you who look into the depths
    from your throne upon the cherubim,
    praiseworthy and exalted above all forever." ℟

"Blessed are you in the firmament of heaven,
   praiseworthy and glorious forever."   ℟

Or: Ps 19:8, 9, 10, 11   Joe Higginbotham

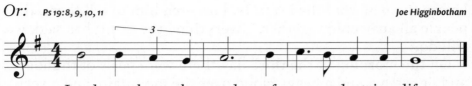

Lord, you have the words   of   ev-er-last-ing life.

The law of the LORD is perfect,
   refreshing the soul;
The decree of the LORD is trustworthy,
   giving wisdom to the simple.   ℟

The precepts of the LORD are right,
   rejoicing the heart;
The command of the LORD is clear,
   enlightening the eye.   ℟

The fear of the LORD is pure,
   enduring forever;
The ordinances of the LORD are true,
   all of them just.   ℟

They are more precious than gold,
   than a heap of purest gold;
Sweeter also than syrup
   or honey from the comb.   ℟

Third Reading: Ez 37: 1–14 The hand of the LORD came upon me,
and he led me out in the spirit of the LORD and set me in the
center of the plain, which was now filled with bones. He made
me walk among the bones in every direction so that I saw how
many they were on the surface of the plain. How dry they
were! He asked me: Son of man, can these bones come to life?
I answered, "Lord GOD, you alone know that." Then he said
to me: Prophesy over these bones, and say to them: Dry bones,
hear the word of the LORD! Thus says the Lord GOD to these

bones: See! I will bring spirit into you, that you may come to life. I will put sinews upon you, make flesh grow over you, cover you with skin, and put spirit in you so that you may come to life and know that I am the LORD. I, Ezekiel, prophesied as I had been told, and even as I was prophesying I heard a noise; it was a rattling as the bones came together, bone joining bone. I saw the sinews and the flesh come upon them, and the skin cover them, but there was no spirit in them. Then the LORD said to me: Prophesy to the spirit, prophesy, son of man, and say to the spirit: Thus says the Lord GOD: From the four winds come, O spirit, and breathe into these slain that they may come to life. I prophesied as he told me, and the spirit came into them; they came alive and stood upright, a vast army. Then he said to me: Son of man, these bones are the whole house of Israel. They have been saying, "Our bones are dried up, our hope is lost, and we are cut off." Therefore, prophesy and say to them: Thus says the Lord GOD: O my people, I will open your graves and have you rise from them, and bring you back to the land of Israel. Then you shall know that I am the LORD, when I open your graves and have you rise from them, O my people! I will put my spirit in you that you may live, and I will settle you upon your land; thus you shall know that I am the LORD. I have promised, and I will do it, says the LORD.

Responsorial Psalm   Ps 107: 2–3, 4–5, 6–7, 8–9   Michael Giszczak

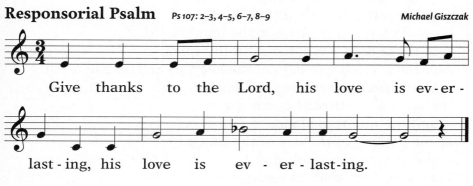

Give thanks to the Lord, his love is ev-er-last-ing, his love is ev-er-last-ing.

Or: **Alleluia.**

Let the redeemed of the LORD say,
   those whom he has redeemed from the hand of the foe

And gathered from the lands,
    from the east and the west, from the north and the
       south.   ℟

They went astray in the desert wilderness;
    the way to an inhabited city they did not find.
Hungry and thirsty,
    their life was wasting away within them.   ℟

They cried to the LORD in their distress;
    from their straits he rescued them.
And he led them by a direct way
    to reach an inhabited city.   ℟

Let them give thanks to the LORD for his mercy
    and his wondrous deeds to the children of men,
Because he satisfied the longing soul
    and filled the hungry soul with good things.   ℟

Fourth Reading   Jl 3: 1–5
Thus says the LORD:
    I will pour out my spirit upon all flesh.
    Your sons and daughters shall prophesy,
        your old men shall dream dreams,
        your young men shall see visions;
    even upon the servants and the handmaids,
        in those days, I will pour out my spirit.
    And I will work wonders in the heavens and on the earth,
        blood, fire, and columns of smoke;
    the sun will be turned to darkness,
        and the moon to blood,
    at the coming of the day of the LORD,
        the great and terrible day.
    Then everyone shall be rescued
        who calls on the name of the LORD;
    for on Mount Zion there shall be a remnant,
        as the LORD has said,
    and in Jerusalem survivors
        whom the LORD shall call.

Responsorial Psalm

Ps 104: 1–2, 24, 35, 27–28, 29, 30 — David Miles

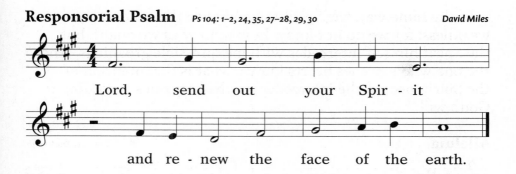

Lord, send out your Spir - it

and re - new the face of the earth.

Or: ℟ **Alleluia.**

Bless the LORD, O my soul!
 O LORD, my God, you are great indeed!
You are clothed with majesty and glory,
 robed in light as with a cloak. ℟

How manifold are your works, O LORD!
 In wisdom you have wrought them all—
the earth is full of your creatures;
 bless the LORD, O my soul! Alleluia. ℟

Creatures all look to you
 to give them food in due time.
When you give it to them, they gather it;
 when you open your hand, they are filled with good
  things. ℟

If you take away their breath, they perish
 and return to their dust.
When you send forth your spirit, they are created,
 and you renew the face of the earth. ℟

Epistle *Rom 8: 22–27* Brothers and sisters: We know that all creation is groaning in labor pains even until now; and not only that, but we ourselves, who have the firstfruits of the Spirit, we also groan within ourselves as we wait for adoption, the redemption of our bodies. For in hope we were saved. Now hope that sees is not hope. For who hopes for what one sees? But if we hope for what we do not see, we wait with endurance.

In the same way, the Spirit too comes to the aid of our weakness; for we do not know how to pray as we ought, but the Spirit himself intercedes with inexpressible groanings. And the one who searches hearts knows what is the intention of the Spirit, because he intercedes for the holy ones according to God's will.

Alleluia

Laura Lea Duckworth

Al - le - lu - ia, al-le-lu - ia.
Al - le - lu - ia, al-le-lu - ia.

Come, Holy Spirit, fill the hearts of the faithful / and kindle in them the fire of your love.   **Alleluia, alleluia.**

Gospel Jn 7:37-39 On the last and greatest day of the feast, Jesus stood up and exclaimed, "Let anyone who thirsts come to me and drink. As Scripture says:
Rivers of living water will flow from within him who believes in me."

He said this in reference to the Spirit that those who came to believe in him were to receive. There was, of course, no Spirit yet, because Jesus had not yet been glorified.

Communion Antiphon Jn 7:37 **On the last day of the festival, Jesus stood and cried out:** ◆ **If anyone is thirsty, let him come to me and drink, alleluia.**

❖   At the Mass During the Day   ❖

Entrance Antiphon Wis 1:7 **The Spirit of the Lord has filled the whole world** ◆ **and that which contains all things** ◆ **understands what is said, alleluia.**

Or: Rom 5: 5; cf. 8: 11   **The love of God has been poured into our hearts • through the Spirit of God dwelling within us, alleluia.**

First Reading Acts 2: 1–11 When the time for Pentecost was fulfilled, they were all in one place together. And suddenly there came from the sky a noise like a strong driving wind, and it filled the entire house in which they were. Then there appeared to them tongues as of fire, which parted and came to rest on each one of them. And they were all filled with the Holy Spirit and began to speak in different tongues, as the Spirit enabled them to proclaim.

Now there were devout Jews from every nation under heaven staying in Jerusalem. At this sound, they gathered in a large crowd, but they were confused because each one heard them speaking in his own language. They were astounded, and in amazement they asked, "Are not all these people who are speaking Galileans? Then how does each of us hear them in his native language? We are Parthians, Medes, and Elamites, inhabitants of Mesopotamia, Judea and Cappadocia, Pontus and Asia, Phrygia and Pamphylia, Egypt and the districts of Libya near Cyrene, as well as travelers from Rome, both Jews and converts to Judaism, Cretans and Arabs, yet we hear them speaking in our own tongues of the mighty acts of God."

Responsorial Psalm   Ps 104: 1, 24, 29–30, 31, 34   David Miles

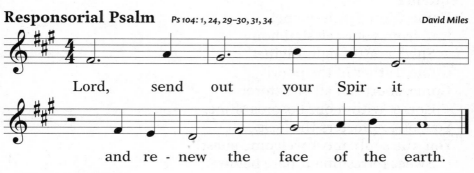

Lord, send out your Spir-it

and re-new the face of the earth.

Or: ℟ **Alleluia.**

Bless the LORD, O my soul!
O LORD, my God, you are great indeed!
How manifold are your works, O LORD!
the earth is full of your creatures; ℟

If you take away their breath, they perish
    and return to their dust.
When you send forth your spirit, they are created,
    and you renew the face of the earth. ℟

May the glory of the LORD endure forever;
    may the LORD be glad in his works!
Pleasing to him be my theme;
    I will be glad in the LORD. ℟

Second Reading 1 Cor 12: 3b–7, 12–13 Brothers and sisters: No one can
say, "Jesus is Lord," except by the Holy Spirit.

There are different kinds of spiritual gifts but the same Spirit;
there are different forms of service but the same Lord; there are
different workings but the same God who produces all of them
in everyone. To each individual the manifestation of the Spirit is
given for some benefit.

As a body is one though it has many parts, and all the parts
of the body, though many, are one body, so also Christ. For in
one Spirit we were all baptized into one body, whether Jews or
Greeks, slaves or free persons, and we were all given to drink of
one Spirit.

Sequence
    Come, Holy Spirit, come!
    And from your celestial home
        Shed a ray of light divine!
    Come, Father of the poor!
    Come, source of all our store!
        Come, within our bosoms shine.
    You, of comforters the best;
    You, the soul's most welcome guest;
        Sweet refreshment here below;
    In our labor, rest most sweet;
    Grateful coolness in the heat;
        Solace in the midst of woe.
    O most blessed Light divine,

Shine within these hearts of yours,
  And our inmost being fill!
Where you are not, we have naught,
Nothing good in deed or thought,
  Nothing free from taint of ill.
Heal our wounds, our strength renew;
On our dryness pour your dew;
  Wash the stains of guilt away:
Bend the stubborn heart and will;
Melt the frozen, warm the chill;
  Guide the steps that go astray.
On the faithful, who adore
And confess you, evermore
  In your sevenfold gift descend;
Give them virtue's sure reward;
Give them your salvation, Lord;
  Give them joys that never end. Amen.
  Alleluia.

Alleluia

Laura Lea Duckworth

Al - le - lu - ia, al-le-lu - ia.

Al - le - lu - ia, al-le-lu - ia.

Come, Holy Spirit, fill the hearts of the faithful / and kindle
in them the fire of your love.   **Alleluia, alleluia.**

Gospel Jn 20: 19–23 On the evening of that first day of the week,
when the doors were locked, where the disciples were, for fear of
the Jews, Jesus came and stood in their midst and said to them,
"Peace be with you." When he had said this, he showed them
his hands and his side. The disciples rejoiced when they saw
the Lord. Jesus said to them again, "Peace be with you. As the

Father has sent me, so I send you." And when he had said this, he breathed on them and said to them, "Receive the Holy Spirit. Whose sins you forgive are forgiven them, and whose sins you retain are retained."

Communion Antiphon *Acts 2: 4, 11* **They were all filled with the Holy Spirit ◆ and spoke of the marvels of God, alleluia.**

Solemnities of the Lord
During Ordinary Time † YEAR A

THE SOLEMNITY OF
THE MOST HOLY TRINITY

Entrance Antiphon   Blest be God the Father, ◆ and the Only Begotten Son of God, ◆ and also the Holy Spirit, ◆ for he has shown us his merciful love.

First Reading   *Ex 34: 4b–6, 8–9*   Early in the morning Moses went up Mount Sinai as the LORD had commanded him, taking along the two stone tablets.

Having come down in a cloud, the LORD stood with Moses there and proclaimed his name, "LORD." Thus the LORD passed before him and cried out, "The LORD, the LORD, a merciful and gracious God, slow to anger and rich in kindness and fidelity." Moses at once bowed down to the ground in worship. Then he said, "If I find favor with you, O LORD, do come along in our company. This is indeed a stiff-necked people; yet pardon our wickedness and sins, and receive us as your own."

Responsorial Psalm   *Dn 3: 52, 53, 54, 55, 56*   *Alexander Young*

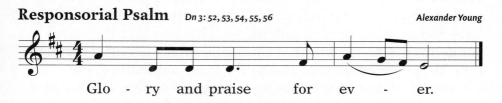

Glo - ry and praise for ev - er.

Blessed are you, O Lord, the God of our fathers,
  praiseworthy and exalted above all forever;

And blessed is your holy and glorious name,
   praiseworthy and exalted above all for all ages.   ℟

Blessed are you in the temple of your holy glory,
   praiseworthy and glorious above all forever.   ℟

Blessed are you on the throne of your kingdom,
   praiseworthy and exalted above all forever.   ℟

Blessed are you who look into the depths
   from your throne upon the cherubim,
   praiseworthy and exalted above all forever.   ℟

Second Reading   *2 Cor 13: 11–13*   Brothers and sisters, rejoice. Mend your ways, encourage one another, agree with one another, live in peace, and the God of love and peace will be with you. Greet one another with a holy kiss. All the holy ones greet you.
   The grace of the Lord Jesus Christ and the love of God and the fellowship of the Holy Spirit be with all of you.

Alleluia   *cf. Rv 1: 8*   *Jim Hughes*

Al-le-lu-ia   Al-le-lu-ia   Al-le-lu - ia.

Glory to the Father, the Son, and the Holy Spirit; / to God who is, who was, and who is to come.   **Alleluia, alleluia.**

Gospel   *Jn 3: 16–18*   God so loved the world that he gave his only Son, so that everyone who believes in him might not perish but might have eternal life. For God did not send his Son into the world to condemn the world, but that the world might be saved through him. Whoever believes in him will not be condemned, but whoever does not believe has already been condemned, because he has not believed in the name of the only Son of God.

Communion Antiphon   *Gal 4: 6*   **Since you are children of God, ◆ God has sent into your hearts the Spirit of his Son, ◆ the Spirit who cries out: Abba, Father.**

THE SOLEMNITY OF THE

MOST HOLY BODY AND BLOOD OF CHRIST

(CORPUS CHRISTI)

Where the Solemnity of the Most Holy Body and Blood of Christ is not a Holyday of Obligation, it is assigned to the Sunday after the Most Holy Trinity as its proper day.

Entrance Antiphon *cf. Ps 81 (80): 17* **He fed them with the finest wheat ◆ and satisfied them with honey from the rock.**

First Reading *Dt 8: 2–3, 14b–16a* Moses said to the people: "Remember how for forty years now the LORD, your God, has directed all your journeying in the desert, so as to test you by affliction and find out whether or not it was your intention to keep his commandments. He therefore let you be afflicted with hunger, and then fed you with manna, a food unknown to you and your fathers, in order to show you that not by bread alone does one live, but by every word that comes forth from the mouth of the LORD.

"Do not forget the LORD, your God, who brought you out of the land of Egypt, that place of slavery; who guided you through the vast and terrible desert with its saraph serpents and scorpions, its parched and waterless ground; who brought forth water for you from the flinty rock and fed you in the desert with manna, a food unknown to your fathers."

Responsorial Psalm   *Ps 147: 12–13, 14–15, 19–20*   Joe Higginbotham

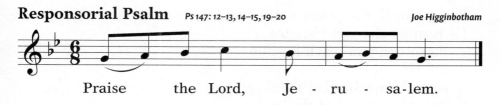

Praise the Lord, Je - ru - sa - lem.

Or: ℟ **Alleluia.**

Glorify the LORD, O Jerusalem;
   praise your God, O Zion.

For he has strengthened the bars of your gates;
   he has blessed your children within you. ℟

He has granted peace in your borders;
   with the best of wheat he fills you.
He sends forth his command to the earth;
   swiftly runs his word! ℟

He has proclaimed his word to Jacob,
   his statutes and his ordinances to Israel.
He has not done thus for any other nation;
   his ordinances he has not made known to them.
     Alleluia. ℟

Second Reading *1 Cor 10:16–17* Brothers and sisters: The cup of
blessing that we bless, is it not a participation in the blood of
Christ? The bread that we break, is it not a participation in the
body of Christ? Because the loaf of bread is one, we, though
many, are one body, for we all partake of the one loaf.

Sequence
The sequence Laud, O Zion (Lauda Sion), *or the shorter form
beginning with the verse* Lo! the angels' food is given *may be sung
optionally before the* Alleluia. *For the shorter form, read only the
parts in brackets.*

Laud, O Zion, your salvation,
Laud with hymns of exultation,
   Christ, your king and shepherd true:

Bring him all the praise you know,
He is more than you bestow.
   Never can you reach his due.

Special theme for glad thanksgiving
Is the quick'ning and the living
   Bread today before you set:

From his hands of old partaken,
As we know, by faith unshaken,

THE MOST HOLY BODY AND BLOOD OF CHRIST   177

Where the Twelve at supper met.

Full and clear ring out your chanting,
Joy nor sweetest grace be wanting,
   From your heart let praises burst:

For today the feast is holden,
When the institution olden
   Of that supper was rehearsed.

Here the new law's new oblation,
By the new king's revelation,
   Ends the form of ancient rite:

Now the new the old effaces,
Truth away the shadow chases,
   Light dispels the gloom of night.

What he did at supper seated,
Christ ordained to be repeated,
   His memorial ne'er to cease:

And his rule for guidance taking,
Bread and wine we hallow, making
   Thus our sacrifice of peace.

This the truth each Christian learns,
Bread into his flesh he turns,
   To his precious blood the wine:

Sight has fail'd, nor thought conceives,
But a dauntless faith believes,
   Resting on a pow'r divine.

Here beneath these signs are hidden
Priceless things to sense forbidden;
   Signs, not things are all we see:

Blood is poured and flesh is broken,
Yet in either wondrous token

Christ entire we know to be.

Whoso of this food partakes,
Does not rend the Lord nor breaks;
   Christ is whole to all that tastes:

Thousands are, as one, receivers,
One, as thousands of believers,
   Eats of him who cannot waste.

Bad and good the feast are sharing,
Of what divers dooms preparing,
   Endless death, or endless life.

Life to these, to those damnation,
See how like participation
   Is with unlike issues rife.

When the sacrament is broken,
Doubt not, but believe 'tis spoken,
   That each sever'd outward token
      doth the very whole contain.

Nought the precious gift divides,
Breaking but the sign betides
   Jesus still the same abides,
      still unbroken does remain.

(*The shorter form of the sequence begins here.*)
   [Lo! the angel's food is given
To the pilgrim who has striven;
   See the children's bread from heaven,
      which on dogs may not be spent.

Truth the ancient types fulfilling,
Isaac bound, a victim willing,
   Paschal lamb, its lifeblood spilling,
      manna to the fathers sent.

Very bread, good shepherd, tend us,
Jesu, of your love befriend us,
   You refresh us, you defend us,
   Your eternal goodness send us
In the land of life to see.

You who all things can and know,
Who on earth such food bestow,
   Grant us with your saints, though lowest,
   Where the heav'nly feast you show,
Fellow heirs and guests to be. Amen. Alleluia.]

Alleluia   *Jn 6: 51*   *Jim Hughes*

Al-le-lu-ia   Al-le-lu-ia   Al - le-lu - ia.

I am the living bread that came down from heaven, says
the Lord; / whoever eats this bread will live forever.
Alleluia, alleluia.

Gospel *Jn 6: 51-58* Jesus said to the Jewish crowds: "I am the living
bread that came down from heaven; whoever eats this bread will
live forever; and the bread that I will give is my flesh for the life
of the world."
    The Jews quarreled among themselves, saying, "How can this
man give us his flesh to eat?" Jesus said to them, "Amen, amen, I
say to you, unless you eat the flesh of the Son of Man and drink
his blood, you do not have life within you. Whoever eats my
flesh and drinks my blood has eternal life, and I will raise him
on the last day. For my flesh is true food, and my blood is true
drink. Whoever eats my flesh and drinks my blood remains in
me and I in him. Just as the living Father sent me and I have
life because of the Father, so also the one who feeds on me will
have life because of me. This is the bread that came down from
heaven. Unlike your ancestors who ate and still died, whoever
eats this bread will live forever."

Communion Antiphon Jn 6: 57 Whoever eats my flesh and drinks my blood ◆ remains in me and I in him, says the Lord.

THE SOLEMNITY OF

THE MOST SACRED HEART OF JESUS

Entrance Antiphon Ps 33 (32): 11, 19 The designs of his Heart are from age to age, ◆ to rescue their souls from death, ◆ and to keep them alive in famine.

First Reading Dt 7: 6–11 Moses said to the people: "You are a people sacred to the LORD, your God; he has chosen you from all the nations on the face of the earth to be a people peculiarly his own. It was not because you are the largest of all nations that the LORD set his heart on you and chose you, for you are really the smallest of all nations. It was because the LORD loved you and because of his fidelity to the oath he had sworn your fathers, that he brought you out with his strong hand from the place of slavery, and ransomed you from the hand of Pharaoh, king of Egypt. Understand, then, that the LORD, your God, is God indeed, the faithful God who keeps his merciful covenant down to the thousandth generation toward those who love him and keep his commandments, but who repays with destruction a person who hates him; he does not dally with such a one, but makes them personally pay for it. You shall therefore carefully observe the commandments, the statutes and the decrees that I enjoin on you today."

Responsorial Psalm Ps 103: 1–2, 3–4, 6–7, 8, 10   *Vince Ambrosetti*

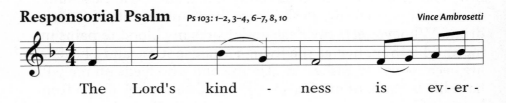

The Lord's kind - ness is ev - er -

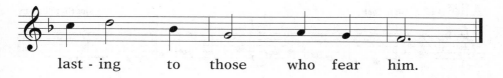

last - ing   to   those   who   fear   him.

Bless the LORD, O my soul;
   all my being, bless his holy name.
Bless the LORD, O my soul;
   and forget not all his benefits. ℟

He pardons all your iniquities,
   heals all your ills.
He redeems your life from destruction,
   crowns you with kindness and compassion. ℟

Merciful and gracious is the LORD,
   slow to anger and abounding in kindness.
Not according to our sins does he deal with us,
   nor does he requite us according to our crimes. ℟

Second Reading 1 Jn 4:7–16 Beloved, let us love one another, because love is of God; everyone who loves is begotten by God and knows God. Whoever is without love does not know God, for God is love. In this way the love of God was revealed to us: God sent his only Son into the world so that we might have life through him. In this is love: not that we have loved God, but that he loved us and sent his Son as expiation for our sins. Beloved, if God so loved us, we also must love one another. No one has ever seen God. Yet, if we love one another, God remains in us, and his love is brought to perfection in us.

This is how we know that we remain in him and he in us, that he has given us of his Spirit. Moreover, we have seen and testify that the Father sent his Son as savior of the world. Whoever acknowledges that Jesus is the Son of God, God remains in him and he in God. We have come to know and to believe in the love God has for us.

God is love, and whoever remains in love remains in God and God in him.

Alleluia   Mt 11: 29ab   *Joe Higginbotham*

Al - le - lu - ia,   al - le - lu - ia,   al - le - lu - ia.

Take my yoke upon you, says the Lord; / and learn from me,
for I am meek and humble of heart.   **Alleluia, alleluia.**

Gospel Mt 11: 25–30 At that time Jesus exclaimed: "I give praise
to you, Father, Lord of heaven and earth, for although you
have hidden these things from the wise and the learned you
have revealed them to little ones. Yes, Father, such has been
your gracious will. All things have been handed over to me by
my Father. No one knows the Son except the Father, and no
one knows the Father except the Son and anyone to whom
the Son wishes to reveal him.

"Come to me, all you who labor and are burdened, and I
will give you rest. Take my yoke upon you and learn from me,
for I am meek and humble of heart; and you will find rest for
yourselves. For my yoke is easy, and my burden light."

Communion Antiphon cf. Jn 7: 37–38 **Thus says the Lord: ♦ Let
whoever is thirsty come to me and drink. ♦ Streams of living
water will flow ♦ from within the one who believes in me.**

Or: Jn 19: 34 **One of the soldiers opened his side with a lance, ♦
and at once there came forth blood and water.**

Ordinary Time † YEAR A

SECOND SUNDAY IN ORDINARY TIME

Entrance Antiphon Ps 66 (65): 4 **All the earth shall bow down before you, O God, ◆ and shall sing to you, ◆ shall sing to your name, O Most High!**

First Reading Is 49: 3, 5–6

The LORD said to me: You are my servant,
    Israel, through whom I show my glory.
Now the LORD has spoken
    who formed me as his servant from the womb,
that Jacob may be brought back to him
    and Israel gathered to him;
and I am made glorious in the sight of the LORD,
    and my God is now my strength!
It is too little, the LORD says, for you to be my servant,
    to raise up the tribes of Jacob,
      and restore the survivors of Israel;
I will make you a light to the nations,
    that my salvation may reach to the ends of the earth.

Responsorial Psalm Ps 40: 2, 4, 7–8, 8–9, 10   *Beverly McDevitt*

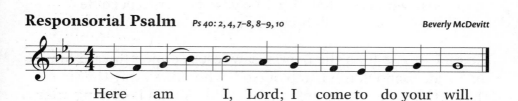

Here am I, Lord; I come to do your will.

I have waited, waited for the LORD,
    and he stooped toward me and heard my cry.
And he put a new song into my mouth,
    a hymn to our God. ℟

◆ 183 ◆

Sacrifice or offering you wished not,
    but ears open to obedience you gave me.
Holocausts or sin-offerings you sought not;
    then said I, "Behold I come." ℟

"In the written scroll it is prescribed for me,
    to do your will, O my God, is my delight,
    and your law is within my heart!" ℟

I announced your justice in the vast assembly;
    I did not restrain my lips, as you, O LORD, know. ℟

Second Reading *1 Cor 1: 1-3* Paul, called to be an apostle of
Christ Jesus by the will of God, and Sosthenes our brother, to
the church of God that is in Corinth, to you who have been
sanctified in Christ Jesus, called to be holy, with all those
everywhere who call upon the name of our Lord Jesus Christ,
their Lord and ours. Grace to you and peace from God our
Father and the Lord Jesus Christ.

Alleluia *Jn 1: 14a, 12a*   *Joe Higginbotham*

Al - le - lu - ia,   al - le - lu - ia,   al - le - lu - ia.

The Word of God became flesh and dwelt among us. /
To those who accepted him, / he gave power to become
children of God. **Alleluia, alleluia.**

Gospel *Jn 1: 29-34* John the Baptist saw Jesus coming toward him
and said, "Behold, the Lamb of God, who takes away the sin of
the world. He is the one of whom I said, 'A man is coming after
me who ranks ahead of me because he existed before me.' I did
not know him, but the reason why I came baptizing with water
was that he might be made known to Israel." John testified
further, saying, "I saw the Spirit come down like a dove from
heaven and remain upon him. I did not know him, but the one
who sent me to baptize with water told me, 'On whomever you

see the Spirit come down and remain, he is the one who will baptize with the Holy Spirit.' Now I have seen and testified that he is the Son of God."

Communion Antiphon *cf. Ps 23 (22): 5* **You have prepared a table before me, ♦ and how precious is the chalice that quenches my thirst.**

Or: *1 Jn 4: 16* **We have come to know and to believe ♦ in the love that God has for us.**

THIRD SUNDAY IN ORDINARY TIME

Entrance Antiphon *cf. Ps 96 (95): 1, 6* **O sing a new song to the Lord; ♦ sing to the Lord, all the earth. ♦ In his presence are majesty and splendor, ♦ strength and honor in his holy place.**

First Reading *Is 8: 23–9: 3* First the LORD degraded the land of Zebulun and the land of Naphtali; but in the end he has glorified the seaward road, the land west of the Jordan, the District of the Gentiles.

> Anguish has taken wing, dispelled is darkness:
>   for there is no gloom where but now there was distress.
> The people who walked in darkness
>   have seen a great light;
> upon those who dwelt in the land of gloom
>   a light has shone.
> You have brought them abundant joy
>   and great rejoicing,
> as they rejoice before you as at the harvest,
>   as people make merry when dividing spoils.
> For the yoke that burdened them,
>   the pole on their shoulder,
> and the rod of their taskmaster
>   you have smashed, as on the day of Midian.

Responsorial Psalm   Ps 27: 1, 4, 13–14

E. Louis Canter, OEF

The Lord is my light and my sal - va - tion.

The Lord is my light and my sal - va - tion.

The LORD is my light and my salvation;
   whom should I fear?
The LORD is my life's refuge;
   of whom should I be afraid? ℟

One thing I ask of the LORD;
   this I seek:
To dwell in the house of the LORD
   all the days of my life,
That I may gaze on the loveliness of the LORD
   and contemplate his temple. ℟

I believe that I shall see the bounty of the LORD
   in the land of the living.
Wait for the LORD with courage;
   be stouthearted, and wait for the LORD. ℟

Second Reading 1 Cor 1: 10–13, 17 I urge you, brothers and sisters, in the name of our Lord Jesus Christ, that all of you agree in what you say, and that there be no divisions among you, but that you be united in the same mind and in the same purpose. For it has been reported to me about you, my brothers and sisters, by Chloe's people, that there are rivalries among you. I mean that each of you is saying, "I belong to Paul," or "I belong to Apollos," or "I belong to Cephas," or "I belong to Christ." Is Christ divided? Was Paul crucified for you? Or were you baptized in the name of Paul? For Christ did not send me to baptize but to preach the gospel, and not with the wisdom of human eloquence, so that the cross of Christ might not be emptied of its meaning.

Alleluia *cf. Mt 4: 23*   *Joe Higginbotham*

Al - le - lu - ia,   al - le - lu - ia,   al - le - lu - ia.

Jesus proclaimed the Gospel of the kingdom / and cured
every disease among the people. **Alleluia, alleluia.**

Gospel Mt 4: 12–23 or 4: 12–17
For the shorter form, read only the parts in brackets.
[When Jesus heard that John had been arrested, he withdrew to
Galilee. He left Nazareth and went to live in Capernaum by the
sea, in the region of Zebulun and Naphtali, that what had been
said through Isaiah the prophet might be fulfilled:
  Land of Zebulun and land of Naphtali,
    the way to the sea, beyond the Jordan,
    Galilee of the Gentiles,
  the people who sit in darkness have seen a great light,
  on those dwelling in a land overshadowed by death
    light has arisen.
From that time on, Jesus began to preach and say, "Repent, for
the kingdom of heaven is at hand."]
  As he was walking by the Sea of Galilee, he saw two brothers,
Simon who is called Peter, and his brother Andrew, casting a net
into the sea; they were fishermen. He said to them, "Come after
me, and I will make you fishers of men." At once they left their
nets and followed him. He walked along from there and saw
two other brothers, James, the son of Zebedee, and his brother
John. They were in a boat, with their father Zebedee, mending
their nets. He called them, and immediately they left their boat
and their father and followed him. He went around all of Galilee,
teaching in their synagogues, proclaiming the gospel of the
kingdom, and curing every disease and illness among the people.

Communion Antiphon *cf. Ps 34 (33): 6* **Look toward the Lord and
be radiant; ◆ let your faces not be abashed.**

Or: Jn 8:12 **I am the light of the world, says the Lord; ◆ whoever follows me will not walk in darkness, ◆ but will have the light of life.**

FOURTH SUNDAY IN ORDINARY TIME

Entrance Antiphon Ps 106 (105): 47 **Save us, O Lord our God! ◆ And gather us from the nations, ◆ to give thanks to your holy name, ◆ and make it our glory to praise you.**

First Reading Zep 2: 3; 3: 12–13

> Seek the LORD, all you humble of the earth,
>> who have observed his law;
> seek justice, seek humility;
>> perhaps you may be sheltered
>> on the day of the LORD's anger.
>
> But I will leave as a remnant in your midst
>> a people humble and lowly,
> who shall take refuge in the name of the LORD:
>> the remnant of Israel.
> They shall do no wrong
>> and speak no lies;
> nor shall there be found in their mouths
>> a deceitful tongue;
> they shall pasture and couch their flocks
>> with none to disturb them.

Responsorial Psalm Ps 146: 6–7, 8–9, 9–10   Joe Higginbotham

Bless - ed are the poor in spir - it;
the king - dom of heav - en is theirs.

Or: ℟ **Alleluia.**

The LORD keeps faith forever,
>secures justice for the oppressed,
>gives food to the hungry.
The LORD sets captives free. ℟

The LORD gives sight to the blind;
>the LORD raises up those who were bowed down.
The LORD loves the just;
>the LORD protects strangers. ℟

The fatherless and the widow the LORD sustains,
>but the way of the wicked he thwarts.
The LORD shall reign forever;
>your God, O Zion, through all generations. Alleluia. ℟

Second Reading *1 Cor 1: 26–31* Consider your own calling, brothers and sisters. Not many of you were wise by human standards, not many were powerful, not many were of noble birth. Rather, God chose the foolish of the world to shame the wise, and God chose the weak of the world to shame the strong, and God chose the lowly and despised of the world, those who count for nothing, to reduce to nothing those who are something, so that no human being might boast before God. It is due to him that you are in Christ Jesus, who became for us wisdom from God, as well as righteousness, sanctification, and redemption, so that, as it is written, "Whoever boasts, should boast in the Lord."

Alleluia   *Mt 5: 12a*   Joe Higginbotham

Al-le-lu-ia,   al-le-lu-ia,   al-le-lu - ia.

Rejoice and be glad; / your reward will be great in heaven. **Alleluia, alleluia.**

Gospel *Mt 5: 1–12a* When Jesus saw the crowds, he went up the mountain, and after he had sat down, his disciples came to him. He began to teach them, saying:
"Blessed are the poor in spirit,
   for theirs is the kingdom of heaven.
Blessed are they who mourn,
   for they will be comforted.
Blessed are the meek,
   for they will inherit the land.
Blessed are they who hunger and thirst for righteousness,
   for they will be satisfied.
Blessed are the merciful,
   for they will be shown mercy.
Blessed are the clean of heart,
   for they will see God.
Blessed are the peacemakers,
   for they will be called children of God.
Blessed are they who are persecuted for the sake of righteousness,
   for theirs is the kingdom of heaven.
Blessed are you when they insult you and persecute you and utter every kind of evil against you falsely because of me. Rejoice and be glad, for your reward will be great in heaven."

Communion Antiphon *cf. Ps 31 (30): 17–18* Let your face shine on your servant. ✦ Save me in your merciful love. ✦ O Lord, let me never be put to shame, for I call on you.

Or: *Mt 5: 3–4* Blessed are the poor in spirit, ✦ for theirs is the Kingdom of Heaven. ✦ Blessed are the meek, for they shall possess the land.

FIFTH SUNDAY IN ORDINARY TIME

Entrance Antiphon *Ps 95 (94): 6–7* O come, let us worship God ✦ and bow low before the God who made us, ✦ for he is the Lord our God.

First Reading   *Is 58: 7–10*

Thus says the LORD:
Share your bread with the hungry,
   shelter the oppressed and the homeless;
clothe the naked when you see them,
   and do not turn your back on your own.
Then your light shall break forth like the dawn,
   and your wound shall quickly be healed;
your vindication shall go before you,
   and the glory of the LORD shall be your rear guard.
Then you shall call, and the LORD will answer,
   you shall cry for help, and he will say: Here I am!
If you remove from your midst
   oppression, false accusation and malicious speech;
if you bestow your bread on the hungry
   and satisfy the afflicted;
then light shall rise for you in the darkness,
   and the gloom shall become for you like midday.

Responsorial Psalm   *Ps 112: 4-5, 6-7, 8-9*   Ann Fons et al.

The just man   is a light in dark-ness   to the up-right.

Or: ℟ **Alleluia.**

Light shines through the darkness for the upright;
   he is gracious and merciful and just.
Well for the man who is gracious and lends,
   who conducts his affairs with justice.   ℟

He shall never be moved;
   the just one shall be in everlasting remembrance.
An evil report he shall not fear;
   his heart is firm, trusting in the LORD.   ℟

His heart is steadfast; he shall not fear.
   Lavishly he gives to the poor;

His justice shall endure forever;
    his horn shall be exalted in glory. ℟

Second Reading *1 Cor 2: 1–5* When I came to you, brothers and
sisters, proclaiming the mystery of God, I did not come with
sublimity of words or of wisdom. For I resolved to know nothing
while I was with you except Jesus Christ, and him crucified.
I came to you in weakness and fear and much trembling, and
my message and my proclamation were not with persuasive
words of wisdom, but with a demonstration of Spirit and power,
so that your faith might rest not on human wisdom but on the
power of God.

Alleluia *Jn 8: 12*   **Joe Higginbotham**

Al - le - lu - ia,   al - le - lu - ia,   al - le - lu - ia.

I am the light of the world, says the Lord; / whoever follows
me will have the light of life. **Alleluia, alleluia.**

Gospel *Mt 5: 13–16* Jesus said to his disciples: "You are the salt of the
earth. But if salt loses its taste, with what can it be seasoned?
It is no longer good for anything but to be thrown out and
trampled underfoot. You are the light of the world. A city set
on a mountain cannot be hidden. Nor do they light a lamp and
then put it under a bushel basket; it is set on a lampstand, where
it gives light to all in the house. Just so, your light must shine
before others, that they may see your good deeds and glorify
your heavenly Father."

Communion Antiphon *cf. Ps 107 (106): 8–9* **Let them thank the Lord
for his mercy, ◆ his wonders for the children of men, ◆ for
he satisfies the thirsty soul, ◆ and the hungry he fills with
good things.**

Or: *Mt 5: 5-6* **Blessed are those who mourn, for they shall be
consoled. ◆ Blessed are those who hunger and thirst for
righteousness, ◆ for they shall have their fill.**

SIXTH SUNDAY IN ORDINARY TIME

Entrance Antiphon *cf. Ps 31 (30): 3-4* **Be my protector, O God, ◆
a mighty stronghold to save me. ◆ For you are my rock, my
stronghold! ◆ Lead me, guide me, for the sake of your name.**

First Reading   *Sir 15: 15-20*

If you choose you can keep the commandments, they will
    save you;
  if you trust in God, you too shall live;
he has set before you fire and water;
  to whichever you choose, stretch forth your hand.
Before man are life and death, good and evil,
  whichever he chooses shall be given him.
Immense is the wisdom of the Lord;
  he is mighty in power, and all-seeing.
The eyes of God are on those who fear him;
  he understands man's every deed.
No one does he command to act unjustly,
  to none does he give license to sin.

Responsorial Psalm   *Ps 119: 1-2, 4-5, 17-18, 33-34*   Dave Bradshaw

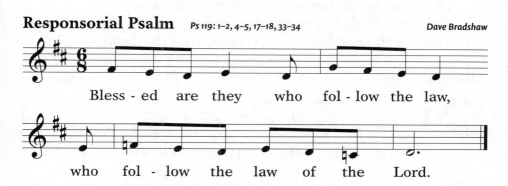

Bless - ed   are   they   who   fol - low   the   law,
who   fol - low   the   law   of   the   Lord.

Blessed are they whose way is blameless,
  who walk in the law of the LORD.
Blessed are they who observe his decrees,
  who seek him with all their heart. ℟

You have commanded that your precepts
  be diligently kept.
Oh, that I might be firm in the ways

of keeping your statutes!   ℟

Be good to your servant, that I may live
    and keep your words.
Open my eyes, that I may consider
    the wonders of your law.   ℟

Instruct me, O LORD, in the way of your statutes,
    that I may exactly observe them.
Give me discernment, that I may observe your law
    and keep it with all my heart.   ℟

Second Reading *1 Cor 2: 6–10* Brothers and sisters: We speak a
wisdom to those who are mature, not a wisdom of this age, nor
of the rulers of this age who are passing away. Rather, we speak
God's wisdom, mysterious, hidden, which God predetermined
before the ages for our glory, and which none of the rulers of
this age knew; for, if they had known it, they would not have
crucified the Lord of glory. But as it is written:
    What eye has not seen, and ear has not heard,
      and what has not entered the human heart,
      what God has prepared for those who love him,
this God has revealed to us through the Spirit.
    For the Spirit scrutinizes everything, even the depths of God.

Alleluia   *cf. Mt 11: 25*   Joe Higginbotham

Al - le - lu - ia,   al - le - lu - ia,   al - le - lu - ia.

Blessed are you, Father, Lord of heaven and earth; / you
have revealed to little ones the mysteries of the kingdom.
Alleluia, alleluia.

Gospel   *Mt 5: 17–37 or 5: 20–22a, 27–28, 33–34a, 37*
For the shorter form, read only the parts in brackets.
[Jesus said to his disciples:] "Do not think that I have come
to abolish the law or the prophets. I have come not to abolish

but to fulfill. Amen, I say to you, until heaven and earth pass away, not the smallest letter or the smallest part of a letter will pass from the law, until all things have taken place. Therefore, whoever breaks one of the least of these commandments and teaches others to do so will be called least in the kingdom of heaven. But whoever obeys and teaches these commandments will be called greatest in the kingdom of heaven. [I tell you, unless your righteousness surpasses that of the scribes and Pharisees, you will not enter the kingdom of heaven.

"You have heard that it was said to your ancestors, *You shall not kill; and whoever kills will be liable to judgment.* But I say to you, whoever is angry with brother will be liable to judgment;] and whoever says to brother, 'Raqa,' will be answerable to the Sanhedrin; and whoever says, 'You fool,' will be liable to fiery Gehenna. Therefore, if you bring your gift to the altar, and there recall that your brother has anything against you, leave your gift there at the altar, go first and be reconciled with your brother, and then come and offer your gift. Settle with your opponent quickly while on the way to court. Otherwise your opponent will hand you over to the judge, and the judge will hand you over to the guard, and you will be thrown into prison. Amen, I say to you, you will not be released until you have paid the last penny.

["You have heard that it was said, *You shall not commit adultery.* But I say to you, everyone who looks at a woman with lust has already committed adultery with her in his heart.] If your right eye causes you to sin, tear it out and throw it away. It is better for you to lose one of your members than to have your whole body thrown into Gehenna. And if your right hand causes you to sin, cut it off and throw it away. It is better for you to lose one of your members than to have your whole body go into Gehenna.

"It was also said, *Whoever divorces his wife must give her a bill of divorce.* But I say to you, whoever divorces his wife—unless the marriage is unlawful—causes her to commit adultery, and whoever marries a divorced woman commits adultery.

["Again you have heard that it was said to your ancestors, *Do not take a false oath, but make good to the Lord all that you vow.* But I say to you, do not swear at all;] not by heaven, for it is God's throne; nor by the earth, for it is his footstool; nor by Jerusalem, for it is the city of the great King. Do not swear by your head, for you cannot make a single hair white or black. [Let your 'Yes' mean 'Yes,' and your 'No' mean 'No.' Anything more is from the evil one."]

Communion Antiphon *cf. Ps 78 (77): 29-30* **They ate and had their fill, ♦ and what they craved the Lord gave them; ♦ they were not disappointed in what they craved.**

Or: *Jn 3: 16* **God so loved the world ♦ that he gave his Only Begotten Son, ♦ so that all who believe in him may not perish, ♦ but may have eternal life.**

SEVENTH SUNDAY IN ORDINARY TIME

Entrance Antiphon *Ps 13 (12): 6* **O Lord, I trust in your merciful love. ♦ My heart will rejoice in your salvation. ♦ I will sing to the Lord who has been bountiful with me.**

First Reading *Lv 19: 1-2, 17-18* The LORD said to Moses, "Speak to the whole Israelite community and tell them: Be holy, for I, the LORD, your God, am holy.

"You shall not bear hatred for your brother or sister in your heart. Though you may have to reprove your fellow citizen, do not incur sin because of him. Take no revenge and cherish no grudge against any of your people. You shall love your neighbor as yourself. I am the LORD."

Responsorial Psalm *Ps 103: 1-2, 3-4, 8, 10, 12-13* *Vince Ambrosetti*

The Lord is kind and mer-ci-ful.

Bless the LORD, O my soul;
   and all my being, bless his holy name.
Bless the LORD, O my soul,
   and forget not all his benefits. ℟

He pardons all your iniquities,
  heals all your ills.
He redeems your life from destruction,
  crowns you with kindness and compassion. ℟

Merciful and gracious is the LORD,
  slow to anger and abounding in kindness.
Not according to our sins does he deal with us,
  nor does he requite us according to our crimes. ℟

As far as the east is from the west,
  so far has he put our transgressions from us.
As a father has compassion on his children,
  so the LORD has compassion on those who fear him. ℟

Second Reading *1 Cor 3: 16–23* Brothers and sisters: Do you not know that you are the temple of God, and that the Spirit of God dwells in you? If anyone destroys God's temple, God will destroy that person; for the temple of God, which you are, is holy.

Let no one deceive himself. If any one among you considers himself wise in this age, let him become a fool, so as to become wise. For the wisdom of this world is foolishness in the eyes of God, for it is written:
God catches the wise in their own ruses,
and again:
The Lord knows the thoughts of the wise,
  that they are vain.
So let no one boast about human beings, for everything belongs to you, Paul or Apollos or Cephas, or the world or life or death, or the present or the future: all belong to you, and you to Christ, and Christ to God.

Alleluia   *1 Jn 2: 5*   Joe Higginbotham

Al - le - lu - ia,   al - le - lu - ia,   al - le - lu - ia.

Whoever keeps the word of Christ, / the love of God is truly perfected in him.   **Alleluia, alleluia.**

Gospel Mt 5: 38–48 Jesus said to his disciples: "You have heard that it was said, A*n eye for an eye and a tooth for a tooth.* But I say to you, offer no resistance to one who is evil. When someone strikes you on your right cheek, turn the other one as well. If anyone wants to go to law with you over your tunic, hand over your cloak as well. Should anyone press you into service for one mile, go for two miles. Give to the one who asks of you, and do not turn your back on one who wants to borrow.

"You have heard that it was said, *You shall love your neighbor and hate your enemy.* But I say to you, love your enemies and pray for those who persecute you, that you may be children of your heavenly Father, for he makes his sun rise on the bad and the good, and causes rain to fall on the just and the unjust. For if you love those who love you, what recompense will you have? Do not the tax collectors do the same? And if you greet your brothers only, what is unusual about that? Do not the pagans do the same? So be perfect, just as your heavenly Father is perfect."

Communion Antiphon Ps 9: 2–3 I will recount all your wonders, ✦ I will rejoice in you and be glad, ✦ and sing psalms to your name, O Most High.

Or: Jn 11: 27 Lord, I have come to believe that you are the Christ, ✦ the Son of the living God, who is coming into this world.

EIGHTH SUNDAY IN ORDINARY TIME

Entrance Antiphon cf. Ps 18 (17): 19–20 The Lord became my protector. ✦ He brought me out to a place of freedom; ✦ he saved me because he delighted in me.

First Reading Is 49: 14–15
Zion said, "The LORD has forsaken me;
    my LORD has forgotten me."
Can a mother forget her infant,

be without tenderness for the child of her womb?
Even should she forget,
   I will never forget you.

Responsorial Psalm   Ps 62: 2–3, 6–7, 8–9   *Stacy Whitfield,* SGL

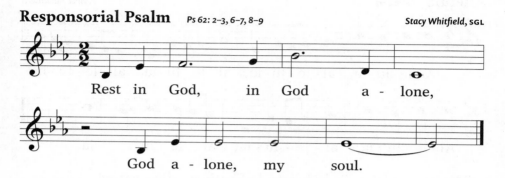

Rest in God, in God a - lone, God a - lone, my soul.

Only in God is my soul at rest;
   from him comes my salvation.
He only is my rock and my salvation,
   my stronghold; I shall not be disturbed at all. ℟

Only in God be at rest, my soul,
   for from him comes my hope.
He only is my rock and my salvation,
   my stronghold; I shall not be disturbed. ℟

With God is my safety and my glory,
   he is the rock of my strength; my refuge is in God.
Trust in him at all times, O my people!
   Pour out your hearts before him. ℟

Second Reading *1 Cor 4: 1–5* Brothers and sisters: Thus should one regard us: as servants of Christ and stewards of the mysteries of God. Now it is of course required of stewards that they be found trustworthy. It does not concern me in the least that I be judged by you or any human tribunal; I do not even pass judgment on myself; I am not conscious of anything against me, but I do not thereby stand acquitted; the one who judges me is the Lord. Therefore do not make any judgment before the appointed time, until the Lord comes, for he will bring to light what is hidden in darkness and will manifest the motives of our hearts, and then everyone will receive praise from God.

Alleluia *Heb 4: 12*   Vince Ambrosetti

Al - le - lu - ia, al - le - lu - ia, al - le - lu - ia, al - le - lu - ia.

Al - le - lu - ia, al - le - lu - ia, al - le - lu - ia.

The word of God is living and effective; / discerning reflections and thoughts of the heart.   **Alleluia, alleluia.**

Gospel *Mt 6: 24-34* Jesus said to his disciples: "No one can serve two masters. He will either hate one and love the other, or be devoted to one and despise the other. You cannot serve God and mammon.

"Therefore I tell you, do not worry about your life, what you will eat or drink, or about your body, what you will wear. Is not life more than food and the body more than clothing? Look at the birds in the sky; they do not sow or reap, they gather nothing into barns, yet your heavenly Father feeds them. Are not you more important than they? Can any of you by worrying add a single moment to your life-span? Why are you anxious about clothes? Learn from the way the wild flowers grow. They do not work or spin. But I tell you that not even Solomon in all his splendor was clothed like one of them. If God so clothes the grass of the field, which grows today and is thrown into the oven tomorrow, will he not much more provide for you, O you of little faith? So do not worry and say, 'What are we to eat?' or 'What are we to drink?' or 'What are we to wear?' All these things the pagans seek. Your heavenly Father knows that you need them all. But seek first the kingdom of God and his righteousness, and all these things will be given you besides. Do not worry about tomorrow; tomorrow will take care of itself. Sufficient for a day is its own evil."

Communion Antiphon *cf. Ps 13 (12): 6* I will sing to the Lord who has been bountiful with me, ◆ sing psalms to the name of the Lord Most High.

Or: *Mt 28: 20* Behold, I am with you always, ◆ even to the end of the age, says the Lord.

NINTH SUNDAY IN ORDINARY TIME

Entrance Antiphon *cf. Ps 25 (24): 16, 18* Turn to me and have mercy on me, O Lord, ◆ for I am alone and poor. ◆ See my lowliness and suffering ◆ and take away all my sins, my God.

First Reading *Dt 11: 18, 26–28, 32* Moses told the people, "Take these words of mine into your heart and soul. Bind them at your wrist as a sign, and let them be a pendant on your forehead.

"I set before you here, this day, a blessing and a curse: a blessing for obeying the commandments of the LORD, your God, which I enjoin on you today; a curse if you do not obey the commandments of the LORD, your God, but turn aside from the way I ordain for you today, to follow other gods, whom you have not known. Be careful to observe all the statutes and decrees that I set before you today."

Responsorial Psalm   *Ps 31: 2–3, 3–4, 17, 25*   *Joe Higginbotham*

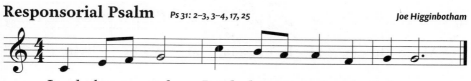

Lord, be my rock, Lord, be my rock of safe-ty.

In you, O LORD, I take refuge;
　let me never be put to shame.
In your justice rescue me,
　incline your ear to me,
　make haste to deliver me!   ℟

Be my rock of refuge,

a stronghold to give me safety.
You are my rock and my fortress;
  for your name's sake you will lead and guide me. ℟

Let your face shine upon your servant;
  save me in your kindness.
Take courage and be stouthearted,
  all you who hope in the LORD. ℟

Second Reading Rom 3: 21–25, 28 Brothers and sisters: Now
the righteousness of God has been manifested apart from the
law, though testified to by the law and the prophets, the
righteousness of God through faith in Jesus Christ for all who
believe. For there is no distinction; all have sinned and are
deprived of the glory of God. They are justified freely by his
grace through the redemption in Christ Jesus, whom God
set forth as an expiation, through faith, by his blood. For we
consider that a person is justified by faith apart from works
of the law.

Alleluia   Jn 15: 5   *Vince Ambrosetti*

Al-le-lu-ia, al-le-lu-ia, al-le-lu-ia, al-le-lu-ia.

Al-le-lu-ia, al-le-lu-ia, al-le-lu - ia.

I am the vine, you are the branches, says the Lord; /
whoever remains in me and I in him will bear much fruit.
Alleluia, alleluia.

Gospel Mt 7: 21–27 Jesus said to his disciples: "Not everyone who
says to me, 'Lord, Lord,' will enter the kingdom of heaven, but
only the one who does the will of my Father in heaven. Many
will say to me on that day, 'Lord, Lord, did we not prophesy in
your name? Did we not drive out demons in your name? Did we

not do mighty deeds in your name?' Then I will declare to them
solemnly, 'I never knew you. Depart from me, you evildoers.'
    "Everyone who listens to these words of mine and acts on
them will be like a wise man who built his house on rock. The
rain fell, the floods came, and the winds blew and buffeted the
house. But it did not collapse; it had been set solidly on rock.
And everyone who listens to these words of mine but does not
act on them will be like a fool who built his house on sand. The
rain fell, the floods came, and the winds blew and buffeted the
house. And it collapsed and was completely ruined."

Communion Antiphon *cf. Ps 17 (16): 6* **To you I call, for you will
surely heed me, O God; ♦ turn your ear to me; hear my words.**

Or: *Mk 11: 23, 24* **Amen, I say to you: Whatever you ask for in
prayer, ♦ believe you will receive it, ♦ and it will be yours,
says the Lord.**

TENTH SUNDAY IN ORDINARY TIME

Entrance Antiphon *cf. Ps 27 (26): 1–2* **The Lord is my light and my
salvation; whom shall I fear? ♦ The Lord is the stronghold
of my life; whom should I dread? ♦ When those who do evil
draw near, they stumble and fall.**

First Reading *Hos 6: 3–6*
In their affliction, people will say:
    "Let us know, let us strive to know the LORD;
        as certain as the dawn is his coming,
        and his judgment shines forth like the light of day!
    He will come to us like the rain,
        like spring rain that waters the earth."

    What can I do with you, Ephraim?
        What can I do with you, Judah?
    Your piety is like a morning cloud,
        like the dew that early passes away.

For this reason I smote them through the prophets,
  I slew them by the words of my mouth;
for it is love that I desire, not sacrifice,
  and knowledge of God rather than holocausts.

Responsorial Psalm   Ps 50: 1, 8, 12–13, 14–15   Joe Higginbotham

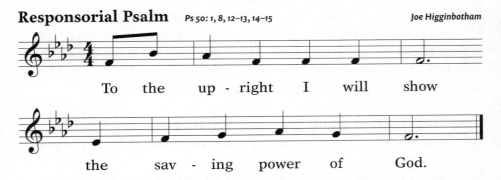

To the up-right I will show the sav-ing power of God.

God the LORD has spoken and summoned the earth,
  from the rising of the sun to its setting.
"Not for your sacrifices do I rebuke you,
  for your holocausts are before me always." ℟

"If I were hungry, I would not tell you,
  for mine are the world and its fullness.
Do I eat the flesh of strong bulls,
  or is the blood of goats my drink?" ℟

"Offer to God praise as your sacrifice
  and fulfill your vows to the Most High;
Then call upon me in time of distress;
  I will rescue you, and you shall glorify me." ℟

Second Reading Rom 4: 18–25 Brothers and sisters: Abraham believed, hoping against hope, that he would become "the father of many nations," according to what was said, "Thus shall your descendants be." He did not weaken in faith when he considered his own body as already dead—for he was almost a hundred years old—and the dead womb of Sarah. He did not doubt God's promise in unbelief; rather, he was strengthened by faith and gave glory to God and was fully convinced that what he had promised he was also able to do. That is why *it was credited to* *him as righteousness.* But it was not for him alone that it was written that *it was credited to him;* it was also for us, to whom it will be credited, who believe in the one who raised Jesus our Lord from the dead, who was handed over for our transgressions and was raised for our justification.

Alleluia   *cf. Lk 4: 18*   *Vince Ambrosetti*

Al - le - lu - ia,   al - le - lu - ia,   al - le - lu - ia,   al - le - lu - ia.

Al - le - lu - ia,   al - le - lu - ia,   al - le - lu - ia.

The Lord sent me to bring glad tidings to the poor, / and to proclaim liberty to captives.   **Alleluia, alleluia.**

Gospel *Mt 9: 9–13* As Jesus passed on from there, he saw a man named Matthew sitting at the customs post. He said to him, "Follow me." And he got up and followed him. While he was at table in his house, many tax collectors and sinners came and sat with Jesus and his disciples. The Pharisees saw this and said to his disciples, "Why does your teacher eat with tax collectors and sinners?" He heard this and said, "Those who are well do not need a physician, but the sick do. Go and learn the meaning of the words, 'I desire mercy, not sacrifice.' I did not come to call the righteous but sinners."

Communion Antiphon *Ps 18 (17): 3* **The Lord is my rock, my fortress, and my deliverer; ✦ my God is my saving strength.**

Or: *1 Jn 4: 16* **God is love, and whoever abides in love ✦ abides in God, and God in him.**

ELEVENTH SUNDAY IN ORDINARY TIME

Entrance Antiphon *cf. Ps 27 (26): 7, 9* O Lord, hear my voice, for I have called to you; be my help. ◆ Do not abandon or forsake me, O God, my Savior!

First Reading *Ex 19: 2–6a* In those days, the Israelites came to the desert of Sinai and pitched camp. While Israel was encamped here in front of the mountain, Moses went up the mountain to God. Then the LORD called to him and said, "Thus shall you say to the house of Jacob; tell the Israelites: You have seen for yourselves how I treated the Egyptians and how I bore you up on eagle wings and brought you here to myself. Therefore, if you hearken to my voice and keep my covenant, you shall be my special possession, dearer to me than all other people, though all the earth is mine. You shall be to me a kingdom of priests, a holy nation."

Responsorial Psalm *Ps 100: 1–2, 3, 5*   Joe Higginbotham

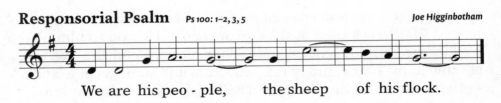

We are his peo - ple,   the sheep   of his flock.

Sing joyfully to the LORD, all you lands;
   serve the LORD with gladness;
   come before him with joyful song. ℟

Know that the LORD is God;
   he made us, his we are;
   his people, the flock he tends. ℟

The LORD is good:
   his kindness endures forever,
   and his faithfulness to all generations. ℟

Second Reading *Rom 5: 6–11* Brothers and sisters: Christ, while we were still helpless, yet died at the appointed time for the ungodly. Indeed, only with difficulty does one die for a just person, though perhaps for a good person one might even find courage to die. But God proves his love for us in that while we were still sinners Christ died for us. How much more then, since we are now justified by his blood, will we be saved through him from the wrath. Indeed, if, while we were enemies, we were reconciled to God through the death of his Son, how much more, once reconciled, will we be saved by his life. Not only that, but we also boast of God through our Lord Jesus Christ, through whom we have now received reconciliation.

Alleluia Mk 1: 15   Vince Ambrosetti

Al-le-lu-ia, al-le-lu-ia, al-le-lu-ia, al-le-lu-ia.

Al-le-lu-ia, al-le-lu-ia, al-le-lu - ia.

The kingdom of God is at hand. / Repent and believe in the Gospel. **Alleluia, alleluia.**

Gospel Mt 9: 36–10: 8 At the sight of the crowds, Jesus' heart was moved with pity for them because they were troubled and abandoned, like sheep without a shepherd. Then he said to his disciples, "The harvest is abundant but the laborers are few; so ask the master of the harvest to send out laborers for his harvest."

Then he summoned his twelve disciples and gave them authority over unclean spirits to drive them out and to cure every disease and every illness. The names of the twelve apostles are these: first, Simon called Peter, and his brother Andrew; James, the son of Zebedee, and his brother John; Philip and Bartholomew, Thomas and Matthew the tax collector; James, the son of Alphaeus, and Thaddeus; Simon from Cana, and Judas Iscariot who betrayed him.

Jesus sent out these twelve after instructing them thus, "Do not go into pagan territory or enter a Samaritan town. Go rather to the lost sheep of the house of Israel. As you go, make this proclamation: 'The kingdom of heaven is at hand.' Cure the sick, raise the dead, cleanse lepers, drive out demons. Without cost you have received; without cost you are to give."

Communion Antiphon Ps 27 (26): 4 There is one thing I ask of the Lord, only this do I seek: ◆ to live in the house of the Lord all the days of my life.

Or: Jn 17: 11 Holy Father, keep in your name those you have given me, ◆ that they may be one as we are one, says the Lord.

TWELFTH SUNDAY IN ORDINARY TIME

Entrance Antiphon cf. Ps 28 (27): 8–9 The Lord is the strength of his people, ◆ a saving refuge for the one he has anointed. ◆ Save your people, Lord, and bless your heritage, ◆ and govern them for ever.

First Reading   Jer 20: 10–13
Jeremiah said:
"I hear the whisperings of many:
    'Terror on every side!
    Denounce! let us denounce him!'
All those who were my friends
    are on the watch for any misstep of mine.
'Perhaps he will be trapped; then we can prevail,
    and take our vengeance on him.'
But the LORD is with me, like a mighty champion:
    my persecutors will stumble, they will not triumph.
In their failure they will be put to utter shame,
    to lasting, unforgettable confusion.
O LORD of hosts, you who test the just,
    who probe mind and heart,
let me witness the vengeance you take on them,
    for to you I have entrusted my cause.

Sing to the LORD,
   praise the LORD,
for he has rescued the life of the poor
   from the power of the wicked!"

Responsorial Psalm   Ps 69: 8–10, 14, 17, 33–35   Roger Holtz

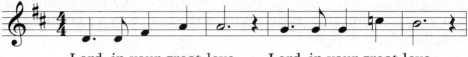

Lord, in your great love,   Lord, in your great love,

an - swer me,   an - swer me.

For your sake I bear insult,
   and shame covers my face.
I have become an outcast to my brothers,
   a stranger to my children,
Because zeal for your house consumes me,
   and the insults of those who blaspheme you fall upon me.   ℟

I pray to you, O LORD,
   for the time of your favor, O God!
In your great kindness answer me
   with your constant help.
Answer me, O LORD, for bounteous is your kindness;
   in your great mercy turn toward me.   ℟

"See, you lowly ones, and be glad;
   you who seek God, may your hearts revive!
For the LORD hears the poor,
   and his own who are in bonds he spurns not.
Let the heavens and the earth praise him,
   the seas and whatever moves in them!"   ℟

Second Reading Rom 5: 12–15 Brothers and sisters: Through one
man sin entered the world, and through sin, death, and thus
death came to all men, inasmuch as all sinned—for up to

the time of the law, sin was in the world, though sin is not accounted when there is no law. But death reigned from Adam to Moses, even over those who did not sin after the pattern of the trespass of Adam, who is the type of the one who was to come.

But the gift is not like the transgression. For if by the transgression of the one the many died, how much more did the grace of God and the gracious gift of the one man Jesus Christ overflow for the many.

Alleluia   Jn 15: 26b, 27a   *Vince Ambrosetti*

Al-le-lu-ia, al-le-lu-ia, al-le-lu-ia, al-le-lu-ia.

Al-le-lu-ia, al-le-lu-ia, al-le-lu - ia.

The Spirit of truth will testify to me, says the Lord; / and you also will testify.   **Alleluia, alleluia.**

Gospel   Mt 10: 26-33 Jesus said to the Twelve: "Fear no one. Nothing is concealed that will not be revealed, nor secret that will not be known. What I say to you in the darkness, speak in the light; what you hear whispered, proclaim on the housetops. And do not be afraid of those who kill the body but cannot kill the soul; rather, be afraid of the one who can destroy both soul and body in Gehenna. Are not two sparrows sold for a small coin? Yet not one of them falls to the ground without your Father's knowledge. Even all the hairs of your head are counted. So do not be afraid; you are worth more than many sparrows. Everyone who acknowledges me before others I will acknowledge before my heavenly Father. But whoever denies me before others, I will deny before my heavenly Father."

Communion Antiphon   Ps 145 (144): 15 **The eyes of all look to you, Lord, ◆ and you give them their food in due season.**

Or: Jn 10: 11, 15 **I am the Good Shepherd, ◆ and I lay down my life for my sheep, says the Lord.**

THIRTEENTH SUNDAY IN ORDINARY TIME

Entrance Antiphon Ps 47 (46): 2 **All peoples, clap your hands. ◆ Cry to God with shouts of joy!**

First Reading 2 Kgs 4: 8–11, 14–16a One day Elisha came to Shunem, where there was a woman of influence, who urged him to dine with her. Afterward, whenever he passed by, he used to stop there to dine. So she said to her husband, "I know that Elisha is a holy man of God. Since he visits us often, let us arrange a little room on the roof and furnish it for him with a bed, table, chair, and lamp, so that when he comes to us he can stay there." Sometime later Elisha arrived and stayed in the room overnight.

Later Elisha asked, "Can something be done for her?" His servant Gehazi answered, "Yes! She has no son, and her husband is getting on in years." Elisha said, "Call her." When the woman had been called and stood at the door, Elisha promised, "This time next year you will be fondling a baby son."

Responsorial Psalm   Ps 89: 2–3, 16–17, 18–19   *Beverly McDevitt*

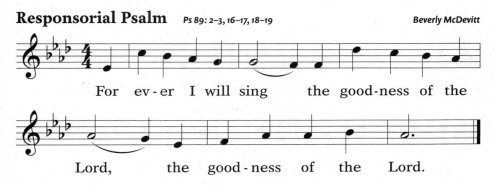

For ev-er I will sing the good-ness of the Lord, the good-ness of the Lord.

The promises of the LORD I will sing forever,
through all generations my mouth shall proclaim your
faithfulness.

For you have said, "My kindness is established forever;"
   in heaven you have confirmed your faithfulness. ℟

Blessed the people who know the joyful shout;
   in the light of your countenance, O LORD, they walk.
At your name they rejoice all the day,
   and through your justice they are exalted. ℟

You are the splendor of their strength,
   and by your favor our horn is exalted.
For to the LORD belongs our shield,
   and the Holy One of Israel, our king. ℟

Second Reading *Rom 6: 3–4, 8–11* Brothers and sisters: Are you
unaware that we who were baptized into Christ Jesus were
baptized into his death? We were indeed buried with him
through baptism into death, so that, just as Christ was raised
from the dead by the glory of the Father, we too might live in
newness of life.

   If, then, we have died with Christ, we believe that we shall
also live with him. We know that Christ, raised from the dead,
dies no more; death no longer has power over him. As to his
death, he died to sin once and for all; as to his life, he lives for
God. Consequently, you too must think of yourselves as dead to
sin and living for God in Christ Jesus.

Alleluia   *1 Pt 2: 9*   *Vince Ambrosetti*

You are a chosen race, a royal priesthood, a holy nation; /
announce the praises of him who called you out of darkness
into his wonderful light.   **Alleluia, alleluia.**

Gospel Mt 10: 37-42 Jesus said to his apostles: "Whoever loves father or mother more than me is not worthy of me, and whoever loves son or daughter more than me is not worthy of me; and whoever does not take up his cross and follow after me is not worthy of me. Whoever finds his life will lose it, and whoever loses his life for my sake will find it.

"Whoever receives you receives me, and whoever receives me receives the one who sent me. Whoever receives a prophet because he is a prophet will receive a prophet's reward, and whoever receives a righteous man because he is a righteous man will receive a righteous man's reward. And whoever gives only a cup of cold water to one of these little ones to drink because the little one is a disciple—amen, I say to you, he will surely not lose his reward."

Communion Antiphon cf. Ps 103 (102): 1 **Bless the Lord, O my soul,** ◆ **and all within me, his holy name.**

Or: Jn 17: 20-21 **O Father, I pray for them, that they may be one in us,** ◆ **that the world may believe that you have sent me, says the Lord.**

FOURTEENTH SUNDAY IN ORDINARY TIME

Entrance Antiphon cf. Ps 48 (47): 10-11 **Your merciful love, O God,** ◆ **we have received in the midst of your temple.** ◆ **Your praise, O God, like your name,** ◆ **reaches the ends of the earth;** ◆ **your right hand is filled with saving justice.**

First Reading Zec 9: 9-10
Thus says the Lord:
    Rejoice heartily, O daughter Zion,
        shout for joy, O daughter Jerusalem!
    See, your king shall come to you;
        a just savior is he,
    meek, and riding on an ass,

on a colt, the foal of an ass.
He shall banish the chariot from Ephraim,
    and the horse from Jerusalem;
the warrior's bow shall be banished,
    and he shall proclaim peace to the nations.
His dominion shall be from sea to sea,
    and from the River to the ends of the earth.

Responsorial Psalm   Ps 145: 1-2, 8-9, 10-11, 13-14   *Bill Svarda*

I will praise your name for ev-er, my king and my God.

Or: ℟ **Alleluia.**

I will extol you, O my God and King,
    and I will bless your name forever and ever.
Every day will I bless you,
    and I will praise your name forever and ever. ℟

The LORD is gracious and merciful,
    slow to anger and of great kindness.
The LORD is good to all
    and compassionate toward all his works. ℟

Let all your works give you thanks, O LORD,
    and let your faithful ones bless you.
Let them discourse of the glory of your kingdom
    and speak of your might. ℟

The LORD is faithful in all his words
    and holy in all his works.
The LORD lifts up all who are falling
    and raises up all who are bowed down. ℟

Second Reading Rom 8: 9, 11–13 Brothers and sisters: You are not in the flesh; on the contrary, you are in the spirit, if only the Spirit of God dwells in you. Whoever does not have the Spirit of Christ does not belong to him. If the Spirit of the one who raised Jesus from the dead dwells in you, the one who raised Christ from the dead will give life to your mortal bodies also, through his Spirit that dwells in you. Consequently, brothers and sisters, we are not debtors to the flesh, to live according to the flesh. For if you live according to the flesh, you will die, but if by the Spirit you put to death the deeds of the body, you will live.

Alleluia   *cf. Mt 11: 25*   *Vince Ambrosetti*

Al-le-lu-ia, al-le-lu-ia, al-le-lu-ia, al-le-lu-ia.

Al-le-lu-ia, al-le-lu-ia, al-le-lu - ia.

Blessed are you, Father, Lord of heaven and earth; / you have revealed to little ones the mysteries of the kingdom. **Alleluia, alleluia.**

Gospel Mt 11: 25-30 At that time Jesus exclaimed: "I give praise to you, Father, Lord of heaven and earth, for although you have hidden these things from the wise and the learned you have revealed them to little ones. Yes, Father, such has been your gracious will. All things have been handed over to me by my Father. No one knows the Son except the Father, and no one knows the Father except the Son and anyone to whom the Son wishes to reveal him."

"Come to me, all you who labor and are burdened, and I will give you rest. Take my yoke upon you and learn from me, for I am meek and humble of heart; and you will find rest for yourselves. For my yoke is easy, and my burden light."

Communion Antiphon Ps 34 (33): 9 Taste and see that the Lord is good; ◆ blessed the man who seeks refuge in him.

Or: Mt 11: 28 **Come to me, all who labor and are burdened, ♦ and I will refresh you, says the Lord.**

FIFTEENTH SUNDAY IN ORDINARY TIME

Entrance Antiphon *cf. Ps 17 (16): 15* **As for me, in justice I shall behold your face; ♦ I shall be filled with the vision of your glory.**

First Reading Is 55: 10–11
Thus says the LORD:
    Just as from the heavens
        the rain and snow come down
    and do not return there
        till they have watered the earth,
        making it fertile and fruitful,
    giving seed to the one who sows
        and bread to the one who eats,
    so shall my word be
        that goes forth from my mouth;
    my word shall not return to me void,
        but shall do my will,
        achieving the end for which I sent it.

Responsorial Psalm Ps 65: 10, 11, 12–13, 14   *based on* DIX

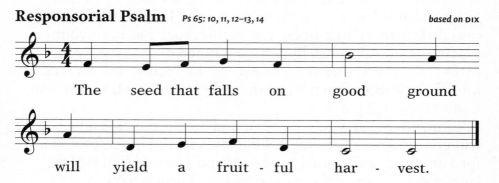

The seed that falls on good ground will yield a fruit-ful har-vest.

You have visited the land and watered it;
    greatly have you enriched it.
God's watercourses are filled;

you have prepared the grain. ℟

Thus have you prepared the land: drenching its furrows,
   breaking up its clods,
Softening it with showers,
   blessing its yield. ℟

You have crowned the year with your bounty,
   and your paths overflow with a rich harvest;
The untilled meadows overflow with it,
   and rejoicing clothes the hills. ℟

The fields are garmented with flocks
   and the valleys blanketed with grain.
They shout and sing for joy. ℟

Second Reading *Rom 8: 18–23* Brothers and sisters: I consider that
the sufferings of this present time are as nothing compared with
the glory to be revealed for us. For creation awaits with eager
expectation the revelation of the children of God; for creation was
made subject to futility, not of its own accord but because of the
one who subjected it, in hope that creation itself would be set free
from slavery to corruption and share in the glorious freedom of
the children of God. We know that all creation is groaning in labor
pains even until now; and not only that, but we ourselves, who
have the firstfruits of the Spirit, we also groan within ourselves as
we wait for adoption, the redemption of our bodies.

Alleluia   *Vince Ambrosetti*

Al - le - lu - ia, al - le - lu - ia, al - le - lu - ia, al - le - lu - ia.

Al - le - lu - ia, al - le - lu - ia, al - le - lu - ia.

The seed is the word of God, Christ is the sower. / All who
come to him will have life for ever. **Alleluia, alleluia.**

Gospel   Mt 13: 1–23 or 13: 1–9

For the shorter form, read only the parts in brackets.

[On that day, Jesus went out of the house and sat down by the sea. Such large crowds gathered around him that he got into a boat and sat down, and the whole crowd stood along the shore. And he spoke to them at length in parables, saying: "A sower went out to sow. And as he sowed, some seed fell on the path, and birds came and ate it up. Some fell on rocky ground, where it had little soil. It sprang up at once because the soil was not deep, and when the sun rose it was scorched, and it withered for lack of roots. Some seed fell among thorns, and the thorns grew up and choked it. But some seed fell on rich soil, and produced fruit, a hundred or sixty or thirtyfold. Whoever has ears ought to hear."]

The disciples approached him and said, "Why do you speak to them in parables?" He said to them in reply, "Because knowledge of the mysteries of the kingdom of heaven has been granted to you, but to them it has not been granted. To anyone who has, more will be given and he will grow rich; from anyone who has not, even what he has will be taken away. This is why I speak to them in parables, because *they look but do not see and hear but do not listen or understand.* Isaiah's prophecy is fulfilled in them, which says:

You shall indeed hear but not understand,
   you shall indeed look but never see.
Gross is the heart of this people,
   they will hardly hear with their ears,
   they have closed their eyes,
   lest they see with their eyes
   and hear with their ears
and understand with their hearts and be converted,
   and I heal them.

"But blessed are your eyes, because they see, and your ears, because they hear. Amen, I say to you, many prophets and righteous people longed to see what you see but did not see it, and to hear what you hear but did not hear it.

"Hear then the parable of the sower. The seed sown on the path is the one who hears the word of the kingdom without understanding it, and the evil one comes and steals away what was sown in his heart. The seed sown on rocky ground is the one who hears the word and receives it at once with joy. But he has no root and lasts only for a time. When some tribulation or persecution comes because of the word, he immediately falls away. The seed sown among thorns is the one who hears the word, but then worldly anxiety and the lure of riches choke the word and it bears no fruit. But the seed sown on rich soil is the one who hears the word and understands it, who indeed bears fruit and yields a hundred or sixty or thirtyfold."

Communion Antiphon *cf. Ps 84 (83): 4–5* **The sparrow finds a home, ◆ and the swallow a nest for her young: ◆ by your altars, O Lord of hosts, my King and my God. ◆ Blessed are they who dwell in your house, ◆ for ever singing your praise.**

Or: *Jn 6: 57* **Whoever eats my flesh and drinks my blood ◆ remains in me and I in him, says the Lord.**

SIXTEENTH SUNDAY IN ORDINARY TIME

Entrance Antiphon *Ps 54 (53): 6, 8* **See, I have God for my help. ◆ The Lord sustains my soul. ◆ I will sacrifice to you with willing heart, ◆ and praise your name, O Lord, for it is good.**

First Reading *Wis 12: 13, 16–19*
There is no god besides you who have the care of all,
    that you need show you have not unjustly condemned.
For your might is the source of justice;
    your mastery over all things makes you lenient to all.
For you show your might when the perfection of your power
        is disbelieved;
    and in those who know you, you rebuke temerity.
But though you are master of might, you judge with clemency,
    and with much lenience you govern us;
    for power, whenever you will, attends you.
And you taught your people, by these deeds,
    that those who are just must be kind;
and you gave your children good ground for hope
    that you would permit repentance for their sins.

Responsorial Psalm

Ps 86: 5–6, 9–10, 15–16

Joe Higginbotham

Lord, you are good and for - giv - ing.

Lord, you are good and for - giv - ing.

You, O LORD, are good and forgiving,
   abounding in kindness to all who call upon you.
Hearken, O LORD, to my prayer
   and attend to the sound of my pleading. ℟

All the nations you have made shall come
   and worship you, O LORD,
   and glorify your name.
For you are great, and you do wondrous deeds;
   you alone are God. ℟

You, O LORD, are a God merciful and gracious,
   slow to anger, abounding in kindness and fidelity.
Turn toward me, and have pity on me;
   give your strength to your servant. ℟

Second Reading *Rom 8: 26–27* Brothers and sisters: The Spirit comes to the aid of our weakness; for we do not know how to pray as we ought, but the Spirit himself intercedes with inexpressible groanings. And the one who searches hearts knows what is the intention of the Spirit, because he intercedes for the holy ones according to God's will.

Alleluia

cf. Mt 11: 25

Jim Hughes

Al-le-lu-ia   Al-le-lu-ia   Al - le-lu - ia.

Blessed are you, Father, Lord of heaven and earth; / you have revealed to little ones the mysteries of the kingdom. **Alleluia, alleluia.**

Gospel   Mt 13: 24-43 or 13: 24-30

For the shorter form, read only the parts in brackets.

[Jesus proposed another parable to the crowds, saying: "The kingdom of heaven may be likened to a man who sowed good seed in his field. While everyone was asleep his enemy came and sowed weeds all through the wheat, and then went off. When the crop grew and bore fruit, the weeds appeared as well. The slaves of the householder came to him and said, 'Master, did you not sow good seed in your field? Where have the weeds come from?' He answered, 'An enemy has done this.' His slaves said to him, 'Do you want us to go and pull them up?' He replied, 'No, if you pull up the weeds you might uproot the wheat along with them. Let them grow together until harvest; then at harvest time I will say to the harvesters, "First collect the weeds and tie them in bundles for burning; but gather the wheat into my barn."'"]

He proposed another parable to them. "The kingdom of heaven is like a mustard seed that a person took and sowed in a field. It is the smallest of all the seeds, yet when full-grown it is the largest of plants. It becomes a large bush, and the 'birds of the sky come and dwell in its branches.'"

He spoke to them another parable. "The kingdom of heaven is like yeast that a woman took and mixed with three measures of wheat flour until the whole batch was leavened."

All these things Jesus spoke to the crowds in parables. He spoke to them only in parables, to fulfill what had been said through the prophet:

I will open my mouth in parables,
   I will announce what has lain hidden from the foundation of the world.

Then, dismissing the crowds, he went into the house. His disciples approached him and said, "Explain to us the parable of the weeds in the field." He said in reply, "He who sows good seed is the Son of Man, the field is the world, the good seed the children of the kingdom. The weeds are the children of the

evil one, and the enemy who sows them is the devil. The harvest
is the end of the age, and the harvesters are angels. Just as
weeds are collected and burned up with fire, so will it be at the
end of the age. The Son of Man will send his angels, and they
will collect out of his kingdom all who cause others to sin and
all evildoers. They will throw them into the fiery furnace, where
there will be wailing and grinding of teeth. Then the righteous
will shine like the sun in the kingdom of their Father. Whoever
has ears ought to hear."

Communion Antiphon Ps 111 (110): 4-5 **The Lord, the gracious, the
merciful, ◆ has made a memorial of his wonders; ◆ he gives
food to those who fear him.**

Or: Rv 3: 20 **Behold, I stand at the door and knock, says the
Lord. ◆ If anyone hears my voice and opens the door to me, ◆
I will enter his house and dine with him, and he with me.**

SEVENTEENTH SUNDAY IN ORDINARY TIME

Entrance Antiphon cf. Ps 68 (67): 6-7, 36 **God is in his holy place, ◆
God who unites those who dwell in his house; ◆ he himself
gives might and strength to his people.**

First Reading 1 Kgs 3: 5, 7-12 The LORD appeared to Solomon in a
dream at night. God said, "Ask something of me and I will give it
to you." Solomon answered: "O LORD, my God, you have made
me, your servant, king to succeed my father David; but I am a
mere youth, not knowing at all how to act. I serve you in the
midst of the people whom you have chosen, a people so vast that
it cannot be numbered or counted. Give your servant, therefore,
an understanding heart to judge your people and to distinguish
right from wrong. For who is able to govern this vast people of
yours?"

The LORD was pleased that Solomon made this request. So
God said to him: "Because you have asked for this—not for

a long life for yourself, nor for riches, nor for the life of your enemies, but for understanding so that you may know what is right—I do as you requested. I give you a heart so wise and understanding that there has never been anyone like you up to now, and after you there will come no one to equal you."

Responsorial Psalm   Ps 119: 57, 72, 76–77, 127–128, 129–130   Joe Higginbotham

Lord, I love your com-mands, I love your com-mands.

I have said, O LORD, that my part
   is to keep your words.
The law of your mouth is to me more precious
   than thousands of gold and silver pieces. ℟

Let your kindness comfort me
   according to your promise to your servants.
Let your compassion come to me that I may live,
   for your law is my delight. ℟

For I love your commands
   more than gold, however fine.
For in all your precepts I go forward;
   every false way I hate. ℟

Wonderful are your decrees;
   therefore I observe them.
The revelation of your words sheds light,
   giving understanding to the simple. ℟

Second Reading Rom 8: 28–30 Brothers and sisters: We know that all things work for good for those who love God, who are called according to his purpose. For those he foreknew he also predestined to be conformed to the image of his Son, so that he might be the firstborn among many brothers and sisters. And those he predestined he also called; and those he called he also justified; and those he justified he also glorified.

Alleluia *cf. Mt 11: 25*

Jim Hughes

Al - le - lu - ia   Al - le - lu - ia   Al - le - lu - ia.

Blessed are you Father, Lord of heaven and earth; / for you have revealed to little ones the mysteries of the kingdom. **Alleluia, alleluia.**

Gospel   Mt 13: 44–52 or 13: 44–46

For the shorter form, read only the parts in brackets.

[Jesus said to his disciples: "The kingdom of heaven is like a treasure buried in a field, which a person finds and hides again, and out of joy goes and sells all that he has and buys that field. Again, the kingdom of heaven is like a merchant searching for fine pearls. When he finds a pearl of great price, he goes and sells all that he has and buys it.] Again, the kingdom of heaven is like a net thrown into the sea, which collects fish of every kind. When it is full they haul it ashore and sit down to put what is good into buckets. What is bad they throw away. Thus it will be at the end of the age. The angels will go out and separate the wicked from the righteous and throw them into the fiery furnace, where there will be wailing and grinding of teeth.

"Do you understand all these things?" They answered, "Yes." And he replied, "Then every scribe who has been instructed in the kingdom of heaven is like the head of a household who brings from his storeroom both the new and the old."

Communion Antiphon Ps 103 (102): 2 **Bless the Lord, O my soul, ◆ and never forget all his benefits.**

Or: Mt 5: 7-8 **Blessed are the merciful, for they shall receive mercy. ◆ Blessed are the clean of heart, for they shall see God.**

EIGHTEENTH SUNDAY IN ORDINARY TIME

Entrance Antiphon Ps 70 (69): 2, 6 **O God, come to my assistance; ◆**

O Lord, make haste to help me! ✦ You are my rescuer, my help;
✦ O Lord, do not delay.

First Reading   Is 55: 1–3
Thus says the LORD:
  All you who are thirsty,
    come to the water!
  You who have no money,
    come, receive grain and eat;
  Come, without paying and without cost,
    drink wine and milk!
  Why spend your money for what is not bread;
    your wages for what fails to satisfy?
  Heed me, and you shall eat well,
    you shall delight in rich fare.
  Come to me heedfully,
    listen, that you may have life.
  I will renew with you the everlasting covenant,
    the benefits assured to David.

Responsorial Psalm   Ps 145: 8–9, 15–16, 17–18   Don Fishel

The hand of the Lord feeds us; he an-swers all our needs.

The LORD is gracious and merciful,
  slow to anger and of great kindness.
The LORD is good to all
  and compassionate toward all his works.   ℟

The eyes of all look hopefully to you,
  and you give them their food in due season;
you open your hand
  and satisfy the desire of every living thing.   ℟

The LORD is just in all his ways
  and holy in all his works.
The LORD is near to all who call upon him,
  to all who call upon him in truth.   ℟

Second Reading *Rom 8: 35,37-39* Brothers and sisters: What will separate us from the love of Christ? Will anguish, or distress, or persecution, or famine, or nakedness, or peril, or the sword? No, in all these things we conquer overwhelmingly through him who loved us. For I am convinced that neither death, nor life, nor angels, nor principalities, nor present things, nor future things, nor powers, nor height, nor depth, nor any other creature will be able to separate us from the love of God in Christ Jesus our Lord.

Alleluia *Mt 4: 4b* Jim Hughes

Al-le-lu-ia   Al-le-lu-ia   Al - le-lu - ia.

One does not live on bread alone, / but on every word that comes forth from the mouth of God. **Alleluia, alleluia.**

Gospel *Mt 14: 13-21* When Jesus heard of the death of John the Baptist, he withdrew in a boat to a deserted place by himself. The crowds heard of this and followed him on foot from their towns. When he disembarked and saw the vast crowd, his heart was moved with pity for them, and he cured their sick. When it was evening, the disciples approached him and said, "This is a deserted place and it is already late; dismiss the crowds so that they can go to the villages and buy food for themselves." Jesus said to them, "There is no need for them to go away; give them some food yourselves." But they said to him, "Five loaves and two fish are all we have here." Then he said, "Bring them here to me," and he ordered the crowds to sit down on the grass. Taking the five loaves and the two fish, and looking up to heaven, he said the blessing, broke the loaves, and gave them to the disciples, who in turn gave them to the crowds. They all ate and were satisfied, and they picked up the fragments left over—twelve wicker baskets full. Those who ate were about five thousand men, not counting women and children.

Communion Antiphon *Wis 16: 20* You have given us, O Lord, bread from heaven, ◆ endowed with all delights and sweetness in every taste.

Or: Jn 6: 35   I am the bread of life, says the Lord; ◆ whoever comes to me will not hunger ◆ and whoever believes in me will not thirst.

NINETEENTH SUNDAY IN ORDINARY TIME

Entrance Antiphon   *cf. Ps 74 (73): 20, 19, 22, 23*   Look to your covenant, O Lord, ◆ and forget not the life of your poor ones for ever. ◆ Arise, O God, and defend your cause, ◆ and forget not the cries of those who seek you.

First Reading   1 Kgs 19: 9a, 11–13a   At the mountain of God, Horeb, Elijah came to a cave where he took shelter. Then the LORD said to him, "Go outside and stand on the mountain before the LORD; the LORD will be passing by." A strong and heavy wind was rending the mountains and crushing rocks before the LORD—but the LORD was not in the wind. After the wind there was an earthquake—but the LORD was not in the earthquake. After the earthquake there was fire—but the LORD was not in the fire. After the fire there was a tiny whispering sound. When he heard this, Elijah hid his face in his cloak and went and stood at the entrance of the cave.

Responsorial Psalm   Ps 85: 9, 10, 11–12, 13–14   *Beverly McDevitt*

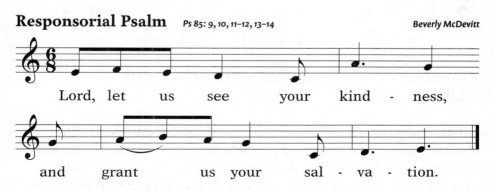

Lord, let us see your kind - ness, and grant us your sal - va - tion.

I will hear what God proclaims;
    the LORD—for he proclaims peace.

Near indeed is his salvation to those who fear him,
  glory dwelling in our land.   ℟

Kindness and truth shall meet;
  justice and peace shall kiss.
Truth shall spring out of the earth,
  and justice shall look down from heaven.   ℟

The LORD himself will give his benefits;
  our land shall yield its increase.
Justice shall walk before him,
  and prepare the way of his steps.   ℟

Second Reading   *Rom 9: 1–5*   Brothers and sisters: I speak the truth
in Christ, I do not lie; my conscience joins with the Holy Spirit
in bearing me witness that I have great sorrow and constant
anguish in my heart. For I could wish that I myself were
accursed and cut off from Christ for the sake of my own people,
my kindred according to the flesh. They are Israelites; theirs
the adoption, the glory, the covenants, the giving of the law, the
worship, and the promises; theirs the patriarchs, and from them,
according to the flesh, is the Christ, who is over all, God blessed
forever. Amen.

Alleluia   *cf. Ps 130: 5*   *Jim Hughes*

Al-le-lu-ia   Al-le-lu-ia   Al - le-lu - ia.

I wait for the Lord; / my soul waits for his word.
Alleluia, alleluia.

Gospel   *Mt 14: 22–33*   After he had fed the people, Jesus made the
disciples get into a boat and precede him to the other side, while
he dismissed the crowds. After doing so, he went up on the
mountain by himself to pray. When it was evening he was there
alone. Meanwhile the boat, already a few miles offshore, was
being tossed about by the waves, for the wind was against it.

During the fourth watch of the night, he came toward them walking on the sea. When the disciples saw him walking on the sea they were terrified. "It is a ghost," they said, and they cried out in fear. At once Jesus spoke to them, "Take courage, it is I; do not be afraid." Peter said to him in reply, "Lord, if it is you, command me to come to you on the water." He said, "Come." Peter got out of the boat and began to walk on the water toward Jesus. But when he saw how strong the wind was he became frightened; and, beginning to sink, he cried out, "Lord, save me!" Immediately Jesus stretched out his hand and caught Peter, and said to him, "O you of little faith, why did you doubt?" After they got into the boat, the wind died down. Those who were in the boat did him homage, saying, "Truly, you are the Son of God."

Communion Antiphon Ps 147 (146): 12, 14 **O Jerusalem, glorify the Lord, ◆ who gives you your fill of finest wheat.**

Or: cf. Jn 6: 51 **The bread that I will give, says the Lord, ◆ is my flesh for the life of the world.**

TWENTIETH SUNDAY IN ORDINARY TIME

Entrance Antiphon Ps 84 (83): 10–11 **Turn your eyes, O God, our shield; ◆ and look on the face of your anointed one; ◆ one day within your courts ◆ is better than a thousand elsewhere.**

First Reading   Is 56: 1, 6–7
Thus says the LORD:
  Observe what is right, do what is just;
    for my salvation is about to come,
    my justice, about to be revealed.

  The foreigners who join themselves to the LORD,
    ministering to him,
  loving the name of the LORD,
    and becoming his servants—
  all who keep the sabbath free from profanation

and hold to my covenant,
them I will bring to my holy mountain
and make joyful in my house of prayer;
their burnt offerings and sacrifices
will be acceptable on my altar,
for my house shall be called
a house of prayer for all peoples.

Responsorial Psalm   Ps 67: 2–3, 5, 6, 8   *Roger Holtz and Jane Terwilliger*

O God, let all the na-tions praise you, let all the na-tions praise you!

May God have pity on us and bless us;
   may he let his face shine upon us.
So may your way be known upon earth;
   among all nations, your salvation.   ℟

May the nations be glad and exult
   because you rule the peoples in equity;
   the nations on the earth you guide.   ℟

May the peoples praise you, O God;
   may all the peoples praise you!
May God bless us,
   and may all the ends of the earth fear him!   ℟

Second Reading   Rom 11: 13–15, 29–32   Brothers and sisters: I am speaking
to you Gentiles. Inasmuch as I am the apostle to the Gentiles,
I glory in my ministry in order to make my race jealous and thus
save some of them. For if their rejection is the reconciliation of
the world, what will their acceptance be but life from the dead?

For the gifts and the call of God are irrevocable. Just as you once disobeyed God but have now received mercy because of their disobedience, so they have now disobeyed in order that, by virtue of the mercy shown to you, they too may now receive mercy. For God delivered all to disobedience, that he might have mercy upon all.

Alleluia   *cf. Mt 4: 23*   *Jim Hughes*

Al-le-lu-ia   Al-le-lu-ia   Al - le-lu - ia.

Jesus proclaimed the Gospel of the kingdom / and cured every disease among the people.   **Alleluia, alleluia.**

Gospel *Mt 15: 21–28* At that time, Jesus withdrew to the region of Tyre and Sidon. And behold, a Canaanite woman of that district came and called out, "Have pity on me, Lord, Son of David! My daughter is tormented by a demon." But Jesus did not say a word in answer to her. Jesus' disciples came and asked him, "Send her away, for she keeps calling out after us." He said in reply, "I was sent only to the lost sheep of the house of Israel." But the woman came and did Jesus homage, saying, "Lord, help me." He said in reply, "It is not right to take the food of the children and throw it to the dogs." She said, "Please, Lord, for even the dogs eat the scraps that fall from the table of their masters." Then Jesus said to her in reply, "O woman, great is your faith! Let it be done for you as you wish." And the woman's daughter was healed from that hour.

Communion Antiphon *Ps 130 (129): 7* **With the Lord there is mercy; ◆ in him is plentiful redemption.**

Or: *Jn 6: 51–52* **I am the living bread that came down from heaven, says the Lord. ◆ Whoever eats of this bread will live for ever.**

TWENTY-FIRST SUNDAY IN ORDINARY TIME

Entrance Antiphon *cf. Ps 86 (85): 1–3* **Turn your ear, O Lord, and answer me; ◆ save the servant who trusts in you, my God. ◆ Have mercy on me, O Lord, for I cry to you all the day long.**

First Reading *Is 22: 19–23*
Thus says the LORD to Shebna, master of the palace:
"I will thrust you from your office
  and pull you down from your station.
On that day I will summon my servant
  Eliakim, son of Hilkiah;
I will clothe him with your robe,
  and gird him with your sash,
  and give over to him your authority.
He shall be a father to the inhabitants of Jerusalem,
  and to the house of Judah.
I will place the key of the House of David on Eliakim's
    shoulder;
  when he opens, no one shall shut;
  when he shuts, no one shall open.
I will fix him like a peg in a sure spot,
  to be a place of honor for his family."

Responsorial Psalm   *Ps 138: 1–2, 2–3, 6, 8*   *Bill Svarda*

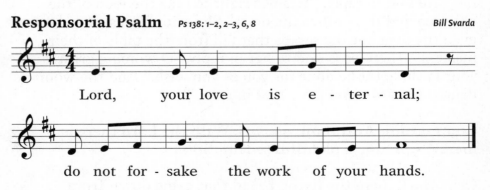

Lord, your love is e - ter - nal; do not for - sake the work of your hands.

I will give thanks to you, O LORD, with all my heart,
  for you have heard the words of my mouth;
  in the presence of the angels I will sing your praise;
I will worship at your holy temple. ℟

I will give thanks to your name,
   because of your kindness and your truth:
When I called, you answered me;
   you built up strength within me. ℟

The LORD is exalted, yet the lowly he sees,
   and the proud he knows from afar.
Your kindness, O LORD, endures forever;
   forsake not the work of your hands. ℟

Second Reading Rom 11: 33–36 Oh, the depth of the riches and
wisdom and knowledge of God! How inscrutable are his
judgments and how unsearchable his ways!
   For who has known the mind of the Lord
     or who has been his counselor?
   Or who has given the Lord anything
     that he may be repaid?
For from him and through him and for him are all things. To him
be glory forever. Amen.

Alleluia   Mt 16: 18   *Jim Hughes*

Al-le-lu-ia   Al-le-lu-ia   Al - le-lu - ia.

You are Peter and upon this rock I will build my Church /
   and the gates of the netherworld shall not prevail against it.
Alleluia, alleluia.

Gospel Mt 16: 13–20 Jesus went into the region of Caesarea Philippi
and he asked his disciples, "Who do people say that the Son of
Man is?" They replied, "Some say John the Baptist, others Elijah,
still others Jeremiah or one of the prophets." He said to them,
"But who do you say that I am?" Simon Peter said in reply, "You
are the Christ, the Son of the living God." Jesus said to him in
reply, "Blessed are you, Simon son of Jonah. For flesh and blood
has not revealed this to you, but my heavenly Father. And so I say
to you, you are Peter, and upon this rock I will build my church,

and the gates of the netherworld shall not prevail against it.
I will give you the keys to the kingdom of heaven. Whatever you
bind on earth shall be bound in heaven; and whatever you loose
on earth shall be loosed in heaven." Then he strictly ordered his
disciples to tell no one that he was the Christ.

Communion Antiphon *cf. Ps 104 (103): 13–15* **The earth is replete with
the fruits of your work, O Lord; ♦ you bring forth bread from
the earth ♦ and wine to cheer the heart.**

Or: *cf. Jn 6: 54* **Whoever eats my flesh and drinks my blood ♦
has eternal life, says the Lord, ♦ and I will raise him up on
the last day.**

TWENTY-SECOND

SUNDAY IN ORDINARY TIME

Entrance Antiphon *cf. Ps 86 (85): 3, 5* **Have mercy on me, O Lord,
for I cry to you all the day long. ♦ O Lord, you are good and
forgiving, ♦ full of mercy to all who call to you.**

First Reading   *Jer 20: 7–9*

You duped me, O LORD, and I let myself be duped;
  you were too strong for me, and you triumphed.
All the day I am an object of laughter;
  everyone mocks me.

Whenever I speak, I must cry out,
  violence and outrage is my message;
the word of the LORD has brought me
  derision and reproach all the day.

I say to myself, I will not mention him,
  I will speak in his name no more.
But then it becomes like fire burning in my heart,
  imprisoned in my bones;
I grow weary holding it in, I cannot endure it.

Responsorial Psalm   *Ps 63: 2, 3–4, 5–6, 8–9*   *Bill Svarda*

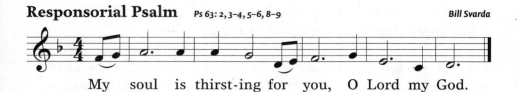

My soul is thirst-ing for you, O Lord my God.

O God, you are my God whom I seek;
   for you my flesh pines and my soul thirsts
   like the earth, parched, lifeless and without water. ℟

Thus have I gazed toward you in the sanctuary
   to see your power and your glory,
For your kindness is a greater good than life;
   my lips shall glorify you. ℟

Thus will I bless you while I live;
   lifting up my hands, I will call upon your name.
As with the riches of a banquet shall my soul be satisfied,
   and with exultant lips my mouth shall praise you. ℟

You are my help,
   and in the shadow of your wings I shout for joy.
My soul clings fast to you;
   your right hand upholds me. ℟

Second Reading   *Rom 12: 1–2*   I urge you, brothers and sisters, by the
mercies of God, to offer your bodies as a living sacrifice, holy
and pleasing to God, your spiritual worship. Do not conform
yourselves to this age but be transformed by the renewal of your
mind, that you may discern what is the will of God, what is good
and pleasing and perfect.

Alleluia   *cf. Eph 1: 17–18*   *Jim Hughes*

Al-le-lu-ia   Al-le-lu-ia   Al - le-lu - ia.

May the Father of our Lord Jesus Christ enlighten the eyes

of our hearts, / that we may know what is the hope that belongs to our call. **Alleluia, alleluia.**

Gospel Mt 16: 21–27 Jesus began to show his disciples that he must go to Jerusalem and suffer greatly from the elders, the chief priests, and the scribes, and be killed and on the third day be raised. Then Peter took Jesus aside and began to rebuke him, "God forbid, Lord! No such thing shall ever happen to you." He turned and said to Peter, "Get behind me, Satan! You are an obstacle to me. You are thinking not as God does, but as human beings do."

Then Jesus said to his disciples, "Whoever wishes to come after me must deny himself, take up his cross, and follow me. For whoever wishes to save his life will lose it, but whoever loses his life for my sake will find it. What profit would there be for one to gain the whole world and forfeit his life? Or what can one give in exchange for his life? For the Son of Man will come with his angels in his Father's glory, and then he will repay all according to his conduct."

Communion Antiphon Ps 31 (30): 20 **How great is the goodness, Lord, ◆ that you keep for those who fear you.**

Or: Mt 5: 9–10 **Blessed are the peacemakers, ◆ for they shall be called children of God. ◆ Blessed are they who are persecuted for the sake of righteousness, ◆ for theirs is the Kingdom of Heaven.**

TWENTY-THIRD

SUNDAY IN ORDINARY TIME

Entrance Antiphon Ps 119 (118): 137, 124 **You are just, O Lord, and your judgment is right; ◆ treat your servant in accord with your merciful love.**

First Reading *Ez 33:7-9* Thus says the LORD: You, son of man,
I have appointed watchman for the house of Israel; when
you hear me say anything, you shall warn them for me. If I tell
the wicked, "O wicked one, you shall surely die," and you do not
speak out to dissuade the wicked from his way, the wicked shall
die for his guilt, but I will hold you responsible for his death.
But if you warn the wicked, trying to turn him from his way,
and he refuses to turn from his way, he shall die for his guilt, but
you shall save yourself.

Responsorial Psalm   *Ps 95: 1-2, 6-7, 8-9*   Joe Higginbotham

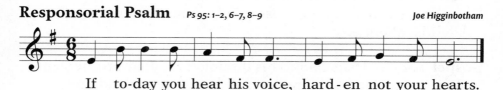

If   to-day you hear his voice, hard-en not your hearts.

Come, let us sing joyfully to the LORD;
   let us acclaim the rock of our salvation.
Let us come into his presence with thanksgiving;
   let us joyfully sing psalms to him. ℟

Come, let us bow down in worship;
   let us kneel before the LORD who made us.
For he is our God,
   and we are the people he shepherds, the flock he guides. ℟

Oh, that today you would hear his voice:
   "Harden not your hearts as at Meribah,
   as in the day of Massah in the desert,
Where your fathers tempted me;
   they tested me though they had seen my works." ℟

Second Reading *Rom 13: 8-10* Brothers and sisters: Owe nothing
to anyone, except to love one another; for the one who loves
another has fulfilled the law. The commandments, "You shall
not commit adultery; you shall not kill; you shall not steal; you
shall not covet," and whatever other commandment there may
be, are summed up in this saying, namely, "You shall love your

neighbor as yourself." Love does no evil to the neighbor; hence, love is the fulfillment of the law.

Alleluia   *2 Cor 5: 19*   *Michael Kissinger*

Al-le - lu-ia, al-le - lu - ia, al - le - lu - ia.

God was reconciling the world to himself in Christ /
and entrusting to us the message of reconciliation.
Alleluia, alleluia.

Gospel *Mt 18: 15–20* Jesus said to his disciples: "If your brother sins against you, go and tell him his fault between you and him alone. If he listens to you, you have won over your brother. If he does not listen, take one or two others along with you, so that 'every fact may be established on the testimony of two or three witnesses.' If he refuses to listen to them, tell the church. If he refuses to listen even to the church, then treat him as you would a Gentile or a tax collector. Amen, I say to you, whatever you bind on earth shall be bound in heaven, and whatever you loose on earth shall be loosed in heaven. Again, amen, I say to you, if two of you agree on earth about anything for which they are to pray, it shall be granted to them by my heavenly Father. For where two or three are gathered together in my name, there am I in the midst of them."

Communion Antiphon *cf. Ps 42 (41): 2–3* **Like the deer that yearns for running streams, ◆ so my soul is yearning for you, my God; ◆ my soul is thirsting for God, the living God.**

Or: *Jn 8: 12* **I am the light of the world, says the Lord; ◆ whoever follows me will not walk in darkness, ◆ but will have the light of life.**

TWENTY-FOURTH

SUNDAY IN ORDINARY TIME

Entrance Antiphon *cf. Sir 36: 18* Give peace, O Lord, to those who wait for you, ◆ that your prophets be found true. ◆ Hear the prayers of your servant, ◆ and of your people Israel.

First Reading   *Sir 27: 30–28: 7*

Wrath and anger are hateful things,
    yet the sinner hugs them tight.
The vengeful will suffer the LORD's vengeance,
    for he remembers their sins in detail
Forgive your neighbor's injustice;
    then when you pray, your own sins will be forgiven.
Could anyone nourish anger against another
    and expect healing from the LORD?
Could anyone refuse mercy to another like himself,
    can he seek pardon for his own sins?
If one who is but flesh cherishes wrath,
    who will forgive his sins?
Remember your last days, set enmity aside;
    remember death and decay, and cease from sin!
Think of the commandments, hate not your neighbor;
    remember the Most High's covenant, and overlook faults.

Responsorial Psalm   *Ps 103: 1–2, 3–4, 9–10, 11–12*   *Bill Svarda*

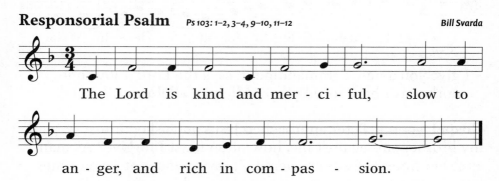

The Lord is kind and mer-ci-ful, slow to an-ger, and rich in com-pas-sion.

Bless the LORD, O my soul;
    and all my being, bless his holy name

Bless the LORD, O my soul,
and forget not all his benefits. ℟

He pardons all your iniquities,
heals all your ills.
redeems your life from destruction,
crowns you with kindness and compassion. ℟

He will not always chide,
nor does he keep his wrath forever.
Not according to our sins does he deal with us,
nor does he requite us according to our crimes. ℟

For as the heavens are high above the earth,
so surpassing is his kindness toward those who fear him.
As far as the east is from the west,
so far has he put our transgressions from us. ℟

Second Reading Rom 14: 7–9 Brothers and sisters: None of us lives for oneself, and no one dies for oneself. For if we live, we live for the Lord, and if we die, we die for the Lord; so then, whether we live or die, we are the Lord's. For this is why Christ died and came to life, that he might be Lord of both the dead and the living.

Alleluia Jn 13: 34   *Michael Kissinger*

Al-le - lu-ia, al-le - lu - ia, al   –   le - lu - ia.

I give you a new commandment, says the Lord; / love one another as I have loved you. **Alleluia, alleluia.**

Gospel Mt 18: 21–35 Peter approached Jesus and asked him, "Lord, if my brother sins against me, how often must I forgive? As many as seven times?" Jesus answered, "I say to you, not seven times but seventy-seven times. That is why the kingdom of heaven may be likened to a king who decided to settle accounts with his servants. When he began the accounting, a debtor was brought before him who owed him a huge amount. Since he had no way of paying it back, his master ordered him to be sold, along with his wife, his children, and all his property, in payment of the debt. At that, the servant fell down, did him homage, and said, 'Be patient with me, and I will pay you back in full.' Moved with compassion the master of that servant let him go and forgave him the loan. When that servant had left, he found one of his fellow servants who owed him a much smaller amount. He seized him and started to choke him, demanding, 'Pay back what you owe.' Falling to his knees, his fellow servant begged him, 'Be patient with me, and I will pay you back.' But he refused. Instead, he had the fellow servant put in prison until he paid back the debt. Now when his fellow servants saw what had happened, they were deeply disturbed, and went to their master and reported the whole affair. His master summoned him and said to him, 'You wicked servant! I forgave you your entire debt because you begged me to. Should you not have had pity on your fellow servant, as I had pity on you?' Then in anger his master handed him over to the torturers until he should pay back the whole debt. So will my heavenly Father do to you, unless each of you forgives your brother from your heart."

Communion Antiphon *cf. Ps 36 (35): 8* How precious is your mercy, O God! ✦ The children of men seek shelter in the shadow of your wings.

Or: *cf. 1 Cor 10: 16* The chalice of blessing that we bless ✦ is a communion in the Blood of Christ; ✦ and the bread that we break ✦ is a sharing in the Body of the Lord.

TWENTY-FIFTH SUNDAY IN ORDINARY TIME

Entrance Antiphon   I am the salvation of the people, says the Lord. ✦ Should they cry to me in any distress, ✦ I will hear them, and I will be their Lord for ever.

First Reading   *Is 55: 6–9*

Seek the LORD while he may be found,
  call him while he is near.
Let the scoundrel forsake his way,
  and the wicked his thoughts;
let him turn to the LORD for mercy;
  to our God, who is generous in forgiving.
For my thoughts are not your thoughts,
  nor are your ways my ways, says the LORD.
As high as the heavens are above the earth,
  so high are my ways above your ways
  and my thoughts above your thoughts.

Responsorial Psalm   *Ps 145: 2–3, 8–9, 17–18*   *Bill Svarda*

The Lord is near to all who call up-on him.

Every day will I bless you,
  and I will praise your name forever and ever.
Great is the LORD and highly to be praised;
  his greatness is unsearchable.   ℟

The LORD is gracious and merciful,
  slow to anger and of great kindness.
The LORD is good to all
  and compassionate toward all his works.   ℟

The LORD is just in all his ways
  and holy in all his works.
The LORD is near to all who call upon him,
  to all who call upon him in truth.   ℟

Second Reading   *Phil 1: 20c–24, 27a*   Brothers and sisters: Christ will
be magnified in my body, whether by life or by death. For to me
life is Christ, and death is gain. If I go on living in the flesh, that
means fruitful labor for me. And I do not know which I shall
choose. I am caught between the two. I long to depart this life

and be with Christ, for that is far better. Yet that I remain in the flesh is more necessary for your benefit.

Only, conduct yourselves in a way worthy of the gospel of Christ.

Alleluia *cf. Acts 16: 14b*   *Michael Kissinger*

Al-le - lu-ia, al-le - lu - ia, al - le - lu - ia.

Open our hearts, O Lord, / to listen to the words of your Son. **Alleluia, alleluia.**

Gospel *Mt 20: 1–16a* Jesus told his disciples this parable: "The kingdom of heaven is like a landowner who went out at dawn to hire laborers for his vineyard. After agreeing with them for the usual daily wage, he sent them into his vineyard. Going out about nine o'clock, the landowner saw others standing idle in the marketplace, and he said to them, 'You too go into my vineyard, and I will give you what is just.' So they went off. And he went out again around noon, and around three o'clock, and did likewise. Going out about five o'clock, the landowner found others standing around, and said to them, 'Why do you stand here idle all day?' They answered, 'Because no one has hired us.' He said to them, 'You too go into my vineyard.' When it was evening the owner of the vineyard said to his foreman, 'Summon the laborers and give them their pay, beginning with the last and ending with the first.' When those who had started about five o'clock came, each received the usual daily wage. So when the first came, they thought that they would receive more, but each of them also got the usual wage. And on receiving it they grumbled against the landowner, saying, 'These last ones worked only one hour, and you have made them equal to us, who bore the day's burden and the heat.' He said to one of them in reply, 'My friend, I am not cheating you. Did you not agree with me for the usual daily wage? Take what is yours and go. What if I wish to give this last one the same as you? Or am I not free to do as I wish with my own money? Are you envious because I am generous?' Thus, the last will be first, and the first will be last."

Communion Antiphon Ps 119 (118): 4–5 You have laid down your precepts to be carefully kept; ♦ may my ways be firm in keeping your statutes.

Or: Jn 10: 14 I am the Good Shepherd, says the Lord; ♦ I know my sheep, and mine know me.

TWENTY-SIXTH SUNDAY IN ORDINARY TIME

Entrance Antiphon Dn 3: 31, 29, 30, 43, 42 All that you have done to us, O Lord, ♦ you have done with true judgment, ♦ for we have sinned against you ♦ and not obeyed your commandments. ♦ But give glory to your name ♦ and deal with us according to the bounty of your mercy.

First Reading Ez 18: 25–28 Thus says the LORD: You say, "The LORD's way is not fair!" Hear now, house of Israel: Is it my way that is unfair, or rather, are not your ways unfair? When someone virtuous turns away from virtue to commit iniquity, and dies, it is because of the iniquity he committed that he must die. But if he turns from the wickedness he has committed, he does what is right and just, he shall preserve his life; since he has turned away from all the sins that he has committed, he shall surely live, he shall not die.

Responsorial Psalm Ps 25: 4–5,6–7, 8–9 Michael Giszczak

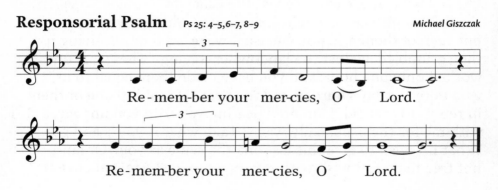

Re-mem-ber your mer-cies, O Lord.

Re-mem-ber your mer-cies, O Lord.

Your ways, O LORD, make known to me;
    teach me your paths,
guide me in your truth and teach me,
    for you are God my savior. ℟

Remember that your compassion, O LORD,
    and your love are from of old.
The sins of my youth and my frailties remember not;
    in your kindness remember me,
    because of your goodness, O LORD. ℟

Good and upright is the LORD;
    thus he shows sinners the way.
He guides the humble to justice,
    and teaches the humble his way. ℟

Second Reading   *Phil 2: 1–11 or 2: 1–5*
For the shorter form, read only the parts in brackets.
[Brothers and sisters: If there is any encouragement in Christ,
any solace in love, any participation in the Spirit, any compassion
and mercy, complete my joy by being of the same mind, with the
same love, united in heart, thinking one thing. Do nothing out
of selfishness or out of vainglory; rather, humbly regard others
as more important than yourselves, each looking out not for his
own interests, but also for those of others.
    Have in you the same attitude that is also in Christ Jesus,]
    Who, though he was in the form of God,
        did not regard equality with God
        something to be grasped.
    Rather, he emptied himself,
        taking the form of a slave,
        coming in human likeness;
        and found human in appearance,
        he humbled himself,
        becoming obedient to the point of death,
        even death on a cross.
    Because of this, God greatly exalted him
        and bestowed on him the name
        which is above every name,

that at the name of Jesus
every knee should bend,
of those in heaven and on earth and under the earth,
and every tongue confess that
Jesus Christ is Lord,
to the glory of God the Father.

Alleluia   Jn 10: 27   *Michael Kissinger*

Al-le - lu-ia, al-le - lu - ia, al - le - lu - ia.

My sheep hear my voice, says the Lord; / I know them, and
they follow me.   **Alleluia, alleluia.**

Gospel Mt 21: 28-32 Jesus said to the chief priests and elders of the
people: "What is your opinion? A man had two sons. He came to
the first and said, 'Son, go out and work in the vineyard today.'
He said in reply, 'I will not,' but afterwards changed his mind
and went. The man came to the other son and gave the same
order. He said in reply, 'Yes, sir,' but did not go. Which of the
two did his father's will?" They answered, "The first." Jesus said
to them, "Amen, I say to you, tax collectors and prostitutes are
entering the kingdom of God before you. When John came to
you in the way of righteousness, you did not believe him; but tax
collectors and prostitutes did. Yet even when you saw that, you
did not later change your minds and believe him."

Communion Antiphon cf. Ps 119 (118): 49-50 **Remember your word to
your servant, O Lord, ◆ by which you have given me hope. ◆
This is my comfort when I am brought low.**

Or: 1 Jn 3: 16 **By this we came to know the love of God: ◆ that
Christ laid down his life for us; ◆ so we ought to lay down our
lives for one another.**

TWENTY-SEVENTH

SUNDAY IN ORDINARY TIME

Entrance Antiphon *cf. Est 4: 17* Within your will, O Lord, all things are established, ✦ and there is none that can resist your will. ✦ For you have made all things, the heaven and the earth, ✦ and all that is held within the circle of heaven; ✦ you are the Lord of all.

First Reading *Is 5: 1–7*

Let me now sing of my friend,
   my friend's song concerning his vineyard.
My friend had a vineyard
   on a fertile hillside;
he spaded it, cleared it of stones,
   and planted the choicest vines;
within it he built a watchtower,
   and hewed out a wine press.
Then he looked for the crop of grapes,
   but what it yielded was wild grapes.

Now, inhabitants of Jerusalem and people of Judah,
   judge between me and my vineyard:
What more was there to do for my vineyard
   that I had not done?
Why, when I looked for the crop of grapes,
   did it bring forth wild grapes?
Now, I will let you know
   what I mean to do with my vineyard:
take away its hedge, give it to grazing,
   break through its wall, let it be trampled!
Yes, I will make it a ruin:
   it shall not be pruned or hoed,
   but overgrown with thorns and briers;
I will command the clouds
   not to send rain upon it.
The vineyard of the LORD of hosts is the house of Israel,

and the people of Judah are his cherished plant;
he looked for judgment, but see, bloodshed!
for justice, but hark, the outcry!

Responsorial Psalm   *Ps 80: 9, 12, 13–14, 15–16, 19–20*   Joe Higginbotham

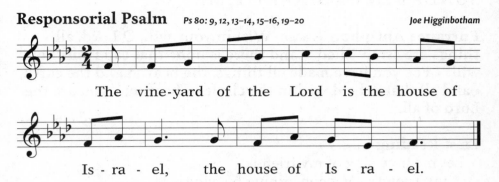

The vine-yard of the Lord is the house of
Is - ra - el, the house of Is - ra - el.

A vine from Egypt you transplanted;
  you drove away the nations and planted it.
It put forth its foliage to the Sea,
  its shoots as far as the River. ℟

Why have you broken down its walls,
  so that every passer-by plucks its fruit,
The boar from the forest lays it waste,
  and the beasts of the field feed upon it? ℟

Once again, O LORD of hosts,
  look down from heaven, and see;
take care of this vine,
  and protect what your right hand has planted,
  the son of man whom you yourself made strong. ℟

Then we will no more withdraw from you;
  give us new life, and we will call upon your name.
O LORD, God of hosts, restore us;
  if your face shine upon us, then we shall be saved. ℟

Second Reading   *Phil 4: 6–9* Brothers and sisters: Have no
anxiety at all, but in everything, by prayer and petition, with
thanksgiving, make your requests known to God. Then the

peace of God that surpasses all understanding will guard your hearts and minds in Christ Jesus.

Finally, brothers and sisters, whatever is true, whatever is honorable, whatever is just, whatever is pure, whatever is lovely, whatever is gracious, if there is any excellence and if there is anything worthy of praise, think about these things. Keep on doing what you have learned and received and heard and seen in me. Then the God of peace will be with you.

Alleluia *cf. Jn 15: 16* *Michael Kissinger*

Al-le - lu-ia, al-le - lu - ia, al - le - lu - ia.

I have chosen you from the world, says the Lord, / to go and bear fruit that will remain. **Alleluia, alleluia.**

Gospel *Mt 21: 33–43* Jesus said to the chief priests and the elders of the people: "Hear another parable. There was a landowner who planted a vineyard, put a hedge around it, dug a wine press in it, and built a tower. Then he leased it to tenants and went on a journey. When vintage time drew near, he sent his servants to the tenants to obtain his produce. But the tenants seized the servants and one they beat, another they killed, and a third they stoned. Again he sent other servants, more numerous than the first ones, but they treated them in the same way. Finally, he sent his son to them, thinking, 'They will respect my son.' But when the tenants saw the son, they said to one another, 'This is the heir. Come, let us kill him and acquire his inheritance.' They seized him, threw him out of the vineyard, and killed him. What will the owner of the vineyard do to those tenants when he comes?" They answered him, "He will put those wretched men to a wretched death and lease his vineyard to other tenants who will give him the produce at the proper times." Jesus said to them, "Did you never read in the Scriptures:

The stone that the builders rejected
has become the cornerstone;

by the Lord has this been done,
and it is wonderful in our eyes?
Therefore, I say to you, the kingdom of God will be taken away
from you and given to a people that will produce its fruit."

Communion Antiphon Lam 3: 25 **The Lord is good to those who
hope in him, ◆ to the soul that seeks him.**

Or: cf. 1 Cor 10: 17 **Though many, we are one bread, one body, ◆ for
we all partake of the one Bread and one Chalice.**

TWENTY-EIGHTH

SUNDAY IN ORDINARY TIME

Entrance Antiphon Ps 130 (129): 3–4 **If you, O Lord, should mark
iniquities, ◆ Lord, who could stand? ◆ But with you is found
forgiveness, ◆ O God of Israel.**

First Reading Is 25: 6–10a
On this mountain the LORD of hosts
    will provide for all peoples
a feast of rich food and choice wines,
    juicy, rich food and pure, choice wines.
On this mountain he will destroy
    the veil that veils all peoples,
the web that is woven over all nations;
    he will destroy death forever.
The Lord GOD will wipe away
    the tears from every face;
the reproach of his people he will remove
    from the whole earth; for the LORD has spoken.
    On that day it will be said:
"Behold our God, to whom we looked to save us!
    This is the LORD for whom we looked;
    let us rejoice and be glad that he has saved us!"
For the hand of the LORD will rest on this mountain.

Responsorial Psalm

Ps 23: 1–3a, 3b–4, 5, 6

Bill Svarda

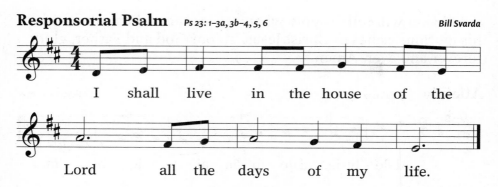

I shall live in the house of the

Lord all the days of my life.

The LORD is my shepherd; I shall not want.
  In verdant pastures he gives me repose;
beside restful waters he leads me;
  he refreshes my soul. ℟

He guides me in right paths
  for his name's sake.
Even though I walk in the dark valley
  I fear no evil; for you are at my side
with your rod and your staff
  that give me courage. ℟

You spread the table before me
  in the sight of my foes;
you anoint my head with oil;
  my cup overflows. ℟

Only goodness and kindness follow me
  all the days of my life;
and I shall dwell in the house of the LORD
  for years to come. ℟

Second Reading

Phil 4: 12–14, 19–20 Brothers and sisters: I know
how to live in humble circumstances; I know also how to live
with abundance. In every circumstance and in all things I have
learned the secret of being well fed and of going hungry, of
living in abundance and of being in need. I can do all things
in him who strengthens me. Still, it was kind of you to share
in my distress.

My God will fully supply whatever you need, in accord with his glorious riches in Christ Jesus. To our God and Father, glory forever and ever. Amen.

Alleluia   *cf. Eph 1: 17–18*   Michael Kissinger

Al-le - lu-ia, al-le - lu - ia, al - le - lu - ia.

May the Father of our Lord Jesus Christ enlighten the eyes of our hearts, so that we may know what is the hope that belongs to our call.   **Alleluia, alleluia.**

Gospel   *Mt 22: 1–14 or 22: 1–10*
For the shorter form, read only the parts in brackets.
[Jesus again in reply spoke to the chief priests and elders of the people in parables, saying, "The kingdom of heaven may be likened to a king who gave a wedding feast for his son. He dispatched his servants to summon the invited guests to the feast, but they refused to come. A second time he sent other servants, saying, 'Tell those invited: "Behold, I have prepared my banquet, my calves and fattened cattle are killed, and everything is ready; come to the feast."' Some ignored the invitation and went away, one to his farm, another to his business. The rest laid hold of his servants, mistreated them, and killed them. The king was enraged and sent his troops, destroyed those murderers, and burned their city. Then he said to his servants, 'The feast is ready, but those who were invited were not worthy to come. Go out, therefore, into the main roads and invite to the feast whomever you find.' The servants went out into the streets and gathered all they found, bad and good alike, and the hall was filled with guests.] But when the king came in to meet the guests, he saw a man there not dressed in a wedding garment. The king said to him, 'My friend, how is it that you came in here without a wedding garment?' But he was reduced to silence. Then the king said to his attendants, 'Bind his hands and feet, and cast him into the darkness outside, where there will be wailing and grinding of teeth.' Many are invited, but few are chosen."

Communion Antiphon   *cf. Ps 34 (33): 11* The rich suffer want and go hungry, ♦ but those who seek the Lord lack no blessing.

Or: *1 Jn 3: 2* When the Lord appears, we shall be like him, ♦ for we shall see him as he is.

TWENTY-NINTH SUNDAY IN ORDINARY TIME

Entrance Antiphon   *cf. Ps 17 (16): 6, 8* To you I call; for you will surely heed me, O God; ♦ turn your ear to me; hear my words. ♦ Guard me as the apple of your eye; ♦ in the shadow of your wings protect me.

First Reading   *Is 45: 1, 4–6*
Thus says the LORD to his anointed, Cyrus,
    whose right hand I grasp,
subduing nations before him,
    and making kings run in his service,
opening doors before him
    and leaving the gates unbarred:
For the sake of Jacob, my servant,
    of Israel, my chosen one,
I have called you by your name,
    giving you a title, though you knew me not.
I am the LORD and there is no other,
    there is no God besides me.
It is I who arm you, though you know me not,
    so that toward the rising and the setting of the sun
    people may know that there is none besides me.
I am the LORD, there is no other.

Responsorial Psalm   Ps 96: 1, 3, 4–5, 7–8, 9–10   *Keith Sammut*

Give the Lord glo-ry and hon - or.

Sing to the LORD a new song;
    sing to the LORD, all you lands.

Tell his glory among the nations;
>among all peoples, his wondrous deeds.   ℟

For great is the LORD and highly to be praised;
>awesome is he, beyond all gods.
For all the gods of the nations are things of nought,
>but the LORD made the heavens.   ℟

Give to the LORD, you families of nations,
>give to the LORD glory and praise;
>give to the LORD the glory due his name!
Bring gifts, and enter his courts.   ℟

Worship the LORD, in holy attire;
>tremble before him, all the earth;
>say among the nations: The LORD is king,
>he governs the peoples with equity.   ℟

Second Reading   *1 Thes 1: 1–5b*   Paul, Silvanus, and Timothy to the church of the Thessalonians in God the Father and the Lord Jesus Christ: grace to you and peace. We give thanks to God always for all of you, remembering you in our prayers, unceasingly calling to mind your work of faith and labor of love and endurance in hope of our Lord Jesus Christ, before our God and Father, knowing, brothers and sisters loved by God, how you were chosen. For our gospel did not come to you in word alone, but also in power and in the Holy Spirit and with much conviction.

Alleluia   *Phil 2: 15d, 16a*   *Michael Kissinger*

Al-le - lu-ia, al-le - lu - ia, al - le - lu - ia.

Shine like lights in the world / as you hold on to the word of life.   **Alleluia, alleluia.**

Gospel   *Mt 22: 15–21*   The Pharisees went off and plotted how they might entrap Jesus in speech. They sent their disciples to him, with the Herodians, saying, "Teacher, we know that you are a truthful man and that you teach the way of God in accordance with the truth. And you are not concerned with anyone's opinion, for you do not regard a person's status. Tell us, then, what is your opinion: Is it lawful to pay the census tax to Caesar or not?" Knowing their malice, Jesus said, "Why are you testing me, you hypocrites? Show me the coin that pays the census tax." Then they handed him the Roman coin. He said to them, "Whose image is this and whose inscription?" They replied, "Caesar's." At that he said to them, "Then repay to Caesar what belongs to Caesar and to God what belongs to God."

Communion Antiphon *cf. Ps 33 (32): 18–19* Behold, the eyes of the Lord ♦ are on those who fear him, ♦ who hope in his merciful love, ♦ to rescue their souls from death, ♦ to keep them alive in famine.

Or: Mk 10: 45 The Son of Man has come ♦ to give his life as a ransom for many.

THIRTIETH SUNDAY IN ORDINARY TIME

Entrance Antiphon *cf. Ps 105 (104): 3–4* Let the hearts that seek the Lord rejoice; ♦ turn to the Lord and his strength; ♦ constantly seek his face.

First Reading Ex 22: 20–26 Thus says the LORD: "You shall not molest or oppress an alien, for you were once aliens yourselves in the land of Egypt. You shall not wrong any widow or orphan. If ever you wrong them and they cry out to me, I will surely hear their cry. My wrath will flare up, and I will kill you with the sword; then your own wives will be widows, and your children orphans.

"If you lend money to one of your poor neighbors among my people, you shall not act like an extortioner toward him by demanding interest from him. If you take your neighbor's cloak as a pledge, you shall return it to him before sunset; for this cloak of his is the only covering he has for his body. What else has he to sleep in? If he cries out to me, I will hear him; for I am compassionate."

Responsorial Psalm   Ps 18: 2–3, 3–4, 47, 51   *Beverly McDevitt*

I love you, Lord, my strength.

I love you, O LORD, my strength,
    O LORD, my rock, my fortress, my deliverer. ℟

My God, my rock of refuge,
    my shield, the horn of my salvation, my stronghold!
Praised be the LORD, I exclaim,
    and I am safe from my enemies.   ℟

The LORD lives and blessed be my rock!
    Extolled be God my savior.
You who gave great victories to your king
    and showed kindness to your anointed.   ℟

Second Reading *1 Thes 1: 5c–10* Brothers and sisters: You know what sort of people we were among you for your sake. And you became imitators of us and of the Lord, receiving the word in great affliction, with joy from the Holy Spirit, so that you became a model for all the believers in Macedonia and in Achaia. For from you the word of the Lord has sounded forth not only in Macedonia and in Achaia, but in every place your faith in God has gone forth, so that we have no need to say anything. For they themselves openly declare about us what sort of reception we had among you, and how you turned to God from idols to serve the living and true God and to await his Son from heaven, whom he raised from the dead, Jesus, who delivers us from the coming wrath.

Alleluia   Jn 14: 23   Brian J. Nelson

Al - le-lu - ia,   al - le - lu - ia,   al-le-lu - ia.

Whoever loves me will keep my word, says the Lord, /
and my Father will love him and we will come to him.
Alleluia, alleluia.

Gospel   Mt 22: 34-40   When the Pharisees heard that Jesus had
silenced the Sadducees, they gathered together, and one of
them, a scholar of the law tested him by asking, "Teacher, which
commandment in the law is the greatest?" He said to him, "You
shall love the Lord, your God, with all your heart, with all
your soul, and with all your mind. This is the greatest and the
first commandment. The second is like it: You shall love your
neighbor as yourself. The whole law and the prophets depend on
these two commandments."

Communion Antiphon   cf. Ps 20 (19): 6   **We will ring out our joy at
your saving help ✦ and exult in the name of our God.**

Or: Eph 5: 2   **Christ loved us and gave himself up for us, ✦ as a
fragrant offering to God.**

THIRTY-FIRST SUNDAY IN ORDINARY TIME

Entrance Antiphon   cf. Ps 38 (37): 22-23   **Forsake me not, O Lord, my
God; ✦ be not far from me! ✦ Make haste and come to my help,
✦ O Lord, my strong salvation!**

First Reading   Mal 1: 14b–2: 2b, 8–10
A great King am I, says the LORD of hosts,
  and my name will be feared among the nations.
And now, O priests, this commandment is for you:
  If you do not listen,

if you do not lay it to heart,
    to give glory to my name, says the LORD of hosts,
I will send a curse upon you
    and of your blessing I will make a curse.
You have turned aside from the way,
    and have caused many to falter by your instruction;
you have made void the covenant of Levi,
    says the LORD of hosts.
I, therefore, have made you contemptible
    and base before all the people,
since you do not keep my ways,
    but show partiality in your decisions.
Have we not all the one father?
    Has not the one God created us?
Why then do we break faith with one another,
    violating the covenant of our fathers?

Responsorial Psalm Ps 131: 1, 2, 3   Tim Wells

In you, Lord, I have found my peace.

In you, Lord, I have found my peace.

O LORD, my heart is not proud,
    nor are my eyes haughty;
I busy not myself with great things,
    nor with things too sublime for me. ℟

Nay rather, I have stilled and quieted
    my soul like a weaned child.
Like a weaned child on its mother's lap,
    so is my soul within me. ℟

O Israel, hope in the LORD,
    both now and forever. ℟

Second Reading *1 Thes 2: 7b–9, 13* Brothers and sisters: We were
gentle among you, as a nursing mother cares for her children.
With such affection for you, we were determined to share
with you not only the gospel of God, but our very selves as well,
so dearly beloved had you become to us. You recall, brothers
and sisters, our toil and drudgery. Working night and day
in order not to burden any of you, we proclaimed to you the
gospel of God.

   And for this reason we too give thanks to God unceasingly,
that, in receiving the word of God from hearing us, you received
not a human word but, as it truly is, the word of God, which is
now at work in you who believe.

Alleluia   *Mt 23: 9b, 10b*   Brian J. Nelson

Al - le-lu - ia,   al - le - lu - ia,   al-le-lu - ia.

You have but one Father in heaven / and one master, the
Christ. **Alleluia, alleluia.**

Gospel *Mt 23: 1–12* Jesus spoke to the crowds and to his disciples,
saying, "The scribes and the Pharisees have taken their seat
on the chair of Moses. Therefore, do and observe all things
whatsoever they tell you, but do not follow their example. For
they preach but they do not practice. They tie up heavy burdens
hard to carry and lay them on people's shoulders, but they will
not lift a finger to move them. All their works are performed
to be seen. They widen their phylacteries and lengthen their
tassels. They love places of honor at banquets, seats of honor in
synagogues, greetings in marketplaces, and the salutation 'Rabbi.'
As for you, do not be called 'Rabbi.' You have but one teacher,
and you are all brothers. Call no one on earth your father; you
have but one Father in heaven. Do not be called 'Master'; you
have but one master, the Christ. The greatest among you must
be your servant. Whoever exalts himself will be humbled; but
whoever humbles himself will be exalted."

Communion Antiphon   *cf. Ps 16 (15): 11*   You will show me the path of life, ✦ the fullness of joy in your presence, O Lord.

Or: *Jn 6: 58*   Just as the living Father sent me ✦ and I have life because of the Father, ✦ so whoever feeds on me ✦ shall have life because of me, says the Lord.

THIRTY-SECOND SUNDAY IN ORDINARY TIME

Entrance Antiphon   *cf. Ps 88 (87): 3*   Let my prayer come into your presence. ✦ Incline your ear to my cry for help, O Lord.

First Reading   *Wis 6: 12–16*

> Resplendent and unfading is wisdom,
>> and she is readily perceived by those who love her,
>> and found by those who seek her.
> She hastens to make herself known in anticipation of their
>> desire;
>> whoever watches for her at dawn shall not be disappointed,
>> for he shall find her sitting by his gate.
> For taking thought of wisdom is the perfection of prudence,
>> and whoever for her sake keeps vigil
>> shall quickly be free from care;
> because she makes her own rounds, seeking those worthy
>> of her,
>> and graciously appears to them in the ways,
>> and meets them with all solicitude.

Responsorial Psalm   *Ps 63: 2, 3–4, 5–6, 7–8*   *Bill Svarda*

My soul is thirst-ing for you, O Lord my God.

> O God, you are my God whom I seek;
>> for you my flesh pines and my soul thirsts
>> like the earth, parched, lifeless and without water. ℟

Thus have I gazed toward you in the sanctuary
   to see your power and your glory,
For your kindness is a greater good than life;
   my lips shall glorify you. ℟

Thus will I bless you while I live;
   lifting up my hands, I will call upon your name.
As with the riches of a banquet shall my soul be satisfied,
   and with exultant lips my mouth shall praise you. ℟

I will remember you upon my couch,
   and through the night-watches I will meditate on you:
You are my help,
   and in the shadow of your wings I shout for joy. ℟

Second Reading   *1 Thes 4: 13–18 or 4: 13–14*
For the shorter form, read only the parts in brackets.
[We do not want you to be unaware, brothers and sisters, about
those who have fallen asleep, so that you may not grieve like
the rest, who have no hope. For if we believe that Jesus died and
rose, so too will God, through Jesus, bring with him those who
have fallen asleep.] Indeed, we tell you this, on the word of the
Lord, that we who are alive, who are left until the coming of the
Lord, will surely not precede those who have fallen asleep. For
the Lord himself, with a word of command, with the voice of an
archangel and with the trumpet of God, will come down from
heaven, and the dead in Christ will rise first. Then we who are
alive, who are left, will be caught up together with them in the
clouds to meet the Lord in the air. Thus we shall always be with
the Lord. Therefore, console one another with these words.

Alleluia   *Mt 24: 42a, 44*   *Brian J. Nelson*

Al - le-lu - ia,   al - le - lu - ia,   al-le-lu - ia.

Stay awake and be ready! / For you do not know on what
day your Lord will come. **Alleluia, alleluia.**

Gospel *Mt 25: 1–13* Jesus told his disciples this parable: "The kingdom of heaven will be like ten virgins who took their lamps and went out to meet the bridegroom. Five of them were foolish and five were wise. The foolish ones, when taking their lamps, brought no oil with them, but the wise brought flasks of oil with their lamps. Since the bridegroom was long delayed, they all became drowsy and fell asleep. At midnight, there was a cry, 'Behold, the bridegroom! Come out to meet him!' Then all those virgins got up and trimmed their lamps. The foolish ones said to the wise, 'Give us some of your oil, for our lamps are going out.' But the wise ones replied, 'No, for there may not be enough for us and you. Go instead to the merchants and buy some for yourselves.' While they went off to buy it, the bridegroom came and those who were ready went into the wedding feast with him. Then the door was locked. Afterwards the other virgins came and said, 'Lord, Lord, open the door for us!' But he said in reply, 'Amen, I say to you, I do not know you.' Therefore, stay awake, for you know neither the day nor the hour."

Communion Antiphon *cf. Ps 23 (22): 1–2* The Lord is my shepherd; there is nothing I shall want. ✦ Fresh and green are the pastures where he gives me repose, ✦ near restful waters he leads me.

Or: *cf. Lk 24: 35* The disciples recognized the Lord Jesus in the breaking of bread.

THIRTY-THIRD SUNDAY IN ORDINARY TIME

Entrance Antiphon *Jer 29: 11, 12, 14* The Lord said: I think thoughts of peace and not of affliction. ✦ You will call upon me, and I will answer you, ✦ and I will lead back your captives from every place.

First Reading *Prv 31: 10–13, 19–20, 30–31*
When one finds a worthy wife,
    her value is far beyond pearls.
Her husband, entrusting his heart to her,

has an unfailing prize.
She brings him good, and not evil,
   all the days of her life.
She obtains wool and flax
   and works with loving hands.
She puts her hands to the distaff,
   and her fingers ply the spindle.
She reaches out her hands to the poor,
   and extends her arms to the needy.
Charm is deceptive and beauty fleeting;
   the woman who fears the LORD is to be praised.
Give her a reward for her labors,
   and let her works praise her at the city gates.

Responsorial Psalm   *Ps 128: 1–2, 3, 4–5*   *Beverly McDevitt*

Bless - ed are those who fear the Lord, who fear the Lord.

Blessed are you who fear the LORD,
   who walk in his ways!
For you shall eat the fruit of your handiwork;
   blessed shall you be, and favored.   ℞

Your wife shall be like a fruitful vine
   in the recesses of your home;
Your children like olive plants
   around your table.   ℞

Behold, thus is the man blessed
   who fears the LORD.
The LORD bless you from Zion:
   may you see the prosperity of Jerusalem
   all the days of your life.   ℞

Second Reading *1 Thes 5: 1–6* Concerning times and seasons, brothers and sisters, you have no need for anything to be written to you. For you yourselves know very well that the day of the Lord will come like a thief at night. When people are saying, "Peace and security," then sudden disaster comes upon them, like labor pains upon a pregnant woman, and they will not escape.

But you, brothers and sisters, are not in darkness, for that day to overtake you like a thief. For all of you are children of the light and children of the day. We are not of the night or of darkness. Therefore, let us not sleep as the rest do, but let us stay alert and sober.

Alleluia *Jn 15: 4a, 5b*   Brian J. Nelson

Al - le-lu - ia,   al - le - lu - ia,   al-le-lu - ia.

Remain in me as I remain in you, says the Lord. / Whoever remains in me bears much fruit. **Alleluia, alleluia.**

Gospel *Mt 25: 14–30 or 25: 14–15, 19–21*
For the shorter form, read only the parts in brackets.
[Jesus told his disciples this parable: "A man going on a journey called in his servants and entrusted his possessions to them. To one he gave five talents; to another, two; to a third, one—to each according to his ability. Then he went away.] Immediately the one who received five talents went and traded with them, and made another five. Likewise, the one who received two made another two. But the man who received one went off and dug a hole in the ground and buried his master's money.

["After a long time the master of those servants came back and settled accounts with them. The one who had received five talents came forward bringing the additional five. He said, 'Master, you gave me five talents. See, I have made five more.' His master said to him, 'Well done, my good and faithful servant. Since you were faithful in small matters, I will give you great responsibilities. Come, share your master's joy.'] Then the one who had received two talents also came forward and said, 'Master, you gave me two talents. See, I have made two more.' His master said to him, 'Well done, my good and faithful servant. Since you were faithful in small matters, I will give you great responsibilities. Come, share your master's joy.' Then the one who had received the one talent came forward and said, 'Master, I knew you were a demanding person, harvesting where you did not plant and gathering where you did not scatter; so out of fear I went off and buried your talent in the ground. Here it is back.' His master said to him in reply, 'You wicked, lazy servant! So you knew that I harvest where I did not plant and gather where I did not scatter? Should you not then have put my money in the bank so that I could have got it back with interest on my return? Now then! Take the talent from him and give it to the one with ten. For to everyone who has, more will be given and he will grow rich; but from the one who has not, even what he has will be taken away. And throw this useless servant into the darkness outside, where there will be wailing and grinding of teeth.'"

Communion Antiphon *cf. Ps 73 (72): 28* To be near God is my happiness, ◆ to place my hope in God the Lord.

Or: Mk 11: 23-24 Amen, I say to you: Whatever you ask in prayer, ◆ believe that you will receive, ◆ and it shall be given to you, says the Lord.

OUR LORD JESUS CHRIST,

KING OF THE UNIVERSE

Entrance Antiphon Rv 5: 12; 1: 6 How worthy is the Lamb who was slain, ◆ to receive power and divinity, ◆ and wisdom and strength and honor. ◆ To him belong glory and power for ever and ever.

First Reading Ez 34: 11-12, 15-17 Thus says the Lord GOD: I myself will look after and tend my sheep. As a shepherd tends his flock when he finds himself among his scattered sheep, so will I tend my sheep. I will rescue them from every place where they were scattered when it was cloudy and dark. I myself will pasture my sheep; I myself will give them rest, says the Lord GOD. The lost I will seek out, the strayed I will bring back, the injured I will bind up, the sick I will heal, but the sleek and the strong I will destroy, shepherding them rightly.

As for you, my sheep, says the Lord GOD, I will judge between one sheep and another, between rams and goats.

Responsorial Psalm   Ps 23: 1–2, 2–3, 5–6   Vince Ambrosetti

The Lord is my shep-herd; there is noth-ing I shall want.

The LORD is my shepherd; I shall not want.
In verdant pastures he gives me repose. ℟

Beside restful waters he leads me;
he refreshes my soul.
He guides me in right paths
for his name's sake. ℟

You spread the table before me
in the sight of my foes;
you anoint my head with oil;
my cup overflows. ℟

Only goodness and kindness follow me
all the days of my life;
and I shall dwell in the house of the LORD
for years to come. ℟

Second Reading 1 Cor 15: 20–26, 28 Brothers and sisters: Christ has been raised from the dead, the firstfruits of those who have fallen asleep. For since death came through man, the resurrection of the dead came also through man. For just as in Adam all die, so too in Christ shall all be brought to life, but each one in proper order: Christ the firstfruits; then, at his coming, those who belong to Christ; then comes the end, when he hands over the kingdom to his God and Father, when he has destroyed every sovereignty and every authority and power. For he must reign until he has put all his enemies under his feet. The last enemy to be destroyed is death. When everything is subjected to him, then the Son himself will also be subjected to the one who subjected everything to him, so that God may be all in all.

Alleluia Mk 11: 9, 10   Brian J. Nelson

Al - le-lu - ia,   al - le - lu - ia,   al-le-lu - ia.

Blessed is he who comes in the name of the Lord! / Blessed is the kingdom of our father David that is to come! **Alleluia, alleluia.**

Gospel Mt 25: 31–46 Jesus said to his disciples: "When the Son of Man comes in his glory, and all the angels with him, he will sit upon his glorious throne, and all the nations will be assembled before him. And he will separate them one from another, as a shepherd separates the sheep from the goats. He will place the sheep on his right and the goats on his left. Then the king will say to those his right, 'Come, you who are blessed by my Father. Inherit the kingdom prepared for you from the foundation of the world. For I was hungry and you gave me food, I was thirsty and you gave me drink, a stranger and you welcomed me, naked and you clothed me, ill and you cared for me, in prison and you visited me.' Then the righteous will answer him and say, 'Lord, when did we see you hungry and feed you, or thirsty and give you drink? When did we see you a stranger and welcome you, or naked and clothe you? When did we see you ill or in prison, and visit you?' And the king will say to them in reply, 'Amen, I say to you, whatever you did for one of the least brothers of mine, you did for me.' Then he will say to those on his left, 'Depart from me, you accursed, into the eternal fire prepared for the devil and his angels. For I was hungry and you gave me no food, I was thirsty and you gave me no drink, a stranger and you gave me no welcome, naked and you gave me no clothing, ill and in prison, and you did not care for me.' Then they will answer and say, 'Lord, when did we see you hungry or thirsty or a stranger or naked or ill or in prison, and not minister to your needs?' He will answer them, 'Amen, I say to you, what you did not do for one of these least ones, you did not do for me.' And these will go off to eternal punishment, but the righteous to eternal life."

Communion Antiphon Ps 29 (28): 10–11 **The Lord sits as King for ever.** ✦ **The Lord will bless his people with peace.**

Advent † YEAR B

FIRST SUNDAY OF ADVENT

Entrance Antiphon *cf. Ps 25 (24): 1–3* To you, I lift up my soul, O my God. ✦ In you, I have trusted; let me not be put to shame. ✦ Nor let my enemies exult over me; ✦ and let none who hope in you be put to shame.

First Reading *Is 63: 16b–17, 19b; 64: 2–7*
You, Lord, are our father,
 our redeemer you are named forever.
Why do you let us wander, O Lord, from your ways,
 and harden our hearts so that we fear you not?
Return for the sake of your servants,
 the tribes of your heritage.
Oh, that you would rend the heavens and come down,
 with the mountains quaking before you,
while you wrought awesome deeds we could not hope for,
 such as they had not heard of from of old.
No ear has ever heard, no eye ever seen, any God but you
 doing such deeds for those who wait for him.
Would that you might meet us doing right,
 that we were mindful of you in our ways!
Behold, you are angry, and we are sinful;
 all of us have become like unclean people,
 all our good deeds are like polluted rags;
we have all withered like leaves,
 and our guilt carries us away like the wind.
There is none who calls upon your name,
 who rouses himself to cling to you;
for you have hidden your face from us
 and have delivered us up to our guilt.

Yet, O LORD, you are our father;
   we are the clay and you the potter:
   we are all the work of your hands.

Responsorial Psalm   Ps 80: 2–3, 15–16, 18–19   Joe Higginbotham

Lord, make us turn to you; let us see your face and we shall be saved.

O shepherd of Israel, hearken,
   from your throne upon the cherubim, shine forth.
Rouse your power,
   and come to save us. ℟

Once again, O LORD of hosts,
   look down from heaven, and see;
take care of this vine,
   and protect what your right hand has planted,
   the son of man whom you yourself made strong. ℟

May your help be with the man of your right hand,
   with the son of man whom you yourself made strong.
Then we will no more withdraw from you;
   give us new life, and we will call upon your name. ℟

Second Reading 1 Cor 1: 3–9 Brothers and sisters: Grace to you and peace from God our Father and the Lord Jesus Christ.
   I give thanks to my God always on your account for the grace of God bestowed on you in Christ Jesus, that in him you were enriched in every way, with all discourse and all knowledge, as the testimony to Christ was confirmed among you, so that you are not lacking in any spiritual gift as you wait for the revelation of our Lord Jesus Christ. He will keep you firm to the end, irreproachable on the day of our Lord Jesus Christ. God is

faithful, and by him you were called to fellowship with his Son, Jesus Christ our Lord.

Alleluia   Ps 85: 8   *Joe Higginbotham*

Al - le - lu - ia,   al - le - lu - ia,   al - le - lu - ia.

Al - le - lu - ia,   al - le - lu - ia,   al - le - lu - ia.

Show us, Lord, your love; / and grant us your salvation. **Alleluia, alleluia.**

Gospel   Mk 13: 33-37   Jesus said to his disciples: "Be watchful! Be alert! You do not know when the time will come. It is like a man traveling abroad. He leaves home and places his servants in charge, each with his own work, and orders the gatekeeper to be on the watch. Watch, therefore; you do not know when the Lord of the house is coming, whether in the evening, or at midnight, or at cockcrow, or in the morning. May he not come suddenly and find you sleeping. What I say to you, I say to all: 'Watch!'"

Communion Antiphon   Ps 85 (84): 13   The Lord will bestow his bounty, and our earth shall yield its increase.

SECOND SUNDAY OF ADVENT

Entrance Antiphon   *cf.* Is 30: 19, 30   O people of Sion, behold, the Lord will come to save the nations, ♦ and the Lord will make the glory of his voice heard in the joy of your heart.

First Reading   Is 40: 1–5, 9–11
   Comfort, give comfort to my people,
      says your God.

Speak tenderly to Jerusalem, and proclaim to her
 that her service is at an end,
  her guilt is expiated;
indeed, she has received from the hand of the LORD
 double for all her sins.

 A voice cries out:
In the desert prepare the way of the LORD!
 Make straight in the wasteland a highway for our God!
Every valley shall be filled in,
 every mountain and hill shall be made low;
the rugged land shall be made a plain,
 the rough country, a broad valley.
Then the glory of the LORD shall be revealed,
 and all people shall see it together;
 for the mouth of the LORD has spoken.
Go up on to a high mountain,
 Zion, herald of glad tidings;
cry out at the top of your voice,
 Jerusalem, herald of good news!
Fear not to cry out
 and say to the cities of Judah:
 Here is your God!
Here comes with power
 the Lord GOD,
 who rules by his strong arm;
here is his reward with him,
 his recompense before him.
Like a shepherd he feeds his flock;
 in his arms he gathers the lambs,
carrying them in his bosom,
 and leading the ewes with care.

Responsorial Psalm   Ps 85: 9–10, 11–12, 13–14   Joe Higginbotham

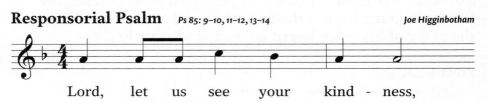

Lord, let us see your kind - ness,

and grant us your sal - va - tion.

I will hear what God proclaims;
the LORD—for he proclaims peace to his people.
Near indeed is his salvation to those who fear him,
glory dwelling in our land. ℟

Kindness and truth shall meet;
justice and peace shall kiss.
Truth shall spring out of the earth,
and justice shall look down from heaven. ℟

The LORD himself will give his benefits;
our land shall yield its increase.
Justice shall walk before him,
and prepare the way of his steps. ℟

Second Reading *2 Pt 3: 8–14* Do not ignore this one fact, beloved, that with the Lord one day is like a thousand years and a thousand years like one day. The Lord does not delay his promise, as some regard "delay," but he is patient with you, not wishing that any should perish but that all should come to repentance. But the day of the Lord will come like a thief, and then the heavens will pass away with a mighty roar and the elements will be dissolved by fire, and the earth and everything done on it will be found out.

Since everything is to be dissolved in this way, what sort of persons ought you to be, conducting yourselves in holiness and devotion, waiting for and hastening the coming of the day of God, because of which the heavens will be dissolved in flames and the elements melted by fire. But according to his promise we await new heavens and a new earth in which righteousness dwells. Therefore, beloved, since you await these things, be eager to be found without spot or blemish before him, at peace.

Alleluia *Lk 3: 4, 6*   *Joe Higginbotham*

Al-le-lu-ia, al-le-lu-ia,   al-le-lu - ia.

Al-le-lu-ia, al-le-lu-ia,   al-le-lu - ia.

Prepare the way of the Lord, make straight his paths: / all
flesh shall see the salvation of God. **Alleluia, alleluia.**

Gospel *Mk 1: 1–8* The beginning of the gospel of Jesus Christ the
Son of God.
As it is written in Isaiah the prophet:
Behold, I am sending my messenger ahead of you;
  he will prepare your way.
A voice of one crying out in the desert:
  "Prepare the way of the Lord,
  make straight his paths."
John the Baptist appeared in the desert proclaiming a baptism
of repentance for the forgiveness of sins. People of the whole
Judean countryside and all the inhabitants of Jerusalem were
going out to him and were being baptized by him in the Jordan
River as they acknowledged their sins. John was clothed in
camel's hair, with a leather belt around his waist. He fed on
locusts and wild honey. And this is what he proclaimed: "One
mightier than I is coming after me. I am not worthy to stoop
and loosen the thongs of his sandals. I have baptized you with
water; he will baptize you with the Holy Spirit."

Communion Antiphon *Bar 5: 5; 4: 36* **Jerusalem, arise and stand
upon the heights, ◆ and behold the joy which comes to
you from God.**

THIRD SUNDAY OF ADVENT

Entrance Antiphon *Phil 4: 4–5* **Rejoice in the Lord always; again I say, rejoice. ◆ Indeed, the Lord is near.**

First Reading   *Is 61: 1–2a, 10–11*

The spirit of the Lord GOD is upon me,
    because the LORD has anointed me;
he has sent me to bring glad tidings to the poor,
    to heal the brokenhearted,
to proclaim liberty to the captives
    and release to the prisoners,
to announce a year of favor from the LORD
    and a day of vindication by our God.

I rejoice heartily in the LORD,
    in my God is the joy of my soul;
for he has clothed me with a robe of salvation
    and wrapped me in a mantle of justice,
like a bridegroom adorned with a diadem,
    like a bride bedecked with her jewels.
As the earth brings forth its plants,
    and a garden makes its growth spring up,
so will the Lord GOD make justice and praise
    spring up before all the nations.

Responsorial Psalm   *Lk 1: 46–48, 49–50, 53–54*   *Roger Holtz and Jane Terwilliger*

My soul re-joic-es, re-joic-es in my God.

My soul proclaims the greatness of the Lord;
    my spirit rejoices in God my Savior,
for he has looked upon his lowly servant.
    From this day all generations will call me blessed. ℟

The Almighty has done great things for me,
    and holy is his Name.

He has mercy on those who fear him
   in every generation.   ℟

He has filled the hungry with good things,
   and the rich he has sent away empty.
He has come to the help of his servant Israel
   for he has remembered his promise of mercy.   ℟

Second Reading   *1 Thes 5: 16–24*   Brothers and sisters: Rejoice always.
Pray without ceasing. In all circumstances give thanks, for this
is the will of God for you in Christ Jesus. Do not quench the
Spirit. Do not despise prophetic utterances. Test everything;
retain what is good. Refrain from every kind of evil.

   May the God of peace make you perfectly holy and may you
entirely, spirit, soul, and body, be preserved blameless for the
coming of our Lord Jesus Christ. The one who calls you is
faithful, and he will also accomplish it.

Alleluia   *Is 61: 1 (cited in Lk 4: 18)*   Joe Higginbotham

Al - le - lu - ia,   al - le - lu - ia,   al - le - lu - ia.

Al - le - lu - ia,   al - le - lu - ia,   al - le - lu - ia.

The Spirit of the Lord is upon me, / because he has anointed
me / to bring glad tidings to the poor.   **Alleluia, alleluia.**

Gospel   *Jn 1: 6–8, 19–28*   A man named John was sent from God. He
came for testimony, to testify to the light, so that all might
believe through him. He was not the light, but came to testify to
the light.

   And this is the testimony of John. When the Jews from
Jerusalem sent priests and Levites to him to ask him, "Who are
you?" He admitted and did not deny it, but admitted, "I am not
the Christ." So they asked him, "What are you then? Are you
Elijah?" And he said, "I am not." "Are you the Prophet?" He

FOURTH SUNDAY OF ADVENT 277

answered, "No." So they said to him, "Who are you, so we can
give an answer to those who sent us? What do you have to say
for yourself?" He said:

"I am *the voice of one crying out in the desert,*
  'make straight the way of the Lord,'
as Isaiah the prophet said." Some Pharisees were also sent. They
asked him, "Why then do you baptize if you are not the Christ
or Elijah or the Prophet?" John answered them, "I baptize with
water; but there is one among you whom you do not recognize,
the one who is coming after me, whose sandal strap I am not
worthy to untie." This happened in Bethany across the Jordan,
where John was baptizing.

Communion Antiphon *cf. Is 35: 4* **Say to the faint of heart: Be
strong and do not fear. ◆ Behold, our God will come, and he
will save us.**

FOURTH SUNDAY OF ADVENT

Entrance Antiphon *cf. Is 45: 8* **Drop down dew from above, you
heavens, ◆ and let the clouds rain down the Just One; ◆ let the
earth be opened and bring forth a Savior.**

First Reading *2 Sm 7: 1–5, 8b–12, 14a, 16* When King David was settled in
his palace, and the LORD had given him rest from his enemies on
every side, he said to Nathan the prophet, "Here I am living in
a house of cedar, while the ark of God dwells in a tent!" Nathan
answered the king, "Go, do whatever you have in mind, for the
LORD is with you." But that night the LORD spoke to Nathan and
said: "Go, tell my servant David, 'Thus says the LORD: Should
you build me a house to dwell in?

"'It was I who took you from the pasture and from the care
of the flock to be commander of my people Israel. I have been
with you wherever you went, and I have destroyed all your
enemies before you. And I will make you famous like the great
ones of the earth. I will fix a place for my people Israel; I will
plant them so that they may dwell in their place without further
disturbance. Neither shall the wicked continue to afflict them
as they did of old, since the time I first appointed judges over

my people Israel. I will give you rest from all your enemies. The
LORD also reveals to you that he will establish a house for you.
And when your time comes and you rest with your ancestors,
I will raise up your heir after you, sprung from your loins, and
I will make his kingdom firm. I will be a father to him, and he
shall be a son to me. Your house and your kingdom shall endure
forever before me; your throne shall stand firm forever.'"

Responsorial Psalm   Ps 89: 2–3, 4–5, 27, 29   Joe Higginbotham

For ev‑er I will sing the good‑ness of the Lord.

The promises of the LORD I will sing forever;
    through all generations my mouth shall proclaim your
        faithfulness.
For you have said, "My kindness is established forever";
    in heaven you have confirmed your faithfulness. ℟

"I have made a covenant with my chosen one,
    I have sworn to David my servant:
Forever will I confirm your posterity
    and establish your throne for all generations." ℟

"He shall say of me, 'You are my father,
    my God, the Rock, my savior.'
Forever I will maintain my kindness toward him,
    and my covenant with him stands firm." ℟

Second Reading   Rom 16: 25–27   Brothers and sisters: To him who can
strengthen you, according to my gospel and the proclamation
of Jesus Christ, according to the revelation of the mystery kept
secret for long ages but now manifested through the prophetic
writings and, according to the command of the eternal God,
made known to all nations to bring about the obedience of faith,
to the only wise God, through Jesus Christ be glory forever and
ever. Amen.

Alleluia   Lk 1: 38

Joe Higginbotham

Al - le - lu - ia,   al - le - lu - ia,   al - le - lu - ia.

Al - le - lu - ia,   al - le - lu - ia,   al - le - lu - ia.

Behold, I am the handmaid of the Lord. / May it be done to me according to your word. **Alleluia, alleluia.**

Gospel Lk 1: 26–38 The angel Gabriel was sent from God to a town of Galilee called Nazareth, to a virgin betrothed to a man named Joseph, of the house of David, and the virgin's name was Mary. And coming to her, he said, "Hail, full of grace! The Lord is with you." But she was greatly troubled at what was said and pondered what sort of greeting this might be. Then the angel said to her, "Do not be afraid, Mary, for you have found favor with God.

"Behold, you will conceive in your womb and bear a son, and you shall name him Jesus. He will be great and will be called Son of the Most High, and the Lord God will give him the throne of David his father, and he will rule over the house of Jacob forever, and of his kingdom there will be no end." But Mary said to the angel, "How can this be, since I have no relations with a man?" And the angel said to her in reply, "The Holy Spirit will come upon you, and the power of the Most High will overshadow you. Therefore the child to be born will be called holy, the Son of God. And behold, Elizabeth, your relative, has also conceived a son in her old age, and this is the sixth month for her who was called barren; for nothing will be impossible for God." Mary said, "Behold, I am the handmaid of the Lord. May it be done to me according to your word." Then the angel departed from her.

Communion Antiphon Is 7: 14 Behold, a Virgin shall conceive and bear a son; ♦ and his name will be called Emmanuel.

Christmas Time † YEAR B

THE NATIVITY OF THE LORD

❖ At the Vigil Mass ❖

Entrance Antiphon *cf. Ex 16: 6–7* **Today you will know that the Lord will come, and he will save us, ◆ and in the morning you will see his glory.**

First Reading *Is 62: 1–5*
For Zion's sake I will not be silent,
    for Jerusalem's sake I will not be quiet,
until her vindication shines forth like the dawn
    and her victory like a burning torch.

Nations shall behold your vindication,
    and all the kings your glory;
you shall be called by a new name
    pronounced by the mouth of the LORD.
You shall be a glorious crown in the hand of the LORD,
    a royal diadem held by your God.
No more shall people call you "Forsaken,"
    or your land "Desolate,"
but you shall be called "My Delight,"
    and your land "Espoused."
For the LORD delights in you
    and makes your land his spouse.
As a young man marries a virgin,
    your Builder shall marry you;

and as a bridegroom rejoices in his bride
   so shall your God rejoice in you.

Responsorial Psalm   Ps 89: 4–5, 16–17, 27, 29   *Joe Higginbotham*

For ev-er I will sing the good-ness of the Lord.

I have made a covenant with my chosen one,
   I have sworn to David my servant:
Forever will I confirm your posterity
   and establish your throne for all generations. ℟

Blessed the people who know the joyful shout;
   in the light of your countenance, O LORD, they walk.
At your name they rejoice all the day,
   and through your justice they are exalted. ℟

He shall say of me, "You are my father,
   my God, the rock, my savior."
Forever I will maintain my kindness toward him,
   and my covenant with him stands firm. ℟

Second Reading Acts 13: 16–17, 22–25 When Paul reached Antioch
in Pisidia and entered the synagogue, he stood up, motioned
with his hand, and said, "Fellow Israelites and you others who
are God-fearing, listen. The God of this people Israel chose our
ancestors and exalted the people during their sojourn in the
land of Egypt. With uplifted arm he led them out of it. Then he
removed Saul and raised up David as king; of him he testified,
'I have found David, son of Jesse, a man after my own heart;
he will carry out my every wish.' From this man's descendants
God, according to his promise, has brought to Israel a savior,
Jesus. John heralded his coming by proclaiming a baptism of
repentance to all the people of Israel; and as John was completing
his course, he would say, 'What do you suppose that I am? I am
not he. Behold, one is coming after me; I am not worthy to
unfasten the sandals of his feet.'"

Alleluia

Joe Higginbotham

Al - le - lu - ia, al - le - lu - ia, al - le - lu - ia.

Al - le - lu - ia, al - le - lu - ia, al - le - lu - ia.

Tomorrow the wickedness of the earth will be destroyed: /
the Savior of the world will reign over us. **Alleluia, alleluia.**

Gospel Mt 1: 1–25 or 1: 18–25 The book of the genealogy of Jesus Christ,
the son of David, the son of Abraham.

Abraham became the father of Isaac, Isaac the father of Jacob,
Jacob the father of Judah and his brothers. Judah became the
father of Perez and Zerah, whose mother was Tamar. Perez
became the father of Hezron, Hezron the father of Ram, Ram
the father of Amminadab. Amminadab became the father of
Nahshon, Nahshon the father of Salmon, Salmon the father of
Boaz, whose mother was Rahab. Boaz became the father of Obed,
whose mother was Ruth. Obed became the father of Jesse, Jesse
the father of David the king.

David became the father of Solomon, whose mother had been
the wife of Uriah. Solomon became the father of Rehoboam,
Rehoboam the father of Abijah, Abijah the father of Asaph.
Asaph became the father of Jehoshaphat, Jehoshaphat the father
of Joram, Joram the father of Uzziah. Uzziah became the father
of Jotham, Jotham the father of Ahaz, Ahaz the father of
Hezekiah. Hezekiah became the father of Manasseh, Manasseh
the father of Amos, Amos the father of Josiah. Josiah became
the father of Jechoniah and his brothers at the time of the
Babylonian exile.

After the Babylonian exile, Jechoniah became the father of
Shealtiel, Shealtiel the father of Zerubbabel, Zerubbabel the
father of Abiud. Abiud became the father of Eliakim, Eliakim
the father of Azor, Azor the father of Zadok. Zadok became the
father of Achim, Achim the father of Eliud, Eliud the father of
Eleazar. Eleazar became the father of Matthan, Matthan the

father of Jacob, Jacob the father of Joseph, the husband of Mary. Of her was born Jesus who is called the Christ.

Thus the total number of generations from Abraham to David is fourteen generations; from David to the Babylonian exile, fourteen generations; from the Babylonian exile to the Christ, fourteen generations.

Now [this is how the birth of Jesus Christ came about. When his mother Mary was betrothed to Joseph, but before they lived together, she was found with child through the Holy Spirit. Joseph her husband, since he was a righteous man, yet unwilling to expose her to shame, decided to divorce her quietly. Such was his intention when, behold, the angel of the Lord appeared to him in a dream and said, "Joseph, son of David, do not be afraid to take Mary your wife into your home. For it is through the Holy Spirit that this child has been conceived in her. She will bear a son and you are to name him Jesus, because he will save his people from their sins." All this took place to fulfill what the Lord had said through the prophet:

Behold, the virgin shall conceive and bear a son,
  and they shall name him Emmanuel,

which means "God is with us." When Joseph awoke, he did as the angel of the Lord had commanded him and took his wife into his home. He had no relations with her until she bore a son, and he named him Jesus.]

During the Creed, all kneel at the words and by the Holy Spirit was incarnate.

Communion Antiphon *cf. Is 40: 5* **The glory of the Lord will be revealed, ◆ and all flesh will see the salvation of our God.**

⁜ At the Mass During the Night ⁜

Entrance Antiphon *Ps 2: 7* **The Lord said to me: You are my Son. ◆ It is I who have begotten you this day.**

Or: **Let us all rejoice in the Lord for our Savior has been born in the world. ◆ Today true peace has come down to us from heaven.**

First Reading   *Is 9: 1–6*

The people who walked in darkness
    have seen a great light;
upon those who dwelt in the land of gloom
    a light has shone.
You have brought them abundant joy
    and great rejoicing,
as they rejoice before you as at the harvest,
    as people make merry when dividing spoils.
For the yoke that burdened them,
    the pole on their shoulder,
and the rod of their taskmaster
    you have smashed, as on the day of Midian.
For every boot that tramped in battle,
    every cloak rolled in blood,
    will be burned as fuel for flames.
For a child is born to us, a son is given us;
    upon his shoulder dominion rests.
They name him Wonder-Counselor, God-Hero,
    Father-Forever, Prince of Peace.
His dominion is vast
    and forever peaceful,
from David's throne, and over his kingdom,
    which he confirms and sustains
by judgment and justice,
    both now and forever.
The zeal of the LORD of hosts will do this!

Responsorial Psalm   *Ps 96: 1–2, 2–3, 11–12, 13*   Joe Higginbotham

Today is born our Savior, our Savior, Christ the Lord.

Sing to the LORD a new song;
    sing to the LORD, all you lands.

Sing to the LORD; bless his name. ℟

Announce his salvation, day after day.
Tell his glory among the nations;
among all peoples, his wondrous deeds. ℟

Let the heavens be glad and the earth rejoice;
let the sea and what fills it resound;
let the plains be joyful and all that is in them!
Then shall all the trees of the forest exult. ℟

They shall exult before the LORD, for he comes;
for he comes to rule the earth.
He shall rule the world with justice
and the peoples with his constancy. ℟

Second Reading *Ti 2: 11–14* Beloved: The grace of God has appeared,
saving all and training us to reject godless ways and worldly
desires and to live temperately, justly, and devoutly in this age,
as we await the blessed hope, the appearance of the glory of
our great God and savior Jesus Christ, who gave himself for us
to deliver us from all lawlessness and to cleanse for himself a
people as his own, eager to do what is good.

Alleluia   *Lk 2: 10–11*   Joe Higginbotham

Al - le - lu - ia, al - le - lu - ia, al - le - lu - ia.

Al - le - lu - ia, al - le - lu - ia, al - le - lu - ia.

I proclaim to you good news of great joy: / today a Savior is
born for us, / Christ the Lord.   **Alleluia, alleluia.**

Gospel *Lk 2: 1–14* In those days a decree went out from Caesar
Augustus that the whole world should be enrolled. This was the
first enrollment, when Quirinius was governor of Syria. So all

went to be enrolled, each to his own town. And Joseph too went up from Galilee from the town of Nazareth to Judea, to the city of David that is called Bethlehem, because he was of the house and family of David, to be enrolled with Mary, his betrothed, who was with child. While they were there, the time came for her to have her child, and she gave birth to her firstborn son. She wrapped him in swaddling clothes and laid him in a manger, because there was no room for them in the inn.

Now there were shepherds in that region living in the fields and keeping the night watch over their flock. The angel of the Lord appeared to them and the glory of the Lord shone around them, and they were struck with great fear. The angel said to them, "Do not be afraid; for behold, I proclaim to you good news of great joy that will be for all the people. For today in the city of David a savior has been born for you who is Christ and Lord. And this will be a sign for you: you will find an infant wrapped in swaddling clothes and lying in a manger." And suddenly there was a multitude of the heavenly host with the angel, praising God and saying:

"Glory to God in the highest
    and on earth peace to those on whom his favor rests."

During the Creed, all kneel at the words and by the Holy Spirit was incarnate.

Communion Antiphon Jn 1:14 The Word became flesh, and we have seen his glory.

❖ At the Mass at Dawn ❖

Entrance Antiphon cf. Is 9: 1, 5; Lk 1: 33 Today a light will shine upon us, for the Lord is born for us; • and he will be called Wondrous God, • Prince of peace, Father of future ages: • and his reign will be without end.

First Reading Is 62: 11–12
    See, the LORD proclaims
        to the ends of the earth:
    say to daughter Zion,

your savior comes!
Here is his reward with him,
   his recompense before him.
They shall be called the holy people,
   the redeemed of the LORD,
and you shall be called "Frequented,"
   a city that is not forsaken.

Responsorial Psalm   *Ps 97: 1, 6, 11–12*   *Bill Svarda*

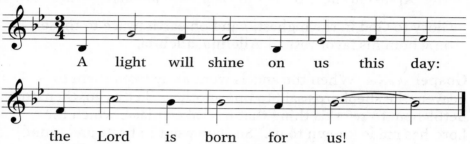

A light will shine on us this day: the Lord is born for us!

The LORD is king; let the earth rejoice;
   let the many isles be glad.
The heavens proclaim his justice,
   and all peoples see his glory. ℟

Light dawns for the just;
   and gladness, for the upright of heart.
Be glad in the LORD, you just,
   and give thanks to his holy name. ℟

Second Reading   *Ti 3: 4–7*
Beloved:
   When the kindness and generous love
      of God our savior appeared,
not because of any righteous deeds we had done
      but because of his mercy,
he saved us through the bath of rebirth
      and renewal by the Holy Spirit,
whom he richly poured out on us
      through Jesus Christ our savior,
so that we might be justified by his grace
      and become heirs in hope of eternal life.

Alleluia   Lk 2: 14   *Joe Higginbotham*

Al-le-lu-ia,   al-le-lu-ia,   al-le-lu - ia.

Al-le-lu-ia,   al-le-lu-ia,   al-le-lu - ia.

Glory to God in the highest, / and on earth peace to those / on whom his favor rests.   **Alleluia, alleluia.**

Gospel Lk 2: 15–20 When the angels went away from them to heaven, the shepherds said to one another, "Let us go, then, to Bethlehem to see this thing that has taken place, which the Lord has made known to us." So they went in haste and found Mary and Joseph, and the infant lying in the manger. When they saw this, they made known the message that had been told them about this child. All who heard it were amazed by what had been told them by the shepherds. And Mary kept all these things, reflecting on them in her heart. Then the shepherds returned, glorifying and praising God for all they had heard and seen, just as it had been told to them.

During the Creed, all kneel at the words and by the Holy Spirit was incarnate.

Communion Antiphon cf. Zec 9: 9 Rejoice, O Daughter Sion; lift up praise, Daughter Jerusalem: ✦ Behold, your King will come, the Holy One and Savior of the world.

❖   At the Mass During the Day   ❖

Entrance Antiphon cf. Is 9: 5 A child is born for us, and a son is given to us; ✦ his scepter of power rests upon his shoulder, ✦ and his name will be called Messenger of great counsel.

First Reading   *Is 52: 7–10*

How beautiful upon the mountains
  are the feet of him who brings glad tidings,
announcing peace, bearing good news,
  announcing salvation, and saying to Zion,
    "Your God is King!"

Hark! Your sentinels raise a cry,
  together they shout for joy,
for they see directly, before their eyes,
  the LORD restoring Zion.
Break out together in song,
  O ruins of Jerusalem!
For the LORD comforts his people,
  he redeems Jerusalem.
The LORD has bared his holy arm
  in the sight of all the nations;
all the ends of the earth will behold
  the salvation of our God.

Responsorial Psalm   *Ps 98: 1, 2–3, 3–4, 5–6*   Don Fishel

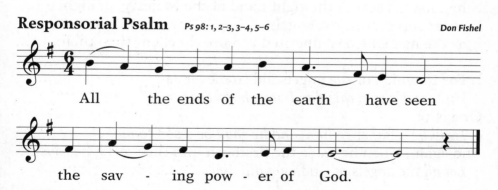

All the ends of the earth have seen the sav - ing pow - er of God.

Sing to the LORD a new song,
  for he has done wondrous deeds;
his right hand has won victory for him,
  his holy arm. ℟

The LORD has made his salvation known:
  in the sight of the nations he has revealed his justice.
He has remembered his kindness and his faithfulness
  toward the house of Israel. ℟

All the ends of the earth have seen
   the salvation by our God.
Sing joyfully to the LORD, all you lands;
   break into song; sing praise. ℟

Sing praise to the LORD with the harp,
   with the harp and melodious song.
With trumpets and the sound of the horn
   sing joyfully before the King, the LORD. ℟

Second Reading *Heb 1: 1–6* Brothers and sisters: In times past, God
spoke in partial and various ways to our ancestors through the
prophets; in these last days, he has spoken to us through the Son,
whom he made heir of all things and through whom he created
the universe,
   who is the refulgence of his glory, the very imprint of his
      being,
   and who sustains all things by his mighty word.
When he had accomplished purification from sins,
   he took his seat at the right hand of the Majesty on high,
   as far superior to the angels
   as the name he has inherited is more excellent than theirs.

For to which of the angels did God ever say:
You are my son; this day I have begotten you?
Or again:
I will be a father to him, and he shall be a son to me?
And again, when he leads the firstborn into the world, he says:
Let all the angels of God worship him.

Alleluia

Joe Higginbotham

Al - le - lu - ia, al - le - lu - ia, al - le - lu - ia.

Al - le - lu - ia, al - le - lu - ia, al - le - lu - ia.

A holy day has dawned upon us. / Come, you nations, and
adore the Lord. / For today a great light has come upon the
earth.   **Alleluia, alleluia.**

Gospel   Jn 1: 1–18 or 1: 1–5, 9–14
For the shorter form, read only the parts in brackets.
[In the beginning was the Word,
  and the Word was with God,
  and the Word was God.
He was in the beginning with God.
All things came to be through him,
  and without him nothing came to be.
What came to be through him was life,
  and this life was the light of the human race;
the light shines in the darkness,
  and the darkness has not overcome it.]
A man named John was sent from God. He came for testimony,
to testify to the light, so that all might believe through him. He
was not the light, but came to testify to the light. [The true light,
which enlightens everyone, was coming into the world.

He was in the world,
  and the world came to be through him,
  but the world did not know him.
He came to what was his own,
  but his own people did not accept him.
But to those who did accept him he gave power to become
children of God, to those who believe in his name, who were
born not by natural generation nor by human choice nor by a
man's decision but of God.
And the Word became flesh
  and made his dwelling among us,
  and we saw his glory,
  the glory as of the Father's only Son,
  full of grace and truth.]
John testified to him and cried out, saying, "This was he of
whom I said, 'The one who is coming after me ranks ahead of
me because he existed before me.'" From his fullness we have
all received, grace in place of grace, because while the law was
given through Moses, grace and truth came through Jesus Christ.

No one has ever seen God. The only Son, God, who is at the Father's side, has revealed him.

During the Creed, all kneel at the words and by the Holy Spirit was incarnate.

Communion Antiphon *cf. Ps 98 (97): 3* **All the ends of the earth have seen the salvation of our God.**

THE HOLY FAMILY

OF JESUS, MARY, AND JOSEPH

When a Sunday does not occur between December 25 and January 1, this feast is celebrated on December 30 with only one reading before the Gospel.

Entrance Antiphon *Lk 2: 16* **The shepherds went in haste, ♦ and found Mary and Joseph and the Infant lying in a manger.**

First Reading   *Sir 3: 2–6, 12–14*
God sets a father in honor over his children;
  a mother's authority he confirms over her sons.
Whoever honors his father atones for sins,
  and preserves himself from them.
When he prays, he is heard;
  he stores up riches who reveres his mother.
Whoever honors his father is gladdened by children,
  and, when he prays, is heard.
Whoever reveres his father will live a long life;
  he who obeys his father brings comfort to his mother.

My son, take care of your father when he is old;
  grieve him not as long as he lives.
Even if his mind fail, be considerate of him;
  revile him not all the days of his life;
kindness to a father will not be forgotten,

firmly planted against the debt of your sins
—a house raised in justice to you.

Responsorial Psalm   *Ps 128: 1–2, 3, 4–5*   *Beverly McDevitt*

Bless - ed   are   those   who fear the   Lord

and   walk   in   his   ways.

Blessed is everyone who fears the LORD,
   who walks in his ways!
For you shall eat the fruit of your handiwork;
   blessed shall you be, and favored. ℟

Your wife shall be like a fruitful vine
   in the recesses of your home;
your children like olive plants
   around your table. ℟

Behold, thus is the man blessed
   who fears the LORD.
The LORD bless you from Zion:
   may you see the prosperity of Jerusalem
   all the days of your life. ℟

Second Reading   *Col 3: 12–21 or 3: 12–17*
For the shorter form, read only the parts in brackets.
[Brothers and sisters: Put on, as God's chosen ones, holy and
beloved, heartfelt compassion, kindness, humility, gentleness,
and patience, bearing with one another and forgiving one
another, if one has a grievance against another; as the Lord has
forgiven you, so must you also do. And over all these put on
love, that is, the bond of perfection. And let the peace of Christ
control your hearts, the peace into which you were also called
in one body. And be thankful. Let the word of Christ dwell in

you richly, as in all wisdom you teach and admonish one another, singing psalms, hymns, and spiritual songs with gratitude in your hearts to God. And whatever you do, in word or in deed, do everything in the name of the Lord Jesus, giving thanks to God the Father through him.]

Wives, be subordinate to your husbands, as is proper in the Lord. Husbands, love your wives, and avoid any bitterness toward them. Children, obey your parents in everything, for this is pleasing to the Lord. Fathers, do not provoke your children, so they may not become discouraged.

Alleluia   Col 3: 15a, 16a   Joe Higginbotham

Al - le - lu - ia,   al - le - lu - ia,   al - le - lu - ia.

Al - le - lu - ia,   al - le - lu - ia,   al - le - lu - ia.

Let the peace of Christ control your hearts; / let the word of Christ dwell in you richly.   **Alleluia, alleluia.**

Gospel   Lk 2: 22-40 or 2:22, 39-40
For the shorter form, read only the parts in brackets.
[When the days were completed for their purification according to the law of Moses, they took him up to Jerusalem to present him to the Lord,] just as it is written in the law of the Lord, *Every male that opens the womb shall be consecrated to the Lord,* and to offer the sacrifice of *a pair of turtledoves or two young pigeons,* in accordance with the dictate in the law of the Lord.

Now there was a man in Jerusalem whose name was Simeon. This man was righteous and devout, awaiting the consolation of Israel, and the Holy Spirit was upon him. It had been revealed to him by the Holy Spirit that he should not see death before he had seen the Christ of the Lord. He came in the Spirit into the temple; and when the parents brought in the child Jesus to perform the custom of the law in regard to him, He took him into his arms and blessed God, saying:

"Now, Master, you may let your servant go
   in peace, according to your word,
for my eyes have seen your salvation,
   which you prepared in sight of all the peoples,
a light for revelation to the Gentiles,
   and glory for your people Israel."
The child's father and mother were amazed at what was said
about him; and Simeon blessed them and said to Mary his
mother, "Behold, this child is destined for the fall and rise of
many in Israel, and to be a sign that will be contradicted—and
you yourself a sword will pierce—so that the thoughts of many
hearts may be revealed." There was also a prophetess, Anna, the
daughter of Phanuel, of the tribe of Asher. She was advanced
in years, having lived seven years with her husband after her
marriage, and then as a widow until she was eighty-four. She
never left the temple, but worshiped night and day with fasting
and prayer. And coming forward at that very time, she gave
thanks to God and spoke about the child to all who were
awaiting the redemption of Jerusalem.

[When they had fulfilled all the prescriptions of the law of the
Lord, they returned to Galilee, to their own town of Nazareth.
The child grew and became strong, filled with wisdom; and the
favor of God was upon him.]

Communion Antiphon Bar 3: 38 **Our God has appeared on the earth, and lived among us.**

❈ Optional Readings ❈

In Year B, these readings may be used:

Entrance Antiphon Lk 2: 16 **The shepherds went in haste, ◆ and found Mary and Joseph and the Infant lying in a manger.**

First Reading Gen 15: 1–6; 21: 1–3 The word of the LORD came to
Abram in a vision, saying:
  "Fear not, Abram!
    I am your shield;
    I will make your reward very great."

But Abram said, "O Lord GOD, what good will your gifts be, if I keep on being childless and have as my heir the steward of my house, Eliezer?" Abram continued, "See, you have given me no offspring, and so one of my servants will be my heir." Then the word of the LORD came to him: "No, that one shall not be your heir; your own issue shall be your heir." The Lord took Abram outside and said, "Look up at the sky and count the stars, if you can." "Just so," he added, "shall your descendants be." Abram put his faith in the LORD, who credited it to him as an act of righteousness.

The LORD took note of Sarah as he had said he would; he did for her as he had promised. Sarah became pregnant and bore Abraham a son in his old age, at the set time that God had stated. Abraham gave the name Isaac to this son of his whom Sarah bore him.

Responsorial Psalm Ps 105: 1–2, 3–4, 5–6, 8–9 Joe Higginbotham

The Lord re-mem-bers his cov-e-nant for-ev-er.

Give thanks to the LORD, invoke his name;
    make known among the nations his deeds.
Sing to him, sing his praise,
    proclaim all his wondrous deeds. ℟

Glory in his holy name;
    rejoice, O hearts that seek the LORD!
Look to the LORD in his strength;
    constantly seek his face. ℟

You descendants of Abraham, his servants,
    sons of Jacob, his chosen ones!
He, the LORD, is our God;
    throughout the earth his judgments prevail. ℟

He remembers forever his covenant
    which he made binding for a thousand generations

which he entered into with Abraham
  and by his oath to Isaac. ℟

Second Reading *Heb 11: 8, 11–12, 17–19* Brothers and sisters: By faith
Abraham obeyed when he was called to go out to a place that
he was to receive as an inheritance; he went out, not knowing
where he was to go. By faith he received power to generate, even
though he was past the normal age – and Sarah herself was
sterile – for he thought that the one who had made the promise
was trustworthy. So it was that there came forth from one man,
himself as good as dead, descendants as numerous as the stars in
the sky and as countless as the sands on the seashore.

  By faith Abraham, when put to the test, offered up Isaac, and
he who had received the promises was ready to offer his only
son, of whom it was said, "Through Isaac descendants shall bear
your name." He reasoned that God was able to raise even from
the dead, and he received Isaac back as a symbol.

Alleluia *Heb 1: 1–2*   *Joe Higginbotham*

Al - le - lu - ia, al - le - lu - ia, al - le - lu - ia.

Al - le - lu - ia, al - le - lu - ia, al - le - lu - ia.

In the past God spoke to our ancestors through the
prophets; / in these last days, he has spoken to us through
the Son. **Alleluia, alleluia.**

Gospel *Lk 2: 22–40 or 2: 22, 39–40*
For the shorter form, read only the parts in brackets.
[When the days were completed for their purification according
to the law of Moses, they took him up to Jerusalem to present
him to the Lord,] just as it is written in the law of the Lord,
Every male that opens the womb shall be consecrated to the Lord,
and to offer the sacrifice of *a pair of turtledoves or two young*

pigeons, in accordance with the dictate in the law of the Lord.

Now there was a man in Jerusalem whose name was Simeon. This man was righteous and devout, awaiting the consolation of Israel, and the Holy Spirit was upon him. It had been revealed to him by the Holy Spirit that he should not see death before he had seen the Christ of the Lord. He came in the Spirit into the temple; and when the parents brought in the child Jesus to perform the custom of the law in regard to him, He took him into his arms and blessed God, saying:

"Now, Master, you may let your servant go
  in peace, according to your word,
for my eyes have seen your salvation,
  which you prepared in sight of all the peoples,
a light for revelation to the Gentiles,
  and glory for your people Israel."

The child's father and mother were amazed at what was said about him; and Simeon blessed them and said to Mary his mother, "Behold, this child is destined for the fall and rise of many in Israel, and to be a sign that will be contradicted—and you yourself a sword will pierce—so that the thoughts of many hearts may be revealed." There was also a prophetess, Anna, the daughter of Phanuel, of the tribe of Asher. She was advanced in years, having lived seven years with her husband after her marriage, and then as a widow until she was eighty-four. She never left the temple, but worshiped night and day with fasting and prayer. And coming forward at that very time, she gave thanks to God and spoke about the child to all who were awaiting the redemption of Jerusalem.

[When they had fulfilled all the prescriptions of the law of the Lord, they returned to Galilee, to their own town of Nazareth. The child grew and became strong, filled with wisdom; and the favor of God was upon him.]

Communion Antiphon *Bar 3:38* **Our God has appeared on the earth, and lived among us.**

SOLEMNITY OF MARY,
THE HOLY MOTHER OF GOD

THE OCTAVE DAY OF THE NATIVITY

Entrance Antiphon   Hail, Holy Mother, who gave birth to the King ◆ who rules heaven and earth for ever.

Or: cf. Is 9: 1, 5; Lk 1: 33 Today a light will shine upon us, for the Lord is born for us; ◆ and he will be called Wondrous God, ◆ Prince of peace, Father of future ages: ◆ and his reign will be without end.

First Reading Nm 6: 22–27 The LORD said to Moses: "Speak to Aaron and his sons and tell them: 'This is how you shall bless the Israelites. Say to them:
The LORD bless you and keep you!
The LORD let his face shine upon you, and be gracious to you!
The LORD look upon you kindly and give you peace!'
So shall they invoke my name upon the Israelites, and I will bless them."

Responsorial Psalm   Ps 67: 2–3, 5, 6, 8   *Bill Svarda*

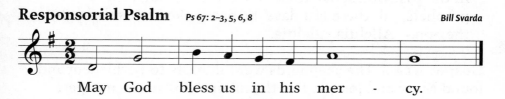

May God bless us in his mer - cy.

May God have pity on us and bless us;
    may he let his face shine upon us.
So may your way be known upon earth;
    among all nations, your salvation. ℟

May the nations be glad and exult
    because you rule the peoples in equity;
    the nations on the earth you guide. ℟

May the peoples praise you, O God;
    may all the peoples praise you!
May God bless us,
    and may all the ends of the earth fear him! ℟

Second Reading *Gal 4: 4-7* Brothers and sisters: When the fullness
of time had come, God sent his Son, born of a woman, born
under the law, to ransom those under the law, so that we might
receive adoption as sons. As proof that you are sons, God sent
the Spirit of his Son into our hearts, crying out, "Abba, Father!"
So you are no longer a slave but a son, and if a son then also an
heir, through God.

Alleluia   *Heb 1: 1-2*   Joe Higginbotham

Al - le - lu - ia, al - le - lu - ia,   al - le - lu - ia.

Al - le - lu - ia, al - le - lu - ia,   al - le - lu - ia.

In the past God spoke to our ancestors through the
prophets; / in these last days, he has spoken to us through
the Son. **Alleluia, alleluia.**

Gospel *Lk 2: 16-21* The shepherds went in haste to Bethlehem and
found Mary and Joseph, and the infant lying in the manger.
When they saw this, they made known the message that had
been told them about this child. All who heard it were amazed
by what had been told them by the shepherds. And Mary kept
all these things, reflecting on them in her heart. Then the
shepherds returned, glorifying and praising God for all they had
heard and seen, just as it had been told to them.

    When eight days were completed for his circumcision, he was
named Jesus, the name given him by the angel before he was
conceived in the womb.

Communion Antiphon *Heb 13: 8* **Jesus Christ is the same
yesterday, today, and for ever.**

THE EPIPHANY OF THE LORD

*Where the Solemnity of the Epiphany is not to be observed as a
Holy day of Obligation, it is assigned to the Sunday occurring
between 2 and 8 January as its proper day.*

Entrance Antiphon

At the Vigil Mass: *cf. Bar 5: 5* **Arise, Jerusalem, and look to the
East ✦ and see your children gathered from the rising to the
setting of the sun.**

At the Mass During the Day: *cf. Mal 3: 1; 1 Chr 29: 12* **Behold, the Lord,
the Mighty One, has come; ✦ and kingship is in his grasp, and
power and dominion.**

First Reading *Is 60: 1–6*
Rise up in splendor, Jerusalem! Your light has come,
    the glory of the Lord shines upon you.
See, darkness covers the earth,
    and thick clouds cover the peoples;
but upon you the LORD shines,
    and over you appears his glory.
Nations shall walk by your light,
    and kings by your shining radiance.
Raise your eyes and look about;
    they all gather and come to you:
your sons come from afar,
    and your daughters in the arms of their nurses.

Then you shall be radiant at what you see,
    your heart shall throb and overflow,
for the riches of the sea shall be emptied out before you,

the wealth of nations shall be brought to you.
Caravans of camels shall fill you,
    dromedaries from Midian and Ephah;
all from Sheba shall come
    bearing gold and frankincense,
    and proclaiming the praises of the LORD.

Responsorial Psalm   Ps 72: 1–2, 7–8, 10–11, 12–13   Brian J. Nelson

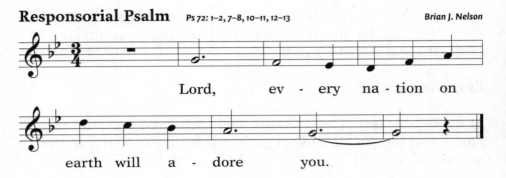

Lord, every nation on earth will adore you.

O God, with your judgment endow the king,
    and with your justice, the king's son;
He shall govern your people with justice
    and your afflicted ones with judgment.   ℟

Justice shall flower in his days,
    and profound peace, till the moon be no more.
May he rule from sea to sea,
    and from the River to the ends of the earth.   ℟

The kings of Tarshish and the Isles shall offer gifts;
    the kings of Arabia and Seba shall bring tribute.
All kings shall pay him homage,
    all nations shall serve him.   ℟

For he shall rescue the poor when he cries out,
    and the afflicted when he has no one to help him.
He shall have pity for the lowly and the poor;
    the lives of the poor he shall save.   ℟

Second Reading Eph 3: 2–3a, 5–6 Brothers and sisters: You have
heard of the stewardship of God's grace that was given to me

for your benefit, namely, that the mystery was made known to me by revelation. It was not made known to people in other generations as it has now been revealed to his holy apostles and prophets by the Spirit: that the Gentiles are coheirs, members of the same body, and copartners in the promise in Christ Jesus through the gospel.

Alleluia Mt 2: 2   Joe Higginbotham

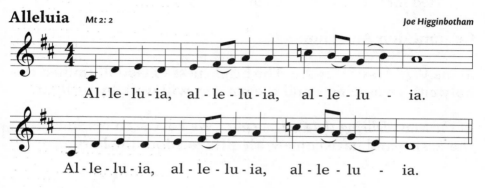

Al - le - lu - ia, al - le - lu - ia, al - le - lu - ia.

Al - le - lu - ia, al - le - lu - ia, al - le - lu - ia.

We saw his star at its rising / and have come to do him homage. **Alleluia, alleluia.**

Gospel Mt 2: 1–12 When Jesus was born in Bethlehem of Judea, in the days of King Herod, behold, magi from the east arrived in Jerusalem, saying, "Where is the newborn king of the Jews? We saw his star at its rising and have come to do him homage." When King Herod heard this, he was greatly troubled, and all Jerusalem with him. Assembling all the chief priests and the scribes of the people, he inquired of them where the Christ was to be born. They said to him, "In Bethlehem of Judea, for thus it has been written through the prophet:
And you, Bethlehem, land of Judah,
   are by no means least among the rulers of Judah;
since from you shall come a ruler,
   who is to shepherd my people Israel."
Then Herod called the magi secretly and ascertained from them the time of the star's appearance. He sent them to Bethlehem and said, "Go and search diligently for the child. When you have found him, bring me word, that I too may go and do him homage." After their audience with the king they set out. And behold, the star that they had seen at its rising preceded them,

until it came and stopped over the place where the child was. They were overjoyed at seeing the star, and on entering the house they saw the child with Mary his mother. They prostrated themselves and did him homage. Then they opened their treasures and offered him gifts of gold, frankincense, and myrrh. And having been warned in a dream not to return to Herod, they departed for their country by another way.

Communion Antiphon

At the Vigil Mass: cf. Rv 21: 23 **The brightness of God illumined the holy city Jerusalem, ◆ and the nations will walk by its light.**

At the Mass During the Day: cf. Mt 2: 2 **We have seen his star in the East, ◆ and have come with gifts to adore the Lord.**

THE BAPTISM OF THE LORD

Sunday after January 6. In dioceses where the Epiphany is transferred to a Sunday that falls on January 7 or 8, the Baptism of the Lord is transferred to the Monday immediately following. Only one reading before the Gospel is used.

Entrance Antiphon cf. Mt 3: 16–17 **After the Lord was baptized, the heavens were opened, ◆ and the Spirit descended upon him like a dove, ◆ and the voice of the Father thundered: ◆ This is my beloved Son, with whom I am well pleased.**

First Reading   Is 42: 1–4, 6–7
  Thus says the LORD:
  Here is my servant whom I uphold,
    my chosen one with whom I am pleased,
  upon whom I have put my spirit;
    he shall bring forth justice to the nations,
  not crying out, not shouting,
    not making his voice heard in the street.
  A bruised reed he shall not break,

and a smoldering wick he shall not quench,
until he establishes justice on the earth;
   the coastlands will wait for his teaching.

I, the LORD, have called you for the victory of justice,
   I have grasped you by the hand;
I formed you, and set you
   as a covenant of the people,
   a light for the nations,
to open the eyes of the blind,
   to bring out prisoners from confinement,
   and from the dungeon, those who live in darkness.

Responsorial Psalm   Ps 29: 1–2, 3–4, 3, 9–10   *based on* EVENTIDE

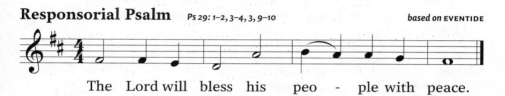

The Lord will bless his peo - ple with peace.

Give to the LORD, you sons of God,
   give to the LORD glory and praise,
Give to the LORD the glory due his name;
   adore the LORD in holy attire. ℟

The voice of the LORD is over the waters,
   the LORD, over vast waters.
The voice of the LORD is mighty;
   the voice of the LORD is majestic. ℟

The God of glory thunders,
   and in his temple all say, "Glory!"
The LORD is enthroned above the flood;
   the LORD is enthroned as king forever. ℟

Second Reading Acts 10: 34–38 Peter proceeded to speak to those
gathered in the house of Cornelius, saying: "In truth, I see that
God shows no partiality. Rather, in every nation whoever fears
him and acts uprightly is acceptable to him. You know the word
that he sent to the Israelites as he proclaimed peace through

Jesus Christ, who is Lord of all, what has happened all over Judea, beginning in Galilee after the baptism that John preached, how God anointed Jesus of Nazareth with the Holy Spirit and power. He went about doing good and healing all those oppressed by the devil, for God was with him."

Alleluia *cf. Mk 9: 7*   *Brian J. Nelson*

Al - le-lu - ia, al - le - lu - ia, al-le-lu - ia.

The heavens were opened and the voice of the Father thundered: / This is my beloved Son, listen to him. **Aleluia, aleluia.**

Gospel *Mk 1: 7–11* This is what John the Baptist proclaimed: "One mightier than I is coming after me. I am not worthy to stoop and loosen the thongs of his sandals. I have baptized you with water; he will baptize you with the Holy Spirit."

It happened in those days that Jesus came from Nazareth of Galilee and was baptized in the Jordan by John. On coming up out of the water he saw the heavens being torn open and the Spirit, like a dove, descending upon him. And a voice came from the heavens, "You are my beloved Son; with you I am well pleased."

Communion Antiphon *Jn 1: 32, 34* Behold the One of whom John said: ✦ I have seen and testified that this is the Son of God.

◈ Optional Readings ◈

In Year B, these readings may be used:

Entrance Antiphon *cf. Mt 3: 16–17* After the Lord was baptized, the heavens were opened, ✦ and the Spirit descended upon him like a dove, ✦ and the voice of the Father thundered: ✦ This is my beloved Son, with whom I am well pleased.

First Reading *Is 55: 1–11*

Thus says the LORD:
All you who are thirsty,
   come to the water!
You who have no money,
   come, receive grain and eat;
come, without paying and without cost,
   drink wine and milk!
Why spend your money for what is not bread,
   your wages for what fails to satisfy?
Heed me, and you shall eat well,
   you shall delight in rich fare.
Come to me heedfully,
   listen, that you may have life.
I will renew with you the everlasting covenant,
   the benefits assured to David.
As I made him a witness to the peoples,
   a leader and commander of nations,
so shall you summon a nation you knew not,
   and nations that knew you not shall run to you,
because of the LORD, your God,
   the Holy One of Israel, who has glorified you.

Seek the LORD while he may be found,
   call him while he is near.
Let the scoundrel forsake his way,
   and the wicked man his thoughts;
let him turn to the LORD for mercy;
   to our God, who is generous in forgiving.
For my thoughts are not your thoughts,
   nor are your ways my ways, says the LORD.
As high as the heavens are above the earth
   so high are my ways above your ways
   and my thoughts above your thoughts.

For just as from the heavens
   the rain and snow come down
and do not return there
   till they have watered the earth,

making it fertile and fruitful,
giving seed to the one who sows
  and bread to the one who eats,
so shall my word be
  that goes forth from my mouth;
my word shall not return to me void,
  but shall do my will,
  achieving the end for which I sent it.

Responsorial Psalm *Is 12: 2–3, 4bcd, 5–6*   *Bill Svarda*

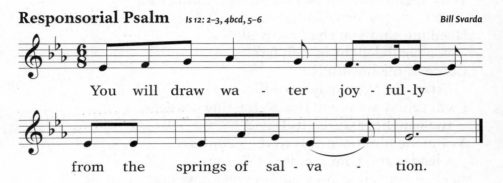

You will draw wa - ter joy - ful-ly
from the springs of sal - va - tion.

God indeed is my savior;
  I am confident and unafraid.
My strength and my courage is the LORD,
  and he has been my savior.
With joy you will draw water
  at the fountain of salvation. ℟

Give thanks to the LORD, acclaim his name;
  among the nations make known his deeds,
  proclaim how exalted is his name. ℟

Sing praise to the LORD for his glorious achievement;
  let this be known throughout all the earth.
Shout with exultation, O city of Zion,
  for great in your midst
  is the Holy One of Israel! ℟

Second Reading *1 Jn 5: 1–9* Beloved: Everyone who believes that
Jesus is the Christ is begotten by God, and everyone who loves
the Father loves also the one begotten by him. In this way we
know that we love the children of God when we love God and

obey his commandments. For the love of God is this, that we keep his commandments. And his commandments are not burdensome, for whoever is begotten by God conquers the world. And the victory that conquers the world is our faith. Who indeed is the victor over the world but the one who believes that Jesus is the Son of God?

This is the one who came through water and blood, Jesus Christ, not by water alone, but by water and blood. The Spirit is the one who testifies, and the Spirit is truth. So there are three that testify, the Spirit, the water, and the blood, and the three are of one accord. If we accept human testimony, the testimony of God is surely greater. Now the testimony of God is this, that he has testified on behalf of his Son.

Alleluia cf. Jn 1: 29   Brian J. Nelson

Al - le-lu - ia, al - le - lu - ia, al-le-lu - ia.

John saw Jesus approaching him, and said: / Behold the Lamb of God who takes away the sin of the world. **Alleluia, alleluia.**

Gospel Mk 1: 7-11 This is what John the Baptist proclaimed: "One mightier than I is coming after me. I am not worthy to stoop and loosen the thongs of his sandals. I have baptized you with water; he will baptize you with the Holy Spirit."

It happened in those days that Jesus came from Nazareth of Galilee and was baptized in the Jordan by John. On coming up out of the water he saw the heavens being torn open and the Spirit, like a dove, descending upon him. And a voice came from the heavens, "You are my beloved Son; with you I am well pleased."

Communion Antiphon Jn 1: 32,34 Behold the One of whom John said: ♦ I have seen and testified that this is the Son of God.

Lent ✝ YEAR B

ASH WEDNESDAY

Entrance Antiphon Wis 11: 23, 24, 26 **You are merciful to all, O Lord, ◆ and despise nothing that you have made. ◆ You overlook people's sins, to bring them to repentance, ◆ and you spare them, for you are the Lord our God.**

The Penitential Act is omitted on Ash Wednesday.

First Reading Jl 2: 12–18
Even now, says the LORD,
    return to me with your whole heart,
    with fasting, and weeping, and mourning;
Rend your hearts, not your garments,
    and return to the LORD, your God.
For gracious and merciful is he,
    slow to anger, rich in kindness,
    and relenting in punishment.
Perhaps he will again relent
    and leave behind him a blessing,
Offerings and libations
    for the LORD, your God.
Blow the trumpet in Zion!
    proclaim a fast,
    call an assembly;
Gather the people,
    notify the congregation;
Assemble the elders,
    gather the children
    and the infants at the breast;
Let the bridegroom quit his room

and the bride her chamber.
Between the porch and the altar
    let the priests, the ministers of the LORD, weep,
And say, "Spare, O LORD, your people,
    and make not your heritage a reproach,
    with the nations ruling over them!
Why should they say among the peoples,
    'Where is their God?'"
Then the LORD was stirred to concern for his land and took
pity on his people.

Responsorial Psalm   Ps 51: 3–4, 5–6, 12–13, 14, 17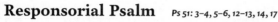

Bill Svarda

Be mer-ci-ful, O Lord,   for we have sinned.

Have mercy on me, O God, in your goodness;
    in the greatness of your compassion wipe out my offense.
Thoroughly wash me from my guilt
    and of my sin cleanse me.   ℟

For I acknowledge my offense,
    and my sin is before me always:
"Against you only have I sinned,
    and done what is evil in your sight."   ℟

A clean heart create for me, O God,
    and a steadfast spirit renew within me.
Cast me not out from your presence,
    and your Holy Spirit take not from me.   ℟

Give me back the joy of your salvation,
    and a willing spirit sustain in me.
O Lord, open my lips,
    and my mouth shall proclaim your praise.   ℟

Second Reading   2 Cor 5: 20–6: 2   Brothers and sisters: We are
ambassadors for Christ, as if God were appealing through us. We

implore you on behalf of Christ, be reconciled to God. For our sake he made him to be sin who did not know sin, so that we might become the righteousness of God in him.

Working together, then, we appeal to you not to receive the grace of God in vain. For he says:

In an acceptable time I heard you,
*   and on the day of salvation I helped you.*

Behold, now is a very acceptable time; behold, now is the day of salvation.

Verse Before the Gospel   Ps 95: 8   Amy Righi

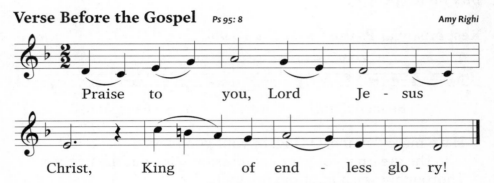

Praise to you, Lord Jesus Christ, King of endless glory!

If today you hear his voice, / harden not your hearts.

Gospel Mt 6: 1–6, 16–18 Jesus said to his disciples: "Take care not to perform righteous deeds in order that people may see them; otherwise, you will have no recompense from your heavenly Father. When you give alms, do not blow a trumpet before you, as the hypocrites do in the synagogues and in the streets to win the praise of others. Amen, I say to you, they have received their reward. But when you give alms, do not let your left hand know what your right is doing, so that your almsgiving may be secret. And your Father who sees in secret will repay you.

"When you pray, do not be like the hypocrites, who love to stand and pray in the synagogues and on street corners so that others may see them. Amen, I say to you, they have received their reward. But when you pray, go to your inner room, close the door, and pray to your Father in secret. And your Father who sees in secret will repay you.

"When you fast, do not look gloomy like the hypocrites. They neglect their appearance, so that they may appear to others to

be fasting. Amen, I say to you, they have received their reward. But when you fast, anoint your head and wash your face, so that you may not appear to be fasting, except to your Father who is hidden. And your Father who sees what is hidden will repay you."

BLESSING AND DISTRIBUTION OF ASHES

After the Homily, the Priest, standing with hands joined, says:
Dear brethren (brothers and sisters),
   let us humbly ask God our Father
that he be pleased to bless with the abundance of his grace
these ashes, which we will put on our heads in penitence.

After a brief prayer in silence, and, with hands extended, he continues:
O God, who are moved by acts of humility
and respond with forgiveness to works of penance,
lend your merciful ear to our prayers
and in your kindness pour out the grace of your + blessing
on your servants who are marked with these ashes,
that, as they follow the Lenten observances,
they may be worthy to come with minds made pure
to celebrate the Paschal Mystery of your Son.
Through Christ our Lord ℟ **Amen.**

Or:
O God, who desire not the death of sinners,
but their conversion,
mercifully hear our prayers
and in your kindness be pleased to bless + these ashes,
which we intend to receive upon our heads,
that we, who acknowledge we are but ashes
and shall return to dust,
may, through a steadfast observance of Lent,
gain pardon for sins and newness of life
after the likeness of your Risen Son.
Who lives and reigns for ever and ever. ℟ **Amen.**

He sprinkles the ashes with holy water, without saying anything.

Then the Priest places ashes on the head of all those present who come to him, and says to each one: Repent, and believe in the Gospel.

Or: Remember that you are dust, and to dust you shall return.

Meanwhile, the following are sung:

Antiphon 1   Let us change our garments to sackcloth and ashes, ✦ let us fast and weep before the Lord, ✦ that our God, rich in mercy, might forgive us our sins.

Antiphon 2   *cf. Jl 2: 17; Est 4: 17*   Let the priests, the ministers of the Lord, ✦ stand between the porch and the altar and weep and cry out: ✦ Spare, O Lord, spare your people; ✦ do not close the mouths of those who sing your praise, O Lord.

Antiphon 3   *Ps 51 (50): 3*   Blot out my transgressions, O Lord.

This may be repeated after each verse of Psalm 51 (50), (Have mercy on me, O God).

Responsory   *cf. Bar 3: 2; Ps 79 (78): 9*
℟ Let us correct our faults which we have committed in ignorance, let us not be taken unawares by the day of our death, looking in vain for leisure to repent. Hear us, O Lord, and show us your mercy, for we have sinned against you.

℣ Help us, O God our Savior; for the sake of your name, O Lord, set us free.
℟ Hear us, O Lord, and show us your mercy, for we have sinned against you.

Another appropriate chant or hymn may also be sung.

After the distribution of ashes, the Priest washes his hands and

proceeds to the Universal Prayer, and continues the Mass in the usual way. The Creed is not said.

Communion Antiphon *cf. Ps 1: 2–3* **He who ponders the law of the Lord day and night ♦ will yield fruit in due season.**

The blessing and distribution of ashes may also take place outside Mass. In this case, the rite is preceded by a Liturgy of the Word, with the Entrance Antiphon, the Collect, and the readings with their chants as at Mass. Then there follow the Homily and the blessing and distribution of ashes. The rite is concluded with the Prayer of the Faithful (Universal Prayer), the Blessing, and the Dismissal of the Faithful.

FIRST SUNDAY OF LENT

Entrance Antiphon *cf. Ps 91 (90): 15–16* **When he calls on me, I will answer him; ♦ I will deliver him and give him glory, ♦ I will grant him length of days.**

First Reading *Gen 9: 8–15* God said to Noah and to his sons with him: "See, I am now establishing my covenant with you and your descendants after you and with every living creature that was with you: all the birds, and the various tame and wild animals that were with you and came out of the ark. I will establish my covenant with you, that never again shall all bodily creatures be destroyed by the waters of a flood; there shall not be another flood to devastate the earth." God added: "This is the sign that I am giving for all ages to come, of the covenant between me and you and every living creature with you: I set my bow in the clouds to serve as a sign of the covenant between me and the earth. When I bring clouds over the earth, and the bow appears in the clouds, I will recall the covenant I have made between me and you and all living beings, so that the waters shall never again become a flood to destroy all mortal beings."

Responsorial Psalm   Ps 25: 4–5, 6–7, 8–9

Michael Giszczak

Your ways, O Lord, are love and truth
to those who keep your cov-e-nant.

Your ways, O LORD, make known to me;
    teach me your paths,
Guide me in your truth and teach me,
    for you are God my savior. ℟

Remember that your compassion, O LORD,
    and your love are from of old.
In your kindness remember me,
    because of your goodness, O LORD. ℟

Good and upright is the LORD,
    thus he shows sinners the way.
He guides the humble to justice,
    and he teaches the humble his way. ℟

Second Reading 1 Pt 3: 18–22 Beloved: Christ suffered for sins once, the righteous for the sake of the unrighteous, that he might lead you to God. Put to death in the flesh, he was brought to life in the Spirit. In it he also went to preach to the spirits in prison, who had once been disobedient while God patiently waited in the days of Noah during the building of the ark, in which a few persons, eight in all, were saved through water. This prefigured baptism, which saves you now. It is not a removal of dirt from the body but an appeal to God for a clear conscience, through the resurrection of Jesus Christ, who has gone into heaven and is at the right hand of God, with angels, authorities, and powers subject to him.

Verse Before the Gospel Mt 4: 4b   Joe Higginbotham

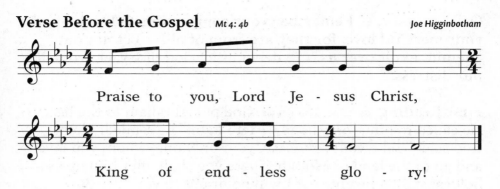

Praise to you, Lord Je-sus Christ,

King of end-less glo-ry!

One does not live on bread alone, / but on every word that
comes forth from the mouth of God.

Gospel Mk 1: 12–15 The Spirit drove Jesus out into the desert, and he
remained in the desert for forty days, tempted by Satan. He was
among wild beasts, and the angels ministered to him.

After John had been arrested, Jesus came to Galilee
proclaiming the gospel of God: "This is the time of fulfillment.
The kingdom of God is at hand. Repent, and believe in the
gospel."

Communion Antiphon Mt 4: 4 One does not live by bread
alone, ◆ but by every word that comes forth from the
mouth of God.

Or: cf. Ps 91 (90): 4 The Lord will conceal you with his pinions, ◆
and under his wings you will trust.

SECOND SUNDAY OF LENT

Entrance Antiphon cf. Ps 27 (26): 8–9 Of you my heart has spoken:
Seek his face. ◆ It is your face, O Lord, that I seek; ◆ hide not
your face from me.

Or: cf. Ps 25 (24): 6, 2, 22 **Remember your compassion, O Lord, ◆ and your merciful love, for they are from of old. ◆ Let not our enemies exult over us. ◆ Redeem us, O God of Israel, from all our distress.**

First Reading Gen 22: 1–2, 9a, 10–13, 15–18 God put Abraham to the test. He called to him, "Abraham!" "Here I am!" he replied. Then God said: "Take your son Isaac, your only one, whom you love, and go to the land of Moriah. There you shall offer him up as a holocaust on a height that I will point out to you."

When they came to the place of which God had told him, Abraham built an altar there and arranged the wood on it. Then he reached out and took the knife to slaughter his son. But the LORD's messenger called to him from heaven, "Abraham, Abraham!" "Here I am!" he answered. "Do not lay your hand on the boy," said the messenger. "Do not do the least thing to him. I know now how devoted you are to God, since you did not withhold from me your own beloved son." As Abraham looked about, he spied a ram caught by its horns in the thicket. So he went and took the ram and offered it up as a holocaust in place of his son.

Again the LORD's messenger called to Abraham from heaven and said: "I swear by myself, declares the LORD, that because you acted as you did in not withholding from me your beloved son, I will bless you abundantly and make your descendants as countless as the stars of the sky and the sands of the seashore; your descendants shall take possession of the gates of their enemies, and in your descendants all the nations of the earth shall find blessing—all this because you obeyed my command."

Responsorial Psalm Ps 116: 10, 15, 16–17, 18–19   Joe Higginbotham

I believed, even when I said,
  "I am greatly afflicted."
Precious in the eyes of the LORD
  is the death of his faithful ones. ℟

O LORD, I am your servant;
  I am your servant, the son of your handmaid;
  you have loosed my bonds.
To you will I offer sacrifice of thanksgiving,
  and I will call upon the name of the LORD. ℟

My vows to the LORD I will pay
  in the presence of all his people,
In the courts of the house of the LORD,
  in your midst, O Jerusalem. ℟

Second Reading Rom 8: 31b–34 Brothers and sisters: If God is for
us, who can be against us? He who did not spare his own Son
but handed him over for us all, how will he not also give us
everything else along with him?
  Who will bring a charge against God's chosen ones? It is God
who acquits us, who will condemn? Christ Jesus it is who died—
or, rather, was raised—who also is at the right hand of God, who
indeed intercedes for us.

Verse Before the Gospel   cf. Mt 17: 5   Joe Higginbotham

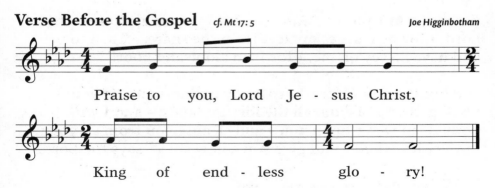

Praise to   you,   Lord   Je - sus   Christ,

King   of   end - less   glo - ry!

From the shining cloud the Father's voice is heard: / This is
my beloved Son, listen to him.

Gospel Mk 9: 2–10 Jesus took Peter, James, and John and led
them up a high mountain apart by themselves. And he was

transfigured before them, and his clothes became dazzling white, such as no fuller on earth could bleach them. Then Elijah appeared to them along with Moses, and they were conversing with Jesus. Then Peter said to Jesus in reply, "Rabbi, it is good that we are here! Let us make three tents: one for you, one for Moses, and one for Elijah." He hardly knew what to say, they were so terrified. Then a cloud came, casting a shadow over them; from the cloud came a voice, "This is my beloved Son. Listen to him." Suddenly, looking around, they no longer saw anyone but Jesus alone with them.

As they were coming down from the mountain, he charged them not to relate what they had seen to anyone, except when the Son of Man had risen from the dead. So they kept the matter to themselves, questioning what rising from the dead meant.

Communion Antiphon Mt 17: 5 This is my beloved Son, with whom I am well pleased; ✦ listen to him.

THIRD SUNDAY OF LENT

The readings given for Year A, page 111, may be used in place of these.

Entrance Antiphon cf. Ps 25 (24): 15–16 My eyes are always on the Lord, ✦ for he rescues my feet from the snare. ✦ Turn to me and have mercy on me, ✦ for I am alone and poor.

Or: cf. Ezekiel 36: 23–26 When I prove my holiness among you, ✦ I will gather you from all the foreign lands; ✦ and I will pour clean water upon you ✦ and cleanse you from all your impurities, ✦ and I will give you a new spirit, says the Lord.

First Reading Ex 20: 1–17 or 20: 1–3, 7–8, 12–17
For the shorter form, read only the parts in brackets.
[In those days, God delivered all these commandments: "I, the LORD, am your God, who brought you out of the land of Egypt, that place of slavery. You shall not have other gods besides me.]

You shall not carve idols for yourselves in the shape of anything in the sky above or on the earth below or in the waters beneath the earth; you shall not bow down before them or worship them. For I, the LORD, your God, am a jealous God, inflicting punishment for their fathers' wickedness on the children of those who hate me, down to the third and fourth generation; but bestowing mercy down to the thousandth generation on the children of those who love me and keep my commandments.

["You shall not take the name of the LORD, your God, in vain. For the LORD will not leave unpunished the one who takes his name in vain.

"Remember to keep holy the sabbath day.] Six days you may labor and do all your work, but the seventh day is the sabbath of the LORD, your God. No work may be done then either by you, or your son or daughter, or your male or female slave, or your beast, or by the alien who lives with you. In six days the LORD made the heavens and the earth, the sea and all that is in them; but on the seventh day he rested. That is why the LORD has blessed the sabbath day and made it holy.

["Honor your father and your mother, that you may have a long life in the land which the LORD, your God, is giving you.

You shall not kill.

You shall not commit adultery.

You shall not steal.

You shall not bear false witness against your neighbor.

You shall not covet your neighbor's house. You shall not covet your neighbor's wife, nor his male or female slave, nor his ox or ass, nor anything else that belongs to him."]

Responsorial Psalm   Ps 19: 8, 9, 10, 11   Joe Higginbotham

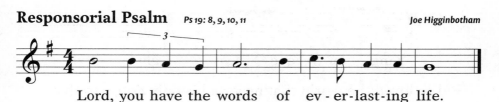

Lord, you have the words of ev - er-last-ing life.

The law of the LORD is perfect,
 refreshing the soul;
The decree of the LORD is trustworthy,
 giving wisdom to the simple. ℟

The precepts of the LORD are right,
    rejoicing the heart;
the command of the LORD is clear,
    enlightening the eye. ℟

The fear of the LORD is pure,
    enduring forever;
the ordinances of the LORD are true,
    all of them just. ℟

They are more precious than gold,
    than a heap of purest gold;
sweeter also than syrup
    or honey from the comb. ℟

Second Reading *1 Cor 1: 22–25* Brothers and sisters: Jews demand
signs and Greeks look for wisdom, but we proclaim Christ
crucified, a stumbling block to Jews and foolishness to Gentiles,
but to those who are called, Jews and Greeks alike, Christ the
power of God and the wisdom of God. For the foolishness of
God is wiser than human wisdom, and the weakness of God is
stronger than human strength.

Verse Before the Gospel   *Jn 3: 16*   Joe Higginbotham

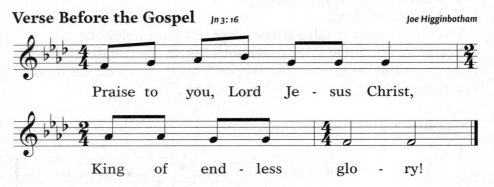

Praise to you, Lord Je - sus Christ,

King of end - less glo - ry!

God so loved the world that he gave his only Son, / so that
everyone who believes in him might have eternal life.

Gospel *Jn 2: 13–25* Since the Passover of the Jews was near, Jesus
went up to Jerusalem. He found in the temple area those who
sold oxen, sheep, and doves, as well as the money changers
seated there. He made a whip out of cords and drove them all

out of the temple area, with the sheep and oxen, and spilled the coins of the money changers and overturned their tables, and to those who sold doves he said, "Take these out of here, and stop making my Father's house a marketplace." His disciples recalled the words of Scripture, *Zeal for your house will consume me.* At this the Jews answered and said to him, "What sign can you show us for doing this?" Jesus answered and said to them, "Destroy this temple and in three days I will raise it up." The Jews said, "This temple has been under construction for forty-six years, and you will raise it up in three days?" But he was speaking about the temple of his body. Therefore, when he was raised from the dead, his disciples remembered that he had said this, and they came to believe the Scripture and the word Jesus had spoken.

While he was in Jerusalem for the feast of Passover, many began to believe in his name when they saw the signs he was doing. But Jesus would not trust himself to them because he knew them all, and did not need anyone to testify about human nature. He himself understood it well.

Communion Antiphon *cf. Ps 84 (83): 4-5* **The sparrow finds a home, ◆ and the swallow a nest for her young: ◆ by your altars, O Lord of hosts, my King and my God. ◆ Blessed are they who dwell in your house, ◆ for ever singing your praise.**

FOURTH SUNDAY OF LENT

The readings given for Year A, page 115, may be used in place of these.

Entrance Antiphon *cf. Is 66: 10-11* **Rejoice, Jerusalem, and all who love her. ◆ Be joyful, all who were in mourning; ◆ exult and be satisfied at her consoling breast.**

First Reading *2 Chr 36: 14-16, 19-23* In those days, all the princes of Judah, the priests, and the people added infidelity to infidelity, practicing all the abominations of the nations and polluting the LORD's temple which he had consecrated in Jerusalem.

Early and often did the LORD, the God of their fathers, send his messengers to them, for he had compassion on his people and his dwelling place. But they mocked the messengers of God, despised his warnings, and scoffed at his prophets, until the anger of the LORD against his people was so inflamed that there was no remedy. Their enemies burnt the house of God, tore down the walls of Jerusalem, set all its palaces afire, and destroyed all its precious objects. Those who escaped the sword were carried captive to Babylon, where they became servants of the king of the Chaldeans and his sons until the kingdom of the Persians came to power. All this was to fulfill the word of the LORD spoken by Jeremiah: "Until the land has retrieved its lost sabbaths, during all the time it lies waste it shall have rest while seventy years are fulfilled."

In the first year of Cyrus, king of Persia, in order to fulfill the word of the LORD spoken by Jeremiah, the LORD inspired King Cyrus of Persia to issue this proclamation throughout his kingdom, both by word of mouth and in writing: "Thus says Cyrus, king of Persia: All the kingdoms of the earth the LORD, the God of heaven, has given to me, and he has also charged me to build him a house in Jerusalem, which is in Judah. Whoever, therefore, among you belongs to any part of his people, let him go up, and may his God be with him!"

Responsorial Psalm   Ps 137: 1–2, 3, 4–5, 6   *Bill Svarda*

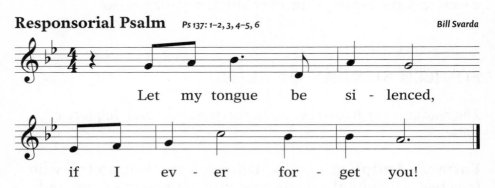

Let my tongue be si - lenced, if I ev - er for - get you!

By the streams of Babylon
  we sat and wept
  when we remembered Zion.
On the aspens of that land
  we hung up our harps. ℟

For there our captors asked of us
    the lyrics of our songs,
And our despoilers urged us to be joyous:
    "Sing for us the songs of Zion!"   ℟

How could we sing a song of the LORD
    in a foreign land?
If I forget you, Jerusalem,
    may my right hand be forgotten!   ℟

May my tongue cleave to my palate
    if I remember you not,
If I place not Jerusalem
    ahead of my joy.   ℟

Second Reading   *Eph 2: 4–10* Brothers and sisters: God, who is rich in mercy, because of the great love he had for us, even when we were dead in our transgressions, brought us to life with Christ—by grace you have been saved—, raised us up with him, and seated us with him in the heavens in Christ Jesus, that in the ages to come he might show the immeasurable riches of his grace in his kindness to us in Christ Jesus. For by grace you have been saved through faith, and this is not from you; it is the gift of God; it is not from works, so no one may boast. For we are his handiwork, created in Christ Jesus for the good works that God has prepared in advance, that we should live in them.

Verse Before the Gospel   *Jn 3: 16*   Jim Hughes

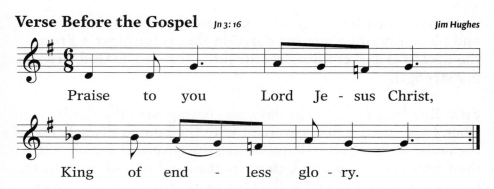

Praise to you Lord Je - sus Christ,

King of end - less glo - ry.

God so loved the world that he gave his only Son, / so everyone who believes in him might have eternal life.

Gospel Jn 3: 14-21 Jesus said to Nicodemus: "Just as Moses lifted up the serpent in the desert, so must the Son of Man be lifted up, so that everyone who believes in him may have eternal life."

For God so loved the world that he gave his only Son, so that everyone who believes in him might not perish but might have eternal life. For God did not send his Son into the world to condemn the world, but that the world might be saved through him. Whoever believes in him will not be condemned, but whoever does not believe has already been condemned, because he has not believed in the name of the only Son of God. And this is the verdict, that the light came into the world, but people preferred darkness to light, because their works were evil. For everyone who does wicked things hates the light and does not come toward the light, so that his works might not be exposed. But whoever lives the truth comes to the light, so that his works may be clearly seen as done in God.

Communion Antiphon cf. Ps 122 (121): 3-4 **Jerusalem is built as a city bonded as one together. ◆ It is there that the tribes go up, the tribes of the Lord, ◆ to praise the name of the Lord.**

FIFTH SUNDAY OF LENT

The readings for Year A, page 119, may be used in place of these.

Entrance Antiphon cf. Ps 43 (42): 1-2 **Give me justice, O God, ◆ and plead my cause against a nation that is faithless. ◆ From the deceitful and cunning rescue me, ◆ for you, O God, are my strength.**

First Reading Jer 31: 31-34 The days are coming, says the LORD, when I will make a new covenant with the house of Israel and the house of Judah. It will not be like the covenant I made with their fathers the day I took them by the hand to lead them forth from the land of Egypt; for they broke my covenant, and I had to show myself their master, says the LORD. But this is the covenant that I will make with the house of Israel after those days, says the LORD. I will place my law within them and write it upon their hearts; I will be their God, and they shall be my people. No longer will they have need to teach their friends and relatives how to know the LORD. All, from least to greatest, shall know me, says the LORD, for I will forgive their evildoing and remember their sin no more.

Responsorial Psalm   Ps 51: 3–4, 12–13, 14–15   Don Fishel

Cre - ate a clean   heart in me, O   God.

Have mercy on me, O God, in your goodness;
    in the greatness of your compassion wipe out my offense.
Thoroughly wash me from my guilt
    and of my sin cleanse me. ℟

A clean heart create for me, O God,
    and a steadfast spirit renew within me.
Cast me not out from your presence,
    and your Holy Spirit take not from me. ℟

Give me back the joy of your salvation,
    and a willing spirit sustain in me.
I will teach transgressors your ways,
    and sinners shall return to you. ℟

Second Reading Heb 5: 7–9 In the days when Christ Jesus was in the flesh, he offered prayers and supplications with loud cries and tears to the one who was able to save him from death, and he was heard because of his reverence. Son though he was, he learned obedience from what he suffered; and when he was made perfect, he became the source of eternal salvation for all who obey him.

Verse Before the Gospel Jn 12: 26

Jim Hughes

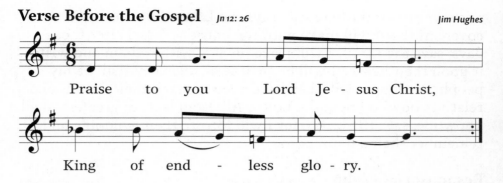

Praise to you Lord Je - sus Christ,

King of end - less glo - ry.

Whoever serves me must follow me, says the Lord; / and where I am, there also will my servant be.

Gospel Jn 12: 20-33 Some Greeks who had come to worship at the Passover Feast came to Philip, who was from Bethsaida in Galilee, and asked him, "Sir, we would like to see Jesus." Philip went and told Andrew; then Andrew and Philip went and told Jesus. Jesus answered them, "The hour has come for the Son of Man to be glorified. Amen, amen, I say to you, unless a grain of wheat falls to the ground and dies, it remains just a grain of wheat; but if it dies, it produces much fruit. Whoever loves his life loses it, and whoever hates his life in this world will preserve it for eternal life. Whoever serves me must follow me, and where I am, there also will my servant be. The Father will honor whoever serves me.

"I am troubled now. Yet what should I say? 'Father, save me from this hour'? But it was for this purpose that I came to this hour. Father, glorify your name." Then a voice came from heaven, "I have glorified it and will glorify it again." The crowd there heard it and said it was thunder; but others said, "An angel has spoken to him." Jesus answered and said, "This voice did not come for my sake but for yours. Now is the time of judgment on this world; now the ruler of this world will be driven out. And when I am lifted up from the earth, I will draw everyone to myself." He said this indicating the kind of death he would die.

Communion Antiphon Jn 12: 24 Amen, Amen I say to you: **Unless a grain of wheat ◆ falls to the ground and dies, it remains a single grain. ◆ But if it dies, it bears much fruit.**

PALM SUNDAY OF THE PASSION OF THE LORD

On this day the Church recalls the entrance of Christ the Lord into Jerusalem to accomplish his Paschal Mystery. Accordingly, the memorial of this entrance of the Lord takes place at all Masses, by means of the Procession or the Solemn Entrance before the principal Mass or the Simple Entrance before other Masses. The Solemn Entrance, but not the Procession, may be repeated before other Masses that are usually celebrated with a large gathering of people.

❖ The Commemoration of the Lord's ❖ Entrance Into Jerusalem

FIRST FORM: THE PROCESSION

At an appropriate hour, a gathering takes place at a smaller church or other suitable place other than inside the church to which the procession will go. The faithful hold branches in their hands.

Wearing the red sacred vestments as for Mass, the Priest and the Deacon, accompanied by other ministers, approach the place where the people are gathered. Meanwhile, the following antiphon or another appropriate chant is sung.

Antiphon Mt 21:9 **Hosanna to the Son of David; ◆ blessed is he who comes in the name of the Lord, ◆ the King of Israel. ◆ Hosanna in the highest.**

The Priest and people sign themselves, while the Priest says: In the name of the Father, and of the Son, and of the Holy Spirit. *Then he greets the people in the usual way. A brief address is given, in which the faithful are invited to participate actively and consciously in the celebration of this day, in these or similar words:*
   Dear brethren (brothers and sisters),
   since the beginning of Lent until now
   we have prepared our hearts by penance and charitable works.
   Today we gather together to herald with the whole Church

the beginning of the celebration
of our Lord's Paschal Mystery,
that is to say, of his Passion and Resurrection.
For it was to accomplish this mystery
that he entered his own city of Jerusalem.
Therefore, with all faith and devotion,
let us commemorate
the Lord's entry into the city for our salvation,
following in his footsteps,
so that, being made by his grace partakers of the Cross,
we may have a share also in his Resurrection and in his life.

After the address, the Priest says one of the following prayers with hands extended.

Let us pray.
Almighty ever-living God,
sanctify + these branches with your blessing,
that we, who follow Christ the King in exultation,
may reach the eternal Jerusalem through him.
Who lives and reigns for ever and ever. ℟ **Amen.**

Or:

Increase the faith of those who place their hope in you, O God,
and graciously hear the prayers of those who call on you,
that we, who today hold high these branches
to hail Christ in his triumph,
may bear fruit for you by good works accomplished in him.
Who lives and reigns for ever and ever. ℟ **Amen.**

The Priest sprinkles the branches with holy water without saying anything. Then a Deacon or, if there is no Deacon, a Priest, proclaims in the usual way the Gospel concerning the Lord's entrance according to one of the four Gospels.

Gospel Mk 11: 1–10 When Jesus and his disciples drew near to Jerusalem, to Bethphage and Bethany at the Mount of Olives, he sent two of his disciples and said to them, "Go into the village opposite you, and immediately on entering it, you will find a colt tethered on which no one has ever sat. Untie it and bring it here.

If anyone should say to you, 'Why are you doing this?' reply,
'The Master has need of it and will send it back here at once.'"
So they went off and found a colt tethered at a gate outside on
the street, and they untied it. Some of the bystanders said to
them, "What are you doing, untying the colt?" They answered
them just as Jesus had told them to, and they permitted them
to do it. So they brought the colt to Jesus and put their cloaks
over it. And he sat on it. Many people spread their cloaks on the
road, and others spread leafy branches that they had cut from
the fields. Those preceding him as well as those following kept
crying out:
  "Hosanna!
    Blessed is he who comes in the name of the Lord!
    Blessed is the kingdom of our father David that is to come!
  Hosanna in the highest!"

Or: Jn 12:12-16 When the great crowd that had come to the feast
heard that Jesus was coming to Jerusalem, they took palm
branches and went out to meet him, and cried out:
  "Hosanna!
  Blessed is he who comes in the name of the Lord,
    the king of Israel."
Jesus found an ass and sat upon it, as is written:
  Fear no more, O daughter Zion;
  see, your king comes, seated upon an ass's colt.
His disciples did not understand this at first, but when Jesus had
been glorified they remembered that these things were written
about him and that they had done this for him.

After the Gospel, a brief homily may be given.

Then, to begin the procession, an invitation may be given by a
Priest or a Deacon or a lay minister, in these or similar words:
  Dear brethren (brothers and sisters),
  like the crowds who acclaimed Jesus in Jerusalem,
  let us go forth in peace.

Or: Let us go forth in peace.
In this latter case, all respond: **In the name of Christ. Amen.**

The procession to the church where Mass will be celebrated then sets off in the usual way. As the procession moves forward, the following or other suitable chants in honor of Christ the King are sung by the choir and people.

Antiphon 1 **The children of the Hebrews, carrying olive branches,** ◆ **went to meet the Lord, crying out and saying:** ◆ **Hosanna in the highest.**

If appropriate, this antiphon is repeated between the strophes of the following Psalm.

Psalm 24 (23)
　　The LORD's is the earth and its fullness,
　　the world, and those who dwell in it.
　　It is he who set it on the seas;
　　on the rivers he made it firm.　　　　(*The antiphon is repeated.*)

　　Who shall climb the mountain of the LORD?
　　The clean of hands and pure of heart,
　　whose soul is not set on vain things,
　　who has not sworn deceitful words. (*The antiphon is repeated.*)

　　Blessings from the LORD shall he receive,
　　and right reward from the God who saves him.
　　Such are the people who seek him,
　　who seek the face of the God of Jacob.
　　　　　　　　　　　　　　　　　(*The antiphon is repeated.*)

　　O gates, lift high your heads;
　　grow higher, ancient doors.
　　Let him enter, the king of glory!
　　Who is this king of glory?
　　The LORD, the mighty, the valiant;
　　the LORD, the valiant in war.　　　(*The antiphon is repeated.*)

　　O gates, lift high your heads;
　　grow higher, ancient doors.

Let him enter, the king of glory!
Who is this king of glory?
He, the LORD of hosts,
he is the king of glory.   (*The antiphon is repeated.*)

Antiphon 2   **The children of the Hebrews spread their
garments on the road, ◆ crying out and saying: Hosanna
to the Son of David; ◆ blessed is he who comes in the name
of the Lord.**

*If appropriate, this antiphon is repeated between the strophes of the
following Psalm.*

Psalm 47 (46)
All peoples, clap your hands.
Cry to God with shouts of joy!
For the LORD, the Most high, is awesome,
the great king over all the earth.   (*The antiphon is repeated.*)

He humbles peoples under us
and nations under our feet.
Our heritage he chose for us,
the pride of Jacob whom he loves.
God goes up with shouts of joy.
The LORD goes up with trumpet blast.
                                      (*The antiphon is repeated.*)

Sing praise for God; sing praise!
Sing praise to king; sing praise!
God is king of all earth.
Sing praise with all your skill.   (*The antiphon is repeated.*)

God reigns over the nations.
God sits upon his holy throne.
The princes of the peoples are assembled
with the people of the God of Abraham.
The rulers of the earth belong to God,
who is greatly exalted.   (*The antiphon is repeated.*)

Hymn to Christ the King

Chorus:
Glory and honor and praise be to you, Christ, King and
    Redeemer,
to whom young children cried out loving Hosannas with joy.

All repeat:
**Glory and honor and praise be to you, Christ, King
    and Redeemer,**
**to whom young children cried out loving
    Hosannas with joy.**

Chorus:
Israel's King are you, King David's magnificent offspring;
you are the ruler who come blest in the name of the Lord.
All repeat: **Glory and honor ...**

Chorus:
Heavenly hosts on high unite in singing your praises;
men and women on earth and all creation join in.
All repeat: **Glory and honor ...**

Chorus:
Bearing branches of palm, Hebrews came crowding to
    greet you;
see how with prayers and hymns we come to pay you
    our vows.
All repeat: **Glory and honor ...**

Chorus:
They offered gifts of praise to you, so near to your Passion;
see how we sing this song now to you reigning on high.
All repeat: **Glory and honor ...**

Chorus:
Those you were pleased to accept; now accept our gifts of
    devotion,
good and merciful King, lover of all that is good.
All repeat: **Glory and honor ...**

As the procession enters the church, there is sung the following responsory or another chant, which should speak of the Lord's entrance.

℟ **As the Lord entered the holy city, the children of the Hebrews proclaimed the resurrection of life. Waving their branches of palm, they cried: Hosanna in the Highest.**

℣ When the people heard that Jesus was coming to Jerusalem, they went out to meet him.

℟ **Waving their branches of palm, they cried: Hosanna in the Highest.**

When the Priest arrives at the altar, he venerates it, and if appropriate, incenses it. Omitting the other Introductory Rites of the Mass and, if appropriate, the Kyrie (Lord, have mercy), *he says the Collect of the Mass, and then continues the Mass in the usual way.*

SECOND FORM: THE SOLEMN ENTRANCE

When a procession outside the church cannot take place, the entrance of the Lord is celebrated inside the church by means of a Solemn Entrance before the principal Mass.

Holding branches in their hands, the faithful gather either outside, in front of the church door, or inside the church itself. The Priest and ministers and a representative group of the faithful go to a suitable place in the church outside the sanctuary, where at least the greater part of the faithful can see the rite.

While the Priest approaches the appointed place, the antiphon Hosanna *(page 329) or another appropriate chant is sung. Then the blessing of branches and the proclamation of the Gospel of the Lord's entrance into Jerusalem take place as in the First Form. After the Gospel, the Priest processes solemnly with the ministers and the representative group of the faithful through the church to the sanctuary, while the responsory,* As the Lord entered, *or another appropriate chant is sung.*

Arriving at the altar, the Priest venerates it. He then goes to the chair and, omitting the Introductory Rites of the Mass and, if appropriate, the Kyrie (Lord, have mercy), *he says the Collect of the Mass, and then continues the Mass in the usual way.*

THIRD FORM: THE SIMPLE ENTRANCE

At all other Masses of this Sunday at which the Solemn Entrance is not held, the memorial of the Lord's entrance into Jerusalem takes place by means of a Simple Entrance.

While the Priest proceeds to the altar, the Entrance Antiphon with its Psalm or another chant on the same theme is sung. Arriving at the altar, the Priest venerates it and goes to the chair. After the Sign of the Cross, he greets the people and continues the Mass in the usual way.

Entrance Antiphon *cf. Jn 12: 1, 12–13; Ps 24 (23): 9–10* Six days before the Passover, / when the Lord came into the city of Jerusalem, / the children ran to meet him; / in their hands they carried palm branches / and with a loud voice cried out: * **Hosanna in the highest! ◆ Blessed are you, who have come in your abundant mercy!**

O gates, lift high your heads; / grow higher, ancient doors. / Let him enter, the king of glory! / Who is this king of glory? / He, the Lord of hosts, he is the king of glory.   * **Hosanna in the highest! ◆ Blessed are you, who have come in your abundant mercy!**

❖ At the Mass ❖

First Reading *Is 50: 4–7*
The Lord GOD has given me
  a well-trained tongue,
that I might know how to speak to the weary
  a word that will rouse them.
Morning after morning

he opens my ear that I may hear;
and I have not rebelled,
    have not turned back.
I gave my back to those who beat me,
    my cheeks to those who plucked my beard;
my face I did not shield
    from buffets and spitting.

The Lord GOD is my help,
    therefore I am not disgraced;
I have set my face like flint,
    knowing that I shall not be put to shame.

Responsorial Psalm   *Ps 22: 8–9, 17–18, 19–20, 23–24*   *Steve Harmon*

My God, my God, why have You a - ban-doned me?

All who see me scoff at me;
    they mock me with parted lips, they wag their heads:
"He relied on the LORD; let him deliver him,
    let him rescue him, if he loves him." ℟

Indeed, many dogs surround me,
    a pack of evildoers closes in upon me;
They have pierced my hands and my feet;
    I can count all my bones. ℟

They divide my garments among them,
    and for my vesture they cast lots.
But you, O LORD, be not far from me;
    O my help, hasten to aid me. ℟

I will proclaim your name to my brethren;
    in the midst of the assembly I will praise you:
"You who fear the LORD, praise him;
    all you descendants of Jacob, give glory to him;
    revere him, all you descendants of Israel!" ℟

Second Reading *Phil 2: 6–11*

Christ Jesus, though he was in the form of God,
   did not regard equality with God
   something to be grasped.
Rather, he emptied himself,
   taking the form of a slave,
   coming in human likeness;
   and found human in appearance,
   he humbled himself,
   becoming obedient to the point of death,
   even death on a cross.
Because of this, God greatly exalted him
   and bestowed on him the name
   which is above every name,
   that at the name of Jesus
   every knee should bend,
   of those in heaven and on earth and under the earth,
   and every tongue confess that
   Jesus Christ is Lord,
   to the glory of God the Father.

Verse Before the Gospel *Phil 2: 8–9*   Jim Hughes

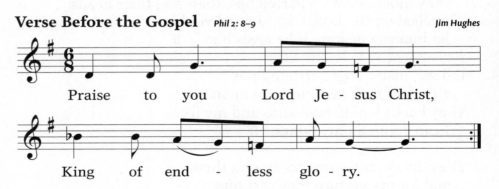

Praise to you Lord Je - sus Christ,

King of end - less glo - ry.

Christ became obedient to the point of death, / even death
on a cross. / Because of this, God greatly exalted him / and
bestowed on him the name which is above every name.

Gospel *Mk 14: 1–15: 47 or 15: 1–39*

*For the shorter form, read only the parts in brackets. The shorter
form begins on page 342. The symbols of the following passion
narrative represent Christ (+), the narrator (N), the voice (V), and
the crowd (C).*

N. The Passion of our Lord Jesus Christ according to Mark.

The Passover and the Feast of Unleavened Bread were to take place in two days' time. So the chief priests and the scribes were seeking a way to arrest him by treachery and put him to death. They said, **V.** "Not during the festival, for fear that there may be a riot among the people."

N. When he was in Bethany reclining at table in the house of Simon the leper, a woman came with an alabaster jar of perfumed oil, costly genuine spikenard. She broke the alabaster jar and poured it on his head. There were some who were indignant. **V.** "Why has there been this waste of perfumed oil? It could have been sold for more than three hundred days' wages and the money given to the poor." **N.** They were infuriated with her. Jesus said, ✝ "Let her alone. Why do you make trouble for her? She has done a good thing for me. The poor you will always have with you, and whenever you wish you can do good to them, but you will not always have me. She has done what she could. She has anticipated anointing my body for burial. Amen, I say to you, wherever the gospel is proclaimed to the whole world, what she has done will be told in memory of her."

N. Then Judas Iscariot, one of the Twelve, went off to the chief priests to hand him over to them. When they heard him they were pleased and promised to pay him money. Then he looked for an opportunity to hand him over.

On the first day of the Feast of Unleavened Bread, when they sacrificed the Passover lamb, his disciples said to him, **V.** "Where do you want us to go and prepare for you to eat the Passover?" **N.** He sent two of his disciples and said to them, ✝ "Go into the city and a man will meet you, carrying a jar of water. Follow him. Wherever he enters, say to the master of the house, 'The Teacher says, "Where is my guest Room where I may eat the Passover with my disciples?"' Then he will show you a large upper room furnished and ready. Make the preparations for us there." **N.** The disciples then went off, entered the city, and found it just as he had told them; and they prepared the Passover.

When it was evening, he came with the Twelve. And as they reclined at table and were eating, Jesus said, ✝ "Amen, I say to you, one of you will betray me, one who is eating with me." **N.** They began to be distressed and to say to him, one by one, **V.** "Surely it is not I?" **N.** He said to them, ✝ "One of the

Twelve, the one who dips with me into the dish. For the Son of Man indeed goes, as it is written of him, but woe to that man by whom the Son of Man is betrayed. It would be better for that man if he had never been born."

N. While they were eating, he took bread, said the blessing, broke it, and gave it to them, and said, ✝ "Take it; this is my body." **N.** Then he took a cup, gave thanks, and gave it to them, and they all drank from it. He said to them, ✝ "This is my blood of the covenant, which will be shed for many. Amen, I say to you, I shall not drink again the fruit of the vine until the day when I drink it new in the kingdom of God." **N.** Then, after singing a hymn, they went out to the Mount of Olives.

Then Jesus said to them, ✝ "All of you will have your faith shaken, for it is written:

I will strike the shepherd,
  and the sheep will be dispersed.

But after I have been raised up, I shall go before you to Galilee." **N.** Peter said to him, **V.** "Even though all should have their faith shaken, mine will not be." **N.** Then Jesus said to him, ✝ "Amen, I say to you, this very night before the cock crows twice you will deny me three times." **N.** But he vehemently replied, **V.** "Even though I should have to die with you, I will not deny you." **N.** And they all spoke similarly.

Then they came to a place named Gethsemane, and he said to his disciples, ✝ "Sit here while I pray." **N.** He took with him Peter, James, and John, and began to be troubled and distressed. Then he said to them, ✝ "My soul is sorrowful even to death. Remain here and keep watch." **N.** He advanced a little and fell to the ground and prayed that if it were possible the hour might pass by him; he said, ✝ "Abba, Father, all things are possible to you. Take this cup away from me, but not what I will but what you will." **N.** When he returned he found them asleep. He said to Peter, ✝ "Simon, are you asleep? Could you not keep watch for one hour? Watch and pray that you may not undergo the test. The spirit is willing but the flesh is weak." **N.** Withdrawing again, he prayed, saying the same thing. Then he returned once more and found them asleep, for they could not keep their eyes open and did not know what to answer him. He returned a third time and said to them, ✝ "Are you still sleeping and taking your rest? It is enough. The hour has come. Behold, the Son of Man is to be handed over to sinners. Get up, let us go. See, my betrayer is at hand."

N. Then, while he was still speaking, Judas, one of the Twelve, arrived, accompanied by a crowd with swords and clubs who had come from the chief priests, the scribes, and the elders. His betrayer had arranged a signal with them, saying, **V.** "The man I shall kiss is the one; arrest him and lead him away securely." **N.** He came and immediately went over to him and said, **V.** "Rabbi." **N.** And he kissed him. At this they laid hands on him and arrested him. One of the bystanders drew his sword, struck the high priest's servant, and cut off his ear. Jesus said to them in reply, **✝** "Have you come out as against a robber, with swords and clubs, to seize me? Day after day I was with you teaching in the temple area, yet you did not arrest me; but that the Scriptures may be fulfilled." **N.** And they all left him and fled. Now a young man followed him wearing nothing but a linen cloth about his body. They seized him, but he left the cloth behind and ran off naked.

They led Jesus away to the high priest, and all the chief priests and the elders and the scribes came together. Peter followed him at a distance into the high priest's courtyard and was seated with the guards, warming himself at the fire. The chief priests and the entire Sanhedrin kept trying to obtain testimony against Jesus in order to put him to death, but they found none. Many gave false witness against him, but their testimony did not agree. Some took the stand and testified falsely against him, alleging, **C. "We heard him say, 'I will destroy this temple made with hands and within three days I will build another not made with hands.'"** **N.** Even so their testimony did not agree. The high priest rose before the assembly and questioned Jesus, saying, **V.** "Have you no answer? What are these men testifying against you?" **N.** But he was silent and answered nothing. Again the high priest asked him and said to him, **V.** "Are you the Christ, the son of the Blessed One?" **N.** Then Jesus answered, **✝** "I am; and 'you will see the Son of Man
seated at the right hand of the Power
and coming with the clouds of heaven.'"
N. At that the high priest tore his garments and said, **V.** "What

further need have we of witnesses? You have heard the blasphemy. What do you think?" **N.** They all condemned him as deserving to die. Some began to spit on him. They blindfolded him and struck him and said to him, **c.** "**Prophesy!**" **N.** And the guards greeted him with blows.

While Peter was below in the courtyard, one of the high priest's maids came along. Seeing Peter warming himself, she looked intently at him and said, **c.** "**You too were with the Nazarene, Jesus.**" **N.** But he denied it saying, **v.** "I neither know nor understand what you are talking about." **N.** So he went out into the outer court. Then the cock crowed. The maid saw him and began again to say to the bystanders, **c.** "**This man is one of them.**" **N.** Once again he denied it. A little later the bystanders said to Peter once more, **c.** "**Surely you are one of them; for you too are a Galilean.**" **N.** He began to curse and to swear, **v.** "I do not know this man about whom you are talking." **N.** And immediately a cock crowed a second time. Then Peter remembered the word that Jesus had said to him, "Before the cock crows twice you will deny me three times." He broke down and wept.

(The shorter form begins here)
[As soon as morning came, the chief priests with the elders and the scribes, that is, the whole Sanhedrin, held a council. They bound Jesus, led him away, and handed him over to Pilate. Pilate questioned him, **v.** "Are you the king of the Jews?" **N.** He said to him in reply, **+** "You say so." **N.** The chief priests accused him of many things. Again Pilate questioned him, **v.** "Have you no answer? See how many things they accuse you of." **N.** Jesus gave him no further answer, so that Pilate was amazed.

Now on the occasion of the feast he used to release to them one prisoner whom they requested. A man called Barabbas was then in prison along with the rebels who had committed murder in a rebellion. The crowd came forward and began to ask him to do for them as he was accustomed. Pilate answered, **v.** "Do you want me to release to you the king of the Jews?" **N.** For he knew that it was out of envy that the chief priests had handed him over. But the chief priests stirred up the crowd to have him release Barabbas for them instead. Pilate again said to them in reply, **V.** "Then what do you want me to do with the man you call the king of the Jews?" **N.** They shouted again, **C. "Crucify him."** **N.** Pilate said to them, **V.** "Why? What evil has he done?" **N.** They only shouted the louder, **C. "Crucify him."** **N.** So Pilate, wishing to satisfy the crowd, released Barabbas to them and, after he had Jesus scourged, handed him over to be crucified.

The soldiers led him away inside the palace, that is, the praetorium, and assembled the whole cohort. They clothed him in purple and, weaving a crown of thorns, placed it on him. They began to salute him with, **C. "Hail, King of the Jews!"** **N.** and kept striking his head with a reed and spitting upon him. They knelt before him in homage. And when they had mocked him, they stripped him of the purple cloak, dressed him in his own clothes, and led him out to crucify him.

They pressed into service a passer-by, Simon, a Cyrenian, who was coming in from the country, the father of Alexander and Rufus, to carry his cross.

They brought him to the place of Golgotha—which is translated Place of the Skull—. They gave him wine drugged with myrrh, but he did not take it. Then they crucified him and divided his garments by casting lots for them to see what each should take. It was nine o'clock in the morning when they crucified him. The inscription of the charge against him read, "The King of the Jews." With him they crucified two revolutionaries, one on his right and one on his left. Those passing by reviled him, shaking their heads and saying, **C. "Aha! You who would destroy the Temple and rebuild it in three days, save yourself by coming down from the cross."** **N.** Likewise the chief priests, with the scribes, mocked him among themselves and said, **C. "He saved others; he cannot save himself. Let the Christ, the King of Israel, come down now from the Cross that we may see and believe."** **N.** Those who were crucified with him also kept abusing him.

At noon darkness came over the whole land until three in the afternoon. And at three o'clock Jesus cried out in a loud voice, ✝ *"Eloi, Eloi, lema sabachthani?"* **N.** which is translated, ✝ "My God, my God, why have you forsaken me?" **N.** Some of the bystanders who heard it said, **C. "Look, he is calling Elijah."** **N.** One of them ran, soaked a sponge with wine, put it on a reed and gave it to him to drink saying, **v.** "Wait, let us see if Elijah comes to take him down." **N.** Jesus gave a loud cry and breathed his last.

Here all kneel and pause for a short time.

The veil of the sanctuary was torn in two from top to bottom. When the centurion who stood facing him saw how he breathed his last he said, **v.** "Truly this man was the Son of God!"] **N.** There were also women looking on from a distance. Among them were Mary Magdalene, Mary the mother of the younger James and of Joses, and Salome. These women had followed him when he was in Galilee and ministered to him. There were also many other women who had come up with him to Jerusalem.

When it was already evening, since it was the day of preparation, the day before the sabbath, Joseph of Arimathea, a distinguished member of the council, who was himself awaiting the kingdom of God, came and courageously went to Pilate and asked for the body of Jesus. Pilate was amazed that he was already dead. He summoned the centurion and asked him if Jesus had already died. And when he learned of it from the centurion, he gave the body to Joseph. Having bought a linen cloth, he took him down, wrapped him in the linen cloth, and laid him in a tomb that had been hewn out of the rock. Then he rolled a stone against the entrance to the tomb. Mary Magdalene and Mary the mother of Joses watched where he was laid.

Communion Antiphon Mt 26: 42 **Father, if this chalice cannot pass without my drinking it, ◆ your will be done.**

The readings for the Sacred Paschal Triduum begin on page 669.

Easter † YEAR B

The readings for Easter Sunday can be found on page 740.

SECOND SUNDAY OF EASTER

DIVINE MERCY SUNDAY

Entrance Antiphon 1 Pt 2: 2 Like newborn infants, you must long for the pure, spiritual milk, ♦ that in him you may grow to salvation, alleluia.

Or: 4 Esdras 2: 36–37 Receive the joy of your glory, giving thanks to God, ♦ who has called you into the heavenly kingdom, alleluia.

First Reading Acts 4: 32–35 The community of believers was of one heart and mind, and no one claimed that any of his possessions was his own, but they had everything in common. With great power the apostles bore witness to the resurrection of the Lord Jesus, and great favor was accorded them all. There was no needy person among them, for those who owned property or houses would sell them, bring the proceeds of the sale, and put them at the feet of the apostles, and they were distributed to each according to need.

Responsorial Psalm   Ps 118: 2–4, 13–15, 22–24   based on ICH WILL DICH LIEBEN

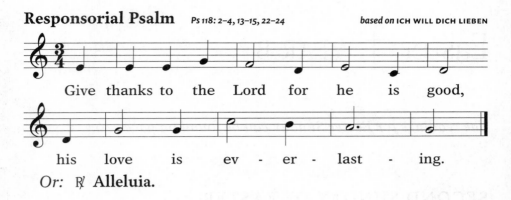

Give thanks to the Lord for he is good,
his love is ev - er - last - ing.

Or: ℟ **Alleluia.**

Let the house of Israel say,
  "His mercy endures forever."
Let the house of Aaron say,
  "His mercy endures forever."
Let those who fear the LORD say,
  "His mercy endures forever." ℟

I was hard pressed and was falling,
  but the LORD helped me.
My strength and my courage is the LORD,
  and he has been my savior.
The joyful shout of victory
  in the tents of the just. ℟

The stone which the builders rejected
  has become the cornerstone.
By the LORD has this been done;
  it is wonderful in our eyes.
This is the day the LORD has made;
  let us be glad and rejoice in it. ℟

Second Reading 1 Jn 5: 1–6 Beloved: Everyone who believes that
Jesus is the Christ is begotten by God, and everyone who loves
the Father loves also the one begotten by him. In this way we
know that we love the children of God when we love God
and obey his commandments. For the love of God is this, that
we keep his commandments. And his commandments are not
burdensome, for whoever is begotten by God conquers the
world. And the victory that conquers the world is our faith.

Who indeed is the victor over the world but the one who
believes that Jesus is the Son of God?

This is the one who came through water and blood, Jesus
Christ, not by water alone, but by water and blood. The Spirit is
the one that testifies, and the Spirit is truth.

Alleluia   *Jn 20: 29*   *Laura Lea Duckworth*

Al - le - lu - ia, al-le-lu - ia.

Al - le - lu - ia, al-le-lu - ia.

You believe in me, Thomas, because you have seen me, says
the Lord; / Blessed are they who have not seen me, but still
believe!   **Alleluia, alleluia.**

Gospel *Jn 20: 19-31* On the evening of that first day of the week,
when the doors were locked, where the disciples were, for fear of
the Jews, Jesus came and stood in their midst and said to them,
"Peace be with you." When he had said this, he showed them
his hands and his side. The disciples rejoiced when they saw
the Lord. Jesus said to them again "Peace be with you. As the
Father has sent me, so I send you." And when he had said this,
he breathed on them and said to them, "Receive the Holy Spirit.
Whose sins you forgive are forgiven them, and whose sins you
retain are retained."

Thomas, called Didymus, one of the Twelve, was not with
them when Jesus came. So the other disciples said to him, "We
have seen the Lord." But he said to them, "Unless I see the mark
of the nails in his hands and put my finger into the nailmarks
and put my hand into his side, I will not believe."

Now a week later his disciples were again inside and Thomas
was with them. Jesus came, although the doors were locked, and
stood in their midst and said, "Peace be with you." Then he said
to Thomas, "Put your finger here and see my hands, and bring
your hand and put it into my side, and do not be unbelieving,
but believe." Thomas answered and said to him, "My Lord and

my God!" Jesus said to him, "Have you come to believe because you have seen me? Blessed are those who have not seen and have believed."

Now, Jesus did many other signs in the presence of his disciples that are not written in this book. But these are written that you may come to believe that Jesus is the Christ, the Son of God, and that through this belief you may have life in his name.

Communion Antiphon *cf. Jn 20: 27* **Bring your hand and feel the place of the nails, ◆ and do not be unbelieving but believing, alleluia.**

THIRD SUNDAY OF EASTER

Entrance Antiphon *cf. Ps 66 (65): 1–2* **Cry out with joy to God, all the earth; ◆ O sing to the glory of his name. ◆ O render him glorious praise, alleluia.**

First Reading *Acts 3: 13–15, 17–19* Peter said to the people: "The God of Abraham, the God of Isaac, and the God of Jacob, the God of our fathers, has glorified his servant Jesus, whom you handed over and denied in Pilate's presence when he had decided to release him. You denied the Holy and Righteous One and asked that a murderer be released to you. The author of life you put to death, but God raised him from the dead; of this we are witnesses. Now I know, brothers, that you acted out of ignorance, just as your leaders did; but God has thus brought to fulfillment what he had announced beforehand through the mouth of all the prophets, that his Christ would suffer. Repent, therefore, and be converted, that your sins may be wiped away."

Responsorial Psalm   Ps 4: 2, 4, 7–8, 9   Joe Higginbotham

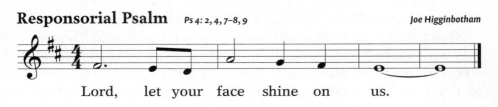

Lord,   let your   face   shine   on   us.

Or: **Alleluia.**

THIRD SUNDAY OF EASTER 349

When I call, answer me, O my just God,
   you who relieve me when I am in distress;
   have pity on me, and hear my prayer! ℟

Know that the LORD does wonders for his faithful one;
   the LORD will hear me when I call upon him. ℟

O LORD, let the light of your countenance shine upon us!
   You put gladness into my heart. ℟

As soon as I lie down, I fall peacefully asleep,
   for you alone, O LORD,
   bring security to my dwelling. ℟

Second Reading *1 Jn 2: 1–5a* My children, I am writing this to you so that you may not commit sin. But if anyone does sin, we have an Advocate with the Father, Jesus Christ the righteous one. He is expiation for our sins, and not for our sins only but for those of the whole world. The way we may be sure that we know him is to keep his commandments. Those who say, "I know him," but do not keep his commandments are liars, and the truth is not in them. But whoever keeps his word, the love of God is truly perfected in him.

Alleluia   *cf. Lk 24: 32*   *Laura Lea Duckworth*

Al - le - lu - ia, al-le-lu - ia.

Al - le - lu - ia, al-le-lu - ia.

Lord Jesus, open the Scriptures to us; / make our hearts burn while you speak to us. **Alleluia, alleluia.**

Gospel *Lk 24: 35–48* The two disciples recounted what had taken place on the way, and how Jesus was made known to them in the breaking of bread.
  While they were still speaking about this, he stood in their

midst and said to them, "Peace be with you." But they were
startled and terrified and thought that they were seeing a ghost.
Then he said to them, "Why are you troubled? And why do
questions arise in your hearts? Look at my hands and my feet,
that it is I myself. Touch me and see, because a ghost does not
have flesh and bones as you can see I have." And as he said this,
he showed them his hands and his feet. While they were still
incredulous for joy and were amazed, he asked them, "Have you
anything here to eat?" They gave him a piece of baked fish; he
took it and ate it in front of them.

He said to them, "These are my words that I spoke to you
while I was still with you, that everything written about me
in the law of Moses and in the prophets and psalms must
be fulfilled." Then he opened their minds to understand the
Scriptures. And he said to them, "Thus it is written that the
Christ would suffer and rise from the dead on the third day and
that repentance, for the forgiveness of sins, would be preached
in his name to all the nations, beginning from Jerusalem. You are
witnesses of these things."

Communion Antiphon *cf. Lk 24: 35* **The disciples recognized the
Lord Jesus ◆ in the breaking of the bread, alleluia.**

Or: *Lk 24: 46–47* **The Christ had to suffer and on the third day
rise from the dead; ◆ in his name repentance and remission of
sins ◆ must be preached to all the nations, alleluia.**

FOURTH SUNDAY OF EASTER

Entrance Antiphon *cf. Ps 33 (32): 5–6* **The merciful love of the Lord
fills the earth; ◆ by the word of the Lord the heavens were
made, alleluia.**

First Reading *Acts 4: 8–12* Peter, filled with the Holy Spirit, said:
"Leaders of the people and elders: If we are being examined today
about a good deed done to a cripple, namely, by what means
he was saved, then all of you and all the people of Israel should
know that it was in the name of Jesus Christ the Nazorean

whom you crucified, whom God raised from the dead; in his name this man stands before you healed. He is *the stone rejected by you, the builders, which has become the cornerstone.* There is no salvation through anyone else, nor is there any other name under heaven given to the human race by which we are to be saved."

Responsorial Psalm   Ps 118: 1, 8–9, 21–23, 26, 28, 29   Jane Terwilliger

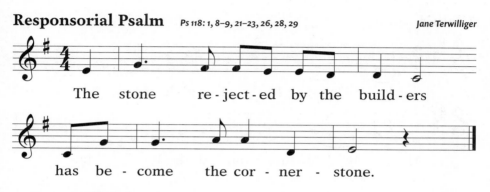

Or: ℟ **Alleluia.**

Give thanks to the LORD, for he is good,
   for his mercy endures forever.
It is better to take refuge in the LORD
   than to trust in man.
It is better to take refuge in the LORD
   than to trust in princes. ℟

I will give thanks to you, for you have answered me
   and have been my savior.
The stone which the builders rejected
   has become the cornerstone.
By the LORD has this been done;
   it is wonderful in our eyes. ℟

Blessed is he who comes in the name of the LORD;
   we bless you from the house of the LORD.
I will give thanks to you, for you have answered me
   and have been my savior.
Give thanks to the LORD, for he is good;
   for his kindness endures forever. ℟

Second Reading *1 Jn 3: 1–2* Beloved: See what love the Father has bestowed on us that we may be called the children of God. Yet so we are. The reason the world does not know us is that it did not know him. Beloved, we are God's children now; what we shall be has not yet been revealed. We do know that when it is revealed we shall be like him, for we shall see him as he is.

Alleluia *Jn 10: 14* Laura Lea Duckworth

Al - le - lu - ia, al-le-lu - ia.

Al - le - lu - ia, al-le-lu - ia.

I am the good shepherd, says the Lord; / I know my sheep, and mine know me.   **Alleluia, alleluia.**

Gospel *Jn 10: 11–18* Jesus said: "I am the good shepherd. A good shepherd lays down his life for the sheep. A hired man, who is not a shepherd and whose sheep are not his own, sees a wolf coming and leaves the sheep and runs away, and the wolf catches and scatters them. This is because he works for pay and has no concern for the sheep. I am the good shepherd, and I know mine and mine know me, just as the Father knows me and I know the Father; and I will lay down my life for the sheep. I have other sheep that do not belong to this fold. These also I must lead, and they will hear my voice, and there will be one flock, one shepherd. This is why the Father loves me, because I lay down my life in order to take it up again. No one takes it from me, but I lay it down on my own. I have power to lay it down, and power to take it up again. This command I have received from my Father."

Communion Antiphon
The Good Shepherd has risen, ◆ who laid down his life for his sheep ◆ and willingly died for his flock, alleluia.

FIFTH SUNDAY OF EASTER

Entrance Antiphon *cf. Ps 98 (97): 1–2* O sing a new song to the Lord, ✦ for he has worked wonders; ✦ in the sight of the nations ✦ he has shown his deliverance, alleluia.

First Reading *Acts 9: 26–31* When Saul arrived in Jerusalem he tried to join the disciples, but they were all afraid of him, not believing that he was a disciple. Then Barnabas took charge of him and brought him to the apostles, and he reported to them how he had seen the Lord, and that he had spoken to him, and how in Damascus he had spoken out boldly in the name of Jesus. He moved about freely with them in Jerusalem, and spoke out boldly in the name of the Lord. He also spoke and debated with the Hellenists, but they tried to kill him. And when the brothers learned of this, they took him down to Caesarea and sent him on his way to Tarsus.

 The church throughout all Judea, Galilee, and Samaria was at peace. It was being built up and walked in the fear of the Lord, and with the consolation of the Holy Spirit it grew in numbers.

Responsorial Psalm   *Ps 22: 26–27, 28, 30, 31–32*   Joe Higginbotham

I will praise you, Lord, in the as-sem-bly of your peo-ple.

Or: ℟ Alleluia.

I will fulfill my vows before those who fear the LORD.
 The lowly shall eat their fill;
they who seek the LORD shall praise him:
  "May your hearts live forever!" ℟

All the ends of the earth
    shall remember and turn to the LORD;
all the families of the nations
    shall bow down before him. ℟

To him alone shall bow down
    all who sleep in the earth;
before him shall bend
    all who go down into the dust. ℟

And to him my soul shall live;
    my descendants shall serve him.
Let the coming generation be told of the LORD
    that they may proclaim to a people yet to be born
    the justice he has shown. ℟

Second Reading *1 Jn 3: 18–24* Children, let us love not in word or speech but in deed and truth.

Now this is how we shall know that we belong to the truth and reassure our hearts before him in whatever our hearts condemn, for God is greater than our hearts and knows everything. Beloved, if our hearts do not condemn us, we have confidence in God and receive from him whatever we ask, because we keep his commandments and do what pleases him. And his commandment is this: we should believe in the name of his Son, Jesus Christ, and love one another just as he commanded us. Those who keep his commandments remain in him, and he in them, and the way we know that he remains in us is from the Spirit he gave us.

Alleluia *Jn 15: 4a, 5b*   *Laura Lea Duckworth*

Al - le - lu - ia, al-le-lu - ia.

Al - le - lu - ia, al-le-lu - ia.

Remain in me as I remain in you, says the Lord. / Whoever remains in me will bear much fruit.   **Alleluia, alleluia.**

Gospel *Jn 15: 1–8* Jesus said to his disciples: "I am the true vine, and my Father is the vine grower. He takes away every branch in me that does not bear fruit, and every one that does he prunes so that it bears more fruit. You are already pruned because of the word that I spoke to you. Remain in me, as I remain in you. Just as a branch cannot bear fruit on its own unless it remains on the vine, so neither can you unless you remain in me. I am the vine, you are the branches. Whoever remains in me and I in him will bear much fruit, because without me you can do nothing. Anyone who does not remain in me will be thrown out like a branch and wither; people will gather them and throw them into a fire and they will be burned. If you remain in me and my words remain in you, ask for whatever you want and it will be done for you. By this is my Father glorified, that you bear much fruit and become my disciples."

Communion Antiphon *cf. Jn 15: 1, 5* **I am the true vine and you are the branches, says the Lord. ✦ Whoever remains in me, and I in him, bears fruit in plenty, alleluia.**

SIXTH SUNDAY OF EASTER

When the Ascension of the Lord is celebrated the following Sunday, the second reading and Gospel from the Seventh Sunday of Easter (page 361) may be read on the Sixth Sunday of Easter.

Entrance Antiphon *cf. Is 48: 20* **Proclaim a joyful sound and let it be heard; ✦ proclaim to the ends of the earth: ✦ The Lord has freed his people, alleluia.**

First Reading *Acts 10: 25–26, 34–35, 44–48* When Peter entered, Cornelius met him and, falling at his feet, paid him homage. Peter, however, raised him up, saying, "Get up. I myself am also a human being."
Then Peter proceeded to speak and said, "In truth, I see that

God shows no partiality. Rather, in every nation whoever fears him and acts uprightly is acceptable to him."

While Peter was still speaking these things, the Holy Spirit fell upon all who were listening to the word. The circumcised believers who had accompanied Peter were astounded that the gift of the Holy Spirit should have been poured out on the Gentiles also, for they could hear them speaking in tongues and glorifying God. Then Peter responded, "Can anyone withhold the water for baptizing these people, who have received the Holy Spirit even as we have?" He ordered them to be baptized in the name of Jesus Christ.

Responsorial Psalm Ps 98: 1, 2–3, 3–4 Don Fishel

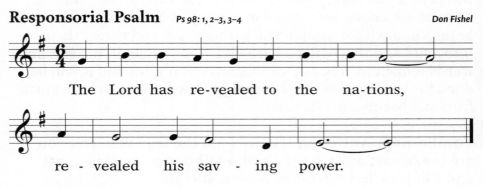

The Lord has re-vealed to the na-tions, re-vealed his sav-ing power.

Or: ℟ **Alleluia.**

Sing to the LORD a new song,
  for he has done wondrous deeds;
His right hand has won victory for him,
  his holy arm. ℟

The LORD has made his salvation known:
  in the sight of the nations he has revealed his justice.
He has remembered his kindness and his faithfulness
  toward the house of Israel. ℟

All the ends of the earth have seen
  the salvation by our God.
Sing joyfully to the LORD, all you lands;
  break into song; sing praise. ℟

Second Reading *1 Jn 4: 7–10* Beloved, let us love one another, because love is of God; everyone who loves is begotten by God and knows God. Whoever is without love does not know God, for God is love. In this way the love of God was revealed to us: God sent his only Son into the world so that we might have life through him. In this is love: not that we have loved God, but that he loved us and sent his Son as expiation for our sins.

Alleluia *Jn 14: 23*   *Laura Lea Duckworth*

Al - le - lu - ia, al-le-lu - ia.
Al - le - lu - ia, al-le-lu - ia.

Whoever loves me will keep my word, says the Lord, /
and my Father will love him and we will come to him.
Alleluia, alleluia.

Gospel *Jn 15: 9–17* Jesus said to his disciples: "As the Father loves me, so I also love you. Remain in my love. If you keep my commandments, you will remain in my love, just as I have kept my Father's commandments and remain in his love.

"I have told you this so that my joy may be in you and your joy might be complete. This is my commandment: love one another as I love you. No one has greater love than this, to lay down one's life for one's friends. You are my friends if you do what I command you. I no longer call you slaves, because a slave does not know what his master is doing. I have called you friends, because I have told you everything I have heard from my Father. It was not you who chose me, but I who chose you and appointed you to go and bear fruit that will remain, so that whatever you ask the Father in my name he may give you. This I command you: love one another."

Communion Antiphon Jn 14: 15–16 **If you love me, keep my commandments, says the Lord,** ✦ **and I will ask the Father and he will send you another Paraclete,** ✦ **to abide with you for ever, alleluia.**

THE ASCENSION OF THE LORD

Where the Solemnity of the Ascension is not to be observed as a Holyday of Obligation, it is assigned to the Seventh Sunday of Easter as its proper day.

Entrance Antiphon

At the Vigil Mass: Psalm 68 (67): 33, 35 **You kingdoms of the earth, sing to God;** ✦ **praise the Lord, who ascends above the highest heavens;** ✦ **his majesty and might are in the skies, alleluia.**

At the Mass During the Day Acts 1: 11 **Men of Galilee, why gaze in wonder at the heavens?** ✦ **This Jesus whom you saw ascending into heaven** ✦ **will return as you saw him go, alleluia.**

First Reading Acts 1: 1–11 In the first book, Theophilus, I dealt with all that Jesus did and taught until the day he was taken up, after giving instructions through the Holy Spirit to the apostles whom he had chosen. He presented himself alive to them by many proofs after he had suffered, appearing to them during forty days and speaking about the kingdom of God. While meeting with the them, he enjoined them not to depart from Jerusalem, but to wait for "the promise of the Father about which you have heard me speak; for John baptized with water, but in a few days you will be baptized with the Holy Spirit."

When they had gathered together they asked him, "Lord, are you at this time going to restore the kingdom to Israel?" He answered them, "It is not for you to know the times or seasons that the Father has established by his own authority. But you will receive power when the Holy Spirit comes upon you, and you will be my witnesses in Jerusalem, throughout Judea and Samaria, and to the ends of the earth." When he had said this, as they were looking on, he was lifted up, and a cloud took him from their sight. While they were looking intently at the sky as he was going, suddenly two men dressed in white garments stood beside them. They said, "Men of Galilee, why are you standing there looking at the sky? This Jesus who has been taken up from you into heaven will return in the same way as you have seen him going into heaven."

Responsorial Psalm   Ps 47: 2–3, 6–7, 8–9   Joe Higginbotham

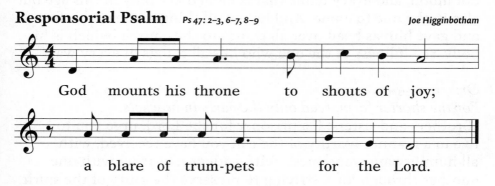

God mounts his throne to shouts of joy; a blare of trum-pets for the Lord.

Or: ℟ **Alleluia.**

All you peoples, clap your hands,
    shout to God with cries of gladness,
For the LORD, the Most High, the awesome,
    is the great king over all the earth. ℟

God mounts his throne amid shouts of joy;
    the LORD, amid trumpet blasts.
Sing praise to God, sing praise;
    sing praise to our king, sing praise. ℟

For king of all the earth is God;
    sing hymns of praise.
God reigns over the nations,
    God sits upon his holy throne. ℟

Second Reading Eph 1: 17–23 Brothers and sisters: May the God
of our Lord Jesus Christ, the Father of glory, give you a Spirit
of wisdom and revelation resulting in knowledge of him. May
the eyes of your hearts be enlightened, that you may know
what is the hope that belongs to his call, what are the riches of
glory in his inheritance among the holy ones, and what is the
surpassing greatness of his power for us who believe, in accord
with the exercise of his great might, which he worked in Christ,
raising him from the dead and seating him at his right hand in
the heavens, far above every principality, authority, power, and
dominion, and every name that is named not only in this age but
also in the one to come. And he put all things beneath his feet
and gave him as head over all things to the church, which is his
body, the fullness of the one who fills all things in every way.

Or: Eph 4: 1–13 or 4: 1–7, 11–13
For the shorter form, read only the parts in brackets.
[Brothers and sisters: I, a prisoner for the Lord, urge you to
live in a manner worthy of the call you have received, with
all humility and gentleness, with patience, bearing with one
another through love, striving to preserve the unity of the spirit
through the bond of peace: one body and one Spirit, as you were
also called to the one hope of your call; one Lord, one faith, one
baptism; one God and Father of all, who is over all and through
all and in all.

But grace was given to each of us according to the measure of
Christ's gift.] Therefore, it says:
He ascended on high and took prisoners captive;
he gave gifts to men.
What does "he ascended" mean except that he also descended
into the lower regions of the earth? The one who descended is
also the one who ascended far above all the heavens, that he
might fill all things.

[And he gave some as apostles, others as prophets, others as
evangelists, others as pastors and teachers, to equip the holy
ones for the work of ministry, for building up the body of Christ,
until we all attain to the unity of faith and knowledge of the Son
of God, to mature manhood, to the extent of the full stature of
Christ.]

Alleluia *Mt 28: 19a, 20b*   *Laura Lea Duckworth*

Al - le - lu - ia, al-le-lu - ia.

Al - le - lu - ia, al-le-lu - ia.

Go and teach all nations, says the Lord; / I am with you
always, until the end of the world.   **Alleluia, alleluia.**

Gospel *Mk 16: 15–20* Jesus said to his disciples: "Go into the whole
world and proclaim the gospel to every creature. Whoever
believes and is baptized will be saved; whoever does not believe
will be condemned. These signs will accompany those who
believe: in my name they will drive out demons, they will speak
new languages. They will pick up serpents with their hands, and
if they drink any deadly thing, it will not harm them. They will
lay hands on the sick, and they will recover."

So then the Lord Jesus, after he spoke to them, was taken up
into heaven and took his seat at the right hand of God. But they
went forth and preached everywhere, while the Lord worked
with them and confirmed the word through accompanying signs.

Communion Antiphon

At the Vigil Mass: *cf. Hebrews 10: 12* **Christ, offering a single sacrifice
for sins,** ◆ **is seated for ever at God's right hand, alleluia.**

At the Mass During the Day: *Matthew 28: 20* **Behold, I am with you
always,** ◆ **even to the end of the age, alleluia.**

SEVENTH SUNDAY OF EASTER

Entrance Antiphon *cf. Ps 27 (26): 7–9* **O Lord, hear my voice, for
I have called to you;** ◆ **of you my heart has spoken: Seek his
face;** ◆ **hide not your face from me, alleluia.**

First Reading *Acts 1: 15–17, 20a, 20c–26* Peter stood up in the midst of the brothers—there was a group of about one hundred and twenty persons in the one place—. He said, "My brothers, the Scripture had to be fulfilled which the Holy Spirit spoke beforehand through the mouth of David, concerning Judas, who was the guide for those who arrested Jesus. He was numbered among us and was allotted a share in this ministry.

"For it is written in the Book of Psalms:
May another take his office.

"Therefore, it is necessary that one of the men who accompanied us the whole time the Lord Jesus came and went among us, beginning from the baptism of John until the day on which he was taken up from us, become with us a witness to his resurrection." So they proposed two, Judas called Barsabbas, who was also known as Justus, and Matthias. Then they prayed, "You, Lord, who know the hearts of all, show which one of these two you have chosen to take the place in this apostolic ministry from which Judas turned away to go to his own place." Then they gave lots to them, and the lot fell upon Matthias, and he was counted with the eleven apostles.

Responsorial Psalm *Ps 103: 1–2, 11–12, 19–20*   *based on* NOËL NOUVELET

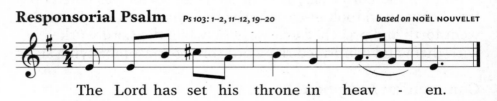

The Lord has set his throne in heav - en.

Or: **Alleluia.**

Bless the LORD, O my soul;
    and all my being, bless his holy name.
Bless the LORD, O my soul,
    and forget not all his benefits. ℟

For as the heavens are high above the earth,
    so surpassing is his kindness toward those who fear him.
As far as the east is from the west,
    so far has he put our transgressions from us. ℟

The LORD has established his throne in heaven,
  and his kingdom rules over all.
Bless the LORD, all you his angels,
  you mighty in strength, who do his bidding.   ℟

Second Reading 1 Jn 4: 11–16 Beloved, if God so loved us, we also must love one another. No one has ever seen God. Yet, if we love one another, God remains in us, and his love is brought to perfection in us.

This is how we know that we remain in him and he in us, that he has given us of his Spirit. Moreover, we have seen and testify that the Father sent his Son as savior of the world. Whoever acknowledges that Jesus is the Son of God, God remains in him and he in God. We have come to know and to believe in the love God has for us.

God is love, and whoever remains in love remains in God and God in him.

Alleluia   *cf. Jn 14: 18*   *Laura Lea Duckworth*

Al - le - lu - ia, al-le-lu - ia.

Al - le - lu - ia, al-le-lu - ia.

I will not leave you orphans, says the Lord. / I will come back to you, and your hearts will rejoice.   **Alleluia, alleluia.**

Gospel Jn 17: 11b–19 Lifting up his eyes to heaven, Jesus prayed saying: "Holy Father, keep them in your name that you have given me, so that they may be one just as we are one. When I was with them I protected them in your name that you gave me, and I guarded them, and none of them was lost except the son of destruction, in order that the Scripture might be fulfilled. But now I am coming to you. I speak this in the world so that they may share my joy completely. I gave them your word, and the world hated them, because they do not belong to the world any more than I belong to the world. I do not ask that you take them out of the world but that you keep them from the evil one. They do not belong to the world any more than I belong to the world. Consecrate them in the truth. Your word is truth. As you sent me into the world, so I sent them into the world. And I consecrate myself for them, so that they also may be consecrated in truth."

Communion Antiphon *Jn 17: 22* **Father, I pray that they may be one ✦ as we also are one, alleluia.**

PENTECOST SUNDAY

The readings for the Vigil Mass can be found on page 161.

❖ At the Mass During the Day ❖

Entrance Antiphon *Wis 1: 7* **The Spirit of the Lord has filled the whole world ✦ and that which contains all things ✦ understands what is said, alleluia.**

Or: *Rom 5: 5; cf. 8: 11* **The love of God has been poured into our hearts ✦ through the Spirit of God dwelling within us, alleluia.**

First Reading *Acts 2: 1–11* When the time for Pentecost was fulfilled, they were all in one place together. And suddenly there came from the sky a noise like a strong driving wind, and it filled the entire house in which they were. Then there appeared to them tongues as of fire, which parted and came to rest on each one of them. And they were all filled with the Holy Spirit and began to speak in different tongues, as the Spirit enabled them to proclaim.

Now there were devout Jews from every nation under heaven staying in Jerusalem. At this sound, they gathered in a large crowd, but they were confused because each one heard them speaking in his own language. They were astounded, and in amazement they asked, "Are not all these people who are speaking Galileans? Then how does each of us hear them in his native language? We are Parthians, Medes, and Elamites, inhabitants of Mesopotamia, Judea and Cappadocia, Pontus and Asia, Phrygia and Pamphylia, Egypt and the districts of Libya near Cyrene, as well as travelers from Rome, both Jews and converts to Judaism, Cretans and Arabs, yet we hear them speaking in our own tongues of the mighty acts of God."

Responsorial Psalm   Ps 104: 1, 24, 29–30, 31, 34   David Miles

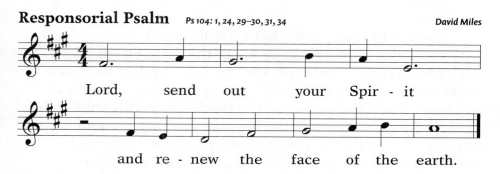

Lord,   send   out   your   Spir - it

and re - new   the   face   of   the   earth.

Or: ℟ **Alleluia.**

Bless the LORD, O my soul!
  O LORD, my God, you are great indeed!
How manifold are your works, O LORD!
  the earth is full of your creatures; ℟

If you take away their breath, they perish
  and return to their dust.
When you send forth your spirit, they are created,
  and you renew the face of the earth. ℟

May the glory of the LORD endure forever;
  may the LORD be glad in his works!
Pleasing to him be my theme;
  I will be glad in the LORD. ℟

Second Reading 1 Cor 12: 3b–7, 12–13 Brothers and sisters: No one can say, "Jesus is Lord," except by the Holy Spirit.

There are different kinds of spiritual gifts but the same Spirit; there are different forms of service but the same Lord; there are different workings but the same God who produces all of them in everyone. To each individual the manifestation of the Spirit is given for some benefit.

As a body is one though it has many parts, and all the parts of the body, though many, are one body, so also Christ. For in one Spirit we were all baptized into one body, whether Jews or Greeks, slaves or free persons, and we were all given to drink of one Spirit.

Or: Gal 5: 16–25   Brothers and sisters, live by the Spirit and you will certainly not gratify the desire of the flesh. For the flesh has desires against the Spirit, and the Spirit against the flesh; these are opposed to each other, so that you may not do what you want. But if you are guided by the Spirit, you are not under the law. Now the works of the flesh are obvious: immorality, impurity, lust, idolatry, sorcery, hatreds, rivalry, jealousy, outbursts of fury, acts of selfishness, dissensions, factions, occasions of envy, drinking bouts, orgies, and the like. I warn you, as I warned you before, that those who do such things will not inherit the kingdom of God. In contrast, the fruit of the Spirit is love, joy, peace, patience, kindness, generosity, faithfulness, gentleness, self-control. Against such there is no law. Now those who belong to Christ Jesus have crucified their flesh with its passions and desires. If we live in the Spirit, let us also follow the Spirit.

Sequence
Come, Holy Spirit, come!
And from your celestial home
    Shed a ray of light divine!
Come, Father of the poor!
Come, source of all our store!
    Come, within our bosoms shine.
You, of comforters the best;
You, the soul's most welcome guest;
    Sweet refreshment here below;
In our labor, rest most sweet;

Grateful coolness in the heat;
  Solace in the midst of woe.
O most blessed Light divine,
Shine within these hearts of yours,
  And our inmost being fill!
Where you are not, we have naught,
Nothing good in deed or thought,
  Nothing free from taint of ill.
Heal our wounds, our strength renew;
On our dryness pour your dew;
  Wash the stains of guilt away:
Bend the stubborn heart and will;
Melt the frozen, warm the chill;
  Guide the steps that go astray.
On the faithful, who adore
And confess you, evermore
  In your sevenfold gift descend;
Give them virtue's sure reward;
Give them your salvation, Lord;
  Give them joys that never end. Amen.
  Alleluia.

Alleluia   *Laura Lea Duckworth*

Al - le - lu - ia, al-le-lu - ia.

Al - le - lu - ia, al-le-lu - ia.

Come, Holy Spirit, fill the hearts of the faithful / and kindle
in them the fire of your love.   **Alleluia, alleluia.**

Gospel *Jn 20: 19–23* On the evening of that first day of the week,
when the doors were locked, where the disciples were, for fear of
the Jews, Jesus came and stood in their midst and said to them,
"Peace be with you." When he had said this, he showed them

his hands and his side. The disciples rejoiced when they saw
the Lord. Jesus said to them again, "Peace be with you. As the
Father has sent me, so I send you." And when he had said this,
he breathed on them and said to them, "Receive the Holy Spirit.
Whose sins you forgive are forgiven them, and whose sins you
retain are retained."

Or: Jn 15: 26–27; 16: 12–15   Jesus said to his disciples: "When the
Advocate comes whom I will send you from the Father, the
Spirit of truth that proceeds from the Father, he will testify to
me. And you also testify, because you have been with me from
the beginning.

  "I have much more to tell you, but you cannot bear it now.
But when he comes, the Spirit of truth, he will guide you to all
truth. He will not speak on his own, but he will speak what he
hears, and will declare to you the things that are coming. He will
glorify me, because he will take from what is mine and declare
it to you. Everything that the Father has is mine; for this reason
I told you that he will take from what is mine and declare it
to you."

Communion Antiphon Acts 2: 4, 11 **They were all filled with the
Holy Spirit ◆ and spoke of the marvels of God, alleluia.**

Solemnities of the Lord During Ordinary Time † YEAR B

THE SOLEMNITY OF

THE MOST HOLY TRINITY

Entrance Antiphon
Blest be God the Father, ◆ and the Only Begotten Son of God, ◆ and also the Holy Spirit, ◆ for he has shown us his merciful love.

First Reading Dt 4: 32-34, 39-40 Moses said to the people: "Ask now of the days of old, before your time, ever since God created man upon the earth; ask from one end of the sky to the other: Did anything so great ever happen before? Was it ever heard of? Did a people ever hear the voice of God speaking from the midst of fire, as you did, and live? Or did any god venture to go and take a nation for himself from the midst of another nation, by testings, by signs and wonders, by war, with strong hand and outstretched arm, and by great terrors, all of which the LORD, your God, did for you in Egypt before your very eyes? This is why you must now know, and fix in your heart, that the LORD is God in the heavens above and on earth below, and that there is no other. You must keep his statutes and commandments that I enjoin on you today, that you and your children after you may prosper, and that you may have long life on the land which the LORD, your God, is giving you forever."

Responsorial Psalm   Ps 33: 4–5, 6, 9, 18–19, 20, 22   Jane Terwilliger

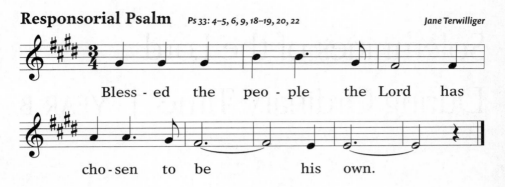

Bless - ed   the   peo - ple   the Lord   has
cho - sen   to   be   his   own.

Upright is the word of the LORD,
  and all his works are trustworthy.
He loves justice and right;
  of the kindness of the LORD the earth is full. ℟

By the word of the LORD the heavens were made;
  by the breath of his mouth all their host.
For he spoke, and it was made;
  he commanded, and it stood forth. ℟

See, the eyes of the LORD are upon those who fear him,
  upon those who hope for his kindness,
To deliver them from death
  and preserve them in spite of famine. ℟

Our soul waits for the LORD,
  who is our help and our shield.
May your kindness, O LORD, be upon us
  who have put our hope in you. ℟

Second Reading Rom 8: 14–17 Brothers and sisters: For those who
are led by the Spirit of God are sons of God. For you did not
receive a spirit of slavery to fall back into fear, but you received
a Spirit of adoption, through whom we cry, "Abba, Father!" The
Spirit himself bears witness with our spirit that we are children
of God, and if children, then heirs, heirs of God and joint heirs
with Christ, if only we suffer with him so that we may also be
glorified with him.

Alleluia Rv 1: 8   *Jim Hughes*

Al-le-lu-ia   Al-le-lu-ia   Al - le-lu - ia.

Glory to the Father, the Son, and the Holy Spirit; / to God who is, who was, and who is to come.   **Alleluia, alleluia.**

Gospel Mt 28: 16–20 The eleven disciples went to Galilee, to the mountain to which Jesus had ordered them. When they all saw him, they worshiped, but they doubted. Then Jesus approached and said to them, "All power in heaven and on earth has been given to me. Go, therefore, and make disciples of all nations, baptizing them in the name of the Father, and of the Son, and of the Holy Spirit, teaching them to observe all that I have commanded you. And behold, I am with you always, until the end of the age."

Communion Antiphon Gal 4: 6 **Since you are children of God, ◆ God has sent into your hearts the Spirit of his Son, ◆ the Spirit who cries out: Abba, Father.**

THE SOLEMNITY OF THE

MOST HOLY BODY AND BLOOD OF CHRIST

(CORPUS CHRISTI)

Where the Solemnity of the Most Holy Body and Blood of Christ is not a Holyday of Obligation, it is assigned to the Sunday after the Most Holy Trinity as its proper day.

Entrance Antiphon cf. Ps 81 (80): 17 **He fed them with the finest wheat ◆ and satisfied them with honey from the rock.**

First Reading Ex 24: 3-8 When Moses came to the people and related all the words and ordinances of the LORD, they all answered with one voice, "We will do everything that the LORD has told us." Moses then wrote down all the words of the LORD and, rising early the next day, he erected at the foot of the mountain an altar and twelve pillars for the twelve tribes of Israel. Then, having sent certain young men of the Israelites to offer holocausts and sacrifice young bulls as peace offerings to the LORD, Moses took half of the blood and put it in large bowls; the other half he splashed on the altar. Taking the book of the covenant, he read it aloud to the people, who answered, "All that the LORD has said, we will heed and do." Then he took the blood and sprinkled it on the people, saying, "This is the blood of the covenant that the LORD has made with you in accordance with all these words of his."

Responsorial Psalm   Ps 116: 12–13, 15–16, 17–18   *based on* ADORO TE DEVOTE

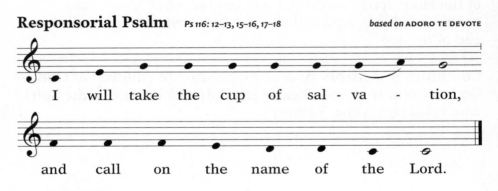

I will take the cup of sal - va - tion, and call on the name of the Lord.

Or: **Alleluia.**

How shall I make a return to the LORD
   for all the good he has done for me?
The cup of salvation I will take up,
   and I will call upon the name of the LORD.   ℟

Precious in the eyes of the LORD
   is the death of his faithful ones.
I am your servant, the son of your handmaid;
   you have loosed my bonds.   ℟

To you will I offer sacrifice of thanksgiving,
   and I will call upon the name of the LORD.

My vows to the LORD I will pay
  in the presence of all his people. ℟

Second Reading Heb 9: 11–15 Brothers and sisters: When Christ
came as high priest of the good things that have come to
be, passing through the greater and more perfect tabernacle
not made by hands, that is, not belonging to this creation, he
entered once for all into the sanctuary, not with the blood
of goats and calves but with his own blood, thus obtaining
eternal redemption. For if the blood of goats and bulls and
the sprinkling of a heifer's ashes can sanctify those who are
defiled so that their flesh is cleansed, how much more will the
blood of Christ, who through the eternal Spirit offered himself
unblemished to God, cleanse our consciences from dead works
to worship the living God.

For this reason he is mediator of a new covenant: since a death
has taken place for deliverance from transgressions under the
first covenant, those who are called may receive the promised
eternal inheritance.

Sequence
The sequence Laud, O Zion (Lauda Sion), *or the shorter form
beginning with the verse* Lo! the angels' food is given *may be sung
optionally before the* Alleluia. *For the shorter form, read only the
parts in brackets.*

Laud, O Zion, your salvation,
Laud with hymns of exultation,
  Christ, your king and shepherd true:

Bring him all the praise you know,
He is more than you bestow.
  Never can you reach his due.

Special theme for glad thanksgiving
Is the quick'ning and the living
  Bread today before you set:

From his hands of old partaken,
As we know, by faith unshaken,

Where the Twelve at supper met.

Full and clear ring out your chanting,
Joy nor sweetest grace be wanting,
    From your heart let praises burst:

For today the feast is holden,
When the institution olden
    Of that supper was rehearsed.

Here the new law's new oblation,
By the new king's revelation,
    Ends the form of ancient rite:

Now the new the old effaces,
Truth away the shadow chases,
    Light dispels the gloom of night.

What he did at supper seated,
Christ ordained to be repeated,
    His memorial ne'er to cease:

And his rule for guidance taking,
Bread and wine we hallow, making
    Thus our sacrifice of peace.

This the truth each Christian learns,
Bread into his flesh he turns,
    To his precious blood the wine:

Sight has fail'd, nor thought conceives,
But a dauntless faith believes,
    Resting on a pow'r divine.

Here beneath these signs are hidden
Priceless things to sense forbidden;
    Signs, not things are all we see:

Blood is poured and flesh is broken,

Yet in either wondrous token
    Christ entire we know to be.

Whoso of this food partakes,
Does not rend the Lord nor breaks;
    Christ is whole to all that tastes:

Thousands are, as one, receivers,
One, as thousands of believers,
    Eats of him who cannot waste.

Bad and good the feast are sharing,
Of what divers dooms preparing,
    Endless death, or endless life.

Life to these, to those damnation,
See how like participation
    Is with unlike issues rife.

When the sacrament is broken,
Doubt not, but believe 'tis spoken,
    That each sever'd outward token
      doth the very whole contain.

Nought the precious gift divides,
Breaking but the sign betides
    Jesus still the same abides,
      still unbroken does remain.

(*The shorter form of the sequence begins here.*)
    [Lo! the angel's food is given
To the pilgrim who has striven;
    See the children's bread from heaven,
      which on dogs may not be spent.

Truth the ancient types fulfilling,
Isaac bound, a victim willing,
    Paschal lamb, its lifeblood spilling,
      manna to the fathers sent.

Very bread, good shepherd, tend us,
Jesu, of your love befriend us,
      You refresh us, you defend us,
      Your eternal goodness send us
In the land of life to see.

You who all things can and know,
Who on earth such food bestow,
      Grant us with your saints, though lowest,
      Where the heav'nly feast you show,
Fellow heirs and guests to be. Amen. Alleluia.]

Alleluia   Jn 6: 51   Jim Hughes

Al-le-lu-ia   Al-le-lu-ia   Al-le-lu - ia.

I am the living bread that came down from heaven, /
says the Lord; whoever eats this bread will live forever.
Alleluia, alleluia.

Gospel Mk 14: 12–16, 22–26 On the first day of the Feast of Unleavened
Bread, when they sacrificed the Passover lamb, Jesus' disciples
said to him, "Where do you want us to go and prepare for you to
eat the Passover?" He sent two of his disciples and said to them,
"Go into the city and a man will meet you, carrying a jar of water.
Follow him. Wherever he enters, say to the master of the house,
'The Teacher says, "Where is my guest room where I may eat
the Passover with my disciples?"' Then he will show you a large
upper room furnished and ready. Make the preparations for us
there." The disciples then went off, entered the city, and found it
just as he had told them; and they prepared the Passover.

While they were eating, he took bread, said the blessing, broke
it, gave it to them, and said, "Take it; this is my body." Then he
took a cup, gave thanks, and gave it to them, and they all drank
from it. He said to them, "This is my blood of the covenant,
which will be shed for many. Amen, I say to you, I shall not

drink again the fruit of the vine until the day when I drink it new in the kingdom of God." Then, after singing a hymn, they went out to the Mount of Olives.

Communion Antiphon *Jn 6: 57* **Whoever eats my flesh and drinks my blood • remains in me and I in him, says the Lord.**

THE SOLEMNITY OF

THE MOST SACRED HEART OF JESUS

Entrance Antiphon *Ps 33 (32): 11, 19* **The designs of his Heart are from age to age, • to rescue their souls from death, • and to keep them alive in famine.**

First Reading *Hos 11: 1, 3–4, 8c–9*
   Thus says the LORD:
When Israel was a child I loved him,
   out of Egypt I called my son.
Yet it was I who taught Ephraim to walk,
   who took them in my arms;
I drew them with human cords,
   with bands of love;
I fostered them like one
   who raises an infant to his cheeks;
Yet, though I stooped to feed my child,
   they did not know that I was their healer.

My heart is overwhelmed,
   my pity is stirred.
I will not give vent to my blazing anger,
   I will not destroy Ephraim again;
For I am God and not a man,
   the Holy One present among you;
   I will not let the flames consume you.

Responsorial Psalm Is 12: 2–3, 4, 5–6 *Bill Svarda*

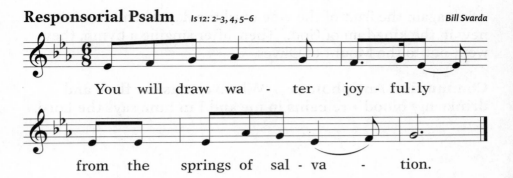

You will draw wa - ter joy - ful-ly
from the springs of sal - va - tion.

God indeed is my savior;
    I am confident and unafraid.
My strength and my courage is the LORD,
    and he has been my savior.
With joy you will draw water
    at the fountain of salvation. ℟

Give thanks to the LORD, acclaim his name;
    among the nations make known his deeds,
    proclaim how exalted is his name. ℟

Sing praise to the LORD for his glorious achievement;
    let this be known throughout all the earth.
Shout with exultation, O city of Zion,
    for great in your midst
    is the Holy One of Israel! ℟

Second Reading Eph 3: 8–12, 14–19 Brothers and sisters: To me, the very least of all the holy ones, this grace was given, to preach to the Gentiles the inscrutable riches of Christ, and to bring to light for all what is the plan of the mystery hidden from ages past in God who created all things, so that the manifold wisdom of God might now be made known through the church to the principalities and authorities in the heavens. This was according to the eternal purpose that he accomplished in Christ Jesus our Lord, in whom we have boldness of speech and confidence of access through faith in him.

For this reason I kneel before the Father, from whom every family in heaven and on earth is named, that he may grant you in accord with the riches of his glory to be strengthened with power through his Spirit in the inner self, and that Christ may dwell in your hearts through faith; that you, rooted and grounded in love, may have strength to comprehend with all the holy ones what is the breadth and length and height and depth, and to know the love of Christ which surpasses knowledge, so that you may be filled with all the fullness of God.

Alleluia Mt 11: 29ab   *Jim Hughes*

Al-le-lu-ia   Al-le-lu-ia   Al - le-lu - ia.

Take my yoke upon you, says the Lord; / and learn from me, for I am meek and humble of heart. **Alleluia, alleluia.**

Or: 1 Jn 4: 10b   *Joe Higginbotham*

Al - le - lu - ia,   al - le - lu - ia,   al - le - lu - ia.

God first loved us / and sent his Son as expiation for our sins. **Alleluia, alleluia.**

Gospel Jn 19: 31–37 Since it was preparation day, in order that the bodies might not remain on the cross on the sabbath, for the sabbath day of that week was a solemn one, the Jews asked Pilate that their legs be broken and they be taken down. So the soldiers came and broke the legs of the first and then of the other one who was crucified with Jesus. But when they came to Jesus and saw that he was already dead, they did not break his legs, but one soldier thrust his lance into his side, and immediately blood and water flowed out. An eyewitness has testified, and his testimony is true; he knows that he is speaking the truth, so that you also may come to believe. For this happened so that the Scripture passage might be fulfilled:
Not a bone of it will be broken.

And again another passage says:
They will look upon him whom they have pierced.

Communion Antiphon *cf. Jn 7: 37-38* Thus says the Lord: ◆ Let whoever is thirsty come to me and drink. ◆ Streams of living water will flow ◆ from within the one who believes in me.

Or: *Jn 19: 34* One of the soldiers opened his side with a lance, ◆ and at once there came forth blood and water.

Ordinary Time † YEAR B

SECOND SUNDAY

IN ORDINARY TIME

Entrance Antiphon *Ps 66 (65): 4* **All the earth shall bow down before you, O God, ◆ and shall sing to you, ◆ shall sing to your name, O Most High!**

First Reading *1 Sm 3: 3b–10,19* Samuel was sleeping in the temple of the LORD where the ark of God was. The LORD called to Samuel, who answered, "Here I am." Samuel ran to Eli and said, "Here I am. You called me." "I did not call you," Eli said. "Go back to sleep." So he went back to sleep. Again the LORD called Samuel, who rose and went to Eli. "Here I am," he said. "You called me." But Eli answered, "I did not call you, my son. Go back to sleep."

At that time Samuel was not familiar with the LORD, because the LORD had not revealed anything to him as yet. The LORD called Samuel again, for the third time. Getting up and going to Eli, he said, "Here I am. You called me." Then Eli understood that the LORD was calling the youth. So he said to Samuel, "Go to sleep, and if you are called, reply, Speak, LORD, for your servant is listening." When Samuel went to sleep in his place, the LORD came and revealed his presence, calling out as before, "Samuel, Samuel!" Samuel answered, "Speak, for your servant is listening."

Samuel grew up, and the LORD was with him, not permitting any word of his to be without effect.

Responsorial Psalm

Ps 40: 2, 4, 7–8, 8–9, 10

Beverly McDevitt

Here am I, Lord; I come to do your will.

I have waited, waited for the LORD,
    and he stooped toward me and heard my cry.
And he put a new song into my mouth,
    a hymn to our God. ℟

Sacrifice or offering you wished not,
    but ears open to obedience you gave me.
Holocausts or sin-offerings you sought not;
    then said I, "Behold I come." ℟

"In the written scroll it is prescribed for me,
    to do your will, O my God, is my delight,
    and your law is within my heart!" ℟

I announced your justice in the vast assembly;
    I did not restrain my lips, as you, O LORD, know. ℟

Second Reading

1 Cor 6: 13c–15a, 17–20 Brothers and sisters: The body is not for immorality, but for the Lord, and the Lord is for the body; God raised the Lord and will also raise us by his power.

Do you not know that your bodies are members of Christ? But whoever is joined to the Lord becomes one Spirit with him. Avoid immorality. Every other sin a person commits is outside the body, but the immoral person sins against his own body. Do you not know that your body is a temple of the Holy Spirit within you, whom you have from God, and that you are not your own? For you have been purchased at a price. Therefore glorify God in your body.

Alleluia

Joe Higginbotham

Al - le - lu - ia, al - le - lu - ia, al - le - lu - ia.

We have found the Messiah: / Jesus Christ, who brings us truth and grace.   **Alleluia, alleluia.**

Gospel *Jn 1: 35–42* John was standing with two of his disciples, and as he watched Jesus walk by, he said, "Behold, the Lamb of God." The two disciples heard what he said and followed Jesus. Jesus turned and saw them following him and said to them, "What are you looking for?" They said to him, "Rabbi"—which translated means Teacher—, "where are you staying?" He said to them, "Come, and you will see." So they went and saw where Jesus was staying, and they stayed with him that day. It was about four in the afternoon. Andrew, the brother of Simon Peter, was one of the two who heard John and followed Jesus. He first found his own brother Simon and told him, "We have found the Messiah"—which is translated Christ. Then he brought him to Jesus. Jesus looked at him and said, "You are Simon the son of John; you will be called Cephas"—which is translated Peter.

Communion Antiphon *cf. Ps 23 (22): 5* **You have prepared a table before me, ◆ and how precious is the chalice that quenches my thirst.**

Or: *1 Jn 4: 16* **We have come to know and to believe ◆ in the love that God has for us.**

THIRD SUNDAY IN ORDINARY TIME

Entrance Antiphon *cf. Ps 96 (95): 1, 6* **O sing a new song to the Lord; ◆ sing to the Lord, all the earth. ◆ In his presence are majesty and splendor, ◆ strength and honor in his holy place.**

First Reading *Jon 3: 1–5, 10* The word of the LORD came to Jonah, saying: "Set out for the great city of Nineveh, and announce to it the message that I will tell you." So Jonah made ready and went to Nineveh, according to the LORD's bidding. Now Nineveh was an enormously large city; it took three days to go through it. Jonah began his journey through the city, and had gone but a single day's walk announcing, "Forty days more and Nineveh shall be destroyed," when the people of Nineveh believed God; they proclaimed a fast and all of them, great and small, put on sackcloth.

When God saw by their actions how they turned from their evil way, he repented of the evil that he had threatened to do to them; he did not carry it out.

Responsorial Psalm   Ps 25: 4–5, 6–7, 8–9   *Michael Giszczak*

Teach me your ways, O Lord.

Teach me your ways, O Lord.

Your ways, O LORD, make known to me;
    teach me your paths,
Guide me in your truth and teach me,
    for you are God my savior. ℟

Remember that your compassion, O LORD,
    and your love are from of old.
In your kindness remember me,
    because of your goodness, O LORD. ℟

Good and upright is the LORD;
    thus he shows sinners the way.
He guides the humble to justice
    and teaches the humble his way. ℟

Second Reading *1 Cor 7: 29–31* I tell you, brothers and sisters, the time is running out. From now on, let those having wives act as not having them, those weeping as not weeping, those rejoicing as not rejoicing, those buying as not owning, those using the world as not using it fully. For the world in its present form is passing away.

Alleluia Mk 1: 15   *Joe Higginbotham*

Al-le-lu-ia, al-le-lu-ia, al-le-lu - ia.

The kingdom of God is at hand. / Repent and believe in the Gospel. **Alleluia, alleluia.**

Gospel Mk 1: 14–20 After John had been arrested, Jesus came to Galilee proclaiming the gospel of God: "This is the time of fulfillment. The kingdom of God is at hand. Repent, and believe in the gospel."

As he passed by the Sea of Galilee, he saw Simon and his brother Andrew casting their nets into the sea; they were fishermen. Jesus said to them, "Come after me, and I will make you fishers of men." Then they abandoned their nets and followed him. He walked along a little farther and saw James, the son of Zebedee, and his brother John. They too were in a boat mending their nets. Then he called them. So they left their father Zebedee in the boat along with the hired men and followed him.

Communion Antiphon cf. Ps 34 (33): 6 **Look toward the Lord and be radiant; ♦ let your faces not be abashed.**

Or: Jn 8: 12 **I am the light of the world, says the Lord; ♦ whoever follows me will not walk in darkness, ♦ but will have the light of life.**

FOURTH SUNDAY IN ORDINARY TIME

Entrance Antiphon Ps 106 (105): 47 **Save us, O Lord our God! ♦ And gather us from the nations, ♦ to give thanks to your holy name, ♦ and make it our glory to praise you.**

First Reading Dt 18: 15–20 Moses spoke to all the people, saying: "A prophet like me will the LORD, your God, raise up for you from among your own kin; to him you shall listen. This is exactly what you requested of the LORD, your God, at Horeb on the day of the assembly, when you said, 'Let us not again hear the voice of the LORD, our God, nor see this great fire any more, lest we die.' And the LORD said to me, 'This was well said. I will raise up for them a prophet like you from among their kin, and will put my words into his mouth; he shall tell them all that I command him. Whoever will not listen to my words which he speaks in my name, I myself will make him answer for it. But if a prophet presumes to speak in my name an oracle that I have not commanded him to speak, or speaks in the name of other gods, he shall die.'"

Responsorial Psalm   Ps 95: 1–2, 6–7, 7–9   Vince Ambrosetti

If to-day you hear his voice, hard-en not your hearts.

Come, let us sing joyfully to the LORD;
   let us acclaim the rock of our salvation.
Let us come into his presence with thanksgiving;
   let us joyfully sing psalms to him. ℟

Come, let us bow down in worship;
   let us kneel before the LORD who made us.
For he is our God,
   and we are the people he shepherds, the flock he guides. ℟

Oh, that today you would hear his voice:
   "Harden not your hearts as at Meribah,

as in the day of Massah in the desert,
  Where your fathers tempted me;
    they tested me though they had seen my works." ℟

Second Reading 1 Cor 7: 32-35 Brothers and sisters: I should like you
to be free of anxieties. An unmarried man is anxious about the
things of the Lord, how he may please the Lord. But a married
man is anxious about the things of the world, how he may
please his wife, and he is divided. An unmarried woman or a
virgin is anxious about the things of the Lord, so that she may
be holy in both body and spirit. A married woman, on the other
hand, is anxious about the things of the world, how she may
please her husband. I am telling you this for your own benefit,
not to impose a restraint upon you, but for the sake of propriety
and adherence to the Lord without distraction.

Alleluia   Mt 4: 16   *Joe Higginbotham*

Al - le - lu - ia,   al - le - lu - ia,   al - le - lu - ia.

The people who sit in darkness have seen a great light; / on
those dwelling in a land overshadowed by death, / light has
arisen.   **Alleluia, alleluia.**

Gospel Mk 1: 21-28 Then they came to Capernaum, and on the
sabbath Jesus entered the synagogue and taught. The people
were astonished at his teaching, for he taught them as one
having authority and not as the scribes. In their synagogue was a
man with an unclean spirit; he cried out, "What have you to do
with us, Jesus of Nazareth? Have you come to destroy us? I know
who you are—the Holy One of God!" Jesus rebuked him and said,
"Quiet! Come out of him!" The unclean spirit convulsed him and
with a loud cry came out of him. All were amazed and asked
one another, "What is this? A new teaching with authority. He
commands even the unclean spirits and they obey him." His
fame spread everywhere throughout the whole region of Galilee.

Communion Antiphon *cf. Ps 31 (30): 17–18* Let your face shine on your servant. ✦ Save me in your merciful love. ✦ O Lord, let me never be put to shame, for I call on you.

Or: *Mt 5: 3–4* Blessed are the poor in spirit, ✦ for theirs is the Kingdom of Heaven. ✦ Blessed are the meek, for they shall possess the land.

FIFTH SUNDAY IN ORDINARY TIME

Entrance Antiphon *Ps 95 (94): 6–7* O come, let us worship God ✦ and bow low before the God who made us, ✦ for he is the Lord our God.

First Reading   *Job 7: 1–4, 6–7*
Job spoke, saying:
    Is not man's life on earth a drudgery?
        Are not his days those of hirelings?
    He is a slave who longs for the shade,
        a hireling who waits for his wages.
    So I have been assigned months of misery,
        and troubled nights have been allotted to me.
    If in bed I say, "When shall I arise?"
        then the night drags on;
    I am filled with restlessness until the dawn.
    My days are swifter than a weaver's shuttle;
        they come to an end without hope.
    Remember that my life is like the wind;
        I shall not see happiness again.

Responsorial Psalm   *Ps 147: 1–2, 3–4, 5–6*   *Beverly McDevitt*

Praise the Lord, who heals the bro-ken-heart-ed.

Or: ℟ **Alleluia.**

Praise the LORD, for he is good;
  sing praise to our God, for he is gracious;
  it is fitting to praise him.
The LORD rebuilds Jerusalem;
  the dispersed of Israel he gathers.   ℟

He heals the brokenhearted
  and binds up their wounds.
He tells the number of the stars;
  he calls each by name.   ℟

Great is our Lord and mighty in power;
  to his wisdom there is no limit.
The LORD sustains the lowly;
  the wicked he casts to the ground   ℟

Second Reading   *1 Cor 9: 16–19, 22–23* Brothers and sisters: If I preach
the gospel, this is no reason for me to boast, for an obligation
has been imposed on me, and woe to me if I do not preach
it! If I do so willingly, I have a recompense, but if unwillingly,
then I have been entrusted with a stewardship. What then is
my recompense? That, when I preach, I offer the gospel free of
charge so as not to make full use of my right in the gospel.

Although I am free in regard to all, I have made myself a
slave to all so as to win over as many as possible. To the weak I
became weak, to win over the weak. I have become all things to
all, to save at least some. All this I do for the sake of the gospel,
so that I too may have a share in it.

Alleluia   *Mt 8: 17*   *Joe Higginbotham*

Al - le - lu - ia,   al - le - lu - ia,   al - le - lu   -   ia.

Christ took away our infirmities / and bore our diseases.
Alleluia, alleluia.

Gospel Mk1: 29-39 On leaving the synagogue Jesus entered the house of Simon and Andrew with James and John. Simon's mother-in-law lay sick with a fever. They immediately told him about her. He approached, grasped her hand, and helped her up. Then the fever left her and she waited on them.

When it was evening, after sunset, they brought to him all who were ill or possessed by demons. The whole town was gathered at the door. He cured many who were sick with various diseases, and he drove out many demons, not permitting them to speak because they knew him.

Rising very early before dawn, he left and went off to a deserted place, where he prayed. Simon and those who were with him pursued him and on finding him said, "Everyone is looking for you." He told them, "Let us go on to the nearby villages that I may preach there also. For this purpose have I come." So he went into their synagogues, preaching and driving out demons throughout the whole of Galilee.

Communion Antiphon cf. Ps 107 (106): 8-9 Let them thank the Lord for his mercy, ◆ his wonders for the children of men, ◆ for he satisfies the thirsty soul, ◆ and the hungry he fills with good things.

Or: Mt 5: 5-6 Blessed are those who mourn, for they shall be consoled. ◆ Blessed are those who hunger and thirst for righteousness, ◆ for they shall have their fill.

SIXTH SUNDAY IN ORDINARY TIME

Entrance Antiphon cf. Ps 31 (30): 3-4 Be my protector, O God, ◆ a mighty stronghold to save me. ◆ For you are my rock, my stronghold! ◆ Lead me, guide me, for the sake of your name.

First Reading Lv 13: 1-2, 44-46 The Lord said to Moses and Aaron, "If someone has on his skin a scab or pustule or blotch which appears to be the sore of leprosy, he shall be brought to Aaron, the priest, or to one of the priests among his descendants. If the man is leprous and unclean, the priest shall declare him unclean by reason of the sore on his head.

"The one who bears the sore of leprosy shall keep his garments rent and his head bare, and shall muffle his beard; he shall cry out, 'Unclean, unclean!' As long as the sore is on him he shall declare himself unclean, since he is in fact unclean. He shall dwell apart, making his abode outside the camp."

Responsorial Psalm *Ps 32: 1–2, 5, 11*   Joe Higginbotham

I turn to you, Lord, in time of trou-ble, and you fill me with the joy of sal - va-tion.

Blessed is he whose fault is taken away,
   whose sin is covered.
Blessed the man to whom the LORD imputes not guilt,
   in whose spirit there is no guile. ℟

Then I acknowledged my sin to you,
   my guilt I covered not.
I said, "I confess my faults to the   LORD,"
   and you took away the guilt of my sin. ℟

Be glad in the LORD and rejoice, you just;
   exult, all you upright of heart. ℟

Second Reading *1 Cor 10: 31–11: 1* Brothers and sisters, whether you eat or drink, or whatever you do, do everything for the glory of God. Avoid giving offense, whether to the Jews or Greeks or the church of God, just as I try to please everyone in every way, not seeking my own benefit but that of the many, that they may be saved. Be imitators of me, as I am of Christ.

Alleluia   Lk 7: 16

Joe Higginbotham

Al-le-lu-ia,   al-le-lu-ia,   al-le-lu - ia.

A great prophet has arisen in our midst, / God has visited his people.   **Alleluia, alleluia.**

Gospel Mk 1: 40–45 A leper came to Jesus and kneeling down begged him and said, "If you wish, you can make me clean." Moved with pity, he stretched out his hand, touched him, and said to him, "I do will it. Be made clean." The leprosy left him immediately, and he was made clean. Then, warning him sternly, he dismissed him at once.

He said to him, "See that you tell no one anything, but go, show yourself to the priest and offer for your cleansing what Moses prescribed; that will be proof for them."

The man went away and began to publicize the whole matter. He spread the report abroad so that it was impossible for Jesus to enter a town openly. He remained outside in deserted places, and people kept coming to him from everywhere.

Communion Antiphon cf. Ps 78 (77): 29–30 **They ate and had their fill, ◆ and what they craved the Lord gave them; ◆ they were not disappointed in what they craved.**

Or: Jn 3: 16 **God so loved the world ◆ that he gave his Only Begotten Son, ◆so that all who believe in him may not perish, ◆ but may have eternal life.**

SEVENTH SUNDAY IN ORDINARY TIME

Entrance Antiphon Ps 13 (12): 6 **O Lord, I trust in your merciful love. ◆ My heart will rejoice in your salvation. ◆ I will sing to the Lord who has been bountiful with me.**

First Reading   Is 43: 18–19, 21–22, 24b–25

Thus says the LORD:
    Remember not the events of the past,
        the things of long ago consider not;
    see, I am doing something new!
        Now it springs forth, do you not perceive it?
    In the desert I make a way,
        in the wasteland, rivers.
    The people I formed for myself,
        that they might announce my praise.
    Yet you did not call upon me, O Jacob,
        for you grew weary of me, O Israel.
    You burdened me with your sins,
        and wearied me with your crimes.
    It is I, I, who wipe out,
        for my own sake, your offenses;
        your sins I remember no more.

Responsorial Psalm   Ps 41: 2–3, 4–5, 13–14   *Bill Svarda*

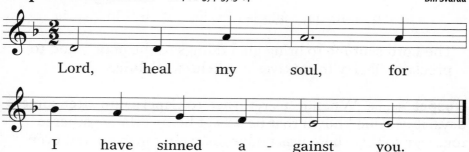

Lord, heal my soul, for I have sinned a - gainst you.

Blessed is the one who has regard for the lowly and the poor;
    in the day of misfortune the LORD will deliver him.
The LORD will keep and preserve him;
    and make him blessed on earth,
    and not give him over to the will of his enemies. ℟

The LORD will help him on his sickbed,
    he will take away all his ailment when he is ill.
Once I said, "O LORD, have pity on me;
    heal me, though I have sinned against you." ℟

But because of my integrity you sustain me
and let me stand before you forever.
Blessed be the LORD, the God of Israel,
from all eternity. Amen. Amen. ℞

Second Reading *2 Cor 1: 18–22* Brothers and sisters: As God is faithful, our word to you is not "yes" and "no." For the Son of God, Jesus Christ, who was proclaimed to you by us, Silvanus and Timothy and me, was not "yes" and "no, " but "yes" has been in him. For however many are the promises of God, their Yes is in him; therefore, the Amen from us also goes through him to God for glory. But the one who gives us security with you in Christ and who anointed us is God; he has also put his seal upon us and given the Spirit in our hearts as a first installment.

Alleluia   *cf. Lk 4: 18*   Joe Higginbotham

Al - le - lu - ia,   al - le - lu - ia,   al - le - lu - ia.

The Lord sent me to bring glad tidings to the poor, / and to proclaim liberty to captives.   **Alleluia, alleluia.**

Gospel *Mk 2: 1–12* When Jesus returned to Capernaum after some days, it became known that he was at home. Many gathered together so that there was no longer room for them, not even around the door, and he preached the word to them. They came bringing to him a paralytic carried by four men. Unable to get near Jesus because of the crowd, they opened up the roof above him. After they had broken through, they let down the mat on which the paralytic was lying. When Jesus saw their faith, he said to the paralytic, "Child, your sins are forgiven." Now some of the scribes were sitting there asking themselves, "Why does this man speak that way? He is blaspheming. Who but God alone can forgive sins?" Jesus immediately knew in his mind what they were thinking to themselves, so he said, "Why are you thinking such things in your hearts? Which is easier, to say to the paralytic, 'Your sins are forgiven,' or to say, 'Rise, pick up your mat and walk?' But that you may know that the Son of Man has authority to forgive sins on earth"—he said to the paralytic, "I say to you, rise, pick up your mat, and go home." He rose, picked up his mat at once, and went away in the sight of everyone. They were all astounded and glorified God, saying, "We have never seen anything like this."

Communion Antiphon *Ps 9: 2–3* I will recount all your wonders, ◆ I will rejoice in you and be glad, ◆ and sing psalms to your name, O Most High.

Or: *Jn 11: 27* Lord, I have come to believe that you are the Christ, ◆ the Son of the living God, who is coming into this world.

EIGHTH SUNDAY

IN ORDINARY TIME

Entrance Antiphon *cf. Ps 18 (17): 19–20* The Lord became my protector. ◆ He brought me out to a place of freedom; ◆ he saved me because he delighted in me.

First Reading *Hos 2: 16b, 17b, 21–22*
Thus says the LORD:
　I will lead her into the desert
　　and speak to her heart.
　She shall respond there as in the days of her youth,
　　when she came up from the land of Egypt.
　I will espouse you to me forever:
　　I will espouse you in right and in justice,
　　in love and in mercy;
　I will espouse you in fidelity,
　　and you shall know the LORD.

Responsorial Psalm   Ps 103: 1–2, 3–4, 8, 10, 12–13   *Beverly McDevitt*

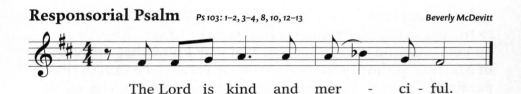

The Lord is kind and mer - ci - ful.

Bless the LORD, O my soul;
  and all my being, bless his holy name.
Bless the LORD, O my soul,
  and forget not all his benefits. ℟

He pardons all your iniquities,
  he heals all your ills.
He redeems your life from destruction,
  crowns you with kindness and compassion. ℟

Merciful and gracious is the LORD,
  slow to anger and abounding in kindness.
Not according to our sins does he deal with us,
  nor does he requite us according to our crimes. ℟

As far as the east is from the west,
  so far has he put our transgressions from us.
As a father has compassion on his children,
  so the LORD has compassion on those who fear him. ℟

Second Reading 2 Cor 3: 1b–6 Brothers and sisters: Do we need, as
some do, letters of recommendation to you or from you? You are
our letter, written on our hearts, known and read by all, shown
to be a letter of Christ ministered by us, written not in ink but
by the Spirit of the living God, not on tablets of stone but on
tablets that are hearts of flesh.

Such confidence we have through Christ toward God. Not
that of ourselves we are qualified to take credit for anything as
coming from us; rather, our qualification comes from God, who
has indeed qualified us as ministers of a new covenant, not of
letter but of spirit; for the letter brings death, but the Spirit
gives life.

Alleluia Jas 1: 18

Vince Ambrosetti

Al-le-lu-ia, al-le-lu-ia, al-le-lu-ia, al-le-lu-ia.

Al-le-lu-ia, al-le-lu-ia, al-le-lu-ia.

The Father willed to give us birth by the word of truth /
that we may be a kind of firstfruits of his creatures.
Alleluia, alleluia.

Gospel Mk 2: 18–22 The disciples of John and of the Pharisees were accustomed to fast. People came to him and objected, "Why do the disciples of John and the disciples of the Pharisees fast, but your disciples do not fast?" Jesus answered them, "Can the wedding guests fast while the bridegroom is with them? As long as they have the bridegroom with them they cannot fast. But the days will come when the bridegroom is taken away from them, and then they will fast on that day. No one sews a piece of unshrunken cloth on an old cloak. If he does, its fullness pulls away, the new from the old, and the tear gets worse. Likewise, no one pours new wine into old wineskins. Otherwise, the wine will burst the skins, and both the wine and the skins are ruined. Rather, new wine is poured into fresh wineskins."

Communion Antiphon cf. Ps 13 (12): 6 **I will sing to the Lord who has been bountiful with me, ◆ sing psalms to the name of the Lord Most High.**

Or: Mt 28: 20 **Behold, I am with you always, ◆ even to the end of the age, says the Lord.**

NINE SUNDAY IN ORDINARY TIME

Entrance Antiphon *cf. Ps 25 (24): 16, 18* **Turn to me and have mercy on me, O Lord, ◆ for I am alone and poor. ◆ See my lowliness and suffering ◆ and take away all my sins, my God.**

First Reading *Dt 5: 12–15* Thus says the LORD: "Take care to keep holy the sabbath day as the LORD, your God, commanded you. Six days you may labor and do all your work; but the seventh day is the sabbath of the LORD, your God. No work may be done then, whether by you, or your son or daughter, or your male or female slave, or your ox or ass or any of your beasts, or the alien who lives with you. Your male and female slave should rest as you do. For remember that you too were once a slave in Egypt, and the LORD, your God, brought you from there with his strong hand and outstretched arm. That is why the LORD, your God, has commanded you to observe the sabbath day."

Responsorial Psalm   Ps 81: 3–4, 5–6, 6–8, 10–11   *Joe Higginbotham*

Sing with joy, sing with joy to God our help.

Take up a melody, and sound the timbrel,
  the pleasant harp and the lyre.
Blow the trumpet at the new moon,
  at the full moon, on our solemn feast. ℟

For it is a statute in Israel,
  an ordinance of the God of Jacob,
Who made it a decree for Joseph
  when he came forth from the land of Egypt. ℟

An unfamiliar speech I hear:
  "I relieved his shoulder of the burden;
  his hands were freed from the basket.
In distress you called, and I rescued you." ℟

"There shall be no strange god among you
    nor shall you worship any alien god.
I, the LORD, am your God
    who led you forth from the land of Egypt." ℟

Second Reading *2 Cor 4: 6–11* Brothers and sisters: God who said,
Let light shine out of darkness, has shone in our hearts to bring
to light the knowledge of the glory of God on the face of Jesus
Christ. But we hold this treasure in earthen vessels, that the
surpassing power may be of God and not from us. We are
afflicted in every way, but not constrained; perplexed, but not
driven to despair; persecuted, but not abandoned; struck down,
but not destroyed; always carrying about in the body the dying
of Jesus, so that the life of Jesus may also be manifested in our
body. For we who live are constantly being given up to death for
the sake of Jesus, so that the life of Jesus may be manifested in
our mortal flesh.

Alleluia   *cf. Jn 17: 17b, 17a*   *Vince Ambrosetti*

Al-le-lu-ia, al-le-lu-ia, al-le-lu-ia, al-le-lu-ia.

Al-le-lu-ia, al-le-lu-ia, al-le-lu - ia.

Your word, O Lord, is truth; / consecrate us in the truth.
Alleluia, alleluia.

Gospel   *Mk 2: 23–3: 6 or 2: 23–28*
For the shorter form, read only the parts in brackets.
[As Jesus was passing through a field of grain on the sabbath,
his disciples began to make a path while picking the heads of
grain. At this the Pharisees said to him, "Look, why are they
doing what is unlawful on the sabbath?" He said to them, "Have
you never read what David did when he was in need and he and
his companions were hungry? How he went into the house of

God when Abiathar was high priest and ate the bread of offering that only the priests could lawfully eat, and shared it with his companions?" Then he said to them, "The sabbath was made for man, not man for the sabbath. That is why the Son of Man is lord even of the sabbath."]

Again he entered the synagogue. There was a man there who had a withered hand. They watched him closely to see if he would cure him on the Sabbath so that they might accuse him. He said to the man with the withered hand, "Come up here before us." Then he said to them, "Is it lawful to do good on the sabbath rather than to do evil, to save life rather than to destroy it?" But they remained silent. Looking around at them with anger and grieved at their hardness of heart, he said to the man, "Stretch out your hand." He stretched it out and his hand was restored. The Pharisees went out and immediately took counsel with the Herodians against him to put him to death.

Communion Antiphon *cf. Ps 17 (16): 6* **To you I call, for you will surely heed me, O God; ◆ turn your ear to me; hear my words.**

Or: Mk 11: 23, 24 **Amen, I say to you: Whatever you ask for in prayer, ◆ believe you will receive it, ◆ and it will be yours, says the Lord.**

TENTH SUNDAY IN ORDINARY TIME

Entrance Antiphon *cf. Ps 27 (26): 1–2* **The Lord is my light and my salvation; whom shall I fear? ◆ The Lord is the stronghold of my life; whom should I dread? ◆ When those who do evil draw near, they stumble and fall.**

First Reading Gen 3: 9–15 After the man, Adam, had eaten of the tree, the LORD God called to the man and asked him, "Where are you?" He answered, "I heard you in the garden; but I was afraid, because I was naked, so I hid myself." Then he asked, "Who told you that you were naked? You have eaten, then, from the tree of which I had forbidden you to eat!" The man replied,

"The woman whom you put here with me—she gave me fruit
from the tree, and so I ate it." The LORD God then asked the
woman, "Why did you do such a thing?" The woman answered,
"The serpent tricked me into it, so I ate it."

Then the LORD God said to the serpent:
"Because you have done this, you shall be banned
    from all the animals
    and from all the wild creatures;
on your belly shall you crawl,
    and dirt shall you eat
    all the days of your life.
I will put enmity between you and the woman,
    and between your offspring and hers;
he will strike at your head,
    while you strike at his heel."

Responsorial Psalm   Ps 130: 1–2, 3–4, 5–6, 7–8   *Bill Svarda*

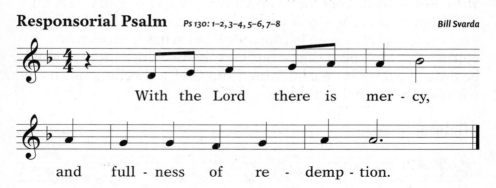

With the Lord there is mer - cy,

and full - ness of re - demp - tion.

Out of the depths I cry to you, O LORD;
    LORD, hear my voice!
Let your ears be attentive
    to my voice in supplication. ℟

If you, O LORD, mark iniquities,
    LORD, who can stand?
But with you is forgiveness,
    that you may be revered. ℟

I trust in the LORD;
    my soul trusts in his word.
More than sentinels wait for the dawn,
    let Israel wait for the LORD. ℟

For with the LORD is kindness
  and with him is plenteous redemption
and he will redeem Israel
  from all their iniquities. ℟

Second Reading *2 Cor 4: 13- 5: 1* Brothers and sisters: Since we
have the same spirit of faith, according to what is written, I
believed, therefore I spoke, we too believe and therefore we speak,
knowing that the one who raised the Lord Jesus will raise us
also with Jesus and place us with you in his presence. Everything
indeed is for you, so that the grace bestowed in abundance on
more and more people may cause the thanksgiving to overflow
for the glory of God. Therefore, we are not discouraged;
rather, although our outer self is wasting away, our inner
self is being renewed day by day. For this momentary light
affliction is producing for us an eternal weight of glory beyond
all comparison, as we look not to what is seen but to what is
unseen; for what is seen is transitory, but what is unseen is
eternal. For we know that if our earthly dwelling, a tent, should
be destroyed, we have a building from God, a dwelling not made
with hands, eternal in heaven.

Alleluia   *Jn 12: 31b–32*   Vince Ambrosetti

Now the ruler of this world will be driven out, says the
Lord; / and when I am lifted up from the earth, I will draw
everyone to myself.   **Alleluia, alleluia**

Gospel *Mk 3: 20–35* Jesus came home with his disciples. Again the
crowd gathered, making it impossible for them even to eat.
When his relatives heard of this they set out to seize him, for
they said, "He is out of his mind." The scribes who had come

from Jerusalem said, "He is possessed by Beelzebul," and "By the prince of demons he drives out demons."

Summoning them, he began to speak to them in parables, "How can Satan drive out Satan? If a kingdom is divided against itself, that kingdom cannot stand. And if a house is divided against itself, that house will not be able to stand. And if Satan has risen up against himself and is divided, he cannot stand; that is the end of him. But no one can enter a strong man's house to plunder his property unless he first ties up the strong man. Then he can plunder the house. Amen, I say to you, all sins and all blasphemies that people utter will be forgiven them. But whoever blasphemes against the Holy Spirit will never have forgiveness, but is guilty of an everlasting sin." For they had said, "He has an unclean spirit."

His mother and his brothers arrived. Standing outside they sent word to him and called him. A crowd seated around him told him, "Your mother and your brothers and your sisters are outside asking for you." But he said to them in reply, "Who are my mother and my brothers?" And looking around at those seated in the circle he said, "Here are my mother and my brothers. For whoever does the will of God is my brother and sister and mother."

Communion Antiphon Ps 18 (17): 3 **The Lord is my rock, my fortress, and my deliverer; ✦ my God is my saving strength.**

Or: 1 Jn 4: 16 **God is love, and whoever abides in love ✦ abides in God, and God in him.**

ELEVENTH SUNDAY IN ORDINARY TIME

Entrance Antiphon cf. Ps 27 (26): 7, 9 **O Lord, hear my voice, for I have called to you; be my help. ✦ Do not abandon or forsake me, O God, my Savior!**

First Reading Ez 17: 22–24
Thus says the Lord God:
    I, too, will take from the crest of the cedar,
        from its topmost branches tear off a tender shoot,

and plant it on a high and lofty mountain;
  on the mountain heights of Israel I will plant it.
It shall put forth branches and bear fruit,
  and become a majestic cedar.
Birds of every kind shall dwell beneath it,
  every winged thing in the shade of its boughs.
And all the trees of the field shall know
  that I, the LORD,
bring low the high tree,
  lift high the lowly tree,
wither up the green tree,
  and make the withered tree bloom.
As I, the LORD, have spoken, so will I do.

Responsorial Psalm   Ps 92: 2–3, 13–14, 15–16   *Bill Svarda*

Lord, it is good   to give thanks to you.

It is good to give thanks to the LORD,
  to sing praise to your name, Most High,
To proclaim your kindness at dawn
  and your faithfulness throughout the night.   ℟

The just one shall flourish like the palm tree,
  like a cedar of Lebanon shall he grow.
They that are planted in the house of the LORD
  shall flourish in the courts of our God.   ℟

They shall bear fruit even in old age;
  vigorous and sturdy shall they be,
Declaring how just is the LORD,
  my rock, in whom there is no wrong.   ℟

Second Reading   2 Cor 5: 6–10   Brothers and sisters: We are always
courageous, although we know that while we are at home in
the body we are away from the Lord, for we walk by faith, not
by sight. Yet we are courageous, and we would rather leave the

body and go home to the Lord. Therefore, we aspire to please him, whether we are at home or away. For we must all appear before the judgment seat of Christ, so that each may receive recompense, according to what he did in the body, whether good or evil.

Alleluia

Vince Ambrosetti

Al-le-lu-ia, al - le - lu - ia, al - le-lu-ia, al - le - lu - ia.

Al - le - lu - ia, al - le - lu - ia, al - le - lu - ia.

The seed is the word of God, Christ is the sower. / All who come to him will live for ever.   **Alleluia, alleluia.**

Gospel Mk 4: 26–34 Jesus said to the crowds: "This is how it is with the kingdom of God; it is as if a man were to scatter seed on the land and would sleep and rise night and day and through it all the seed would sprout and grow, he knows not how. Of its own accord the land yields fruit, first the blade, then the ear, then the full grain in the ear. And when the grain is ripe, he wields the sickle at once, for the harvest has come."

He said, "To what shall we compare the kingdom of God, or what parable can we use for it? It is like a mustard seed that, when it is sown in the ground, is the smallest of all the seeds on the earth. But once it is sown, it springs up and becomes the largest of plants and puts forth large branches, so that the birds of the sky can dwell in its shade." With many such parables he spoke the word to them as they were able to understand it. Without parables he did not speak to them, but to his own disciples he explained everything in private.

Communion Antiphon Ps 27 (26): 4 **There is one thing I ask of the Lord, only this do I seek: ✦ to live in the house of the Lord all the days of my life.**

Or: Jn 17: 11 **Holy Father, keep in your name those you have given me, ♦ that they may be one as we are one, says the Lord.**

TWELFTH SUNDAY IN ORDINARY TIME

Entrance Antiphon cf. Ps 28 (27): 8–9 **The Lord is the strength of his people, ♦ a saving refuge for the one he has anointed. ♦ Save your people, Lord, and bless your heritage, ♦ and govern them for ever.**

First Reading   Job 38: 1, 8–11

The Lord addressed Job out of the storm and said:
  Who shut within doors the sea,
    when it burst forth from the womb;
  when I made the clouds its garment
    and thick darkness its swaddling bands?
  When I set limits for it
    and fastened the bar of its door,
  and said: Thus far shall you come but no farther,
    and here shall your proud waves be stilled!

Responsorial Psalm   Ps 107: 23–24, 25–26, 28–29, 30–31   *Michael Giszczak*

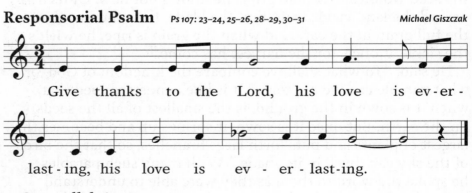

Give thanks to the Lord, his love is ev-er-last-ing, his love is ev-er-last-ing.

Or: **Alleluia.**

They who sailed the sea in ships,
  trading on the deep waters,
These saw the works of the LORD
  and his wonders in the abyss. ℟

His command raised up a storm wind
    which tossed its waves on high.
They mounted up to heaven; they sank to the depths;
    their hearts melted away in their plight. ℟

They cried to the LORD in their distress;
    from their straits he rescued them,
He hushed the storm to a gentle breeze,
    and the billows of the sea were stilled. ℟

They rejoiced that they were calmed,
    and he brought them to their desired haven.
Let them give thanks to the LORD for his kindness
    and his wondrous deeds to the children of men. ℟

Second Reading *2 Cor 5: 14–17* Brothers and sisters: The love of Christ impels us, once we have come to the conviction that one died for all; therefore, all have died. He indeed died for all, so that those who live might no longer live for themselves but for him who for their sake died and was raised.

Consequently, from now on we regard no one according to the flesh; even if we once knew Christ according to the flesh, yet now we know him so no longer. So whoever is in Christ is a new creation: the old things have passed away; behold, new things have come.

Alleluia   *Lk 7: 16*   *Vince Ambrosetti*

Al-le-lu-ia, al-le-lu-ia, al-le-lu-ia, al-le-lu-ia.

Al-le-lu-ia, al-le-lu-ia, al-le-lu-ia.

A great prophet has risen in our midst. / God has visited his people. **Alleluia, alleluia.**

Gospel Mk 4: 35–41 On that day, as evening drew on, Jesus said to his disciples: "Let us cross to the other side." Leaving the crowd, they took Jesus with them in the boat just as he was. And other boats were with him. A violent squall came up and waves were breaking over the boat, so that it was already filling up. Jesus was in the stern, asleep on a cushion. They woke him and said to him, "Teacher, do you not care that we are perishing?" He woke up, rebuked the wind, and said to the sea, "Quiet! Be still!" The wind ceased and there was great calm. Then he asked them, "Why are you terrified? Do you not yet have faith?" They were filled with great awe and said to one another, "Who then is this whom even wind and sea obey?"

Communion Antiphon Ps 145 (144): 15 The eyes of all look to you, Lord, ◆ and you give them their food in due season.

Or: Jn 10: 11, 15 I am the Good Shepherd, ◆ and I lay down my life for my sheep, says the Lord.

THIRTEENTH SUNDAY IN ORDINARY TIME

Entrance Antiphon Ps 47 (46): 2 All peoples, clap your hands. ◆ Cry to God with shouts of joy!

First Reading Wis 1: 13–15; 2: 23–24
God did not make death,
    nor does he rejoice in the destruction of the living.
For he fashioned all things that they might have being;
    and the creatures of the world are wholesome,
and there is not a destructive drug among them
    nor any domain of the netherworld on earth,
    for justice is undying.
For God formed man to be imperishable;
    the image of his own nature he made him.
But by the envy of the devil, death entered the world,
    and they who belong to his company experience it.

Responsorial Psalm

Ps 30: 2, 4, 5–6, 11, 12, 13

Roger Holtz

I will praise you, Lord, I will praise you, Lord, for you have res-cued me.

I will extol you, O LORD, for you drew me clear
and did not let my enemies rejoice over me.
O LORD, you brought me up from the netherworld;
you preserved me from among those going down into
the pit. ℟

Sing praise to the LORD, you his faithful ones,
and give thanks to his holy name.
For his anger lasts but a moment;
a lifetime, his good will.
At nightfall, weeping enters in,
but with the dawn, rejoicing. ℟

Hear, O LORD, and have pity on me;
O LORD, be my helper.
You changed my mourning into dancing;
O LORD, my God, forever will I give you thanks. ℟

Second Reading 2 Cor 8: 7, 9, 13–15 Brothers and sisters: As you excel
in every respect, in faith, discourse, knowledge, all earnestness,
and in the love we have for you, may you excel in this gracious
act also.

For you know the gracious act of our Lord Jesus Christ, that
though he was rich, for your sake he became poor, so that by
his poverty you might become rich. Not that others should have
relief while you are burdened, but that as a matter of equality
your abundance at the present time should supply their needs,
so that their abundance may also supply your needs, that there
may be equality. As it is written:

Whoever had much did not have more,
and whoever had little did not have less.

Alleluia   cf. 2 Tm 1:10   *Vince Ambrosetti*

Al - le - lu - ia,   al - le - lu - ia,   al - le - lu - ia,   al - le - lu - ia.

Al - le - lu - ia,   al - le - lu - ia,   al - le - lu - ia.

Our Savior Jesus Christ destroyed death / and brought life to
light through the Gospel.   **Alleluia, alleluia.**

Gospel   Mk 5: 21–43 or 5: 21–24, 35b–43

For the shorter form, read only the parts in brackets.
[When Jesus had crossed again in the boat to the other side, a
large crowd gathered around him, and he stayed close to the
sea. One of the synagogue officials, named Jairus, came forward.
Seeing him he fell at his feet and pleaded earnestly with him,
saying, "My daughter is at the point of death. Please, come lay
your hands on her that she may get well and live." He went
off with him, and a large crowd followed him and pressed
upon him.]

There was a woman afflicted with hemorrhages for twelve
years. She had suffered greatly at the hands of many doctors
and had spent all that she had. Yet she was not helped but only
grew worse. She had heard about Jesus and came up behind him
in the crowd and touched his cloak. She said, "If I but touch his
clothes, I shall be cured." Immediately her flow of blood dried
up. She felt in her body that she was healed of her affliction.
Jesus, aware at once that power had gone out from him, turned
around in the crowd and asked, "Who has touched my clothes?"
But his disciples said to Jesus, "You see how the crowd is
pressing upon you, and yet you ask, 'Who touched me?'" And
he looked around to see who had done it. The woman, realizing
what had happened to her, approached in fear and trembling.
She fell down before Jesus and told him the whole truth. He said

to her, "Daughter, your faith has saved you. Go in peace and be cured of your affliction."

[While he was still speaking, people from the synagogue official's house arrived and said, "Your daughter has died; why trouble the teacher any longer?" Disregarding the message that was reported, Jesus said to the synagogue official, "Do not be afraid; just have faith." He did not allow anyone to accompany him inside except Peter, James, and John, the brother of James. When they arrived at the house of the synagogue official, he caught sight of a commotion, people weeping and wailing loudly. So he went in and said to them, "Why this commotion and weeping? The child is not dead but asleep." And they ridiculed him. Then he put them all out. He took along the child's father and mother and those who were with him and entered the room where the child was. He took the child by the hand and said to her, *Talitha koum,*" which means, "Little girl, I say to you, arise!" The girl, a child of twelve, arose immediately and walked around. At that they were utterly astounded. He gave strict orders that no one should know this and said that she should be given something to eat.]

Communion Antiphon *cf. Ps 103 (102): 1* **Bless the Lord, O my soul, ✦ and all within me, his holy name.**

Or: *Jn 17: 20–21* **O Father, I pray for them, that they may be one in us, ✦ that the world may believe that you have sent me, says the Lord.**

FOURTEENTH SUNDAY IN ORDINARY TIME

Entrance Antiphon *cf. Ps 48 (47): 10–11* **Your merciful love, O God, ✦ we have received in the midst of your temple. ✦ Your praise, O God, like your name, ✦ reaches the ends of the earth; ✦ your right hand is filled with saving justice.**

First Reading *Ez 2: 2–5* As the LORD spoke to me, the spirit entered into me and set me on my feet, and I heard the one who was speaking say to me: Son of man, I am sending you to the

Israelites, rebels who have rebelled against me; they and their ancestors have revolted against me to this very day. Hard of face and obstinate of heart are they to whom I am sending you. But you shall say to them: Thus says the Lord GOD! And whether they heed or resist—for they are a rebellious house—they shall know that a prophet has been among them.

Responsorial Psalm   Ps 123: 1–2, 2, 3–4   Joe Higginbotham

Our eyes are fixed on the Lord, plead - ing for his mer - cy.

To you I lift up my eyes
   who are enthroned in heaven—
As the eyes of servants
   are on the hands of their masters. ℟

As the eyes of a maid
   are on the hands of her mistress,
So are our eyes on the LORD, our God,
   till he have pity on us. ℟

Have pity on us, O LORD, have pity on us,
   for we are more than sated with contempt;
our souls are more than sated
    with the mockery of the arrogant,
    with the contempt of the proud. ℟

Second Reading 2 Cor 12: 7–10 Brothers and sisters: That I, Paul, might not become too elated, because of the abundance of the revelations, a thorn in the flesh was given to me, an angel of Satan, to beat me, to keep me from being too elated. Three times I begged the Lord about this, that it might leave me, but he said to me, "My grace is sufficient for you, for power is made perfect in weakness." I will rather boast most gladly of my weaknesses, in order that the power of Christ may dwell with me. Therefore, I am content with weaknesses, insults, hardships, persecutions, and constraints, for the sake of Christ; for when I am weak, then I am strong.

Alleluia *cf. Lk 4: 18*   *Vince Ambrosetti*

Al-le-lu-ia, al - le - lu-ia, al - le - lu-ia, al - le - lu - ia.

Al - le - lu - ia, al - le - lu - ia, al - le - lu - ia.

The Spirit of the Lord is upon me, / for he sent me to bring glad tidings to the poor.   **Alleluia, alleluia.**

Gospel Mk 6: 1–6 Jesus departed from there and came to his native place, accompanied by his disciples. When the sabbath came he began to teach in the synagogue, and many who heard him were astonished. They said, "Where did this man get all this? What kind of wisdom has been given him? What mighty deeds are wrought by his hands! Is he not the carpenter, the son of Mary, and the brother of James and Joses and Judas and Simon? And are not his sisters here with us?" And they took offense at him. Jesus said to them, "A prophet is not without honor except in his native place and among his own kin and in his own house." So he was not able to perform any mighty deed there, apart from curing a few sick people by laying his hands on them. He was amazed at their lack of faith.

Communion Antiphon Ps 34 (33): 9 Taste and see that the Lord is good; ◆ blessed the man who seeks refuge in him.

Or: Mt 11: 28 **Come to me, all who labor and are burdened, ◆ and I will refresh you, says the Lord.**

FIFTEENTH SUNDAY IN ORDINARY TIME

Entrance Antiphon *cf. Ps 17 (16): 15* As for me, in justice I shall behold your face; ♦ I shall be filled with the vision of your glory.

First Reading *Am 7: 12–15* Amaziah, priest of Bethel, said to Amos, "Off with you, visionary, flee to the land of Judah! There earn your bread by prophesying, but never again prophesy in Bethel; for it is the king's sanctuary and a royal temple." Amos answered Amaziah, "I was no prophet, nor have I belonged to a company of prophets; I was a shepherd and a dresser of sycamores. The LORD took me from following the flock, and said to me, Go, prophesy to my people Israel."

Responsorial Psalm   *Ps 85: 9–10, 11–12, 13–14*   Brian J. Nelson

Lord, let us see your kind-ness, and grant us your sal-va-tion.

I will hear what God proclaims;
   the LORD—for he proclaims peace.
Near indeed is his salvation to those who fear him,
   glory dwelling in our land. ℟

Kindness and truth shall meet;
   justice and peace shall kiss.
Truth shall spring out of the earth,
   and justice shall look down from heaven. ℟

The LORD himself will give his benefits;
   our land shall yield its increase.
Justice shall walk before him,
   and prepare the way of his steps. ℟

Second Reading Eph 1: 3–14 or 1: 3–10

For the shorter form, read only the parts in brackets.

[Blessed be the God and Father of our Lord Jesus Christ, who has blessed us in Christ with every spiritual blessing in the heavens, as he chose us in him, before the foundation of the world, to be holy and without blemish before him. In love he destined us for adoption to himself through Jesus Christ, in accord with the favor of his will, for the praise of the glory of his grace that he granted us in the beloved.

In him we have redemption by his blood, the forgiveness of transgressions, in accord with the riches of his grace that he lavished upon us. In all wisdom and insight, he has made known to us the mystery of his will in accord with his favor that he set forth in him as a plan for the fullness of times, to sum up all things in Christ, in heaven and on earth.]

In him we were also chosen, destined in accord with the purpose of the One who accomplishes all things according to the intention of his will, so that we might exist for the praise of his glory, we who first hoped in Christ. In him you also, who have heard the word of truth, the gospel of your salvation, and have believed in him, were sealed with the promised Holy Spirit, which is the first installment of our inheritance toward redemption as God's possession, to the praise of his glory.

Alleluia cf. Eph 1: 17–18   Vince Ambrosetti

Al-le-lu-ia, al-le-lu-ia, al-le-lu-ia, al-le-lu-ia.

Al-le-lu-ia, al-le-lu-ia, al-le-lu-ia.

May the Father of our Lord Jesus Christ / enlighten the eyes of our hearts, / that we may know what is the hope that / belongs to our call.   **Alleluia, alleluia.**

Gospel Mk 6: 7–13 Jesus summoned the Twelve and began to send them out two by two and gave them authority over unclean spirits. He instructed them to take nothing for the journey but a walking stick—no food, no sack, no money in their belts. They were, however, to wear sandals but not a second tunic. He said to them, "Wherever you enter a house, stay there until you leave. Whatever place does not welcome you or listen to you, leave there and shake the dust off your feet in testimony against them." So they went off and preached repentance. The Twelve drove out many demons, and they anointed with oil many who were sick and cured them.

Communion Antiphon *cf. Ps 84 (83): 4-5* **The sparrow finds a home, ◆ and the swallow a nest for her young: ◆ by your altars, O Lord of hosts, my King and my God. ◆ Blessed are they who dwell in your house, ◆ for ever singing your praise.**

Or: *Jn 6: 57* **Whoever eats my flesh and drinks my blood ◆ remains in me and I in him, says the Lord.**

SIXTEENTH SUNDAY

IN ORDINARY TIME

Entrance Antiphon *Ps 54 (53): 6, 8* **See, I have God for my help. ◆ The Lord sustains my soul. ◆ I will sacrifice to you with willing heart, ◆ and praise your name, O Lord, for it is good.**

First Reading *Jer 23: 1-6* Woe to the shepherds who mislead and scatter the flock of my pasture, says the LORD. Therefore, thus says the LORD, the God of Israel, against the shepherds who shepherd my people: You have scattered my sheep and driven them away. You have not cared for them, but I will take care to punish your evil deeds. I myself will gather the remnant of my flock from all the lands to which I have driven them and bring them back to their meadow; there they shall increase and multiply. I will appoint shepherds for them who will shepherd them so that they need no longer fear and tremble; and none shall be missing, says the LORD.

Behold, the days are coming, says the LORD,
  when I will raise up a righteous shoot to David;
as king he shall reign and govern wisely,
  he shall do what is just and right in the land.
In his days Judah shall be saved,
  Israel shall dwell in security.
This is the name they give him:
  "The LORD our justice."

Responsorial Psalm   Ps 23: 1–3, 3–4, 5, 6   Elissa Krieg

The Lord is my shep - herd; there is noth - ing I shall want.

The LORD is my shepherd; I shall not want.
  In verdant pastures he gives me repose;
beside restful waters he leads me;
  he refreshes my soul. ℟

He guides me in right paths
  for his name's sake.
Even though I walk in the dark valley
  I fear no evil; for you are at my side
with your rod and your staff
  that give me courage. ℟

You spread the table before me
  in the sight of my foes;
you anoint my head with oil;
  my cup overflows. ℟

Only goodness and kindness follow me
  all the days of my life;

and I shall dwell in the house of the LORD
   for years to come.   ℟

Second Reading *Eph 2: 13–18* Brothers and sisters: In Christ Jesus
you who once were far off have become near by the blood of
Christ.

   For he is our peace, he who made both one and broke down
the dividing wall of enmity, through his flesh, abolishing the law
with its commandments and legal claims, that he might create
in himself one new person in place of the two, thus establishing
peace, and might reconcile both with God, in one body, through
the cross, putting that enmity to death by it. He came and
preached peace to you who were far off and peace to those who
were near, for through him we both have access in one Spirit to
the Father.

Alleluia   *Jn 10: 27*   *Jim Hughes*

Al-le-lu-ia   Al-le-lu-ia   Al - le-lu - ia.

My sheep hear my voice, says the Lord; / I know them, and
they follow me.   **Alleluia, alleluia.**

Gospel *Mk 6: 30–34* The apostles gathered together with Jesus
and reported all they had done and taught. He said to them,
"Come away by yourselves to a deserted place and rest a while."
People were coming and going in great numbers, and they had
no opportunity even to eat. So they went off in the boat by
themselves to a deserted place. People saw them leaving and
many came to know about it. They hastened there on foot from
all the towns and arrived at the place before them.

   When he disembarked and saw the vast crowd, his heart was
moved with pity for them, for they were like sheep without a
shepherd; and he began to teach them many things.

Communion Antiphon *Ps 111 (110): 4–5* **The Lord, the gracious, the
merciful, ◆ has made a memorial of his wonders; ◆ he gives
food to those who fear him.**

Or: Rv 3: 20   **Behold, I stand at the door and knock, says the Lord. ◆ If anyone hears my voice and opens the door to me, ◆ I will enter his house and dine with him, and he with me.**

SEVENTEENTH SUNDAY IN ORDINARY TIME

Entrance Antiphon   *cf. Ps 68 (67): 6–7, 36*   **God is in his holy place, ◆ God who unites those who dwell in his house; ◆ he himself gives might and strength to his people.**

First Reading   2 Kgs 4: 42–44   A man came from Baal-shalishah bringing to Elisha, the man of God, twenty barley loaves made from the firstfruits, and fresh grain in the ear. Elisha said, "Give it to the people to eat." But his servant objected, "How can I set this before a hundred people?" Elisha insisted, "Give it to the people to eat. For thus says the LORD, 'They shall eat and there shall be some left over.'" And when they had eaten, there was some left over, as the LORD had said.

Responsorial Psalm   Ps 145: 10–11, 15–16, 17–18   David Mann

The hand of the Lord feeds us; he an-swers all our needs.

Let all your works give you thanks, O LORD,
  and let your faithful ones bless you.
Let them discourse of the glory of your kingdom
  and speak of your might. ℟

The eyes of all look hopefully to you,
  and you give them their food in due season;
you open your hand
  and satisfy the desire of every living thing. ℟

The LORD is just in all his ways
and holy in all his works.
The LORD is near to all who call upon him,
to all who call upon him in truth. ℟

Second Reading Eph 4:1–6 Brothers and sisters: I, a prisoner for the Lord, urge you to live in a manner worthy of the call you have received, with all humility and gentleness, with patience, bearing with one another through love, striving to preserve the unity of the spirit through the bond of peace: one body and one Spirit, as you were also called to the one hope of your call; one Lord, one faith, one baptism; one God and Father of all, who is over all and through all and in all.

Alleluia   Lk 7:16   Jim Hughes

Al-le-lu-ia   Al-le-lu-ia   Al-le-lu - ia.

A great prophet has risen in our midst. / God has visited his people. **Alleluia, alleluia.**

Gospel Jn 6:1–15 Jesus went across the Sea of Galilee. A large crowd followed him, because they saw the signs he was performing on the sick. Jesus went up on the mountain, and there he sat down with his disciples. The Jewish feast of Passover was near. When Jesus raised his eyes and saw that a large crowd was coming to him, he said to Philip, "Where can we buy enough food for them to eat?" He said this to test him, because he himself knew what he was going to do. Philip answered him, "Two hundred days' wages worth of food would not be enough for each of them to have a little." One of his disciples, Andrew, the brother of Simon Peter, said to him, "There is a boy here who has five barley loaves and two fish; but what good are these for so many?" Jesus said, "Have the people recline." Now there was a great deal of grass in that place. So the men reclined, about five thousand in number. Then Jesus took the loaves, gave thanks, and distributed them to those who were reclining, and also as much of the fish as they wanted. When they had had their fill, he said to his disciples, "Gather the fragments left over, so that nothing will be wasted." So they collected them, and filled twelve wicker baskets with fragments from the five barley loaves that had been more than they could eat. When the people saw the sign he had done, they said, "This is truly the Prophet, the one who is to come into the world." Since Jesus knew that they were going to come and carry him off to make him king, he withdrew again to the mountain alone.

Communion Antiphon Ps 103 (102): 2 **Bless the Lord, O my soul, ◆ and never forget all his benefits.**

Or: Mt 5: 7–8 **Blessed are the merciful, for they shall receive mercy. ◆ Blessed are the clean of heart, for they shall see God.**

EIGHTEENTH SUNDAY IN ORDINARY TIME

Entrance Antiphon Ps 70 (69): 2, 6 **O God, come to my assistance; ◆ O Lord, make haste to help me! ◆ You are my rescuer, my help; ◆ O Lord, do not delay.**

First Reading Ex 16: 2–4, 12–15 The whole Israelite community grumbled against Moses and Aaron. The Israelites said to them, "Would that we had died at the LORD's hand in the land of Egypt, as we sat by our fleshpots and ate our fill of bread! But you had to lead us into this desert to make the whole community die of famine!"

Then the LORD said to Moses, "I will now rain down bread from heaven for you. Each day the people are to go out and gather their daily portion; thus will I test them, to see whether they follow my instructions or not.

"I have heard the grumbling of the Israelites. Tell them: In the evening twilight you shall eat flesh, and in the morning you shall have your fill of bread, so that you may know that I, the LORD, am your God."

In the evening quail came up and covered the camp. In the morning a dew lay all about the camp, and when the dew evaporated, there on the surface of the desert were fine flakes like hoarfrost on the ground. On seeing it, the Israelites asked one another, "What is this?" for they did not know what it was. But Moses told them, "This is the bread that the LORD has given you to eat."

Responsorial Psalm *Ps 78: 3–4, 23–24, 25, 54* Joe Higginbotham

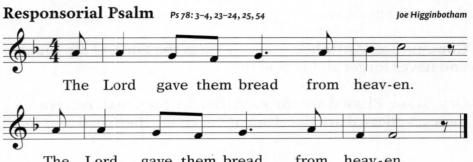

The Lord gave them bread from heav-en.

The Lord gave them bread from heav-en.

What we have heard and know,
    and what our fathers have declared to us,
We will declare to the generation to come
    the glorious deeds of the LORD and his strength
    and the wonders that he wrought. ℟

He commanded the skies above
    and opened the doors of heaven;
he rained manna upon them for food
    and gave them heavenly bread. ℟

Man ate the bread of angels,
    food he sent them in abundance.
And he brought them to his holy land,
    to the mountains his right hand had won. ℟

Second Reading *Eph 4: 17, 20–24* Brothers and sisters: I declare and testify in the Lord that you must no longer live as the Gentiles do, in the futility of their minds; that is not how you learned Christ, assuming that you have heard of him and were taught in him, as truth is in Jesus, that you should put away the old self of your former way of life, corrupted through deceitful desires, and be renewed in the spirit of your minds, and put on the new self, created in God's way in righteousness and holiness of truth.

Alleluia   Mt 4: 4b   Jim Hughes

Al-le-lu-ia   Al-le-lu-ia   Al - le-lu - ia.

One does not live on bread alone, but by every word that comes forth from the mouth of God.   **Alleluia, alleluia.**

Gospel Jn 6: 24-35 When the crowd saw that neither Jesus nor his disciples were there, they themselves got into boats and came to Capernaum looking for Jesus. And when they found him across the sea they said to him, "Rabbi, when did you get here?" Jesus answered them and said, "Amen, amen, I say to you, you are looking for me not because you saw signs but because you ate the loaves and were filled. Do not work for food that perishes but for the food that endures for eternal life, which the Son of Man will give you. For on him the Father, God, has set his seal." So they said to him, "What can we do to accomplish the works of God?" Jesus answered and said to them, "This is the work of God, that you believe in the one he sent." So they said to him, "What sign can you do, that we may see and believe in you? What can you do? Our ancestors ate manna in the desert, as it is written:

He gave them bread from heaven to eat."
So Jesus said to them, "Amen, amen, I say to you, it was not Moses who gave the bread from heaven; my Father gives you the true bread from heaven. For the bread of God is that which comes down from heaven and gives life to the world."

So they said to him, "Sir, give us this bread always." Jesus said to them, "I am the bread of life; whoever comes to me will never hunger, and whoever believes in me will never thirst."

Communion Antiphon Wis 16: 20 You have given us, O Lord, **bread from heaven,** ◆ **endowed with all delights and sweetness in every taste.**

Or: _{Jn 6: 35} **I am the bread of life, says the Lord; ◆ whoever comes to me will not hunger ◆ and whoever believes in me will not thirst.**

NINETEENTH SUNDAY IN ORDINARY TIME

Entrance Antiphon *cf. Ps 74 (73): 20, 19, 22, 23* **Look to your covenant, O Lord, ◆ and forget not the life of your poor ones for ever. ◆ Arise, O God, and defend your cause, ◆ and forget not the cries of those who seek you.**

First Reading *1 Kgs 19: 4–8* Elijah went a day's journey into the desert, until he came to a broom tree and sat beneath it. He prayed for death saying: "This is enough, O LORD! Take my life, for I am no better than my fathers." He lay down and fell asleep under the broom tree, but then an angel touched him and ordered him to get up and eat. Elijah looked and there at his head was a hearth cake and a jug of water. After he ate and drank, he lay down again, but the angel of the LORD came back a second time, touched him, and ordered, "Get up and eat, else the journey will be too long for you!" He got up, ate, and drank; then strengthened by that food, he walked forty days and forty nights to the mountain of God, Horeb.

Responsorial Psalm   Ps 34: 2–3, 4–5, 6–7, 8–9   *Roger Holtz*

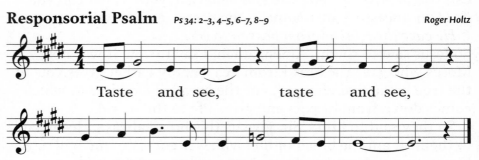

Taste and see, taste and see, taste and see the good-ness of the Lord.

I will bless the LORD at all times;
   his praise shall be ever in my mouth.
Let my soul glory in the LORD;

the lowly will hear me and be glad.   ℟

Glorify the LORD with me,
　　let us together extol his name.
I sought the LORD, and he answered me
　　and delivered me from all my fears.   ℟

Look to him that you may be radiant with joy,
　　and your faces may not blush with shame.
When the afflicted man called out, the LORD heard,
　　and from all his distress he saved him.   ℟

The angel of the LORD encamps
　　around those who fear him and delivers them.
Taste and see how good the LORD is;
　　blessed the man who takes refuge in him.   ℟

Second Reading *Eph 4: 30–5: 2* Brothers and sisters: Do not grieve
the Holy Spirit of God, with which you were sealed for the day
of redemption. All bitterness, fury, anger, shouting, and reviling
must be removed from you, along with all malice. And be kind
to one another, compassionate, forgiving one another as God has
forgiven you in Christ.
　　So be imitators of God, as beloved children, and live in love,
as Christ loved us and handed himself over for us as a sacrificial
offering to God for a fragrant aroma.

Alleluia　　*Jn 6: 51*　　　　　　　　　　　　　　　　*Jim Hughes*

Al-le-lu-ia　　　Al-le-lu-ia　　　Al - le-lu - ia.

I am the living bread that came down from heaven, says
the Lord; / whoever eats this bread will live forever.
Alleluia, alleluia.

Gospel *Jn 6: 41–51* The Jews murmured about Jesus because he said,
"I am the bread that came down from heaven," and they said, "Is

this not Jesus, the son of Joseph? Do we not know his father
and mother? Then how can he say, 'I have come down from
heaven?'" Jesus answered and said to them, "Stop murmuring
among yourselves. No one can come to me unless the Father
who sent me draw him, and I will raise him on the last day. It is
written in the prophets:

They shall all be taught by God.

Everyone who listens to my Father and learns from him comes
to me. Not that anyone has seen the Father except the one who
is from God; he has seen the Father. Amen, amen, I say to you,
whoever believes has eternal life. I am the bread of life. Your
ancestors ate the manna in the desert, but they died; this is the
bread that comes down from heaven so that one may eat it and
not die. I am the living bread that came down from heaven;
whoever eats this bread will live forever; and the bread that I
will give is my flesh for the life of the world."

Communion Antiphon Ps 147 (146): 12, 14 O Jerusalem, glorify the
Lord, ♦ who gives you your fill of finest wheat.

Or: cf. Jn 6: 51 The bread that I will give, says the Lord, ♦ is my
flesh for the life of the world.

TWENTIETH SUNDAY IN ORDINARY TIME

Entrance Antiphon Ps 84 (83): 10–11 Turn your eyes, O God, our
shield; ♦ and look on the face of your anointed one; ♦ one day
within your courts ♦ is better than a thousand elsewhere.

First Reading *Proverbs 9: 1–6*
Wisdom has built her house,
    she has set up her seven columns;
she has dressed her meat, mixed her wine,
    yes, she has spread her table.
She has sent out her maidens; she calls
    from the heights out over the city:

"Let whoever is simple turn in here;"
    to the one who lacks understanding, she says,
"Come, eat of my food,
    and drink of the wine I have mixed!
Forsake foolishness that you may live;
    advance in the way of understanding."

Responsorial Psalm   Ps 34: 2–3, 4–5, 6–7   Roger Holtz

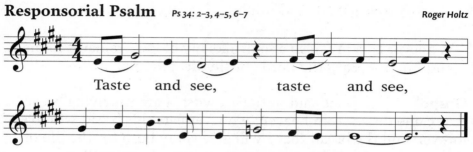

Taste and see, taste and see,
taste and see the good-ness of the Lord.

I will bless the LORD at all times;
    his praise shall be ever in my mouth.
Let my soul glory in the LORD;
    the lowly will hear me and be glad. ℟

Glorify the LORD with me,
    let us together extol his name.
I sought the LORD, and he answered me
    and delivered me from all my fears. ℟

Look to him that you may be radiant with joy,
    and your faces may not blush with shame.
When the poor one called out, the LORD heard,
    and from all his distress he saved him. ℟

Second Reading Eph 5: 15–20 Brothers and sisters: Watch carefully
how you live, not as foolish persons but as wise, making the
most of the opportunity, because the days are evil. Therefore,
do not continue in ignorance, but try to understand what is the
will of the Lord. And do not get drunk on wine, in which lies
debauchery, but be filled with the Spirit, addressing one another
in psalms and hymns and spiritual songs, singing and playing to

the Lord in your hearts, giving thanks always and for everything in the name of our Lord Jesus Christ to God the Father.

Alleluia   *Jn 5: 56*   *Jim Hughes*

Al-le-lu-ia   Al-le-lu-ia   Al - le-lu - ia.

Whoever eats my flesh and drinks my blood / remains in me and I in him, says the Lord.   **Alleluia, alleluia.**

Gospel *Jn 6: 51–58* Jesus said to the crowds: "I am the living bread that came down from heaven; whoever eats this bread will live forever; and the bread that I will give is my flesh for the life of the world."

The Jews quarreled among themselves, saying, "How can this man give us his flesh to eat?" Jesus said to them, "Amen, amen, I say to you, unless you eat the flesh of the Son of Man and drink his blood, you do not have life within you. Whoever eats my flesh and drinks my blood has eternal life, and I will raise him on the last day. For my flesh is true food, and my blood is true drink. Whoever eats my flesh and drinks my blood remains in me and I in him. Just as the living Father sent me and I have life because of the Father, so also the one who feeds on me will have life because of me. This is the bread that came down from heaven. Unlike your ancestors who ate and still died, whoever eats this bread will live forever."

Communion Antiphon *Ps 130 (129): 7* **With the Lord there is mercy ◆ in him is plentiful redemption.**

Or: *Jn 6: 51–52* **I am the living bread that came down from heaven, says the Lord. ◆ Whoever eats of this bread will live for ever.**

TWENTY-FIRST SUNDAY IN ORDINARY TIME

Entrance Antiphon *cf. Ps 86 (85): 1–3* **Turn your ear, O Lord, and
answer me; ◆ save the servant who trusts in you, my God. ◆
Have mercy on me, O Lord, for I cry to you all the day long.**

First Reading *Joshua 24: 1–2a, 15–17, 18b* Joshua gathered together all
the tribes of Israel at Shechem, summoning their elders, their
leaders, their judges, and their officers. When they stood in
ranks before God, Joshua addressed all the people: "If it does not
please you to serve the LORD, decide today whom you will serve,
the gods your fathers served beyond the River or the gods of the
Amorites in whose country you are now dwelling. As for me and
my household, we will serve the LORD."

But the people answered, "Far be it from us to forsake the
LORD for the service of other gods. For it was the LORD, our
God, who brought us and our fathers up out of the land of Egypt,
out of a state of slavery. He performed those great miracles
before our very eyes and protected us along our entire journey
and among the peoples through whom we passed. Therefore we
also will serve the LORD, for he is our God."

Responsorial Psalm *Ps 34: 2–3, 16–17, 18–19, 20–21*   *Roger Holtz*

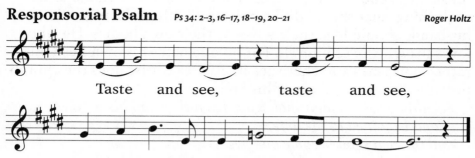

Taste and see, taste and see, taste and see the good-ness of the Lord.

I will bless the LORD at all times;
   his praise shall be ever in my mouth.
Let my soul glory in the LORD;
   the lowly will hear me and be glad. ℟

The LORD has eyes for the just,
   and ears for their cry.

The LORD confronts the evildoers,
  to destroy remembrance of them from the earth. ℟

When the just cry out, the LORD hears them,
  and from all their distress he rescues them.
The LORD is close to the brokenhearted;
  and those who are crushed in spirit he saves. ℟

Many are the troubles of the just one,
  but out of them all the LORD delivers him;
he watches over all his bones;
  not one of them shall be broken. ℟

Second Reading *Eph 5: 21–32* Brothers and sisters: Be subordinate
to one another out of reverence for Christ. Wives should be
subordinate to their husbands as to the Lord. For the husband is
head of his wife just as Christ is head of the church, he himself
the savior of the body. As the church is subordinate to Christ,
so wives should be subordinate to their husbands in everything.
Husbands, love your wives, even as Christ loved the church
and handed himself over for her to sanctify her, cleansing her
by the bath of water with the word, that he might present to
himself the church in splendor, without spot or wrinkle or any
such thing, that she might be holy and without blemish. So also
husbands should love their wives as their own bodies. He who
loves his wife loves himself. For no one hates his own flesh but
rather nourishes and cherishes it, even as Christ does the church,
because we are members of his body.
  For this reason a man shall leave his father and his mother
    and be joined to his wife,
  and the two shall become one flesh.
This is a great mystery, but I speak in reference to Christ and the
church.

Or (shorter form): *Eph 5: 2a, 25–32* Brothers and sisters: Live in love,
as Christ loved us. Husbands, love your wives, even as Christ
loved the church and handed himself over for her to sanctify
her, cleansing her by the bath of water with the word, that he
might present to himself the church in splendor, without spot or
wrinkle or any such thing, that she might be holy and without

blemish. So also husbands should love their wives as their own bodies. He who loves his wife loves himself. For no one hates his own flesh but rather nourishes and cherishes it, even as Christ does the church, because we are members of his body.

For this reason a man shall leave his father and his mother
*   and be joined to his wife,*
and the two shall become one flesh.

This is a great mystery, but I speak in reference to Christ and the church.

Alleluia   *Jn 6: 63c, 68c*   *Jim Hughes*

Al-le-lu-ia   Al-le-lu-ia   Al-le-lu - ia.

Your words, Lord, are Spirit and life; / you have the words of everlasting life.   **Alleluia, alleluia.**

Gospel   *Jn 6: 60–69*   Many of Jesus' disciples who were listening said, "This saying is hard; who can accept it?" Since Jesus knew that his disciples were murmuring about this, he said to them, "Does this shock you? What if you were to see the Son of Man ascending to where he was before? It is the spirit that gives life, while the flesh is of no avail. The words I have spoken to you are Spirit and life. But there are some of you who do not believe." Jesus knew from the beginning the ones who would not believe and the one who would betray him. And he said, "For this reason I have told you that no one can come to me unless it is granted him by my Father."

As a result of this, many of his disciples returned to their former way of life and no longer accompanied him. Jesus then said to the Twelve, "Do you also want to leave?" Simon Peter answered him, "Master, to whom shall we go? You have the words of eternal life. We have come to believe and are convinced that you are the Holy One of God."

Communion Antiphon   *cf. Ps 104 (103): 13–15*   **The earth is replete with the fruits of your work, O Lord; ✦ you bring forth bread from the earth ✦ and wine to cheer the heart.**

Or: *cf. Jn 6: 54* **Whoever eats my flesh and drinks my blood ◆ has eternal life, says the Lord, ◆ and I will raise him up on the last day.**

TWENTY-SECOND

SUNDAY IN ORDINARY TIME

Entrance Antiphon *cf. Ps 86 (85): 3, 5* **Have mercy on me, O Lord, for I cry to you all the day long. ◆ O Lord, you are good and forgiving, ◆ full of mercy to all who call to you.**

First Reading *Dt 4: 1–2, 6–8* Moses said to the people: "Now, Israel, hear the statutes and decrees which I am teaching you to observe, that you may live, and may enter in and take possession of the land which the LORD, the God of your fathers, is giving you. In your observance of the commandments of the LORD, your God, which I enjoin upon you, you shall not add to what I command you nor subtract from it. Observe them carefully, for thus will you give evidence of your wisdom and intelligence to the nations, who will hear of all these statutes and say, 'This great nation is truly a wise and intelligent people.' For what great nation is there that has gods so close to it as the LORD, our God, is to us whenever we call upon him? Or what great nation has statutes and decrees that are as just as this whole law which I am setting before you today?"

Responsorial Psalm *Ps 15: 2–3, 3–4, 4–5*   Jim Cowan

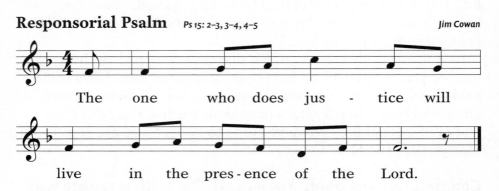

The one who does jus-tice will live in the pres-ence of the Lord.

Whoever walks blamelessly and does justice;

who thinks the truth in his heart
and slanders not with his tongue. ℟

Who harms not his fellow man,
nor takes up a reproach against his neighbor;
by whom the reprobate is despised,
while he honors those who fear the LORD. ℟

Who lends not his money at usury
and accepts no bribe against the innocent.
Whoever does these things
shall never be disturbed. ℟

Second Reading *Jas 1: 17–18, 21b–22, 27* Dearest brothers and sisters: All good giving and every perfect gift is from above, coming down from the Father of lights, with whom there is no alteration or shadow caused by change. He willed to give us birth by the word of truth that we may be a kind of firstfruits of his creatures.

Humbly welcome the word that has been planted in you and is able to save your souls.

Be doers of the word and not hearers only, deluding yourselves.

Religion that is pure and undefiled before God and the Father is this: to care for orphans and widows in their affliction and to keep oneself unstained by the world.

Alleluia   *Jas 1: 18*   *Jim Hughes*

Al-le-lu-ia   Al-le-lu-ia   Al - le-lu - ia.

The Father willed to give us birth by the word of truth
/ that we may be a kind of firstfruits of his creatures.
Alleluia, alleluia.

Gospel *Mk 7: 1–8, 14–15, 21–23* When the Pharisees with some scribes who had come from Jerusalem gathered around Jesus, they observed that some of his disciples ate their meals with unclean,

that is, unwashed, hands.—For the Pharisees and, in fact, all
Jews, do not eat without carefully washing their hands, keeping
the tradition of the elders. And on coming from the marketplace
they do not eat without purifying themselves. And there are
many other things that they have traditionally observed, the
purification of cups and jugs and kettles and beds.—So the
Pharisees and scribes questioned him, "Why do your disciples
not follow the tradition of the elders but instead eat a meal with
unclean hands?" He responded, "Well did Isaiah prophesy about
you hypocrites, as it is written:

This people honors me with their lips,
but their hearts are far from me;
in vain do they worship me,
teaching as doctrines human precepts.

You disregard God's commandment but cling to human
tradition."

He summoned the crowd again and said to them, "Hear me,
all of you, and understand. Nothing that enters one from outside
can defile that person; but the things that come out from within
are what defile.

"From within people, from their hearts, come evil thoughts,
unchastity, theft, murder, adultery, greed, malice, deceit,
licentiousness, envy, blasphemy, arrogance, folly. All these evils
come from within and they defile."

Communion Antiphon Ps 31 (30): 20 **How great is the goodness,
Lord, ◆ that you keep for those who fear you.**

Or: Mt 5: 9–10 **Blessed are the peacemakers, ◆ for they shall be
called children of God. ◆ Blessed are they who are persecuted
for the sake of righteousness, ◆ for theirs is the Kingdom
of Heaven.**

TWENTY-THIRD SUNDAY IN ORDINARY TIME

Entrance Antiphon *Ps 119 (118): 137, 124* You are just, O Lord, and your judgment is right; ◆ treat your servant in accord with your merciful love.

First Reading *Is 35: 4–7a*
Thus says the LORD:
  Say to those whose hearts are frightened:
    Be strong, fear not!
  Here is your God,
    he comes with vindication;
  with divine recompense
    he comes to save you.
  Then will the eyes of the blind be opened,
    the ears of the deaf be cleared;
  then will the lame leap like a stag,
    then the tongue of the mute will sing.
  Streams will burst forth in the desert,
    and rivers in the steppe.
  The burning sands will become pools,
    and the thirsty ground, springs of water.

Responsorial Psalm *Ps 146: 6–7, 8–9, 9–10*   Joe Higginbotham

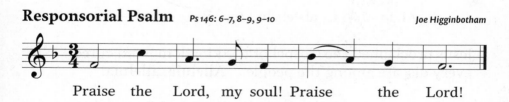

Praise the Lord, my soul! Praise the Lord!

Or: ℟ Alleluia.

The God of Jacob keeps faith forever,
    secures justice for the oppressed,
    gives food to the hungry.
The LORD sets captives free. ℟

The LORD gives sight to the blind;
    the LORD raises up those who were bowed down.

The LORD loves the just;
  the LORD protects strangers. ℟

The fatherless and the widow the LORD sustains,
  but the way of the wicked he thwarts.
The LORD shall reign forever;
  your God, O Zion, through all generations. Alleluia. ℟

Second Reading *Jas 2: 1–5* My brothers and sisters, show no partiality as you adhere to the faith in our glorious Lord Jesus Christ. For if a man with gold rings and fine clothes comes into your assembly, and a poor person in shabby clothes also comes in, and you pay attention to the one wearing the fine clothes and say, "Sit here, please," while you say to the poor one, "Stand there," or "Sit at my feet," have you not made distinctions among yourselves and become judges with evil designs?

Listen, my beloved brothers and sisters. Did not God choose those who are poor in the world to be rich in faith and heirs of the kingdom that he promised to those who love him?

Alleluia   *cf. Mt 4: 23*   *Michael Kissinger*

Al-le - lu-ia, al-le - lu - ia, al - le - lu - ia.

Jesus proclaimed the Gospel of the kingdom / and cured
  every disease among the people. **Alleluia, alleluia.**

Gospel *Mk 7: 31–37* Again Jesus left the district of Tyre and went by way of Sidon to the Sea of Galilee, into the district of the Decapolis. And people brought to him a deaf man who had a speech impediment and begged him to lay his hand on him. He took him off by himself away from the crowd. He put his finger into the man's ears and, spitting, touched his tongue; then he looked up to heaven and groaned, and said to him, *"Ephphatha!"*—that is, "Be opened!"—And immediately the man's ears were opened, his speech impediment was removed, and he spoke plainly. He ordered them not to tell anyone. But the more he ordered them not to, the more they proclaimed it. They were exceedingly astonished and they said, "He has done all things well. He makes the deaf hear and the mute speak."

Communion Antiphon *cf. Ps 42 (41): 2-3* **Like the deer that yearns for running streams, ◆ so my soul is yearning for you, my God; ◆ my soul is thirsting for God, the living God.**

Or: *Jn 8: 12* **I am the light of the world, says the Lord; ◆ whoever follows me will not walk in darkness, ◆ but will have the light of life.**

TWENTY-FOURTH

SUNDAY IN ORDINARY TIME

Entrance Antiphon *cf. Sir 36: 18* **Give peace, O Lord, to those who wait for you, ◆ that your prophets be found true. ◆ Hear the prayers of your servant, ◆ and of your people Israel.**

First Reading   *Is 50: 5-9a*
The Lord GOD opens my ear that I may hear;
   and I have not rebelled,
   have not turned back.
I gave my back to those who beat me,
   my cheeks to those who plucked my beard;
my face I did not shield
   from buffets and spitting.

The Lord GOD is my help,
   therefore I am not disgraced;
I have set my face like flint,
   knowing that I shall not be put to shame.
He is near who upholds my right;
   if anyone wishes to oppose me,
   let us appear together.

Who disputes my right?
Let that man confront me.
See, the Lord GOD is my help;
who will prove me wrong?

Responsorial Psalm Ps 116: 1–2, 3–4, 5–6, 8–9 Beverly McDevitt

I will walk be-fore the Lord, in the land of the liv-ing.

Or: ℟ **Alleluia.**

I love the LORD because he has heard
my voice in supplication,
Because he has inclined his ear to me
the day I called. ℟

The cords of death encompassed me;
the snares of the netherworld seized upon me;
I fell into distress and sorrow,
And I called upon the name of the LORD,
"O LORD, save my life!" ℟

Gracious is the LORD and just;
yes, our God is merciful.
The LORD keeps the little ones;
I was brought low, and he saved me. ℟

For he has freed my soul from death,
my eyes from tears, my feet from stumbling.
I shall walk before the LORD
in the land of the living. ℟

Second Reading Jas 2: 14–18 What good is it, my brothers and
sisters, if someone says he has faith but does not have works?
Can that faith save him? If a brother or sister has nothing to
wear and has no food for the day, and one of you says to them,
"Go in peace, keep warm, and eat well," but you do not give them

the necessities of the body, what good is it? So also faith of itself, if it does not have works, is dead.

Indeed someone might say, "You have faith and I have works." Demonstrate your faith to me without works, and I will demonstrate my faith to you from my works.

Alleluia   *Gal 6: 14*   *Michael Kissinger*

Al-le - lu-ia, al-le - lu - ia, al - le - lu - ia.

May I never boast except in the cross of our Lord / through which the world has been crucified to me and I to the world. **Alleluia, alleluia.**

Gospel *Mk 8: 27-35* Jesus and his disciples set out for the villages of Caesarea Philippi. Along the way he asked his disciples, "Who do people say that I am?" They said in reply, "John the Baptist, others Elijah, still others one of the prophets." And he asked them, "But who do you say that I am?" Peter said to him in reply, "You are the Christ." Then he warned them not to tell anyone about him.

He began to teach them that the Son of Man must suffer greatly and be rejected by the elders, the chief priests, and the scribes, and be killed, and rise after three days. He spoke this openly. Then Peter took him aside and began to rebuke him. At this he turned around and, looking at his disciples, rebuked Peter and said, "Get behind me, Satan. You are thinking not as God does, but as human beings do."

He summoned the crowd with his disciples and said to them, "Whoever wishes to come after me must deny himself, take up his cross, and follow me. For whoever wishes to save his life will lose it, but whoever loses his life for my sake and that of the gospel will save it."

Communion Antiphon   *cf. Ps 36 (35): 8* **How precious is your mercy, O God! ◆ The children of men seek shelter in the shadow of your wings.**

Or: cf. 1 Cor 10: 16   **The chalice of blessing that we bless ◆ is a communion in the Blood of Christ; ◆ and the bread that we break ◆ is a sharing in the Body of the Lord.**

TWENTY-FIFTH SUNDAY IN ORDINARY TIME

Entrance Antiphon
I am the salvation of the people, says the Lord. ◆ Should they cry to me in any distress, ◆ I will hear them, and I will be their Lord for ever.

First Reading   Wis 2: 12, 17–20
The wicked say:
Let us beset the just one, because he is obnoxious to us;
  he sets himself against our doings,
reproaches us for transgressions of the law
  and charges us with violations of our training.
Let us see whether his words be true;
  let us find out what will happen to him.
For if the just one be the son of God, God will defend him
  and deliver him from the hand of his foes.
With revilement and torture let us put the just one to the test
  that we may have proof of his gentleness
  and try his patience.
Let us condemn him to a shameful death;
  for according to his own words, God will take care of him.

Responsorial Psalm   Ps 54: 3–4, 5, 6–8   Tim Wells

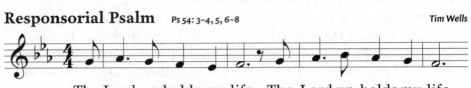

The Lord up-holds my life. The Lord up-holds my life.

The Lord up-holds my life, up-holds my life.

O God, by your name save me,
 and by your might defend my cause.
O God, hear my prayer;
 hearken to the words of my mouth. ℟

For the haughty men have risen up against me,
 the ruthless seek my life;
 they set not God before their eyes. ℟

Behold, God is my helper;
 the Lord sustains my life.
Freely will I offer you sacrifice;
 I will praise your name, O LORD, for its goodness. ℟

Second Reading *Jas 3: 16–4: 3* Beloved: Where jealousy and selfish ambition exist, there is disorder and every foul practice. But the wisdom from above is first of all pure, then peaceable, gentle, compliant, full of mercy and good fruits, without inconstancy or insincerity. And the fruit of righteousness is sown in peace for those who cultivate peace.

 Where do the wars and where do the conflicts among you come from? Is it not from your passions that make war within your members? You covet but do not possess. You kill and envy but you cannot obtain; you fight and wage war. You do not possess because you do not ask. You ask but do not receive, because you ask wrongly, to spend it on your passions.

Alleluia *cf. 2 Thes 2: 14*   *Michael Kissinger*

Al-le - lu-ia, al-le - lu - ia, al - le - lu - ia.

God has called us through the Gospel / to possess the glory of our Lord Jesus Christ. **Alleluia, alleluia.**

Gospel *Mk 9: 30–37* Jesus and his disciples left from there and began a journey through Galilee, but he did not wish anyone to know about it. He was teaching his disciples and telling them, "The

Son of Man is to be handed over to men and they will kill him, and three days after his death the Son of Man will rise." But they did not understand the saying, and they were afraid to question him.

They came to Capernaum and, once inside the house, he began to ask them, "What were you arguing about on the way?" But they remained silent. They had been discussing among themselves on the way who was the greatest. Then he sat down, called the Twelve, and said to them, "If anyone wishes to be first, he shall be the last of all and the servant of all." Taking a child, he placed it in the their midst, and putting his arms around it, he said to them, "Whoever receives one child such as this in my name, receives me; and whoever receives me, receives not me but the One who sent me."

Communion Antiphon Ps 119 (118): 4-5 You have laid down your precepts to be carefully kept; ◆ may my ways be firm in keeping your statutes.

Or: Jn 10: 14 I am the Good Shepherd, says the Lord; ◆ I know my sheep, and mine know me.

TWENTY-SIXTH SUNDAY IN ORDINARY TIME

Entrance Antiphon Dn 3: 31, 29, 30, 43, 42 All that you have done to us, O Lord, ◆ you have done with true judgment, ◆ for we have sinned against you ◆ and not obeyed your commandments. ◆ But give glory to your name ◆ and deal with us according to the bounty of your mercy.

First Reading Nm 11: 25-29 The LORD came down in the cloud and spoke to Moses. Taking some of the spirit that was on Moses, the LORD bestowed it on the seventy elders; and as the spirit came to rest on them, they prophesied.

Now two men, one named Eldad and the other Medad, were not in the gathering but had been left in the camp. They too had been on the list, but had not gone out to the tent; yet the spirit came to rest on them also, and they prophesied in the camp. So, when a young man quickly told Moses, "Eldad and Medad are prophesying in the camp," Joshua, son of Nun, who from his youth had been Moses' aide, said, "Moses, my lord, stop them." But Moses answered him, "Are you jealous for my sake? Would that all the people of the LORD were prophets! Would that the LORD might bestow his spirit on them all!"

Responsorial Psalm   Ps 19: 8, 10, 12–13, 14   *Joe Higginbotham*

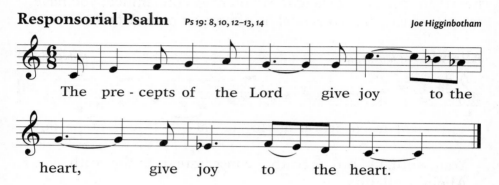

The pre-cepts of the Lord give joy to the heart, give joy to the heart.

The law of the LORD is perfect,
   refreshing the soul;
the decree of the LORD is trustworthy,
   giving wisdom to the simple. ℟

The fear of the LORD is pure,
   enduring forever;
the ordinances of the LORD are true,
   all of them just. ℟

Though your servant is careful of them,
   very diligent in keeping them,
Yet who can detect failings?
   Cleanse me from my unknown faults! ℟

From wanton sin especially, restrain your servant;
   let it not rule over me.
Then shall I be blameless and innocent
   of serious sin. ℟

Second Reading Jas 5: 1–6 Come now, you rich, weep and wail over your impending miseries. Your wealth has rotted away, your clothes have become moth-eaten, your gold and silver have corroded, and that corrosion will be a testimony against you; it will devour your flesh like a fire. You have stored up treasure for the last days. Behold, the wages you withheld from the workers who harvested your fields are crying aloud; and the cries of the harvesters have reached the ears of the Lord of hosts. You have lived on earth in luxury and pleasure; you have fattened your hearts for the day of slaughter. You have condemned; you have murdered the righteous one; he offers you no resistance.

Alleluia   cf. Jn 17: 17b, 17a   *Michael Kissinger*

Al-le - lu-ia, al-le - lu - ia, al - le - lu - ia.

Your word, O Lord, is truth; / consecrate us in the truth.
Alleluia, alleluia.

Gospel Mk 9: 38–43, 45, 47–48 At that time, John said to Jesus, "Teacher, we saw someone driving out demons in your name, and we tried to prevent him because he does not follow us." Jesus replied, "Do not prevent him. There is no one who performs a mighty deed in my name who can at the same time speak ill of me. For whoever is not against us is for us. Anyone who gives you a cup of water to drink because you belong to Christ, amen, I say to you, will surely not lose his reward.

"Whoever causes one of these little ones who believe in me to sin, it would be better for him if a great millstone were put around his neck and he were thrown into the sea. If your hand causes you to sin, cut it off. It is better for you to enter into life maimed than with two hands to go into Gehenna, into the unquenchable fire. And if your foot causes you to sin, cut if off. It is better for you to enter into life crippled than with two feet to be thrown into Gehenna. And if your eye causes you to sin, pluck it out. Better for you to enter into the kingdom of God with one eye than with two eyes to be thrown into Gehenna, where 'their worm does not die, and the fire is not quenched.'"

Communion Antiphon *cf. Ps 119 (118): 49–50* Remember your word to your servant, O Lord, ♦ by which you have given me hope. ♦ This is my comfort when I am brought low.

Or: *1 Jn 3: 16* By this we came to know the love of God: ♦ that Christ laid down his life for us; ♦ so we ought to lay down our lives for one another.

TWENTY-SEVENTH

SUNDAY IN ORDINARY TIME

Entrance Antiphon *cf. Est 4: 17* Within your will, O Lord, all things are established, ♦ and there is none that can resist your will. ♦ For you have made all things, the heaven and the earth, ♦ and all that is held within the circle of heaven; ♦ you are the Lord of all.

First Reading *Gen 2: 18–24* The LORD God said: "It is not good for the man to be alone. I will make a suitable partner for him." So the LORD God formed out of the ground various wild animals and various birds of the air, and he brought them to the man to see what he would call them; whatever the man called each of them would be its name. The man gave names to all the cattle, all the birds of the air, and all wild animals; but none proved to be the suitable partner for the man.

So the LORD God cast a deep sleep on the man, and while he was asleep, he took out one of his ribs and closed up its place with flesh. The LORD God then built up into a woman the rib that he had taken from the man. When he brought her to the man, the man said:

"This one, at last, is bone of my bones
 and flesh of my flesh;
this one shall be called 'woman,'
 for out of 'her man' this one has been taken."

That is why a man leaves his father and mother and clings to his wife, and the two of them become one flesh.

Responsorial Psalm Ps 128: 1–2, 3, 4–5, 6   *Beverly McDevitt*

May the Lord bless us all the days of our lives.

Blessed are you who fear the LORD,
  who walk in his ways!
For you shall eat the fruit of your handiwork;
  blessed shall you be, and favored. ℟

Your wife shall be like a fruitful vine
  in the recesses of your home;
your children like olive plants
  around your table. ℟

Behold, thus is the man blessed
  who fears the LORD.
The LORD bless you from Zion:
  may you see the prosperity of Jerusalem
  all the days of your life. ℟

May you see your children's children.
  Peace be upon Israel! ℟

Second Reading Heb 2: 9–11 Brothers and sisters: He "for a little while" was made "lower than the angels," that by the grace of God he might taste death for everyone.

For it was fitting that he, for whom and through whom all things exist, in bringing many children to glory, should make the leader to their salvation perfect through suffering. He who consecrates and those who are being consecrated all have one origin. Therefore, he is not ashamed to call them "brothers."

Alleluia 1 Jn 4: 12   *Michael Kissinger*

Al-le - lu-ia, al-le - lu - ia, al – le - lu - ia.

If we love one another, God remains in us / and his love is brought to perfection in us. **Alleluia, alleluia.**

Gospel *Mk 10: 2–16 or 10: 2–12*
For the shorter form, read only the parts in brackets.
[The Pharisees approached Jesus and asked, "Is it lawful for a husband to divorce his wife?" They were testing him. He said to them in reply, "What did Moses command you?" They replied, "Moses permitted a husband to write a bill of divorce and dismiss her." But Jesus told them, "Because of the hardness of your hearts he wrote you this commandment. But from the beginning of creation, *God made them male and female. For this reason a man shall leave his father and mother and be joined to his wife, and the two shall become one flesh.* So they are no longer two but one flesh. Therefore what God has joined together, no human being must separate." In the house the disciples again questioned Jesus about this. He said to them, "Whoever divorces his wife and marries another commits adultery against her; and if she divorces her husband and marries another, she commits adultery."]

And people were bringing children to him that he might touch them, but the disciples rebuked them. When Jesus saw this he became indignant and said to them, "Let the children come to me; do not prevent them, for the kingdom of God belongs to such as these. Amen, I say to you, whoever does not accept the kingdom of God like a child will not enter it." Then he embraced them and blessed them, placing his hands on them.

Communion Antiphon *Lam 3: 25* The Lord is good to those who hope in him, ✦ to the soul that seeks him.

Or: *cf. 1 Cor 10: 17* **Though many, we are one bread, one body, ✦ for we all partake of the one Bread and one Chalice.**

TWENTY-EIGHTH SUNDAY IN ORDINARY TIME

Entrance Antiphon *Ps 130 (129): 3–4* If you, O Lord, should mark iniquities, ◆ Lord, who could stand? ◆ But with you is found forgiveness, ◆ O God of Israel.

First Reading   *Wis 7: 7–11*

I prayed, and prudence was given me;
   I pleaded, and the spirit of wisdom came to me.
I preferred her to scepter and throne,
and deemed riches nothing in comparison with her,
   nor did I liken any priceless gem to her;
because all gold, in view of her, is a little sand,
   and before her, silver is to be accounted mire.
Beyond health and comeliness I loved her,
and I chose to have her rather than the light,
   because the splendor of her never yields to sleep.
Yet all good things together came to me in her company,
   and countless riches at her hands.

Responsorial Psalm   *Ps 90: 12–13, 14–15, 16–17*   *Tim Wells*

Fill us with your love, O Lord and we will sing for joy!

Teach us to number our days aright,
   that we may gain wisdom of heart.
Return, O LORD! How long?
   Have pity on your servants! ℟

Fill us at daybreak with your kindness,
   that we may shout for joy and gladness all our days.
Make us glad, for the days when you afflicted us,

for the years when we saw evil. ℟

Let your work be seen by your servants
    and your glory by their children;
and may the gracious care of the Lord our God be ours;
    prosper the work of our hands for us!
    Prosper the work of our hands! ℟

Second Reading *Heb 4: 12–13* Brothers and sisters: Indeed the word
of God is living and effective, sharper than any two-edged sword,
penetrating even between soul and spirit, joints and marrow,
and able to discern reflections and thoughts of the heart. No
creature is concealed from him, but everything is naked and
exposed to the eyes of him to whom we must render an account.

Alleluia *Mt 5: 3* Michael Kissinger

Al-le - lu-ia, al-le - lu - ia, al - le - lu - ia.

Blessed are the poor in spirit, / for theirs is the kingdom of
heaven. **Alleluia, alleluia.**

Gospel *Mk 10: 17–30 or 10: 17–27*
For the shorter form, read only the parts in brackets.
[As Jesus was setting out on a journey, a man ran up, knelt
down before him, and asked him, "Good teacher, what must I
do to inherit eternal life?" Jesus answered him, "Why do you
call me good? No one is good but God alone. You know the
commandments: *You shall not kill; you shall not commit adultery;
you shall not steal; you shall not bear false witness; you shall not
defraud; honor your father and your mother.*" He replied and said
to him, "Teacher, all of these I have observed from my youth."
Jesus, looking at him, loved him and said to him, "You are
lacking in one thing. Go, sell what you have, and give to the poor
and you will have treasure in heaven; then come, follow me." At
that statement his face fell, and he went away sad, for he had
many possessions.

Jesus looked around and said to his disciples, "How hard it is for those who have wealth to enter the kingdom of God!" The disciples were amazed at his words. So Jesus again said to them in reply, "Children, how hard it is to enter the kingdom of God! It is easier for a camel to pass through the eye of a needle than for one who is rich to enter the kingdom of God." They were exceedingly astonished and said among themselves, "Then who can be saved?" Jesus looked at them and said, "For human beings it is impossible, but not for God. All things are possible for God."] Peter began to say to him, "We have given up everything and followed you." Jesus said, "Amen, I say to you, there is no one who has given up house or brothers or sisters or mother or father or children or lands for my sake and for the sake of the gospel who will not receive a hundred times more now in this present age: houses and brothers and sisters and mothers and children and lands, with persecutions, and eternal life in the age to come."

Communion Antiphon *cf. Ps 34 (33): 11* **The rich suffer want and go hungry, ◆ but those who seek the Lord lack no blessing.**

Or: *1 Jn 3: 2* **When the Lord appears, we shall be like him, ◆ for we shall see him as he is.**

TWENTY-NINTH SUNDAY IN ORDINARY TIME

Entrance Antiphon *cf. Ps 17 (16): 6, 8* **To you I call; for you will surely heed me, O God; ◆ turn your ear to me; hear my words. ◆ Guard me as the apple of your eye; ◆ in the shadow of your wings protect me.**

First Reading   *Is 53: 10–11*

The LORD was pleased
  to crush him in infirmity.

If he gives his life as an offering for sin,
  he shall see his descendants in a long life,

and the will of the LORD shall be accomplished through him.

Because of his affliction
    he shall see the light in fullness of days;
through his suffering, my servant shall justify many,
    and their guilt he shall bear.

Responsorial Psalm   Ps 33: 4–5, 18–19, 20, 22   *Beverly McDevitt*

Lord, let your mer-cy be on us, as we place our trust in you.

Upright is the word of the LORD,
    and all his works are trustworthy.
He loves justice and right;
    of the kindness of the LORD the earth is full. ℟

See, the eyes of the LORD are upon those who fear him,
    upon those who hope for his kindness,
to deliver them from death
    and preserve them in spite of famine. ℟

Our soul waits for the LORD,
    who is our help and our shield.
May your kindness, O LORD, be upon us
    who have put our hope in you. ℟

Second Reading *Heb 4: 14–16* Brothers and sisters: Since we have a great high priest who has passed through the heavens, Jesus, the Son of God, let us hold fast to our confession. For we do not have a high priest who is unable to sympathize with our weaknesses, but one who has similarly been tested in every way, yet without sin. So let us confidently approach the throne of grace to receive mercy and to find grace for timely help.

Alleluia   Mk 10: 45

Michael Kissinger

Al-le - lu-ia, al-le - lu - ia, al - le - lu - ia.

The Son of Man came to serve / and to give his life as a
ransom for many.   **Alleluia, alleluia.**

Gospel   Mk 10: 35–45 or 10: 42–45

For the shorter form, read only the parts in brackets.

James and John, the sons of Zebedee, came to Jesus and said to
him, "Teacher, we want you to do for us whatever we ask of
you." He replied, "What do you wish me to do for you?" They
answered him, "Grant that in your glory we may sit one at your
right and the other at your left." Jesus said to them, "You do not
know what you are asking. Can you drink the cup that I drink
or be baptized with the baptism with which I am baptized?"
They said to him, "We can." Jesus said to them, "The cup that
I drink, you will drink, and with the baptism with which I am
baptized, you will be baptized; but to sit at my right or at my
left is not mine to give but is for those for whom it has been
prepared." When the ten heard this, they became indignant at
James and John. [Jesus summoned them [the Twelve] and said
to them, "You know that those who are recognized as rulers
over the Gentiles lord it over them, and their great ones make
their authority over them felt. But it shall not be so among you.
Rather, whoever wishes to be great among you will be your
servant; whoever wishes to be first among you will be the slave
of all. For the Son of Man did not come to be served but to serve
and to give his life as a ransom for many."]

Communion Antiphon   *cf. Ps 33 (32): 18–19*   **Behold, the eyes of the
Lord ◆ are on those who fear him, ◆ who hope in his merciful
love, ◆ to rescue their souls from death, ◆ to keep them alive
in famine.**

Or: Mk 10: 45   **The Son of Man has come ◆ to give his life as a
ransom for many.**

THIRTIETH SUNDAY IN ORDINARY TIME

Entrance Antiphon *cf. Ps 105 (104): 3-4* **Let the hearts that seek the Lord rejoice; ◆ turn to the Lord and his strength; ◆ constantly seek his face.**

First Reading   *Jer 31: 7–9*
Thus says the LORD:
Shout with joy for Jacob,
    exult at the head of the nations;
    proclaim your praise and say:
The LORD has delivered his people,
    the remnant of Israel.
Behold, I will bring them back
    from the land of the north;
I will gather them from the ends of the world,
    with the blind and the lame in their midst,
the mothers and those with child;
    they shall return as an immense throng.
They departed in tears,
    but I will console them and guide them;
I will lead them to brooks of water,
    on a level road, so that none shall stumble.
For I am a father to Israel,
    Ephraim is my first-born.

Responsorial Psalm   *Ps 126: 1–2, 2–3, 4–5, 6*   Joe Higginbotham

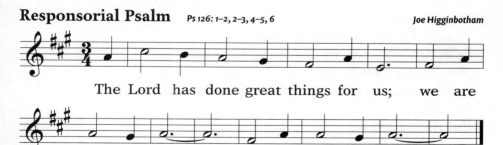

The Lord has done great things for us; we are filled with joy. We are filled with joy.

When the LORD brought back the captives of Zion,
    we were like men dreaming.

Then our mouth was filled with laughter,
  and our tongue with rejoicing. ℟

Then they said among the nations,
  "The LORD has done great things for them."
The LORD has done great things for us;
  we are glad indeed. ℟

Restore our fortunes, O LORD,
  like the torrents in the southern desert.
Those that sow in tears
  shall reap rejoicing. ℟

Although they go forth weeping,
  carrying the seed to be sown,
They shall come back rejoicing,
  carrying their sheaves. ℟

Second Reading *Heb 5: 1–6* Brothers and sisters: Every high priest
is taken from among men and made their representative before
God, to offer gifts and sacrifices for sins. He is able to deal
patiently with the ignorant and erring, for he himself is beset
by weakness and so, for this reason, must make sin offerings for
himself as well as for the people. No one takes this honor upon
himself but only when called by God, just as Aaron was. In the
same way, it was not Christ who glorified himself in becoming
high priest, but rather the one who said to him:
  You are my son:
    this day I have begotten you;
just as he says in another place:
  You are a priest forever
    according to the order of Melchizedek.

Alleluia *cf. 2 Tm 1: 10*   *Brian J. Nelson*

Al - le-lu - ia, al - le - lu - ia, al-le -lu - ia.

Our Savior Jesus Christ destroyed death / and brought life to light through the Gospel.   **Alleluia, alleluia.**

Gospel Mk 10: 46–52 As Jesus was leaving Jericho with his disciples and a sizable crowd, Bartimaeus, a blind man, the son of Timaeus, sat by the roadside begging. On hearing that it was Jesus of Nazareth, he began to cry out and say, "Jesus, son of David, have pity on me." And many rebuked him, telling him to be silent. But he kept calling out all the more, "Son of David, have pity on me." Jesus stopped and said, "Call him." So they called the blind man, saying to him, "Take courage; get up, Jesus is calling you." He threw aside his cloak, sprang up, and came to Jesus. Jesus said to him in reply, "What do you want me to do for you?" The blind man replied to him, "Master, I want to see." Jesus told him, "Go your way; your faith has saved you." Immediately he received his sight and followed him on the way.

Communion Antiphon cf. Ps 20 (19): 6 **We will ring out our joy at your saving help ◆ and exult in the name of our God.**

Or: Eph 5: 2 **Christ loved us and gave himself up for us, ◆ as a fragrant offering to God.**

THIRTY-FIRST SUNDAY IN ORDINARY TIME

Entrance Antiphon cf. Ps 38 (37): 22–23 **Forsake me not, O Lord, my God; ◆ be not far from me! ◆ Make haste and come to my help, ◆ O Lord, my strong salvation!**

First Reading Dt 6: 2–6 Moses spoke to the people, saying: "Fear the LORD, your God, and keep, throughout the days of your lives, all his statutes and commandments which I enjoin on you, and thus have long life. Hear then, Israel, and be careful to observe them, that you may grow and prosper the more, in keeping with the promise of the LORD, the God of your fathers, to give you a land flowing with milk and honey.

"Hear, O Israel! The LORD is our God, the LORD alone!

Therefore, you shall love the LORD, your God, with all your heart, and with all your soul, and with all your strength. Take to heart these words which I enjoin on you today."

Responsorial Psalm   Ps 18: 2–3, 3–4, 47, 51   *Beverly McDevitt*

I love you, Lord, my strength.

I love you, Lord, my strength.

I love you, O LORD, my strength,
  O LORD, my rock, my fortress, my deliverer. ℟

My God, my rock of refuge,
  my shield, the horn of my salvation, my stronghold!
Praised be the LORD, I exclaim,
  and I am safe from my enemies. ℟

The LORD lives! And blessed be my rock!
  Extolled be God my savior.
You who gave great victories to your king
  and showed kindness to your anointed. ℟

Second Reading Heb 7: 23–28 Brothers and sisters: The levitical priests were many because they were prevented by death from remaining in office, but Jesus, because he remains forever, has a priesthood that does not pass away. Therefore, he is always able to save those who approach God through him, since he lives forever to make intercession for them.

It was fitting that we should have such a high priest: holy, innocent, undefiled, separated from sinners, higher than the heavens. He has no need, as did the high priests, to offer sacrifice day after day, first for his own sins and then for those of the people; he did that once for all when he offered himself. For the law appoints men subject to weakness to be high priests, but the word of the oath, which was taken after the law, appoints a son, who has been made perfect forever.

Alleluia   *Jn 14: 23*   *Brian J. Nelson*

Al - le-lu - ia,   al - le - lu - ia,   al-le-lu - ia.

Whoever loves me will keep my word, says the Lord; /
and my Father will love him and we will come to him.
Alleluia, alleluia.

Gospel *Mk 12: 28b–34* One of the scribes came to Jesus and asked him, "Which is the first of all the commandments?" Jesus replied, "The first is this: *Hear, O Israel! The Lord our God is Lord alone! You shall love the Lord your God with all your heart, with all your soul, with all your mind, and with all your strength.* The second is this: *You shall love your neighbor as yourself.* There is no other commandment greater than these." The scribe said to him, "Well said, teacher. You are right in saying, 'He is One and there is no other than he.' And 'to love him with all your heart, with all your understanding, with all your strength, and to love your neighbor as yourself' is worth more than all burnt offerings and sacrifices." And when Jesus saw that he answered with understanding, he said to him, "You are not far from the kingdom of God." And no one dared to ask him any more questions.

Communion Antiphon *cf. Ps 16 (15): 11* **You will show me the path of life, ◆ the fullness of joy in your presence, O Lord.**

Or: *Jn 6: 58* **Just as the living Father sent me ◆ and I have life because of the Father, ◆ so whoever feeds on me ◆ shall have life because of me, says the Lord.**

THIRTY-SECOND SUNDAY IN ORDINARY TIME

Entrance Antiphon *cf. Ps 88 (87): 3* **Let my prayer come into your presence. ◆ Incline your ear to my cry for help, O Lord.**

First Reading *1 Kgs 17: 10–16* In those days, Elijah the prophet went to Zarephath. As he arrived at the entrance of the city, a widow was gathering sticks there; he called out to her, "Please bring me a small cupful of water to drink." She left to get it, and he called out after her, "Please bring along a bit of bread." She answered, "As the LORD, your God, lives, I have nothing baked; there is only a handful of flour in my jar and a little oil in my jug. Just now I was collecting a couple of sticks, to go in and prepare something for myself and my son; when we have eaten it, we shall die." Elijah said to her, "Do not be afraid. Go and do as you propose. But first make me a little cake and bring it to me. Then you can prepare something for yourself and your son. For the LORD, the God of Israel, says, 'The jar of flour shall not go empty, nor the jug of oil run dry, until the day when the LORD sends rain upon the earth.'" She left and did as Elijah had said. She was able to eat for a year, and he and her son as well; the jar of flour did not go empty, nor the jug of oil run dry, as the LORD had foretold through Elijah.

Responsorial Psalm   Ps 146: 7, 8–9, 9–10   Don Fishel

Praise   the   Lord,   my   soul!

Praise the   Lord,   my   soul!

Or: ℟ **Alleluia.**

The LORD keeps faith forever,
    secures justice for the oppressed,

gives food to the hungry.
   The LORD sets captives free. ℟

The LORD gives sight to the blind;
   the LORD raises up those who were bowed down.
The LORD loves the just;
   the LORD protects strangers. ℟

The fatherless and the widow he sustains,
   but the way of the wicked he thwarts.
The LORD shall reign forever;
   your God, O Zion, through all generations. Alleluia. ℟

Second Reading *Heb 9: 24–28* Christ did not enter into a sanctuary made by hands, a copy of the true one, but heaven itself, that he might now appear before God on our behalf. Not that he might offer himself repeatedly, as the high priest enters each year into the sanctuary with blood that is not his own; if that were so, he would have had to suffer repeatedly from the foundation of the world. But now once for all he has appeared at the end of the ages to take away sin by his sacrifice. Just as it is appointed that human beings die once, and after this the judgment, so also Christ, offered once to take away the sins of many, will appear a second time, not to take away sin but to bring salvation to those who eagerly await him.

Alleluia *Mt 5: 3*   Brian J. Nelson

Al - le-lu - ia, al - le - lu - ia, al-le-lu - ia.

Blessed are the poor in spirit, / for theirs is the kingdom of heaven. **Alleluia, alleluia.**

Gospel *Mk 12: 38–44* In the course of his teaching Jesus said to the crowds, "Beware of the scribes, who like to go around in long robes and accept greetings in the marketplaces, seats of honor in synagogues, and places of honor at banquets. They devour the houses of widows and, as a pretext recite lengthy prayers. They will receive a very severe condemnation."

He sat down opposite the treasury and observed how the crowd put money into the treasury. Many rich people put in large sums. A poor widow also came and put in two small coins worth a few cents. Calling his disciples to himself, he said to them, "Amen, I say to you, this poor widow put in more than all the other contributors to the treasury. For they have all contributed from their surplus wealth, but she, from her poverty, has contributed all she had, her whole livelihood."

Or (shorter form): Mk 12: 41-44 Jesus sat down opposite the treasury and observed how the crowd put money into the treasury. Many rich people put in large sums. A poor widow also came and put in two small coins worth a few cents. Calling his disciples to himself, he said to them, "Amen, I say to you, this poor widow put in more than all the other contributors to the treasury. For they have all contributed from their surplus wealth, but she, from her poverty, has contributed all she had, her whole livelihood."

Communion Antiphon cf. Ps 23 (22): 1-2 **The Lord is my shepherd; there is nothing I shall want. ◆ Fresh and green are the pastures where he gives me repose, ◆ near restful waters he leads me.**

Or: cf. Lk 24: 35 **The disciples recognized the Lord Jesus in the breaking of bread.**

THIRTY-THIRD

SUNDAY IN ORDINARY TIME

Entrance Antiphon Jer 29: 11, 12, 14 **The Lord said: I think thoughts of peace and not of affliction. ◆ You will call upon me, and I will answer you, ◆ and I will lead back your captives from every place.**

First Reading   Dn 12: 1–3

In those days, I, Daniel, heard this word of the Lord:
  "At that time there shall arise
        Michael, the great prince,
        guardian of your people;
    it shall be a time unsurpassed in distress
        since nations began until that time.
    At that time your people shall escape,
        everyone who is found written in the book.

  "Many of those who sleep in the dust of the earth shall awake;
        some shall live forever,
        others shall be an everlasting horror and disgrace.

  "But the wise shall shine brightly
        like the splendor of the firmament,
    and those who lead the many to justice
        shall be like the stars forever."

Responsorial Psalm   Ps 16: 5, 8, 9–10, 11   Joe Higginbotham

You are my in - her - i - tance, O   Lord.

O LORD, my allotted portion and my cup,
    you it is who hold fast my lot.
I set the LORD ever before me;
    with him at my right hand I shall not be disturbed. ℟

Therefore my heart is glad and my soul rejoices,
    my body, too, abides in confidence;
because you will not abandon my soul to the netherworld,
    nor will you suffer your faithful one to undergo
        corruption. ℟

You will show me the path to life,
    fullness of joys in your presence,
    the delights at your right hand forever. ℟

Second Reading Heb 10: 11–14, 18 Brothers and sisters: Every priest stands daily at his ministry, offering frequently those same sacrifices that can never take away sins. But this one offered one sacrifice for sins, and took his seat forever at the right hand of God; now he waits until his enemies are made his footstool. For by one offering he has made perfect forever those who are being consecrated.

Where there is forgiveness of these, there is no longer offering for sin.

Alleluia   Lk 21: 36   Brian J. Nelson

Al - le-lu - ia,   al - le - lu - ia,   al-le-lu - ia.

Be vigilant at all times / and pray that you have the strength to stand before the Son of Man.   **Alleluia, alleluia.**

Gospel Mk 13: 24–32 Jesus said to his disciples: "In those days after that tribulation
the sun will be darkened,
and the moon will not give its light,
and the stars will be falling from the sky,
and the powers in the heavens will be shaken.
"And then they will see 'the Son of Man coming in the clouds' with great power and glory, and then he will send out the angels and gather his elect from the four winds, from the end of the earth to the end of the sky.

"Learn a lesson from the fig tree. When its branch becomes tender and sprouts leaves, you know that summer is near. In the same way, when you see these things happening, know that he is near, at the gates. Amen, I say to you, this generation will not pass away until all these things have taken place. Heaven and earth will pass away, but my words will not pass away.

"But of that day or hour, no one knows, neither the angels in heaven, nor the Son, but only the Father."

Communion Antiphon cf. Ps 73 (72): 28 To be near God is my happiness, ◆ to place my hope in God the Lord.

Or: Mk 11: 23-24 **Amen, I say to you: Whatever you ask in prayer, ◆ believe that you will receive, ◆ and it shall be given to you, says the Lord.**

THE SOLEMNITY OF OUR LORD JESUS CHRIST, KING OF THE UNIVERSE

Entrance Antiphon Rv 5: 12; 1: 6 **How worthy is the Lamb who was slain, ◆to receive power and divinity, ◆ and wisdom and strength and honor. ◆ To him belong glory and power for ever and ever.**

First Reading   Dn 7: 13-14

As the visions during the night continued, I saw
   one like a Son of man coming,
on the clouds of heaven;
   when he reached the Ancient One
and was presented before him,
   the one like a Son of man received dominion, glory, and
     kingship;
   all peoples, nations, and languages serve him.
His dominion is an everlasting dominion
   that shall not be taken away,
   his kingship shall not be destroyed.

Responsorial Psalm   Ps 93: 1, 1-2, 5   *Roger Holtz*

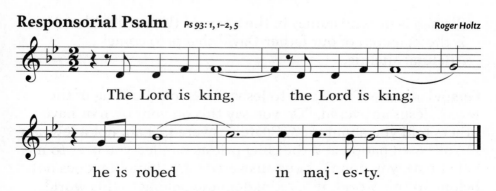

The Lord is king, the Lord is king; he is robed in maj-es-ty.

The LORD is king, in splendor robed;
   robed is the LORD and girt about with strength. ℟

And he has made the world firm,
    not to be moved.
Your throne stands firm from of old;
    from everlasting you are, O LORD. ℟

Your decrees are worthy of trust indeed;
    holiness befits your house,
    O LORD, for length of days. ℟

Second Reading Rv 1: 5–8 Jesus Christ is the faithful witness, the
firstborn of the dead and ruler of the kings of the earth. To him
who loves us and has freed us from our sins by his blood, who
has made us into a kingdom, priests for his God and Father, to
him be glory and power forever and ever. Amen.
    Behold, he is coming amid the clouds,
        and every eye will see him,
        even those who pierced him.
All the peoples of the earth will lament him.
    Yes. Amen.
"I am the Alpha and the Omega," says the Lord God, "the one
who is and who was and who is to come, the almighty."

Alleluia   Mk 11: 9, 10   Brian J. Nelson

Al - le-lu - ia, al - le - lu - ia, al-le-lu - ia.

Blessed is he who comes in the name of the Lord! / Blessed
is the kingdom of our father David that is to come!
Alleluia, alleluia.

Gospel Jn 18: 33b–37 Pilate said to Jesus, "Are you the King of the
Jews?" Jesus answered, "Do you say this on your own or have
others told you about me?" Pilate answered, "I am not a Jew, am
I? Your own nation and the chief priests handed you over to me.
What have you done?" Jesus answered, "My kingdom does not
belong to this world. If my kingdom did belong to this world,
my attendants would be fighting to keep me from being handed

over to the Jews. But as it is, my kingdom is not here." So Pilate said to him, "Then you are a king?" Jesus answered, "You say I am a king. For this I was born and for this I came into the world, to testify to the truth. Everyone who belongs to the truth listens to my voice."

Communion Antiphon Ps 29 (28): 10–11 **The Lord sits as King for ever. ◆ The Lord will bless his people with peace.**

Advent † YEAR C

FIRST SUNDAY OF ADVENT

Entrance Antiphon *cf. Ps 25 (24): 1–3* To you, I lift up my soul, O my God. ✦ In you, I have trusted; let me not be put to shame. ✦ Nor let my enemies exult over me; ✦ and let none who hope in you be put to shame.

First Reading *Jer 33: 14–16*

The days are coming, says the LORD,
    when I will fulfill the promise
    I made to the house of Israel and Judah.
In those days, in that time,
    I will raise up for David a just shoot;
    he shall do what is right and just in the land.
In those days Judah shall be safe
    and Jerusalem shall dwell secure;
    this is what they shall call her:
"The LORD our justice."

Responsorial Psalm   *Ps 25: 4–5, 8–9, 10, 14*   *Brian J. Nelson*

To you, O Lord, I lift my soul.

Your ways, O LORD, make known to me;
    teach me your paths,
Guide me in your truth and teach me,
    for you are God my savior,
    and for you I wait all the day. ℟

Good and upright is the L<small>ORD</small>;
   thus he shows sinners the way.
He guides the humble to justice,
   and teaches the humble his way. ℟

All the paths of the L<small>ORD</small> are kindness and constancy
   toward those who keep his covenant and his decrees.
The friendship of the L<small>ORD</small> is with those who fear him,
   and his covenant, for their instruction. ℟

Second Reading *1 Thes 3: 12- 4: 2* Brothers and sisters: May the Lord make you increase and abound in love for one another and for all, just as we have for you, so as to strengthen your hearts, to be blameless in holiness before our God and Father at the coming of our Lord Jesus with all his holy ones. Amen.

Finally, brothers and sisters, we earnestly ask and exhort you in the Lord Jesus that, as you received from us how you should conduct yourselves to please God—and as you are conducting yourselves—you do so even more. For you know what instructions we gave you through the Lord Jesus.

Alleluia   *Ps 85: 8*   *Joe Higginbotham*

Al - le - lu - ia,   al - le - lu - ia,   al - le - lu - ia.

Al - le - lu - ia,   al - le - lu - ia,   al - le - lu - ia.

Show us, Lord, your love; / and grant us your salvation.
Alleluia, alleluia.

Gospel *Lk 21: 25–28, 34–36* Jesus said to his disciples: "There will be signs in the sun, the moon, and the stars, and on earth nations will be in dismay, perplexed by the roaring of the sea and the waves. People will die of fright in anticipation of what is coming upon the world, for the powers of the heavens will be shaken. And then they will see the Son of Man coming in a cloud with power and great glory. But when these signs begin to happen, stand erect and raise your heads because your redemption is at hand.

"Beware that your hearts do not become drowsy from carousing and drunkenness and the anxieties of daily life, and that day catch you by surprise like a trap. For that day will assault everyone who lives on the face of the earth. Be vigilant at all times and pray that you have the strength to escape the tribulations that are imminent and to stand before the Son of Man."

Communion Antiphon Ps 85 (84): 13 The Lord will bestow his bounty, and our earth shall yield its increase.

SECOND SUNDAY OF ADVENT

Entrance Antiphon cf. Is 30: 19, 30 O people of Sion, behold, the Lord will come to save the nations, ◆ and the Lord will make the glory of his voice heard in the joy of your heart.

First Reading   Bar 5: 1–9
Jerusalem, take off your robe of mourning and misery;
    put on the splendor of glory from God forever:
wrapped in the cloak of justice from God,
    bear on your head the mitre
    that displays the glory of the eternal name.
For God will show all the earth your splendor:
    you will be named by God forever
    the peace of justice, the glory of God's worship.

Up, Jerusalem! stand upon the heights;
    look to the east and see your children
gathered from the east and the west

at the word of the Holy One,
  rejoicing that they are remembered by God.
Led away on foot by their enemies they left you:
  but God will bring them back to you
  borne aloft in glory as on royal thrones.
For God has commanded
  that every lofty mountain be made low,
and that the age-old depths and gorges
  be filled to level ground,
  that Israel may advance secure in the glory of God.
The forests and every fragrant kind of tree
  have overshadowed Israel at God's command;
for God is leading Israel in joy
  by the light of his glory,
  with his mercy and justice for company.

Responsorial Psalm   *Ps 126: 1–2, 2–3, 4–5, 6*   *Joe Higginbotham*

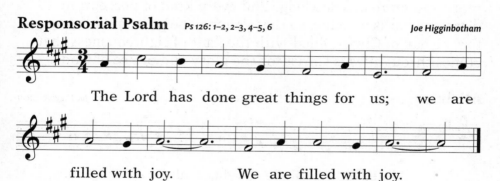

The Lord has done great things for us; we are filled with joy. We are filled with joy.

When the LORD brought back the captives of Zion,
  we were like men dreaming.
Then our mouth was filled with laughter,
  and our tongue with rejoicing. ℟

Then they said among the nations,
  "The LORD has done great things for them."
The LORD has done great things for us;
  we are glad indeed. ℟

Restore our fortunes, O LORD,
  like the torrents in the southern desert.

Those who sow in tears
    shall reap rejoicing. ℟

Although they go forth weeping,
    carrying the seed to be sown,
they shall come back rejoicing,
    carrying their sheaves. ℟

Second Reading *Phil 1: 4–6, 8–11* Brothers and sisters: I pray always with joy in my every prayer for all of you, because of your partnership for the gospel from the first day until now. I am confident of this, that the one who began a good work in you will continue to complete it until the day of Christ Jesus. God is my witness, how I long for all of you with the affection of Christ Jesus. And this is my prayer: that your love may increase ever more and more in knowledge and every kind of perception, to discern what is of value, so that you may be pure and blameless for the day of Christ, filled with the fruit of righteousness that comes through Jesus Christ for the glory and praise of God.

Alleluia *Lk 3: 4, 6*   Joe Higginbotham

Al-le-lu-ia, al-le-lu-ia, al-le-lu - ia.

Al-le-lu-ia, al-le-lu-ia, al-le-lu - ia.

Prepare the way of the Lord, make straight his paths: / all flesh shall see the salvation of God. **Alleluia, alleluia.**

Gospel *Lk 3: 1–6* In the fifteenth year of the reign of Tiberius Caesar, when Pontius Pilate was governor of Judea, and Herod was tetrarch of Galilee, and his brother Philip tetrarch of the region of Ituraea and Trachonitis, and Lysanias was tetrarch of Abilene, during the high priesthood of Annas and Caiaphas, the word of God came to John the son of Zechariah in the desert. John went throughout the whole region of the Jordan, proclaiming a baptism of repentance for the forgiveness of sins, as it is written in the book of the words of the prophet Isaiah:

> *A voice of one crying out in the desert:*
> *"Prepare the way of the Lord,*
>   *make straight his paths.*
> *Every valley shall be filled*
>   *and every mountain and hill shall be made low.*
> *The winding roads shall be made straight,*
>   *and the rough ways made smooth,*
> *and all flesh shall see the salvation of God."*

Communion Antiphon *Bar 5: 5; 4: 36* **Jerusalem, arise and stand upon the heights,** ◆ **and behold the joy which comes to you from God.**

THIRD SUNDAY OF ADVENT

Entrance Antiphon *Phil 4: 4–5* **Rejoice in the Lord always; again I say, rejoice.** ◆ **Indeed, the Lord is near.**

First Reading *Zep 3: 14–18a*

> Shout for joy, O daughter Zion!
>   Sing joyfully, O Israel!
> Be glad and exult with all your heart,
>   O daughter Jerusalem!
> The LORD has removed the judgment against you,
>   he has turned away your enemies;
> the King of Israel, the LORD, is in your midst,
>   you have no further misfortune to fear.
> On that day, it shall be said to Jerusalem:
>   Fear not, O Zion, be not discouraged!
> The LORD, your God, is in your midst,

a mighty savior;
he will rejoice over you with gladness,
   and renew you in his love,
he will sing joyfully because of you,
   as one sings at festivals.

Responsorial Psalm Is 12: 2–3, 4, 5–6 *Jim Cowan*

Cry out with joy and glad-ness, for a-mong you is the great and Ho-ly One of Is-ra-el.

God indeed is my savior;
   I am confident and unafraid.
My strength and my courage is the LORD,
   and he has been my savior.
With joy you will draw water
   at the fountain of salvation. ℟

Give thanks to the LORD, acclaim his name;
   among the nations make known his deeds,
   proclaim how exalted is his name. ℟

Sing praise to the LORD for his glorious achievement;
   let this be known throughout all the earth.
Shout with exultation, O city of Zion,
   for great in your midst
   is the Holy One of Israel! ℟

Second Reading Phil 4: 4–7 Brothers and sisters: Rejoice in the
Lord always. I shall say it again: rejoice! Your kindness should
be known to all. The Lord is near. Have no anxiety at all, but
in everything, by prayer and petition, with thanksgiving, make
your requests known to God. Then the peace of God that

surpasses all understanding will guard your hearts and minds in
Christ Jesus.

Alleluia   Is 61: 1 (cited in Lk 4: 18)   Joe Higginbotham

Al - le - lu - ia,   al - le - lu - ia,   al - le - lu - ia.

Al - le - lu - ia,   al - le - lu - ia,   al - le - lu - ia.

The Spirit of the Lord is upon me, / because he has anointed
me / to bring glad tidings to the poor.   **Alleluia, alleluia.**

Gospel Lk 3: 10–18 The crowds asked John the Baptist, "What
should we do?" He said to them in reply, "Whoever has two
cloaks should share with the person who has none. And
whoever has food should do likewise." Even tax collectors came
to be baptized and they said to him, "Teacher, what should we
do?" He answered them, "Stop collecting more than what is
prescribed." Soldiers also asked him, "And what is it that we
should do?" He told them, "Do not practice extortion, do not
falsely accuse anyone, and be satisfied with your wages."

Now the people were filled with expectation, and all were
asking in their hearts whether John might be the Christ. John
answered them all, saying, "I am baptizing you with water, but
one mightier than I is coming. I am not worthy to loosen the
thongs of his sandals. He will baptize you with the Holy Spirit
and fire. His winnowing fan is in his hand to clear his threshing
floor and to gather the wheat into his barn, but the chaff he will
burn with unquenchable fire." Exhorting them in many other
ways, he preached good news to the people.

Communion Antiphon cf. Is 35: 4 **Say to the faint of heart: Be
strong and do not fear. ◆ Behold, our God will come, and he
will save us.**

FOURTH SUNDAY OF ADVENT

Entrance Antiphon *cf. Is 45: 8* **Drop down dew from above, you heavens, ◆ and let the clouds rain down the Just One; ◆ let the earth be opened and bring forth a Savior.**

First Reading *Mi 5: 1–4a*

Thus says the LORD:
You, Bethlehem-Ephrathah,
   too small to be among the clans of Judah,
from you shall come forth for me
   one who is to be ruler in Israel;
whose origin is from of old,
   from ancient times.
Therefore the Lord will give them up, until the time
   when she who is to give birth has borne,
and the rest of his kindred shall return
   to the children of Israel.
He shall stand firm and shepherd his flock
   by the strength of the LORD,
   in the majestic name of the LORD, his God;
and they shall remain, for now his greatness
   shall reach to the ends of the earth;
   he shall be peace.

Responsorial Psalm *Ps 80: 2–3, 15–16, 18–19*   Joe Higginbotham

Lord, make us turn to you; let us see your face and we shall be saved.

O shepherd of Israel, hearken,
   from your throne upon the cherubim, shine forth.
Rouse your power,
   and come to save us. ℟

Once again, O LORD of hosts,
>> look down from heaven, and see;
take care of this vine,
>> and protect what your right hand has planted,
>> the son of man whom you yourself made strong.   ℟

May your help be with the man of your right hand,
>> with the son of man whom you yourself made strong.
Then we will no more withdraw from you;
>> give us new life, and we will call upon your name.   ℟

Second Reading *Heb 10: 5–10* Brothers and sisters: When Christ
came into the world, he said:
>> "Sacrifice and offering you did not desire,
>> but a body you prepared for me;
in holocausts and sin offerings you took no delight.
Then I said, 'As is written of me in the scroll,
behold, I come to do your will, O God.'"
First he says, "Sacrifices and offerings, holocausts and sin
offerings, you neither desired nor delighted in." These are
offered according to the law. Then he says, "Behold, I come to
do your will." He takes away the first to establish the second. By
this "will," we have been consecrated through the offering of the
body of Jesus Christ once for all.

Alleluia   *Lk 1: 38*   *Joe Higginbotham*

Al-le-lu-ia, al-le-lu-ia, al-le-lu - ia.

Al-le-lu-ia, al-le-lu-ia, al-le-lu - ia.

Behold, I am the handmaid of the Lord. / May it be done to
me according to your word.   **Alleluia, alleluia.**

Gospel *Lk 1: 39–45* Mary set out and traveled to the hill country
in haste to a town of Judah, where she entered the house of

Zechariah and greeted Elizabeth. When Elizabeth heard Mary's greeting, the infant leaped in her womb, and Elizabeth, filled with the Holy Spirit, cried out in a loud voice and said, "Blessed are you among women, and blessed is the fruit of your womb. And how does this happen to me, that the mother of my Lord should come to me? For at the moment the sound of your greeting reached my ears, the infant in my womb leaped for joy. Blessed are you who believed that what was spoken to you by the Lord would be fulfilled."

Communion Antiphon Is 7:14 **Behold, a Virgin shall conceive and bear a son; ◆ and his name will be called Emmanuel.**

Christmas Time † YEAR C

THE NATIVITY OF THE LORD

❖ At the Vigil Mass ❖

Entrance Antiphon *cf. Ex 16: 6–7* Today you will know that the Lord will come, and he will save us, ◆ and in the morning you will see his glory.

First Reading *Is 62: 1–5*

For Zion's sake I will not be silent,
    for Jerusalem's sake I will not be quiet,
until her vindication shines forth like the dawn
    and her victory like a burning torch.

Nations shall behold your vindication,
    and all the kings your glory;
you shall be called by a new name
    pronounced by the mouth of the LORD.
You shall be a glorious crown in the hand of the LORD,
    a royal diadem held by your God.
No more shall people call you "Forsaken,"
    or your land "Desolate,"
but you shall be called "My Delight,"
    and your land "Espoused."
For the LORD delights in you
    and makes your land his spouse.
As a young man marries a virgin,
    your Builder shall marry you;

and as a bridegroom rejoices in his bride
  so shall your God rejoice in you.

Responsorial Psalm   Ps 89: 4–5, 16–17, 27, 29   Joe Higginbotham

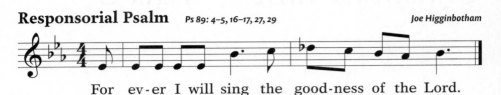

For ev-er I will sing the good-ness of the Lord.

I have made a covenant with my chosen one,
  I have sworn to David my servant:
Forever will I confirm your posterity
  and establish your throne for all generations.   ℟

Blessed the people who know the joyful shout;
  in the light of your countenance, O LORD, they walk.
At your name they rejoice all the day,
  and through your justice they are exalted.   ℟

He shall say of me, "You are my father,
  my God, the rock, my savior."
Forever I will maintain my kindness toward him,
  and my covenant with him stands firm.   ℟

Second Reading   Acts 13: 16–17, 22–25   When Paul reached Antioch in
Pisidia and entered the synagogue, he stood up, motioned with
his hand, and said, "Fellow Israelites and you others who
are God-fearing, listen. The God of this people Israel chose
our ancestors and exalted the people during their sojourn in
the land of Egypt. With uplifted arm he led them out of it.
Then he removed Saul and raised up David as king; of him
he testified, 'I have found David, son of Jesse, a man after my
own heart; he will carry out my every wish.' From this man's
descendants God, according to his promise, has brought to
Israel a savior, Jesus. John heralded his coming by proclaiming
a baptism of repentance to all the people of Israel; and as John
was completing his course, he would say, 'What do you suppose
that I am? I am not he. Behold, one is coming after me; I am
not worthy to unfasten the sandals of his feet.'"

Alleluia

Jim Hughes

Al-le-lu-ia   Al-le-lu-ia   Al - le-lu - ia.

Tomorrow the wickedness of the earth will be destroyed: /
the Savior of the world will reign over us. **Alleluia, alleluia.**

Gospel Mt 1: 1–25 or 1: 18–25 The book of the genealogy of Jesus Christ,
the son of David, the son of Abraham.

Abraham became the father of Isaac, Isaac the father of Jacob,
Jacob the father of Judah and his brothers. Judah became the
father of Perez and Zerah, whose mother was Tamar. Perez
became the father of Hezron, Hezron the father of Ram, Ram
the father of Amminadab. Amminadab became the father of
Nahshon, Nahshon the father of Salmon, Salmon the father of
Boaz, whose mother was Rahab. Boaz became the father of Obed,
whose mother was Ruth. Obed became the father of Jesse, Jesse
the father of David the king.

David became the father of Solomon, whose mother had been
the wife of Uriah. Solomon became the father of Rehoboam,
Rehoboam the father of Abijah, Abijah the father of Asaph.
Asaph became the father of Jehoshaphat, Jehoshaphat the father
of Joram, Joram the father of Uzziah. Uzziah became the father
of Jotham, Jotham the father of Ahaz, Ahaz the father of
Hezekiah. Hezekiah became the father of Manasseh, Manasseh
the father of Amos, Amos the father of Josiah. Josiah became
the father of Jechoniah and his brothers at the time of the
Babylonian exile.

After the Babylonian exile, Jechoniah became the father of
Shealtiel, Shealtiel the father of Zerubbabel, Zerubbabel the
father of Abiud. Abiud became the father of Eliakim, Eliakim
the father of Azor, Azor the father of Zadok. Zadok became the
father of Achim, Achim the father of Eliud, Eliud the father of
Eleazar. Eleazar became the father of Matthan, Matthan the
father of Jacob, Jacob the father of Joseph, the husband of Mary.
Of her was born Jesus who is called the Christ.

Thus the total number of generations from Abraham to David

is fourteen generations; from David to the Babylonian exile, fourteen generations; from the Babylonian exile to the Christ, fourteen generations.

Now [this is how the birth of Jesus Christ came about. When his mother Mary was betrothed to Joseph, but before they lived together, she was found with child through the Holy Spirit. Joseph her husband, since he was a righteous man, yet unwilling to expose her to shame, decided to divorce her quietly. Such was his intention when, behold, the angel of the Lord appeared to him in a dream and said, "Joseph, son of David, do not be afraid to take Mary your wife into your home. For it is through the Holy Spirit that this child has been conceived in her. She will bear a son and you are to name him Jesus, because he will save his people from their sins." All this took place to fulfill what the Lord had said through the prophet:

Behold, the virgin shall conceive and bear a son,
 and they shall name him Emmanuel,

which means "God is with us." When Joseph awoke, he did as the angel of the Lord had commanded him and took his wife into his home. He had no relations with her until she bore a son, and he named him Jesus.]

During the Creed, all kneel at the words and by the Holy Spirit was incarnate.

Communion Antiphon *cf. Is 40: 5* The glory of the Lord will be revealed, ◆ and all flesh will see the salvation of our God.

❖   At the Mass During the Night   ❖

Entrance Antiphon *Ps 2: 7* The Lord said to me: You are my Son. ◆ It is I who have begotten you this day.

Or:
Let us all rejoice in the Lord for our Savior has been born in the world. ◆ Today true peace has come down to us from heaven.

First Reading Is 9: 1–6

The people who walked in darkness
 have seen a great light;
upon those who dwelt in the land of gloom
 a light has shone.
You have brought them abundant joy
 and great rejoicing,
as they rejoice before you as at the harvest,
 as people make merry when dividing spoils.
For the yoke that burdened them,
 the pole on their shoulder,
and the rod of their taskmaster
 you have smashed, as on the day of Midian.
For every boot that tramped in battle,
 every cloak rolled in blood,
 will be burned as fuel for flames.
For a child is born to us, a son is given us;
 upon his shoulder dominion rests.
They name him Wonder-Counselor, God-Hero,
 Father-Forever, Prince of Peace.
His dominion is vast
 and forever peaceful,
from David's throne, and over his kingdom,
 which he confirms and sustains
by judgment and justice,
 both now and forever.
The zeal of the LORD of hosts will do this!

Responsorial Psalm   Ps 96: 1–2, 2–3, 11–12, 13   Joe Higginbotham

To - day is born our Sav - ior,

our Sav - ior, Christ the Lord.

Sing to the LORD a new song;

sing to the LORD, all you lands.
Sing to the LORD; bless his name. ℟

Announce his salvation, day after day.
Tell his glory among the nations;
among all peoples, his wondrous deeds. ℟

Let the heavens be glad and the earth rejoice;
let the sea and what fills it resound;
let the plains be joyful and all that is in them!
Then shall all the trees of the forest exult. ℟

They shall exult before the LORD, for he comes;
for he comes to rule the earth.
He shall rule the world with justice
and the peoples with his constancy. ℟

Second Reading *Ti 2: 11–14* Beloved: The grace of God has appeared, saving all and training us to reject godless ways and worldly desires and to live temperately, justly, and devoutly in this age, as we await the blessed hope, the appearance of the glory of our great God and savior Jesus Christ, who gave himself for us to deliver us from all lawlessness and to cleanse for himself a people as his own, eager to do what is good.

Alleluia *Lk 2: 10–11*   *Jim Hughes*

Al-le-lu-ia   Al-le-lu-ia   Al-le-lu - ia.

I proclaim to you good news of great joy: / today a Savior is born for us, / Christ the Lord. **Alleluia, alleluia.**

Gospel *Lk 2: 1–14* In those days a decree went out from Caesar Augustus that the whole world should be enrolled. This was the first enrollment, when Quirinius was governor of Syria. So all went to be enrolled, each to his own town. And Joseph too went up from Galilee from the town of Nazareth to Judea, to the city

of David that is called Bethlehem, because he was of the house
and family of David, to be enrolled with Mary, his betrothed,
who was with child. While they were there, the time came for
her to have her child, and she gave birth to her firstborn son.
She wrapped him in swaddling clothes and laid him in a manger,
because there was no room for them in the inn.

Now there were shepherds in that region living in the fields
and keeping the night watch over their flock. The angel of the
Lord appeared to them and the glory of the Lord shone around
them, and they were struck with great fear. The angel said to
them, "Do not be afraid; for behold, I proclaim to you good news
of great joy that will be for all the people. For today in the city
of David a savior has been born for you who is Christ and Lord.
And this will be a sign for you: you will find an infant wrapped
in swaddling clothes and lying in a manger." And suddenly there
was a multitude of the heavenly host with the angel, praising
God and saying:
   "Glory to God in the highest
      and on earth peace to those on whom his favor rests."

During the Creed, all kneel at the words and by the Holy Spirit
was incarnate.

Communion Antiphon *Jn 1: 14* **The Word became flesh, and we
have seen his glory.**

✧   At the Mass at Dawn   ✧

Entrance Antiphon *cf. Is 9: 1, 5; Lk 1: 33* **Today a light will shine
upon us, for the Lord is born for us; ✦ and he will be
called Wondrous God, ✦ Prince of peace, Father of future ages:
✦ and his reign will be without end.**

First Reading *Is 62: 11–12*
   See, the LORD proclaims
      to the ends of the earth:
   say to daughter Zion,
      your savior comes!

Here is his reward with him,
    his recompense before him.
They shall be called the holy people,
    the redeemed of the LORD,
and you shall be called "Frequented,"
    a city that is not forsaken.

Responsorial Psalm   Ps 97: 1, 6, 11–12   *Bill Svarda*

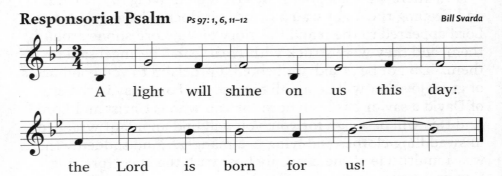

A light will shine on us this day: the Lord is born for us!

The LORD is king; let the earth rejoice;
    let the many isles be glad.
The heavens proclaim his justice,
    and all peoples see his glory. ℟

Light dawns for the just;
    and gladness, for the upright of heart.
Be glad in the LORD, you just,
    and give thanks to his holy name. ℟

Second Reading   Ti 3: 4–7
Beloved:
    When the kindness and generous love
        of God our savior appeared,
not because of any righteous deeds we had done
    but because of his mercy,
he saved us through the bath of rebirth
    and renewal by the Holy Spirit,
whom he richly poured out on us
    through Jesus Christ our savior,
so that we might be justified by his grace
    and become heirs in hope of eternal life.

Alleluia Lk 2: 14   Jim Hughes

Al-le-lu-ia   Al-le-lu-ia   Al - le-lu - ia.

Glory to God in the highest, / and on earth peace to those / on whom his favor rests.   **Alleluia, alleluia.**

Gospel Lk 2: 15–20 When the angels went away from them to heaven, the shepherds said to one another, "Let us go, then, to Bethlehem to see this thing that has taken place, which the Lord has made known to us." So they went in haste and found Mary and Joseph, and the infant lying in the manger. When they saw this, they made known the message that had been told them about this child. All who heard it were amazed by what had been told them by the shepherds. And Mary kept all these things, reflecting on them in her heart. Then the shepherds returned, glorifying and praising God for all they had heard and seen, just as it had been told to them.

During the Creed, all kneel at the words and by the Holy Spirit was incarnate.

Communion Antiphon cf. Zec 9: 9 Rejoice, O Daughter Sion; lift up praise, Daughter Jerusalem: ♦ Behold, your King will come, the Holy One and Savior of the world.

❖   At the Mass During the Day   ❖

Entrance Antiphon cf. Is 9: 5 A child is born for us, and a son is given to us; ♦ his scepter of power rests upon his shoulder, ♦ and his name will be called Messenger of great counsel.

First Reading Is 52: 7–10
How beautiful upon the mountains
  are the feet of him who brings glad tidings,

announcing peace, bearing good news,
   announcing salvation, and saying to Zion,
   "Your God is King!"

Hark! Your sentinels raise a cry,
   together they shout for joy,
for they see directly, before their eyes,
   the LORD restoring Zion.
Break out together in song,
   O ruins of Jerusalem!
For the LORD comforts his people,
   he redeems Jerusalem.
The LORD has bared his holy arm
   in the sight of all the nations;
all the ends of the earth will behold
   the salvation of our God.

Responsorial Psalm   Ps 98: 1, 2–3, 3–4, 5–6   Don Fishel

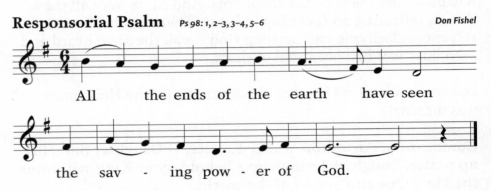

All the ends of the earth have seen the sav-ing pow-er of God.

Sing to the LORD a new song,
   for he has done wondrous deeds;
his right hand has won victory for him,
   his holy arm. ℟

The LORD has made his salvation known:
   in the sight of the nations he has revealed his justice.
He has remembered his kindness and his faithfulness
   toward the house of Israel. ℟

All the ends of the earth have seen

the salvation by our God.
Sing joyfully to the LORD, all you lands;
   break into song; sing praise. ℟

Sing praise to the LORD with the harp,
   with the harp and melodious song.
With trumpets and the sound of the horn
   sing joyfully before the King, the LORD. ℟

Second Reading *Heb 1: 1–6* Brothers and sisters: In times past, God
spoke in partial and various ways to our ancestors through the
prophets; in these last days, he has spoken to us through the Son,
whom he made heir of all things and through whom he created
the universe,
   who is the refulgence of his glory, the very imprint of his
      being,
   and who sustains all things by his mighty word.
   When he had accomplished purification from sins,
   he took his seat at the right hand of the Majesty on high,
   as far superior to the angels
   as the name he has inherited is more excellent than theirs.

   For to which of the angels did God ever say:
   You are my son; this day I have begotten you?
Or again:
   I will be a father to him, and he shall be a son to me?
And again, when he leads the firstborn into the world, he says:
   Let all the angels of God worship him.

Alleluia
Jim Hughes

Al-le-lu-ia   Al-le-lu-ia   Al - le-lu - ia.

A holy day has dawned upon us. / Come, you nations, and
adore the Lord. / For today a great light has come upon the
earth. **Alleluia, alleluia.**

Gospel   Jn 1: 1–18 or 1: 1–5, 9–14

For the shorter form, read only the parts in brackets.

[In the beginning was the Word,
   and the Word was with God,
   and the Word was God.
He was in the beginning with God.
All things came to be through him,
   and without him nothing came to be.
What came to be through him was life,
   and this life was the light of the human race;
the light shines in the darkness,
   and the darkness has not overcome it.]
A man named John was sent from God. He came for testimony,
to testify to the light, so that all might believe through him. He
was not the light, but came to testify to the light. [The true light,
which enlightens everyone, was coming into the world.

He was in the world,
   and the world came to be through him,
   but the world did not know him.
He came to what was his own,
   but his own people did not accept him.
But to those who did accept him he gave power to become
children of God, to those who believe in his name, who were
born not by natural generation nor by human choice nor by a
man's decision but of God.
And the Word became flesh
   and made his dwelling among us,
   and we saw his glory,
   the glory as of the Father's only Son,
   full of grace and truth.]
John testified to him and cried out, saying, "This was he of
whom I said, 'The one who is coming after me ranks ahead of
me because he existed before me.'" From his fullness we have
all received, grace in place of grace, because while the law was
given through Moses, grace and truth came through Jesus
Christ. No one has ever seen God. The only Son, God, who is at
the Father's side, has revealed him.

During the Creed, all kneel at the words and by the Holy Spirit was incarnate.

Communion Antiphon *cf. Ps 98 (97): 3* **All the ends of the earth have seen the salvation of our God.**

THE HOLY FAMILY

OF JESUS, MARY, AND JOSEPH

When a Sunday does not occur between December 25 and January 1, this feast is celebrated on December 30 with only one reading before the Gospel.

Entrance Antiphon *Lk 2:16* **The shepherds went in haste, ♦ and found Mary and Joseph and the Infant lying in a manger.**

First Reading *Sir 3: 2–6, 12–14*
God sets a father in honor over his children;
  a mother's authority he confirms over her sons.
Whoever honors his father atones for sins,
  and preserves himself from them.
When he prays, he is heard;
  he stores up riches who reveres his mother.
Whoever honors his father is gladdened by children,
  and, when he prays, is heard.
Whoever reveres his father will live a long life;
  he who obeys his father brings comfort to his mother.

My son, take care of your father when he is old;
  grieve him not as long as he lives.
Even if his mind fail, be considerate of him;
  revile him not all the days of his life;
kindness to a father will not be forgotten,
  firmly planted against the debt of your sins
    —a house raised in justice to you.

Responsorial Psalm

Ps 128: 1–2, 3, 4–5

Beverly McDevitt

Bless - ed are those who fear the Lord
and walk in his ways.

Blessed is everyone who fears the LORD,
who walks in his ways!
For you shall eat the fruit of your handiwork;
blessed shall you be, and favored. ℟

Your wife shall be like a fruitful vine
in the recesses of your home;
your children like olive plants
around your table. ℟

Behold, thus is the man blessed
who fears the LORD.
The LORD bless you from Zion:
may you see the prosperity of Jerusalem
all the days of your life. ℟

Second Reading

Col 3: 12–21 or 3: 12–17

For the shorter form, read only the parts in brackets.
[Brothers and sisters: Put on, as God's chosen ones, holy and beloved, heartfelt compassion, kindness, humility, gentleness, and patience, bearing with one another and forgiving one another, if one has a grievance against another; as the Lord has forgiven you, so must you also do. And over all these put on love, that is, the bond of perfection. And let the peace of Christ control your hearts, the peace into which you were also called in one body. And be thankful. Let the word of Christ dwell in you richly, as in all wisdom you teach and admonish one another, singing psalms, hymns, and spiritual songs with gratitude in your hearts to God. And whatever you do, in word or in deed, do

everything in the name of the Lord Jesus, giving thanks to God the Father through him.]

Wives, be subordinate to your husbands, as is proper in the Lord. Husbands, love your wives, and avoid any bitterness toward them. Children, obey your parents in everything, for this is pleasing to the Lord. Fathers, do not provoke your children, so they may not become discouraged.

Alleluia   Col 3: 15a, 16a   Joe Higginbotham

Al-le-lu-ia, al - le - lu-ia, al - le - lu - ia.

Al-le-lu-ia, al - le - lu-ia, al - le - lu - ia.

Let the peace of Christ control your hearts; / let the word of Christ dwell in you richly.   **Alleluia, alleluia.**

Gospel Lk 2: 41-52 Each year Jesus' parents went to Jerusalem for the feast of Passover, and when he was twelve years old, they went up according to festival custom. After they had completed its days, as they were returning, the boy Jesus remained behind in Jerusalem, but his parents did not know it. Thinking that he was in the caravan, they journeyed for a day and looked for him among their relatives and acquaintances, but not finding him, they returned to Jerusalem to look for him. After three days they found him in the temple, sitting in the midst of the teachers, listening to them and asking them questions, and all who heard him were astounded at his understanding and his answers. When his parents saw him, they were astonished, and his mother said to him, "Son, why have you done this to us? Your father and I have been looking for you with great anxiety." And he said to them, "Why were you looking for me? Did you not know that I must be in my Father's house?" But they did not understand what he said to them. He went down with them and came to Nazareth, and was obedient to them; and his mother kept all these things in her heart. And Jesus advanced in wisdom and age and favor before God and man.

Communion Antiphon *Bar 3:38* **Our God has appeared on the earth, and lived among us.**

❖ Optional Readings ❖

In Year C, these readings may be used:

Entrance Antiphon *Lk 2:16* **The shepherds went in haste, ◆ and found Mary and Joseph and the Infant lying in a manger.**

First Reading *1 Sm 1: 20–22, 24–28* In those days Hannah conceived, and at the end of her term bore a son whom she called Samuel, since she had asked the LORD for him. The next time her husband Elkanah was going up with the rest of his household to offer the customary sacrifice to the LORD and to fulfill his vows, Hannah did not go, explaining to her husband, "Once the child is weaned, I will take him to appear before the LORD and to remain there forever; I will offer him as a perpetual nazirite."

Once Samuel was weaned, Hannah brought him up with her, along with a three-year-old bull, an ephah of flour, and a skin of wine, and presented him at the temple of the LORD in Shiloh. After the boy's father had sacrificed the young bull, Hannah, his mother, approached Eli and said: "Pardon, my lord! As you live, my lord, I am the woman who stood near you here, praying to the LORD. I prayed for this child, and the LORD granted my request. Now I, in turn, give him to the LORD; as long as he lives, he shall be dedicated to the LORD." Hannah left Samuel there.

Responsorial Psalm *Ps 84: 2–3, 5–6, 9–10*   Joe Higginbotham

Bless-ed are they who dwell in your house, O Lord.

How lovely is your dwelling place, O LORD of hosts!
    My soul yearns and pines for the courts of the LORD.
My heart and my flesh cry out for the living God. ℟

Happy they who dwell in your house!
  Continually they praise you.
Happy the men whose strength you are!
  Their hearts are set upon the pilgrimage. ℟

O LORD of hosts, hear our prayer;
  hearken, O God of Jacob!
O God, behold our shield,
  and look upon the face of your anointed. ℟

Second Reading *1 Jn 3: 1–2, 21–24* Beloved: See what love the Father
has bestowed on us that we may be called the children of God.
And so we are. The reason the world does not know us is that it
did not know him. Beloved, we are God's children now; what we
shall be has not yet been revealed. We do know that when it is
revealed we shall be like him, for we shall see him as he is.

Beloved, if our hearts do not condemn us, we have confidence
in God and receive from him whatever we ask, because we
keep his commandments and do what pleases him. And his
commandment is this: we should believe in the name of his
Son, Jesus Christ, and love one another just as he commanded
us. Those who keep his commandments remain in him, and he
in them, and the way we know that he remains in us is from the
Spirit he gave us.

Alleluia *cf. Acts 16: 14b*   *Joe Higginbotham*

Al - le - lu - ia, al - le - lu - ia, al - le - lu - ia.

Al - le - lu - ia, al - le - lu - ia, al - le - lu - ia.

Open our hearts, O Lord, / to listen to the words of your Son.
Alleluia, alleluia.

Gospel *Lk 2: 41–52* Each year Jesus' parents went to Jerusalem for
the feast of Passover, and when he was twelve years old, they

went up according to festival custom. After they had completed its days, as they were returning, the boy Jesus remained behind in Jerusalem, but his parents did not know it. Thinking that he was in the caravan, they journeyed for a day and looked for him among their relatives and acquaintances, but not finding him, they returned to Jerusalem to look for him. After three days they found him in the temple, sitting in the midst of the teachers, listening to them and asking them questions, and all who heard him were astounded at his understanding and his answers. When his parents saw him, they were astonished, and his mother said to him, "Son, why have you done this to us? Your father and I have been looking for you with great anxiety." And he said to them, "Why were you looking for me? Did you not know that I must be in my Father's house?" But they did not understand what he said to them. He went down with them and came to Nazareth, and was obedient to them; and his mother kept all these things in her heart. And Jesus advanced in wisdom and age and favor before God and man.

SOLEMNITY OF MARY,

THE HOLY MOTHER OF GOD

THE OCTAVE DAY OF THE NATIVITY

Entrance Antiphon   Hail, Holy Mother, who gave birth to the King ◆ who rules heaven and earth for ever.

Or: *cf. Is 9: 1, 5; Lk 1: 33*   Today a light will shine upon us, for the Lord is born for us; ◆ and he will be called Wondrous God, ◆ Prince of peace, Father of future ages: ◆ and his reign will be without end.

First Reading   *Nm 6: 22-27*   The LORD said to Moses: "Speak to Aaron and his sons and tell them: 'This is how you shall bless the Israelites. Say to them:
   The LORD bless you and keep you!
   The LORD let his face shine upon you, and be gracious to you!
   The LORD look upon you kindly and give you peace!'

So shall they invoke my name upon the Israelites, and I will bless them."

Responsorial Psalm Ps 67: 2–3, 5, 6, 8   Bill Svarda

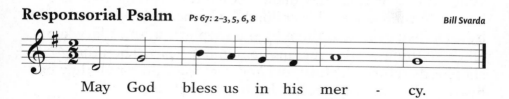

May God bless us in his mer - cy.

May God have pity on us and bless us;
  may he let his face shine upon us.
So may your way be known upon earth;
  among all nations, your salvation. ℟

May the nations be glad and exult
  because you rule the peoples in equity;
  the nations on the earth you guide. ℟

May the peoples praise you, O God;
  may all the peoples praise you!
May God bless us,
  and may all the ends of the earth fear him! ℟

Second Reading Gal 4: 4–7 Brothers and sisters: When the fullness of time had come, God sent his Son, born of a woman, born under the law, to ransom those under the law, so that we might receive adoption as sons. As proof that you are sons, God sent the Spirit of his Son into our hearts, crying out, "Abba, Father!" So you are no longer a slave but a son, and if a son then also an heir, through God.

Alleluia Heb 1: 1–2   Brian J. Nelson

Al - le-lu - ia, al - le - lu - ia, al-le-lu - ia.

In the past God spoke to our ancestors through the prophets; / in these last days, he has spoken to us through the Son. **Alleluia, alleluia.**

Gospel Lk 2: 16–21 The shepherds went in haste to Bethlehem and found Mary and Joseph, and the infant lying in the manger. When they saw this, they made known the message that had been told them about this child. All who heard it were amazed by what had been told them by the shepherds. And Mary kept all these things, reflecting on them in her heart. Then the shepherds returned, glorifying and praising God for all they had heard and seen, just as it had been told to them.

When eight days were completed for his circumcision, he was named Jesus, the name given him by the angel before he was conceived in the womb.

Communion Antiphon Heb 13: 8 **Jesus Christ is the same yesterday, today, and for ever.**

THE EPIPHANY OF THE LORD

Where the Solemnity of the Epiphany is not to be observed as a Holy day of Obligation, it is assigned to the Sunday occurring between 2 and 8 January as its proper day.

Entrance Antiphon

At the Vigil Mass: cf. Bar 5: 5 **Arise, Jerusalem, and look to the East ◆ and see your children gathered from the rising to the setting of the sun.**

At the Mass During the Day: cf. Mal 3: 1; 1 Chr 29: 12 **Behold, the Lord, the Mighty One, has come; ◆ and kingship is in his grasp, and power and dominion.**

First Reading Is 60: 1–6
Rise up in splendor, Jerusalem! Your light has come,
  the glory of the Lord shines upon you.
See, darkness covers the earth,
  and thick clouds cover the peoples;
but upon you the LORD shines,

and over you appears his glory.
Nations shall walk by your light,
   and kings by your shining radiance.
Raise your eyes and look about;
   they all gather and come to you:
your sons come from afar,
   and your daughters in the arms of their nurses.

Then you shall be radiant at what you see,
   your heart shall throb and overflow,
for the riches of the sea shall be emptied out before you,
   the wealth of nations shall be brought to you.
Caravans of camels shall fill you,
   dromedaries from Midian and Ephah;
all from Sheba shall come
   bearing gold and frankincense,
 and proclaiming the praises of the LORD.

Responsorial Psalm   Ps 72: 1–2, 7–8, 10–11, 12–13   Brian J. Nelson

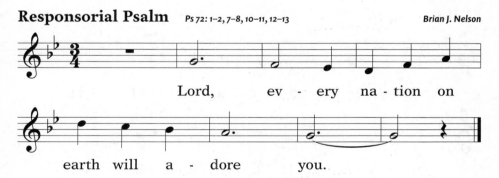

Lord, every nation on earth will adore you.

O God, with your judgment endow the king,
   and with your justice, the king's son;
He shall govern your people with justice
   and your afflicted ones with judgment.   ℟

Justice shall flower in his days,
   and profound peace, till the moon be no more.
May he rule from sea to sea,
   and from the River to the ends of the earth.   ℟

The kings of Tarshish and the Isles shall offer gifts;

the kings of Arabia and Seba shall bring tribute.
All kings shall pay him homage,
   all nations shall serve him. ℟

For he shall rescue the poor when he cries out,
   and the afflicted when he has no one to help him.
He shall have pity for the lowly and the poor;
   the lives of the poor he shall save. ℟

Second Reading *Eph 3: 2–3a, 5–6* Brothers and sisters: You have heard of the stewardship of God's grace that was given to me for your benefit, namely, that the mystery was made known to me by revelation. It was not made known to people in other generations as it has now been revealed to his holy apostles and prophets by the Spirit: that the Gentiles are coheirs, members of the same body, and copartners in the promise in Christ Jesus through the gospel.

Alleluia   *Mt 2: 2*   Joe Higginbotham

Al - le - lu - ia, al - le - lu - ia,   al - le - lu - ia.

Al - le - lu - ia, al - le - lu - ia,   al - le - lu - ia.

We saw his star at its rising / and have come to do him homage.   **Alleluia, alleluia.**

Gospel *Mt 2: 1–12* When Jesus was born in Bethlehem of Judea, in the days of King Herod, behold, magi from the east arrived in Jerusalem, saying, "Where is the newborn king of the Jews? We saw his star at its rising and have come to do him homage." When King Herod heard this, he was greatly troubled, and all Jerusalem with him. Assembling all the chief priests and the scribes of the people, he inquired of them where the Christ was to be born. They said to him, "In Bethlehem of Judea, for thus it has been written through the prophet:

And you, Bethlehem, land of Judah,
*   are by no means least among the rulers of Judah;*
since from you shall come a ruler,
*   who is to shepherd my people Israel."*

Then Herod called the magi secretly and ascertained from them the time of the star's appearance. He sent them to Bethlehem and said, "Go and search diligently for the child. When you have found him, bring me word, that I too may go and do him homage." After their audience with the king they set out. And behold, the star that they had seen at its rising preceded them, until it came and stopped over the place where the child was. They were overjoyed at seeing the star, and on entering the house they saw the child with Mary his mother. They prostrated themselves and did him homage. Then they opened their treasures and offered him gifts of gold, frankincense, and myrrh. And having been warned in a dream not to return to Herod, they departed for their country by another way.

Communion Antiphon

At the Vigil Mass: cf. Rv 21: 23 **The brightness of God illumined the holy city Jerusalem, ✦ and the nations will walk by its light.**

At the Mass During the Day: cf. Mt 2: 2 **We have seen his star in the East, ✦ and have come with gifts to adore the Lord.**

THE BAPTISM OF THE LORD

SUNDAY AFTER JANUARY 6 | FIRST SUNDAY IN ORDINARY TIME

In dioceses where the Epiphany is transferred to a Sunday that falls on January 7 or 8, the Baptism of the Lord is transferred to the Monday immediately following. Only one reading before the Gospel is used.

Entrance Antiphon *cf. Mt 3: 16–17* After the Lord was baptized, the heavens were opened, ✦ and the Spirit descended upon him like a dove, ✦ and the voice of the Father thundered: ✦ This is my beloved Son, with whom I am well pleased.

First Reading   *Is 42: 1–4, 6–7*

Thus says the LORD:
Here is my servant whom I uphold,
   my chosen one with whom I am pleased,
upon whom I have put my spirit;
   he shall bring forth justice to the nations,
not crying out, not shouting,
   not making his voice heard in the street.
A bruised reed he shall not break,
   and a smoldering wick he shall not quench,
until he establishes justice on the earth;
   the coastlands will wait for his teaching.

I, the LORD, have called you for the victory of justice,
   I have grasped you by the hand;
I formed you, and set you
   as a covenant of the people,
   a light for the nations,
to open the eyes of the blind,
   to bring out prisoners from confinement,
   and from the dungeon, those who live in darkness.

Responsorial Psalm   *Ps 29: 1–2, 3–4, 3, 9–10*   based on EVENTIDE

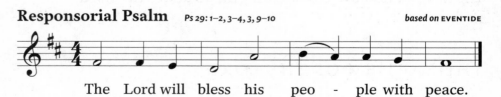

The Lord will bless his peo - ple with peace.

Give to the LORD, you sons of God,
   give to the LORD glory and praise,
Give to the LORD the glory due his name;
   adore the LORD in holy attire. ℟

The voice of the LORD is over the waters,

the LORD, over vast waters.
The voice of the LORD is mighty;
   the voice of the LORD is majestic. ℟

The God of glory thunders,
   and in his temple all say, "Glory!"
The LORD is enthroned above the flood;
   the LORD is enthroned as king forever. ℟

Second Reading Acts 10: 34-38 Peter proceeded to speak to those
gathered in the house of Cornelius, saying: "In truth, I see that
God shows no partiality. Rather, in every nation whoever fears
him and acts uprightly is acceptable to him. You know the word
that he sent to the Israelites as he proclaimed peace through
Jesus Christ, who is Lord of all, what has happened all over Judea,
beginning in Galilee after the baptism that John preached, how
God anointed Jesus of Nazareth with the Holy Spirit and power.
He went about doing good and healing all those oppressed by
the devil, for God was with him."

Alleluia   *cf. Mk 9: 7*   *Laura Lea Duckworth*

Al-le - lu-ia, al-le - lu-ia, al   -   le - lu - ia.

The heavens were opened and the voice of the Father
thundered: / This is my beloved Son, listen to him.
Alleluia, alleluia.

Gospel Lk 3: 15-16, 21-22 The people were filled with expectation, and
all were asking in their hearts whether John might be the Christ.
John answered them all, saying, "I am baptizing you with water,
but one mightier than I is coming. I am not worthy to loosen
the thongs of his sandals. He will baptize you with the Holy
Spirit and fire."

    After all the people had been baptized and Jesus also had been
baptized and was praying, heaven was opened and the Holy
Spirit descended upon him in bodily form like a dove. And a

voice came from heaven, "You are my beloved Son; with you I
am well pleased."

Communion Antiphon Jn 1: 32, 34 Behold the One of whom John
said: ◆ I have seen and testified that this is the Son of God.

⸙   Optional Readings   ⸙

In Year C, these readings may be used:

Entrance Antiphon cf. Mt 3: 16–17 After the Lord was baptized, the
heavens were opened, ◆ and the Spirit descended upon him
like a dove, ◆ and the voice of the Father thundered: ◆ This is
my beloved Son, with whom I am well pleased.

First Reading   Is 40: 1–5, 9–11
Comfort, give comfort to my people,
    says your God.
Speak tenderly to Jerusalem, and proclaim to her
    that her service is at an end,
        her guilt is expiated;
indeed, she has received from the hand of the LORD
    double for all her sins.

        A voice cries out:
In the desert prepare the way of the LORD!
    Make straight in the wasteland a highway for our God!
Every valley shall be filled in,
    every mountain and hill shall be made low;
the rugged land shall be made a plain,
    the rough country, a broad valley.
Then the glory of the LORD shall be revealed,
    and all people shall see it together;
    for the mouth of the LORD has spoken.

Go up on to a high mountain,
    Zion, herald of glad tidings;
cry out at the top of your voice,

Jerusalem, herald of good news!
Fear not to cry out
   and say to the cities of Judah:
   Here is your God!
Here comes with power
   the Lord GOD,
   who rules by a strong arm;
here is his reward with him,
   his recompense before him.
Like a shepherd he feeds his flock;
   in his arms he gathers the lambs,
carrying them in his bosom,
   and leading the ewes with care.

Responsorial Psalm   Ps 104: 1b–2, 3–4, 24–25, 27–28, 29–30   *David Mann*

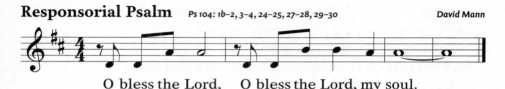

O bless the Lord,   O bless the Lord, my soul.

O LORD, my God, you are great indeed!
   You are clothed with majesty and glory,
robed in light as with a cloak.
   You have spread out the heavens like a tent-cloth; ℟

You have constructed your palace upon the waters.
   You make the clouds your chariot;
you travel on the wings of the wind.
   You make the winds your messengers,
and flaming fire your ministers. ℟

How manifold are your works, O LORD!
   In wisdom you have wrought them all—
the earth is full of your creatures;
   the sea also, great and wide,
in which are schools without number
   of living things both small and great. ℟

They look to you to give them food in due time.

When you give it to them, they gather it;
when you open your hand, they are filled with good things.   ℟

If you take away their breath, they perish and return to
      the dust.
When you send forth your spirit, they are created,
and you renew the face of the earth.   ℟

Second Reading *Ti 2: 11–14; 3: 4–7* Beloved: The grace of God has
appeared, saving all and training us to reject godless ways and
worldly desires and to live temperately, justly, and devoutly in
this age, as we await the blessed hope, the appearance of the
glory of our great God and savior Jesus Christ, who gave himself
for us to deliver us from all lawlessness and to cleanse for
himself a people as his own, eager to do what is good.
      When the kindness and generous love
            of God our savior appeared,
      not because of any righteous deeds we had done
            but because of his mercy,
      he saved us through the bath of rebirth
            and renewal by the Holy Spirit,
      whom he richly poured out on us
            through Jesus Christ our savior,
      so that we might be justified by his grace
            and become heirs in hope of eternal life.

Alleluia   *cf. Lk 3: 16*   *Laura Lea Duckworth*

Al-le - lu-ia, al-le - lu-ia, al - le - lu - ia.

John said: One mightier than I is coming; / he will baptize
you with the Holy Spirit and with fire.   **Alleluia, alleluia.**

Gospel *Lk 3: 15–16, 21–22* The people were filled with expectation, and
all were asking in their hearts whether John might be the Christ.
John answered them all, saying, "I am baptizing you with water,
but one mightier than I is coming. I am not worthy to loosen

the thongs of his sandals. He will baptize you with the Holy Spirit and fire."

After all the people had been baptized and Jesus also had been baptized and was praying, heaven was opened and the Holy Spirit descended upon him in bodily form like a dove. And a voice came from heaven, "You are my beloved Son; with you I am well pleased."

Communion Antiphon *Jn 1: 32, 34* **Behold the One of whom John said: ♦ I have seen and testified that this is the Son of God.**

Lent † YEAR C

ASH WEDNESDAY

Entrance Antiphon <small>Wis 11: 23, 24, 26</small> You are merciful to all, O Lord,
✦ and despise nothing that you have made. ✦ You overlook
people's sins, to bring them to repentance, ✦ and you spare
them, for you are the Lord our God.

The Penitential Act is omitted on Ash Wednesday.

First Reading <small>Jl 2: 12–18</small>
Even now, says the LORD,
    return to me with your whole heart,
    with fasting, and weeping, and mourning;
Rend your hearts, not your garments,
    and return to the LORD, your God.
For gracious and merciful is he,
    slow to anger, rich in kindness,
    and relenting in punishment.
Perhaps he will again relent
    and leave behind him a blessing,
Offerings and libations
    for the LORD, your God.
Blow the trumpet in Zion!
    proclaim a fast,
    call an assembly;
Gather the people,
    notify the congregation;
Assemble the elders,
    gather the children
    and the infants at the breast;
Let the bridegroom quit his room
    and the bride her chamber.

Between the porch and the altar
  let the priests, the ministers of the LORD, weep,
And say, "Spare, O LORD, your people,
  and make not your heritage a reproach,
  with the nations ruling over them!
Why should they say among the peoples,
  'Where is their God?'"
Then the LORD was stirred to concern for his land and took
pity on his people.

Responsorial Psalm Ps 51: 3–4, 5–6, 12–13, 14, 17   *Bill Svarda*

Be mer-ci-ful, O Lord,   for we have sinned.

Have mercy on me, O God, in your goodness;
  in the greatness of your compassion wipe out my offense.
Thoroughly wash me from my guilt
  and of my sin cleanse me. ℟

For I acknowledge my offense,
  and my sin is before me always:
"Against you only have I sinned,
  and done what is evil in your sight." ℟

A clean heart create for me, O God,
  and a steadfast spirit renew within me.
Cast me not out from your presence,
  and your Holy Spirit take not from me. ℟

Give me back the joy of your salvation,
  and a willing spirit sustain in me.
O Lord, open my lips,
  and my mouth shall proclaim your praise. ℟

Second Reading 2 Cor 5: 20–6: 2 Brothers and sisters: We are
ambassadors for Christ, as if God were appealing through us. We
implore you on behalf of Christ, be reconciled to God. For our

sake he made him to be sin who did not know sin, so that we might become the righteousness of God in him.

Working together, then, we appeal to you not to receive the grace of God in vain. For he says:

In an acceptable time I heard you,
and on the day of salvation I helped you.

Behold, now is a very acceptable time; behold, now is the day of salvation.

Verse Before the Gospel   Ps 95: 8   Amy Righi

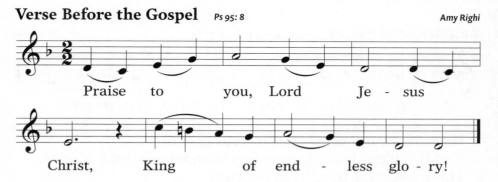

Praise to you, Lord Je - sus Christ, King of end - less glo - ry!

If today you hear his voice, / harden not your hearts.

Gospel Mt 6: 1–6, 16–18 Jesus said to his disciples: "Take care not to perform righteous deeds in order that people may see them; otherwise, you will have no recompense from your heavenly Father. When you give alms, do not blow a trumpet before you, as the hypocrites do in the synagogues and in the streets to win the praise of others. Amen, I say to you, they have received their reward. But when you give alms, do not let your left hand know what your right is doing, so that your almsgiving may be secret. And your Father who sees in secret will repay you.

"When you pray, do not be like the hypocrites, who love to stand and pray in the synagogues and on street corners so that others may see them. Amen, I say to you, they have received their reward. But when you pray, go to your inner room, close the door, and pray to your Father in secret. And your Father who sees in secret will repay you.

"When you fast, do not look gloomy like the hypocrites. They neglect their appearance, so that they may appear to others to

be fasting. Amen, I say to you, they have received their reward. But when you fast, anoint your head and wash your face, so that you may not appear to be fasting, except to your Father who is hidden. And your Father who sees what is hidden will repay you."

BLESSING AND DISTRIBUTION OF ASHES

After the Homily, the Priest, standing with hands joined, says:
Dear brethren (brothers and sisters),
   let us humbly ask God our Father
that he be pleased to bless with the abundance of his grace
these ashes, which we will put on our heads in penitence.

After a brief prayer in silence, and, with hands extended, he continues:
O God, who are moved by acts of humility
and respond with forgiveness to works of penance,
lend your merciful ear to our prayers
and in your kindness pour out the grace of your + blessing
on your servants who are marked with these ashes,
that, as they follow the Lenten observances,
they may be worthy to come with minds made pure
to celebrate the Paschal Mystery of your Son.
Through Christ our Lord   ℟ **Amen.**

Or:
O God, who desire not the death of sinners,
but their conversion,
mercifully hear our prayers
and in your kindness be pleased to bless + these ashes,
which we intend to receive upon our heads,
that we, who acknowledge we are but ashes
and shall return to dust,
may, through a steadfast observance of Lent,
gain pardon for sins and newness of life
after the likeness of your Risen Son.
Who lives and reigns for ever and ever.   ℟ **Amen.**

He sprinkles the ashes with holy water, without saying anything.

Then the Priest places ashes on the head of all those present who come to him, and says to each one: Repent, and believe in the Gospel.

Or: Remember that you are dust, and to dust you shall return.

Meanwhile, the following are sung:

Antiphon 1   Let us change our garments to sackcloth and ashes, ✦ let us fast and weep before the Lord, ✦ that our God, rich in mercy, might forgive us our sins.

Antiphon 2   *cf. Jl 2: 17; Est 4: 17*   Let the priests, the ministers of the Lord, ✦ stand between the porch and the altar and weep and cry out: ✦ Spare, O Lord, spare your people; ✦ do not close the mouths of those who sing your praise, O Lord.

Antiphon 3   *Ps 51 (50): 3*   Blot out my transgressions, O Lord.

This may be repeated after each verse of Psalm 51 (50), (Have mercy on me, O God).

Responsory   *cf. Bar 3: 2; Ps 79 (78): 9*
℞ Let us correct our faults which we have committed in ignorance, let us not be taken unawares by the day of our death, looking in vain for leisure to repent. Hear us, O Lord, and show us your mercy, for we have sinned against you.

℣ Help us, O God our Savior; for the sake of your name, O Lord, set us free.
℞ Hear us, O Lord, and show us your mercy, for we have sinned against you.

Another appropriate chant or hymn may also be sung.

After the distribution of ashes, the Priest washes his hands and

proceeds to the Universal Prayer, and continues the Mass in the usual way. The Creed is not said.

Communion Antiphon *cf. Ps 1: 2–3* He who ponders the law of the Lord day and night ✦ will yield fruit in due season.

The blessing and distribution of ashes may also take place outside Mass. In this case, the rite is preceded by a Liturgy of the Word, with the Entrance Antiphon, the Collect, and the readings with their chants as at Mass. Then there follow the Homily and the blessing and distribution of ashes. The rite is concluded with the Prayer of the Faithful (Universal Prayer), the Blessing, and the Dismissal of the Faithful.

FIRST SUNDAY OF LENT

Entrance Antiphon *cf. Ps 91 (90): 15–16* When he calls on me, I will answer him; ✦ I will deliver him and give him glory, ✦ I will grant him length of days.

First Reading *Dt 26: 4–10* Moses spoke to the people, saying: "The priest shall receive the basket from you and shall set it in front of the altar of the LORD, your God. Then you shall declare before the LORD, your God, 'My father was a wandering Aramean who went down to Egypt with a small household and lived there as an alien. But there he became a nation great, strong, and numerous. When the Egyptians maltreated and oppressed us, imposing hard labor upon us, we cried to the LORD, the God of our fathers, and he heard our cry and saw our affliction, our toil, and our oppression. He brought us out of Egypt with his strong hand and outstretched arm, with terrifying power, with signs and wonders; and bringing us into this country, he gave us this land flowing with milk and honey. Therefore, I have now brought you the firstfruits of the products of the soil which you, O LORD, have given me.' And having set them before the LORD, your God, you shall bow down in his presence."

Responsorial Psalm Ps 91: 1–2, 10–11, 12–13, 14–15   Joe Higginbotham

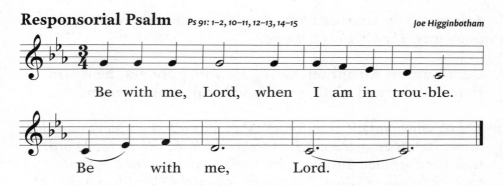

Be with me, Lord, when I am in trou-ble.

Be with me, Lord.

You who dwell in the shelter of the Most High,
   who abide in the shadow of the Almighty,
say to the LORD, "My refuge and fortress,
   my God in whom I trust." ℟

No evil shall befall you,
   nor shall affliction come near your tent,
For to his angels he has given command about you,
   that they guard you in all your ways. ℟

Upon their hands they shall bear you up,
   lest you dash your foot against a stone.
You shall tread upon the asp and the viper;
   you shall trample down the lion and the dragon. ℟

Because he clings to me, I will deliver him;
   I will set him on high because he acknowledges my name.
He shall call upon me, and I will answer him;
   I will be with him in distress;
   I will deliver him and glorify him. ℟

Second Reading Rom 10: 8–13 Brothers and sisters: What does
Scripture say?
   The word is near you,
      in your mouth and in your heart
—that is, the word of faith that we preach—, for, if you confess
with your mouth that Jesus is Lord and believe in your heart
that God raised him from the dead, you will be saved. For one
believes with the heart and so is justified, and one confesses

with the mouth and so is saved. For the Scripture says, *No one who believes in him will be put to shame.* For there is no distinction between Jew and Greek; the same Lord is Lord of all, enriching all who call upon him. For "everyone who calls on the name of the Lord will be saved."

Verse Before the Gospel   Mt 4: 4b   Laura Lea Duckworth

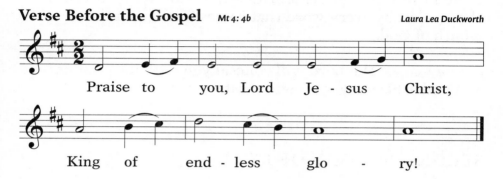

Praise to you, Lord Je-sus Christ,

King of end-less glo-ry!

One does not live on bread alone, / but on every word that comes forth from the mouth of God.

Gospel Lk 4: 1–13 Filled with the Holy Spirit, Jesus returned from the Jordan and was led by the Spirit into the desert for forty days, to be tempted by the devil. He ate nothing during those days, and when they were over he was hungry. The devil said to him, "If you are the Son of God, command this stone to become bread." Jesus answered him, "It is written, *One does not live on bread alone.*" Then he took him up and showed him all the kingdoms of the world in a single instant. The devil said to him, "I shall give to you all this power and glory; for it has been handed over to me, and I may give it to whomever I wish. All this will be yours, if you worship me." Jesus said to him in reply, "It is written:
You shall worship the Lord, your God,
   and him alone shall you serve."
Then he led him to Jerusalem, made him stand on the parapet of the temple, and said to him, "If you are the Son of God, throw yourself down from here, for it is written:
He will command his angels concerning you, to guard you,
and:
With their hands they will support you,

lest you dash your foot against a stone."
Jesus said to him in reply, "It also says, *You shall not put the Lord, your God, to the test."* When the devil had finished every temptation, he departed from him for a time.

Communion Antiphon Mt 4: 4 **One does not live by bread alone, ◆ but by every word that comes forth from the mouth of God.**

Or: cf. Ps 91 (90): 4 **The Lord will conceal you with his pinions, ◆ and under his wings you will trust.**

SECOND SUNDAY OF LENT

Entrance Antiphon cf. Ps 27 (26): 8–9 **Of you my heart has spoken: Seek his face. ◆ It is your face, O Lord, that I seek; ◆ hide not your face from me.**

Or: cf. Ps 25 (24): 6, 2, 22 **Remember your compassion, O Lord, ◆ and your merciful love, for they are from of old. ◆ Let not our enemies exult over us. ◆ Redeem us, O God of Israel, from all our distress.**

First Reading Gen 15: 5–12, 17–18 The Lord God took Abram outside and said, "Look up at the sky and count the stars, if you can. Just so," he added, "shall your descendants be." Abram put his faith in the LORD, who credited it to him as an act of righteousness.
He then said to him, "I am the LORD who brought you from Ur of the Chaldeans to give you this land as a possession." "O Lord GOD," he asked, "how am I to know that I shall possess it?" He answered him, "Bring me a three-year-old heifer, a three-year-old she-goat, a three-year-old ram, a turtledove, and a young pigeon." Abram brought him all these, split them in two, and placed each half opposite the other; but the birds he did not cut up. Birds of prey swooped down on the carcasses, but Abram stayed with them. As the sun was about to set, a trance fell upon Abram, and a deep, terrifying darkness enveloped him.

When the sun had set and it was dark, there appeared a smoking fire pot and a flaming torch, which passed between those pieces. It was on that occasion that the LORD made a covenant with Abram, saying: "To your descendants I give this land, from the Wadi of Egypt to the Great River, the Euphrates."

Responsorial Psalm   *Ps 27: 1, 7-8, 8-9, 13-14*   *Ann Fons et al.*

The Lord is my light and my salvation.

The LORD is my light and my salvation;
   whom should I fear?
The LORD is my life's refuge;
   of whom should I be afraid? ℟

Hear, O LORD, the sound of my call;
   have pity on me, and answer me.
Of you my heart speaks; you my glance seeks. ℟

Your presence, O LORD, I seek.
   Hide not your face from me;
do not in anger repel your servant.
   You are my helper: cast me not off. ℟

I believe that I shall see the bounty of the LORD
   in the land of the living.
Wait for the LORD with courage;
   be stouthearted, and wait for the LORD. ℟

Second Reading   *Phil 3: 17–4: 1 or 3: 20–4: 1*
For the shorter form, read only the parts in brackets.
Join with others in being imitators of me, [brothers and sisters,] and observe those who thus conduct themselves according to

the model you have in us. For many, as I have often told you and now tell you even in tears, conduct themselves as enemies of the cross of Christ. Their end is destruction. Their God is their stomach; their glory is in their "shame." Their minds are occupied with earthly things. But [our citizenship is in heaven, and from it we also await a savior, the Lord Jesus Christ. He will change our lowly body to conform with his glorified body by the power that enables him also to bring all things into subjection to himself.

Therefore, my brothers and sisters, whom I love and long for, my joy and crown, in this way stand firm in the Lord.]

Verse Before the Gospel   cf. Mt 17: 5

Laura Lea Duckworth

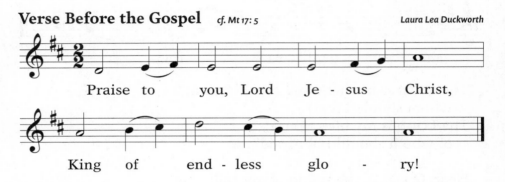

Praise to you, Lord Je - sus Christ,

King of end - less glo - ry!

From the shining cloud the Father's voice is heard: / This is my beloved Son, hear him.

Gospel Lk 9: 28b–36 Jesus took Peter, John, and James and went up the mountain to pray. While he was praying his face changed in appearance and his clothing became dazzling white. And behold, two men were conversing with him, Moses and Elijah, who appeared in glory and spoke of his exodus that he was going to accomplish in Jerusalem. Peter and his companions had been overcome by sleep, but becoming fully awake, they saw his glory and the two men standing with him. As they were about to part from him, Peter said to Jesus, "Master, it is good that we are here; let us make three tents, one for you, one for Moses, and one for Elijah." But he did not know what he was saying. While he was still speaking, a cloud came and cast a shadow over them, and they became frightened when they entered the cloud. Then from the cloud came a voice that said, "This is my chosen Son;

listen to him." After the voice had spoken, Jesus was found alone. They fell silent and did not at that time tell anyone what they had seen.

Communion Antiphon Mt 17:5 This is my beloved Son, with whom I am well pleased; ◆ listen to him.

THIRD SUNDAY OF LENT

The readings given for Year A, page 111, may be used in place of these.

Entrance Antiphon cf. Ps 25 (24): 15-16 My eyes are always on the Lord, ◆ for he rescues my feet from the snare. ◆ Turn to me and have mercy on me, ◆ for I am alone and poor.

Or: cf. Ezekiel 36: 23-26 When I prove my holiness among you, ◆ I will gather you from all the foreign lands; ◆ and I will pour clean water upon you ◆ and cleanse you from all your impurities, ◆ and I will give you a new spirit, says the Lord.

First Reading Ex 3: 1-8a, 13-15 Moses was tending the flock of his father-in-law Jethro, the priest of Midian. Leading the flock across the desert, he came to Horeb, the mountain of God. There an angel of the LORD appeared to Moses in fire flaming out of a bush. As he looked on, he was surprised to see that the bush, though on fire, was not consumed. So Moses decided, "I must go over to look at this remarkable sight, and see why the bush is not burned."

When the LORD saw him coming over to look at it more closely, God called out to him from the bush, "Moses! Moses!" He answered, "Here I am." God said, "Come no nearer! Remove the sandals from your feet, for the place where you stand is holy ground. I am the God of your fathers," he continued, "the God of Abraham, the God of Isaac, the God of Jacob." Moses hid his face, for he was afraid to look at God. But the LORD said, "I have witnessed the affliction of my people in Egypt and have heard their cry of complaint against their slave drivers, so I know well what they are suffering. Therefore I have come down to rescue them from the hands of the Egyptians and lead them out of that land into a good and spacious land, a land flowing with milk and honey."

Moses said to God, "But when I go to the Israelites and say to them, 'The God of your fathers has sent me to you,' if they ask me, 'What is his name?' what am I to tell them?" God replied, "I am who am." Then he added, "This is what you shall tell the Israelites: I AM sent me to you."

God spoke further to Moses, "Thus shall you say to the Israelites: The LORD, the God of your fathers, the God of Abraham, the God of Isaac, the God of Jacob, has sent me to you.

"This is my name forever;
      thus am I to be remembered through all generations."

Responsorial Psalm   Ps 103: 1–2, 3–4, 6–7, 8, 11   *Beverly McDevitt*

The Lord is kind and mer - ci - ful.

Bless the LORD, O my soul;
    and all my being, bless his holy name.
Bless the LORD, O my soul,
    and forget not all his benefits. ℟

He pardons all your iniquities,
    heals all your ills.
He redeems your life from destruction,
    crowns you with kindness and compassion. ℟

The LORD secures justice
    and the rights of all the oppressed.
He has made known his ways to Moses,
    and his deeds to the children of Israel. ℟

Merciful and gracious is the LORD,

slow to anger and abounding in kindness.
For as the heavens are high above the earth,
so surpassing is his kindness toward those who fear him. ℟

Second Reading *1 Cor 10: 1–6, 10–12* I do not want you to be unaware, brothers and sisters, that our ancestors were all under the cloud and all passed through the sea, and all of them were baptized into Moses in the cloud and in the sea. All ate the same spiritual food, and all drank the same spiritual drink, for they drank from a spiritual rock that followed them, and the rock was the Christ. Yet God was not pleased with most of them, for they were struck down in the desert.

These things happened as examples for us, so that we might not desire evil things, as they did. Do not grumble as some of them did, and suffered death by the destroyer. These things happened to them as an example, and they have been written down as a warning to us, upon whom the end of the ages has come. Therefore, whoever thinks he is standing secure should take care not to fall.

Verse Before the Gospel *Mt 4: 17*   *Laura Lea Duckworth*

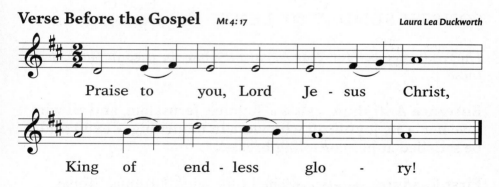

Praise to you, Lord Je - sus Christ,

King of end - less glo - ry!

Repent, says the Lord; / the kingdom of heaven is at hand.

Gospel *Lk 13: 1–9* Some people told Jesus about the Galileans whose blood Pilate had mingled with the blood of their sacrifices. Jesus said to them in reply, "Do you think that because these Galileans suffered in this way they were greater sinners than all other Galileans? By no means! But I tell you, if you do not repent, you will all perish as they did! Or those eighteen people who were killed when the tower at Siloam fell on them— do you think they were more guilty than everyone else who lived in Jerusalem? By no means! But I tell you, if you do not repent, you will all perish as they did!"

And he told them this parable: "There once was a person who had a fig tree planted in his orchard, and when he came in search of fruit on it but found none, he said to the gardener, 'For three years now I have come in search of fruit on this fig tree but have found none. So cut it down. Why should it exhaust the soil?' He said to him in reply, 'Sir, leave it for this year also, and I shall cultivate the ground around it and fertilize it; it may bear fruit in the future. If not you can cut it down.'"

Communion Antiphon *cf. Ps 84 (83): 4–5* **The sparrow finds a home, ✦ and the swallow a nest for her young: ✦ by your altars, O Lord of hosts, my King and my God. ✦ Blessed are they who dwell in your house, ✦ for ever singing your praise.**

FOURTH SUNDAY OF LENT

The readings given for Year A, page 115, may be used in place of these.

Entrance Antiphon *cf. Is 66: 10–11* **Rejoice, Jerusalem, and all who love her. ✦ Be joyful, all who were in mourning; ✦ exult and be satisfied at her consoling breast.**

First Reading *Joshua 5: 9a, 10–12* The LORD said to Joshua, "Today I have removed the reproach of Egypt from you."

While the Israelites were encamped at Gilgal on the plains of Jericho, they celebrated the Passover on the evening of the fourteenth of the month. On the day after the Passover, they ate of the produce of the land in the form of unleavened cakes and parched grain. On that same day after the Passover, on which they ate of the produce of the land, the manna ceased. No longer was there manna for the Israelites, who that year ate of the yield of the land of Canaan.

Responsorial Psalm Ps 34: 2–3, 4–5, 6–7   Roger Holtz

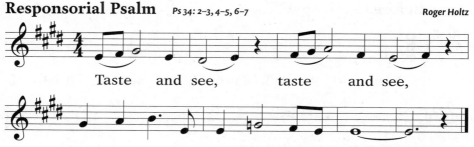

Taste and see, taste and see, taste and see the good-ness of the Lord.

I will bless the LORD at all times;
  his praise shall be ever in my mouth.
Let my soul glory in the LORD;
  the lowly will hear me and be glad. ℟

Glorify the LORD with me,
  let us together extol his name.
I sought the LORD, and he answered me
  and delivered me from all my fears. ℟

Look to him that you may be radiant with joy,
  and your faces may not blush with shame.
When the poor one called out, the LORD heard,
  and from all his distress he saved him. ℟

Second Reading 2 Cor 5: 17–21 Brothers and sisters: Whoever is in Christ is a new creation: the old things have passed away; behold, new things have come. And all this is from God, who has reconciled us to himself through Christ and given us the ministry of reconciliation, namely, God was reconciling the world to himself in Christ, not counting their trespasses against them and entrusting to us the message of reconciliation. So we are ambassadors for Christ, as if God were appealing through us. We implore you on behalf of Christ, be reconciled to God. For our sake he made him to be sin who did not know sin, so that we might become the righteousness of God in him.

Verse Before the Gospel   Lk 15: 18   *Laura Lea Duckworth*

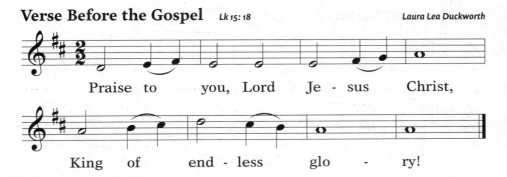

Praise to you, Lord Je-sus Christ, King of end-less glo - ry!

I will get up and go to my Father and shall say to him: / Father, I have sinned against heaven and against you.

Gospel Lk 15: 1–3, 11–32 Tax collectors and sinners were all drawing near to listen to Jesus, but the Pharisees and scribes began to complain, saying, "This man welcomes sinners and eats with them." So to them Jesus addressed this parable: "A man had two sons, and the younger son said to his father, 'Father give me the share of your estate that should come to me.' So the father divided the property between them. After a few days, the younger son collected all his belongings and set off to a distant country where he squandered his inheritance on a life of dissipation. When he had freely spent everything, a severe famine struck that country, and he found himself in dire need. So he hired himself out to one of the local citizens who sent him to his farm to tend the swine. And he longed to eat his fill of the pods on which the swine fed, but nobody gave him any. Coming to his senses he thought, 'How many of my father's hired workers have more than enough food to eat, but here am I, dying from hunger. I shall get up and go to my father and I shall say to him, "Father, I have sinned against heaven and against you. I no longer deserve to be called your son; treat me as you would treat one of your hired workers."' So he got up and went back to his father. While he was still a long way off, his father caught sight of him, and was filled with compassion. He ran to his son, embraced him and kissed him. His son said to him, 'Father, I have sinned against heaven and against you; I no longer deserve to be called your son.' But his father ordered his servants, 'Quickly bring the finest robe and put it on him; put a ring on his finger and sandals on his feet. Take the fattened calf and slaughter it. Then let us celebrate with a feast, because this son of mine was dead, and has come to life again; he was lost, and has been found.' Then the celebration began. Now the older son had been out in the field and, on his way back, as he neared the house, he heard the sound of music and dancing. He called one of the servants and asked what this might mean. The servant said to him, 'Your brother has returned and your father has slaughtered the fattened calf because he has him back safe and sound.' He became angry, and when he refused to enter the house, his father came out and pleaded with him. He said to his father in reply, 'Look, all these years I served you and not once did I disobey your orders; yet you never gave me even a young goat to feast on with my friends. But when your son returns who swallowed up your property with prostitutes, for him you slaughter the fattened calf.' He said to him, 'My son, you are here with me always; everything I have is yours. But now we must celebrate and rejoice, because your brother was dead and has come to life again; he was lost and has been found.'"

Communion Antiphon Lk 15: 32 **You must rejoice, my son, ◆ for your brother was dead and has come to life; ◆ he was lost and is found.**

FIFTH SUNDAY OF LENT

The readings given for Year A, page 111, may be used in place of these.

Entrance Antiphon cf. Ps 43 (42): 1–2 **Give me justice, O God, ◆ and plead my cause against a nation that is faithless. ◆ From the deceitful and cunning rescue me, ◆ for you, O God, are my strength.**

First Reading Is 43: 16–21
Thus says the LORD,
  who opens a way in the sea

and a path in the mighty waters,
who leads out chariots and horsemen,
  a powerful army,
till they lie prostrate together, never to rise,
  snuffed out and quenched like a wick.
Remember not the events of the past,
  the things of long ago consider not;
see, I am doing something new!
  Now it springs forth, do you not perceive it?
In the desert I make a way,
  in the wasteland, rivers.
Wild beasts honor me,
  jackals and ostriches,
for I put water in the desert
  and rivers in the wasteland
  for my chosen people to drink,
the people whom I formed for myself,
  that they might announce my praise.

Responsorial Psalm   Ps 126: 1–2, 2–3, 4–5, 6   Joe Higginbotham

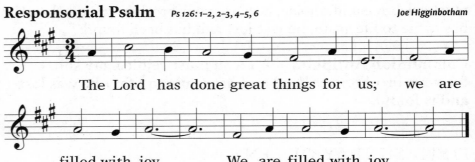

The Lord has done great things for us; we are filled with joy. We are filled with joy.

When the LORD brought back the captives of Zion,
  we were like men dreaming.
Then our mouth was filled with laughter,
  and our tongue with rejoicing. ℟

Then they said among the nations,
  "The LORD has done great things for them."
The LORD has done great things for us;
  we are glad indeed. ℟

Restore our fortunes, O LORD,

like the torrents in the southern desert.
Those that sow in tears
    shall reap rejoicing. ℟

Although they go forth weeping,
    carrying the seed to be sown,
They shall come back rejoicing,
    carrying their sheaves. ℟

Second Reading *Phil 3: 8–14* Brothers and sisters: I consider
everything as a loss because of the supreme good of knowing
Christ Jesus my Lord. For his sake I have accepted the loss of
all things and I consider them so much rubbish, that I may gain
Christ and be found in him, not having any righteousness of my
own based on the law but that which comes through faith in
Christ, the righteousness from God, depending on faith to know
him and the power of his resurrection and the sharing of his
sufferings by being conformed to his death, if somehow I may
attain the resurrection from the dead.

It is not that I have already taken hold of it or have already
attained perfect maturity, but I continue my pursuit in hope that
I may possess it, since I have indeed been taken possession of by
Christ Jesus. Brothers and sisters, I for my part do not consider
myself to have taken possession. Just one thing: forgetting what
lies behind but straining forward to what lies ahead, I continue
my pursuit toward the goal, the prize of God's upward calling, in
Christ Jesus.

Verse Before the Gospel *Joel 2: 12–13*   Laura Lea Duckworth

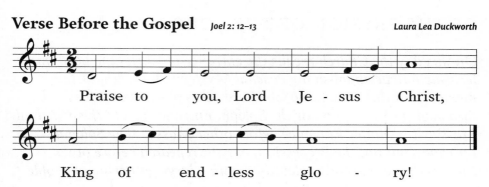

Praise to you, Lord Je - sus Christ,
King of end - less glo - ry!

Even now, says the Lord, / return to me with your whole
heart; / for I am gracious and merciful.

Gospel *Jn 8: 1–11* Jesus went to the Mount of Olives. But early in the morning he arrived again in the temple area, and all the people started coming to him, and he sat down and taught them. Then the scribes and the Pharisees brought a woman who had been caught in adultery and made her stand in the middle. They said to him, "Teacher, this woman was caught in the very act of committing adultery. Now in the law, Moses commanded us to stone such women. So what do you say?" They said this to test him, so that they could have some charge to bring against him. Jesus bent down and began to write on the ground with his finger. But when they continued asking him, he straightened up and said to them, "Let the one among you who is without sin be the first to throw a stone at her." Again he bent down and wrote on the ground. And in response, they went away one by one, beginning with the elders. So he was left alone with the woman before him. Then Jesus straightened up and said to her, "Woman, where are they? Has no one condemned you?" She replied, "No one, sir." Then Jesus said, "Neither do I condemn you. Go, and from now on do not sin any more."

Communion Antiphon *Jn 8: 10–11* Has no one condemned you, woman? No one, Lord. ✦ Neither shall I condemn you. From now on, sin no more.

PALM SUNDAY

OF THE PASSION OF THE LORD

On this day the Church recalls the entrance of Christ the Lord into Jerusalem to accomplish his Paschal Mystery. Accordingly, the memorial of this entrance of the Lord takes place at all Masses, by means of the Procession or the Solemn Entrance before the principal Mass or the Simple Entrance before other Masses. The Solemn Entrance, but not the Procession, may be repeated before other Masses that are usually celebrated with a large gathering of people.

✠ The Commemoration of the Lord's ✠ Entrance Into Jerusalem

FIRST FORM: THE PROCESSION

At an appropriate hour, a gathering takes place at a smaller church or other suitable place other than inside the church to which the procession will go. The faithful hold branches in their hands.

The Priest and the Deacon, accompanied by other ministers, approach the place where the people are gathered. Meanwhile, the following Antiphon or another appropriate chant is sung.

Antiphon Mt 21: 9 **Hosanna to the Son of David; blessed is he who comes in the name of the Lord, the King of Israel. Hosanna in the highest.**

The Priest and people sign themselves, while the Priest says: In the name of the Father, and of the Son, and of the Holy Spirit. *Then he greets the people in the usual way. A brief address is given, in which the faithful are invited to participate actively and consciously in the celebration of this day, in these or similar words:*
Dear brethren (brothers and sisters),
since the beginning of Lent until now
we have prepared our hearts by penance and charitable works.
Today we gather together to herald with the whole Church
the beginning of the celebration
of our Lord's Paschal Mystery,
that is to say, of his Passion and Resurrection.
For it was to accomplish this mystery
that he entered his own city of Jerusalem.
Therefore, with all faith and devotion,
let us commemorate
the Lord's entry into the city for our salvation,
following in his footsteps,
so that, being made by his grace partakers of the Cross,
we may have a share also in his Resurrection and in his life.

After the address, the Priest says one of the following prayers with hands extended.

Let us pray.
Almighty ever-living God,
sanctify + these branches with your blessing,
that we, who follow Christ the King in exultation,
may reach the eternal Jerusalem through him.
Who lives and reigns for ever and ever. ℟ **Amen**

Or:

Increase the faith of those who place their hope in you, O God,
and graciously hear the prayers of those who call on you,
that we, who today hold high these branches
to hail Christ in his triumph,
may bear fruit for you by good works accomplished in him.
Who lives and reigns for ever and ever. ℟ **Amen.**

The Priest sprinkles the branches with holy water without saying anything. Then a Deacon or, if there is no Deacon, a Priest, proclaims in the usual way the Gospel concerning the Lord's entrance according to one of the four Gospels.

Gospel Lk 19: 28-40 Jesus proceeded on his journey up to Jerusalem. As he drew near to Bethphage and Bethany at the place called the Mount of Olives, he sent two of his disciples. He said, "Go into the village opposite you, and as you enter it you will find a colt tethered on which no one has ever sat. Untie it and bring it here. And if anyone should ask you, 'Why are you untying it?' you will answer, 'The Master has need of it.'" So those who had been sent went off and found everything just as he had told them. And as they were untying the colt, its owners said to them, "Why are you untying this colt?" They answered, "The Master has need of it." So they brought it to Jesus, threw their cloaks over the colt, and helped Jesus to mount. As he rode along, the people were spreading their cloaks on the road; and now as he was approaching the slope of the Mount of Olives, the whole multitude of his disciples began to praise God aloud with joy for all the mighty deeds they had seen. They proclaimed:

"Blessed is the king who comes
   in the name of the Lord.

Peace in heaven
    and glory in the highest."
Some of the Pharisees in the crowd said to him, "Teacher,
rebuke your disciples." He said in reply, "I tell you, if they keep
silent, the stones will cry out!"

After the Gospel, a brief homily may be given.

*Then, to begin the procession, an invitation may be given by a
Priest or a Deacon or a lay minister, in these or similar words:*
    Dear brethren (brothers and sisters),
    like the crowds who acclaimed Jesus in Jerusalem,
    let us go forth in peace.

Or: Let us go forth in peace.
In this latter case, all respond: **In the name of Christ. Amen.**

*The procession to the church where Mass will be celebrated then
begins in the usual way. As the procession moves forward, the
following or other suitable chants in honor of Christ the King are
sung by the choir and people.*

**Antiphon 1   The children of the Hebrews, carrying olive
branches, ♦ went to meet the Lord, crying out and saying: ♦
Hosanna in the highest.**

*If appropriate, this Antiphon is repeated between the strophes of
the following Psalm.*

Psalm 24 (23)
    The LORD's is the earth and its fullness,
    the world, and those who dwell in it.
    It is he who set it on the seas;
    on the rivers he made it firm.   (*The Antiphon is repeated.*)

    Who shall climb the mountain of the LORD?
    The clean of hands and pure of heart,
    whose soul is not set on vain things,
    who has not sworn deceitful words.
                                          (*The Antiphon is repeated.*)

Blessings from the LORD shall he receive,
and right reward from the God who saves him.
Such are the people who seek him,
who seek the face of the God of Jacob.

(The Antiphon is repeated.)

O gates, lift high your heads;
grow higher, ancient doors.
Let him enter, the king of glory!
Who is this king of glory?
The LORD, the mighty, the valiant;
the LORD, the valiant in war.   *(The Antiphon is repeated.)*

O gates, lift high your heads;
grow higher, ancient doors.
Let him enter, the king of glory!
Who is this king of glory?
He, the LORD of hosts,
he is the king of glory.   *(The Antiphon is repeated.)*

Antiphon 2   The children of the Hebrews spread their garments on the road, ◆ crying out and saying: Hosanna to the Son of David; ◆ blesssed is he who comes in the name of the Lord.

If appropriate, this Antiphon is repeated between the strophes of the following Psalm.

Psalm 47 (46)
All peoples, clap your hands.
Cry to God with shouts of joy!
For the LORD, the Most high, is awesome,
the great king over all the earth.   *(The Antiphon is repeated.)*

He humbles peoples under us
and nations under our feet.
Our heritage he chose for us,
the pride of Jacob whom he loves.
God goes up with shouts of joy.
The LORD goes up with trumpet blast.

(The Antiphon is repeated.)

Sing praise for God; sing praise!
Sing praise to king; sing praise!
God is king of all earth.
Sing praise with all your skill.   *(The Antiphon is repeated.)*

God reigns over the nations.
God sits upon his holy throne.
The princes of the peoples are assembled
with the people of the God of Abraham.
The rulers of the earth belong to God,
who is greatly exalted.   *(The Antiphon is repeated.)*

Hymn to Christ the King

Chorus:
Glory and honor and praise be to you, Christ, King and
    Redeemer,
to whom young children cried out loving Hosannas with joy.

All repeat:
**Glory and honor and praise be to you, Christ, King
    and Redeemer,
to whom young children cried out loving
    Hosannas with joy.**

Chorus:
Israel's King are you, King David's magnificent offspring;
you are the ruler who come blest in the name of the Lord.
All repeat: **Glory and honor ...**

Chorus:
Heavenly hosts on high unite in singing your praises;
men and women on earth and all creation join in.
All repeat: **Glory and honor ...**

Chorus:
Bearing branches of palm, Hebrews came crowding to
    greet you;

see how with prayers and hymns we come to pay you
our vows.
All repeat: **Glory and honor ...**

Chorus:
They offered gifts of praise to you, so near to your Passion;
see how we sing this song now to you reigning on high.
All repeat: **Glory and honor ...**

Chorus:
Those you were pleased to accept; now accept our gifts of
devotion,
good and merciful King, lover of all that is good.
All repeat: **Glory and honor ...**

*As the procession enters the church, there is sung the following
responsory or another chant, which should speak of the Lord's
entrance.*
℞ **As the Lord entered the holy city, the children of the
Hebrews proclaimed the resurrection of life. Waving their
branches of palm, they cried: Hosanna in the Highest.**

℣ When the people heard that Jesus was coming to Jerusalem,
they went out to meet him.
℞ **Waving their branches of palm, they cried: Hosanna in
the Highest.**

*When the Priest arrives at the altar, he venerates it. Omitting the
other Introductory Rites of the Mass and, if appropriate, the* Kyrie
(Lord, have mercy), *he says the Collect of the Mass, and then
continues the Mass in the usual way.*

SECOND FORM: THE SOLEMN ENTRANCE

*When a procession outside the church cannot take place, the
entrance of the Lord is celebrated inside the church by means of a
Solemn Entrance before the principal Mass.*

Holding branches in their hands, the faithful gather either outside, in front of the church door, or inside the church itself. The Priest and ministers and a representative group of the faithful go to a suitable place in the church outside the sanctuary, where at least the greater part of the faithful can see the rite.

While the Priest approaches the appointed place, the antiphon Hosanna *(page 125) or another appropriate chant is sung. Then the blessing of branches and the proclamation of the Gospel of the Lord's entrance into Jerusalem take place as in the First Form. After the Gospel, the Priest processes solemnly with the ministers and the representative group of the faithful through the church to the sanctuary, while the responsory,* As the Lord entered, *or another appropriate chant is sung.*

Arriving at the altar, the Priest venerates it. He then goes to the chair and, omitting the Introductory Rites of the Mass and, if appropriate, the Kyrie *(Lord, have mercy), he says the Collect of the Mass, and then continues the Mass in the usual way.*

THIRD FORM: THE SIMPLE ENTRANCE

At all other Masses of this Sunday at which the Solemn Entrance is not held, the memorial of the Lord's entrance into Jerusalem takes place by means of a Simple Entrance.

While the Priest proceeds to the altar, the Entrance Antiphon with its Psalm or another chant on the same theme is sung. Arriving at the altar, the Priest venerates it and goes to the chair. After the Sign of the Cross, he greets the people and continues the Mass in the usual way.

Entrance Antiphon *cf. Jn 12: 1, 12–13; Ps 24 (23): 9–10* Six days before the Passover, / when the Lord came into the city of Jerusalem, / the children ran to meet him; / in their hands they carried palm branches / and with a loud voice cried out: * **Hosanna in the highest!** ◆ **Blessed are you, who have come in your abundant mercy!**

O gates, lift high your heads; / grow higher, ancient doors. /
Let him enter, the king of glory! / Who is this king of glory? /
He, the Lord of hosts, he is the king of glory.   *** Hosanna
in the highest! ◆ Blessed are you, who have come in your
abundant mercy!**

❖ At the Mass ❖

First Reading   *Is 50: 4–7*

The Lord GOD has given me
   a well-trained tongue,
that I might know how to speak to the weary
   a word that will rouse them.
Morning after morning
   he opens my ear that I may hear;
and I have not rebelled,
   have not turned back.
I gave my back to those who beat me,
   my cheeks to those who plucked my beard;
my face I did not shield
   from buffets and spitting.

The Lord GOD is my help,
   therefore I am not disgraced;
I have set my face like flint,
   knowing that I shall not be put to shame.

Responsorial Psalm   *Ps 22: 8–9, 17–18, 19–20, 23–24*   *Steve Harmon*

My God, my God, why have You a - ban-doned me?

All who see me scoff at me;
   they mock me with parted lips, they wag their heads:

"He relied on the LORD; let him deliver him,
    let him rescue him, if he loves him." ℟

Indeed, many dogs surround me,
    a pack of evildoers closes in upon me;
They have pierced my hands and my feet;
    I can count all my bones. ℟

They divide my garments among them,
    and for my vesture they cast lots.
But you, O LORD, be not far from me;
    O my help, hasten to aid me. ℟

I will proclaim your name to my brethren;
    in the midst of the assembly I will praise you:
"You who fear the LORD, praise him;
    all you descendants of Jacob, give glory to him;
    revere him, all you descendants of Israel!" ℟

Second Reading   *Phil 2: 6–11*
Christ Jesus, though he was in the form of God,
    did not regard equality with God
    something to be grasped.
Rather, he emptied himself,
    taking the form of a slave,
    coming in human likeness;
    and found human in appearance,
    he humbled himself,
    becoming obedient to the point of death,
    even death on a cross.
Because of this, God greatly exalted him
    and bestowed on him the name
    which is above every name,
    that at the name of Jesus
    every knee should bend,
    of those in heaven and on earth and under the earth,
    and every tongue confess that

Jesus Christ is Lord,
to the glory of God the Father.

Verse Before the Gospel   *Phil 2:8-9*   *Laura Lea Duckworth*

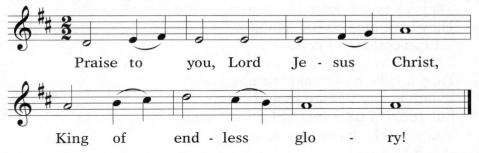

Praise to you, Lord Je - sus Christ,

King of end - less glo - ry!

Christ became obedient to the point of death, / even death
on a cross. / Because of this, God greatly exalted him / and
bestowed on him the name which is above every name.

Gospel   *Lk 22: 14–23: 56 or 23: 1–49*
*For the shorter form, read only the parts in brackets. The shorter
form begins on page 539. The symbols of the following passion
narrative represent Christ (+), the narrator (N), the voice (V), and
the crowd (C).*

N. The Passion of the Lord Jesus Christ according to Luke.
When the hour came, Jesus took his place at table with the
apostles. He said to them, **+** "I have eagerly desired to eat this
Passover with you before I suffer, for, I tell you, I shall not
eat it again until there is fulfillment in the kingdom of God."
N. Then he took a cup, gave thanks, and said, **+** "Take this and
share it among yourselves; for I tell you that from this time on
I shall not drink of the fruit of the vine until the kingdom of
God comes." **N.** Then he took the bread, said the blessing, broke
it, and gave it to them, saying, **+** "This is my body, which will
be given for you; do this in memory of me." **N.** And likewise
the cup after they had eaten, saying, **+** "This cup is the new
covenant in my blood, which will be shed for you.
"And yet behold, the hand of the one who is to betray me is
with me on the table; for the Son of Man indeed goes as it has
been determined; but woe to that man by whom he is betrayed."

N. And they began to debate among themselves who among them would do such a deed.

Then an argument broke out among them about which of them should be regarded as the greatest. He said to them, ✝ "The kings of the Gentiles lord it over them and those in authority over them are addressed as 'Benefactors'; but among you it shall not be so. Rather, let the greatest among you be as the youngest, and the leader as the servant. For who is greater: the one seated at table or the one who serves? Is it not the one seated at table? I am among you as the one who serves. It is you who have stood by me in my trials; and I confer a kingdom on you, just as my Father has conferred one on me, that you may eat and drink at my table in my kingdom; and you will sit on thrones judging the twelve tribes of Israel.

"Simon, Simon, behold Satan has demanded to sift all of you like wheat, but I have prayed that your own faith may not fail; and once you have turned back, you must strengthen your brothers." **N.** He said to him, **V.** "Lord, I am prepared to go to prison and to die with you." **N.** But he replied, ✝ "I tell you, Peter, before the cock crows this day, you will deny three times that you know me." **N.** He said to them, ✝ "When I sent you forth without a money bag or a sack or sandals, were you in need of anything?" **C. "No, nothing,"** **N.** they replied. He said to them, ✝ "But now one who has a money bag should take it, and likewise a sack, and one who does not have a sword should sell his cloak and buy one. For I tell you that this Scripture must be fulfilled in me, namely, *He was counted among the wicked*; and indeed what is written about me is coming to fulfillment." **N.** Then they said, **V.** "Lord, look, there are two swords here." **N.** But he replied, ✝ "It is enough!"

N. Then going out, he went, as was his custom, to the Mount of Olives, and the disciples followed him. When he arrived at the place he said to them, ✝ "Pray that you may not undergo the test." **N.** After withdrawing about a stone's throw from them and kneeling, he prayed, saying, ✝ "Father, if you are willing, take this cup away from me; still, not my will but yours be done." **N.** And to strengthen him an angel from heaven appeared to him. He was in such agony and he prayed so fervently that his sweat became like drops of blood falling on the ground. When he rose from prayer and returned to his disciples, he found them sleeping from grief. He said to them, ✛ "Why are you sleeping? Get up and pray that you may not undergo the test."

N. While he was still speaking, a crowd approached and in front was one of the Twelve, a man named Judas. He went up to Jesus to kiss him. Jesus said to him, ✛ "Judas, are you betraying the Son of Man with a kiss?" **N.** His disciples realized what was about to happen, and they asked, **V.** "Lord, shall we strike with a sword?" **N.** And one of them struck the high priest's servant and cut off his right ear. But Jesus said in reply, ✛ "Stop, no more of this!" **N.** Then he touched the servant's ear and healed him. And Jesus said to the chief priests and temple guards and elders who had come for him, ✛ "Have you come out as against a robber, with swords and clubs? Day after day I was with you in the temple area, and you did not seize me; but this is your hour, the time for the power of darkness."

N. After arresting him they led him away and took him into the house of the high priest; Peter was following at a distance. They lit a fire in the middle of the courtyard and sat around it, and Peter sat down with them. When a maid saw him seated in the light, she looked intently at him and said, **C.** **"This man too was with him."** **N.** But he denied it saying, **V.** "Woman, I do not know him." **N.** A short while later someone else saw him and said, **C.** **"You too are one of them"**; **N.** but Peter answered, **V.** "My friend, I am not." **N.** About an hour later, still another insisted, **C.** **"Assuredly, this man too was with him, for he also is a Galilean."** **N.** But Peter said, **V.** "My friend, I do not know what you are talking about." **N.** Just as he was saying this, the cock crowed, and the Lord turned and looked at Peter; and Peter remembered the word of the Lord, how he had said to him, "Before the cock crows today, you will deny me three times." He went out and began to weep bitterly. The men who held Jesus in custody were ridiculing and beating him. They blindfolded him and questioned him, saying, **C.** **"Prophesy! Who is it that struck you?"** **N.** And they reviled him in saying many other things against him.

When day came the council of elders of the people met, both chief priests and scribes, and they brought him before their Sanhedrin. They said, **C.** **"If you are the Christ, tell us,"** **N.** but he replied to them, ✛ "If I tell you, you will not believe, and if I question, you will not respond. But from this time on the Son of Man will be seated at the right hand of the power of God." **N.** They all asked, **C. "Are you then the Son of God?" N.** He replied to them, **✝** "You say that I am." **N.** Then they said, **C. "What further need have we for testimony? We have heard it from his own mouth."**

N. Then the whole assembly of them arose and brought him before Pilate.

(*The shorter form begins here*)
[(*Shorter form:* The elders of the peoples, chief priests and scribes, arose and brought Jesus before Pilate.) They brought charges against him, saying, **C. "We found this man misleading our people; he opposes the payment of taxes to Caesar and maintains that he is the Christ, a king." N.** Pilate asked him, **V.** "Are you the king of the Jews?" **N.** He said to him in reply, **✝** "You say so." **N.** Pilate then addressed the chief priests and the crowds, **V.** "I find this man not guilty." **N.** But they were adamant and said, **C. "He is inciting the people with his teaching throughout all Judea, from Galilee where he began even to here."**

N. On hearing this Pilate asked if the man was a Galilean; and upon learning that he was under Herod's jurisdiction, he sent him to Herod who was in Jerusalem at that time. Herod was very glad to see Jesus; he had been wanting to see him for a long time, for he had heard about him and had been hoping to see him perform some sign. He questioned him at length, but he gave him no answer. The chief priests and scribes, meanwhile, stood by accusing him harshly. Herod and his soldiers treated him contemptuously and mocked him, and after clothing him in resplendent garb, he sent him back to Pilate. Herod and Pilate became friends that very day, even though they had been enemies formerly. Pilate then summoned the chief priests, the rulers, and the people and said to them, **V.** "You brought this man to me and accused him of inciting the people to revolt. I have conducted my investigation in your presence and have not found this man guilty of the charges you have brought against him, nor did Herod, for he sent him back to us. So no capital crime has been committed by him. Therefore I shall have him flogged and then release him."

N. But all together they shouted out, **c.** **"Away with this man! Release Barabbas to us."** **N.** —Now Barabbas had been imprisoned for a rebellion that had taken place in the city and for murder.— Again Pilate addressed them, still wishing to release Jesus, but they continued their shouting, **c.** **"Crucify him! Crucify him!"** **N.** Pilate addressed them a third time, **v.** "What evil has this man done? I found him guilty of no capital crime. Therefore I shall have him flogged and then release him." **N.** With loud shouts, however, they persisted in calling for his crucifixion, and their voices prevailed. The verdict of Pilate was that their demand should be granted. So he released the man who had been imprisoned for rebellion and murder, for whom they asked, and he handed Jesus over to them to deal with as they wished.

As they led him away they took hold of a certain Simon, a Cyrenian, who was coming in from the country; and after laying the cross on him, they made him carry it behind Jesus. A large crowd of people followed Jesus, including many women who mourned and lamented him. Jesus turned to them and said, ✝ "Daughters of Jerusalem, do not weep for me; weep instead for yourselves and for your children for indeed, the days are coming when people will say, 'Blessed are the barren, the wombs that never bore and the breasts that never nursed.' At that time people will say to the mountains, 'Fall upon us!' and to the hills, 'Cover us!' for if these things are done when the wood is green what will happen when it is dry?" **N.** Now two others, both criminals, were led away with him to be executed.

When they came to the place called the Skull, they crucified him and the criminals there, one on his right, the other on his left. Then Jesus said, ✝ "Father, forgive them, they know not what they do." **N.** They divided his garments by casting lots. The people stood by and watched; the rulers, meanwhile, sneered at him and said, **c.** **"He saved others, let him save himself if he is the chosen one, the Christ of God."** **N.** Even the soldiers jeered at him. As they approached to offer him wine they called out, **c.** **"If you are King of the Jews, save yourself."** **N.** Above him there was an inscription that read, "This is the King of the Jews."

Now one of the criminals hanging there reviled Jesus, saying, **v.** "Are you not the Christ? Save yourself and us." **N.** The other, however, rebuking him, said in reply, **v.** "Have you no fear of God, for you are subject to the same condemnation? And indeed, we have been condemned justly, for the sentence we received corresponds to our crimes, but this man has done nothing criminal." **N.** Then he said, **v.** "Jesus, remember me when you come into your kingdom." **N.** He replied to him, ✚ "Amen, I say to you, today you will be with me in Paradise."

N. It was now about noon and darkness came over the whole land until three in the afternoon because of an eclipse of the sun. Then the veil of the temple was torn down the middle. Jesus cried out in a loud voice, ✚ "Father, into your hands I commend my spirit"; **N.** and when he had said this he breathed his last.

Here all kneel and pause for a short time.

N. The centurion who witnessed what had happened glorified God and said, **v.** "This man was innocent beyond doubt." **N.** When all the people who had gathered for this spectacle saw what had happened, they returned home beating their breasts; but all his acquaintances stood at a distance, including the women who had followed him from Galilee and saw these events.]

Now there was a virtuous and righteous man named Joseph who, though he was a member of the council, had not consented to their plan of action. He came from the Jewish town of Arimathea and was awaiting the kingdom of God. He went to Pilate and asked for the body of Jesus. After he had taken the body down, he wrapped it in a linen cloth and laid him in a rock-hewn tomb in which no one had yet been buried. It was the day of preparation, and the sabbath was about to begin. The women who had come from Galilee with him followed behind, and when they had seen the tomb and the way in which his body was laid in it, they returned and prepared spices and perfumed oils. Then they rested on the sabbath according to the commandment.

Communion Antiphon Mt 26:42 **Father, if this chalice cannot pass without my drinking it, ◆ your will be done.**

The readings for the Sacred Paschal Triduum begin on page 669.

Easter Time † YEAR C

The readings for Easter Sunday can be found on page 740.

SECOND SUNDAY OF EASTER

(DIVINE MERCY SUNDAY)

Entrance Antiphon 1 Pt 2: 2 **Like newborn infants, you must long for the pure, spiritual milk, ♦ that in him you may grow to salvation, alleluia.**

Or: 4 Esdr 2: 36–37 **Receive the joy of your glory, giving thanks to God, ♦ who has called you into the heavenly kingdom, alleluia.**

First Reading Acts 5: 12–16 Many signs and wonders were done among the people at the hands of the apostles. They were all together in Solomon's portico. None of the others dared to join them, but the people esteemed them. Yet more than ever, believers in the Lord, great numbers of men and women, were added to them. Thus they even carried the sick out into the streets and laid them on cots and mats so that when Peter came by, at least his shadow might fall on one or another of them. A large number of people from the towns in the vicinity of Jerusalem also gathered, bringing the sick and those disturbed by unclean spirits, and they were all cured.

Responsorial Psalm Ps 118: 2–4, 13–15, 22–24   *based on* ICH WILL DICH LIEBEN

Give thanks to the Lord for he is good,

his love is ev - er - last - ing.

Or: ℟ **Alleluia.**

Let the house of Israel say,
   "His mercy endures forever."
Let the house of Aaron say,
   "His mercy endures forever."
Let those who fear the LORD say,
   "His mercy endures forever." ℟

I was hard pressed and was falling,
   but the LORD helped me.
My strength and my courage is the LORD,
   and he has been my savior.
The joyful shout of victory
   in the tents of the just. ℟

The stone which the builders rejected
   has become the cornerstone.
By the LORD has this been done;
   it is wonderful in our eyes.
This is the day the LORD has made;
   let us be glad and rejoice in it. ℟

Second Reading Rv 1: 9–11a, 12–13, 17–19 I, John, your brother, who share with you the distress, the kingdom, and the endurance we have in Jesus, found myself on the island called Patmos because I proclaimed God's word and gave testimony to Jesus. I was caught up in spirit on the Lord's day and heard behind me a voice as loud as a trumpet, which said, "Write on a scroll what you see." Then I turned to see whose voice it was that spoke to me, and when I turned, I saw seven gold lampstands and in the midst of the lampstands one like a son of man, wearing an ankle-length robe, with a gold sash around his chest.
   When I caught sight of him, I fell down at his feet as though

dead. He touched me with his right hand and said, "Do not be afraid. I am the first and the last, the one who lives. Once I was dead, but now I am alive forever and ever. I hold the keys to death and the netherworld. Write down, therefore, what you have seen, and what is happening, and what will happen afterwards."

Alleluia   *Jn 20: 29*   *Laura Lea Duckworth*

You believe in me, Thomas, because you have seen me, says the Lord; / Blessed are they who have not seen me, but still believe!   **Alleluia, alleluia.**

Gospel *Jn 20: 19–31* On the evening of that first day of the week, when the doors were locked, where the disciples were, for fear of the Jews, Jesus came and stood in their midst and said to them, "Peace be with you." When he had said this, he showed them his hands and his side. The disciples rejoiced when they saw the Lord. Jesus said to them again, "Peace be with you. As the Father has sent me, so I send you." And when he had said this, he breathed on them and said to them, "Receive the Holy Spirit. Whose sins you forgive are forgiven them, and whose sins you retain are retained."

Thomas, called Didymus, one of the Twelve, was not with them when Jesus came. So the other disciples said to him, "We have seen the Lord." But he said to them, "Unless I see the mark of the nails in his hands and put my finger into the nailmarks and put my hand into his side, I will not believe."

Now a week later his disciples were again inside and Thomas was with them. Jesus came, although the doors were locked, and stood in their midst and said, "Peace be with you." Then he said to Thomas, "Put your finger here and see my hands, and bring your hand and put it into my side, and do not be unbelieving, but believe." Thomas answered and said to him, "My Lord and my God!" Jesus said to him, "Have you come to believe because you have seen me? Blessed are those who have not seen and have believed."

Now, Jesus did many other signs in the presence of his disciples that are not written in this book. But these are written that you may come to believe that Jesus is the Christ, the Son of God, and that through this belief you may have life in his name.

Communion Antiphon *cf. Jn 20: 27* **Bring your hand and feel the place of the nails, ♦ and do not be unbelieving but believing, alleluia.**

THIRD SUNDAY OF EASTER

Entrance Antiphon *cf. Ps 66 (65): 1–2* **Cry out with joy to God, all the earth; ♦ O sing to the glory of his name. ♦ O render him glorious praise, alleluia.**

First Reading *Acts 5: 27–32, 40b–41* When the captain and the court officers had brought the apostles in and made them stand before the Sanhedrin, the high priest questioned them, "We gave you strict orders, did we not, to stop teaching in that name? Yet you have filled Jerusalem with your teaching and want to bring this man's blood upon us." But Peter and the apostles said in reply, "We must obey God rather than men. The God of our ancestors raised Jesus, though you had him killed by hanging him on a tree. God exalted him at his right hand as leader and savior to grant Israel repentance and forgiveness of sins. We are witnesses of these things, as is the Holy Spirit whom God has given to those who obey him."

The Sanhedrin ordered the apostles to stop speaking in the name of Jesus, and dismissed them. So they left the presence of the Sanhedrin, rejoicing that they had been found worthy to suffer dishonor for the sake of the name.

Responsorial Psalm   Ps 30: 2, 4, 5–6, 11–12, 13   *Joe Higginbotham*

I will praise you, Lord, for you have res-cued me.

Or: ℟ **Alleluia.**

I will extol you, O LORD, for you drew me clear
   and did not let my enemies rejoice over me.
O LORD, you brought me up from the netherworld;
   you preserved me from among those going down into
      the pit.   ℟

Sing praise to the LORD, you his faithful ones,
   and give thanks to his holy name.
For his anger lasts but a moment;
   a lifetime, his good will.
At nightfall, weeping enters in,
   but with the dawn, rejoicing.   ℟

Hear, O LORD, and have pity on me;
   O LORD, be my helper.
You changed my mourning into dancing;
   O LORD, my God, forever will I give you thanks.   ℟

Second Reading Rv 5: 11–14 I, John, looked and heard the voices of
many angels who surrounded the throne and the living creatures
and the elders. They were countless in number, and they cried
out in a loud voice:
  "Worthy is the Lamb that was slain
    to receive power and riches, wisdom and strength,
    honor and glory and blessing."
Then I heard every creature in heaven and on earth and under
the earth and in the sea, everything in the universe, cry out:
  "To the one who sits on the throne and to the Lamb
    be blessing and honor, glory and might,
    forever and ever."
The four living creatures answered, "Amen," and the elders fell
down and worshiped.

Alleluia

Laura Lea Duckworth

Al - le - lu - ia, al-le-lu - ia.

Al - le - lu - ia, al-le-lu - ia.

Christ is risen, creator of all; / he has shown pity on all people.
Alleluia, alleluia.

Gospel *Jn 21: 1–19 or 21: 1–14*

For the shorter form, read only the parts in brackets.

[At that time, Jesus revealed himself again to his disciples at the
Sea of Tiberias. He revealed himself in this way. Together were
Simon Peter, Thomas called Didymus, Nathanael from Cana in
Galilee, Zebedee's sons, and two others of his disciples. Simon
Peter said to them, "I am going fishing." They said to him, "We
also will come with you." So they went out and got into the boat,
but that night they caught nothing. When it was already dawn,
Jesus was standing on the shore; but the disciples did not realize
that it was Jesus. Jesus said to them, "Children, have you caught
anything to eat?" They answered him, "No." So he said to
them, "Cast the net over the right side of the boat and you will
find something." So they cast it, and were not able to pull it in
because of the number of fish. So the disciple whom Jesus loved
said to Peter, "It is the Lord." When Simon Peter heard that it
was the Lord, he tucked in his garment, for he was lightly clad,
and jumped into the sea. The other disciples came in the boat,
for they were not far from shore, only about a hundred yards,
dragging the net with the fish. When they climbed out on shore,
they saw a charcoal fire with fish on it and bread. Jesus said to
them, "Bring some of the fish you just caught." So Simon Peter
went over and dragged the net ashore full of one hundred fifty-
three large fish. Even though there were so many, the net was
not torn. Jesus said to them, "Come, have breakfast." And none
of the disciples dared to ask him, "Who are you?" because they
realized it was the Lord. Jesus came over and took the bread and

gave it to them, and in like manner the fish. This was now the third time Jesus was revealed to his disciples after being raised from the dead.]

When they had finished breakfast, Jesus said to Simon Peter, "Simon, son of John, do you love me more than these?" Simon Peter answered him, "Yes, Lord, you know that I love you." Jesus said to him, "Feed my lambs." He then said to Simon Peter a second time, "Simon, son of John, do you love me?" Simon Peter answered him, "Yes, Lord, you know that I love you." Jesus said to him, "Tend my sheep." Jesus said to him the third time, "Simon, son of John, do you love me?" Peter was distressed that Jesus had said to him a third time, "Do you love me?" and he said to him, "Lord, you know everything; you know that I love you." Jesus said to him, "Feed my sheep. Amen, amen, I say to you, when you were younger, you used to dress yourself and go where you wanted; but when you grow old, you will stretch out your hands, and someone else will dress you and lead you where you do not want to go." He said this signifying by what kind of death he would glorify God. And when he had said this, he said to him, "Follow me."

Communion Antiphon *cf. Lk 24: 35* **The disciples recognized the Lord Jesus ✦ in the breaking of the bread, alleluia.**

Or: *cf. Jn 21: 12–13* **Jesus said to his disciples: Come and eat. ✦ And he took bread and gave it to them, alleluia.**

FOURTH SUNDAY OF EASTER

Entrance Antiphon *cf. Ps 33 (32): 5-6* **The merciful love of the Lord fills the earth; ✦ by the word of the Lord the heavens were made, alleluia.**

First Reading *Acts 13: 14, 43-52* Paul and Barnabas continued on from Perga and reached Antioch in Pisidia. On the sabbath they entered the synagogue and took their seats. Many Jews and worshipers who were converts to Judaism followed Paul and

Barnabas, who spoke to them and urged them to remain faithful to the grace of God.

On the following sabbath almost the whole city gathered to hear the word of the Lord. When the Jews saw the crowds, they were filled with jealousy and with violent abuse contradicted what Paul said. Both Paul and Barnabas spoke out boldly and said, "It was necessary that the word of God be spoken to you first, but since you reject it and condemn yourselves as unworthy of eternal life, we now turn to the Gentiles. For so the Lord has commanded us, *I have made you a light to the Gentiles, that you may be an instrument of salvation to the ends of the earth.*"

The Gentiles were delighted when they heard this and glorified the word of the Lord. All who were destined for eternal life came to believe, and the word of the Lord continued to spread through the whole region. The Jews, however, incited the women of prominence who were worshipers and the leading men of the city, stirred up a persecution against Paul and Barnabas, and expelled them from their territory. So they shook the dust from their feet in protest against them, and went to Iconium. The disciples were filled with joy and the Holy Spirit.

Responsorial Psalm   Ps 100: 1–2, 3, 5   *Joe Higginbotham*

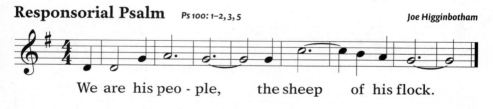

We are his peo - ple, the sheep of his flock.

Or: ℟ **Alleluia.**

Sing joyfully to the LORD, all you lands;
  serve the LORD with gladness;
  come before him with joyful song. ℟

Know that the LORD is God;
  he made us, his we are;
  his people, the flock he tends. ℟

The LORD is good:

his kindness endures forever,
and his faithfulness, to all generations.   ℟

Second Reading Rv 7: 9, 14b–17 I, John, had a vision of a great
multitude, which no one could count, from every nation, race,
people, and tongue. They stood before the throne and before the
Lamb, wearing white robes and holding palm branches in their
hands.

Then one of the elders said to me, "These are the ones who
have survived the time of great distress; they have washed their
robes and made them white in the blood of the Lamb.

"For this reason they stand before God's throne
    and worship him day and night in his temple.
The one who sits on the throne will shelter them.
They will not hunger or thirst anymore,
    nor will the sun or any heat strike them.
For the Lamb who is in the center of the throne
    will shepherd them
    and lead them to springs of life-giving water,
    and God will wipe away every tear from their eyes."

Alleluia   Jn 10: 14   *Laura Lea Duckworth*

Al - le - lu - ia, al-le-lu - ia.

Al - le - lu - ia, al-le-lu - ia.

I am the good shepherd, says the Lord; / I know my sheep,
and mine know me.   **Alleluia, alleluia.**

Gospel Jn 10: 27–30 Jesus said: "My sheep hear my voice; I know
them, and they follow me. I give them eternal life, and they shall
never perish. No one can take them out of my hand. My Father,
who has given them to me, is greater than all, and no one can
take them out of the Father's hand. The Father and I are one."

Communion Antiphon
The Good Shepherd has risen, ♦ who laid down his life for his sheep ♦ and willingly died for his flock, alleluia.

FIFTH SUNDAY OF EASTER

Entrance Antiphon *cf. Ps 98 (97): 1–2* O sing a new song to the Lord, ♦ for he has worked wonders; ♦ in the sight of the nations ♦ he has shown his deliverance, alleluia.

First Reading *Acts 14: 21–27* After Paul and Barnabas had proclaimed the good news to that city and made a considerable number of disciples, they returned to Lystra and to Iconium and to Antioch. They strengthened the spirits of the disciples and exhorted them to persevere in the faith, saying, "It is necessary for us to undergo many hardships to enter the kingdom of God." They appointed elders for them in each church and, with prayer and fasting, commended them to the Lord in whom they had put their faith. Then they traveled through Pisidia and reached Pamphylia. After proclaiming the word at Perga they went down to Attalia. From there they sailed to Antioch, where they had been commended to the grace of God for the work they had now accomplished. And when they arrived, they called the church together and reported what God had done with them and how he had opened the door of faith to the Gentiles.

Responsorial Psalm *Ps 145: 8–9, 10–11, 12–13* *Bill Svarda*

I will praise your name for ev- er,

my king and my God.

Or: **Alleluia.**

The LORD is gracious and merciful,
   slow to anger and of great kindness.
The LORD is good to all
   and compassionate toward all his works.   ℟

Let all your works give you thanks, O LORD,
   and let your faithful ones bless you.
Let them discourse of the glory of your kingdom
   and speak of your might.   ℟

Let them make known your might to the children of Adam,
   and the glorious splendor of your kingdom.
Your kingdom is a kingdom for all ages,
   and your dominion endures through all generations.   ℟

Second Reading Rv 21: 1–5a Then I, John, saw a new heaven and a
new earth. The former heaven and the former earth had passed
away, and the sea was no more. I also saw the holy city, a new
Jerusalem, coming down out of heaven from God, prepared as
a bride adorned for her husband. I heard a loud voice from the
throne saying, "Behold, God's dwelling is with the human race.
He will dwell with them and they will be his people and God
himself will always be with them as their God. He will wipe
every tear from their eyes, and there shall be no more death or
mourning, wailing or pain, for the old order has passed away."
   The One who sat on the throne said, "Behold, I make all
things new."

Alleluia   Jn 13: 34   *Laura Lea Duckworth*

I give you a new commandment, says the Lord: / love one
another as I have loved you.   **Alleluia, alleluia**

Gospel Jn 13: 31–33a, 34–35 When Judas had left them, Jesus said, "Now is the Son of Man glorified, and God is glorified in him. If God is glorified in him, God will also glorify him in himself, and God will glorify him at once. My children, I will be with you only a little while longer. I give you a new commandment: love one another. As I have loved you, so you also should love one another. This is how all will know that you are my disciples, if you have love for one another."

Communion Antiphon cf. Jn 15: 1, 5 I am the true vine and you are the branches, says the Lord. ✦ Whoever remains in me, and I in him, bears fruit in plenty, alleluia.

SIXTH SUNDAY OF EASTER

When the Ascension of the Lord is celebrated the following Sunday, the second reading and Gospel from the Seventh Sunday of Easter (page 559) may be read on the Sixth Sunday of Easter.

Entrance Antiphon cf. Is 48: 20 Proclaim a joyful sound and let it be heard; ✦ proclaim to the ends of the earth: ✦ The Lord has freed his people, alleluia.

First Reading Acts 15: 1–2, 22–29 Some who had come down from Judea were instructing the brothers, "Unless you are circumcised according to the Mosaic practice, you cannot be saved." Because there arose no little dissension and debate by Paul and Barnabas with them, it was decided that Paul, Barnabas, and some of the others should go up to Jerusalem to the apostles and elders about this question.

The apostles and elders, in agreement with the whole church, decided to choose representatives and to send them to Antioch with Paul and Barnabas. The ones chosen were Judas, who was called Barsabbas, and Silas, leaders among the brothers. This is the letter delivered by them:

"The apostles and the elders, your brothers, to the brothers in Antioch, Syria, and Cilicia of Gentile origin: greetings. Since we have heard that some of our number who went out without any mandate from us have upset you with their teachings and disturbed your peace of mind, we have with one accord decided to choose representatives and to send them to you along with our beloved Barnabas and Paul, who have dedicated their lives to the name of our Lord Jesus Christ. So we are sending Judas and Silas who will also convey this same message by word of mouth: 'It is the decision of the Holy Spirit and of us not to place on you any burden beyond these necessities, namely, to abstain from meat sacrificed to idols, from blood, from meats of strangled animals, and from unlawful marriage. If you keep free of these, you will be doing what is right. Farewell.'"

Responsorial Psalm   Ps 67: 2–3, 5, 6, 8   *Roger Holtz and Jane Terwilliger*

O God, let all the na-tions praise you, let all the na-tions praise you!

Or: ℟ **Alleluia.**

May God have pity on us and bless us;
   may he let his face shine upon us.
So may your way be known upon earth;
   among all nations, your salvation. ℟

May the nations be glad and exult
   because you rule the peoples in equity;
   the nations on the earth you guide. ℟

May the peoples praise you, O God;
   may all the peoples praise you!
May God bless us,
   and may all the ends of the earth fear him! ℟

Second Reading Rv 21: 10–14, 22–23 The angel took me in spirit to a great, high mountain and showed me the holy city Jerusalem coming down out of heaven from God. It gleamed with the splendor of God. Its radiance was like that of a precious stone, like jasper, clear as crystal. It had a massive, high wall, with twelve gates where twelve angels were stationed and on which names were inscribed, the names of the twelve tribes of the Israelites. There were three gates facing east, three north, three south, and three west. The wall of the city had twelve courses of stones as its foundation, on which were inscribed the twelve names of the twelve apostles of the Lamb.

I saw no temple in the city for its temple is the Lord God almighty and the Lamb. The city had no need of sun or moon to shine on it, for the glory of God gave it light, and its lamp was the Lamb.

Alleluia *Jn 14: 23* Laura Lea Duckworth

Al - le - lu - ia, al-le-lu - ia.

Al - le - lu - ia, al-le-lu - ia.

Whoever loves me will keep my word, says the Lord, /
and my Father will love him and we will come to him.
Alleluia, alleluia.

Gospel *Jn 14: 23-29* Jesus said to his disciples: "Whoever loves me will keep my word, and my Father will love him, and we will come to him and make our dwelling with him. Whoever does not love me does not keep my words; yet the word you hear is not mine but that of the Father who sent me.

"I have told you this while I am with you. The Advocate, the Holy Spirit, whom the Father will send in my name, will teach you everything and remind you of all that I told you. Peace I leave with you; my peace I give to you. Not as the world gives do I give it to you. Do not let your hearts be troubled or afraid. You heard me tell you, 'I am going away and I will come back to you.' If you loved me, you would rejoice that I am going to the Father;

for the Father is greater than I. And now I have told you this before it happens, so that when it happens you may believe."

Communion Antiphon Jn 14: 15–16 **If you love me, keep my commandments, says the Lord, ◆ and I will ask the Father and he will send you another Paraclete, ◆ to abide with you for ever, alleluia.**

THE ASCENSION OF THE LORD

Where the Solemnity of the Ascension is not to be observed as a Holyday of Obligation, it is assigned to the Seventh Sunday of Easter as its proper day.

Entrance Antiphon

At the Vigil Mass: Ps 68 (67): 33, 35 **You kingdoms of the earth, sing to God; ◆ praise the Lord, who ascends above the highest heavens; ◆ his majesty and might are in the skies, alleluia.**

At the Mass During the Day: Acts 1: 11 **Men of Galilee, why gaze in wonder at the heavens? ◆ This Jesus whom you saw ascending into heaven ◆will return as you saw him go, alleluia.**

First Reading Acts 1: 1–11 In the first book, Theophilus, I dealt with all that Jesus did and taught until the day he was taken up, after giving instructions through the Holy Spirit to the apostles whom he had chosen. He presented himself alive to them by many proofs after he had suffered, appearing to them during forty days and speaking about the kingdom of God. While meeting with the them, he enjoined them not to depart from Jerusalem, but to wait for "the promise of the Father about which you have heard me speak; for John baptized with water, but in a few days you will be baptized with the Holy Spirit."
When they had gathered together they asked him, "Lord, are

you at this time going to restore the kingdom to Israel?" He answered them, "It is not for you to know the times or seasons that the Father has established by his own authority. But you will receive power when the Holy Spirit comes upon you, and you will be my witnesses in Jerusalem, throughout Judea and Samaria, and to the ends of the earth." When he had said this, as they were looking on, he was lifted up, and a cloud took him from their sight. While they were looking intently at the sky as he was going, suddenly two men dressed in white garments stood beside them. They said, "Men of Galilee, why are you standing there looking at the sky? This Jesus who has been taken up from you into heaven will return in the same way as you have seen him going into heaven."

Responsorial Psalm   Ps 47: 2–3, 6–7, 8–9   Joe Higginbotham

God mounts his throne to shouts of joy; a blare of trum-pets for the Lord.

Or: ℟ **Alleluia.**

All you peoples, clap your hands,
    shout to God with cries of gladness,
For the LORD, the Most High, the awesome,
    is the great king over all the earth. ℟

God mounts his throne amid shouts of joy;
    the LORD, amid trumpet blasts.
Sing praise to God, sing praise;
    sing praise to our king, sing praise. ℟

For king of all the earth is God;

sing hymns of praise.
God reigns over the nations,
God sits upon his holy throne. ℟

Second Reading *Eph 1: 17–23* Brothers and sisters: May the God
of our Lord Jesus Christ, the Father of glory, give you a Spirit
of wisdom and revelation resulting in knowledge of him. May
the eyes of your hearts be enlightened, that you may know
what is the hope that belongs to his call, what are the riches of
glory in his inheritance among the holy ones, and what is the
surpassing greatness of his power for us who believe, in accord
with the exercise of his great might, which he worked in Christ,
raising him from the dead and seating him at his right hand in
the heavens, far above every principality, authority, power, and
dominion, and every name that is named not only in this age but
also in the one to come. And he put all things beneath his feet
and gave him as head over all things to the church, which is his
body, the fullness of the one who fills all things in every way.

Or: *Heb 9: 24–28; 10: 19–23* Christ did not enter into a sanctuary made
by hands, a copy of the true one, but heaven itself, that he might
now appear before God on our behalf. Not that he might offer
himself repeatedly, as the high priest enters each year into the
sanctuary with blood that is not his own; if that were so, he
would have had to suffer repeatedly from the foundation of the
world. But now once for all he has appeared at the end of the
ages to take away sin by his sacrifice. Just as it is appointed that
men and women die once, and after this the judgment, so also
Christ, offered once to take away the sins of many, will appear a
second time, not to take away sin but to bring salvation to those
who eagerly await him.

Therefore, brothers and sisters, since through the blood of
Jesus we have confidence of entrance into the sanctuary by the
new and living way he opened for us through the veil, that is,
his flesh, and since we have "a great priest over the house of
God," let us approach with a sincere heart and in absolute trust,
with our hearts sprinkled clean from an evil conscience and our
bodies washed in pure water. Let us hold unwaveringly to our
confession that gives us hope, for he who made the promise is
trustworthy.

Alleluia   *Mt 28: 19a, 20b*   *Jim Hughes*

Al-le-lu-ia   Al-le-lu-ia   Al - le-lu - ia.

Go and teach all nations, says the Lord; / I am with you
always, until the end of the world.   **Alleluia, alleluia.**

Gospel *Lk 24: 46-53* Jesus said to his disciples: "Thus it is written
that the Christ would suffer and rise from the dead on the third
day and that repentance, for the forgiveness of sins, would
be preached in his name to all the nations, beginning from
Jerusalem. You are witnesses of these things. And behold I am
sending the promise of my Father upon you; but stay in the city
until you are clothed with power from on high."

Then he led them out as far as Bethany, raised his hands, and
blessed them. As he blessed them he parted from them and was
taken up to heaven. They did him homage and then returned
to Jerusalem with great joy, and they were continually in the
temple praising God.

Communion Antiphon

At the Vigil Mass: *cf. Heb 10: 12* **Christ, offering a single sacrifice
for sins, ✦ is seated for ever at God's right hand, alleluia.**

At th Mass During the Day: *Mt 28: 20* **Behold, I am with you
always, ✦ even to the end of the age, alleluia.**

SEVENTH SUNDAY OF EASTER

Entrance Antiphon *cf. Ps 27 (26): 7-9* **O Lord, hear my voice, for I
have called to you; ✦ of you my heart has spoken: Seek his
face; ✦ hide not your face from me, alleluia.**

First Reading *Acts 7: 55-60* Stephen, filled with the Holy Spirit,
looked up intently to heaven and saw the glory of God and Jesus

standing at the right hand of God, and Stephen said, "Behold, I see the heavens opened and the Son of Man standing at the right hand of God." But they cried out in a loud voice, covered their ears, and rushed upon him together. They threw him out of the city, and began to stone him. The witnesses laid down their cloaks at the feet of a young man named Saul. As they were stoning Stephen, he called out, "Lord Jesus, receive my spirit." Then he fell to his knees and cried out in a loud voice, "Lord, do not hold this sin against them"; and when he said this, he fell asleep.

Responsorial Psalm   Ps 97: 1–2, 6–7, 9   *Jane Terwilliger*

The Lord is king, the Most High over all the earth.

Or: ℟ **Alleluia.**

The LORD is king; let the earth rejoice;
  let the many islands be glad.
Justice and judgment are the foundation of his throne. ℟

The heavens proclaim his justice,
  and all peoples see his glory.
All gods are prostrate before him. ℟

You, O LORD, are the Most High over all the earth,
  exalted far above all gods. ℟

Second Reading Rv 22: 12–14, 16–17, 20 I, John, heard a voice saying to me: "Behold, I am coming soon. I bring with me the recompense I will give to each according to his deeds. I am the Alpha and the Omega, the first and the last, the beginning and the end."
    Blessed are they who wash their robes so as to have the right to the tree of life and enter the city through its gates.
    "I, Jesus, sent my angel to give you this testimony for the

churches. I am the root and offspring of David, the bright morning star."

The Spirit and the bride say, "Come." Let the hearer say, "Come." Let the one who thirsts come forward, and the one who wants it receive the gift of life-giving water.

The one who gives this testimony says, "Yes, I am coming soon." Amen! Come, Lord Jesus!

Alleluia   *cf. Jn 14: 18*   Laura Lea Duckworth

Al - le - lu - ia, al-le-lu - ia.
Al - le - lu - ia, al-le-lu - ia.

I will not leave you orphans, says the Lord. / I will come back to you, and your hearts will rejoice.   **Alleluia, alleluia.**

Gospel *Jn 17: 20–26* Lifting up his eyes to heaven, Jesus prayed saying: "Holy Father, I pray not only for them, but also for those who will believe in me through their word, so that they may all be one, as you, Father, are in me and I in you, that they also may be in us, that the world may believe that you sent me. And I have given them the glory you gave me, so that they may be one, as we are one, I in them and you in me, that they may be brought to perfection as one, that the world may know that you sent me, and that you loved them even as you loved me. Father, they are your gift to me. I wish that where I am they also may be with me, that they may see my glory that you gave me, because you loved me before the foundation of the world. Righteous Father, the world also does not know you, but I know you, and they know that you sent me. I made known to them your name and I will make it known, that the love with which you loved me may be in them and I in them."

Communion Antiphon *Jn 17: 22* Father, I pray that they may be one ✦ as we also are one, alleluia.

PENTECOST SUNDAY

The readings for the Vigil Mass can be found on page 161.

The readings for the Vigil Mass can be found on page 161.

❖ At the Mass During the Day ❖

Entrance Antiphon *Wis 1: 7* **The Spirit of the Lord has filled the whole world ◆ and that which contains all things ◆ understands what is said, alleluia.**

Or: *Rom 5: 5; cf. 8: 11* **The love of God has been poured into our hearts ◆ through the Spirit of God dwelling within us, alleluia.**

First Reading *Acts 2: 1–11* When the time for Pentecost was fulfilled, they were all in one place together. And suddenly there came from the sky a noise like a strong driving wind, and it filled the entire house in which they were. Then there appeared to them tongues as of fire, which parted and came to rest on each one of them. And they were all filled with the Holy Spirit and began to speak in different tongues, as the Spirit enabled them to proclaim.

Now there were devout Jews from every nation under heaven staying in Jerusalem. At this sound, they gathered in a large crowd, but they were confused because each one heard them speaking in his own language. They were astounded, and in amazement they asked, "Are not all these people who are speaking Galileans? Then how does each of us hear them in his native language? We are Parthians, Medes, and Elamites, inhabitants of Mesopotamia, Judea and Cappadocia, Pontus and Asia, Phrygia and Pamphylia, Egypt and the districts of Libya near Cyrene, as well as travelers from Rome, both Jews and converts to Judaism, Cretans and Arabs, yet we hear them speaking in our own tongues of the mighty acts of God."

Responsorial Psalm *Ps 104: 1, 24, 29–30, 31, 34*   David Miles

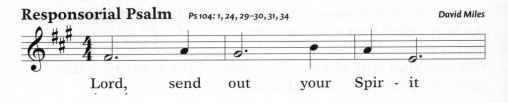

Lord,   send   out   your   Spir - it

and re - new the face of the earth.

Or: **Alleluia.**

Bless the LORD, O my soul!
 O LORD, my God, you are great indeed!
How manifold are your works, O LORD!
 the earth is full of your creatures; ℟

If you take away their breath, they perish
 and return to their dust.
When you send forth your spirit, they are created,
 and you renew the face of the earth. ℟

May the glory of the LORD endure forever;
 may the LORD be glad in his works!
Pleasing to him be my theme;
 I will be glad in the LORD. ℟

Second Reading *1 Cor 12: 3b–7, 12–13* Brothers and sisters: No one can
say, "Jesus is Lord," except by the Holy Spirit.
 There are different kinds of spiritual gifts but the same Spirit;
there are different forms of service but the same Lord; there are
different workings but the same God who produces all of them
in everyone. To each individual the manifestation of the Spirit is
given for some benefit.
 As a body is one though it has many parts, and all the parts
of the body, though many, are one body, so also Christ. For in
one Spirit we were all baptized into one body, whether Jews or
Greeks, slaves or free persons, and we were all given to drink of
one Spirit.

Or: *Rom 8: 8–17* Brothers and sisters: Those who are in the flesh
cannot please God. But you are not in the flesh; on the contrary,
you are in the spirit, if only the Spirit of God dwells in you.
Whoever does not have the Spirit of Christ does not belong to
him. But if Christ is in you, although the body is dead because

of sin, the spirit is alive because of righteousness. If the Spirit of the one who raised Jesus from the dead dwells in you, the one who raised Christ from the dead will give life to your mortal bodies also, through his Spirit that dwells in you. Consequently, brothers and sisters, we are not debtors to the flesh, to live according to the flesh. For if you live according to the flesh, you will die, but if by the Spirit you put to death the deeds of the body, you will live.

For those who are led by the Spirit of God are sons of God. For you did not receive a spirit of slavery to fall back into fear, but you received a Spirit of adoption, through whom we cry, "Abba, Father!" The Spirit himself bears witness with our spirit that we are children of God, and if children, then heirs, heirs of God and joint heirs with Christ, if only we suffer with him so that we may also be glorified with him.

Sequence
    Come, Holy Spirit, come!
    And from your celestial home
        Shed a ray of light divine!
    Come, Father of the poor!
    Come, source of all our store!
        Come, within our bosoms shine.
    You, of comforters the best;
    You, the soul's most welcome guest;
        Sweet refreshment here below;
    In our labor, rest most sweet;
    Grateful coolness in the heat;
        Solace in the midst of woe.
    O most blessed Light divine,
    Shine within these hearts of yours,
        And our inmost being fill!
    Where you are not, we have naught,
    Nothing good in deed or thought,
        Nothing free from taint of ill.
    Heal our wounds, our strength renew;
    On our dryness pour your dew;
        Wash the stains of guilt away:
    Bend the stubborn heart and will;

Melt the frozen, warm the chill;
   Guide the steps that go astray.
On the faithful, who adore
And confess you, evermore
   In your sevenfold gift descend;
Give them virtue's sure reward;
Give them your salvation, Lord;
   Give them joys that never end. Amen.
   Alleluia.

Alleluia
Laura Lea Duckworth

Al - le - lu - ia, al-le-lu - ia.

Al - le - lu - ia, al-le-lu - ia.

Come, Holy Spirit, fill the hearts of your faithful / and
kindle in them the fire of your love.   **Alleluia, alleluia.**

Gospel *Jn 20: 19–23* On the evening of that first day of the week,
when the doors were locked, where the disciples were, for fear of
the Jews, Jesus came and stood in their midst and said to them,
"Peace be with you." When he had said this, he showed them
his hands and his side. The disciples rejoiced when they saw
the Lord. Jesus said to them again, "Peace be with you. As the
Father has sent me, so I send you." And when he had said this,
he breathed on them and said to them, "Receive the Holy Spirit.
Whose sins you forgive are forgiven them, and whose sins you
retain are retained."

Or: *Jn 14: 15–16, 23b–26* Jesus said to his disciples: "If you love me, you
will keep my commandments. And I will ask the Father, and he
will give you another Advocate to be with you always.

   "Whoever loves me will keep my word, and my Father will
love him, and we will come to him and make our dwelling with

him. Those who do not love me do not keep my words; yet the word you hear is not mine but that of the Father who sent me.

"I have told you this while I am with you. The Advocate, the Holy Spirit whom the Father will send in my name, will teach you everything and remind you of all that I told you."

Communion Antiphon Acts 2: 4, 11 **They were all filled with the Holy Spirit ◆ and spoke of the marvels of God, alleluia.**

Solemnities of the Lord
During Ordinary Time † YEAR C

THE SOLEMNITY OF

THE MOST HOLY TRINITY

Entrance Antiphon
**Blest be God the Father, ◆ and the Only Begotten Son of
God, ◆ and also the Holy Spirit, ◆ for he has shown us his
merciful love.**

First Reading   *Prv 8: 22–31*
Thus says the wisdom of God:
"The LORD possessed me, the beginning of his ways,
   the forerunner of his prodigies of long ago;
from of old I was poured forth,
   at the first, before the earth.
When there were no depths I was brought forth,
   when there were no fountains or springs of water;
before the mountains were settled into place,
   before the hills, I was brought forth;
while as yet the earth and fields were not made,
   nor the first clods of the world.

"When the Lord established the heavens I was there,
   when he marked out the vault over the face of the deep;
when he made firm the skies above,
   when he fixed fast the foundations of the earth;
when he set for the sea its limit,
   so that the waters should not transgress his command;
then was I beside him as his craftsman,

and I was his delight day by day,
  playing before him all the while,
    playing on the surface of his earth;
    and I found delight in the human race."

Responsorial Psalm   Ps 8: 4–5, 6–7, 8–9   based on SINE NOMINE

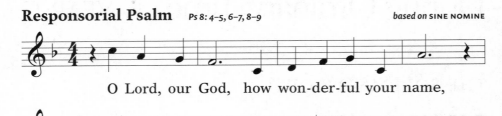

O Lord, our God, how won-der-ful your name,

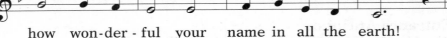

how won-der-ful your name in all the earth!

When I behold your heavens, the work of your fingers,
  the moon and the stars which you set in place—
What is man that you should be mindful of him,
  or the son of man that you should care for him? ℟

You have made him little less than the angels,
  and crowned him with glory and honor.
You have given him rule over the works of your hands,
  putting all things under his feet. ℟

All sheep and oxen,
  yes, and the beasts of the field,
The birds of the air, the fishes of the sea,
  and whatever swims the paths of the seas. ℟

Second Reading Rom 5: 1–5 Brothers and sisters: Therefore, since
we have been justified by faith, we have peace with God through
our Lord Jesus Christ, through whom we have gained access
by faith to this grace in which we stand, and we boast in hope
of the glory of God. Not only that, but we even boast of our
afflictions, knowing that affliction produces endurance, and
endurance, proven character, and proven character, hope, and
hope does not disappoint, because the love of God has been
poured out into our hearts through the Holy Spirit that has been
given to us.

Alleluia   cf. Rv 1: 8   Jim Hughes

Al-le-lu-ia   Al-le-lu-ia   Al - le-lu - ia.

Glory to the Father, the Son, and the Holy Spirit; / to God who is, who was, and who is to come.   **Alleluia, alleluia.**

Gospel Jn 16: 12–15 Jesus said to his disciples: "I have much more to tell you, but you cannot bear it now. But when he comes, the Spirit of truth, he will guide you to all truth. He will not speak on his own, but he will speak what he hears, and will declare to you the things that are coming. He will glorify me, because he will take from what is mine and declare it to you. Everything that the Father has is mine; for this reason I told you that he will take from what is mine and declare it to you."

Communion Antiphon Gal 4: 6 **Since you are children of God, ◆ God has sent into your hearts the Spirit of his Son, ◆ the Spirit who cries out: Abba, Father.**

THE SOLEMNITY OF THE

MOST HOLY BODY AND BLOOD OF CHRIST

(CORPUS CHRISTI)

Where the Solemnity of the Most Holy Body and Blood of Christ is not a Holyday of Obligation, it is assigned to the Sunday after the Most Holy Trinity as its proper day.

Entrance Antiphon cf. Ps 81 (80): 17 **He fed them with the finest wheat ◆ and satisfied them with honey from the rock.**

First Reading Gen 14: 18–20 In those days, Melchizedek, king of Salem, brought out bread and wine, and being a priest of God Most High, he blessed Abram with these words:

"Blessed be Abram by God Most High,
  the creator of heaven and earth;
and blessed be God Most High,
  who delivered your foes into your hand."
Then Abram gave him a tenth of everything.

Responsorial Psalm   Ps 110: 1, 2, 3, 4   Roger Holtz

You are a priest for ev - er,
in the line of Mel - chiz - e - dek.

The LORD said to my Lord: "Sit at my right hand
    till I make your enemies your footstool."   ℟

The scepter of your power the LORD will stretch forth
        from Zion:
    "Rule in the midst of your enemies."   ℟

"Yours is princely power in the day of your birth, in holy
        splendor;
    before the daystar, like the dew, I have begotten you."   ℟

The LORD has sworn, and he will not repent:
    "You are a priest forever, according to the order of
        Melchizedek."   ℟

Second Reading   1 Cor 11: 23–26   Brothers and sisters: I received from
the Lord what I also handed on to you, that the Lord Jesus, on
the night he was handed over, took bread, and, after he had
given thanks, broke it and said, "This is my body that is for you.
Do this in remembrance of me." In the same way also the cup,
after supper, saying, "This cup is the new covenant in my blood.
Do this, as often as you drink it, in remembrance of me." For as
often as you eat this bread and drink the cup, you proclaim the
death of the Lord until he comes.

Sequence

The sequence Laud, O Zion (Lauda Sion), *or the shorter form
beginning with the verse* Lo! the angels' food is given *may be sung
optionally before the* Alleluia. *For the shorter form, read only the
parts in brackets.*

Laud, O Zion, your salvation,
Laud with hymns of exultation,
   Christ, your king and shepherd true:

Bring him all the praise you know,
He is more than you bestow.
   Never can you reach his due.

Special theme for glad thanksgiving
Is the quick'ning and the living
   Bread today before you set:

From his hands of old partaken,
As we know, by faith unshaken,
   Where the Twelve at supper met.

Full and clear ring out your chanting,
Joy nor sweetest grace be wanting,
   From your heart let praises burst:

For today the feast is holden,
When the institution olden
   Of that supper was rehearsed.

Here the new law's new oblation,
By the new king's revelation,
   Ends the form of ancient rite:

Now the new the old effaces,
Truth away the shadow chases,
   Light dispels the gloom of night.

What he did at supper seated,
Christ ordained to be repeated,

His memorial ne'er to cease:

And his rule for guidance taking,
Bread and wine we hallow, making
   Thus our sacrifice of peace.

This the truth each Christian learns,
Bread into his flesh he turns,
   To his precious blood the wine:

Sight has fail'd, nor thought conceives,
But a dauntless faith believes,
   Resting on a pow'r divine.

Here beneath these signs are hidden
Priceless things to sense forbidden;
   Signs, not things are all we see:

Blood is poured and flesh is broken,
Yet in either wondrous token
   Christ entire we know to be.

Whoso of this food partakes,
Does not rend the Lord nor breaks;
   Christ is whole to all that tastes:

Thousands are, as one, receivers,
One, as thousands of believers,
   Eats of him who cannot waste.

Bad and good the feast are sharing,
Of what divers dooms preparing,
   Endless death, or endless life.

Life to these, to those damnation,
See how like participation
   Is with unlike issues rife.

When the sacrament is broken,
Doubt not, but believe 'tis spoken,

That each sever'd outward token
   doth the very whole contain.

Nought the precious gift divides,
Breaking but the sign betides
   Jesus still the same abides,
     still unbroken does remain.

(The shorter form of the sequence begins here.)
   [Lo! the angel's food is given
To the pilgrim who has striven;
   See the children's bread from heaven,
     which on dogs may not be spent.

Truth the ancient types fulfilling,
Isaac bound, a victim willing,
   Paschal lamb, its lifeblood spilling,
     manna to the fathers sent.

Very bread, good shepherd, tend us,
Jesu, of your love befriend us,
   You refresh us, you defend us,
   Your eternal goodness send us
In the land of life to see.

You who all things can and know,
Who on earth such food bestow,
   Grant us with your saints, though lowest,
   Where the heav'nly feast you show,
Fellow heirs and guests to be. Amen. Alleluia.]

Alleluia   Jn 6: 51   **Jim Hughes**

Al-le-lu-ia   Al-le-lu-ia   Al - le-lu - ia.

I am the living bread that came down from heaven, says
the Lord; / whoever eats this bread will live for ever.
Alleluia, alleluia.

Gospel Lk 9: 11b–17 Jesus spoke to the crowds about the kingdom of God, and he healed those who needed to be cured. As the day was drawing to a close, the Twelve approached him and said, "Dismiss the crowd so that they can go to the surrounding villages and farms and find lodging and provisions; for we are in a deserted place here." He said to them, "Give them some food yourselves." They replied, "Five loaves and two fish are all we have, unless we ourselves go and buy food for all these people." Now the men there numbered about five thousand. Then he said to his disciples, "Have them sit down in groups of about fifty." They did so and made them all sit down. Then taking the five loaves and the two fish, and looking up to heaven, he said the blessing over them, broke them, and gave them to the disciples to set before the crowd. They all ate and were satisfied. And when the leftover fragments were picked up, they filled twelve wicker baskets.

Communion Antiphon Jn 6: 57 Whoever eats my flesh and drinks my blood ◆ remains in me and I in him, says the Lord.

THE SOLEMNITY OF

THE MOST SACRED HEART OF JESUS

Entrance Antiphon Ps 33 (32): 11, 19 The designs of his Heart are from age to age, ◆ to rescue their souls from death, ◆ and to keep them alive in famine.

First Reading Ezekiel 34: 11–16 Thus says the Lord GOD: I myself will look after and tend my sheep. As a shepherd tends his flock when he finds himself among his scattered sheep, so will I tend my sheep. I will rescue them from every place where they were scattered when it was cloudy and dark. I will lead them out from among the peoples and gather them from the foreign lands; I will bring them back to their own country and pasture them upon the mountains of Israel in the land's ravines and all its inhabited places. In good pastures will I pasture them, and on the mountain heights of Israel shall be their grazing ground. There they shall lie down on good grazing ground, and in rich pastures shall they be pastured on the mountains of Israel. I myself will pasture my sheep; I myself will give them rest, says the Lord GOD. The lost I will seek out, the strayed I will bring back, the injured I will bind up, the sick I will heal, but the sleek and the strong I will destroy, shepherding them rightly.

Responsorial Psalm   Ps 23: 1–3a, 3b–4, 5, 6   *Elissa Krieg*

The Lord is my shep - herd; there is noth - ing I shall want.

The LORD is my shepherd; I shall not want.
  In verdant pastures he gives me repose;
beside restful waters he leads me;
  he refreshes my soul. ℟

He guides me in right paths
  for his name's sake.
Even though I walk in the dark valley
  I fear no evil; for you are at my side
with your rod and your staff
  that give me courage. ℟

You spread the table before me
  in the sight of my foes;
you anoint my head with oil;
  my cup overflows. ℟

Only goodness and kindness follow me
  all the days of my life;
and I shall dwell in the house of the LORD
  for years to come. ℟

Second Reading *Rom 5: 5b–11* Brothers and sisters: The love of God has been poured out into our hearts through the Holy Spirit that has been given to us. For Christ, while we were still helpless, died at the appointed time for the ungodly. Indeed, only with difficulty does one die for a just person, though perhaps for a good person one might even find courage to die. But God proves his love for us in that while we were still sinners Christ died for us. How much more then, since we are now justified by his blood, will we be saved through him from the wrath. Indeed, if, while we were enemies, we were reconciled to God through the death of his Son, how much more, once reconciled, will we be saved by his life. Not only that, but we also boast of God through our Lord Jesus Christ, through whom we have now received reconciliation.

Alleluia   Mt 11: 29ab   Jim Hughes

Al-le-lu-ia   Al-le-lu-ia   Al - le-lu - ia.

Take my yoke upon you, says the Lord; / and learn from me, for I am meek and humble of heart.   **Alleluia, alleluia.**

Or: Jn 10: 14   Joe Higginbotham

Al-le-lu - ia,   al - le - lu-ia,   al - le - lu - ia.

I am the good shepherd, says the Lord, / I know my sheep, and mine know me.   **Alleluia, alleluia.**

Gospel *Lk 15: 3–7* Jesus addressed this parable to the Pharisees and scribes: "What man among you having a hundred sheep and losing one of them would not leave the ninety-nine in the desert and go after the lost one until he finds it? And when he does find it, he sets it on his shoulders with great joy and, upon his arrival home, he calls together his friends and neighbors and says to them, 'Rejoice with me because I have found my lost sheep.' I tell you, in just the same way there will be more joy in heaven over one sinner who repents than over ninety-nine righteous people who have no need of repentance."

Communion Antiphon *cf. Jn 7: 37–38* **Thus says the Lord: ◆ Let whoever is thirsty come to me and drink. ◆ Streams of living water will flow ◆ from within the one who believes in me.**

Or: *Jn 19: 34* **One of the soldiers opened his side with a lance, ◆ and at once there came forth blood and water.**

Ordinary Time † YEAR C

SECOND SUNDAY IN ORDINARY TIME

Entrance Antiphon *Ps 66 (65): 4* **All the earth shall bow down before you, O God, ◆ and shall sing to you, ◆ shall sing to your name, O Most High!**

First Reading *Is 62: 1–5*
For Zion's sake I will not be silent,
    for Jerusalem's sake I will not be quiet,
until her vindication shines forth like the dawn
    and her victory like a burning torch.

Nations shall behold your vindication,
    and all the kings your glory;
you shall be called by a new name
    pronounced by the mouth of the Lord.
You shall be a glorious crown in the hand of the Lord,
    a royal diadem held by your God.
No more shall people call you "Forsaken,"
    or your land "Desolate,"
but you shall be called "My Delight,"
    and your land "Espoused."
For the Lord delights in you
    and makes your land his spouse.
As a young man marries a virgin,
    your Builder shall marry you;
and as a bridegroom rejoices in his bride
    so shall your God rejoice in you.

Responsorial Psalm   Ps 96: 1–2, 2–3, 7–8, 9–10

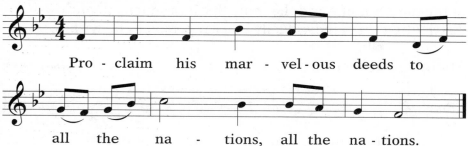

Pro - claim his mar - vel - ous deeds to all the na - tions, all the na - tions.

Sing to the LORD a new song;
  sing to the LORD, all you lands.
Sing to the LORD; bless his name.   ℟

Announce his salvation, day after day.
Tell his glory among the nations;
  among all peoples, his wondrous deeds.   ℟

Give to the LORD, you families of nations,
  give to the LORD glory and praise;
  give to the LORD the glory due his name!   ℟

Worship the LORD in holy attire.
  Tremble before him, all the earth;
say among the nations: The LORD is king.
  He governs the peoples with equity.   ℟

Second Reading   1 Cor 12: 4–11   Brothers and sisters: There are different kinds of spiritual gifts but the same Spirit; there are different forms of service but the same Lord; there are different workings but the same God who produces all of them in everyone. To each individual the manifestation of the Spirit is given for some benefit. To one is given through the Spirit the expression of wisdom; to another, the expression of knowledge according to the same Spirit; to another, faith by the same Spirit; to another, gifts of healing by the one Spirit; to another, mighty deeds; to another, prophecy; to another, discernment of spirits; to another, varieties of tongues; to another, interpretation of tongues. But one and the same Spirit produces all of these, distributing them individually to each person as he wishes.

Alleluia   *cf. 2 Thes 2: 14*   *Joe Higginbotham*

Al - le - lu - ia,   al - le - lu - ia,   al - le - lu - ia.

God has called us through the Gospel / to possess the glory of our Lord Jesus Christ.   **Alleluia alleluia.**

Gospel *Jn 2: 1–11* There was a wedding at Cana in Galilee, and the mother of Jesus was there. Jesus and his disciples were also invited to the wedding. When the wine ran short, the mother of Jesus said to him, "They have no wine." And Jesus said to her, "Woman, how does your concern affect me? My hour has not yet come." His mother said to the servers, "Do whatever he tells you." Now there were six stone water jars there for Jewish ceremonial washings, each holding twenty to thirty gallons. Jesus told the them, "Fill the jars with water." So they filled them to the brim. Then he told them, "Draw some out now and take it to the headwaiter." So they took it. And when the headwaiter tasted the water that had become wine, without knowing where it came from—although the servers who had drawn the water knew—, the headwaiter called the bridegroom and said to him, "Everyone serves good wine first, and then when people have drunk freely, an inferior one; but you have kept the good wine until now." Jesus did this as the beginning of his signs at Cana in Galilee and so revealed his glory, and his disciples began to believe in him.

Communion Antiphon *cf. Ps 23 (22): 5* **You have prepared a table before me, ◆ and how precious is the chalice that quenches my thirst.**

Or: *1 Jn 4: 16* **We have come to know and to believe ◆ in the love that God has for us.**

THIRD SUNDAY IN ORDINARY TIME

Entrance Antiphon *cf. Ps 96 (95): 1, 6* O sing a new song to the Lord;
♦ sing to the Lord, all the earth. ♦ In his presence are majesty
and splendor, ♦ strength and honor in his holy place.

First Reading *Neh 8: 2–4a, 5–6, 8–10* Ezra the priest brought the law
before the assembly, which consisted of men, women, and those
children old enough to understand. Standing at one end of the
open place that was before the Water Gate, he read out of the
book from daybreak till midday, in the presence of the men, the
women, and those children old enough to understand; and all the
people listened attentively to the book of the law. Ezra the scribe
stood on a wooden platform that had been made for the occasion.
He opened the scroll so that all the people might see it—for he was
standing higher up than any of the people—; and, as he opened
it, all the people rose. Ezra blessed the LORD, the great God, and
all the people, their hands raised high, answered, "Amen, amen!"
Then they bowed down and prostrated themselves before the
LORD, their faces to the ground. Ezra read plainly from the book
of the law of God, interpreting it so that all could understand what
was read. Then Nehemiah, that is, His Excellency, and Ezra the
priest-scribe and the Levites who were instructing the people said
to all the people: "Today is holy to the LORD your God. Do not be
sad, and do not weep"—for all the people were weeping as they
heard the words of the law. He said further: "Go, eat rich foods and
drink sweet drinks, and allot portions to those who had nothing
prepared; for today is holy to our LORD. Do not be saddened this
day, for rejoicing in the LORD must be your strength!"

Responsorial Psalm *Ps 19: 8, 9, 10, 15* *Beverly McDevitt*

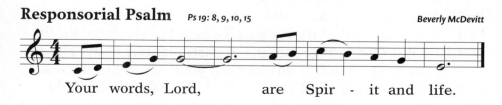

Your words, Lord, are Spir - it and life.

The law of the LORD is perfect,
    refreshing the soul;

The decree of the LORD is trustworthy,
   giving wisdom to the simple.   ℟

The precepts of the LORD are right,
   rejoicing the heart;
The command of the LORD is clear,
   enlightening the eye.   ℟

The fear of the LORD is pure,
   enduring forever;
The ordinances of the LORD are true,
   all of them just.   ℟

Let the words of my mouth and the thought of my heart
   find favor before you,
O LORD, my rock and my redeemer.   ℟

Second Reading   *1 Cor 12: 12–30 or 12: 12–14, 27*

For the shorter form, read only the parts in brackets.

[Brothers and sisters: As a body is one though it has many parts, and all the parts of the body, though many, are one body, so also Christ. For in one Spirit we were all baptized into one body, whether Jews or Greeks, slaves or free persons, and we were all given to drink of one Spirit.

Now the body is not a single part, but many.] If a foot should say, "Because I am not a hand I do not belong to the body," it does not for this reason belong any less to the body. Or if an ear should say, "Because I am not an eye I do not belong to the body," it does not for this reason belong any less to the body. If the whole body were an eye, where would the hearing be? If the whole body were hearing, where would the sense of smell be? But as it is, God placed the parts, each one of them, in the body as he intended. If they were all one part, where would the body be? But as it is, there are many parts, yet one body. The eye cannot say to the hand, "I do not need you," nor again the head to the feet, "I do not need you." Indeed, the parts of the body that seem to be weaker are all the more necessary, and those parts of the body that we consider less honorable we surround with greater honor, and our less presentable parts are treated with greater propriety, whereas our more presentable parts do not need this. But God has so constructed the body as to give greater honor to a part that is without it, so that there may be no division in the body, but that the parts may have the same concern for one another. If one part suffers, all the parts suffer with it; if one part is honored, all the parts share its joy.

Now [you are Christ's body, and individually parts of it.] Some people God has designated in the church to be, first, apostles; second, prophets; third, teachers; then, mighty deeds; then gifts of healing, assistance, administration, and varieties of tongues. Are all apostles? Are all prophets? Are all teachers? Do all work mighty deeds? Do all have gifts of healing? Do all speak in tongues? Do all interpret?

Alleluia   *cf. Lk 4: 18*   *Joe Higginbotham*

Al - le - lu - ia,   al - le - lu - ia,   al - le - lu - ia.

The Lord sent me to bring glad tidings to the poor, / and to proclaim liberty to captives. **Alleluia, alleluia.**

Gospel *Lk 1: 1–4; 4: 14–21* Since many have undertaken to compile a narrative of the events that have been fulfilled among us, just as those who were eyewitnesses from the beginning and ministers of the word have handed them down to us, I too have decided, after investigating everything accurately anew, to write it down in an orderly sequence for you, most excellent Theophilus, so that you may realize the certainty of the teachings you have received.

Jesus returned to Galilee in the power of the Spirit, and news of him spread throughout the whole region. He taught in their synagogues and was praised by all. He came to Nazareth, where he had grown up, and went according to his custom into the synagogue on the sabbath day. He stood up to read and was handed a scroll of the prophet Isaiah. He unrolled the scroll and found the passage where it was written:

The Spirit of the Lord is upon me,

because he has anointed me
to bring glad tidings to the poor.
He has sent me to proclaim liberty to captives
and recovery of sight to the blind,
to let the oppressed go free,
and to proclaim a year acceptable to the Lord.

Rolling up the scroll, he handed it back to the attendant and sat down, and the eyes of all in the synagogue looked intently at him. He said to them, "Today this Scripture passage is fulfilled in your hearing."

Communion Antiphon *cf. Ps 34 (33): 6* Look toward the Lord and be radiant; ✦ let your faces not be abashed.

Or: *Jn 8: 12* I am the light of the world, says the Lord; ✦ whoever follows me will not walk in darkness, ✦ but will have the light of life.

FOURTH SUNDAY IN ORDINARY TIME

Entrance Antiphon *Ps 106 (105): 47* Save us, O Lord our God! ✦ And gather us from the nations, ✦ to give thanks to your holy name, ✦ and make it our glory to praise you.

First Reading *Jer 1: 4–5, 17–19*
The word of the LORD came to me, saying:
    Before I formed you in the womb I knew you,
        before you were born I dedicated you,
        a prophet to the nations I appointed you.

    But do you gird your loins;
        stand up and tell them
        all that I command you.
    Be not crushed on their account,
        as though I would leave you crushed before them;
    for it is I this day
        who have made you a fortified city,

a pillar of iron, a wall of brass,
  against the whole land:
against Judah's kings and princes,
  against its priests and people.
They will fight against you but not prevail over you,
  for I am with you to deliver you, says the LORD.

Responsorial Psalm   Ps 71: 1–2, 3–4, 5–6, 15–17   *Joe Higginbotham*

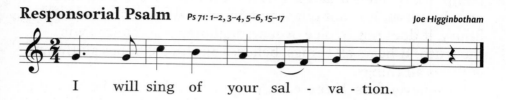

I   will sing of   your sal - va - tion.

In you, O LORD, I take refuge;
  let me never be put to shame.
In your justice rescue me, and deliver me;
  incline your ear to me, and save me. ℟

Be my rock of refuge,
  a stronghold to give me safety,
  for you are my rock and my fortress.
O my God, rescue me from the hand of the wicked. ℟

For you are my hope, O Lord;
  my trust, O God, from my youth.
On you I depend from birth;
  from my mother's womb you are my strength. ℟

My mouth shall declare your justice,
  day by day your salvation.
O God, you have taught me from my youth,
  and till the present I proclaim your wondrous deeds. ℟

Second Reading   1 Cor 12: 31- 13: 13 or 13: 4–13
For the shorter form, read only the parts in brackets.
[Brothers and sisters:] Strive eagerly for the greatest spiritual
gifts. But I shall show you a still more excellent way.
   If I speak in human and angelic tongues, but do not have
love, I am a resounding gong or a clashing cymbal. And if I

have the gift of prophecy, and comprehend all mysteries and all knowledge; if I have all faith so as to move mountains, but do not have love, I am nothing. If I give away everything I own, and if I hand my body over so that I may boast, but do not have love, I gain nothing.

[Love is patient, love is kind. It is not jealous, it is not pompous, It is not inflated, it is not rude, it does not seek its own interests, it is not quick-tempered, it does not brood over injury, it does not rejoice over wrongdoing but rejoices with the truth. It bears all things, believes all things, hopes all things, endures all things.

Love never fails. If there are prophecies, they will be brought to nothing; if tongues, they will cease; if knowledge, it will be brought to nothing. For we know partially and we prophesy partially, but when the perfect comes, the partial will pass away. When I was a child, I used to talk as a child, think as a child, reason as a child; when I became a man, I put aside childish things. At present we see indistinctly, as in a mirror, but then face to face. At present I know partially; then I shall know fully, as I am fully known. So faith, hope, love remain, these three; but the greatest of these is love.]

Alleluia Lk 4: 18   *Joe Higginbotham*

Al - le - lu - ia,   al - le - lu - ia,   al - le - lu - ia.

The Lord sent me to bring glad tidings to the poor, / to proclaim liberty to captives. **Alleluia, alleluia.**

Gospel Lk 4: 21–30 Jesus began speaking in the synagogue, saying: "Today this Scripture passage is fulfilled in your hearing." And all spoke highly of him and were amazed at the gracious words that came from his mouth. They also asked, "Isn't this the son of Joseph?" He said to them, "Surely you will quote me this proverb, 'Physician, cure yourself,' and say, 'Do here in your native place the things that we heard were done in Capernaum.'" And he said, "Amen, I say to you, no prophet is accepted in his own native place. Indeed, I tell you, there were many widows in Israel in the days of Elijah when the sky was closed for three and a half years and a severe famine spread over the entire land. It was to none of these that Elijah was sent, but only to a widow in Zarephath in the land of Sidon. Again, there were many lepers in Israel during the time of Elisha the prophet; yet not one of them was cleansed, but only Naaman the Syrian." When the people in the synagogue heard this, they were all filled with fury. They rose up, drove him out of the town, and led him to the brow of the hill on which their town had been built, to hurl him down headlong. But Jesus passed through the midst of them and went away.

Communion Antiphon *cf. Ps 31 (30): 17–18* **Let your face shine on your servant. ◆ Save me in your merciful love. ◆ O Lord, let me never be put to shame, for I call on you.**

Or: *Mt 5: 3–4* **Blessed are the poor in spirit, ◆ for theirs is the Kingdom of Heaven. ◆ Blessed are the meek, for they shall possess the land.**

FIFTH SUNDAY IN ORDINARY TIME

Entrance Antiphon *Ps 95 (94): 6–7* **O come, let us worship God ◆ and bow low before the God who made us, ◆ for he is the Lord our God.**

First Reading *Is 6: 1–2a, 3–8* In the year King Uzziah died, I saw the Lord seated on a high and lofty throne, with the train of his garment filling the temple. Seraphim were stationed above.

They cried one to the other, "Holy, holy, holy is the LORD of hosts! All the earth is filled with his glory!" At the sound of that cry, the frame of the door shook and the house was filled with smoke.

Then I said, "Woe is me, I am doomed! For I am a man of unclean lips, living among a people of unclean lips; yet my eyes have seen the King, the LORD of hosts!" Then one of the seraphim flew to me, holding an ember that he had taken with tongs from the altar.

He touched my mouth with it, and said, "See, now that this has touched your lips, your wickedness is removed, your sin purged."

Then I heard the voice of the Lord saying, "Whom shall I send? Who will go for us?" "Here I am," I said; "send me!"

Responsorial Psalm   Ps 138: 1–2, 2–3, 4–5, 7–8   *Tim Wells*

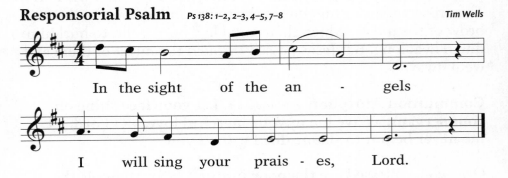

In the sight of the an - gels I will sing your prais - es, Lord.

I will give thanks to you, O LORD, with all my heart,
    for you have heard the words of my mouth;
    in the presence of the angels I will sing your praise;
I will worship at your holy temple
    and give thanks to your name. ℟

Because of your kindness and your truth;
    for you have made great above all things
    your name and your promise.
When I called, you answered me;
    you built up strength within me. ℟

All the kings of the earth shall give thanks to you, O LORD,
    when they hear the words of your mouth;
and they shall sing of the ways of the LORD:
    "Great is the glory of the LORD." ℟

Your right hand saves me.
    The LORD will complete what he has done for me;
your kindness, O LORD, endures forever;
    forsake not the work of your hands. ℟

Second Reading   *1 Cor 15: 1–11 or 15: 3–8, 11*

For the shorter form, read only the parts in brackets.
I am reminding you, [brothers and sisters,] of the gospel I
preached to you, which you indeed received and in which you
also stand. Through it you are also being saved, if you hold fast
to the word I preached to you, unless you believed in vain. For
[I handed on to you as of first importance what I also received:
that Christ died for our sins in accordance with the Scriptures;
that he was buried; that he was raised on the third day in
accordance with the Scriptures; that he appeared to Cephas,
then to the Twelve. After that, Christ appeared to more than five
hundred brothers at once, most of whom are still living, though
some have fallen asleep. After that he appeared to James, then
to all the apostles. Last of all, as to one born abnormally, he
appeared to me.] For I am the least of the apostles, not fit to be
called an apostle, because I persecuted the church of God. But
by the grace of God I am what I am, and his grace to me has not
been ineffective. Indeed, I have toiled harder than all of them;
not I, however, but the grace of God that is with me. [Therefore,
whether it be I or they, so we preach and so you believed.]

Alleluia   *Mt 4: 19*   *Joe Higginbotham*

Al - le - lu - ia,   al - le - lu - ia,   al - le - lu - ia.

Come after me / and I will make you fishers of men.
Alleluia, alleluia.

Gospel   *Lk 5: 1–11*   While the crowd was pressing in on Jesus and
listening to the word of God, he was standing by the Lake
of Gennesaret. He saw two boats there alongside the lake;
the fishermen had disembarked and were washing their nets.
Getting into one of the boats, the one belonging to Simon, he
asked him to put out a short distance from the shore. Then he
sat down and taught the crowds from the boat. After he had
finished speaking, he said to Simon, "Put out into deep water
and lower your nets for a catch." Simon said in reply, "Master,

we have worked hard all night and have caught nothing, but at your command I will lower the nets." When they had done this, they caught a great number of fish and their nets were tearing. They signaled to their partners in the other boat to come to help them. They came and filled both boats so that the boats were in danger of sinking. When Simon Peter saw this, he fell at the knees of Jesus and said, "Depart from me, Lord, for I am a sinful man." For astonishment at the catch of fish they had made seized him and all those with him, and likewise James and John, the sons of Zebedee, who were partners of Simon. Jesus said to Simon, "Do not be afraid; from now on you will be catching men." When they brought their boats to the shore, they left everything and followed him.

Communion Antiphon *cf. Ps 107 (106): 8-9* Let them thank the Lord for his mercy, ◆ his wonders for the children of men, ◆ for he satisfies the thirsty soul, ◆ and the hungry he fills with good things.

Or: *Mt 5: 5-6* Blessed are those who mourn, for they shall be consoled. ◆ Blessed are those who hunger and thirst for righteousness, ◆ for they shall have their fill.

SIXTH SUNDAY IN ORDINARY TIME

Entrance Antiphon *cf. Ps 31 (30): 3-4* Be my protector, O God, ◆ a mighty stronghold to save me. ◆ For you are my rock, my stronghold! ◆ Lead me, guide me, for the sake of your name.

First Reading *Jer 17: 5-8*
Thus says the LORD:
   Cursed is the one who trusts in human beings,
      who seeks his strength in flesh,
      whose heart turns away from the LORD.
   He is like a barren bush in the desert
      that enjoys no change of season,

but stands in a lava waste,
   a salt and empty earth.
Blessed is the one who trusts in the LORD,
   whose hope is the LORD.
He is like a tree planted beside the waters
   that stretches out its roots to the stream:
it fears not the heat when it comes;
   its leaves stay green;
in the year of drought it shows no distress,
   but still bears fruit.

Responsorial Psalm   *Ps 1: 1–2, 3, 4, 6*   *Joe Higginbotham*

Bless - ed are they who hope in the Lord.

Blessed the man who follows not
   the counsel of the wicked,
nor walks in the way of sinners,
   nor sits in the company of the insolent,
but delights in the law of the LORD
   and meditates on his law day and night. ℟

He is like a tree
   planted near running water,
that yields its fruit in due season,
   and whose leaves never fade.
Whatever he does, prospers. ℟

Not so the wicked, not so;
   they are like chaff which the wind drives away.
For the LORD watches over the way of the just,
   but the way of the wicked vanishes. ℟

Second Reading   *1 Cor 15: 12, 16–20*   Brothers and sisters: If Christ is preached as raised from the dead, how can some among you say there is no resurrection of the dead? If the dead are not raised, neither has Christ been raised, and if Christ has not been raised, your faith is vain; you are still in your sins. Then those who have fallen asleep in Christ have perished. If for this life only we have hoped in Christ, we are the most pitiable people of all.

But now Christ has been raised from the dead, the firstfruits of those who have fallen asleep.

Alleluia *Lk 6: 23ab*   *Joe Higginbotham*

Al - le - lu - ia,   al - le - lu - ia,   al - le - lu - ia.

Rejoice and be glad; / your reward will be great in heaven.
Alleluia, alleluia.

Gospel *Lk 6: 17, 20–26* Jesus came down with the Twelve and stood on a stretch of level ground with a great crowd of his disciples and a large number of the people from all Judea and Jerusalem and the coastal region of Tyre and Sidon. And raising his eyes toward his disciples he said:
    "Blessed are you who are poor,
        for the kingdom of God is yours.
    Blessed are you who are now hungry,
        for you will be satisfied.
    Blessed are you who are now weeping,
        for you will laugh.
    Blessed are you when people hate you,
        and when they exclude and insult you,
        and denounce your name as evil
        on account of the Son of Man.
Rejoice and leap for joy on that day! Behold, your reward will be great in heaven. For their ancestors treated the prophets in the same way.
    But woe to you who are rich,
        for you have received your consolation.
    Woe to you who are filled now,
        for you will be hungry.
    Woe to you who laugh now,

for you will grieve and weep.
Woe to you when all speak well of you,
for their ancestors treated the false prophets in this way."

Communion Antiphon *cf. Ps 78 (77): 29–30* **They ate and had their fill,
◆ and what they craved the Lord gave them; ◆ they were not
disappointed in what they craved.**

Or: *Jn 3: 16* **God so loved the world ◆ that he gave his Only
Begotten Son, ◆ so that all who believe in him may not perish,
◆ but may have eternal life.**

SEVENTH SUNDAY IN ORDINARY TIME

Entrance Antiphon *Ps 13 (12): 6* **O Lord, I trust in your merciful
love. ◆ My heart will rejoice in your salvation. ◆ I will sing to
the Lord who has been bountiful with me.**

First Reading *1 Sm 26: 2, 7–9, 12–13, 22–23* In those days, Saul went down
to the desert of Ziph with three thousand picked men of Israel,
to search for David in the desert of Ziph. So David and Abishai
went among Saul's soldiers by night and found Saul lying asleep
within the barricade, with his spear thrust into the ground at his
head and Abner and his men sleeping around him.

Abishai whispered to David: "God has delivered your enemy
into your grasp this day. Let me nail him to the ground with one
thrust of the spear; I will not need a second thrust!" But David
said to Abishai, "Do not harm him, for who can lay hands on the
LORD's anointed and remain unpunished?" So David took the
spear and the water jug from their place at Saul's head, and they
got away without anyone's seeing or knowing or awakening. All
remained asleep, because the LORD had put them into a deep
slumber.

Going across to an opposite slope, David stood on a remote
hilltop at a great distance from Abner, son of Ner, and the
troops. He said: "Here is the king's spear. Let an attendant come
over to get it. The LORD will reward each man for his justice

and faithfulness. Today, though the LORD delivered you into my grasp, I would not harm the LORD's anointed."

Responsorial Psalm   Ps 103: 1–2, 3–4, 8, 10, 12–13   Vince Ambrosetti

The Lord is kind and mer-ci-ful.

Bless the LORD, O my soul;
  and all my being, bless his holy name.
Bless the LORD, O my soul,
  and forget not all his benefits. ℟

He pardons all your iniquities,
  heals all your ills.
He redeems your life from destruction,
  crowns you with kindness and compassion. ℟

Merciful and gracious is the LORD,
  slow to anger and abounding in kindness.
Not according to our sins does he deal with us,
  nor does he requite us according to our crimes. ℟

As far as the east is from the west,
  so far has he put our transgressions from us.
As a father has compassion on his children,
  so the LORD has compassion on those who fear him. ℟

Second Reading 1 Cor 15: 45–49 Brothers and sisters: It is written, *The first man, Adam, became a living being,* the last Adam a life-giving spirit. But the spiritual was not first; rather the natural and then the spiritual. The first man was from the earth, earthly; the second man, from heaven. As was the earthly one, so also are the earthly, and as is the heavenly one, so also are the heavenly. Just as we have borne the image of the earthly one, we shall also bear the image of the heavenly one.

Alleluia *Jn 13: 34*   *Joe Higginbotham*

Al - le - lu - ia,   al - le - lu - ia,   al - le - lu - ia.

I give you a new commandment, says the Lord: / love one another as I have loved you.   **Alleluia, alleluia.**

Gospel *Lk 6: 27–38* Jesus said to his disciples: "To you who hear I say, love your enemies, do good to those who hate you, bless those who curse you, pray for those who mistreat you. To the person who strikes you on one cheek, offer the other one as well, and from the person who takes your cloak, do not withhold even your tunic. Give to everyone who asks of you, and from the one who takes what is yours do not demand it back. Do to others as you would have them do to you. For if you love those who love you, what credit is that to you? Even sinners love those who love them. And if you do good to those who do good to you, what credit is that to you? Even sinners do the same. If you lend money to those from whom you expect repayment, what credit is that to you? Even sinners lend to sinners, and get back the same amount. But rather, love your enemies and do good to them, and lend expecting nothing back; then your reward will be great and you will be children of the Most High, for he himself is kind to the ungrateful and the wicked. Be merciful, just as your Father is merciful.

"Stop judging and you will not be judged. Stop condemning and you will not be condemned. Forgive and you will be forgiven. Give, and gifts will be given to you; a good measure, packed together, shaken down, and overflowing, will be poured into your lap. For the measure with which you measure will in return be measured out to you."

Communion Antiphon *Ps 9: 2–3* I will recount all your wonders, ◆ I will rejoice in you and be glad, ◆ and sing psalms to your name, O Most High.

Or: Jn 11: 27 **Lord, I have come to believe that you are the Christ,**
◆ the Son of the living God, who is coming into this world.

EIGHTH SUNDAY IN ORDINARY TIME

Entrance Antiphon *cf. Ps 18 (17): 19–20* **The Lord became my**
protector. ◆ He brought me out to a place of freedom; ◆ he
saved me because he delighted in me.

First Reading *Sir 27: 4–7*

When a sieve is shaken, the husks appear;
    so do one's faults when one speaks.
As the test of what the potter molds is in the furnace,
    so in tribulation is the test of the just.
The fruit of a tree shows the care it has had;
    so too does one's speech disclose the bent of one's mind.
Praise no one before he speaks,
    for it is then that people are tested.

Responsorial Psalm *Ps 92: 2–3, 13–14, 15–16*   *Bill Svarda*

Lord, it is good to give thanks to you.

It is good to give thanks to the LORD,
    to sing praise to your name, Most High,
To proclaim your kindness at dawn
    and your faithfulness throughout the night. ℟

The just one shall flourish like the palm tree,
    like a cedar of Lebanon shall he grow.
They that are planted in the house of the LORD
    shall flourish in the courts of our God. ℟

They shall bear fruit even in old age;
    vigorous and sturdy shall they be,
Declaring how just is the LORD,
    my rock, in whom there is no wrong. ℟

Second Reading *1 Cor 15: 54-58* Brothers and sisters: When this which is corruptible clothes itself with incorruptibility and this which is mortal clothes itself with immortality, then the word that is written shall come about:
Death is swallowed up in victory.
    Where, O death, is your victory?
    Where, O death, is your sting?
The sting of death is sin, and the power of sin is the law. But thanks be to God who gives us the victory through our Lord Jesus Christ.

Therefore, my beloved brothers and sisters, be firm, steadfast, always fully devoted to the work of the Lord, knowing that in the Lord your labor is not in vain.

Alleluia   *Phil 2: 15d, 16a*   *Vince Ambrosetti*

Al-le-lu-ia, al - le - lu - ia, al - le - lu - ia, al - le - lu - ia.

Al - le - lu - ia, al - le - lu - ia, al - le - lu - ia.

Shine like lights in the world / as you hold on to the word of life. **Alleluia, alleluia.**

Gospel *Lk 6: 39-45* Jesus told his disciples a parable, "Can a blind person guide a blind person? Will not both fall into a pit? No disciple is superior to the teacher; but when fully trained, every disciple will be like his teacher. Why do you notice the splinter in your brother's eye, but do not perceive the wooden beam in your own? How can you say to your brother, 'Brother, let me remove that splinter in your eye,' when you do not even notice the wooden beam in your own eye? You hypocrite! Remove the wooden beam from your eye first; then you will see clearly to remove the splinter in your brother's eye.

"A good tree does not bear rotten fruit, nor does a rotten tree bear good fruit. For every tree is known by its own fruit. For people do not pick figs from thorn bushes, nor do they gather grapes from brambles. A good person out of the store of goodness in his heart produces good, but an evil person out of a store of evil produces evil; for from the fullness of the heart the mouth speaks."

Communion Antiphon *cf. Ps 13 (12): 6* I will sing to the Lord who has been bountiful with me, ◆ sing psalms to the name of the Lord Most High.

Or: *Mt 28: 20* Behold, I am with you always, ◆ even to the end of the age, says the Lord.

NINTH SUNDAY IN ORDINARY TIME

Entrance Antiphon *cf. Ps 25 (24): 16, 18* Turn to me and have mercy on me, O Lord, ◆ for I am alone and poor. ◆ See my lowliness and suffering ◆ and take away all my sins, my God.

First Reading *1 Kgs 8: 41-43* In those days, Solomon prayed in the temple, saying, "To the foreigner, who is not of your people Israel, but comes from a distant land to honor you—since they will learn of your great name and your mighty hand and your outstretched arm—, when he comes and prays toward this temple, listen from your heavenly dwelling. Do all that foreigner asks of you, that all the peoples of the earth may know your name, may fear you as do your people Israel, and may acknowledge that this temple which I have built is dedicated to your honor."

Responsorial Psalm *Ps 117: 1, 2*   Joe Higginbotham

Go out to all the world and tell the Good News.

Go out to all the world and tell the Good News.

Or: ℟ **Alleluia.**

Praise the LORD, all you nations;
 glorify him, all you peoples! ℟

For steadfast is his kindness toward us,
 and the fidelity of the LORD endures forever. ℟

Second Reading *Gal 1: 1–2, 6–10* Paul, an apostle not from human beings nor through a human being but through Jesus Christ and God the Father who raised him from the dead, and all the brothers who are with me, to the churches of Galatia.

I am amazed that you are so quickly forsaking the one who called you by the grace of Christ for a different gospel—not that there is another. But there are some who are disturbing you and wish to pervert the gospel of Christ. But even if we or an angel from heaven should preach to you a gospel other than the one that we preached to you, let that one be accursed! As we have said before, and now I say again, if anyone preaches to you a gospel other than what you have received, let that one be accursed!

Am I now currying favor with humans or with God? Or am I seeking to please people? If I were still trying to please people, I would not be a slave of Christ.

Alleluia   Jn 3:16

Vince Ambrosetti

Al-le-lu-ia, al-le-lu-ia, al-le-lu-ia, al-le-lu-ia.

Al-le-lu-ia, al-le-lu-ia, al-le-lu - ia.

God so loved the world that he gave his only Son, / so
that everyone who believes in him might have eternal life.
Alleluia alleluia.

Gospel Lk 7: 1–10 When Jesus had finished all his words to the
people, he entered Capernaum. A centurion there had a slave
who was ill and about to die, and he was valuable to him. When
he heard about Jesus, he sent elders of the Jews to him, asking
him to come and save the life of his slave. They approached
Jesus and strongly urged him to come, saying, "He deserves to
have you do this for him, for he loves our nation and built the
synagogue for us." And Jesus went with them, but when he was
only a short distance from the house, the centurion sent friends
to tell him, "Lord, do not trouble yourself, for I am not worthy
to have you enter under my roof. Therefore, I did not consider
myself worthy to come to you; but say the word and let my
servant be healed. For I too am a person subject to authority,
with soldiers subject to me. And I say to one, 'Go,' and he goes;
and to another, 'Come here,' and he comes; and to my slave, 'Do
this,' and he does it." When Jesus heard this he was amazed at
him and, turning, said to the crowd following him, "I tell you,
not even in Israel have I found such faith." When the messengers
returned to the house, they found the slave in good health.

Communion Antiphon cf. Ps 17 (16): 6 To you I call, for you will
surely heed me, O God; ◆ turn your ear to me; hear my words.

Or: Mk 11: 23, 24 Amen, I say to you: Whatever you ask for in prayer, ◆ believe you will receive it, ◆ and it will be yours, says the Lord.

TENTH SUNDAY IN ORDINARY TIME

Entrance Antiphon *cf. Ps 27 (26): 1–2* The Lord is my light and my salvation; whom shall I fear? ◆ The Lord is the stronghold of my life; whom should I dread? ◆ When those who do evil draw near, they stumble and fall.

First Reading *1 Kgs 17: 17–24* Elijah went to Zarephath of Sidon to the house of a widow. The son of the mistress of the house fell sick, and his sickness grew more severe until he stopped breathing. So she said to Elijah, "Why have you done this to me, O man of God? Have you come to me to call attention to my guilt and to kill my son?" Elijah said to her, "Give me your son." Taking him from her lap, he carried the son to the upper room where he was staying, and put him on his bed. Elijah called out to the LORD: "O LORD, my God, will you afflict even the widow with whom I am staying by killing her son?" Then he stretched himself out upon the child three times and called out to the LORD: "O LORD, my God, let the life breath return to the body of this child." The LORD heard the prayer of Elijah; the life breath returned to the child's body and he revived. Taking the child, Elijah brought him down into the house from the upper room and gave him to his mother. Elijah said to her, "See! Your son is alive." The woman replied to Elijah, "Now indeed I know that you are a man of God. The word of the LORD comes truly from your mouth."

Responsorial Psalm   Ps 30: 2, 4, 5–6, 11, 12, 13   Joe Higginbotham

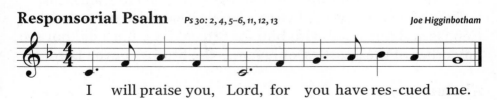

I will praise you, Lord, for you have res-cued me.

I will extol you, O LORD, for you drew me clear
and did not let my enemies rejoice over me.

O LORD, you brought me up from the netherworld;
   you preserved me from among those going down into
     the pit. ℟

Sing praise to the LORD, you his faithful ones,
   and give thanks to his holy name.
For his anger lasts but a moment;
   a lifetime, his good will.
At nightfall, weeping enters in,
   but with the dawn, rejoicing. ℟

Hear, O LORD, and have pity on me;
   O LORD, be my helper.
You changed my mourning into dancing;
   O LORD, my God, forever will I give you thanks. ℟

Second Reading *Gal 1: 11–19* I want you to know, brothers and
sisters, that the gospel preached by me is not of human origin.
For I did not receive it from a human being, nor was I taught it,
but it came through a revelation of Jesus Christ.

For you heard of my former way of life in Judaism, how
I persecuted the church of God beyond measure and tried to
destroy it, and progressed in Judaism beyond many of my
contemporaries among my race, since I was even more a zealot
for my ancestral traditions. But when God, who from my
mother's womb had set me apart and called me through his grace,
was pleased to reveal his Son to me, so that I might proclaim him
to the Gentiles, I did not immediately consult flesh and blood,
nor did I go up to Jerusalem to those who were apostles before
me; rather, I went into Arabia and then returned to Damascus.

Then after three years I went up to Jerusalem to confer with
Cephas and remained with him for fifteen days. But I did not see
any other of the apostles, only James the brother of the Lord.

Alleluia   *Lk 7: 16*   *Vince Ambrosetti*

Al-le-lu-ia,   al - le - lu - ia,   al - le - lu - ia,   al - le - lu - ia.

Al - le - lu - ia, al - le - lu - ia, al - le - lu - ia.

A great prophet has risen in our midst. / God has visited his people. **Alleluia, alleluia.**

Gospel Lk 7: 11–17 Jesus journeyed to a city called Nain, and his disciples and a large crowd accompanied him. As he drew near to the gate of the city, a man who had died was being carried out, the only son of his mother, and she was a widow. A large crowd from the city was with her. When the Lord saw her, he was moved with pity for her and said to her, "Do not weep." He stepped forward and touched the coffin; at this the bearers halted, and he said, "Young man, I tell you, arise!" The dead man sat up and began to speak, and Jesus gave him to his mother. Fear seized them all, and they glorified God, exclaiming, "A great prophet has arisen in our midst," and "God has visited his people." This report about him spread through the whole of Judea and in all the surrounding region.

Communion Antiphon Ps 18 (17): 3 **The Lord is my rock, my fortress, and my deliverer; ✦ my God is my saving strength.**

Or: 1 Jn 4: 16 **God is love, and whoever abides in love ✦ abides in God, and God in him.**

ELEVENTH SUNDAY IN ORDINARY TIME

Entrance Antiphon cf. Ps 27 (26): 7, 9 **O Lord, hear my voice, for I have called to you; be my help. ✦ Do not abandon or forsake me, O God, my Savior!**

First Reading 2 Sm 12: 7–10, 13 Nathan said to David: "Thus says the LORD God of Israel: 'I anointed you king of Israel. I rescued you from the hand of Saul. I gave you your lord's house and your lord's wives for your own. I gave you the house of Israel and of Judah. And if this were not enough, I could count up for you still more. Why have you spurned the LORD and done evil in his sight? You have cut down Uriah the Hittite with the sword; you took his wife as your own, and him you killed with the sword of the Ammonites. Now, therefore, the sword shall never depart from your house, because you have despised me and have taken the wife of Uriah to be your wife.'" Then David said to Nathan, "I have sinned against the LORD." Nathan answered David: "The LORD on his part has forgiven your sin: you shall not die."

Responsorial Psalm   Ps 32: 1–2, 5, 7, 11   Joe Higginbotham

Lord, for - give the wrong I have done.

Blessed is the one whose fault is taken away,
     whose sin is covered.
Blessed the man to whom the LORD imputes not guilt,
     in whose spirit there is no guile. ℟

I acknowledged my sin to you,
     my guilt I covered not.
I said, "I confess my faults to the LORD,"
     and you took away the guilt of my sin. ℟

You are my shelter; from distress you will preserve me;
     with glad cries of freedom you will ring me round. ℟

Be glad in the LORD and rejoice, you just;
     exult, all you upright of heart. ℟

Second Reading Gal 2: 16, 19–21 Brothers and sisters: We who know that a person is not justified by works of the law but through faith in Jesus Christ, even we have believed in Christ Jesus that we may be justified by faith in Christ and not by works of the law, because by works of the law no one will be justified. For through the law I died to the law, that I might live for God. I have been crucified with Christ; yet I live, no longer I, but Christ lives in me; insofar as I now live in the flesh, I live by faith in the Son of God who has loved me and given himself up for me. I do not nullify the grace of God; for if justification comes through the law, then Christ died for nothing.

Alleluia   *1 Jn 4: 10b*   *Vince Ambrosetti*

Al-le-lu-ia, al-le-lu-ia, al-le-lu-ia, al-le-lu-ia.

Al-le-lu-ia, al-le-lu-ia, al-le-lu - ia.

God loved us and sent his Son / as expiation for our sins. **Alleluia, alleluia.**

Gospel   *Lk 7: 36–8: 3 or 7: 36–50*
For the shorter form, read only the parts in brackets.
[A Pharisee invited Jesus to dine with him, and he entered the Pharisee's house and reclined at table. Now there was a sinful woman in the city who learned that he was at table in the house of the Pharisee. Bringing an alabaster flask of ointment, she stood behind him at his feet weeping and began to bathe his feet with her tears. Then she wiped them with her hair, kissed them, and anointed them with the ointment. When the Pharisee who had invited him saw this he said to himself, "If this man were a prophet, he would know who and what sort of woman this is who is touching him, that she is a sinner." Jesus said to him in reply, "Simon, I have something to say to you." "Tell me, teacher," he said. "Two people were in debt to a certain creditor; one owed five hundred days' wages and the other owed fifty. Since they were unable to repay the debt, he forgave it for both. Which of them will love him more?" Simon said in reply, "The one, I suppose, whose larger debt was forgiven." He said to him, "You have judged rightly."

Then he turned to the woman and said to Simon, "Do you

see this woman? When I entered your house, you did not give me water for my feet, but she has bathed them with her tears and wiped them with her hair. You did not give me a kiss, but she has not ceased kissing my feet since the time I entered. You did not anoint my head with oil, but she anointed my feet with ointment. So I tell you, her many sins have been forgiven because she has shown great love. But the one to whom little is forgiven, loves little." He said to her, "Your sins are forgiven." The others at table said to themselves, "Who is this who even forgives sins?" But he said to the woman, "Your faith has saved you; go in peace."]

Afterward he journeyed from one town and village to another, preaching and proclaiming the good news of the kingdom of God. Accompanying him were the Twelve and some women who had been cured of evil spirits and infirmities, Mary, called Magdalene, from whom seven demons had gone out, Joanna, the wife of Herod's steward Chuza, Susanna, and many others who provided for them out of their resources.

Communion Antiphon Ps 27 (26): 4 There is one thing I ask of the Lord, only this do I seek: ◆ to live in the house of the Lord all the days of my life.

Or: Jn 17: 11 Holy Father, keep in your name those you have given me, ◆ that they may be one as we are one, says the Lord.

TWELFTH SUNDAY IN ORDINARY TIME

Entrance Antiphon cf. Ps 28 (27): 8–9 The Lord is the strength of his people, ◆ a saving refuge for the one he has anointed. ◆ Save your people, Lord, and bless your heritage, ◆and govern them for ever.

First Reading Zec 12: 10–11; 13: 1 Thus says the LORD: I will pour out on the house of David and on the inhabitants of Jerusalem a spirit of grace and petition; and they shall look on him whom they have pierced, and they shall mourn for him as one mourns for an only son, and they shall grieve over him as one grieves over a firstborn.

On that day the mourning in Jerusalem shall be as great as the mourning of Hadadrimmon in the plain of Megiddo.

On that day there shall be open to the house of David and to the inhabitants of Jerusalem, a fountain to purify from sin and uncleanness.

Responsorial Psalm Ps 63: 2, 3–4, 5–6, 8–9   *Bill Svarda*

My soul is thirst-ing for you, O Lord my God.

O God, you are my God whom I seek;
   for you my flesh pines and my soul thirsts
   like the earth, parched, lifeless and without water. ℟

Thus have I gazed toward you in the sanctuary
   to see your power and your glory,
For your kindness is a greater good than life;
   my lips shall glorify you. ℟

Thus will I bless you while I live;
   lifting up my hands, I will call upon your name.
As with the riches of a banquet shall my soul be satisfied,
   and with exultant lips my mouth shall praise you. ℟

You are my help,
   and in the shadow of your wings I shout for joy.
My soul clings fast to you;
   your right hand upholds me. ℟

Second Reading Gal 3: 26–29 Brothers and sisters: Through faith you are all children of God in Christ Jesus. For all of you who were baptized into Christ have clothed yourselves with Christ. There is neither Jew nor Greek, there is neither slave nor free person, there is not male and female; for you are all one in Christ Jesus. And if you belong to Christ, then you are Abraham's descendant, heirs according to the promise.

Alleluia　Jn 10: 27　　　　　　　　　　　　　　　　　　　*Vince Ambrosetti*

Al - le - lu - ia,　al - le - lu - ia,　al - le - lu - ia,　al - le - lu - ia.

Al - le - lu - ia,　al - le - lu - ia,　al - le - lu - ia.

My sheep hear my voice, says the Lord; / I know them, and they follow me. **Alleluia, alleluia.**

Gospel Lk 9: 18–24 Once when Jesus was praying in solitude, and the disciples were with him, he asked them, "Who do the crowds say that I am?" They said in reply, "John the Baptist; others, Elijah; still others, 'One of the ancient prophets has arisen.'" Then he said to them, "But who do you say that I am?" Peter said in reply, "The Christ of God." He rebuked them and directed them not to tell this to anyone.

He said, "The Son of Man must suffer greatly and be rejected by the elders, the chief priests, and the scribes, and be killed and on the third day be raised." Then he said to all, "If anyone wishes to come after me, he must deny himself and take up his cross daily and follow me. For whoever wishes to save his life will lose it, but whoever loses his life for my sake will save it."

Communion Antiphon Ps 145 (144): 15 **The eyes of all look to you, Lord, ◆ and you give them their food in due season.**

Or: Jn 10: 11, 15 **I am the Good Shepherd, ◆ and I lay down my life for my sheep, says the Lord.**

THIRTEENTH SUNDAY IN ORDINARY TIME

Entrance Antiphon Ps 47 (46): 2 **All peoples, clap your hands. ◆ Cry to God with shouts of joy!**

First Reading *1 Kgs 19: 16b, 19–21* The LORD said to Elijah: "You shall anoint Elisha, son of Shaphat of Abel-meholah, as prophet to succeed you."

Elijah set out and came upon Elisha, son of Shaphat, as he was plowing with twelve yoke of oxen; he was following the twelfth. Elijah went over to him and threw his cloak over him. Elisha left the oxen, ran after Elijah, and said, "Please, let me kiss my father and mother goodbye, and I will follow you." Elijah answered, "Go back! Have I done anything to you?" Elisha left him, and taking the yoke of oxen, slaughtered them; he used the plowing equipment for fuel to boil their flesh, and gave it to his people to eat. Then Elisha left and followed Elijah as his attendant.

Responsorial Psalm *Ps 16: 1–2, 5, 7–8, 9–10, 11*   Joe Higginbotham

You are my in - her - i - tance, O Lord.

Keep me, O God, for in you I take refuge;
  I say to the LORD, "My Lord are you.
O LORD, my allotted portion and my cup,
  you it is who hold fast my lot." ℟

I bless the LORD who counsels me;
  even in the night my heart exhorts me.
I set the LORD ever before me;
  with him at my right hand I shall not be disturbed. ℟

Therefore my heart is glad and my soul rejoices,
  my body, too, abides in confidence
because you will not abandon my soul to the netherworld,
  nor will you suffer your faithful one to undergo
    corruption. ℟

You will show me the path to life,
  fullness of joys in your presence,
  the delights at your right hand forever. ℟

Second Reading *Gal 5: 1, 13–18* Brothers and sisters: For freedom Christ set us free; so stand firm and do not submit again to the yoke of slavery.

For you were called for freedom, brothers and sisters. But do not use this freedom as an opportunity for the flesh; rather, serve one another through love. For the whole law is fulfilled in one statement, namely, *You shall love your neighbor as yourself.* But if you go on biting and devouring one another, beware that you are not consumed by one another.

I say, then: live by the Spirit and you will certainly not gratify the desire of the flesh. For the flesh has desires against the Spirit, and the Spirit against the flesh; these are opposed to each other, so that you may not do what you want. But if you are guided by the Spirit, you are not under the law.

Alleluia *1 Sm 3: 9; Jn 6: 68c*   *Vince Ambrosetti*

Al-le-lu-ia, al - le - lu - ia, al - le - lu - ia, al - le - lu - ia.

Al - le - lu - ia, al - le - lu - ia, al - le - lu - ia.

Speak, Lord, your servant is listening; / you have the words of everlasting life.   **Alleluia, alleluia.**

Gospel *Lk 9: 51–62* When the days for Jesus' being taken up were fulfilled, he resolutely determined to journey to Jerusalem, and he sent messengers ahead of him. On the way they entered a Samaritan village to prepare for his reception there, but they would not welcome him because the destination of his journey was Jerusalem. When the disciples James and John saw this they asked, "Lord, do you want us to call down fire from heaven to consume them?" Jesus turned and rebuked them, and they journeyed to another village.

As they were proceeding on their journey someone said to him, "I will follow you wherever you go." Jesus answered him,

"Foxes have dens and birds of the sky have nests, but the Son of Man has nowhere to rest his head."

And to another he said, "Follow me." But he replied, "Lord, let me go first and bury my father." But he answered him, "Let the dead bury their dead. But you, go and proclaim the kingdom of God." And another said, "I will follow you, Lord, but first let me say farewell to my family at home." To him Jesus said, "No one who sets a hand to the plow and looks to what was left behind is fit for the kingdom of God."

Communion Antiphon   *cf. Ps 103 (102): 1*   Bless the Lord, O my soul, ◆ and all within me, his holy name.

Or: *Jn 17: 20–21*   O Father, I pray for them, that they may be one in us, ◆ that the world may believe that you have sent me, says the Lord.

FOURTEENTH SUNDAY IN ORDINARY TIME

Entrance Antiphon   *cf. Ps 48 (47): 10–11*   Your merciful love, O God, ◆ we have received in the midst of your temple. ◆ Your praise, O God, like your name, ◆ reaches the ends of the earth; ◆ your right hand is filled with saving justice.

First Reading   *Is 66: 10–14c*
Thus says the LORD:
Rejoice with Jerusalem and be glad because of her,
    all you who love her;
exult, exult with her,
    all you who were mourning over her!
Oh, that you may suck fully
    of the milk of her comfort,
that you may nurse with delight
    at her abundant breasts!
    For thus says the LORD:
Lo, I will spread prosperity over Jerusalem like a river,
    and the wealth of the nations like an overflowing torrent.

As nurslings, you shall be carried in her arms,
  and fondled in her lap;
as a mother comforts her child,
  so will I comfort you;
  in Jerusalem you shall find your comfort.

When you see this, your heart shall rejoice
  and your bodies flourish like the grass;
the LORD's power shall be known to his servants.

Responsorial Psalm Ps 66: 1–3, 4–5, 6–7, 16, 20   Bill Svarda

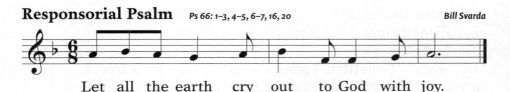

Let all the earth cry out to God with joy.

Shout joyfully to God, all the earth,
  sing praise to the glory of his name;
  proclaim his glorious praise.
Say to God, "How tremendous are your deeds!" ℞

"Let all on earth worship and sing praise to you,
  sing praise to your name!"
Come and see the works of God,
  his tremendous deeds among the children of Adam. ℞

He has changed the sea into dry land;
  through the river they passed on foot;
  therefore let us rejoice in him.
He rules by his might forever. ℞

Hear now, all you who fear God, while I declare
  what he has done for me.
Blessed be God who refused me not
  my prayer or his kindness! ℞

Second Reading Gal 6: 14–18 Brothers and sisters: May I never boast
except in the cross of our Lord Jesus Christ, through which the
world has been crucified to me, and I to the world. For neither

does circumcision mean anything, nor does uncircumcision, but only a new creation. Peace and mercy be to all who follow this rule and to the Israel of God.

From now on, let no one make troubles for me; for I bear the marks of Jesus on my body.

The grace of our Lord Jesus Christ be with your spirit, brothers and sisters. Amen.

Alleluia   *Col 3: 15a, 16a*   *Vince Ambrosetti*

Al-le-lu-ia, al-le-lu-ia, al-le-lu-ia, al-le-lu-ia.

Al-le-lu-ia, al-le-lu-ia, al-le-lu-ia.

Let the peace of Christ control your hearts; / let the word of Christ dwell in you richly. **Alleluia, alleluia.**

Gospel   *Lk 10: 1–12, 17–20 or 10: 19*

For the shorter form, read only the parts in brackets.

[At that time the Lord appointed seventy-two others whom he sent ahead of him in pairs to every town and place he intended to visit. He said to them, "The harvest is abundant but the laborers are few; so ask the master of the harvest to send out laborers for his harvest. Go on your way; behold, I am sending you like lambs among wolves. Carry no money bag, no sack, no sandals; and greet no one along the way. Into whatever house you enter, first say, 'Peace to this household.' If a peaceful person lives there, your peace will rest on him; but if not, it will return to you. Stay in the same house and eat and drink what is offered to you, for the laborer deserves his payment. Do not move about from one house to another. Whatever town you enter and they welcome you, eat what is set before you, cure the sick in it and say to them, 'The kingdom of God is at hand for you.'] Whatever town you enter and they do not receive you, go out into the streets and say, 'The dust of your town that clings to our feet, even that we shake

off against you.' Yet know this: the kingdom of God is at hand.
I tell you, it will be more tolerable for Sodom on that day than for
that town."

The seventy-two returned rejoicing, and said, "Lord, even
the demons are subject to us because of your name." Jesus said,
"I have observed Satan fall like lightning from the sky. Behold,
I have given you the power to 'tread upon serpents' and scorpions
and upon the full force of the enemy and nothing will harm you.
Nevertheless, do not rejoice because the spirits are subject to you,
but rejoice because your names are written in heaven."

Communion Antiphon Ps 34 (33): 9 Taste and see that the Lord is
good; ✦ blessed the man who seeks refuge in him.

Or: Mt 11: 28 Come to me, all who labor and are burdened, ✦ and
I will refresh you, says the Lord.

FIFTEENTH SUNDAY

IN ORDINARY TIME

Entrance Antiphon cf. Ps 17 (16): 15 As for me, in justice I shall
behold your face; ✦ I shall be filled with the vision of
your glory.

First Reading Dt 30: 10–14 Moses said to the people: "If only you
would heed the voice of the LORD, your God, and keep his
commandments and statutes that are written in this book of the
law, when you return to the LORD, your God, with all your heart
and all your soul.

"For this command that I enjoin on you today is not too
mysterious and remote for you. It is not up in the sky, that you
should say, 'Who will go up in the sky to get it for us and tell us
of it, that we may carry it out?' Nor is it across the sea, that you
should say, 'Who will cross the sea to get it for us and tell us of
it, that we may carry it out?' No, it is something very near to
you, already in your mouths and in your hearts; you have only to
carry it out."

Responsorial Psalm   Ps 69: 14, 17, 30–31, 33–34, 36, 37   *Joe Higginbotham*

Turn to the Lord in your need, and you will live.

I pray to you, O LORD,
  for the time of your favor, O God!
In your great kindness answer me
  with your constant help.
Answer me, O LORD, for bounteous is your kindness:
  in your great mercy turn toward me. ℟

I am afflicted and in pain;
  let your saving help, O God, protect me.
I will praise the name of God in song,
  and I will glorify him with thanksgiving. ℟

"See, you lowly ones, and be glad;
  you who seek God, may your hearts revive!
For the LORD hears the poor,
  and his own who are in bonds he spurns not." ℟

For God will save Zion
  and rebuild the cities of Judah.
The descendants of his servants shall inherit it,
  and those who love his name shall inhabit it. ℟

Or: Ps 19: 8, 9, 10, 11   *Jim Hughes*

Your words, Lord, are Spir-it and life.

Your words, Lord, are Spir-it and life.

The law of the LORD is perfect,
  refreshing the soul;

The decree of the LORD is trustworthy,
  giving wisdom to the simple. ℟

The precepts of the LORD are right,
  rejoicing the heart;
the command of the LORD is clear,
  enlightening the eye. ℟

The fear of the LORD is pure,
  enduring forever;
the ordinances of the LORD are true,
  all of them just. ℟

They are more precious than gold,
  than a heap of purest gold;
sweeter also than syrup
  or honey from the comb. ℟

Second Reading   *Col 1: 15–20*
  Christ Jesus is the image of the invisible God,
    the firstborn of all creation.
  For in him were created all things in heaven and on earth,
    the visible and the invisible,
      whether thrones or dominions or principalities or powers;
    all things were created through him and for him.
  He is before all things,
    and in him all things hold together.
  He is the head of the body, the church.
  He is the beginning, the firstborn from the dead,
    that in all things he himself might be preeminent.
  For in him all the fullness was pleased to dwell,
    and through him to reconcile all things for him,
    making peace by the blood of his cross
      through him, whether those on earth or those in heaven.

Alleluia   *cf. Jn 6: 63c, 68c*   *Vince Ambrosetti*

Al-le-lu-ia, al-le-lu-ia, al-le-lu-ia, al-le-lu-ia.

Al - le - lu - ia, al - le - lu - ia, al - le - lu - ia.

Your words, Lord, are Spirit and life; / you have the words of everlasting life. **Alleluia, alleluia.**

Gospel Lk 10: 25-37 There was a scholar of the law who stood up to test Jesus and said, "Teacher, what must I do to inherit eternal life?" Jesus said to him, "What is written in the law? How do you read it?" He said in reply, "*You shall love the Lord, your God, with all your heart, with all your being, with all your strength, and with all your mind, and your neighbor as yourself.*" He replied to him, "You have answered correctly; do this and you will live."

But because he wished to justify himself, he said to Jesus, "And who is my neighbor?" Jesus replied, "A man fell victim to robbers as he went down from Jerusalem to Jericho. They stripped and beat him and went off leaving him half-dead. A priest happened to be going down that road, but when he saw him, he passed by on the opposite side. Likewise a Levite came to the place, and when he saw him, he passed by on the opposite side. But a Samaritan traveler who came upon him was moved with compassion at the sight. He approached the victim, poured oil and wine over his wounds and bandaged them. Then he lifted him up on his own animal, took him to an inn, and cared for him. The next day he took out two silver coins and gave them to the innkeeper with the instruction, 'Take care of him. If you spend more than what I have given you, I shall repay you on my way back.' Which of these three, in your opinion, was neighbor to the robbers' victim?" He answered, "The one who treated him with mercy." Jesus said to him, "Go and do likewise."

Communion Antiphon cf. Ps 84 (83): 4-5 The sparrow finds a home, ◆ and the swallow a nest for her young: ◆ by your altars, O Lord of hosts, my King and my God. ◆ Blessed are they who dwell in your house, ◆ for ever singing your praise.

Or: Jn 6: 57 Whoever eats my flesh and drinks my blood ◆ remains in me and I in him, says the Lord.

SIXTEENTH SUNDAY IN ORDINARY TIME

Entrance Antiphon *Ps 54 (53): 6, 8* See, I have God for my help.
♦ The Lord sustains my soul. ♦ I will sacrifice to you with
willing heart, ♦ and praise your name, O Lord, for it is good.

First Reading *Gen 18: 1–10a* The LORD appeared to Abraham by the
terebinth of Mamre, as he sat in the entrance of his tent, while
the day was growing hot. Looking up, Abraham saw three men
standing nearby. When he saw them, he ran from the entrance
of the tent to greet them; and bowing to the ground, he said:
"Sir, if I may ask you this favor, please do not go on past your
servant. Let some water be brought, that you may bathe your
feet, and then rest yourselves under the tree. Now that you have
come this close to your servant, let me bring you a little food,
that you may refresh yourselves; and afterward you may go on
your way." The men replied, "Very well, do as you have said."

Abraham hastened into the tent and told Sarah, "Quick, three
measures of fine flour! Knead it and make rolls." He ran to the
herd, picked out a tender, choice steer, and gave it to a servant,
who quickly prepared it. Then Abraham got some curds and
milk, as well as the steer that had been prepared, and set these
before the three men; and he waited on them under the tree
while they ate.

They asked Abraham, "Where is your wife Sarah?" He replied,
"There in the tent." One of them said, "I will surely return to you
about this time next year, and Sarah will then have a son."

Responsorial Psalm *Ps 15: 2–3, 3–4, 5*   Jim Cowan

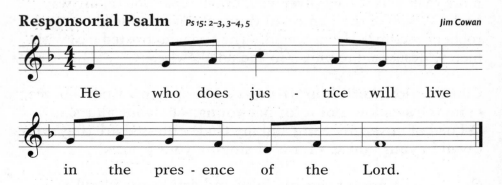

He who does jus - tice will live
in the pres - ence of the Lord.

One who walks blamelessly and does justice;
  who thinks the truth in his heart
  and slanders not with his tongue. ℟

Who harms not his fellow man,
  nor takes up a reproach against his neighbor;
by whom the reprobate is despised,
  while he honors those who fear the LORD. ℟

Who lends not his money at usury
  and accepts no bribe against the innocent.
One who does these things
  shall never be disturbed. ℟

Second Reading *Col 1: 24–28* Brothers and sisters: Now I rejoice in my sufferings for your sake, and in my flesh I am filling up what is lacking in the afflictions of Christ on behalf of his body, which is the church, of which I am a minister in accordance with God's stewardship given to me to bring to completion for you the word of God, the mystery hidden from ages and from generations past. But now it has been manifested to his holy ones, to whom God chose to make known the riches of the glory of this mystery among the Gentiles; it is Christ in you, the hope for glory. It is he whom we proclaim, admonishing everyone and teaching everyone with all wisdom, that we may present everyone perfect in Christ.

Alleluia *cf. Lk 8: 15*   Jim Hughes

Al-le-lu-ia   Al-le-lu-ia   Al - le-lu - ia.

Blessed are they who have kept the word with a generous heart / and yield a harvest through perseverance.
Alleluia, allelua.

Gospel *Lk 10: 38–42* Jesus entered a village where a woman whose name was Martha welcomed him. She had a sister named

Mary who sat beside the Lord at his feet listening to him speak. Martha, burdened with much serving, came to him and said, "Lord, do you not care that my sister has left me by myself to do the serving? Tell her to help me." The Lord said to her in reply, "Martha, Martha, you are anxious and worried about many things. There is need of only one thing. Mary has chosen the better part and it will not be taken from her."

Communion Antiphon Ps 111 (110): 4–5 **The Lord, the gracious, the merciful, ◆ has made a memorial of his wonders; ◆ he gives food to those who fear him.**

Or: Rv 3: 20 **Behold, I stand at the door and knock, says the Lord. ◆ If anyone hears my voice and opens the door to me, ◆ I will enter his house and dine with him, and he with me.**

SEVENTEENTH SUNDAY IN ORDINARY TIME

Entrance Antiphon   cf. Ps 68 (67): 6–7, 36 **God is in his holy place, ◆ God who unites those who dwell in his house; ◆ he himself gives might and strength to his people.**

First Reading   Gen 18: 20–32 In those days, the LORD said: "The outcry against Sodom and Gomorrah is so great, and their sin so grave, that I must go down and see whether or not their actions fully correspond to the cry against them that comes to me. I mean to find out."

    While Abraham's visitors walked on farther toward Sodom, the LORD remained standing before Abraham. Then Abraham drew nearer and said: "Will you sweep away the innocent with the guilty? Suppose there were fifty innocent people in the city; would you wipe out the place, rather than spare it for the sake of the fifty innocent people within it? Far be it from you to do such a thing, to make the innocent die with the guilty so that the innocent and the guilty would be treated alike! Should not the judge of all the world act with justice?" The LORD replied,

"If I find fifty innocent people in the city of Sodom, I will spare the whole place for their sake." Abraham spoke up again: "See how I am presuming to speak to my Lord, though I am but dust and ashes! What if there are five less than fifty innocent people? Will you destroy the whole city because of those five?" He answered, "I will not destroy it, if I find forty-five there." But Abraham persisted, saying "What if only forty are found there?" He replied, "I will forbear doing it for the sake of the forty." Then Abraham said, "Let not my Lord grow impatient if I go on. What if only thirty are found there?" He replied, "I will forbear doing it if I can find but thirty there." Still Abraham went on, "Since I have thus dared to speak to my Lord, what if there are no more than twenty?" The LORD answered, "I will not destroy it, for the sake of the twenty." But he still persisted: "Please, let not my Lord grow angry if I speak up this last time. What if there are at least ten there?" He replied, "For the sake of those ten, I will not destroy it."

Responsorial Psalm

Ps 138: 1–2, 2–3, 6–7, 7–8

Vince Ambrosetti

Lord, on the day I called for help, you an - swered me.

I will give thanks to you, O LORD, with all my heart,
    for you have heard the words of my mouth;
      in the presence of the angels I will sing your praise;
I will worship at your holy temple
    and give thanks to your name. ℟

Because of your kindness and your truth;
    for you have made great above all things
      your name and your promise.
When I called you answered me;
    you built up strength within me. ℟

The LORD is exalted, yet the lowly he sees,
and the proud he knows from afar.
Though I walk amid distress, you preserve me;
against the anger of my enemies you raise your hand. ℟

Your right hand saves me.
The LORD will complete what he has done for me;
your kindness, O LORD, endures forever;
forsake not the work of your hands. ℟

Second Reading *Col 2: 12–14* Brothers and sisters: You were buried with him in baptism, in which you were also raised with him through faith in the power of God, who raised him from the dead. And even when you were dead in transgressions and the uncircumcision of your flesh, he brought you to life along with him, having forgiven us all our transgressions; obliterating the bond against us, with its legal claims, which was opposed to us, he also removed it from our midst, nailing it to the cross.

Alleluia   *Rom 8: 15bc*   Jim Hughes

Al-le-lu-ia   Al-le-lu-ia   Al - le-lu - ia.

You have received a Spirit of adoption, / through which we cry, Abba, Father. **Alleluia, alleluia.**

Gospel *Lk 11: 1–13* Jesus was praying in a certain place, and when he had finished, one of his disciples said to him, "Lord, teach us to pray just as John taught his disciples." He said to them, "When you pray, say:
Father, hallowed be your name,
your kingdom come.
Give us each day our daily bread
and forgive us our sins
for we ourselves forgive everyone in debt to us,
and do not subject us to the final test."
And he said to them, "Suppose one of you has a friend to

whom he goes at midnight and says, 'Friend, lend me three loaves of bread, for a friend of mine has arrived at my house from a journey and I have nothing to offer him,' and he says in reply from within, 'Do not bother me; the door has already been locked and my children and I are already in bed. I cannot get up to give you anything.' I tell you, if he does not get up to give the visitor the loaves because of their friendship, he will get up to give him whatever he needs because of his persistence.

"And I tell you, ask and you will receive; seek and you will find; knock and the door will be opened to you. For everyone who asks, receives; and the one who seeks, finds; and to the one who knocks, the door will be opened. What father among you would hand his son a snake when he asks for a fish? Or hand him a scorpion when he asks for an egg? If you then, who are wicked, know how to give good gifts to your children, how much more will the Father in heaven give the Holy Spirit to those who ask him?"

Communion Antiphon *Ps 103 (102): 2* **Bless the Lord, O my soul, ◆ and never forget all his benefits.**

Or: *Mt 5: 7–8* **Blessed are the merciful, for they shall receive mercy. ◆ Blessed are the clean of heart, for they shall see God.**

EIGHTEENTH SUNDAY IN ORDINARY TIME

Entrance Antiphon *Ps 70 (69): 2, 6* **O God, come to my assistance; ◆ O Lord, make haste to help me! ◆ You are my rescuer, my help; ◆ O Lord, do not delay.**

First Reading *Eccl 1: 2, 2: 21–23*

Vanity of vanities, says Qoheleth,
   vanity of vanities! All things are vanity!

Here is one who has labored with wisdom and knowledge and skill, and yet to another who has not labored over it, he must leave property. This also is vanity and a great misfortune. For what profit comes to man from all the toil and anxiety of heart with which he has labored under the sun? All his days sorrow and grief are his occupation; even at night his mind is not at rest. This also is vanity.

Responsorial Psalm   *Ps 90: 3–4, 5–6, 12–13, 14 & 17*   *Joe Higginbotham*

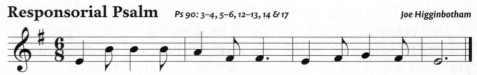

If to-day you hear his voice, hard-en not your hearts.

You turn man back to dust,
 saying, "Return, O children of men."
For a thousand years in your sight
 are as yesterday, now that it is past,
 or as a watch of the night.   ℟

You make an end of them in their sleep;
 the next morning they are like the changing grass,
Which at dawn springs up anew,
 but by evening wilts and fades.   ℟

Teach us to number our days aright,
 that we may gain wisdom of heart.
Return, O LORD! How long?
 Have pity on your servants!   ℟

Fill us at daybreak with your kindness,
 that we may shout for joy and gladness all our days.
And may the gracious care of the LORD our God be ours;
 prosper the work of our hands for us!
 Prosper the work of our hands!   ℟

Second Reading *Col 3: 1–5, 9–11* Brothers and sisters: If you were raised with Christ, seek what is above, where Christ is seated at the right hand of God. Think of what is above, not of what is on earth. For you have died, and your life is hidden with Christ in God. When Christ your life appears, then you too will appear with him in glory.

Put to death, then, the parts of you that are earthly: immorality, impurity, passion, evil desire, and the greed that is idolatry. Stop lying to one another, since you have taken off the old self with its practices and have put on the new self, which is being renewed, for knowledge, in the image of its creator. Here there is not Greek and Jew, circumcision and uncircumcision, barbarian, Scythian, slave, free; but Christ is all and in all.

Alleluia Mt 5: 3   Jim Hughes

Al-le-lu-ia   Al-le-lu-ia   Al - le-lu - ia.

Blessed are the poor in spirit, / for theirs is the kingdom of heaven. **Alleluia, alleluia.**

Gospel Lk 12: 13–21 Someone in the crowd said to Jesus, "Teacher, tell my brother to share the inheritance with me." He replied to him, "Friend, who appointed me as your judge and arbitrator?" Then he said to the crowd, "Take care to guard against all greed, for though one may be rich, one's life does not consist of possessions."

Then he told them a parable. "There was a rich man whose land produced a bountiful harvest. He asked himself, 'What shall I do, for I do not have space to store my harvest?' And he said, 'This is what I shall do: I shall tear down my barns and build larger ones. There I shall store all my grain and other goods and I shall say to myself, "Now as for you, you have so many good things stored up for many years, rest, eat, drink, be merry!"' But God said to him, 'You fool, this night your life will be demanded of you; and the things you have prepared, to whom will they belong?' Thus will it be for all who store up treasure for themselves but are not rich in what matters to God."

Communion Antiphon Wis 16: 20 You have given us, O Lord, bread from heaven, ♦ endowed with all delights and sweetness in every taste.

Or: Jn 6: 35 **I am the bread of life, says the Lord;** ◆ **whoever comes to me will not hunger** ◆ **and whoever believes in me will not thirst.**

NINETEENTH SUNDAY IN ORDINARY TIME

Entrance Antiphon *cf. Ps 74 (73): 20, 19, 22, 23* **Look to your covenant, O Lord,** ◆ **and forget not the life of your poor ones for ever.** ◆ **Arise, O God, and defend your cause,** ◆ **and forget not the cries of those who seek you.**

First Reading *Wis 18: 6–9*

The night of the passover was known beforehand to our
  fathers,
    that, with sure knowledge of the oaths in which they put
      their faith,
    they might have courage.
Your people awaited the salvation of the just
  and the destruction of their foes.
For when you punished our adversaries,
  in this you glorified us whom you had summoned.
For in secret the holy children of the good were offering
  sacrifice
    and putting into effect with one accord the divine
      institution.

Responsorial Psalm *Ps 33: 1, 12, 18–19, 20–22*   Jane Terwilliger

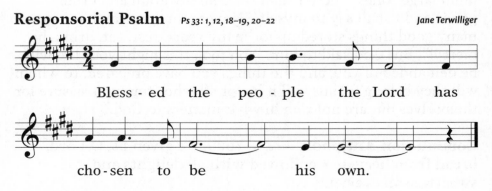

Bless - ed the peo - ple the Lord has cho-sen to be his own.

Exult, you just, in the LORD;
  praise from the upright is fitting.

Blessed the nation whose God is the LORD,
   the people he has chosen for his own inheritance. ℟

See, the eyes of the LORD are upon those who fear him,
upon those who hope for his kindness,
To deliver them from death
   and preserve them in spite of famine. ℟

Our soul waits for the LORD,
   who is our help and our shield.
May your kindness, O LORD, be upon us
   who have put our hope in you. ℟

Second Reading   *Heb 11: 1–2, 8–19 or 11: 1–2, 8–12*

For the shorter form, read only the parts in brackets.
[Brothers and sisters: Faith is the realization of what is hoped for
and evidence of things not seen. Because of it the ancients were
well attested.

By faith Abraham obeyed when he was called to go out to
a place that he was to receive as an inheritance; he went out,
not knowing where he was to go. By faith he sojourned in the
promised land as in a foreign country, dwelling in tents with
Isaac and Jacob, heirs of the same promise; for he was looking
forward to the city with foundations, whose architect and
maker is God. By faith he received power to generate, even
though he was past the normal age—and Sarah herself was
sterile—for he thought that the one who had made the promise
was trustworthy. So it was that there came forth from one man,
himself as good as dead, descendants as numerous as the stars in
the sky and as countless as the sands on the seashore.]

All these died in faith. They did not receive what had been
promised but saw it and greeted it from afar and acknowledged
themselves to be strangers and aliens on earth, for those who
speak thus show that they are seeking a homeland. If they had
been thinking of the land from which they had come, they
would have had opportunity to return. But now they desire a
better homeland, a heavenly one. Therefore, God is not ashamed
to be called their God, for he has prepared a city for them.

By faith Abraham, when put to the test, offered up Isaac, and
he who had received the promises was ready to offer his only

son, of whom it was said, "Through Isaac descendants shall bear your name." He reasoned that God was able to raise even from the dead, and he received Isaac back as a symbol.

Alleluia   Mt 24: 42a, 44   *Jim Hughes*

Al-le-lu-ia   Al-le-lu-ia   Al - le-lu - ia.

Stay awake and be ready! / For you do not know on what day your Lord will come.   **Alleluia, alleluia.**

Gospel   Lk 12: 32–48 or 12: 35–40
For the shorter form, read only the parts in brackets.
[Jesus said to his disciples:] "Do not be afraid any longer, little flock, for your Father is pleased to give you the kingdom. Sell your belongings and give alms. Provide money bags for yourselves that do not wear out, an inexhaustible treasure in heaven that no thief can reach nor moth destroy. For where your treasure is, there also will your heart be.

  ["Gird your loins and light your lamps and be like servants who await their master's return from a wedding, ready to open immediately when he comes and knocks. Blessed are those servants whom the master finds vigilant on his arrival. Amen, I say to you, he will gird himself, have them recline at table, and proceed to wait on them. And should he come in the second or third watch and find them prepared in this way, blessed are those servants. Be sure of this: if the master of the house had known the hour when the thief was coming, he would not have let his house be broken into. You also must be prepared, for at an hour you do not expect, the Son of Man will come."]

  Then Peter said, "Lord, is this parable meant for us or for everyone?" And the Lord replied, "Who, then, is the faithful and prudent steward whom the master will put in charge of his servants to distribute the food allowance at the proper time? Blessed is that servant whom his master on arrival finds doing so. Truly, I say to you, the master will put the servant in charge of all his property. But if that servant says to himself, 'My master is delayed in coming,' and begins to beat the menservants and the maidservants, to eat and drink and get drunk, then that servant's master will come on an unexpected day and at an unknown hour and will punish the servant severely and assign him a place with the unfaithful. That servant who knew his master's will but did not make preparations nor act in accord with his will shall be beaten severely; and the servant who was ignorant of his master's will but acted in a way deserving of a severe beating shall be beaten only lightly. Much will be required of the person entrusted with much, and still more will be demanded of the person entrusted with more."

Communion Antiphon Ps 147 (146): 12, 14 O Jerusalem, glorify the Lord, ✦ who gives you your fill of finest wheat.

Or: cf. Jn 6: 51 The bread that I will give, says the Lord, ✦ is my flesh for the life of the world.

TWENTIETH SUNDAY IN ORDINARY TIME

Entrance Antiphon Ps 84 (83): 10–11 Turn your eyes, O God, our shield; ✦ and look on the face of your anointed one; ✦ one day within your courts ✦ is better than a thousand elsewhere.

First Reading Jer 38: 4–6, 8–10 In those days, the princes said to the king: "Jeremiah ought to be put to death; he is demoralizing the soldiers who are left in this city, and all the people, by speaking such things to them; he is not interested in the welfare of our people, but in their ruin." King Zedekiah answered: "He is in your power"; for the king could do nothing with them. And so they took Jeremiah and threw him into the cistern of Prince Malchiah, which was in the quarters of the guard, letting him down with ropes. There was no water in the cistern, only mud, and Jeremiah sank into the mud.

Ebed-melech, a court official, went there from the palace and said to him: "My lord king, these men have been at fault in all they have done to the prophet Jeremiah, casting him into the cistern. He will die of famine on the spot, for there is no more food in the city." Then the king ordered Ebed-melech the

Cushite to take three men along with him, and draw the prophet Jeremiah out of the cistern before he should die.

Responsorial Psalm Ps 40: 2, 3, 4, 18   *Vince Ambrosetti and Debra Lee Williamson*

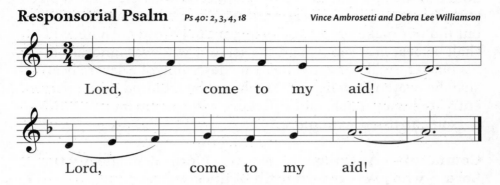

Lord, come to my aid!

Lord, come to my aid!

I have waited, waited for the LORD,
   and he stooped toward me. ℟

The LORD heard my cry.
He drew me out of the pit of destruction,
   out of the mud of the swamp;
he set my feet upon a crag;
   he made firm my steps. ℟

And he put a new song into my mouth,
   a hymn to our God.
Many shall look on in awe
   and trust in the LORD. ℟

Though I am afflicted and poor,
   yet the LORD thinks of me.
You are my help and my deliverer;
   O my God, hold not back! ℟

Second Reading *Heb 12: 1–4* Brothers and sisters: Since we are surrounded by so great a cloud of witnesses, let us rid ourselves of every burden and sin that clings to us and persevere in running the race that lies before us while keeping our eyes fixed on Jesus, the leader and perfecter of faith. For the sake of the joy that lay before him he endured the cross, despising its shame, and has taken his seat at the right of the throne of God. Consider how he endured such opposition from sinners, in order that you may not grow weary and lose heart. In your struggle against sin you have not yet resisted to the point of shedding blood.

Alleluia   Jn 10: 27   *Jim Hughes*

Al-le-lu-ia   Al-le-lu-ia   Al - le-lu - ia.

My sheep hear my voice, says the Lord; / I know them, and they follow me.   **Alleluia, alleluia.**

Gospel Lk 12: 49–53 Jesus said to his disciples: "I have come to set the earth on fire, and how I wish it were already blazing! There is a baptism with which I must be baptized, and how great is my anguish until it is accomplished! Do you think that I have come to establish peace on the earth? No, I tell you, but rather division. From now on a household of five will be divided, three against two and two against three; a father will be divided against his son and a son against his father, a mother against her daughter and a daughter against her mother, a mother-in-law against her daughter-in-law and a daughter-in-law against her mother-in-law."

Communion Antiphon Ps 130 (129): 7 With the Lord there is mercy; ◆ in him is plentiful redemption.

Or: Jn 6: 51–52 I am the living bread that came down from heaven, says the Lord. ◆ Whoever eats of this bread will live for ever.

TWENTY-FIRST SUNDAY IN ORDINARY TIME

Entrance Antiphon cf. Ps 86 (85): 1–3 Turn your ear, O Lord, and answer me; ◆ save the servant who trusts in you, my God. ◆ Have mercy on me, O Lord, for I cry to you all the day long.

First Reading *Is 66: 18–21* Thus says the LORD: I know their works and their thoughts, and I come to gather nations of every language; they shall come and see my glory. I will set a sign among them; from them I will send fugitives to the nations: to Tarshish, Put and Lud, Mosoch, Tubal and Javan, to the distant coastlands that have never heard of my fame, or seen my glory; and they shall proclaim my glory among the nations. They shall bring all your brothers and sisters from all the nations as an offering to the LORD, on horses and in chariots, in carts, upon mules and dromedaries, to Jerusalem, my holy mountain, says the LORD, just as the Israelites bring their offering to the house of the LORD in clean vessels. Some of these I will take as priests and Levites, says the LORD.

Responsorial Psalm   *Ps 117: 1, 2*   Joe Higginbotham

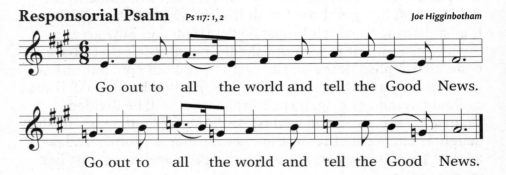

Go out to all the world and tell the Good News.

Go out to all the world and tell the Good News.

Or: ℞ **Alleluia.**

Praise the LORD all you nations;
    glorify him, all you peoples! ℞

For steadfast is his kindness toward us,
    and the fidelity of the LORD endures forever. ℞

Second Reading *Heb 12: 5–7, 11–13* Brothers and sisters: You have forgotten the exhortation addressed to you as children:
  "My son, do not disdain the discipline of the Lord
      or lose heart when reproved by him;
    for whom the Lord loves, he disciplines;
      he scourges every son he acknowledges."
Endure your trials as "discipline"; God treats you as sons. For

what "son" is there whom his father does not discipline? At the time, all discipline seems a cause not for joy but for pain, yet later it brings the peaceful fruit of righteousness to those who are trained by it.

So strengthen your drooping hands and your weak knees. Make straight paths for your feet, that what is lame may not be disjointed but healed.

Alleluia Jn 14: 6   Jim Hughes

Al-le-lu-ia   Al-le-lu-ia   Al - le-lu - ia.

I am the way, the truth and the life, says the Lord; / no one comes to the Father, except through me. **Alleluia, alleluia.**

Gospel Lk 13: 22–30 Jesus passed through towns and villages, teaching as he went and making his way to Jerusalem. Someone asked him, "Lord, will only a few people be saved?" He answered them, "Strive to enter through the narrow gate, for many, I tell you, will attempt to enter but will not be strong enough. After the master of the house has arisen and locked the door, then will you stand outside knocking and saying, 'Lord, open the door for us.' He will say to you in reply, 'I do not know where you are from.' And you will say, 'We ate and drank in your company and you taught in our streets.' Then he will say to you, 'I do not know where you are from. Depart from me, all you evildoers!' And there will be wailing and grinding of teeth when you see Abraham, Isaac, and Jacob and all the prophets in the kingdom of God and you yourselves cast out. And people will come from the east and the west and from the north and the south and will recline at table in the kingdom of God. For behold, some are last who will be first, and some are first who will be last."

Communion Antiphon cf. Ps 104 (103): 13–15 **The earth is replete with the fruits of your work, O Lord;** ✦ **you bring forth bread from the earth** ✦ **and wine to cheer the heart.**

Or: *cf. Jn 6: 54* **Whoever eats my flesh and drinks my blood ◆ has eternal life, says the Lord, ◆ and I will raise him up on the last day.**

TWENTY-SECOND

SUNDAY IN ORDINARY TIME

Entrance Antiphon *cf. Ps 86 (85): 3, 5* **Have mercy on me, O Lord, for I cry to you all the day long. ◆ O Lord, you are good and forgiving, ◆ full of mercy to all who call to you.**

First Reading *Sir 3: 17–18, 20, 28–29*

My child, conduct your affairs with humility,
    and you will be loved more than a giver of gifts.
Humble yourself the more, the greater you are,
    and you will find favor with God.
What is too sublime for you, seek not,
    into things beyond your strength search not.
The mind of a sage appreciates proverbs,
    and an attentive ear is the joy of the wise.
Water quenches a flaming fire,
    and alms atone for sins.

Responsorial Psalm Ps 68: 4–5, 6–7, 10–11 *based on* KINGSFOLD

God, in your good-ness, you have made a home for the poor.

The just rejoice and exult before God;
    they are glad and rejoice.
Sing to God, chant praise to his name;

whose name is the LORD. ℟

The father of orphans and the defender of widows
   is God in his holy dwelling.
God gives a home to the forsaken;
   he leads forth prisoners to prosperity. ℟

A bountiful rain you showered down, O God, upon your
     inheritance;
   you restored the land when it languished;
your flock settled in it;
   in your goodness, O God, you provided it for the needy. ℟

Second Reading *Heb 12: 18–19, 22–24a* Brothers and sisters: You have
not approached that which could be touched and a blazing fire
and gloomy darkness and storm and a trumpet blast and a voice
speaking words such that those who heard begged that no
message be further addressed to them. No, you have approached
Mount Zion and the city of the living God, the heavenly
Jerusalem, and countless angels in festal gathering, and the
assembly of the firstborn enrolled in heaven, and God the judge
of all, and the spirits of the just made perfect, and Jesus, the
mediator of a new covenant, and the sprinkled blood that speaks
more eloquently than that of Abel.

Alleluia   *Mt 11: 29ab*   *Jim Hughes*

Al-le-lu-ia   Al-le-lu-ia   Al - le-lu - ia.

Take my yoke upon you, says the Lord, / and learn from me,
for I am meek and humble of heart.   **Alleluia, alleluia.**

Gospel *Lk 14: 1, 7–14* On a sabbath Jesus went to dine at the home
of one of the leading Pharisees, and the people there were
observing him carefully.
   He told a parable to those who had been invited, noticing how
they were choosing the places of honor at the table. "When you

are invited by someone to a wedding banquet, do not recline at table in the place of honor. A more distinguished guest than you may have been invited by him, and the host who invited both of you may approach you and say, 'Give your place to this man,' and then you would proceed with embarrassment to take the lowest place. Rather, when you are invited, go and take the lowest place so that when the host comes to you he may say, 'My friend, move up to a higher position.' Then you will enjoy the esteem of your companions at the table. For every one who exalts himself will be humbled, but the one who humbles himself will be exalted." Then he said to the host who invited him, "When you hold a lunch or a dinner, do not invite your friends or your brothers or your relatives or your wealthy neighbors, in case they may invite you back and you have repayment. Rather, when you hold a banquet, invite the poor, the crippled, the lame, the blind; blessed indeed will you be because of their inability to repay you. For you will be repaid at the resurrection of the righteous."

Communion Antiphon Ps 31 (30): 20 How great is the goodness, Lord, ♦ that you keep for those who fear you.

Or: Mt 5: 9–10 Blessed are the peacemakers, ♦ for they shall be called children of God. ♦ Blessed are they who are persecuted for the sake of righteousness, ♦ for theirs is the Kingdom of Heaven.

TWENTY-THIRD SUNDAY IN ORDINARY TIME

Entrance Antiphon Ps 119 (118): 137, 124 You are just, O Lord, and your judgment is right; ♦ treat your servant in accord with your merciful love.

First Reading Wis 9: 13–18b

Who can know God's counsel,
  or who can conceive what the LORD intends?

For the deliberations of mortals are timid,
 and unsure are our plans.
For the corruptible body burdens the soul
 and the earthen shelter weighs down the mind that has
  many concerns.
And scarce do we guess the things on earth,
 and what is within our grasp we find with difficulty;
 but when things are in heaven, who can search them out?
Or who ever knew your counsel, except you had given
  wisdom
 and sent your holy spirit from on high?
And thus were the paths of those on earth made straight.

Responsorial Psalm   Ps 90: 3–4, 5–6, 12–13, 14 & 17   Jim Cowan

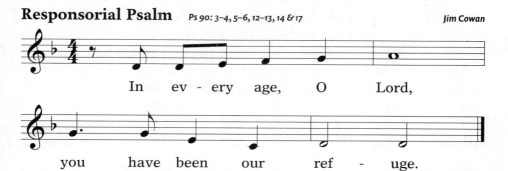

In ev - ery age, O Lord, you have been our ref - uge.

You turn man back to dust,
 saying, "Return, O children of men."
For a thousand years in your sight
 are as yesterday, now that it is past,
 or as a watch of the night. ℟

You make an end of them in their sleep;
 the next morning they are like the changing grass,
Which at dawn springs up anew,
 but by evening wilts and fades. ℟

Teach us to number our days aright,
 that we may gain wisdom of heart.
Return, O LORD! How long?
 Have pity on your servants! ℟

Fill us at daybreak with your kindness,
   that we may shout for joy and gladness all our days.
And may the gracious care of the LORD our God be ours;
   prosper the work of our hands for us!
   Prosper the work of our hands!   ℟

Second Reading *Phlm 9–10, 12–17* I, Paul, an old man, and now also
a prisoner for Christ Jesus, urge you on behalf of my child
Onesimus, whose father I have become in my imprisonment; I
am sending him, that is, my own heart, back to you. I should
have liked to retain him for myself, so that he might serve me
on your behalf in my imprisonment for the gospel, but I did not
want to do anything without your consent, so that the good you
do might not be forced but voluntary. Perhaps this is why he
was away from you for a while, that you might have him back
forever, no longer as a slave but more than a slave, a brother,
beloved especially to me, but even more so to you, as a man and
in the Lord. So if you regard me as a partner, welcome him as
you would me.

Alleluia   *Ps 119: 135*   *Michael Kissinger*

Al-le - lu-ia, al-le - lu - ia, al - le - lu - ia.

Let your face shine upon your servant; / and teach me
your laws.   **Alleluia, alleluia.**

Gospel *Lk 14: 25–33* Great crowds were traveling with Jesus, and he
turned and addressed them, "If anyone comes to me without
hating his father and mother, wife and children, brothers and
sisters, and even his own life, he cannot be my disciple. Whoever
does not carry his own cross and come after me cannot be my
disciple. Which of you wishing to construct a tower does not
first sit down and calculate the cost to see if there is enough
for its completion? Otherwise, after laying the foundation and
finding himself unable to finish the work the onlookers should
laugh at him and say, 'This one began to build but did not have

the resources to finish.' Or what king marching into battle would not first sit down and decide whether with ten thousand troops he can successfully oppose another king advancing upon him with twenty thousand troops? But if not, while he is still far away, he will send a delegation to ask for peace terms. In the same way, anyone of you who does not renounce all his possessions cannot be my disciple."

Communion Antiphon *cf. Ps 42 (41): 2-3* **Like the deer that yearns for running streams, ◆ so my soul is yearning for you, my God; ◆ my soul is thirsting for God, the living God.**

Or: *Jn 8:12* **I am the light of the world, says the Lord; ◆ whoever follows me will not walk in darkness, ◆ but will have the light of life.**

TWENTY-FOURTH

SUNDAY IN ORDINARY TIME

Entrance Antiphon *cf. Sir 36:18* **Give peace, O Lord, to those who wait for you, ◆ that your prophets be found true. ◆ Hear the prayers of your servant, ◆ and of your people Israel.**

First Reading *Ex 32:7-11, 13-14* The LORD said to Moses, "Go down at once to your people, whom you brought out of the land of Egypt, for they have become depraved. They have soon turned aside from the way I pointed out to them, making for themselves a molten calf and worshiping it, sacrificing to it and crying out, 'This is your God, O Israel, who brought you out of the land of Egypt!' I see how stiff-necked this people is," continued the LORD to Moses. "Let me alone, then, that my wrath may blaze up against them to consume them. Then I will make of you a great nation."

But Moses implored the LORD, his God, saying, "Why, O LORD, should your wrath blaze up against your own people, whom you brought out of the land of Egypt with such great power and with so strong a hand? Remember your servants Abraham, Isaac, and Israel, and how you swore to them by your own self, saying, 'I will make your descendants as numerous as the stars in the sky; and all this land that I promised, I will give your descendants as their perpetual heritage.'" So the LORD relented in the punishment he had threatened to inflict on his people.

Responsorial Psalm   Ps 51: 3–4, 12–13, 17, 19   *Roger Holtz*

I will rise and go, I will rise and go to my Fa-ther.

Have mercy on me, O God, in your goodness;
in the greatness of your compassion wipe out my offense.
Thoroughly wash me from my guilt
and of my sin cleanse me. ℟

A clean heart create for me, O God,
and a steadfast spirit renew within me.
Cast me not out from your presence,
and your Holy Spirit take not from me. ℟

O Lord, open my lips,
and my mouth shall proclaim your praise.
My sacrifice, O God, is a contrite spirit;
a heart contrite and humbled, O God, you will not spurn. ℟

Second Reading 1 Tm 1: 12–17 Beloved: I am grateful to him who has strengthened me, Christ Jesus our Lord, because he considered me trustworthy in appointing me to the ministry. I was once a blasphemer and a persecutor and arrogant, but I have been

mercifully treated because I acted out of ignorance in my
unbelief. Indeed, the grace of our Lord has been abundant, along
with the faith and love that are in Christ Jesus. This saying is
trustworthy and deserves full acceptance: Christ Jesus came
into the world to save sinners. Of these I am the foremost.
But for that reason I was mercifully treated, so that in me, as
the foremost, Christ Jesus might display all his patience as
an example for those who would come to believe in him for
everlasting life. To the king of ages, incorruptible, invisible, the
only God, honor and glory forever and ever. Amen.

Alleluia   2 Cor 5: 19   Michael Kissinger

Al-le - lu-ia, al-le - lu - ia, al - le - lu - ia.

God was reconciling the world to himself in Christ /
and entrusting to us the message of reconciliation.
Alleluia, alleluia.

Gospel   Lk 15: 1–32 or 15: 1–10
For the shorter form, read only the parts in brackets.
[Tax collectors and sinners were all drawing near to listen to
Jesus, but the Pharisees and scribes began to complain, saying,
"This man welcomes sinners and eats with them." So to them
he addressed this parable. "What man among you having a
hundred sheep and losing one of them would not leave the
ninety-nine in the desert and go after the lost one until he finds
it? And when he does find it, he sets it on his shoulders with
great joy and, upon his arrival home, he calls together his friends
and neighbors and says to them, 'Rejoice with me because I have
found my lost sheep.' I tell you, in just the same way there will
be more joy in heaven over one sinner who repents than over
ninety-nine righteous people who have no need of repentance.
     "Or what woman having ten coins and losing one would not
light a lamp and sweep the house, searching carefully until she
finds it? And when she does find it, she calls together her friends

and neighbors and says to them, 'Rejoice with me because I have found the coin that I lost.' In just the same way, I tell you, there will be rejoicing among the angels of God over one sinner who repents."]

Then he said, "A man had two sons, and the younger son said to his father, 'Father give me the share of your estate that should come to me.' So the father divided the property between them. After a few days, the younger son collected all his belongings and set off to a distant country where he squandered his inheritance on a life of dissipation. When he had freely spent everything, a severe famine struck that country, and he found himself in dire need. So he hired himself out to one of the local citizens who sent him to his farm to tend the swine. And he longed to eat his fill of the pods on which the swine fed, but nobody gave him any. Coming to his senses he thought, 'How many of my father's hired workers have more than enough food to eat, but here am I, dying from hunger. I shall get up and go to my father and I shall say to him, "Father, I have sinned against heaven and against you. I no longer deserve to be called your son; treat me as you would treat one of your hired workers."' So he got up and went back to his father. While he was still a long way off, his father caught sight of him, and was filled with compassion. He ran to his son, embraced him and kissed him. His son said to him, 'Father, I have sinned against heaven and against you; I no longer deserve to be called your son.' But his father ordered his servants, 'Quickly bring the finest robe and put it on him; put a ring on his finger and sandals on his feet. Take the fattened calf and slaughter it. Then let us celebrate with a feast, because this son of mine was dead, and has come to life again; he was lost, and has been found.' Then the celebration began. Now the older son had been out in the field and, on his way back, as he neared the house, he heard the sound of music and dancing. He called one of the servants and asked what this might mean. The servant said to him, 'Your brother has returned and your father has slaughtered the fattened calf because he has him back safe and sound.' He became angry, and when he refused to enter the house, his father came out and pleaded with him. He said to his father in reply, 'Look, all these years I served you and not once did I disobey your orders; yet you never gave me even a young goat to feast on with my friends. But when your son returns, who swallowed up your property with prostitutes, for him you slaughter the fattened calf.' He said to him, 'My son, you are here with me always; everything I have is yours. But now we must celebrate and rejoice, because your brother was dead and has come to life again; he was lost and has been found.'"

Communion Antiphon *cf. Ps 36 (35): 8* How precious is your mercy, O God! • The children of men seek shelter in the shadow of your wings.

Or: *cf. 1 Cor 10: 16* The chalice of blessing that we bless • is a communion in the Blood of Christ; • and the bread that we break • is a sharing in the Body of the Lord.

TWENTY-FIFTH SUNDAY IN ORDINARY TIME

Entrance Antiphon
I am the salvation of the people, says the Lord. • Should they cry to me in any distress, • I will hear them, and I will be their Lord for ever.

First Reading *Am 8: 4–7*
Hear this, you who trample upon the needy
    and destroy the poor of the land!
"When will the new moon be over," you ask,
    "that we may sell our grain,
    and the sabbath, that we may display the wheat?
We will diminish the ephah,
    add to the shekel,
    and fix our scales for cheating!
We will buy the lowly for silver,
    and the poor for a pair of sandals;
    even the refuse of the wheat we will sell!"
The LORD has sworn by the pride of Jacob:
    Never will I forget a thing they have done!

Responsorial Psalm Ps 113: 1–2, 4–6, 7–8   *Joe Higginbotham*

Praise the Lord, who lifts up the poor.

Praise the Lord, who lifts up the poor.

Or: ℟ **Alleluia.**

Praise, you servants of the LORD,
    praise the name of the LORD.
Blessed be the name of the LORD
    both now and forever. ℟

High above all nations is the LORD;
    above the heavens is his glory.
Who is like the LORD, our God, who is enthroned on high
    and looks upon the heavens and the earth below? ℟

He raises up the lowly from the dust;
    from the dunghill he lifts up the poor
to seat them with princes,
    with the princes of his own people. ℟

Second Reading 1 Tm 2: 1–8 Beloved: First of all, I ask that
supplications, prayers, petitions, and thanksgivings be offered
for everyone, for kings and for all in authority, that we may lead
a quiet and tranquil life in all devotion and dignity. This is good
and pleasing to God our savior, who wills everyone to be saved
and to come to knowledge of the truth.
    For there is one God.
    There is also one mediator between God and men,
    the man Christ Jesus,
    who gave himself as ransom for all.
This was the testimony at the proper time. For this I was

appointed preacher and apostle—I am speaking the truth, I am not lying—, teacher of the Gentiles in faith and truth.

It is my wish, then, that in every place the men should pray, lifting up holy hands, without anger or argument.

Alleluia   *cf. 2 Cor 8: 9*   *Michael Kissinger*

Al-le - lu-ia, al-le - lu - ia, al   -   le - lu - ia.

Though our Lord Jesus Christ was rich, he became poor, / so that by his poverty you might become rich. **Alleluia, alleluia.**

Gospel   Lk 16: 1–13 or 16: 10–13
For the shorter form, read only the parts in brackets.
[Jesus said to his disciples,] "A rich man had a steward who was reported to him for squandering his property. He summoned him and said, 'What is this I hear about you? Prepare a full account of your stewardship, because you can no longer be my steward.' The steward said to himself, 'What shall I do, now that my master is taking the position of steward away from me? I am not strong enough to dig and I am ashamed to beg. I know what I shall do so that, when I am removed from the stewardship, they may welcome me into their homes.' He called in his master's debtors one by one. To the first he said, 'How much do you owe my master?' He replied, 'One hundred measures of olive oil.' He said to him, 'Here is your promissory note. Sit down and quickly write one for fifty.' Then to another the steward said, 'And you, how much do you owe?' He replied, 'One hundred kors of wheat.' The steward said to him, 'Here is your promissory note; write one for eighty.' And the master commended that dishonest steward for acting prudently.

"For the children of this world are more prudent in dealing with their own generation than are the children of light. I tell you, make friends for yourselves with dishonest wealth, so that when it fails, you will be welcomed into eternal dwellings.

[The person who is trustworthy in very small matters is also trustworthy in great ones; and the person who is dishonest in very small matters is also dishonest in great ones. If, therefore, you are not trustworthy with dishonest wealth, who will trust you with true wealth? If you are not trustworthy with what belongs to another, who will give you what is yours? No servant can serve two masters. He will either hate one and love the other, or be devoted to one and despise the other. You cannot serve both God and mammon."]

Communion Antiphon Ps 119 (118): 4–5 **You have laid down your precepts to be carefully kept; ◆ may my ways be firm in keeping your statutes.**

Or: Jn 10: 14 **I am the Good Shepherd, says the Lord; ◆ I know my sheep, and mine know me.**

TWENTY-SIXTH

SUNDAY IN ORDINARY TIME

Entrance Antiphon Dn 3: 31, 29, 30, 43, 42 **All that you have done to us, O Lord, ◆ you have done with true judgment, ◆ for we have sinned against you ◆ and not obeyed your commandments. ◆ But give glory to your name ◆ and deal with us according to the bounty of your mercy.**

First Reading   Am 6: 1a, 4–7
Thus says the LORD the God of hosts:
  Woe to the complacent in Zion!
  Lying upon beds of ivory,
    stretched comfortably on their couches,
  they eat lambs taken from the flock,
    and calves from the stall!
  Improvising to the music of the harp,
    like David, they devise their own accompaniment.

They drink wine from bowls
   and anoint themselves with the best oils;
   yet they are not made ill by the collapse of Joseph!
Therefore, now they shall be the first to go into exile,
   and their wanton revelry shall be done away with.

Responsorial Psalm *Ps 146: 7, 8–9, 9–10*   *Joe Higginbotham*

Praise the Lord, my soul! Praise the Lord!

Or: ℟ **Alleluia.**

Blessed is he who keeps faith forever,
   secures justice for the oppressed,
   gives food to the hungry.
The Lord sets captives free. ℟

The Lord gives sight to the blind;
   the Lord raises up those who were bowed down.
The Lord loves the just;
   The Lord protects strangers. ℟

The fatherless and the widow he sustains,
   but the way of the wicked he thwarts.
The Lord shall reign forever;
   your God, O Zion, through all generations. Alleluia. ℟

Second Reading *1 Tm 6: 11–16* But you, man of God, pursue
righteousness, devotion, faith, love, patience, and gentleness.
Compete well for the faith. Lay hold of eternal life, to which
you were called when you made the noble confession in the
presence of many witnesses. I charge you before God, who gives
life to all things, and before Christ Jesus, who gave testimony
under Pontius Pilate for the noble confession, to keep the
commandment without stain or reproach until the appearance
of our Lord Jesus Christ that the blessed and only ruler will

make manifest at the proper time, the King of kings and Lord of lords, who alone has immortality, who dwells in unapproachable light, and whom no human being has seen or can see. To him be honor and eternal power. Amen.

Alleluia   *cf. 2 Cor 8: 9*   Michael Kissinger

Al-le - lu-ia, al-le - lu - ia, al - le - lu - ia.

Though our Lord Jesus Christ was rich, he became poor, / so that by his poverty you might become rich. **Alleluia, alleluia.**

Gospel *Lk 16: 19–31* Jesus said to the Pharisees: "There was a rich man who dressed in purple garments and fine linen and dined sumptuously each day. And lying at his door was a poor man named Lazarus, covered with sores, who would gladly have eaten his fill of the scraps that fell from the rich man's table. Dogs even used to come and lick his sores. When the poor man died, he was carried away by angels to the bosom of Abraham. The rich man also died and was buried, and from the netherworld, where he was in torment, he raised his eyes and saw Abraham far off and Lazarus at his side. And he cried out, 'Father Abraham, have pity on me. Send Lazarus to dip the tip of his finger in water and cool my tongue, for I am suffering torment in these flames.' Abraham replied, 'My child, remember that you received what was good during your lifetime while Lazarus likewise received what was bad; but now he is comforted here, whereas you are tormented. Moreover, between us and you a great chasm is established to prevent anyone from crossing who might wish to go from our side to yours or from your side to ours.' He said, 'Then I beg you, father, send him to my father's house, for I have five brothers, so that he may warn them, lest they too come to this place of torment.' But Abraham replied, 'They have Moses and the prophets. Let them listen to them.' He said, 'Oh no, father Abraham, but if someone from the dead goes to them, they will repent.' Then Abraham said, 'If they will not listen to Moses and the prophets, neither will they be persuaded if someone should rise from the dead.'"

Communion Antiphon *cf. Ps 119 (118): 49–50* **Remember your word to your servant, O Lord, ✦ by which you have given me hope. ✦ This is my comfort when I am brought low.**

Or: *1 Jn 3: 16* **By this we came to know the love of God: ✦ that Christ laid down his life for us; ✦ so we ought to lay down our lives for one another.**

TWENTY-SEVENTH

SUNDAY IN ORDINARY TIME

Entrance Antiphon *cf. Est 4: 17* **Within your will, O Lord, all things are established, ✦ and there is none that can resist your will. ✦ For you have made all things, the heaven and the earth, ✦ and all that is held within the circle of heaven; ✦ you are the Lord of all.**

First Reading *Hab 1: 2–3; 2: 2–4*
How long, O LORD? I cry for help
    but you do not listen!
I cry out to you, "Violence!"
    but you do not intervene.
Why do you let me see ruin;
    why must I look at misery?
Destruction and violence are before me;
    there is strife, and clamorous discord.
Then the LORD answered me and said:
    Write down the vision clearly upon the tablets,
    so that one can read it readily.
For the vision still has its time,

presses on to fulfillment, and will not disappoint;
if it delays, wait for it,
  it will surely come, it will not be late.
The rash one has no integrity;
  but the just one, because of his faith, shall live.

Responsorial Psalm   Ps 95: 1–2, 6–7, 8–9

Vince Ambrosetti

If to-day you hear his voice, hard-en not your hearts.

Come, let us sing joyfully to the LORD;
  let us acclaim the Rock of our salvation.
Let us come into his presence with thanksgiving;
  let us joyfully sing psalms to him.   ℟

Come, let us bow down in worship;
  let us kneel before the LORD who made us.
For he is our God,
  and we are the people he shepherds, the flock he guides.   ℟

Oh, that today you would hear his voice:
  "Harden not your hearts as at Meribah,
  as in the day of Massah in the desert,
where your fathers tempted me;
  they tested me though they had seen my works."   ℟

Second Reading   2 Tm 1: 6–8, 13–14   Beloved: I remind you to stir into
flame the gift of God that you have through the imposition of
my hands. For God did not give us a spirit of cowardice but
rather of power and love and self-control. So do not be ashamed
of your testimony to our Lord, nor of me, a prisoner for his sake;
but bear your share of hardship for the gospel with the strength
that comes from God.
  Take as your norm the sound words that you heard from me,

in the faith and love that are in Christ Jesus. Guard this rich trust with the help of the Holy Spirit that dwells within us.

Alleluia   *1 Pt 1: 25*   *Michael Kissinger*

Al-le - lu-ia, al-le - lu - ia, al - le - lu - ia.

The word of the Lord remains for ever. / This is the word that has been proclaimed to you.   **Alleluia, alleluia.**

Gospel *Lk 17: 5–10* The apostles said to the Lord, "Increase our faith." The Lord replied, "If you have faith the size of a mustard seed, you would say to this mulberry tree, 'Be uprooted and planted in the sea,' and it would obey you.

"Who among you would say to your servant who has just come in from plowing or tending sheep in the field, 'Come here immediately and take your place at table?' Would he not rather say to him, 'Prepare something for me to eat. Put on your apron and wait on me while I eat and drink. You may eat and drink when I am finished?' Is he grateful to that servant because he did what was commanded? So should it be with you. When you have done all you have been commanded, say, 'We are unprofitable servants; we have done what we were obliged to do.'"

Communion Antiphon *Lam 3: 25* **The Lord is good to those who hope in him, ◆ to the soul that seeks him.**

Or: *cf. 1 Cor 10: 17* **Though many, we are one bread, one body, ◆ for we all partake of the one Bread and one Chalice.**

TWENTY-EIGHTH SUNDAY IN ORDINARY TIME

Entrance Antiphon *Ps 130 (129): 3–4* **If you, O Lord, should mark iniquities, ◆ Lord, who could stand? ◆ But with you is found forgiveness, ◆ O God of Israel.**

First Reading *2 Kgs 5: 14–17* Naaman went down and plunged into the Jordan seven times at the word of Elisha, the man of God. His flesh became again like the flesh of a little child, and he was clean of his leprosy.

Naaman returned with his whole retinue to the man of God. On his arrival he stood before Elisha and said, "Now I know that there is no God in all the earth, except in Israel. Please accept a gift from your servant."

Elisha replied, "As the LORD lives whom I serve, I will not take it;" and despite Naaman's urging, he still refused. Naaman said: "If you will not accept, please let me, your servant, have two mule-loads of earth, for I will no longer offer holocaust or sacrifice to any other god except to the LORD."

Responsorial Psalm   *Ps 98: 1, 2–3, 3–4*   Don Fishel

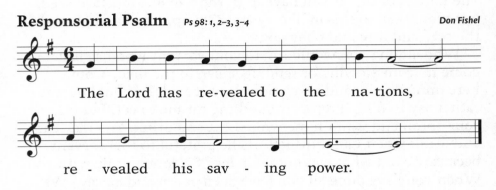

The Lord has re-vealed to the na-tions, re-vealed his sav-ing power.

Sing to the LORD a new song,
   for he has done wondrous deeds;
his right hand has won victory for him,
   his holy arm. ℟

The LORD has made his salvation known:
   in the sight of the nations he has revealed his justice.
He has remembered his kindness and his faithfulness
   toward the house of Israel. ℟

All the ends of the earth have seen
   the salvation by our God.
Sing joyfully to the LORD, all you lands:
   break into song; sing praise. ℟

Second Reading *2 Tm 2: 8–13* Beloved: Remember Jesus Christ, raised from the dead, a descendant of David: such is my gospel, for which I am suffering, even to the point of chains, like a criminal. But the word of God is not chained. Therefore, I bear with everything for the sake of those who are chosen, so that they too may obtain the salvation that is in Christ Jesus, together with eternal glory. This saying is trustworthy:

If we have died with him
    we shall also live with him;
if we persevere
    we shall also reign with him.
But if we deny him
    he will deny us.
If we are unfaithful
    he remains faithful,
    for he cannot deny himself.

Alleluia   *1 Thes 5: 18*   *Michael Kissinger*

Al-le - lu-ia, al-le - lu - ia, al - le - lu - ia.

In all circumstances, give thanks, / for this is the will of God for you in Christ Jesus.   **Alleluia, alleluia.**

Gospel *Lk 17: 11–19* As Jesus continued his journey to Jerusalem, he traveled through Samaria and Galilee. As he was entering a village, ten lepers met him. They stood at a distance from him and raised their voices, saying, "Jesus, Master! Have pity on us!" And when he saw them, he said, "Go show yourselves to the priests." As they were going they were cleansed. And one of them, realizing he had been healed, returned, glorifying God in a loud voice; and he fell at the feet of Jesus and thanked him. He was a Samaritan. Jesus said in reply, "Ten were cleansed, were they not? Where are the other nine? Has none but this foreigner returned to give thanks to God?" Then he said to him, "Stand up and go; your faith has saved you."

Communion Antiphon *cf. Ps 34 (33): 11* **The rich suffer want and go hungry,** ◆ **but those who seek the Lord lack no blessing.**

Or: *1 Jn 3: 2* **When the Lord appears, we shall be like him,** ◆ **for we shall see him as he is.**

TWENTY-NINTH SUNDAY IN ORDINARY TIME

Entrance Antiphon *cf. Ps 17 (16): 6, 8* **To you I call; for you will surely heed me, O God;** ◆ **turn your ear to me; hear my words.** ◆ **Guard me as the apple of your eye;** ◆ **in the shadow of your wings protect me.**

First Reading *Ex 17: 8–13* In those days, Amalek came and waged war against Israel. Moses, therefore, said to Joshua, "Pick out certain men, and tomorrow go out and engage Amalek in battle. I will be standing on top of the hill with the staff of God in my hand." So Joshua did as Moses told him: he engaged Amalek in battle after Moses had climbed to the top of the hill with Aaron and Hur. As long as Moses kept his hands raised up, Israel had the better of the fight, but when he let his hands rest, Amalek had the better of the fight. Moses' hands, however, grew tired; so they put a rock in place for him to sit on. Meanwhile Aaron and Hur supported his hands, one on one side and one on the other, so that his hands remained steady till sunset. And Joshua mowed down Amalek and his people with the edge of the sword.

Responsorial Psalm   *Ps 121: 1–2, 3–4, 5–6, 7–8*   Ann Fons and Roger Holtz

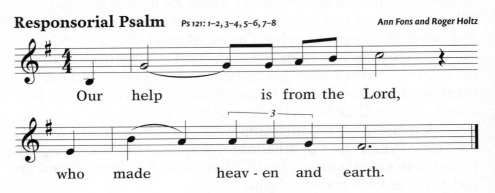

Our help is from the Lord, who made heav-en and earth.

I lift up my eyes toward the mountains;
whence shall help come to me?

My help is from the LORD,
   who made heaven and earth. ℟

May he not suffer your foot to slip;
   may he slumber not who guards you:
indeed he neither slumbers nor sleeps,
   the guardian of Israel. ℟

The LORD is your guardian; the LORD is your shade;
   he is beside you at your right hand.
The sun shall not harm you by day,
   nor the moon by night. ℟

The LORD will guard you from all evil;
   he will guard your life.
The LORD will guard your coming and your going,
   both now and forever. ℟

Second Reading *2 Tm 3: 14- 4: 2* Beloved: Remain faithful to what you
have learned and believed, because you know from whom you
learned it, and that from infancy you have known the sacred
Scriptures, which are capable of giving you wisdom for salvation
through faith in Christ Jesus. All Scripture is inspired by God
and is useful for teaching, for refutation, for correction, and for
training in righteousness, so that one who belongs to God may
be competent, equipped for every good work.

   I charge you in the presence of God and of Christ Jesus, who
will judge the living and the dead, and by his appearing and his
kingly power: proclaim the word; be persistent whether it is
convenient or inconvenient; convince, reprimand, encourage
through all patience and teaching.

Alleluia   *Heb 4: 12*   Brian J. Nelson

Al - le-lu - ia, al - le - lu - ia, al-le-lu - ia.

The word of God is living and effective, / discerning
reflections and thoughts of the heart.   **Alleluia, alleluia.**

Gospel Lk 18: 1–8 Jesus told his disciples a parable about the necessity for them to pray always without becoming weary. He said, "There was a judge in a certain town who neither feared God nor respected any human being. And a widow in that town used to come to him and say, 'Render a just decision for me against my adversary.' For a long time the judge was unwilling, but eventually he thought, 'While it is true that I neither fear God nor respect any human being, because this widow keeps bothering me I shall deliver a just decision for her lest she finally come and strike me.'" The Lord said, "Pay attention to what the dishonest judge says. Will not God then secure the rights of his chosen ones who call out to him day and night? Will he be slow to answer them? I tell you, he will see to it that justice is done for them speedily. But when the Son of Man comes, will he find faith on earth?"

Communion Antiphon cf. Ps 33 (32): 18–19 Behold, the eyes of the Lord ✦ are on those who fear him, ✦ who hope in his merciful love, ✦ to rescue their souls from death, ✦ to keep them alive in famine.

Or: Mk 10: 45 The Son of Man has come ✦ to give his life as a ransom for many.

THIRTIETH SUNDAY IN ORDINARY TIME

Entrance Antiphon cf. Ps 105 (104): 3–4 Let the hearts that seek the Lord rejoice; ✦ turn to the Lord and his strength; ✦ constantly seek his face.

First Reading Sir 35: 12–14, 16–18
The LORD is a God of justice,
 who knows no favorites.
Though not unduly partial toward the weak,
 yet he hears the cry of the oppressed.
The LORD is not deaf to the wail of the orphan,
 nor to the widow when she pours out her complaint.

The one who serves God willingly is heard;
  his petition reaches the heavens.
The prayer of the lowly pierces the clouds;
  it does not rest till it reaches its goal,
nor will it withdraw till the Most High responds,
  judges justly and affirms the right,
and the Lord will not delay.

Responsorial Psalm   Ps 34: 2–3, 17–18, 19, 23   Joe Higginbotham

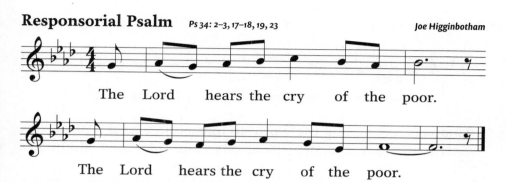

The Lord hears the cry of the poor.

The Lord hears the cry of the poor.

I will bless the LORD at all times;
  his praise shall be ever in my mouth.
Let my soul glory in the LORD;
  the lowly will hear me and be glad. ℟

The LORD confronts the evildoers,
  to destroy remembrance of them from the earth.
When the just cry out, the LORD hears them,
  and from all their distress he rescues them. ℟

The LORD is close to the brokenhearted;
  and those who are crushed in spirit he saves.
The LORD redeems the lives of his servants;
  no one incurs guilt who takes refuge in him. ℟

Second Reading 2 Tm 4: 6–8, 16–18 Beloved: I am already being poured
out like a libation, and the time of my departure is at hand. I
have competed well; I have finished the race; I have kept the
faith. From now on the crown of righteousness awaits me,
which the Lord, the just judge, will award to me on that day, and
not only to me, but to all who have longed for his appearance.

At my first defense no one appeared on my behalf, but everyone deserted me. May it not be held against them! But the Lord stood by me and gave me strength, so that through me the proclamation might be completed and all the Gentiles might hear it. And I was rescued from the lion's mouth. The Lord will rescue me from every evil threat and will bring me safe to his heavenly kingdom. To him be glory forever and ever. Amen.

Alleluia   2 Cor 5: 19   Brian J. Nelson

Al - le-lu - ia,   al - le - lu - ia,   al-le-lu - ia.

God was reconciling the world to himself in Christ, / and entrusting to us the message of salvation.   **Alleluia, alleluia.**

Gospel Lk 18: 9–14 Jesus addressed this parable to those who were convinced of their own righteousness and despised everyone else. "Two people went up to the temple area to pray; one was a Pharisee and the other was a tax collector. The Pharisee took up his position and spoke this prayer to himself, 'O God, I thank you that I am not like the rest of humanity—greedy, dishonest, adulterous—or even like this tax collector. I fast twice a week, and I pay tithes on my whole income.' But the tax collector stood off at a distance and would not even raise his eyes to heaven but beat his breast and prayed, 'O God, be merciful to me a sinner.' I tell you, the latter went home justified, not the former; for whoever exalts himself will be humbled, and the one who humbles himself will be exalted."

Communion Antiphon cf. Ps 20 (19): 6 **We will ring out our joy at your saving help ◆ and exult in the name of our God.**

Or: Eph 5: 2 **Christ loved us and gave himself up for us, ◆ as a fragrant offering to God.**

THIRTY-FIRST SUNDAY IN ORDINARY TIME

Entrance Antiphon *cf. Ps 38 (37): 22–23* **Forsake me not, O Lord, my God; ◆ be not far from me! ◆ Make haste and come to my help, ◆ O Lord, my strong salvation!**

First Reading *Wis 11: 22–12: 2*

Before the LORD the whole universe is as a grain from a balance
or a drop of morning dew come down upon the earth.
But you have mercy on all, because you can do all things;
and you overlook people's sins that they may repent.
For you love all things that are
and loathe nothing that you have made;
for what you hated, you would not have fashioned.
And how could a thing remain, unless you willed it;
or be preserved, had it not been called forth by you?
But you spare all things, because they are yours,
O LORD and lover of souls,
for your imperishable spirit is in all things!
Therefore you rebuke offenders little by little,
warn them and remind them of the sins they are committing,
that they may abandon their wickedness and believe in you,
O LORD!

Responsorial Psalm *Ps 145: 1–2, 8–9, 10–11, 13, 14*   Bill Svarda

I will praise your name for ev - er,

my king and my God.

I will extol you, O my God and King,
and I will bless your name forever and ever.
Every day will I bless you,
and I will praise your name forever and ever. ℟

The LORD is gracious and merciful,
  slow to anger and of great kindness.
The LORD is good to all
  and compassionate toward all his works. ℟

Let all your works give you thanks, O LORD,
  and let your faithful ones bless you.
Let them discourse of the glory of your kingdom
  and speak of your might. ℟

The LORD is faithful in all his words
  and holy in all his works.
The LORD lifts up all who are falling
  and raises up all who are bowed down. ℟

Second Reading *2 Thes 1: 11–2: 2* Brothers and sisters: We always pray for you, that our God may make you worthy of his calling and powerfully bring to fulfillment every good purpose and every effort of faith, that the name of our Lord Jesus may be glorified in you, and you in him, in accord with the grace of our God and Lord Jesus Christ.

  We ask you, brothers and sisters, with regard to the coming of our Lord Jesus Christ and our assembling with him, not to be shaken out of your minds suddenly, or to be alarmed either by a "spirit," or by an oral statement, or by a letter allegedly from us to the effect that the day of the Lord is at hand.

Alleluia *Jn 3: 16*   Brian J. Nelson

Al - le-lu - ia, al - le - lu - ia, al-le-lu - ia.

God so loved the world that he gave his only Son, / so
that everyone who believes in him might have eternal life.
Alleluia, alleluia.

Gospel *Lk 19: 1–10* At that time, Jesus came to Jericho and intended to pass through the town. Now a man there named Zacchaeus, who was a chief tax collector and also a wealthy man, was seeking to see who Jesus was; but he could not see him because of the crowd, for he was short in stature. So he ran ahead and climbed a sycamore tree in order to see Jesus, who was about to pass that way. When he reached the place, Jesus looked up and said, "Zacchaeus, come down quickly, for today I must stay at your house." And he came down quickly and received him with joy. When they all saw this, they began to grumble, saying, "He has gone to stay at the house of a sinner." But Zacchaeus stood there and said to the Lord, "Behold, half of my possessions, Lord, I shall give to the poor, and if I have extorted anything from anyone I shall repay it four times over." And Jesus said to him, "Today salvation has come to this house because this man too is a descendant of Abraham. For the Son of Man has come to seek and to save what was lost."

Communion Antiphon *cf. Ps 16 (15): 11* You will show me the path of life, ◆ the fullness of joy in your presence, O Lord.

Or: *Jn 6: 58* Just as the living Father sent me ◆ and I have life because of the Father, ◆ so whoever feeds on me ◆ shall have life because of me, says the Lord.

THIRTY-SECOND SUNDAY IN ORDINARY TIME

Entrance Antiphon *cf. Ps 88 (87): 3* Let my prayer come into your presence. ◆ Incline your ear to my cry for help, O Lord.

First Reading *2 Mc 7: 1-2, 9-14* It happened that seven brothers with their mother were arrested and tortured with whips and scourges by the king, to force them to eat pork in violation of God's law. One of the brothers, speaking for the others, said: "What do you expect to achieve by questioning us? We are ready to die rather than transgress the laws of our ancestors."

At the point of death he said: "You accursed fiend, you are depriving us of this present life, but the King of the world will raise us up to live again forever. It is for his laws that we are dying."

After him the third suffered their cruel sport. He put out his tongue at once when told to do so, and bravely held out his hands, as he spoke these noble words: "It was from Heaven that I received these; for the sake of his laws I disdain them; from him I hope to receive them again." Even the king and his attendants marveled at the young man's courage, because he regarded his sufferings as nothing.

After he had died, they tortured and maltreated the fourth brother in the same way. When he was near death, he said, "It is my choice to die at the hands of men with the hope God gives of being raised up by him; but for you, there will be no resurrection to life."

Responsorial Psalm   Ps 17: 1, 5–6, 8, 15   Amy Righi

Lord, when your glo - ry ap - pears, my joy will be full, my joy will be full.

Hear, O LORD, a just suit;
　　attend to my outcry;
　　hearken to my prayer from lips without deceit. ℟

My steps have been steadfast in your paths,
　　my feet have not faltered.
I call upon you, for you will answer me, O God;
　　incline your ear to me; hear my word. ℟

Keep me as the apple of your eye,
　　hide me in the shadow of your wings.
But I in justice shall behold your face;
　　on waking I shall be content in your presence. ℟

Second Reading 2 Thes 2: 16–3: 5 Brothers and sisters: May our Lord Jesus Christ himself and God our Father, who has loved us and given us everlasting encouragement and good hope through his grace, encourage your hearts and strengthen them in every good deed and word.

Finally, brothers and sisters, pray for us, so that the word of the Lord may speed forward and be glorified, as it did among you, and that we may be delivered from perverse and wicked people, for not all have faith. But the Lord is faithful; he will strengthen you and guard you from the evil one. We are confident of you in the Lord that what we instruct you, you are doing and will continue to do. May the Lord direct your hearts to the love of God and to the endurance of Christ.

Alleluia   Rv 1: 5a, 6b

Brian J. Nelson

Al - le-lu - ia,   al - le - lu - ia,   al-le-lu - ia.

Jesus Christ is the firstborn of the dead; ◆ to him be glory and power, forever and ever.   **Alleluia, alleluia.**

Gospel   Lk 20: 27–38 or 20: 27, 34–38
For the shorter form, read only the parts in brackets.
[Some Sadducees, those who deny that there is a resurrection, came forward] and put this question to Jesus, saying, "Teacher, Moses wrote for us, *If someone's brother dies leaving a wife but no child, his brother must take the wife and raise up descendants for his brother.* Now there were seven brothers; the first married a woman but died childless. Then the second and the third married her, and likewise all the seven died childless. Finally the woman also died. Now at the resurrection whose wife will that woman be? For all seven had been married to her." [Jesus said to them, "The children of this age marry and remarry; but those who are deemed worthy to attain to the coming age and to the resurrection of the dead neither marry nor are given in marriage. They can no longer die, for they are like angels; and they are the children of God because they are the ones who will rise. That the dead will rise even Moses made known in the passage about the bush, when he called out 'Lord,' the God of Abraham, the God of Isaac, and the God of Jacob; and he is not God of the dead, but of the living, for to him all are alive."]

Communion Antiphon *cf. Ps 23 (22): 1–2* The Lord is my shepherd; there is nothing I shall want. ◆ Fresh and green are the pastures where he gives me repose, ◆ near restful waters he leads me.

Or: *cf. Lk 24: 35* The disciples recognized the Lord Jesus in the breaking of bread.

THIRTY-THIRD SUNDAY IN ORDINARY TIME

Entrance Antiphon *Jer 29: 11, 12, 14* The Lord said: I think thoughts of peace and not of affliction. ◆ You will call upon me, and I will answer you, and I will lead back your captives from every place.

First Reading *Mal 3: 19–20a*

Lo, the day is coming, blazing like an oven,
    when all the proud and all evildoers will be stubble,
and the day that is coming will set them on fire,
    leaving them neither root nor branch,
    says the LORD of hosts.
But for you who fear my name, there will arise
    the sun of justice with its healing rays.

Responsorial Psalm *Ps 98: 5–6, 7–8, 9*   *Roger Holtz and Jane Terwilliger*

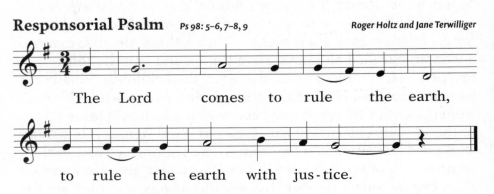

The Lord comes to rule the earth, to rule the earth with jus-tice.

Sing praise to the LORD with the harp,
    with the harp and melodious song.
With trumpets and the sound of the horn
    sing joyfully before the King, the LORD. ℟

Let the sea and what fills it resound,
  the world and those who dwell in it;
let the rivers clap their hands, the
  mountains shout with them for joy. ℟

Before the LORD, for he comes,
  for he comes to rule the earth,
He will rule the world with justice and
  the peoples with equity. ℟

Second Reading *2 Thes 3: 7–12* Brothers and sisters: You know how one must imitate us. For we did not act in a disorderly way among you, nor did we eat food received free from anyone. On the contrary, in toil and drudgery, night and day we worked, so as not to burden any of you. Not that we do not have the right. Rather, we wanted to present ourselves as a model for you, so that you might imitate us. In fact, when we were with you, we instructed you that if anyone was unwilling to work, neither should that one eat. We hear that some are conducting themselves among you in a disorderly way, by not keeping busy but minding the business of others. Such people we instruct and urge in the Lord Jesus Christ to work quietly and to eat their own food.

Alleluia   Lk 21: 28   Brian J. Nelson

Al - le-lu - ia, al - le - lu - ia, al-le-lu - ia.

Stand erect and raise your heads / because your redemption is at hand. **Alleluia, alleluia.**

Gospel *Lk 21: 5–19* While some people were speaking about how the temple was adorned with costly stones and votive offerings, Jesus said, "All that you see here—the days will come when there will not be left a stone upon another stone that will not be thrown down."
  Then they asked him, "Teacher, when will this happen?

And what sign will there be when all these things are about to happen?" He answered, "See that you not be deceived, for many will come in my name, saying, 'I am he,' and 'The time has come.' Do not follow them! When you hear of wars and insurrections, do not be terrified; for such things must happen first, but it will not immediately be the end." Then he said to them, "Nation will rise against nation, and kingdom against kingdom. There will be powerful earthquakes, famines, and plagues from place to place; and awesome sights and mighty signs will come from the sky.

"Before all this happens, however, they will seize and persecute you, they will hand you over to the synagogues and to prisons, and they will have you led before kings and governors because of my name. It will lead to your giving testimony. Remember, you are not to prepare your defense beforehand, for I myself shall give you a wisdom in speaking that all your adversaries will be powerless to resist or refute. You will even be handed over by parents, brothers, relatives, and friends, and they will put some of you to death. You will be hated by all because of my name, but not a hair on your head will be destroyed. By your perseverance you will secure your lives."

Communion Antiphon *cf. Ps 73 (72): 28* To be near God is my happiness, ◆ to place my hope in God the Lord.

Or: *Mk 11: 23–24* Amen, I say to you: Whatever you ask in prayer, ◆ believe that you will receive, ◆ and it shall be given to you, says the Lord.

OUR LORD JESUS CHRIST,

KING OF THE UNIVERSE

Entrance Antiphon *Rv 5: 12; 1: 6* How worthy is the Lamb who was slain, ◆ to receive power and divinity, ◆ and wisdom and strength and honor. ◆ To him belong glory and power for ever and ever.

First Reading *2 Sm 5: 1–3* In those days, all the tribes of Israel came to David in Hebron and said: "Here we are, your bone and your flesh. In days past, when Saul was our king, it was you who led the Israelites out and brought them back. And the LORD said to you, 'You shall shepherd my people Israel and shall be commander of Israel.'" When all the elders of Israel came to David in Hebron, King David made an agreement with them there before the LORD, and they anointed him king of Israel.

Responsorial Psalm   Ps 122: 1–2, 3–4, 4–5   Brian J. Nelson

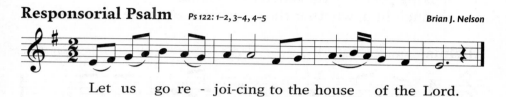

Let us go re - joi-cing to the house of the Lord.

I rejoiced because they said to me,
    "We will go up to the house of the LORD."
And now we have set foot
    within your gates, O Jerusalem. ℟

Jerusalem, built as a city
    with compact unity.
To it the tribes go up,
    the tribes of the LORD. ℟

According to the decree for Israel,
    to give thanks to the name of the LORD.
In it are set up judgment seats,
    seats for the house of David. ℟

Second Reading   Col 1: 12–20   Brothers and sisters: Let us give thanks to the Father, who has made you fit to share in the inheritance of the holy ones in light. He delivered us from the power of darkness and transferred us to the kingdom of his beloved Son, in whom we have redemption, the forgiveness of sins.
    He is the image of the invisible God,
        the firstborn of all creation.
    For in him were created all things in heaven and on earth,
        the visible and the invisible,
        whether thrones or dominions or principalities or powers;
        all things were created through him and for him.
    He is before all things,

and in him all things hold together.
He is the head of the body, the church.
He is the beginning, the firstborn from the dead,
    that in all things he himself might be preeminent.
For in him all the fullness was pleased to dwell,
    and through him to reconcile all things for him,
    making peace by the blood of his cross
    through him, whether those on earth or those in heaven.

Alleluia   Mk 11: 9, 10   Brian J. Nelson

Al - le-lu - ia,   al - le - lu - ia,   al-le-lu - ia.

Blessed is he who comes in the name of the Lord! / Blessed
is the kingdom of our father David that is to come!
Alleluia, alleluia.

Gospel Lk 23: 35-43 The rulers sneered at Jesus and said, "He saved
others, let him save himself if he is the chosen one, the Christ
of God." Even the soldiers jeered at him. As they approached to
offer him wine they called out, "If you are King of the Jews, save
yourself." Above him there was an inscription that read, "This is
the King of the Jews."

   Now one of the criminals hanging there reviled Jesus, saying,
"Are you not the Christ? Save yourself and us." The other,
however, rebuking him, said in reply, "Have you no fear of God,
for you are subject to the same condemnation? And indeed,
we have been condemned justly, for the sentence we received
corresponds to our crimes, but this man has done nothing
criminal." Then he said, "Jesus, remember me when you come
into your kingdom." He replied to him, "Amen, I say to you,
today you will be with me in Paradise.

Communion Antiphon Ps 29 (28): 10-11 **The Lord sits as King for
ever. ⬧ The Lord will bless his people with peace.**

The Sacred Paschal Triduum

In the Sacred Triduum, the Church solemnly celebrates the greatest mysteries of our redemption, keeping by means of special celebrations the memorial of her Lord, crucified, buried, and risen.

The Paschal Fast should also be kept sacred. It is to be celebrated everywhere on the Friday of the Lord's Passion and, where appropriate, prolonged also through Holy Saturday as a way of coming, with spirit uplifted, to the joys of the Lord's Resurrection.

HOLY THURSDAY

❖ Mass of the Lord's Supper ❖

The Mass of the Lord's Supper is celebrated in the evening, at a convenient time, with the full participation of the whole local community and with all the Priests and ministers exercising their office.

Entrance Antiphon *cf. Gal 6: 14* **We should glory in the Cross of our Lord Jesus Christ, ◆ in whom is our salvation, life and resurrection, ◆ through whom we are saved and delivered.**

The Gloria in Excelsis *(Glory to God in the Highest) is said. While the hymn is being sung, bells are rung, and when it is finished, they remain silent until the* Gloria in Excelsis *of the Easter Vigil. Likewise, during this same period, the organ and other musical instruments may be used only so as to support the singing.*

First Reading *Ex 12: 1–8, 11–14* The LORD said to Moses and Aaron in the land of Egypt, "This month shall stand at the head of your calendar; you shall reckon it the first month of the year. Tell the whole community of Israel: On the tenth of this month every one of your families must procure for itself a lamb, one apiece for each household. If a family is too small for a whole lamb, it shall join the nearest household in procuring one and shall share in the lamb in proportion to the number of persons who partake of it. The lamb must be a year-old male and without blemish. You may take it from either the sheep or the goats. You shall keep it until the fourteenth day of this month, and then, with the whole assembly of Israel present, it shall be slaughtered during the evening twilight. They shall take some of its blood and apply it to the two doorposts and the lintel of every house in which they partake of the lamb. That same night they shall eat its roasted flesh with unleavened bread and bitter herbs.

"This is how you are to eat it: with your loins girt, sandals on your feet and your staff in hand, you shall eat like those who are in flight. It is the Passover of the LORD. For on this same night I will go through Egypt, striking down every firstborn of the land, both man and beast, and executing judgment on all the gods of Egypt—I, the LORD! But the blood will mark the houses where you are. Seeing the blood, I will pass over you; thus, when I strike the land of Egypt, no destructive blow will come upon you.

"This day shall be a memorial feast for you, which all your generations shall celebrate with pilgrimage to the LORD, as a perpetual institution."

Responsorial Psalm   Ps 116: 12–13, 15–16bc, 17–18   Joe Higginbotham

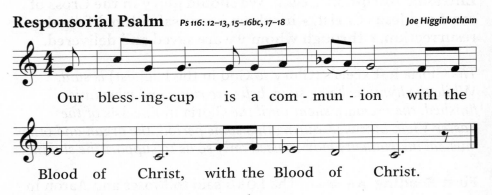

Our bless-ing-cup is a com-mun-ion with the Blood of Christ, with the Blood of Christ.

How shall I make a return to the LORD
for all the good he has done for me?

The cup of salvation I will take up,
  and I will call upon the name of the LORD.   ℟

Precious in the eyes of the LORD
  is the death of his faithful ones.
I am your servant, the son of your handmaid;
  you have loosed my bonds.   ℟

To you will I offer sacrifice of thanksgiving,
  and I will call upon the name of the LORD.
My vows to the LORD I will pay
  in the presence of all his people.   ℟

Second Reading *1 Cor 11: 23–26* Brothers and sisters: I received from the Lord what I also handed on to you, that the Lord Jesus, on the night he was handed over, took bread, and, after he had given thanks, broke it and said, "This is my body that is for you. Do this in remembrance of me." In the same way also the cup, after supper, saying, "This cup is the new covenant in my blood. Do this, as often as you drink it, in remembrance of me." For as often as you eat this bread and drink the cup, you proclaim the death of the Lord until he comes.

Verse Before the Gospel   *Jn 13: 34*   *Amy Righi*

Praise to you, Lord Jesus Christ, King of endless glory!

I give you a new commandment, says the Lord: / love one another as I have loved you.

Gospel *Jn 13: 1–15* Before the feast of Passover, Jesus knew that his hour had come to pass from this world to the Father. He loved his own in the world and he loved them to the end. The devil had already induced Judas, son of Simon the Iscariot, to hand him over. So, during supper, fully aware that the Father had put everything into his power and that he had come from God and was returning to God, he rose from supper and took off his outer garments. He took a towel and tied it around his waist. Then he poured water into a basin and began to wash the disciples' feet and dry them with the towel around his waist. He came to Simon Peter, who said to him, "Master, are you going to wash my feet?" Jesus answered and said to him, "What I am doing, you do not understand now, but you will understand later." Peter said to him, "You will never wash my feet." Jesus answered him, "Unless I wash you, you will have no inheritance with me." Simon Peter said to him, "Master, then not only my feet, but my hands and head as well." Jesus said to him, "Whoever has bathed has no need except to have his feet washed, for he is clean all over; so you are clean, but not all." For he knew who would betray him; for this reason, he said, "Not all of you are clean."

So when he had washed their feet and put his garments back on and reclined at table again, he said to them, "Do you realize what I have done for you? You call me 'teacher' and 'master,' and rightly so, for indeed I am. If I, therefore, the master and teacher, have washed your feet, you ought to wash one another's feet. I have given you a model to follow, so that as I have done for you, you should also do."

After the proclamation of the Gospel, the Priest gives a homily in which light is shed on the principal mysteries that are commemorated in this Mass, namely, the institution of the Holy Eucharist and of the Priestly Order, and the commandment of the Lord concerning fraternal charity.

THE WASHING OF FEET

After the Homily, where a pastoral reason suggests it, the Washing of Feet follows.

Those who are chosen from among the people of God are led by the ministers to seats prepared in a suitable place. Then the Priest goes

*to each one and, with the help of the ministers, pours water over
each one's feet and then dries them.*

*Meanwhile some of the following antiphons or other appropriate
chants are sung.*

Antiphon 1 *cf. Jn 13: 4, 5, 15* **After the Lord had risen from supper, ◆
he poured water into a basin ◆ and began to wash the feet of
his disciples: ◆ he left them this example.**

Antiphon 2 *cf. Jn 13: 12, 13, 15* **The Lord Jesus, after eating supper
with his disciples, ◆ washed their feet and said to them: ◆ Do
you know what I, your Lord and Master, have done for you? ◆
I have given you an example, that you should do likewise.**

Antiphon 3 *Jn 13: 6, 7, 8*
℟ **Lord, are you to wash my feet? Jesus said to him in
answer: ◆ If I do not wash your feet, you will have no
share with me.**

℣ So he came to Simon Peter and Peter said to him:
℟ **Lord, are you to wash my feet? Jesus said to him in
answer: ◆ If I do not wash your feet, you will have no
share with me.**

℣ What I am doing, you do not know for now, / but later you
will come to know.
℟ **Lord, are you to wash my feet? Jesus said to him in
answer: ◆ If I do not wash your feet, you will have no
share with me.**

Antiphon 4 *cf. Jn 13: 14* **If I, your Lord and Master, have
washed your feet, ◆ how much more should you wash each
other's feet?**

Antiphon 5 *Jn 13: 35*
℟ **This is how all will know that you are my disciples: ◆
if you have love for one another.**

℣ Jesus said to his disciples:
℟ **This is how all will know that you are my disciples:** ◆
if you have love for one another.

Antiphon 6 Jn 13:34 **I give you a new commandment, ◆ that you**
love one another ◆ as I have loved you, says the Lord.

Antiphon 7   1 Cor 13: 13
℟ **Let faith, hope and charity, these three, remain among**
you, ◆ but the greatest of these is charity.

℣ Now faith, hope and charity, these three, remain; / but the
greatest of these is charity.
℟ **Let faith, hope and charity, these three, remain among**
you, ◆ but the greatest of these is charity.

After the Washing of Feet, the Priest washes and dries his hands,
and returns to the chair, and from there he directs the Universal
Prayer.

The Creed *is not said.*

THE LITURGY OF THE EUCHARIST

At the beginning of the Liturgy of the Eucharist, there may be
a procession of the faithful in which gifts for the poor may be
presented with the bread and wine.

Meanwhile the following, or another appropriate chant, is sung.
  Ant. Where true charity is dwelling, God is present there.
  ℣ By the love of Christ we have been brought together:
  ℣ let us find in him our gladness and our pleasure;
  ℣ may we love him and revere him, God the living,
  ℣ and in love respect each other with sincere hearts.

  Ant. Where true charity is dwelling, God is present there.
  ℣ So when we as one are gathered all together,
  ℣ let us strive to keep our minds free of division;
  ℣ may there be an end to malice, strife and quarrels,

℣ and let Christ our God be dwelling here among us.

Ant. Where true charity is dwelling, God is present there.
℣ May your face thus be our vision, bright in glory,
℣ Christ our God, with all the blessed Saints in heaven:
℣ such delight is pure and faultless, joy unbounded,
℣ which endures through countless ages world without
end. Amen.

*At an appropriate time during Communion, the Priest entrusts the
Eucharist from the table of the altar to Deacons or acolytes or other
extraordinary ministers, so that afterwards it may be brought to
the sick who are to receive Holy Communion at home.*

Communion Antiphon 1 Cor 11: 24-25 **This is the Body that will be
given up for you; ♦ this is the Chalice of the new covenant in
my Blood, says the Lord; ♦ do this, whenever you receive it, in
memory of me.**

TRANSFER OF THE MOST BLESSED SACRAMENT

*After the Prayer after Communion, the Priest puts incense in
the thurible, blesses it and then, kneeling, incenses the Blessed
Sacrament three times. Then, having put on a white humeral veil, he
rises, takes the ciborium, and covers it with the ends of the veil.*

*A procession is formed in which the Blessed Sacrament,
accompanied by torches and incense, is carried through the church
to a place of repose prepared in a part of the church or in a chapel
suitably decorated. Meanwhile the hymn* Pange, lingua [Sing, my
tongue*] *(exclusive of the last two stanzas) or another eucharistic
chant is sung.*

Pange lingua gloriósi	Sing, my tongue, the Savior's
Córporis mystérium,	glory
Sanguinísque pretiósi	Of his Flesh the mystery sing;
Quem in mundi prétium	Of the Blood, all price exceeding,

* tr. Edward Caswall, 1814–1878, *Lyra Catholica*, 1851

Fructus ventris generósi
Rex effúdit géntium.

Shed by our immortal King,
Destined, for the world's
    redemption,
From a noble womb to spring.

Nobis datus, nobis natus
Ex intácta Vírgine,
Et in mundo conversátus,
Sparso verbi semine,
Sui moras incolátus
Miro clausit órdine.

Of a pure and spotless Virgin
Born for us on earth below,
He, as Man with man conversing,
Stayed, the seeds of truth to sow;
Then he closed in solemn order
Wondrously his life of woe.

In suprémae nocte cenae
Recúmbens cum
    frátribus,
Observáta lege plene
Cibis in legálibus,
Cibum turbae duodénae
Se dat suis mánibus.

On the night of that Last Supper,
Seated with his chosen band,
He the Paschal victim eatine,
First fulfills the Law's command;
Then, as Food to all his brethen
Gives Himself with his own hand.

Verbum caro, panem
    verum
Verbo carnem éfficit:
Fitque sanguis Christi
    merum,
Et si sensus déficit,
Ad firmándum cor
    sincérum
Sola fides súfficit.

Word made Flesh, the bread of
    nature
By his word to Flesh He turns;
Wine into his Blood He changes—
What though sense no change
    discerns?
Only be the heart in earnest,
Faith her lesson quickly learns.

When the procession reaches the place of repose, the Priest places the ciborium in the tabernacle, the door of which remains open. Then he puts incense in the thurible and, kneeling, incenses the Blessed Sacrament, while Tantum ergo Sacramentum *or another eucharistic chant is sung. Then the Deacon or the Priest himself places the Sacrament in the tabernacle and closes the door.*

Tantum ergo Sacraméntum
Venerémur cérnui,

Down in adoration falling,
Lo! the sacred Host we hail;

Et antíquum documéntum Novo cedat rítui; Praestet fides suppleméntum sénsuum deféctui.	Lo! o'er ancient forms departing, Newer rites of grace prevail; Faith, for all defects supplying, Where the feeble senses fail.

Genitóri Genitóque
Laus et jubilátio,
Salus, honor, virtus quoque
Sit et benedíctio;
Procedénti ab utróque
Compar sit laudátio.
Amen.
	To the Everlasting Father,
	And the Son who reigns on
	    high,
	With the Holy Ghost
	    proceeding
	Forth from Each eternally,
	Be salvation, honor, blessing,
	Might, and endless majesty.
	Amen.

After a period of adoration in silence, the Priest and ministers genuflect and return to the sacristy.

At an appropriate time, the altar is stripped and, if possible, the crosses are removed from the church. It is expedient that any crosses which remain in the church be veiled.

Vespers (Evening Prayer) is not celebrated by those who have attended the Mass of the Lord's Supper.

The faithful are invited to continue adoration before the Blessed Sacrament for a suitable length of time during the night, according to local circumstances, but after midnight the adoration should take place without solemnity.

FRIDAY OF THE PASSION OF THE LORD

On this and the following day, by a most ancient tradition, the Church does not celebrate the Sacraments at all, except for Penance and the Anointing of the Sick.

*On the afternoon of this day there takes place the celebration of the
Lord's Passion consisting of three parts, namely, the Liturgy of the
Word, the Adoration of the Cross, and Holy Communion.*

*The Priest and the Deacon, if a Deacon is present, wearing red
vestments as for Mass, go to the altar in silence and, after making a
reverence to the altar, prostrate themselves or, if appropriate, kneel
and pray in silence for a while. All others kneel.*

*Then the Priest, with the ministers, goes to the chair where, facing
the people, who are standing, he says one of the following prayers,
omitting the invitation* Let us pray.

Prayer
Remember your mercies, O Lord,
and with your eternal protection sanctify your servants,
for whom Christ your Son,
by the shedding of his Blood,
established the Paschal Mystery.
Who lives and reigns for ever and ever.   ℞ **Amen.**

Or:
O God, who by the Passion of Christ your Son, our Lord,
abolished the death inherited from ancient sin
by every succeeding generation,
grant that just as, being conformed to him,
we have borne by the law of nature
the image of the man of earth,
so by the sanctification of grace
we may bear the image of the Man of heaven.
Through Christ our Lord.   ℞ **Amen.**

❖ First Part: The Liturgy of the Word ❖

First Reading *Is 52: 13–53: 12*
See, my servant shall prosper,
he shall be raised high and greatly exalted.
Even as many were amazed at him—

so marred was his look beyond human semblance
and his appearance beyond that of the sons of man—
so shall he startle many nations,
because of him kings shall stand speechless;
for those who have not been told shall see,
those who have not heard shall ponder it.

Who would believe what we have heard?
To whom has the arm of the LORD been revealed?
He grew up like a sapling before him,
like a shoot from the parched earth;
there was in him no stately bearing to make us look at him,
nor appearance that would attract us to him.
He was spurned and avoided by people,
a man of suffering, accustomed to infirmity,
one of those from whom people hide their faces,
spurned, and we held him in no esteem.

Yet it was our infirmities that he bore,
our sufferings that he endured,
while we thought of him as stricken,
as one smitten by God and afflicted.
But he was pierced for our offenses,
crushed for our sins;
upon him was the chastisement that makes us whole,
by his stripes we were healed.
We had all gone astray like sheep,
each following his own way;
but the LORD laid upon him
the guilt of us all.

Though he was harshly treated, he submitted
and opened not his mouth;
like a lamb led to the slaughter
or a sheep before the shearers,
he was silent and opened not his mouth.
Oppressed and condemned, he was taken away,
and who would have thought any more of his destiny?
When he was cut off from the land of the living,
and smitten for the sin of his people,

a grave was assigned him among the wicked
 and a burial place with evildoers,
though he had done no wrong
 nor spoken any falsehood.
But the LORD was pleased
 to crush him in infirmity.

If he gives his life as an offering for sin,
 he shall see his descendants in a long life,
 and the will of the LORD shall be accomplished
  through him.

Because of his affliction
 he shall see the light in fullness of days;
through his suffering, my servant shall justify many,
 and their guilt he shall bear.
Therefore I will give him his portion among the great,
 and he shall divide the spoils with the mighty,
because he surrendered himself to death
 and was counted among the wicked;
and he shall take away the sins of many,
 and win pardon for their offenses.

Responsorial Psalm Ps 31: 2, 6, 12–13, 15–16, 17, 25   Joe Higginbotham

Fa - ther, in-to your hands, I com-mend my spir-it.

In you, O LORD, I take refuge;
 let me never be put to shame.
In your justice rescue me.
Into your hands I commend my spirit;
 you will redeem me, O LORD, O faithful God. ℟

For all my foes I am an object of reproach,
 a laughingstock to my neighbors, and a dread to my friends;
 they who see me abroad flee from me.
I am forgotten like the unremembered dead;

I am like a dish that is broken. ℟

But my trust is in you, O LORD;
  I say, "You are my God.
In your hands is my destiny; rescue me
  from the clutches of my enemies and my persecutors." ℟

Let your face shine upon your servant;
  save me in your kindness.
Take courage and be stouthearted,
  all you who hope in the LORD. ℟

Second Reading *Heb 4: 14–16; 5: 7–9* Brothers and sisters: Since we
have a great high priest who has passed through the heavens,
Jesus, the Son of God, let us hold fast to our confession. For we
do not have a high priest who is unable to sympathize with our
weaknesses, but one who has similarly been tested in every way,
yet without sin. So let us confidently approach the throne of
grace to receive mercy and to find grace for timely help.
  In the days when Christ was in the flesh, he offered prayers
and supplications with loud cries and tears to the one who was
able to save him from death, and he was heard because of his
reverence. Son though he was, he learned obedience from what
he suffered; and when he was made perfect, he became the
source of eternal salvation for all who obey him.

Verse Before the Gospel *Phil 2: 8–9* Amy Righi

Praise to you, Lord Je - sus Christ, King of end - less glo - ry!

Christ became obedient to the point of death, / even death
on a cross. / Because of this, God greatly exalted him / and
bestowed on him the name which is above every other name.

Gospel   *Jn 18: 1–19: 42*
The symbols of the following passion narrative represent:
+ Christ;   **N.** *narrator;*   **V.** *voice;*   **C.** *crowd.*

N. The Passion of our Lord Jesus Christ according to John.

Jesus went out with his disciples across the Kidron valley to where there was a garden, into which he and his disciples entered. Judas his betrayer also knew the place, because Jesus had often met there with his disciples. So Judas got a band of soldiers and guards from the chief priests and the Pharisees and went there with lanterns, torches, and weapons. Jesus, knowing everything that was going to happen to him, went out and said to them, **+** "Whom are you looking for?" **N.** They answered him, **C.** "**Jesus the Nazorean.**" **N.** He said to them, **+** "I AM." **N.** Judas his betrayer was also with them. When he said to them, "I AM," they turned away and fell to the ground. So he again asked them, **+** "Whom are you looking for?" **N.** They said, **C.** "**Jesus the Nazorean.**" **N.** Jesus answered, **+** "I told you that I AM. So if you are looking for me, let these men go." **N.** This was to fulfill what he had said, "I have not lost any of those you gave me." Then Simon Peter, who had a sword, drew it, struck the high priest's slave, and cut off his right ear. The slave's name was Malchus. Jesus said to Peter, **+** "Put your sword into its scabbard. Shall I not drink the cup that the Father gave me?"

N. So the band of soldiers, the tribune, and the Jewish guards seized Jesus, bound him, and brought him to Annas first. He was the father-in-law of Caiaphas, who was high priest that year. It was Caiaphas who had counseled the Jews that it was better that one man should die rather than the people.

Simon Peter and another disciple followed Jesus. Now the other disciple was known to the high priest, and he entered the courtyard of the high priest with Jesus. But Peter stood at the gate outside. So the other disciple, the acquaintance of the high priest, went out and spoke to the gatekeeper and brought Peter in. Then the maid who was the gatekeeper said to Peter, **C.** "**You are not one of this man's disciples, are you?**" **N.** He said, **V.** "I am not." **N.** Now the slaves and the guards were standing around a charcoal fire that they had made, because it was cold, and were warming themselves. Peter was also standing there keeping warm.

The high priest questioned Jesus about his disciples and about his doctrine. Jesus answered him, **+** "I have spoken publicly to the world. I have always taught in a synagogue or in the temple area where all the Jews gather, and in secret I have said nothing. Why ask me? Ask those who heard me what I said to them. They know what I said." **N.** When he had said this, one of the temple guards standing there struck Jesus and said, **V.** "Is this the way you answer the high priest?" **N.** Jesus answered him, **+** "If I have spoken wrongly, testify to the wrong; but if I have spoken rightly, why do you strike me?" **N.** Then Annas sent him bound to Caiaphas the high priest.

Now Simon Peter was standing there keeping warm. And they said to him, **C.** **"You are not one of his disciples, are you?"** **N.** He denied it and said, **V.** "I am not." **N.** One of the slaves of the high priest, a relative of the one whose ear Peter had cut off, said, **C.** **"Didn't I see you in the garden with him?"** **N.** Again Peter denied it. And immediately the cock crowed.

Then they brought Jesus from Caiaphas to the praetorium. It was morning. And they themselves did not enter the praetorium, in order not to be defiled so that they could eat the Passover. So Pilate came out to them and said, **V.** "What charge do you bring against this man?" **N.** They answered and said to him, **C.** **"If he were not a criminal, we would not have handed him over to you."** **N.** At this, Pilate said to them, **V.** "Take him yourselves, and judge him according to your law." **N.** The Jews answered him, **C.** **"We do not have the right to execute anyone,"** **N.** in order that the word of Jesus might be fulfilled that he said indicating the kind of death he would die. So Pilate went back into the praetorium and summoned Jesus and said to him, **V.** "Are you the King of the Jews?" **N.** Jesus answered, **+** "Do you say this on your own or have others told you about me?" **N.** Pilate answered, **V.** "I am not a Jew, am I? Your own nation and the chief priests handed you over to me. What have you done?" **N.** Jesus answered, **+** "My kingdom does not belong to this world. If my kingdom did belong to this world, my attendants would be fighting to keep me from being handed over to the Jews. But as it is, my kingdom is not here." **N.** So Pilate said to him, **V.** "Then you are a king?" **N.** Jesus answered, **+** "You say I am a king. For this I was born and for this I came into the world, to testify to the truth. Everyone who

belongs to the truth listens to my voice." **N.** Pilate said to him,
V. "What is truth?"

N. When he had said this, he again went out to the Jews and
said to them, **V.** "I find no guilt in him. But you have a custom
that I release one prisoner to you at Passover. Do you want
me to release to you the King of the Jews?" **N.** They cried out
again, **C. "Not this one but Barabbas!"** **N.** Now Barabbas was a
revolutionary.

Then Pilate took Jesus and had him scourged. And the soldiers
wove a crown out of thorns and placed it on his head, and
clothed him in a purple cloak, and they came to him and said,
C. "Hail, King of the Jews!" **N.** And they struck him repeatedly.
Once more Pilate went out and said to them, **V.** "Look, I am
bringing him out to you, so that you may know that I find no
guilt in him." **N.** So Jesus came out, wearing the crown of thorns
and the purple cloak. And Pilate said to them, **V.** "Behold,
the man!" **N.** When the chief priests and the guards saw him
they cried out, **C. "Crucify him, crucify him!"** **N.** Pilate said
to them, **V.** "Take him yourselves and crucify him. I find no
guilt in him." **N.** The Jews answered, **C. "We have a law, and
according to that law he ought to die, because he made
himself the Son of God."** **N.** Now when Pilate heard this
statement, he became even more afraid, and went back into the
praetorium and said to Jesus, **V.** "Where are you from?" **N.** Jesus
did not answer him. So Pilate said to him, **V.** "Do you not speak
to me? Do you not know that I have power to release you and
I have power to crucify you?" **N.** Jesus answered him, **✝** "You
would have no power over me if it had not been given to you
from above. For this reason the one who handed me over to
you has the greater sin." **N.** Consequently, Pilate tried to release
him; but the Jews cried out, **C. "If you release him, you are
not a Friend of Caesar. Everyone who makes himself a king
opposes Caesar."**

N. When Pilate heard these words he brought Jesus out
and seated him on the judge's bench in the place called Stone
Pavement, in Hebrew, Gabbatha. It was preparation day for
Passover, and it was about noon. And he said to the Jews,
V. "Behold, your king!" **N.** They cried out, **C. "Take him away,
take him away! Crucify him!"** **N.** Pilate said to them, **V.** "Shall
I crucify your king?" **N.** The chief priests answered, **C. "We**

have no king but Caesar." N. Then he handed him over to
them to be crucified.

So they took Jesus, and, carrying the cross himself, he
went out to what is called the Place of the Skull, in Hebrew,
Golgotha. There they crucified him, and with him two others,
one on either side, with Jesus in the middle. Pilate also had an
inscription written and put on the cross. It read, "Jesus the
Nazorean, the King of the Jews." Now many of the Jews read
this inscription, because the place where Jesus was crucified was
near the city; and it was written in Hebrew, Latin, and Greek.
So the chief priests of the Jews said to Pilate, **c. "Do not write
'The King of the Jews,' but that he said, 'I am the King of
the Jews.'" N.** Pilate answered, **v.** "What I have written, I have
written."

N. When the soldiers had crucified Jesus, they took his clothes
and divided them into four shares, a share for each soldier. They
also took his tunic, but the tunic was seamless, woven in one
piece from the top down. So they said to one another, **c. "Let's
not tear it, but cast lots for it to see whose it will be," N.** in
order that the passage of Scripture might be fulfilled that says:
They divided my garments among them,
and for my vesture they cast lots.
This is what the soldiers did. Standing by the cross of Jesus were
his mother and his mother's sister, Mary the wife of Clopas, and
Mary of Magdala. When Jesus saw his mother and the disciple
there whom he loved he said to his mother, **+** "Woman, behold,
your son." **N.** Then he said to the disciple, **+** "Behold, your
mother." **N.** And from that hour the disciple took her into his
home.

After this, aware that everything was now finished, in order
that the Scripture might be fulfilled, Jesus said, **+** "I thirst."
N. There was a vessel filled with common wine. So they put
a sponge soaked in wine on a sprig of hyssop and put it up to
his mouth. When Jesus had taken the wine, he said, **+** "It is
finished." **N.** And bowing his head, he handed over the spirit.

Here all kneel and pause for a short time.

Now since it was preparation day, in order that the bodies
might not remain on the cross on the sabbath, for the sabbath

day of that week was a solemn one, the Jews asked Pilate that
their legs be broken and that they be taken down. So the soldiers
came and broke the legs of the first and then of the other one
who was crucified with Jesus. But when they came to Jesus
and saw that he was already dead, they did not break his legs,
but one soldier thrust his lance into his side, and immediately
blood and water flowed out. An eyewitness has testified, and
his testimony is true; he knows that he is speaking the truth, so
that you also may come to believe. For this happened so that the
Scripture passage might be fulfilled:
 Not a bone of it will be broken.
And again another passage says:
 They will look upon him whom they have pierced.
 After this, Joseph of Arimathea, secretly a disciple of Jesus
for fear of the Jews, asked Pilate if he could remove the body of
Jesus. And Pilate permitted it. So he came and took his body.
Nicodemus, the one who had first come to him at night, also
came bringing a mixture of myrrh and aloes weighing about
one hundred pounds. They took the body of Jesus and bound it
with burial cloths along with the spices, according to the Jewish
burial custom. Now in the place where he had been crucified
there was a garden, and in the garden a new tomb, in which no
one had yet been buried. So they laid Jesus there because of the
Jewish preparation day; for the tomb was close by.

*After the reading of the Lord's Passion, the Priest gives a brief
homily and, at its end, the faithful may be invited to spend a short
time in prayer.*

THE SOLEMN INTERCESSIONS

*The Liturgy of the Word concludes with the Solemn Intercessions,
which take place in this way: the Deacon, if a Deacon is present, or
if he is not, a lay minister, stands at the ambo, and sings or says
the invitation in which the intention is expressed. Then all pray in
silence for a while, and afterwards the Priest, standing at the chair
or, if appropriate, at the altar, sings or says the prayer.*

*The faithful may remain either kneeling or standing throughout the
entire period of the prayers.*

Before the Priest's prayer, in accord with tradition, it is permissible to use the Deacon's invitations Let us kneel—Let us stand, *with all kneeling for silent prayer.*

I. For the Holy Church

Let us pray, dearly beloved, for the holy Church of God,
that our God and Lord be pleased to give her peace,
to guard her and to unite her throughout the whole world
and grant that, leading our life in tranquility and quiet,
we may glorify God the Father almighty.

Prayer in silence. Then the Priest says:
Almighty ever-living God,
who in Christ revealed your glory to all the nations,
watch over the works of your mercy,
that your Church, spread throughout all the world,
may persevere with steadfast faith in confessing your name.
Through Christ our Lord. ℟ **Amen.**

II. For the Pope

Let us pray also for our most Holy Father Pope N.,
that our God and Lord,
who chose him for the Order of Bishops,
may keep him safe and unharmed for the Lord's holy Church,
to govern the holy People of God.

Prayer in silence. Then the Priest says:
Almighty ever-living God,
by whose decree all things are founded,
look with favor on our prayers
and in your kindness protect the Pope chosen for us,
that, under him, the Christian people,
governed by you their maker,
may grow in merit by reason of their faith.
Through Christ our Lord. ℟ **Amen.**

III. For all orders and degrees of the faithful

Let us pray also for our Bishop N.,
for all Bishops, Priests, and Deacons of the Church
and for the whole of the faithful people.

Prayer in silence. Then the Priest says:
Almighty ever-living God,
by whose Spirit the whole body of the Church
is sanctified and governed,
hear our humble prayer for your ministers,
that, by the gift of your grace,
all may serve you faithfully.
Through Christ our Lord.   ℟ **Amen.**

IV. For catechumens

Let us pray also for (our) catechumens,
that our God and Lord
may open wide the ears of their inmost hearts
and unlock the gates of his mercy,
that, having received forgiveness of all their sins
through the waters of rebirth,
they, too, may be one with Christ Jesus our Lord.

Prayer in silence. Then the Priest says:
Almighty ever-living God,
who make your Church ever fruitful with new offspring,
increase the faith and understanding of (our) catechumens,
that, reborn in the font of Baptism,
they may be added to the number of your adopted children.
Through Christ our Lord.   ℟ **Amen.**

V. For the unity of Christians

Let us pray also for all our brothers and sisters who believe in
    Christ,
that our God and Lord may be pleased,
as they live the truth,
to gather them together and keep them in his one Church.

Prayer in silence. Then the Priest says:
Almighty ever-living God,
who gather what is scattered
and keep together what you have gathered,
look kindly on the flock of your Son,
that those whom one Baptism has consecrated

may be joined together by integrity of faith
and united in the bond of charity.
Through Christ our Lord.   ℟ **Amen.**

VI. For the Jewish people
Let us pray also for the Jewish people,
to whom the Lord our God spoke first,
that he may grant them to advance in love of his name
and in faithfulness to his covenant.

Prayer in silence. Then the Priest says:
Almighty ever-living God,
who bestowed your promises on Abraham and his
descendants,
graciously hear the prayers of your Church,
that the people you first made your own
may attain the fullness of redemption.
Through Christ our Lord.   ℟ **Amen.**

VII. For those who do not believe in Christ
Let us pray also for those who do not believe in Christ,
that, enlightened by the Holy Spirit,
they, too, may enter on the way of salvation.

Prayer in silence. Then the Priest says:
Almighty ever-living God,
grant to those who do not confess Christ
that, by walking before you with a sincere heart,
they may find the truth
and that we ourselves, being constant in mutual love
and striving to understand more fully the mystery of your life,
may be made more perfect witnesses to your love in the
  world.
Through Christ our Lord.   ℟ **Amen.**

VIII. For those who do not believe in God
Let us pray also for those who do not acknowledge God,
that, following what is right in sincerity of heart,
they may find the way to God himself.

Prayer in silence. Then the Priest says:
Almighty ever-living God,
who created all people
to seek you always by desiring you
and, by finding you, come to rest,
grant, we pray,
that, despite every harmful obstacle,
all may recognize the signs of your fatherly love
and the witness of the good works
done by those who believe in you,
and so in gladness confess you,
the one true God and Father of our human race.
Through Christ our Lord.   ℟ **Amen.**

IX. For those in public office

Let us pray also for those in public office,
that our God and Lord
may direct their minds and hearts according to his will
for the true peace and freedom of all.

Prayer in silence. Then the Priest says:
Almighty ever-living God,
in whose hand lies every human heart
and the rights of peoples,
look with favor, we pray,
on those who govern with authority over us,
that throughout the whole world,
the prosperity of peoples,
the assurance of peace,
and freedom of religion
may through your gift be made secure.
Through Christ our Lord.   ℟ **Amen.**

X. For those in tribulation

Let us pray, dearly beloved,
to God the Father almighty,
that he may cleanse the world of all errors,
banish disease, drive out hunger,
unlock prisons, loosen fetters,

granting to travelers safety, to pilgrims return,
health to the sick, and salvation to the dying.

Prayer in silence. Then the Priest says:
Almighty ever-living God,
comfort of mourners, strength of all who toil,
may the prayers of those who cry out in any tribulation
come before you,
that all may rejoice,
because in their hour of need
your mercy was at hand.
Through Christ our Lord.   ℟ **Amen.**

☼   Second Part: The Adoration of the Holy Cross   ☼

*After the Solemn Intercessions, the solemn Adoration of the Holy
Cross takes place. Of the two forms of the showing of the Cross
presented here, the more appropriate one, according to pastoral
needs, should be chosen.*

THE SHOWING OF THE HOLY CROSS

First Form   *The Deacon, or another suitable minister, goes to the
sacristy, from which, in procession, accompanied by two ministers
with lighted candles, he carries the Cross, covered with a violet veil,
through the church to the middle of the sanctuary.*

*The Priest, standing before the altar and facing the people, receives
the Cross, uncovers a little of its upper part and elevates it while
beginning the* Ecce lignum Crucis *(Behold the wood of the
Cross). All respond,* **Come, let us adore.** *At the end of the singing,
all kneel and for a brief moment adore in silence, while the Priest
stands and holds the Cross raised.*

Behold the wood of the Cross, / on which hung the salvation
of the world.   ℟ **Come, let us adore.**

Then the Priest uncovers the right arm of the Cross and again, raising up the Cross, begins, Behold the wood of the Cross *and everything takes place as above. Finally, he uncovers the Cross entirely and, raising it up, he begins the invitation* Behold the wood of the Cross *a third time and everything takes place like the first time.*

Second Form   *The Priest or the Deacon accompanied by ministers, or another suitable minister, goes to the door of the church, where he receives the unveiled Cross, and the ministers take lighted candles; then the procession sets off through the church to the sanctuary. Near the door, in the middle of the church and before the entrance of the sanctuary, the one who carries the Cross elevates it, singing,* Behold the wood of the Cross, *to which all respond,* Come, let us adore. *After each response all kneel and for a brief moment adore in silence, as above.*

THE ADORATION OF THE HOLY CROSS

Then the Priest or Deacon carries the Cross to the entrance of the Sanctuary or to another suitable place and there puts it down or hands it over to the ministers to hold. Candles are places on the right and left sides of the Cross.

For the Adoration of the Cross, first the Priest Celebrant alone approaches. Then the clergy, the lay ministers, and the faithful approach, moving as if in procession, and showing reverence to the Cross by a simple genuflection or by some other sign appropriate to the usage of the region, for example, by kissing the Cross.

While the adoration of the Holy Cross is taking place, the antiphon Crucem tuam adoramus (We adore your Cross, O Lord), *the Reproaches, the hymn* Crux fidelis (Faithful Cross), *or other suitable chants are sung, during which all who have already adored the Cross remain seated.*

CHANTS TO BE SUNG DURING THE ADORATION OF THE HOLY CROSS

Antiphon   *cf. Ps 67 (66): 2*
We adore your Cross, O Lord, ✦ we praise and glorify your

holy Resurrection, ✦ for behold, because of the wood of a
tree ✦ joy has come to the whole world.

℣ May God have mercy on us and bless us; / may he let his
face shed its light upon us / and have mercy on us.
And the antiphon is repeated: **We adore ...**

The Reproaches

*Parts assigned to one of the two choirs separately are indicated by
the numbers 1 (first choir) and 2 (second choir); parts sung by both
choirs together are marked: 1 and 2. Some of the verses may also be
sung by two cantors.*

✦ I ✦

1 and 2
My people, what have I done to you?
Or how have I grieved you? Answer me!

1
Because I led you out of the land of Egypt,
you have prepared a Cross for your Savior.

1 *Hagios o Theos,*
2 Holy is God,
1 *Hagios Ischyros,*
2 Holy and Mighty,
1 *Hagios Athanatos, eleison himas.*
2 Holy and Immortal One, have mercy on us.

1 and 2
Because I led you out through the desert forty years
and fed you with manna and brought you into a land of plenty,
you have prepared a Cross for your Savior.

The choirs respond, alternating: Hágios o Theós, *etc.,* Holy is God,
etc., in such a way that the first choir always repeats Hágios, *as
above.*

1 and 2
What more should I have done for you and have not done?
Indeed, I planted you as my most beautiful chosen vine
and you have turned very bitter for me,
for in my thirst you gave me vinegar to drink
and with a lance you pierced your Savior's side.

The choirs respond in the same way, alternating Hágios o Theós,
Holy is God.

◆ II ◆

Cantors:
I scourged Egypt for your sake with its firstborn sons,
and you scourged me and handed me over.

1 and 2 repeat:
My people, what have I done to you?
Or how have I grieved you? Answer me!

Cantors:
I led you out from Egypt as Pharoah lay sunk in the Red Sea,
and you handed me over to the chief priests.
    1 and 2 repeat: My people ...

Cantors:
I opened up the sea before you,
and you opened my side with a lance.
    1 and 2 repeat: My people ...

Cantors:
I went before you in a pillar of cloud,
and you led me into Pilate's palace.
    1 and 2 repeat: My people ...

Cantors:
I fed you with manna in the desert,
and on me you rained blows and lashes.
    1 and 2 repeat: My people ...

Cantors:
I gave you saving water from the rock to drink,
and for drink you gave me gall and vinegar.
   1 and 2 repeat: My people ...

Cantors:
I struck down for you the kings of the Canaanites,
and you struck my head with a reed.
   1 and 2 repeat: My people ...

Cantors:
I put in your hand a royal scepter,
and you put on my head a crown of thorns.
   1 and 2 repeat: My people ...

Cantors:
I exalted you with great power,
and you hung me on the scaffold of the Cross.
   1 and 2 repeat: My people ...

Hymn

Faithful Cross the Saints rely on,
Noble tree beyond compare!
Never was there such a scion,
Never leaf or flower so rare.
Sweet the timber, sweet the iron,
Sweet the burden that they bear!

Sing, my tongue, in exultation
Of our banner and device!
Make a solemn proclamation
Of a triumph and its price:
How the Savior of creation
Conquered by his sacrifice!

Faithful Cross the Saints rely on,
Noble tree beyond compare!

Never was there such a scion,
Never leaf or flower so rare.

For, when Adam first offended,
Eating that forbidden fruit,
Not all hopes of glory ended
With the serpent at the root:
Broken nature would be mended
By a second tree and shoot.

Sweet the timber, sweet the iron,
Sweet the burden that they bear!

Thus the tempter was outwitted
By a wisdom deeper still:
Remedy and ailment fitted,
Means to cure and means to kill;
That the world might be acquitted,
Christ would do his Father's will.
    Faithful Cross ...

So the Father, out of pity
For our self-inflicted doom,
Sent him from the heavenly city
When the holy time had come:
He, the Son and the Almighty,
Took our flesh in Mary's womb.
    Sweet the timber ...

Hear a tiny baby crying,
Founder of the seas and strands;
See his virgin Mother tying
Cloth around his feet and hands;
Find him in a manger lying
Tightly wrapped in swaddling-bands!
    Faithful Cross ...

So he came, the long-expected,
Not in glory, not to reign;

Only born to be rejected,
Choosing hunger, toil and pain,
Till the scaffold was erected
And the Paschal Lamb was slain.
　Sweet the timber ...

No disgrace was too abhorrent:
Nailed and mocked and parched he died;
Blood and water, double warrant,
Issue from his wounded side,
Washing in a mighty torrent
Earth and stars and oceantide.
　Faithful Cross ...

Lofty timber, smooth your roughness,
Flex your boughs for blossoming;
Let your fibers lose their toughness,
Gently let your tendrils cling;
Lay aside your native gruffness,
Clasp the body of your King!
　Sweet the timber ...

Noblest tree of all created,
Richly jeweled and embossed:
Post by Lamb's blood consecrated;
Spar that saves the tempest-tossed;
Scaffold-beam which, elevated,
Carries what the world has cost!
　Faithful Cross ...

The following conclusion is never to be omitted:

Wisdom, power, and adoration
To the blessed Trinity
For redemption and salvation
Through the Paschal Mystery,
Now, in every generation,
And for all eternity. Amen.
　Sweet the timber ...

In accordance with local circumstances or popular traditions and if it is pastorally appropriate, the Stabat Mater *may be sung, as found in the* Graduale Romanum, *or another suitable chant in memory of the compassion of the Blessed Virgin Mary.*

When the adoration has been concluded, the Cross is carried by the Deacon or a minister to its place at the altar. Lighted candles are placed around or on the altar or near the Cross.

❖ Third Part: Holy Communion ❖

A cloth is spread on the altar, and a corporal and the Missal are put in place. Meanwhile the Deacon or, if there is no Deacon, the Priest himself, brings the Blessed Sacrament back from the place of repose to the altar, while all stand in silence.

When the Deacon has placed the Blessed Sacrament upon the altar and uncovered the ciborium, the Priest goes to the altar and genuflects.

Then the Priest says aloud:
At the Savior's command
and formed by divine teaching,
we dare to say:

The Priest and all present continue:
Our Father ...

The Priest continues alone:
Deliver us, Lord ...

The people conclude the prayer, acclaiming:
For the kingdom, the power and the glory are yours now and for ever.

The Priest then genuflects, takes a particle, and, holding it slightly raised over the ciborium, says aloud:
Behold the Lamb of God,

behold him who takes away the sins of the world.
Blessed are those called to the supper of the Lamb.

And together with the people he adds once:
Lord, I am not worthy
that you should enter under my roof,
But only say the word
and my soul shall be healed.

And facing the altar, he reverently consumes the Body of Christ.

He then proceeds to distribute Communion to the faithful. During Communion, Psalm 22 (21) or another appropriate chant may be sung.

When the distribution of Communion has been completed, the ciborium is taken by the Deacon or another suitable minister to a place prepared outside the church or, if circumstances so require, it is placed in the tabernacle.

Then the Priest says: Let us pray, *and, after a period of sacred silence has been observed, he says the Prayer after Communion, to which the people respond:*   **Amen.**

For the Dismissal the Deacon or, if there is no Deacon, the Priest himself, may say the invitation Bow down for the blessing. *Then the Priest says the Prayer over the People. And all, after genuflecting to the Cross, depart in silence.*

Vespers (Evening Prayer) is not celebrated by those who have been present at the solemn afternoon liturgical celebration.

THE EASTER VIGIL IN THE HOLY NIGHT

By most ancient tradition, this is the night of keeping vigil for the Lord (Exodus 12: 42) in which, following the Gospel admonition (Luke 12: 35–37), the faithful, carrying lighted lamps in their hands, should be like those looking for the Lord when he returns, so that at his coming he may find them awake and have them sit at his table.

Of this night's Vigil, which is the greatest and most noble of all solemnities, there is to be only one celebration in each church. It is arranged, moreover, in such a way that after the Lucernarium and Easter Proclamation (which constitutes the first part of this Vigil), Holy Church meditates on the wonders the Lord God has done for his people from the beginning, trusting in his word and promise (the second part, that is, the Liturgy of the Word) until, as day approaches, with new members reborn in Baptism (the third part), the Church is called to the table the Lord has prepared for his people, the memorial of his Death and Resurrection until he comes again (the fourth part).

The entire celebration of the Easter Vigil must take place during the night, so that it begins after nightfall and ends before daybreak on the Sunday.

Candles should be prepared for all who participate in the Vigil. The lights of the church are extinguished.

First Part:
❖ The Solemn Beginning of the Vigil or Lucenarium ❖

THE BLESSING OF THE FIRE
AND PREPARATION OF THE CANDLE

A blazing fire is prepared in a suitable place outside the church. When the people are gathered there, the Priest approaches with the ministers, one of whom carries the paschal candle.

The Priest and faithful sign themselves while the Priest says: In the name of the Father, and of the Son, and of the Holy Spirit, *and then he greets the assembled people in the usual way and briefly instructs them about the night vigil in these or similar words:*
 Dear brethren (brothers and sisters),

on this most sacred night,
in which our Lord Jesus Christ
passed over from death to life,
the Church calls upon her sons and daughters,
scattered throughout the world,
to come together to watch and pray.
If we keep the memorial
of the Lord's paschal solemnity in this way,
listening to his word and celebrating his mysteries,
then we shall have the sure hope
of sharing his triumph over death
and living with him in God.

Then the Priest blesses the fire, saying:
Let us pray.

O God, who through your Son
bestowed upon the faithful the fire of your glory,
sanctify + this new fire, we pray,
and grant that,
by these paschal celebrations,
we may be so inflamed with heavenly desires,
that with minds made pure
we may attain festivities of unending splendor.
Through Christ our Lord.   ℟ **Amen.**

*After the blessing of the new fire, one of the ministers brings the
paschal candle to the Priest, who cuts a cross into the candle with
a stylus. Then he makes the Greek letter Alpha above the cross,
the letter Omega below, and the four numerals of the current year
between the arms of the cross, saying meanwhile:*

1 Christ yesterday and today
2 the Beginning and the End
3 the Alpha
4 and the Omega
5 All time belongs to him
6 and all the ages
7 To him be glory and power
8 through every age and for ever. Amen

A
2 | 0
1 | 7
Ω

When the cutting of the cross and of the other signs has been completed, the Priest may insert five grains of incense into the candle in the form of a cross, meanwhile saying:

1 By his holy		1	
2 and glorious wounds,	4	2	5
3 may Christ the Lord		3	
4 guard us			
5 and protect us. Amen.			

The Priest lights the paschal candle from the new fire, saying:
May the light of Christ rising in glory
dispel the darkness of our hearts and minds.

PROCESSION

When the candle has been lit, one of the ministers takes burning coals from the fire and places them in the thurible, and the Priest puts incense into it in the usual way. The Deacon or, if there is no Deacon, another suitable minister, takes the paschal candle and a procession forms. The thurifer with the smoking thurible precedes the Deacon or other minister who carries the paschal candle. After them follows the Priest with the ministers and the people, all holding in their hands unlit candles.

At the door of the church the Deacon, standing and raising up the candle, sings: The Light of Christ. *Or:* Lumen Christi.
And all reply: **Thanks be to God.** *Or:* **Deo grátias.**

The Priest lights his candle from the flame of the paschal candle.

Then the Deacon moves forward to the middle of the church and, standing and raising up the candle, sings a second time: The Light of Christ.
And all reply: **Thanks be to God.**

All light their candles from the flame of the paschal candle and continue in procession.

When the Deacon arrives before the altar, he stands facing the people, raises up the candle and sings a third time: The Light of Christ.
And all reply: **Thanks be to God.**

Then the Deacon places the paschal candle in a large candlestand. And lights are lit throughout the church, except for the altar candles.

THE EASTER PROCLAMATION
(EXULTET)

The Deacon, after incensing the book and the candle, proclaims the Easter Proclamation (Exultet) at the ambo or at the lectern, with all standing and holding lighted candles in their hands.

The Easter Proclamation may be made, in the absence of a Deacon, by the Priest himself or by another concelebrating Priest. If, however, because of necessity, a lay cantor sings the Proclamation, the words Therefore, dearest friends *up to the end of the invitation are omitted, along with the greeting* The Lord be with you. *The sections to be omitted by a lay minister are marked with parentheses.*

The proclamation may also be sung in the shorter form, consisting of the sections in brackets.

[Exult, let them exult, the hosts of heaven,
exult, let Angel ministers of God exult,
let the trumpet of salvation
sound aloud our mighty King's triumph!
Be glad, let earth be glad, as glory floods her,
ablaze with light from her eternal King,
let all corners of the earth be glad,
knowing an end to gloom and darkness.
Rejoice, let Mother Church also rejoice,
arrayed with the lightning of his glory,
let this holy building shake with joy,

filled with the mighty voices of the peoples.]
(Therefore, dearest friends,
standing in the awesome glory of this holy light,
invoke with me, I ask you,
the mercy of God almighty,
that he, who has been pleased to number me,
though unworthy, among the Levites,
may pour into me his light unshadowed,
that I may sing this candle's perfect praises.)

[(℣ The Lord be with you.
℟ **And with your spirit.**)

℣ Lift up your hearts.
℟ **We lift them up to the Lord.**

℣ Let us give thanks to the Lord our God.
℟ **It is right and just.**

It is truly right and just,
with ardent love of mind and heart
and with devoted service of our voice,
to acclaim our God invisible, the almighty Father,
and Jesus Christ, our Lord, his Son, his Only Begotten.

Who for our sake paid Adam's debt to the eternal Father,
and, pouring out his own dear Blood,
wiped clean the record of our ancient sinfulness.

These, then, are the feasts of Passover,
in which is slain the Lamb, the one true Lamb,
whose Blood anoints the doorposts of believers.

This is the night,
when once you led our forebears, Israel's children,
from slavery in Egypt
and made them pass dry-shod through the Red Sea.

This is the night

that with a pillar of fire
banished the darkness of sin.

This is the night
that even now, throughout the world,
sets Christian believers apart from worldly vices
and from the gloom of sin,
leading them to grace
and joining them to his holy ones.

This is the night,
when Christ broke the prison-bars of death
and rose victorious from the underworld.]

Our birth would have been no gain,
had we not been redeemed.
[O wonder of your humble care for us!
O love, O charity beyond all telling,
to ransom a slave you gave away your Son!

O truly necessary sin of Adam,
destroyed completely by the Death of Christ!

O happy fault
that earned so great, so glorious a Redeemer!]

O truly blessed night,
worthy alone to know the time and hour
when Christ rose from the underworld!

This is the night
of which it is written:
The night shall be as bright as day,
dazzling is the night for me,
and full of gladness.

[The sanctifying power of this night
dispels wickedness, washes faults away,
restores innocence to the fallen, and joy to mourners,]

drives out hatred, fosters concord, and brings down the
   mighty.

[On this, your night of grace, O holy Father,
accept this candle, a solemn offering,
the work of bees and of your servants' hands,
an evening sacrifice of praise,
this gift from your most holy Church.]

But now we know the praises of this pillar,
which glowing fire ignites for God's honor,
a fire into many flames divided,
yet never dimmed by sharing of its light,
for it is fed by melting wax,
drawn out by mother bees
to build a torch so precious.

[O truly blessed night,
when things of heaven are wed to those of earth,
and divine to the human.

The following stanza is sung in the shorter form only:
   On this, your night of grace, O holy Father,
   accept this candle, a solemn offering,
   the work of bees and of your servants' hands,
   an evening sacrifice of praise,
   this gift from your most holy Church.

Therefore, O Lord,
we pray you that this candle,
hallowed to the honor of your name,
may persevere undimmed,
to overcome the darkness of this night.
Receive it as a pleasing fragrance,
and let it mingle with the lights of heaven.
May this flame be found still burning
by the Morning Star:
the one Morning Star who never sets,
Christ your Son,

who, coming back from death's domain,
has shed his peaceful light on humanity,
and lives and reigns for ever and ever.   ℟ **Amen.**]

✦ Second Part: The Liturgy of the Word ✦

*In this Vigil, the mother of all Vigils, nine readings are provided,
namely seven from the Old Testament and two from the New (the
Epistle and Gospel), all of which should be read whenever this
can be done, so that the character of the Vigil, which demands an
extended period of time, may be preserved.*

*Nevertheless, where more serious pastoral circumstances demand
it, the number of readings from the Old Testament may be reduced,
always bearing in mind that the reading of the Word of God is a
fundamental part of this Easter Vigil. At least three readings should
be read from the Old Testament, both from the Law and from the
Prophets, and their respective Responsorial Psalms should be sung.
Never, moreover, should the reading of chapter 14 of Exodus with
its canticle be omitted.*

*After setting aside their candles, all sit. Before the readings begin,
the Priest instructs the people in these or similar words:*
Dear brethren (brothers and sisters),
now that we have begun our solemn Vigil,
let us listen with quiet hearts to the Word of God.
Let us meditate on how God in times past saved his people
and in these, the last days, has sent us his Son as our
Redeemer.
Let us pray that our God may complete this paschal work of
salvation
by the fullness of redemption.

*Then the readings follow. A reader goes to the ambo and proclaims
the reading. Afterwards a psalmist or a cantor sings or says the
Psalm with the people making the response. Then all rise, the Priest
says,* Let us pray *and, after all have prayed for a while in silence, he
says the prayer corresponding to the reading.*

In place of the Responsorial Psalm a period of sacred silence may be observed, in which case the pause after Let us pray *is omitted.*

First Reading Gen 1: 1–2: 2 In the beginning, when God created the heavens and the earth, the earth was a formless wasteland, and darkness covered the abyss, while a mighty wind swept over the waters.

Then God said, "Let there be light," and there was light. God saw how good the light was. God then separated the light from the darkness. God called the light "day," and the darkness he called "night." Thus evening came, and morning followed—the first day.

Then God said, "Let there be a dome in the middle of the waters, to separate one body of water from the other." And so it happened: God made the dome, and it separated the water above the dome from the water below it. God called the dome "the sky." Evening came, and morning followed—the second day.

Then God said, "Let the water under the sky be gathered into a single basin, so that the dry land may appear." And so it happened: the water under the sky was gathered into its basin, and the dry land appeared. God called the dry land "the earth," and the basin of the water he called "the sea." God saw how good it was. Then God said, "Let the earth bring forth vegetation: every kind of plant that bears seed and every kind of fruit tree on earth that bears fruit with its seed in it." And so it happened: the earth brought forth every kind of plant that bears seed and every kind of fruit tree on earth that bears fruit with its seed in it. God saw how good it was. Evening came, and morning followed—the third day.

Then God said: "Let there be lights in the dome of the sky, to separate day from night. Let them mark the fixed times, the days and the years, and serve as luminaries in the dome of the sky, to shed light upon the earth." And so it happened: God made the two great lights, the greater one to govern the day, and the lesser one to govern the night; and he made the stars. God set them in the dome of the sky, to shed light upon the earth, to govern the day and the night, and to separate the light from the darkness. God saw how good it was. Evening came, and morning followed—the fourth day.

Then God said, "Let the water teem with an abundance of living creatures, and on the earth let birds fly beneath the dome of the sky." And so it happened: God created the great sea monsters and all kinds of swimming creatures with which the water teems, and all kinds of winged birds. God saw how good it was, and God blessed them, saying, "Be fertile, multiply, and fill the water of the seas; and let the birds multiply on the earth." Evening came, and morning followed—the fifth day.

Then God said, "Let the earth bring forth all kinds of living creatures: cattle, creeping things, and wild animals of all kinds." And so it happened: God made all kinds of wild animals, all kinds of cattle, and all kinds of creeping things of the earth. God saw how good it was. Then God said: "Let us make man in our image, after our likeness. Let them have dominion over the fish of the sea, the birds of the air, and the cattle, and over all the wild animals and all the creatures that crawl on the ground."

God created man in his image;
in the image of God he created him;
male and female he created them.

God blessed them, saying: "Be fertile and multiply; fill the earth and subdue it. Have dominion over the fish of the sea, the birds of the air, and all the living things that move on the earth." God also said: "See, I give you every seed-bearing plant all over the earth and every tree that has seed-bearing fruit on it to be your food; and to all the animals of the land, all the birds of the air, and all the living creatures that crawl on the ground, I give all the green plants for food." And so it happened. God looked at everything he had made, and he found it very good. Evening came, and morning followed—the sixth day.

Thus the heavens and the earth and all their array were completed. Since on the seventh day God was finished with the work he had been doing, he rested on the seventh day from all the work he had undertaken.

Or (short form): Gen 1: 1, 26–31a In the beginning, when God created the heavens and the earth, God said: "Let us make man in our image, after our likeness. Let them have dominion over the fish of the sea, the birds of the air, and the cattle, and over all the wild animals and all the creatures that crawl on the ground."

God created man in his image;
  in the image of God he created him;
  male and female he created them.
God blessed them, saying: "Be fertile and multiply; fill the earth
and subdue it. Have dominion over the fish of the sea, the birds
of the air, and all the living things that move on the earth." God
also said: "See, I give you every seed-bearing plant all over the
earth and every tree that has seed-bearing fruit on it to be your
food; and to all the animals of the land, all the birds of the air,
and all the living creatures that crawl on the ground, I give all
the green plants for food." And so it happened. God looked at
everything he had made, and he found it very good.

Responsorial Psalm   Ps 104: 1–2, 5–6, 10, 12, 13–14, 24, 35   Joe Higginbotham

Lord, send out your Spir-it, and re-new the face of the earth.

Bless the LORD, O my soul!
  O LORD, my God, you are great indeed!
You are clothed with majesty and glory,
  robed in light as with a cloak.   ℟

You fixed the earth upon its foundation,
  not to be moved forever;
with the ocean, as with a garment, you covered it;
  above the mountains the waters stood.   ℟

You send forth springs into the watercourses
  that wind among the mountains.
Beside them the birds of heaven dwell;
  from among the branches they send forth their song.   ℟

You water the mountains from your palace;

the earth is replete with the fruit of your works.
You raise grass for the cattle,
   and vegetation for man's use,
Producing bread from the earth. ℟

How manifold are your works, O LORD!
   In wisdom you have wrought them all—
the earth is full of your creatures.
   Bless the LORD, O my soul! ℟

Or: Ps 33: 4–5, 6–7, 12–13, 20 and 22   **Ann Fons**

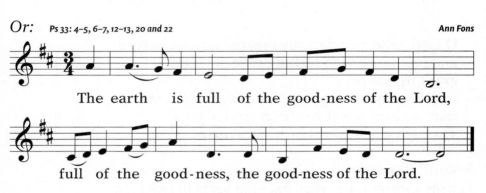

The earth is full of the good-ness of the Lord,
full of the good-ness, the good-ness of the Lord.

Upright is the word of the LORD,
   and all his works are trustworthy.
He loves justice and right;
   of the kindness of the LORD the earth is full. ℟

By the word of the LORD the heavens were made;
   by the breath of his mouth all their host.
He gathers the waters of the sea as in a flask;
   in cellars he confines the deep. ℟

Blessed the nation whose God is the LORD,
   the people he has chosen for his own inheritance.
From heaven the LORD looks down;
   he sees all mankind. ℟

Our soul waits for the LORD,
   who is our help and our shield.
May your kindness, O LORD, be upon us
   who have put our hope in you. ℟

Prayer
> Almighty ever-living God,
> who are wonderful in the ordering of all your works,
> may those you have redeemed understand
> that there exists nothing more marvelous
> than the world's creation in the beginning
> except that, at the end of the ages,
> Christ our Passover has been sacrificed.
> Who lives and reigns for ever and ever.   ℟ **Amen.**

Or:
> O God, who wonderfully created human nature
> and still more wonderfully redeemed it,
> grant us, we pray,
> to set our minds against the enticements of sin,
> that we may merit to attain eternal joys.
> Through Christ our Lord.   ℟ **Amen.**

Second Reading   Gen 22: 1–18 or 22: 1–2, 9a, 10–13, 15–18
For the shorter form, read only the parts in brackets.
[God put Abraham to the test. He called to him, "Abraham!"
"Here I am," he replied. Then God said: "Take your son Isaac,
your only one, whom you love, and go to the land of Moriah.
There you shall offer him up as a holocaust on a height that
I will point out to you."] Early the next morning Abraham
saddled his donkey, took with him his son Isaac and two of
his servants as well, and with the wood that he had cut for the
holocaust, set out for the place of which God had told him.

On the third day Abraham got sight of the place from afar.
Then he said to his servants: "Both of you stay here with the
donkey, while the boy and I go on over yonder. We will worship
and then come back to you." Thereupon Abraham took the
wood for the holocaust and laid it on his son Isaac's shoulders,
while he himself carried the fire and the knife. As the two
walked on together, Isaac spoke to his father Abraham: "Father!"
Isaac said. "Yes, son," he replied. Isaac continued, "Here are the
fire and the wood, but where is the sheep for the holocaust?"
"Son," Abraham answered, "God himself will provide the sheep

for the holocaust." Then the two continued going forward.

[When they came to the place of which God had told him, Abraham built an altar there and arranged the wood on it.] Next he tied up his son Isaac, and put him on top of the wood on the altar. [Then he reached out and took the knife to slaughter his son. But the LORD's messenger called to him from heaven, "Abraham, Abraham!" "Here I am!" he answered. "Do not lay your hand on the boy," said the messenger. "Do not do the least thing to him. I know now how devoted you are to God, since you did not withhold from me your own beloved son." As Abraham looked about, he spied a ram caught by its horns in the thicket. So he went and took the ram and offered it up as a holocaust in place of his son.] Abraham named the site Yahweh-yireh; hence people now say, "On the mountain the LORD will see."

[Again the LORD's messenger called to Abraham from heaven and said: "I swear by myself, declares the LORD, that because you acted as you did in not withholding from me your beloved son, I will bless you abundantly and make your descendants as countless as the stars of the sky and the sands of the seashore; your descendants shall take possession of the gates of their enemies, and in your descendants all the nations of the earth shall find blessing—all this because you obeyed my command."]

Responsorial Psalm   Ps 16: 5, 8, 9–10, 11   *Joe Higginbotham*

You are my in - her - i - tance, O Lord.

O LORD, my allotted portion and my cup,
  you it is who hold fast my lot.
I set the LORD ever before me;
  with him at my right hand I shall not be disturbed.   ℟

Therefore my heart is glad and my soul rejoices,
  my body, too, abides in confidence;
because you will not abandon my soul to the netherworld,

nor will you suffer your faithful one to undergo
   corruption.   ℟

You will show me the path to life,
   fullness of joys in your presence,
   the delights at your right hand forever.   ℟

Prayer
   O God, supreme Father of the faithful,
   who increase the children of your promise
   by pouring out the grace of adoption
   throughout the whole world
   and who through the Paschal Mystery
   make your servant Abraham father of nations,
   as once you swore,
   grant, we pray,
   that your peoples may enter worthily
   into the grace to which you call them.
   Through Christ our Lord.   ℟ **Amen.**

Third Reading Ex 14: 15–15: 1 The LORD said to Moses, "Why are you
crying out to me? Tell the Israelites to go forward. And you, lift
up your staff and, with hand outstretched over the sea, split the
sea in two, that the Israelites may pass through it on dry land.
But I will make the Egyptians so obstinate that they will go in
after them. Then I will receive glory through Pharaoh and all
his army, his chariots and charioteers. The Egyptians shall know
that I am the LORD, when I receive glory through Pharaoh and
his chariots and charioteers."
   The angel of God, who had been leading Israel's camp, now
moved and went around behind them. The column of cloud
also, leaving the front, took up its place behind them, so that it
came between the camp of the Egyptians and that of Israel. But
the cloud now became dark, and thus the night passed without
the rival camps coming any closer together all night long. Then
Moses stretched out his hand over the sea, and the LORD swept
the sea with a strong east wind throughout the night and so
turned it into dry land. When the water was thus divided, the

Israelites marched into the midst of the sea on dry land, with the water like a wall to their right and to their left.

The Egyptians followed in pursuit; all Pharaoh's horses and chariots and charioteers went after them right into the midst of the sea. In the night watch just before dawn the LORD cast through the column of the fiery cloud upon the Egyptian force a glance that threw it into a panic; and he so clogged their chariot wheels that they could hardly drive. With that the Egyptians sounded the retreat before Israel, because the LORD was fighting for them against the Egyptians.

Then the LORD told Moses, "Stretch out your hand over the sea, that the water may flow back upon the Egyptians, upon their chariots and their charioteers." So Moses stretched out his hand over the sea, and at dawn the sea flowed back to its normal depth. The Egyptians were fleeing head on toward the sea, when the LORD hurled them into its midst. As the water flowed back, it covered the chariots and the charioteers of Pharaoh's whole army which had followed the Israelites into the sea. Not a single one of them escaped. But the Israelites had marched on dry land through the midst of the sea, with the water like a wall to their right and to their left. Thus the LORD saved Israel on that day from the power of the Egyptians. When Israel saw the Egyptians lying dead on the seashore and beheld the great power that the LORD had shown against the Egyptians, they feared the LORD and believed in him and in his servant Moses.

Then Moses and the Israelites sang this song to the LORD:
I will sing to the LORD, for he is gloriously triumphant;
horse and chariot he has cast into the sea.

Responsorial Psalm   Ex 15: 1–2, 3–4, 5–6, 17–18   *Joe Higginbotham*

Let us sing to the Lord; he has cov-ered him-self in glo-ry.

I will sing to the LORD, for he is gloriously triumphant;
   horse and chariot he has cast into the sea.
My strength and my courage is the LORD,

and he has been my savior.
He is my God, I praise him;
    the God of my father, I extol him.   ℟

The LORD is a warrior,
    LORD is his name!
Pharaoh's chariots and army he hurled into the sea;
    the elite of his officers were submerged in the Red Sea.   ℟

The flood waters covered them,
    they sank into the depths like a stone.
Your right hand, O LORD, magnificent in power,
    your right hand, O LORD, has shattered the enemy.   ℟

You brought in the people you redeemed
    and planted them on the mountain of your inheritance—
the place where you made your seat, O LORD,
    the sanctuary, LORD, which your hands established.
The LORD shall reign forever and ever.   ℟

Prayer
O God, whose ancient wonders
remain undimmed in splendor even in our day,
for what you once bestowed on a single people,
freeing them from Pharaoh's persecution
by the power of your right hand,
now you bring about as the salvation of the nations
through the waters of rebirth,
grant, we pray, that the whole world
may become children of Abraham
and inherit the dignity of Israel's birthright.
Through Christ our Lord.   ℟ **Amen.**

Or:
O God, who by the light of the New Testament
have unlocked the meaning
of wonders worked in former times,
so that the Red Sea prefigures the sacred font

and the nation delivered from slavery
foreshadows the Christian people,
grant, we pray, that all nations,
obtaining the privilege of Israel by merit of faith,
may be reborn by partaking of your Spirit.
Through Christ our Lord. ℟ **Amen.**

Fourth Reading Is 54: 5–14

The One who has become your husband is your Maker;
   his name is the LORD of hosts;
your redeemer is the Holy One of Israel,
   called God of all the earth.
The LORD calls you back,
   like a wife forsaken and grieved in spirit,
   a wife married in youth and then cast off,
   says your God.
For a brief moment I abandoned you,
   but with great tenderness I will take you back.
In an outburst of wrath, for a moment
   I hid my face from you;
but with enduring love I take pity on you,
   says the LORD, your redeemer.
This is for me like the days of Noah,
   when I swore that the waters of Noah
   should never again deluge the earth;
so I have sworn not to be angry with you,
   or to rebuke you.
Though the mountains leave their place
   and the hills be shaken,
my love shall never leave you
   nor my covenant of peace be shaken,
   says the LORD, who has mercy on you.
O afflicted one, storm-battered and unconsoled,
   I lay your pavements in carnelians,
   and your foundations in sapphires;
I will make your battlements of rubies,
   your gates of carbuncles,
   and all your walls of precious stones.

All your children shall be taught by the LORD,
   and great shall be the peace of your children.
In justice shall you be established,
   far from the fear of oppression,
   where destruction cannot come near you.

Responsorial Psalm   Ps 30: 2, 4, 5–6, 11–12, 13   Joe Higginbotham

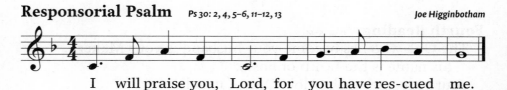

I will praise you, Lord, for you have res-cued me.

I will extol you, O LORD, for you drew me clear
   and did not let my enemies rejoice over me.
O LORD, you brought me up from the netherworld;
   you preserved me from among those going down into
      the pit.   ℟

Sing praise to the LORD, you his faithful ones,
   and give thanks to his holy name.
For his anger lasts but a moment;
   a lifetime, his good will.
At nightfall, weeping enters in,
   but with the dawn, rejoicing.   ℟

Hear, O LORD, and have pity on me;
   O LORD, be my helper.
You changed my mourning into dancing;
   O LORD, my God, forever will I give you thanks.   ℟

Prayer
   Almighty ever-living God,
   surpass, for the honor of your name,
   what you pledged to the Patriarchs by reason of their faith,
   and through sacred adoption increase the children of your
      promise,
   so that what the Saints of old never doubted would come
      to pass
   your Church may now see in great part fulfilled.
   Through Christ our Lord.   ℟ **Amen.**

Fifth Reading Is 55: 1–11
> Thus says the LORD:
> All you who are thirsty,
>> come to the water!
> You who have no money,
>> come, receive grain and eat;
> come, without paying and without cost,
>> drink wine and milk!
> Why spend your money for what is not bread,
>> your wages for what fails to satisfy?
> Heed me, and you shall eat well,
>> you shall delight in rich fare.
> Come to me heedfully,
>> listen, that you may have life.
> I will renew with you the everlasting covenant,
>> the benefits assured to David.
> As I made him a witness to the peoples,
>> a leader and commander of nations,
> so shall you summon a nation you knew not,
>> and nations that knew you not shall run to you,
> because of the LORD, your God,
>> the Holy One of Israel, who has glorified you.
>
> Seek the LORD while he may be found,
>> call him while he is near.
> Let the scoundrel forsake his way,
>> and the wicked man his thoughts;
> let him turn to the LORD for mercy;
>> to our God, who is generous in forgiving.
> For my thoughts are not your thoughts,
>> nor are your ways my ways, says the LORD.
> As high as the heavens are above the earth,
>> so high are my ways above your ways
>> and my thoughts above your thoughts.
>
> For just as from the heavens
>> the rain and snow come down
> and do not return there
>> till they have watered the earth,
>> making it fertile and fruitful,

giving seed to the one who sows
　　and bread to the one who eats,
so shall my word be
　　that goes forth from my mouth;
my word shall not return to me void,
　　but shall do my will,
　　achieving the end for which I sent it.

Responsorial Psalm   Is 12: 2–3, 4, 5–6   *Bill Svarda*

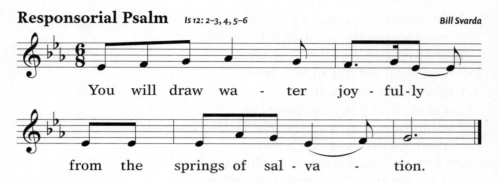

You will draw wa - ter joy - ful-ly from the springs of sal - va - tion.

God indeed is my savior;
　　I am confident and unafraid.
My strength and my courage is the LORD,
　　and he has been my savior.
With joy you will draw water
　　at the fountain of salvation.   ℟

Give thanks to the LORD, acclaim his name;
　　among the nations make known his deeds,
　　proclaim how exalted is his name.   ℟

Sing praise to the LORD for his glorious achievement;
　　let this be known throughout all the earth.
Shout with exultation, O city of Zion,
　　for great in your midst
　　is the Holy One of Israel!   ℟

Prayer
　　Almighty ever-living God,
　　sole hope of the world,

who by the preaching of your Prophets
unveiled the mysteries of this present age,
graciously increase the longing of your people,
for only at the prompting of your grace
do the faithful progress in any kind of virtue.
Through Christ our Lord.   ℟ **Amen.**

Sixth Reading   Bar 3: 9–15, 32–4: 4

Hear, O Israel, the commandments of life:
     listen, and know prudence!
How is it, Israel,
     that you are in the land of your foes,
     grown old in a foreign land,
defiled with the dead,
     accounted with those destined for the netherworld?
You have forsaken the fountain of wisdom!
     Had you walked in the way of God,
     you would have dwelt in enduring peace.
Learn where prudence is,
     where strength, where understanding;
that you may know also
     where are length of days, and life,
     where light of the eyes, and peace.
Who has found the place of wisdom,
     who has entered into her treasuries?

The One who knows all things knows her;
     he has probed her by his knowledge—
The One who established the earth for all time,
     and filled it with four-footed beasts;
he who dismisses the light, and it departs,
     calls it, and it obeys him trembling;
before whom the stars at their posts
     shine and rejoice;
when he calls them, they answer, "Here we are!"
     shining with joy for their Maker.
Such is our God;
     no other is to be compared to him:

723 THE SACRED PASCHAL TRIDUUM

he has traced out the whole way of understanding,
  and has given her to Jacob, his servant,
  to Israel, his beloved son.

Since then she has appeared on earth,
  and moved among people.
She is the book of the precepts of God,
  the law that endures forever;
all who cling to her will live,
  but those will die who forsake her.
Turn, O Jacob, and receive her:
  walk by her light toward splendor.
Give not your glory to another,
  your privileges to an alien race.
Blessed are we, O Israel;
  for what pleases God is known to us!

Responsorial Psalm Ps 19: 8, 9, 10, 11 Joe Higginbotham

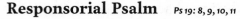

Lord, you have the words of ev-er-last-ing life.

The law of the LORD is perfect,
  refreshing the soul;
the decree of the LORD is trustworthy,
  giving wisdom to the simple. ℟

The precepts of the LORD are right,
  rejoicing the heart;
the command of the LORD is clear,
  enlightening the eye. ℟

The fear of the LORD is pure,
  enduring forever;
the ordinances of the LORD are true,
  all of them just. ℟

They are more precious than gold,
  than a heap of purest gold;

sweeter also than syrup
    or honey from the comb.   ℟

Prayer

O God, who constantly increase your Church
by your call to the nations,
graciously grant
to those you wash clean in the waters of Baptism
the assurance of your unfailing protection.
Through Christ our Lord.   ℟ **Amen.**

Seventh Reading *Ez 36: 16–17a, 18–28* The word of the LORD came to me, saying: Son of man, when the house of Israel lived in their land, they defiled it by their conduct and deeds. Therefore I poured out my fury upon them because of the blood that they poured out on the ground, and because they defiled it with idols. I scattered them among the nations, dispersing them over foreign lands; according to their conduct and deeds I judged them. But when they came among the nations wherever they came, they served to profane my holy name, because it was said of them: "These are the people of the LORD, yet they had to leave their land." So I have relented because of my holy name which the house of Israel profaned among the nations where they came. Therefore say to the house of Israel: Thus says the Lord GOD: Not for your sakes do I act, house of Israel, but for the sake of my holy name, which you profaned among the nations to which you came. I will prove the holiness of my great name, profaned among the nations, in whose midst you have profaned it. Thus the nations shall know that I am the LORD, says the Lord GOD, when in their sight I prove my holiness through you. For I will take you away from among the nations, gather you from all the foreign lands, and bring you back to your own land. I will sprinkle clean water upon you to cleanse you from all your impurities, and from all your idols I will cleanse you. I will give you a new heart and place a new spirit within you, taking from your bodies your stony hearts and giving you natural hearts. I will put my spirit within you and make you live by my statutes, careful to observe my decrees. You shall live in the land I gave your fathers; you shall be my people, and I will be your God.

Responsorial Psalm

When baptism is celebrated, responsorial psalm (a) is used; when baptism is not celebrated, responsorial psalm (b) or (c) is used.

(a) When baptism is celebrated   Ps 42: 3, 5; 43: 3, 4   **Keith Sammut and Steve Wolpert**

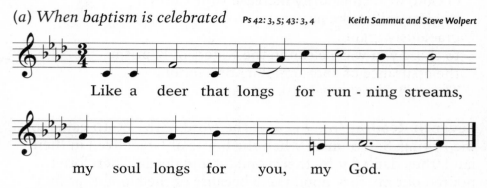

Like a deer that longs for run - ning streams,
my soul longs for you, my God.

Athirst is my soul for God, the living God.
    When shall I go and behold the face of God?   ℟

I went with the throng
    and led them in procession to the house of God,
Amid loud cries of joy and thanksgiving,
    with the multitude keeping festival.   ℟

Send forth your light and your fidelity;
    they shall lead me on
And bring me to your holy mountain,
    to your dwelling-place.   ℟

Then will I go in to the altar of God,
    the God of my gladness and joy;
Then will I give you thanks upon the harp,
    O God, my God!   ℟

(b) When baptism is not celebrated   Is 12: 2–3, 4bcd, 5–6   **Bill Svarda**

You will draw wa - ter joy - ful-ly

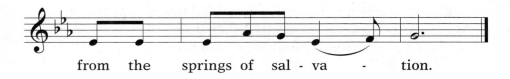

from   the   springs of sal - va - - tion.

God indeed is my savior;
    I am confident and unafraid.
My strength and my courage is the LORD,
    and he has been my savior.
With joy you will draw water
    at the fountain of salvation.   ℟

Give thanks to the LORD, acclaim his name;
    among the nations make known his deeds,
    proclaim how exalted is his name.   ℟

Sing praise to the LORD for his glorious achievement;
    let this be known throughout all the earth.
Shout with exultation, O city of Zion,
    for great in your midst
    is the Holy One of Israel!   ℟

(c) When baptism is not celebrated   Ps 51: 12–13, 14–15, 18–19   **Don Fishel**

Cre - ate a clean   heart in me, O   God.

A clean heart create for me, O God,
    and a steadfast spirit renew within me.
Cast me not out from your presence,
    and your Holy Spirit take not from me.   ℟

Give me back the joy of your salvation,
    and a willing spirit sustain in me.
I will teach transgressors your ways,
    and sinners shall return to you.   ℟

For you are not pleased with sacrifices;

should I offer a holocaust, you would not accept it.
My sacrifice, O God, is a contrite spirit;
a heart contrite and humbled, O God, you will not
spurn. ℟

Prayer
O God of unchanging power and eternal light,
look with favor on the wondrous mystery of the whole
Church
and serenely accomplish the work of human salvation,
which you planned from all eternity;
may the whole world know and see
that what was cast down is raised up,
what had become old is made new,
and all things are restored to integrity through Christ,
just as by him they came into being.
Who lives and reigns for ever and ever. ℟ **Amen.**

Or:
O God, who by the pages of both Testaments
instruct and prepare us to celebrate the Paschal Mystery,
grant that we may comprehend your mercy,
so that the gifts we receive from you this night
may confirm our hope of the gifts to come.
Through Christ our Lord. ℟ **Amen.**

*After the last reading from the Old Testament with its Responsorial
Psalm and its prayer, the altar candles are lit, and the Priest intones
the hymn* Gloria in Excelsis Deo (*Glory to God in the Highest*),
*page 11 which is taken up by all, while bells are rung, according
to local custom.*

*When the hymn is concluded, the Priest says the Collect in the
usual way:*
Let us pray.

O God, who make this most sacred night radiant
with the glory of the Lord's Resurrection,
stir up in your Church a spirit of adoption,
so that, renewed in body and mind,

we may render you undivided service.
Through our Lord Jesus Christ, your Son,
who lives and reigns with you in the unity of the Holy Spirit,
one God, for ever and ever.   ℟ **Amen.**

Epistle *Rom 6:3–11* Brothers and sisters: Are you unaware that
we who were baptized into Christ Jesus were baptized into his
death? We were indeed buried with him through baptism into
death, so that, just as Christ was raised from the dead by the
glory of the Father, we too might live in newness of life.

For if we have grown into union with him through a death
like his, we shall also be united with him in the resurrection. We
know that our old self was crucified with him, so that our sinful
body might be done away with, that we might no longer be in
slavery to sin. For a dead person has been absolved from sin. If,
then, we have died with Christ, we believe that we shall also
live with him. We know that Christ, raised from the dead, dies
no more; death no longer has power over him. As to his death,
he died to sin once and for all; as to his life, he lives for God.
Consequently, you too must think of yourselves as being dead to
sin and living for God in Christ Jesus.

*After the Epistle has been read, all rise, then the Priest solemnly
intones the* Alleluia *three times, raising his voice by a step each
time, with all repeating it. If necessary, the psalmist intones the*
Alleluia.

*Then the psalmist or cantor proclaims Psalm 118 (117) with the
people responding* Alleluia.

Responsorial Psalm   *Ps 118: 1–2, 16–17, 22–23*   *Laura Lea Duckworth*

Al-le - lu-ia, al-le - lu-ia, al   -   le - lu - ia.

Give thanks to the LORD, for he is good,
   for his mercy endures forever.
Let the house of Israel say,
   "His mercy endures forever."   ℟

"The right hand of the LORD has struck with power;
    the right hand of the LORD is exalted.
I shall not die, but live,
    and declare the works of the LORD."   ℟

he stone which the builders rejected
    has become the cornerstone.
By the LORD has this been done;
    it is wonderful in our eyes.   ℟

Gospel (Year A) Mt 28: 1–10 After the sabbath, as the first day of
the week was dawning, Mary Magdalene and the other Mary
came to see the tomb. And behold, there was a great earthquake;
for an angel of the Lord descended from heaven, approached,
rolled back the stone, and sat upon it. His appearance was like
lightning and his clothing was white as snow. The guards were
shaken with fear of him and became like dead men. Then the
angel said to the women in reply, "Do not be afraid! I know that
you are seeking Jesus the crucified. He is not here, for he has
been raised just as he said. Come and see the place where he lay.
Then go quickly and tell his disciples, 'He has been raised from
the dead, and he is going before you to Galilee; there you will
see him.' Behold, I have told you." Then they went away quickly
from the tomb, fearful yet overjoyed, and ran to announce this
to his disciples. And behold, Jesus met them on their way and
greeted them. They approached, embraced his feet, and did him
homage. Then Jesus said to them, "Do not be afraid. Go tell my
brothers to go to Galilee, and there they will see me."

Gospel (Year B) Mk 16: 1–7 When the sabbath was over, Mary
Magdalene, Mary, the mother of James, and Salome bought
spices so that they might go and anoint him. Very early when
the sun had risen, on the first day of the week, they came to
the tomb. They were saying to one another, "Who will roll
back the stone for us from the entrance to the tomb?" When
they looked up, they saw that the stone had been rolled back;
it was very large. On entering the tomb they saw a young man
sitting on the right side, clothed in a white robe, and they were
utterly amazed. He said to them, "Do not be amazed! You seek

Jesus of Nazareth, the crucified. He has been raised; he is not here. Behold the place where they laid him. But go and tell his disciples and Peter, 'He is going before you to Galilee; there you will see him, as he told you.'"

Gospel (Year C) Lk 24: 1–12 At daybreak on the first day of the week the women who had come from Galilee with Jesus took the spices they had prepared and went to the tomb. They found the stone rolled away from the tomb; but when they entered, they did not find the body of the Lord Jesus. While they were puzzling over this, behold, two men in dazzling garments appeared to them. They were terrified and bowed their faces to the ground. They said to them, "Why do you seek the living one among the dead? He is not here, but he has been raised. Remember what he said to you while he was still in Galilee, that the Son of Man must be handed over to sinners and be crucified, and rise on the third day." And they remembered his words. Then they returned from the tomb and announced all these things to the eleven and to all the others. The women were Mary Magdalene, Joanna, and Mary the mother of James; the others who accompanied them also told this to the apostles, but their story seemed like nonsense and they did not believe them. But Peter got up and ran to the tomb, bent down, and saw the burial cloths alone; then he went home amazed at what had happened.

After the Gospel, the Homily, even if brief, is not to be omitted.

❖ Third Part: Baptismal Liturgy ❖

After the Homily the Baptismal Liturgy begins. The Priest goes with the ministers to the baptismal font. Catechumens, if there are any, are called forward and presented by their godparents in front of the assembled Church.

Then, if there is to be a procession to the baptistry or to the font, it forms immediately. During the procession, the Litany of the Saints is sung. When the Litany is completed, the Priest gives the address.

If however, the Baptismal Liturgy takes place in the sanctuary, the Priest immediately makes an introductory statement in these or similar words:

If there are candidates to be baptized:
Dearly beloved,
with one heart and one soul, let us by our prayers
come to the aid of these our brothers and sisters in their
blessed hope,
so that, as they approach the font of rebirth,
the almighty Father may bestow on them
all his merciful help.

If the font is to be blessed, but no one is to be baptized:
Dearly beloved,
let us humbly invoke upon this font
the grace of God the almighty Father,
that those who from it are born anew
may be numbered among the children of adoption in Christ.

The Litany is sung by two cantors, with all standing and responding.

If no one is to be baptized and the font is not to be blessed, the Litany is omitted, and the Blessing of Water (page 735) takes place at once.

In the Litany the names of some Saints may be added, especially the Titular Saint of the church and the Patron Saints of the place and of those to be baptized.

Lord, have mercy.	**Lord, have mercy.**
Christ, have mercy.	**Christ, have mercy.**
Lord, have mercy.	**Lord, have mercy.**
Holy Mary, Mother of God,	**pray for us.**
Saint Michael,	**pray for us.**
Holy Angels of God,	**pray for us.**
Saint John the Baptist,	**pray for us.**

Saint Joseph,	**pray for us.**
Saint Peter and Saint Paul,	**pray for us.**
Saint Andrew,	**pray for us.**
Saint John,	**pray for us.**
Saint Mary Magdalene,	**pray for us.**
Saint Stephen,	**pray for us.**
Saint Ignatius of Antioch,	**pray for us.**
Saint Lawrence,	**pray for us.**
Saint Perpetua and Saint Felicity,	**pray for us.**
Saint Agnes,	**pray for us.**
Saint Gregory,	**pray for us.**
Saint Augustine,	**pray for us.**
Saint Athanatius,	**pray for us.**
Saint Basil,	**pray for us.**
Saint Martin,	**pray for us.**
Saint Benedict,	**pray for us.**
Saint Francis and Saint Dominic,	**pray for us.**
Saint Francis Xavier,	**pray for us.**
Saint John Vianney,	**pray for us.**
Saint Catherine of Siena,	**pray for us.**
Saint Teresa of Jesus,	**pray for us.**
All holy men and women, Saints of God,	**pray for us.**

Lord, be merciful,	**Lord, deliver us, we pray.**
From all evil,	**Lord, deliver us, we pray.**
From every sin,	**Lord, deliver us, we pray.**
From everlasting death,	**Lord, deliver us, we pray.**
By your incarnation,	**Lord, deliver us, we pray.**
By your Death and Resurrection,	
	Lord, deliver us, we pray.
By the outpouring of the Holy Spirit,	
	Lord, deliver us, we pray.

Be merciful to us sinners,
Lord, we ask you, hear our prayer.

If there are candidates to be baptized:
Bring these chosen ones to new birth through the grace
of Baptism,   **Lord, we ask you, hear our prayer.**

If there is no one to be baptized:
Make this font holy by your grace for the new birth of
your children,   **Lord, we ask you, hear our prayer.**

Jesus, Son of the living God,
Lord, we ask you, hear our prayer.

Christ, hear us.   **Christ, hear us.**
Christ, graciously hear us,   **Christ, graciously hear us.**

If there are candidates to be baptized, the Priest says the following prayer:
Almighty ever-living God,
be present by the mysteries of your great love
and send forth the spirit of adoption
to create the new peoples
brought to birth for you in the font of Baptism,
so that what is to be carried out by our humble service
may be brought to fulfillment by your mighty power.
Through Christ our Lord.   ℟ **Amen.**

BLESSING OF BAPTISMAL WATER

The Priest then blesses the baptismal water, saying the following prayer with hands extended:
O God, who by invisible power
accomplish a wondrous effect
through sacramental signs
and who in many ways have prepared water, your creation,
to show forth the grace of Baptism;

O God, whose Spirit
in the first moments of the world's creation
hovered over the waters,
so that the very substance of water
would even then take to itself the power to sanctify;

O God, who by the outpouring of the flood
foreshadowed regeneration,

so that from the mystery of one and the same element
    of water
would come an end to vice and a beginning of virtue;

O God, who caused the children of Abraham
to pass dry-shod through the Red Sea,
so that the chosen people,
set free from slavery to Pharaoh,
would prefigure the people of the baptized;

O God, whose Son,
baptized by John in the waters of the Jordan,
was anointed with the Holy Spirit,
and, as he hung upon the Cross,
gave forth water from his side along with blood,
and after his Resurrection, commanded his disciples:
"Go forth, teach all nations, baptizing them
in the name of the Father and of the Son and of the Holy
    Spirit,"
look now, we pray, upon the face of your Church
and graciously unseal for her the fountain of Baptism.

May this water receive by the Holy Spirit
the grace of your Only Begotten Son,
so that human nature, created in your image
and washed clean through the Sacrament of Baptism
from all the squalor of the life of old,
may be found worthy to rise to the life of newborn children
through water and the Holy Spirit.

*And, if appropriate, lowering the paschal candle into the water
either once or three times, he continues:*
   May the power of the Holy Spirit,
   O Lord, we pray,
   come down through your Son
   into the fullness of this font,

and, holding the candle in the water, he continues:
   so that all who have been buried with Christ

by Baptism into death
may rise again to life with him.
Who lives and reigns with you in the unity of the Holy Spirit,
one God, for ever and ever.   ℟ **Amen.**

Then the candle is lifted out of the water, as the people acclaim:
Springs of water, bless the Lord;
praise and exalt him above all for ever.

*After the blessing of baptismal water and the acclamation of the
people, the Priest, standing, puts the prescribed questions to the
adults and the parents or godparents of the children, as is set out in
the respective Rites of the Roman Ritual, in order for them to make
the required renunciation.*

*If the anointing of the adults with the Oil of Catechumens has not
taken place beforehand, it occurs at this moment.*

*Then the Priest questions the adults individually about the faith
and, if there are children to be baptized, he requests the triple
profession of faith from all the parents and godparents together, as
is indicated in the respective Rites.*

*Where there are many to be baptized on this night, it is possible
to arrange the rite so that, immediately after the response of those
to be baptized, the Celebrant asks for and receives the renewal of
baptismal promises of all present (page 736).*

*When the interrogation is concluded, the Priest baptizes the adult
elect and the children.*

*After the Baptism, the Priest anoints the infants with chrism. A
white garment is given to each, whether adults or children. Then the
Priest or Deacon receives the paschal candle from the hand of the
minister, and the candles of the newly baptized are lighted.*

*Afterwards, unless the baptismal washing and the other
explanatory rites have occurred in the sanctuary, a procession
returns to the sanctuary, formed as before, with the newly baptized*

or the godparents or parents carrying lighted candles. During this procession, the baptismal canticle Vidi aquam (I saw water) *or another appropriate chant is sung (page 58).*

If adults have been baptized, the Bishop or, in his absence, the Priest who has conferred Baptism, should at once administer the Sacrament of Confirmation to them in the sanctuary, as is indicated in the Roman Pontifical or Roman Ritual.

THE BLESSING OF WATER

If no one present is to be baptized and the font is not to be blessed, the Priest introduces the faithful to the blessing of water, saying:
Dear brothers and sisters,
let us humbly beseech the Lord our God
to bless this water he has created,
which will be sprinkled upon us
as a memorial of our Baptism.
May he graciously renew us,
that we may remain faithful to the Spirit
whom we have received.

And after a brief pause in silence, he proclaims the following prayer:
Lord our God,
in your mercy be present to your people
who keep vigil on this most sacred night,
and, for us who recall the wondrous work of our creation
and the still greater work of our redemption,
graciously bless this water.
For you created water to make the fields fruitful
and to refresh and cleanse our bodies.
You also made water the instrument of your mercy:
for through water you freed your people from slavery
and quenched their thirst in the desert;
through water the Prophets proclaimed the new covenant
you were to enter upon with the human race;
and last of all,

through water, which Christ made holy in the Jordan,
you have renewed our corrupted nature
in the bath of regeneration.
Therefore, may this water be for us
a memorial of the Baptism we have received,
and grant that we may share
in the gladness of our brothers and sisters,
who at Easter have received their Baptism.
Through Christ our Lord.   ℞ **Amen.**

THE RENEWAL OF BAPTISMAL PROMISES

*When the Rite of Baptism (and Confirmation) has been completed
or, if this has not taken place, after the blessing of water, all stand,
holding lighted candles in their hands, and renew the promise of
baptismal faith, unless this has already been done together with
those to be baptized.*

The Priest addresses the faithful in these or similar words:
Dear brethren (brothers and sisters), through the Paschal
Mystery
we have been buried with Christ in Baptism,
so that we may walk with him in newness of life.
And so, now that our Lenten observance is concluded,
let us renew the promises of Holy Baptism,
by which we once renounced Satan and his works
and promised to serve God in the holy Catholic Church.
And so I ask you:

Priest: Do you renounce Satan?
All: **I do.**

Priest: And all his works?
All: **I do.**

Priest: And all his empty show?
All: **I do.**

Or:

Priest:
    Do you renounce sin,
      so as to live in the freedom of the children of God?
All: **I do.**

Priest:
    Do you renounce the lure of evil,
      so that sin may have no mastery over you?
All: **I do.**

Priest:
    Do you renounce Satan,
      the author and prince of sin?
All: **I do.**

Then the Priest continues:

Priest:
    Do you believe in God,
      the Father almighty,
      Creator of heaven and earth?
All: **I do.**

Priest:
    Do you believe in Jesus Christ, his only Son, our Lord,
      who was born of the Virgin Mary,
      suffered death and was buried,
      rose again from the dead
      and is seated at the right hand of the Father?
All: **I do.**

Priest:
    Do you believe in the Holy Spirit,
      the holy Catholic Church,
      the communion of saints,
      the forgiveness of sins,

the resurrection of the body,
and life everlasting?
All: **I do.**

And the Priest concludes:
And may almighty God, the Father of our Lord Jesus Christ,
who has given us new birth by water and the Holy Spirit
and bestowed on us forgiveness of our sins,
keep us by his grace,
in Christ Jesus our Lord,
for eternal life.
All: **Amen.**

The Priest sprinkles the people with the blessed water, while all sing or say:

Antiphon   **I saw water flowing from the Temple, ♦ from its right-hand side, alleluia; ♦ and all to whom this water came were saved ♦ and shall say: Alleluia, alleluia.**

Another chant that is baptismal in character may also be sung.

Meanwhile the newly baptized are led to their place among the faithful.

After the sprinkling, the Priest returns to the chair where, omitting the Creed, he directs the Universal prayer, in which the newly baptized participate for the first time.

❖   Fourth Part: The Liturgy of the Eucharist   ❖

The Priest goes to the altar and begins the Liturgy of the Eucharist in the usual way (page 19).

In the Eucharistic Prayer, a commemoration is made of the

*baptized and their godparents in accord with the formulas which
are found in the Roman Missal and Roman Ritual for each of the
Eucharistic Prayers.*

Before the Ecce Angus Dei (Behold the Lamb of God), *the Priest
may briefly address the newly baptized about receiving their
first Communion and about the excellence of this great mystery,
which is the climax of Initiation and the center of the whole of
Christian life.*

Communion Antiphon *1 Cor 5: 7–8* **Christ our Passover has
been sacrificed; ◆ therefore let us keep the feast ◆ with the
unleavened bread of purity and truth, alleluia.**

Psalm 118 (117) may appropriately be sung.

Solemn Blessing
May almighty God bless you
through today's Easter Solemnity
and, in his compassion,
defend you from every assault of sin.   ℟ **Amen.**

And may he, who restores you to eternal life
in the Resurrection of his Only Begotten,
endow you with the prize of immortality.   ℟ **Amen.**

Now that the days of the Lord's Passion have drawn to a close,
may you who celebrate the gladness of the Paschal Feast
come with Christ's help, and exulting in spirit,
to those feasts that are celebrated in eternal joy.   ℟ **Amen.**

And may the blessing of almighty God,
the Father, and the Son, + and the Holy Spirit,
come down on you and remain with you for ever.   ℟ **Amen.**

*The final blessing formula from the Rite of Baptism of Adults or of
Children may also be used, according to circumstances.*

To dismiss the people the Deacon or, if there is no Deacon, the Priest himself sings or says:
 Go forth, the Mass is ended, alleluia, alleluia.
 Or: Go in peace, alleluia, alleluia.

All reply: **Thanks be to God, alleluia, alleluia.**

This practice is observed throughout the Octave of Easter.

EASTER SUNDAY

OF THE RESURRECTION OF THE LORD

❖ At the Mass During the Day ❖

Entrance Antiphon *cf. Ps 139 (138): 18, 5-6* **I have risen, and I am with you still, alleluia. ◆ You have laid your hand upon me, alleluia. ◆ Too wonderful for me, this knowledge, alleluia, alleluia.**

Or: *Lk 24: 34; cf. Rev 1: 6* **The Lord is truly risen, alleluia. ◆ To him be glory and power ◆ for all the ages of eternity, alleluia, alleluia.**

First Reading *Acts 10: 34a, 37-43* Peter proceeded to speak and said: "You know what has happened all over Judea, beginning in Galilee after the baptism that John preached, how God anointed Jesus of Nazareth with the Holy Spirit and power. He went about doing good and healing all those oppressed by the devil, for God was with him. We are witnesses of all that he did both in the country of the Jews and in Jerusalem. They put him to death by hanging him on a tree. This man God raised on the third day and granted that he be visible, not to all the people, but to us, the witnesses chosen by God in advance, who ate and drank with him after he rose from the dead. He commissioned us to preach to the people and testify that he is the one appointed by God as judge of the living and the dead. To him all the prophets bear witness, that everyone who believes in him will receive forgiveness of sins through his name."

Responsorial Psalm Ps 118: 1–2, 16–17, 22–23   *Bill Svarda*

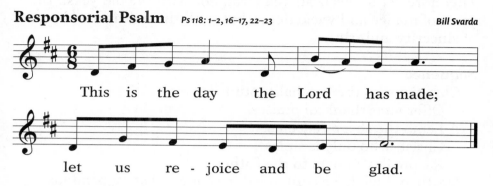

This is the day the Lord has made;

let us re - joice and be glad.

Or: ℟ **Alleluia.**

Give thanks to the LORD, for he is good,
  for his mercy endures forever.
Let the house of Israel say,
  "His mercy endures forever." ℟

"The right hand of the LORD has struck with power;
  the right hand of the LORD is exalted.
I shall not die, but live,
  and declare the works of the LORD." ℟

The stone which the builders rejected
  has become the cornerstone.
By the LORD has this been done;
  it is wonderful in our eyes. ℟

Second Reading Col 3: 1–4 Brothers and sisters: If then you were raised with Christ, seek what is above, where Christ is seated at the right hand of God. Think of what is above, not of what is on earth. For you have died, and your life is hidden with Christ in God. When Christ your life appears, then you too will appear with him in glory.

Or: 1 Cor 5: 6b–8 Brothers and sisters: Do you not know that a little yeast leavens all the dough? Clear out the old yeast, so that you may become a fresh batch of dough, inasmuch as you are unleavened. For our paschal lamb, Christ, has been sacrificed. Therefore, let us celebrate the feast, not with the old yeast, the yeast of malice and wickedness, but with the unleavened bread of sincerity and truth.

Sequence

Christians, to the Paschal Victim
    Offer your thankful praises!
A Lamb the sheep redeems;
    Christ, who only is sinless,
    Reconciles sinners to the Father.
Death and life have contended in that combat stupendous:
    The Prince of life, who died, reigns immortal.
Speak, Mary, declaring
    What you saw, wayfaring.
"The tomb of Christ, who is living,
    The glory of Jesus' resurrection;
Bright angels attesting,
    The shroud and napkin resting.
Yes, Christ my hope is arisen;
    to Galilee he goes before you."
Christ indeed from death is risen, our new life obtaining.
    Have mercy, victor King, ever reigning!
    Amen. Alleluia.

Alleluia   <small>cf. 1 Cor 5: 7b–8a</small>   <small>Laura Lea Duckworth</small>

Al - le - lu - ia, al-le-lu - ia.

Al - le - lu - ia, al-le-lu - ia.

Christ, our paschal lamb, has been sacrificed; / let us then feast with joy in the Lord.   **Alleluia, alleluia.**

*At an afternoon or evening Mass, another Gospel may be
read: Luke 24: 13–35—Stay with us since it is almost evening
(page 146).*

*The Gospel from the Easter Vigil (page 728) may also be read in
place of the following Gospel at any time of the day.*

Gospel *Jn 20: 1–9* On the first day of the week, Mary of Magdala
came to the tomb early in the morning, while it was still dark,
and saw the stone removed from the tomb. So she ran and went
to Simon Peter and to the other disciple whom Jesus loved, and
told them, "They have taken the Lord from the tomb, and we
don't know where they put him." So Peter and the other disciple
went out and came to the tomb. They both ran, but the other
disciple ran faster than Peter and arrived at the tomb first; he
bent down and saw the burial cloths there, but did not go in.
When Simon Peter arrived after him, he went into the tomb and
saw the burial cloths there, and the cloth that had covered his
head, not with the burial cloths but rolled up in a separate place.
Then the other disciple also went in, the one who had arrived
at the tomb first, and he saw and believed. For they did not yet
understand the Scripture that he had to rise from the dead.

Communion Antiphon *1 Cor 5: 7–8* **Christ our Passover has been
sacrificed, alleluia; ✦ therefore let us keep the feast with the
unleavened bread ✦ of purity and truth, alleluia, alleluia.**

*To dismiss the people the Deacon or, if there is no Deacon, the
Priest himself sings or says:*
   Go forth, the Mass is ended, alleluia, alleluia.
   Or: Go in peace, alleluia, alleluia.

All reply: **Thanks be to God, alleluia, alleluia.**

This practice is observed throughout the Octave of Easter.

Solemnities, Feasts, and Various Occasions

FEBRUARY 2:

THE PRESENTATION OF THE LORD

✤ The Blessing of Candles and the Procession ✤

FIRST FORM: THE PROCESSION

At an appropriate hour, a gathering takes place at a smaller church or other suitable place other than inside the church to which the procession will go. The faithful hold in their hands unlighted candles.

While the candles are being lit, the following antiphon or another appropriate chant is sung.

Behold, our Lord will come with power, to enlighten the eyes of his servants, alleluia.

When the chant is concluded, the Priest, facing the people, says: In the name of the Father, and of the Son, and of the Holy Spirit. *Then the Priest greets the people in the usual way, and next he gives an introductory address, encouraging the faithful to celebrate the rite of this feast day acticely and conscously.*

After the address the Priest blesses the candles, and all respond: **Amen.** *He sprinkles the candles with holy water* *without saying anything, and puts incense in the thurible for the procession.*

Then the procession begins, with the Deacon announcing (or if there is no Deacon, the Priest himself):   Let us go forth in peace to meet the Lord.

Or: Let us go forth in peace.
In this case all respond: **In the name of Christ. Amen.**

All carry lighted candles. As the procession moves forward, one or other of the antiphons that follow is sung, namely the antiphon A light for revelation *with the canticle (Luke 2: 29–32), or the antiphon* Sion, adorn your bridal chamber *or another appropriate chant.*

I   Lk 2: 29–32

ANTIPHON
**A light for revelation to the Gentiles
and the glory of your people Israel.**

Lord, now let your servant go in peace,
in accordance with your word.   ANT.

For my eyes have seen your salvation.   ANT.

Which you have prepared in the sight of all peoples.   ANT.

**II   Sion, adorn your bridal chamber and welcome Christ
the King; take Mary in your arms, who is the gate of heaven,
for she herself is carrying the King of glory and new light.
A Virgin she remains, though bringing in her hands the Son
before the morning star begotten, whom Simeon, taking in his
arms announced to the peoples as Lord of life and death and
Savior of the world.**

As the procession enters the church, the Entrance Antiphon of the Mass is sung. After the singing of the hymn Gloria in excelsis

(Glory to God in the highest), *the Mass continues in the usual manner.*

SECOND FORM: THE SOLEMN ENTRANCE

Whenever a procession cannot take place, the faithful gather in church, holding candles in their hands. The Priest, together with the ministers and a representative group of the faithful, goes to a suitable place, either in front of the church door or inside the church itself.

When the Priest reaches the place appointed for the blessing of the candles, candles are lit while the antiphon Behold, our Lord *or another appropriate chant is sung.*

Then, after the greeting and address, the Priest blesses the candles, and then the procession to the altar takes place, with singing.

As the procession enters the church, the Entrance Antiphon of the Mass is sung. After the singing of the hymn Gloria in excelsis (Glory to God in the highest), *the mass continues in the usual manner.*

⚜ At the Mass ⚜

Entrance Antiphon *cf. Ps 48 (47): 10–11* Your merciful love, O God, ✦ we have received in the midst of your temple. ✦ Your praise, O God, like your name, ✦ reaches the ends of the earth; ✦ your right hand is filled with saving justice.

First Reading *Mal 3: 1–4*
Thus says the Lord GOD:
Lo, I am sending my messenger
  to prepare the way before me;
And suddenly there will come to the temple
  the LORD whom you seek,
And the messenger of the covenant whom you desire.
  Yes, he is coming, says the LORD of hosts.

But who will endure the day of his coming?
    And who can stand when he appears?
For he is like the refiner's fire,
    or like the fuller's lye.
He will sit refining and purifying silver,
    and he will purify the sons of Levi,
Refining them like gold or like silver
    that they may offer due sacrifice to the LORD.
Then the sacrifice of Judah and Jerusalem
    will please the LORD,
    as in the days of old, as in years gone by.

Responsorial Psalm   *Ps 24: 7, 8, 9, 10*   *Vince Ambrosetti and Debra Lee Williamson*

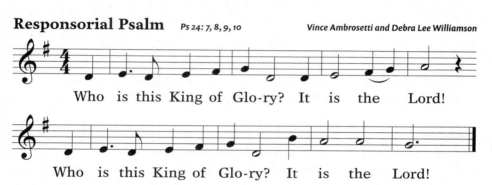

Who is this King of Glo-ry? It is the Lord!

Who is this King of Glo-ry? It is the Lord!

Lift up, O gates, your lintels;
    reach up, you ancient portals,
    that the king of glory may come in! ℟

Who is this king of glory?
    The LORD, strong and mighty,
    the LORD, mighty in battle. ℟

Lift up, O gates, your lintels;
    reach up, you ancient portals,
    that the king of glory may come in! ℟

Who is this king of glory?
    The LORD of hosts; he is the king of glory. ℟

Second Reading *Heb 2: 14–18* Since the children share in blood and
flesh, Jesus likewise shared in them, that through death he might

destroy the one who has the power of death, that is, the Devil, and free those who through fear of death had been subject to slavery all their life. Surely he did not help angels but rather the descendants of Abraham; therefore, he had to become like his brothers and sisters in every way, that he might be a merciful and faithful high priest before God to expiate the sins of the people. Because he himself was tested through what he suffered, he is able to help those who are being tested.

Alleluia   Lk 2: 32   Laura Lea Duckworth

Al-le - lu-ia, al-le - lu-ia, al - le - lu - ia.

A light of revelation to the Gentiles, / and glory for your people Israel.   **Alleluia, alleluia.**

Gospel   Lk 2: 22–40 or 2: 22–32

For the shorter form, read only the parts in brackets.

[When the days were completed for their purification according to the law of Moses, Mary and Joseph took Jesus up to Jerusalem to present him to the Lord, just as it is written in the law of the Lord, *Every male that opens the womb shall be consecrated to the Lord,* and to offer the sacrifice of *a pair of turtledoves or two young pigeons,* in accordance with the dictate in the law of the Lord.

Now there was a man in Jerusalem whose name was Simeon. This man was righteous and devout, awaiting the consolation of Israel, and the Holy Spirit was upon him. It had been revealed to him by the Holy Spirit that he should not see death before he had seen the Christ of the Lord. He came in the Spirit into the temple; and when the parents brought in the child Jesus to perform the custom of the law in regard to him, he took him into his arms and blessed God, saying:

"Now, Master, you may let your servant go
    in peace, according to your word,
for my eyes have seen your salvation,
    which you prepared in the sight of all the peoples:

a light for revelation to the Gentiles,
    and glory for your people Israel."]
The child's father and mother were amazed at what was said
about him; and Simeon blessed them and said to Mary his
mother, "Behold, this child is destined for the fall and rise of
many in Israel, and to be a sign that will be contradicted—and
you yourself a sword will pierce—so that the thoughts of many
hearts may be revealed." There was also a prophetess, Anna, the
daughter of Phanuel, of the tribe of Asher. She was advanced
in years, having lived seven years with her husband after her
marriage, and then as a widow until she was eighty-four.
She never left the temple, but worshiped night and day with
fasting and prayer. And coming forward at that very time, she
gave thanks to God and spoke about the child to all who were
awaiting the redemption of Jerusalem.

When they had fulfilled all the prescriptions of the law of the
Lord, they returned to Galilee, to their own town of Nazareth.
The child grew and became strong, filled with wisdom; and the
favor of God was upon him.

Communion Antiphon Lk 2: 30-31 **My eyes have seen your
salvation, ◆ which you prepared in the sight of all the peoples.**

MARCH 19: SAINT JOSEPH,

SPOUSE OF THE BLESSED VIRGIN MARY

Entrance Antiphon cf. Lk 12: 42 **Behold, a faithful and prudent
steward, ◆ whom the Lord set over his household.**

First Reading 2 Sm 7: 4–5a, 12–14a, 16 The LORD spoke to Nathan and
said: "Go, tell my servant David, 'When your time comes and
you rest with your ancestors, I will raise up your heir after you,
sprung from your loins, and I will make his kingdom firm. It is
he who shall build a house for my name. And I will make his
royal throne firm forever. I will be a father to him, and he shall

be a son to me. Your house and your kingdom shall endure forever before me; your throne shall stand firm forever.'"

Responsial Psalm   Ps 89: 2–3, 4–5, 27, 29   based on IRBY

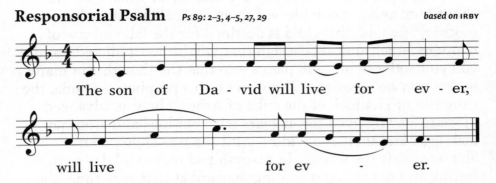

The son of Da - vid will live for ev - er, will live for ev - er.

The promises of the LORD I will sing forever;
    through all generations my mouth shall proclaim your
        faithfulness,
For you have said, "My kindness is established forever;"
    in heaven you have confirmed your faithfulness. ℟

"I have made a covenant with my chosen one,
    I have sworn to David my servant:
Forever will I confirm your posterity
    and establish your throne for all generations." ℟

He shall say of me, 'You are my father,
    my God, the Rock, my savior.'
Forever I will maintain my kindness toward him,
    and my covenant with him stands firm." ℟

Second Reading   Rom 4: 13, 16–18, 22   Brothers and sisters: It was not through the law that the promise was made to Abraham and his descendants that he would inherit the world, but through the righteousness that comes from faith. For this reason, it depends on faith, so that it may be a gift, and the promise may be guaranteed to all his descendants, not to those who only adhere to the law but to those who follow the faith of Abraham, who is the father of all of us, as it is written, *I have made you father of many nations*. He is our father in the sight of God, in whom he believed, who gives life to the dead and calls into being what does not exist. He believed, hoping against hope, that he would become *the father of many nations,* according to what was said, *Thus shall your descendants be.* That is why *it was credited to him as righteousness.*

Alleluia   Ps 84: 5   *Jim Hughes*

Al-le-lu-ia   Al-le-lu-ia   Al - le-lu - ia.

During Lent: *Amy Righi*

Praise   to   you,   Lord   Je - sus

Christ,   King   of   end - less glo - ry!

Blessed are those who dwell in your house, O Lord; / they never cease to praise you. **[Alleluia, alleluia]**

Gospel Mt 1: 16, 18–21, 24a Jacob was the father of Joseph, the husband of Mary. Of her was born Jesus who is called the Christ.

Now this is how the birth of Jesus Christ came about. When his mother Mary was betrothed to Joseph, but before they lived together, she was found with child through the Holy Spirit. Joseph her husband, since he was a righteous man, yet unwilling to expose her to shame, decided to divorce her quietly. Such was his intention when, behold, the angel of the Lord appeared to him in a dream and said, "Joseph, son of David, do not be afraid to take Mary your wife into your home. For it is through the Holy Spirit that this child has been conceived in her. She will bear a son and you are to name him Jesus, because he will save his people from their sins." When Joseph awoke, he did as the angel of the Lord had commanded him and took his wife into his home.

Or: Luke 2: 41–51a   Each year Jesus' parents went to Jerusalem for
the feast of Passover, and when he was twelve years old, they
went up according to festival custom. After they had completed
its days, as they were returning, the boy Jesus remained behind
in Jerusalem, but his parents did not know it. Thinking that
he was in the caravan, they journeyed for a day and looked for
him among their relatives and acquaintances, but not finding
him, they returned to Jerusalem to look for him. After three
days they found him in the temple, sitting in the midst of the
teachers, listening to them and asking them questions, and all
who heard him were astounded at his understanding and his
answers. When his parents saw him, they were astonished, and
his mother said to him, "Son, why have you done this to us?
Your father and I have been looking for you with great anxiety."
And he said to them, "Why were you looking for me? Did you
not know that I must be in my Father's house?" But they did not
understand what he said to them. He went down with them and
came to Nazareth, and was obedient to them.

Communion Antiphon   Mt 25: 21   Well done, good and faithful
servant. ◆ Come, share your master's joy.

MARCH 25: THE ANNUNCIATION OF THE LORD

*Whenever this Solemnity occurs during Holy Week, it is
transferred to the Monday after the Second Sunday of Easter.*

Entrance Antiphon   Heb 10: 5, 7   The Lord said, as he entered the
world: ◆ Behold, I come to do your will, O God.

First Reading   Is 7: 10–14; 8: 10   The LORD spoke to Ahaz, saying: Ask
for a sign from the LORD, your God; let it be deep as the nether
world, or high as the sky! But Ahaz answered, "I will not ask!
I will not tempt the LORD!" Then Isaiah said: Listen, O house of
David! Is it not enough for you to weary people, must you also
weary my God? Therefore the Lord himself will give you this

sign: the virgin shall be with child, and bear a son, and shall name him Emmanuel, which means "God is with us!"

Responsorial Psalm Ps 40: 7–8a, 8b–9, 10, 11   *Beverly McDevitt*

Here am I, Lord; I come to do your will.

Sacrifice or oblation you wished not,
    but ears open to obedience you gave me.
Holocausts or sin-offerings you sought not;
    then said I, "Behold I come." ℟

"In the written scroll it is prescribed for me,
To do your will, O my God, is my delight,
    and your law is within my heart!" ℟

I announced your justice in the vast assembly;
    I did not restrain my lips, as you, O LORD, know. ℟

Your justice I kept not hid within my heart;
    your faithfulness and your salvation I have spoken of;
I have made no secret of your kindness and your truth
    in the vast assembly. ℟

Second Reading Heb 10: 4–10 Brothers and sisters: It is impossible that the blood of bulls and goats take away sins. For this reason, when Christ came into the world, he said:
    "Sacrifice and offering you did not desire,
        but a body you prepared for me;
    in holocausts and sin offerings you took no delight.
    Then I said, 'As is written of me in the scroll,
    behold, I come to do your will, O God.'"

First he says, "Sacrifices and offerings, holocausts and sin offerings, you neither desired nor delighted in." These are offered according to the law. Then he says, "Behold, I come to do your will." He takes away the first to establish the second. By this "will," we have been consecrated through the offering of the Body of Jesus Christ once for all.

Alleluia Jn 1: 14ab   *Jim Hughes*

Al-le-lu-ia   Al-le-lu-ia   Al - le-lu - ia.

During Lent: *Amy Righi*

Praise   to   you,   Lord   Je - sus

Christ,   King   of   end - less glo - ry!

The Word of God became flesh and made his dwelling among us; / and we saw his glory.   **[Alleluia, alleluia.]**

Gospel Lk 1: 26–38 The angel Gabriel was sent from God to a town of Galilee called Nazareth, to a virgin betrothed to a man named Joseph, of the house of David, and the virgin's name was Mary. And coming to her, he said, "Hail, full of grace! The Lord is with you." But she was greatly troubled at what was said and pondered what sort of greeting this might be. Then the angel said to her, "Do not be afraid, Mary, for you have found favor with God. Behold, you will conceive in your womb and bear a son, and you shall name him Jesus. He will be great and will be called Son of the Most High, and the Lord God will give him the throne of David his father, and he will rule over the house of Jacob forever, and of his Kingdom there will be no end." But Mary said to the angel, "How can this be, since I have no relations with a man?" And the angel said to her in reply, "The Holy Spirit will come upon you, and the power of the Most High will overshadow you. Therefore the child to be born will be called holy, the Son of God. And behold, Elizabeth, your relative, has also conceived a son in her old age, and this is the sixth month for her who was called barren; for nothing will be impossible for God." Mary said, "Behold, I am the handmaid of the Lord. May it be done to me according to your word." Then the angel departed from her.

The Creed is said. At the words and was incarnate *all genuflect.*

Communion Antiphon Is 7:14 **Behold, a Virgin shall conceive and bear a son; ♦ and his name will be called Emmanuel.**

JUNE 24: THE NATIVITY
OF SAINT JOHN THE BAPTIST

❖ At the Vigil Mass ❖

Entrance Antiphon Lk 1:15,14 **He will be great in the sight of the Lord ♦ and will be filled with the Holy Spirit, ♦ even from his mother's womb; ♦ and many will rejoice at his birth.**

First Reading Jer 1:4-10 In the days of King Josiah, the word of the LORD came to me, saying:
    Before I formed you in the womb I knew you,
        before you were born I dedicated you,
        a prophet to the nations I appointed you.

    "Ah, Lord GOD!" I said,
        "I know not how to speak; I am too young."
    But the LORD answered me,
    Say not, "I am too young."
        To whomever I send you, you shall go;
        whatever I command you, you shall speak.
    Have no fear before them,
        because I am with you to deliver you, says the LORD.
    Then the LORD extended his hand and touched my mouth,
saying,

See, I place my words in your mouth!
    This day I set you
    over nations and over kingdoms,
to root up and to tear down,
    to destroy and to demolish,
    to build and to plant.

Responsorial Psalm   *Ps 71: 1–2, 3–4a, 5–6ab, 15ab, 17*   Joe Higginbotham

Since my moth-er's womb, you have been my strength.

In you, O Lord, I take refuge;
    let me never be put to shame.
In your justice rescue me, and deliver me;
    incline your ear to me, and save me. ℟

Be my rock of refuge,
    a stronghold to give me safety,
    for you are my rock and my fortress.
O my God, rescue me from the hand of the wicked. ℟

For you are my hope, O Lord;
    my trust, O Lord, from my youth.
On you I depend from birth;
    from my mother's womb you are my strength. ℟

My mouth shall declare your justice,
    day by day your salvation.
O God, you have taught me from my youth,
    and till the present I proclaim your wondrous deeds. ℟

Second Reading *Peter 1: 8–12* Beloved: Although you have not seen
Jesus Christ you love him; even though you do not see him now
yet believe in him, you rejoice with an indescribable and glorious
joy, as you attain the goal of your faith, the salvation of your
souls.
    Concerning this salvation, prophets who prophesied about

the grace that was to be yours searched and investigated it, investigating the time and circumstances that the Spirit of Christ within them indicated when he testified in advance to the sufferings destined for Christ and the glories to follow them. It was revealed to them that they were serving not themselves but you with regard to the things that have now been announced to you by those who preached the Good News to you through the Holy Spirit sent from heaven, things into which angels longed to look.

Alleluia   *cf. Jn 1: 7; Lk 1: 17*   *Vince Ambrosetti*

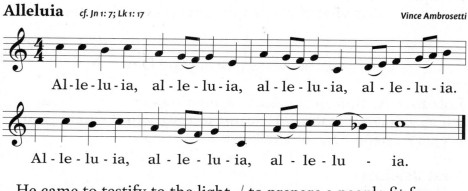

Al-le-lu-ia, al - le - lu - ia, al - le - lu - ia, al - le - lu - ia.

Al - le - lu - ia, al - le - lu - ia, al - le - lu - ia.

He came to testify to the light, / to prepare a people fit for the Lord. **Alleluia, alleluia.**

Gospel *Lk 1: 5–17* In the days of Herod, King of Judea, there was a priest named Zechariah of the priestly division of Abijah; his wife was from the daughters of Aaron, and her name was Elizabeth. Both were righteous in the eyes of God, observing all the commandments and ordinances of the Lord blamelessly. But they had no child, because Elizabeth was barren and both were advanced in years. Once when he was serving as priest in his division's turn before God, according to the practice of the priestly service, he was chosen by lot to enter the sanctuary of the Lord to burn incense. Then, when the whole assembly of the people was praying outside at the hour of the incense offering, the angel of the Lord appeared to him, standing at the right of the altar of incense. Zechariah was troubled by what he saw, and fear came upon him. But the angel said to him, "Do not be afraid, Zechariah, because your prayer has been heard. Your wife Elizabeth will bear you a son, and you shall name him

John. And you will have joy and gladness, and many will rejoice at his birth, for he will be great in the sight of the Lord. John will drink neither wine nor strong drink. He will be filled with the Holy Spirit even from his mother's womb, and he will turn many of the children of Israel to the Lord their God. He will go before him in the spirit and power of Elijah to turn their hearts toward their children and the disobedient to the understanding of the righteous, to prepare a people fit for the Lord."

Communion Antiphon Lk 1: 68 Blessed be the Lord, the God of Israel! ◆ He has visited his people and redeemed them.

❖   At the Mass During the Day   ❖

Entrance Antiphon Jn 1: 6–7; Lk 1, 17 A man was sent from God, whose name was John. ◆ He came to testify to the light, ◆ to prepare a people fit for the Lord.

First Reading Is 49: 1–6
> Hear me, O coastlands,
>   listen, O distant peoples.
> The LORD called me from birth,
>   from my mother's womb he gave me my name.
> He made of me a sharp-edged sword
>   and concealed me in the shadow of his arm.
> He made me a polished arrow,
>   in his quiver he hid me.
> You are my servant, he said to me,
>   Israel, through whom I show my glory.
>
> Though I thought I had toiled in vain,
>   and for nothing, uselessly, spent my strength,
> yet my reward is with the LORD,
>   my recompense is with my God.
> For now the LORD has spoken
>   who formed me as his servant from the womb,
> that Jacob may be brought back to him
>   and Israel gathered to him;

and I am made glorious in the sight of the LORD,
    and my God is now my strength!
It is too little, he says, for you to be my servant,
    to raise up the tribes of Jacob,
    and restore the survivors of Israel;
I will make you a light to the nations,
    that my salvation may reach to the ends of the earth.

Responsorial Psalm   Ps 139: 1b–3, 13–14ab, 14c–15   *Joe Higginbotham*

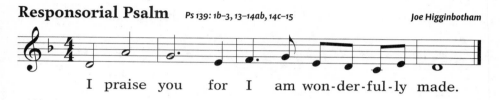

I praise you for I am won-der-ful-ly made.

O LORD, you have probed me, you know me:
    you know when I sit and when I stand;
    you understand my thoughts from afar.
My journeys and my rest you scrutinize,
    with all my ways you are familiar. ℟

Truly you have formed my inmost being;
    you knit me in my mother's womb.
I give you thanks that I am fearfully, wonderfully made;
    wonderful are your works. ℟

My soul also you knew full well;
    nor was my frame unknown to you
When I was made in secret,
    when I was fashioned in the depths of the earth. ℟

Second Reading Acts 13: 22–26 In those days, Paul said: "God raised up David as king; of him God testified, *I have found David, son of Jesse, a man after my own heart; he will carry out my every wish.* From this man's descendants God, according to his promise, has brought to Israel a savior, Jesus. John heralded his coming by proclaiming a baptism of repentance to all the people of Israel; and as John was completing his course, he would say, 'What do you suppose that I am? I am not he. Behold, one is coming after me; I am not worthy to unfasten the sandals of his feet.'

"My brothers, sons of the family of Abraham, and those others among you who are God-fearing, to us this word of salvation has been sent."

Alleluia *Lk 1: 76*   *Vince Ambrosetti*

Al-le-lu-ia, al - le - lu - ia, al - le - lu - ia, al - le - lu - ia.

Al - le - lu - ia, al - le - lu - ia, al - le - lu - ia.

You, child, will be called prophet of the Most High, /
for you will go before the Lord to prepare his way.
Alleluia, alleluia.

Gospel *Lk 1: 57–66, 80* When the time arrived for Elizabeth to have her child she gave birth to a son. Her neighbors and relatives heard that the Lord had shown his great mercy toward her, and they rejoiced with her. When they came on the eighth day to circumcise the child, they were going to call him Zechariah after his father, but his mother said in reply, "No. He will be called John." But they answered her, "There is no one among your relatives who has this name." So they made signs, asking his father what he wished him to be called. He asked for a tablet and wrote, "John is his name," and all were amazed. Immediately his mouth was opened, his tongue freed, and he spoke blessing God. Then fear came upon all their neighbors, and all these matters were discussed throughout the hill country of Judea. All who heard these things took them to heart, saying, "What, then, will this child be?" For surely the hand of the Lord was with him.

The child grew and became strong in spirit, and he was in the desert until the day of his manifestation to Israel.

Communion Antiphon *cf. Lk 1: 78* **Through the tender mercy of our God, ◆ the Dawn from on high will visit us.**

JUNE 29: SAINTS PETER AND PAUL, APOSTLES

❖   At the Vigil Mass   ❖

Entrance Antiphon   Peter the Apostle, and Paul the teacher of the Gentiles, ✦ these have taught us your law, O Lord.

First Reading Acts 3: 1–10 Peter and John were going up to the temple area for the three o'clock hour of prayer. And a man crippled from birth was carried and placed at the gate of the temple called "the Beautiful Gate" every day to beg for alms from the people who entered the temple. When he saw Peter and John about to go into the temple, he asked for alms. But Peter looked intently at him, as did John, and said, "Look at us." He paid attention to them, expecting to receive something from them. Peter said, "I have neither silver nor gold, but what I do have I give you: in the name of Jesus Christ the Nazorean, rise and walk." Then Peter took him by the right hand and raised him up, and immediately his feet and ankles grew strong. He leaped up, stood, and walked around, and went into the temple with them, walking and jumping and praising God. When all the people saw the man walking and praising God, they recognized him as the one who used to sit begging at the Beautiful Gate of the temple, and they were filled with amazement and astonishment at what had happened to him.

Responsorial Psalm   Ps 19: 2–3, 4–5   *Roger Holtz*

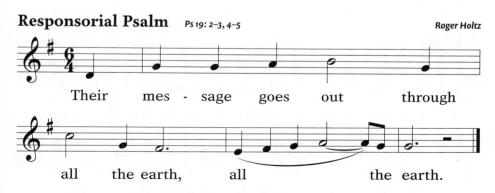

Their mes - sage goes out through all the earth, all the earth.

The heavens declare the glory of God;
  and the firmament proclaims his handiwork.

Day pours out the word to day;
and night to night imparts knowledge. ℟

Not a word nor a discourse
whose voice is not heard;
through all the earth their voice resounds,
and to the ends of the world, their message. ℟

Second Reading *Gal 1: 11–20* I want you to know, brothers and
sisters, that the Gospel preached by me is not of human origin.
For I did not receive it from a human being, nor was I taught it,
but it came through a revelation of Jesus Christ.

For you heard of my former way of life in Judaism, how I
persecuted the Church of God beyond measure and tried to
destroy it, and progressed in Judaism beyond many of my
contemporaries among my race, since I was even more a
zealot for my ancestral traditions. But when God, who from
my mother's womb had set me apart and called me through
his grace, was pleased to reveal his Son to me, so that I might
proclaim him to the Gentiles, I did not immediately consult
flesh and blood, nor did I go up to Jerusalem to those who were
Apostles before me; rather, I went into Arabia and then returned
to Damascus.

Then after three years I went up to Jerusalem to confer with
Cephas and remained with him for fifteen days. But I did not
see any other of the Apostles, only James the brother of the
Lord.—As to what I am writing to you, behold, before God, I am
not lying.

Alleluia   *Jn 21: 17*   *Vince Ambrosetti*

Al-le-lu-ia, al-le-lu-ia, al-le-lu-ia, al-le-lu-ia.

Al-le-lu-ia, al-le-lu-ia, al-le-lu - ia.

Lord, you know everything; / you know that I love you.
Alleluia, alleluia.

Gospel *Jn 21: 15–19* Jesus had revealed himself to his disciples and, when they had finished breakfast, said to Simon Peter, "Simon, son of John, do you love me more than these?" Simon Peter answered him, "Yes, Lord, you know that I love you." Jesus said to him, "Feed my lambs." He then said to Simon Peter a second time, "Simon, son of John, do you love me?" Simon Peter answered him, "Yes, Lord, you know that I love you." He said to him, "Tend my sheep." He said to him the third time, "Simon, son of John, do you love me?" Peter was distressed that he had said to him a third time, "Do you love me?" and he said to him, "Lord, you know everything; you know that I love you." Jesus said to him, "Feed my sheep. Amen, amen, I say to you, when you were younger, you used to dress yourself and go where you wanted; but when you grow old, you will stretch out your hands, and someone else will dress you and lead you where you do not want to go." He said this signifying by what kind of death he would glorify God. And when he had said this, he said to him, "Follow me."

Communion Antiphon *cf. Jn 21: 15, 17* Simon, Son of John, do you love me more than these? ✦ Lord, you know everything; you know that I love you.

✧ At the Mass During the Day ✧

Entrance Antiphon These are the ones who, living in the flesh, ✦ planted the Church with their blood; ✦ they drank the chalice of the Lord ✦ and became the friends of God.

First Reading *Acts 12: 1–11* In those days, King Herod laid hands upon some members of the Church to harm them. He had James, the brother of John, killed by the sword, and when he saw that this was pleasing to the Jews he proceeded to arrest Peter also.—It was the feast of Unleavened Bread.—He had him taken into custody and put in prison under the guard of four squads of four soldiers each. He intended to bring him before the people after Passover. Peter thus was being kept in prison, but prayer by the Church was fervently being made to God on his behalf.

On the very night before Herod was to bring him to trial, Peter, secured by double chains, was sleeping between two soldiers, while outside the door guards kept watch on the prison. Suddenly the angel of the Lord stood by him and a light shone in the cell. He tapped Peter on the side and awakened him, saying, "Get up quickly." The chains fell from his wrists. The angel said to him, "Put on your belt and your sandals." He did so. Then he said to him, "Put on your cloak and follow me." So he followed him out, not realizing that what was happening through the angel was real; he thought he was seeing a vision. They passed the first guard, then the second, and came to the iron gate leading out to the city, which opened for them by itself. They emerged and made their way down an alley, and suddenly the angel left him. Then Peter recovered his senses and said, "Now I know for certain that the Lord sent his angel and rescued me from the hand of Herod and from all that the Jewish people had been expecting."

Responsorial Psalm   *Ps 34: 2–3, 4–5, 6–7, 8–9*   *Joe Higginbotham*

The an-gel of the Lord will res-cue those who fear him.

I will bless the LORD at all times;
　　his praise shall be ever in my mouth.
Let my soul glory in the LORD;
　　the lowly will hear me and be glad.　℟

Glorify the LORD with me,
　　let us together extol his name.
I sought the LORD, and he answered me

and delivered me from all my fears. ℟

Look to him that you may be radiant with joy,
  and your faces may not blush with shame.
When the poor one called out, the LORD heard,
  and from all his distress he saved him. ℟

The angel of the LORD encamps
  around those who fear him, and delivers them.
Taste and see how good the LORD is;
  blessed the man who takes refuge in him. ℟

Second Reading *2 Tim 4: 6–8, 17–18* I, Paul, am already being poured
out like a libation, and the time of my departure is at hand. I
have competed well; I have finished the race; I have kept the
faith. From now on the crown of righteousness awaits me, which
the Lord, the just judge, will award to me on that day, and not
only to me, but to all who have longed for his appearance.

   The Lord stood by me and gave me strength, so that through
me the proclamation might be completed and all the Gentiles
might hear it. And I was rescued from the lion's mouth. The
Lord will rescue me from every evil threat and will bring me
safe to his heavenly Kingdom. To him be glory forever and
ever. Amen.

Alleluia   *Mt 16: 18*   *Laura Lea Duckworth*

Al-le - lu-ia, al-le - lu-ia, al   -   le - lu - ia.

You are Peter and upon this rock I will build my Church, /
and the gates of the netherworld shall not prevail against it.
Alleluia, alleluia.

Gospel *Mt 16: 13–19* When Jesus went into the region of Caesarea
Philippi he asked his disciples, "Who do people say that the Son

of Man is?" They replied, "Some say John the Baptist, others Elijah, still others Jeremiah or one of the prophets." He said to them, "But who do you say that I am?" Simon Peter said in reply, "You are the Christ, the Son of the living God." Jesus said to him in reply, "Blessed are you, Simon son of Jonah. For flesh and blood has not revealed this to you, but my heavenly Father. And so I say to you, you are Peter, and upon this rock I will build my Church, and the gates of the netherworld shall not prevail against it. I will give you the keys to the Kingdom of heaven. Whatever you bind on earth shall be bound in heaven; and whatever you loose on earth shall be loosed in heaven."

Communion Antiphon *cf. Mt 16: 16, 18* **Peter said to Jesus: You are the Christ, the Son of the living God. ◆ And Jesus replied: You are Peter, ◆ and upon this rock I will build my Church.**

JULY 4: INDEPENDENCE DAY

Entrance Antiphon *cf. Sir 36: 18, 19* **Give peace, O Lord, to those who wait for you; ◆ hear the prayers of your servants ◆ and guide us in the way of justice.**

First Reading *Nm 6: 22-27* The LORD said to Moses: "Speak to Aaron and his sons and tell them: This is how you shall bless the children of Israel. Say to them:
   The LORD bless you and keep you!
   The LORD let his face shine upon you, and be gracious to you!
   The LORD look upon you kindly and give you peace!
   So shall they invoke my name upon the children of Israel, and I will bless them."

Responsorial Psalm   *Ps 8: 4-5, 6-7a, 7b-9*   *based on* SINE NOMINE

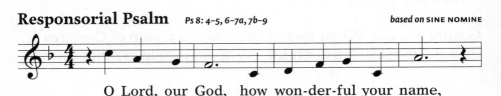

O Lord, our God, how won-der-ful your name,

how won-der-ful your name in all the earth!

When I behold your heavens, the work of your fingers,
   the moon and the stars which you set in place—
What is man that you should be mindful of him,
   or the son of man that you should care for him? ℟

You have made him little less than the angels,
   you have crowned him with glory and honor.
You have given him rule over the works of your hands,
   putting all things under his feet. ℟

All sheep and oxen,
   yes, and the beasts of the field,
The birds of the air, the fishes of the sea,
   and whatever swims in the paths of the sea. ℟

Second Reading *Col 3: 9b–17* Brothers and sisters: You have taken off the old self with its practices and have put on the new self, which is being renewed, for knowledge, in the image of its creator. Here there is not Greek and Jew, circumcision and uncircumcision, barbarian, Scythian, slave, free; but Christ is all and in all.

   Put on then, as God's chosen ones, holy and beloved, heartfelt compassion, kindness, humility, gentleness, and patience, bearing with one another and forgiving one another, if one has a grievance against another; as the Lord has forgiven you, so must you also do. And over all these put on love, that is, the bond of perfection. And let the peace of Christ control your hearts, the peace into which you were also called in one Body. And be thankful. Let the word of Christ dwell in you richly, as in all wisdom you each and admonish one another, singing psalms, hymns, and spiritual songs with gratitude in your hearts to God. And whatever you do, in word or in deed, do everything in the name of the Lord Jesus, giving thanks to God the Father through him.

Alleluia Mt 5: 9

Vince Ambrosetti

Al-le-lu-ia, al-le-lu-ia, al-le-lu-ia, al-le-lu-ia.

Al-le-lu-ia, al-le-lu-ia, al-le-lu - ia.

Blessed are the peacemakers; / they shall be called children of God. **Alleluia, alleluia.**

Gospel Mt 5: 1–12a When Jesus saw the crowds, he went up the mountain, and after he had sat down, his disciples came to him. He began to teach them, saying:
"Blessed are the poor in spirit,
    for theirs is the Kingdom of heaven.
Blessed are they who mourn,
    for they will be comforted.
Blessed are the meek,
    for they will inherit the land.
Blessed are they who hunger and thirst for righteousness,
    for they will be satisfied.
Blessed are the merciful,
    for they will be shown mercy.
Blessed are the clean of heart,
    for they will see God.
Blessed are the peacemakers,
    for they will be called children of God.
Blessed are they who are persecuted for the sake of
        righteousness,
    for theirs is the Kingdom of heaven.
Blessed are you when they insult you and persecute you and utter every kind of evil against you falsely because of me. Rejoice and be glad, for your reward will be great in heaven."

Communion Antiphon Ps 36 (35): 10 **With you, O Lord, is the fountain of life, ◆ and in your light, we see light.**

Additional readings are available in the Lectionary for Mass, nos. 882–886, "For the Country or a City or for Those Who Serve in Public Office," or nos. 887–891, "For Peace and Justice."

AUGUST 6:

THE TRANSFIGURATION OF THE LORD

Entrance Antiphon *cf. Mt 17: 5* **In a resplendent cloud the Holy Spirit appeared.** ◆ **The Father's voice was heard: This is my beloved Son,** ◆ **with whom I am well pleased. Listen to him.**

First Reading   *Dn 7: 9–10, 13–14*
As I watched:
Thrones were set up
  and the Ancient One took his throne.
His clothing was bright as snow,
  and the hair on his head as white as wool;
his throne was flames of fire,
  with wheels of burning fire.
A surging stream of fire
  flowed out from where he sat;
Thousands upon thousands were ministering to him,
  and myriads upon myriads attended him.
The court was convened and the books were opened.

As the visions during the night continued, I saw:
One like a Son of man coming,
  on the clouds of heaven;
When he reached the Ancient One
  and was presented before him,
The one like a Son of man received dominion, glory, and
      kingship;
  all peoples, nations, and languages serve him.
His dominion is an everlasting dominion
  that shall not be taken away,
  his kingship shall not be destroyed.

Responsorial Psalm   Ps 97: 1–2, 5–6, 9   *Jane Terwilliger*

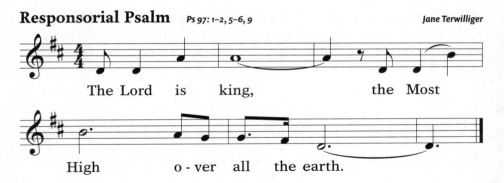

The Lord is king, the Most High o-ver all the earth.

The LORD is king; let the earth rejoice;
  let the many islands be glad.
Clouds and darkness are round about him,
  justice and judgment are the foundation of his throne ℟

The mountains melt like wax before the LORD,
  before the LORD of all the earth.
The heavens proclaim his justice,
  and all peoples see his glory. ℟

Because you, O LORD, are the Most High over all the earth,
  exalted far above all gods. ℟

Second Reading 2 Pt 1: 16–19 Beloved: We did not follow cleverly
devised myths when we made known to you the power and
coming of our Lord Jesus Christ, but we had been eyewitnesses
of his majesty. For he received honor and glory from God the
Father when that unique declaration came to him from the
majestic glory, "This is my Son, my beloved, with whom I am
well pleased." We ourselves heard this voice come from heaven
while we were with him on the holy mountain. Moreover, we
possess the prophetic message that is altogether reliable. You
will do well to be attentive to it, as to a lamp shining in a dark
place, until day dawns and the morning star rises in your hearts.

Alleluia Mt 17: 5c   *Laura Lea Duckworth*

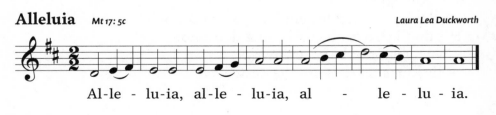

Al-le - lu-ia, al-le - lu-ia, al - le - lu - ia.

This is my beloved Son, with whom I am well pleased; /
listen to him.   **Alleluia, alleluia.**

Gospel (Year A) Mt 17:1–9 Jesus took Peter, James, and his brother,
John, and led them up a high mountain by themselves. And he
was transfigured before them; his face shone like the sun and
his clothes became white as light. And behold, Moses and Elijah
appeared to them, conversing with him. Then Peter said to Jesus
in reply, "Lord, it is good that we are here. If you wish, I will
make three tents here, one for you, one for Moses, and one for
Elijah." While he was still speaking, behold, a bright cloud cast
a shadow over them, then from the cloud came a voice that said,
"This is my beloved Son, with whom I am well pleased; listen to
him." When the disciples heard this, they fell prostrate and were
very much afraid. But Jesus came and touched them, saying,
"Rise, and do not be afraid." And when the disciples raised their
eyes, they saw no one else but Jesus alone.

As they were coming down from the mountain, Jesus charged
them, "Do not tell the vision to anyone until the Son of Man has
been raised from the dead."

Gospel (Year B) Mk 9:2–10 Jesus took Peter, James, and his brother
John, and led them up a high mountain apart by themselves.
And he was transfigured before them, and his clothes became
dazzling white, such as no fuller on earth could bleach them.
Then Elijah appeared to them along with Moses, and they were
conversing with Jesus. Then Peter said to Jesus in reply, "Rabbi,
it is good that we are here! Let us make three tents: one for you,
one for Moses, and one for Elijah." He hardly knew what to say,
they were so terrified. Then a cloud came, casting a shadow over
them; from the cloud came a voice, "This is my beloved Son.
Listen to him." Suddenly, looking around, they no longer saw
anyone but Jesus alone with them.

As they were coming down from the mountain, he charged
them not to relate what they had seen to anyone, except when
the Son of Man had risen from the dead. So they kept the matter
to themselves, questioning what rising from the dead meant.

Gospel (Year C) Lk 9:28b–36 Jesus took Peter, John, and James and
went up a mountain to pray. While he was praying his face

changed in appearance and his clothing became dazzling white. And behold, two men were conversing with him, Moses and Elijah, who appeared in glory and spoke of his exodus that he was going to accomplish in Jerusalem. Peter and his companions had been overcome by sleep, but becoming fully awake, they saw his glory and the two men standing with him. As they were about to part from him, Peter said to Jesus, "Master, it is good that we are here; let us make three tents, one for you, one for Moses, and one for Elijah." But he did not know what he was saying. While he was still speaking, a cloud came and cast a shadow over them, and they became frightened when they entered the cloud. Then from the cloud came a voice that said, "This is my chosen Son; listen to him." After the voice had spoken, Jesus was found alone. They fell silent and did not at that time tell anyone what they had seen.

Communion Antiphon *cf. 1 Jn 3: 2* **When Christ appears, we shall be like him, ◆ for we shall see him as he is.**

AUGUST 15: THE ASSUMPTION
OF THE BLESSED VIRGIN MARY

❧ At the Vigil Mass ❧

Entrance Antiphon **Glorious things are spoken of you, O Mary, ◆ who today were exalted above the choirs of Angels ◆ into eternal triumph with Christ.**

First Reading *1 Chr 15: 3–4, 15–16; 16: 1–2* David assembled all Israel in Jerusalem to bring the ark of the LORD to the place which he had prepared for it. David also called together the sons of Aaron and the Levites.

The Levites bore the ark of God on their shoulders with poles, as Moses had ordained according to the word of the LORD.

David commanded the chiefs of the Levites to appoint their

kinsmen as chanters, to play on musical instruments, harps, lyres, and cymbals, to make a loud sound of rejoicing.

They brought in the ark of God and set it within the tent which David had pitched for it. Then they offered up burnt offerings and peace offerings to God. When David had finished offering up the burnt offerings and peace offerings, he blessed the people in the name of the LORD.

Responsorial Psalm   Ps 132: 6–7, 9–10, 13–14   Joe Higginbotham

Lord, go up to the place of your rest, you and the ark of your ho-li-ness.

Behold, we heard of it in Ephrathah;
  we found it in the fields of Jaar.
Let us enter his dwelling,
  let us worship at his footstool. ℟

May your priests be clothed with justice;
  let your faithful ones shout merrily for joy.
For the sake of David your servant,
  reject not the plea of your anointed. ℟

For the LORD has chosen Zion;
  he prefers her for her dwelling.
"Zion is my resting place forever;
  in her will I dwell, for I prefer her." ℟

Second Reading 1 Cor 15: 54b–57 Brothers and sisters: When that which is mortal clothes itself with immortality, then the word that is written shall come about:
  Death is swallowed up in victory.
  Where, O death, is your victory?
  Where, O death, is your sting?

The sting of death is sin, and the power of sin is the law. But thanks be to God who gives us the victory through our Lord Jesus Christ.

Alleluia *Lk 11: 28*   *Laura Lea Duckworth*

Al - le - lu - ia, al-le-lu - ia.

Al - le - lu - ia, al-le-lu - ia.

Blessed are they who hear the word of God / and observe it. **Alleluia, alleluia.**

Gospel *Lk 11: 27–28* While Jesus was speaking, a woman from the crowd called out and said to him, "Blessed is the womb that carried you and the breasts at which you nursed." He replied, "Rather, blessed are those who hear the word of God and observe it."

Communion Antiphon *cf. Lk 11: 27* Blessed is the womb of the Virgin Mary, ◆ which bore the Son of the eternal Father.

❖ At the Mass During the Day ❖

Entrance Antiphon *cf. Rv 12: 1* A great sign appeared in heaven: ◆ a woman clothed with the sun, and the moon beneath her feet, ◆ and on her head a crown of twelve stars.

Or: Let us all rejoice in the Lord, ◆ as we celebrate the feast day in honor of the Virgin Mary, ◆ at whose Assumption the Angels rejoice ◆ and praise the Son of God.

First Reading *Rv 11: 19a; 12: 1–6a, 10ab* God's temple in heaven was opened, and the ark of his covenant could be seen in the temple.

A great sign appeared in the sky, a woman clothed with the sun, with the moon under her feet, and on her head a crown of twelve stars. She was with child and wailed aloud in pain as she labored to give birth. Then another sign appeared in the sky; it was a huge red dragon, with seven heads and ten horns, and on its heads were seven diadems. Its tail swept away a third of the stars in the sky and hurled them down to the earth. Then the dragon stood before the woman about to give birth, to devour her child when she gave birth. She gave birth to a son, a male child, destined to rule all the nations with an iron rod. Her child was caught up to God and his throne. The woman herself fled into the desert where she had a place prepared by God.

Then I heard a loud voice in heaven say:
"Now have salvation and power come,
     and the Kingdom of our God
     and the authority of his Anointed One."

Responsorial Psalm   Ps 45: 10, 11, 12, 16   Joe Higginbotham

The queen stands at your right hand, ar-rayed in   gold.

The queen takes her place at your right hand in gold of
     Ophir. ℟

Hear, O daughter, and see; turn your ear,
     forget your people and your father's house. ℟

So shall the king desire your beauty;
     for he is your lord. ℟

They are borne in with gladness and joy;
     they enter the palace of the king. ℟

Second Reading   1 Cor 15: 20–27   Brothers and sisters: Christ has been raised from the dead, the firstfruits of those who have fallen asleep. For since death came through man, the resurrection of the dead came also through man. For just as in Adam all die, so

too in Christ shall all be brought to life, but each one in proper order: Christ the firstfruits; then, at his coming, those who belong to Christ; then comes the end, when he hands over the Kingdom to his God and Father, when he has destroyed every sovereignty and every authority and power. For he must reign until he has put all his enemies under his feet. The last enemy to be destroyed is death, for "he subjected everything under his feet."

Alleluia

Laura Lea Duckworth

Al - le - lu - ia, al-le-lu - ia.

Al - le - lu - ia, al-le-lu - ia.

Mary is taken up to heaven; / a chorus of angels exults. **Alleluia, alleluia.**

Gospel Lk 1: 39–56 Mary set out and traveled to the hill country in haste to a town of Judah, where she entered the house of Zechariah and greeted Elizabeth. When Elizabeth heard Mary's greeting, the infant leaped in her womb, and Elizabeth, filled with the Holy Spirit, cried out in a loud voice and said, "Blessed are you among women, and blessed is the fruit of your womb. And how does this happen to me, that the mother of my Lord should come to me? For at the moment the sound of your greeting reached my ears, the infant in my womb leaped for joy. Blessed are you who believed that what was spoken to you by the Lord would be fulfilled."

And Mary said:
"My soul proclaims the greatness of the Lord;
    my spirit rejoices in God my Savior
    for he has looked with favor on his lowly servant.
From this day all generations will call me blessed:
    the Almighty has done great things for me

and holy is his Name.
He has mercy on those who fear him
in every generation.
He has shown the strength of his arm,
and has scattered the proud in their conceit.
He has cast down the mighty from their thrones,
and has lifted up the lowly.
He has filled the hungry with good things,
and the rich he has sent away empty.
He has come to the help of his servant Israel
for he has remembered his promise of mercy,
the promise he made to our fathers,
to Abraham and his children forever."
Mary remained with her about three months and then
returned to her home.

Communion Antiphon Lk 1: 48–49 **All generations will call me blessed, ◆ for he who is mighty has done great things for me.**

SEPTEMBER 14:

THE EXALTATION OF THE HOLY CROSS

Entrance Antiphon cf. Gal 6: 14 **We should glory in the Cross of our Lord Jesus Christ, ◆ in whom is our salvation, life and resurrection, ◆ through whom we are saved and delivered.**

First Reading Nm 21: 4b–9 With their patience worn out by the journey, the people complained against God and Moses, "Why have you brought us up from Egypt to die in this desert, where there is no food or water? We are disgusted with this wretched food!"

In punishment the LORD sent among the people saraph serpents, which bit the people so that many of them died. Then the people came to Moses and said, "We have sinned in complaining against the LORD and you. Pray the LORD to take the serpents from us." So Moses prayed for the people, and the

LORD said to Moses, "Make a saraph and mount it on a pole, and if any who have been bitten look at it, they will live." Moses accordingly made a bronze serpent and mounted it on a pole, and whenever anyone who had been bitten by a serpent looked at the bronze serpent, he lived.

Responsorial Psalm   Ps 78: 1bc–2, 34–35, 36–37, 38   Joe Higginbotham

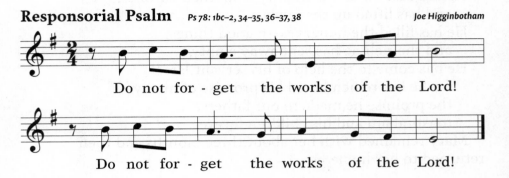

Do not for - get   the works   of   the   Lord!

Do not for - get   the works   of   the   Lord!

Hearken, my people, to my teaching;
    incline your ears to the words of my mouth.
I will open my mouth in a parable,
    I will utter mysteries from of old. ℟

While he slew them they sought him
    and inquired after God again,
Remembering that God was their rock
    and the Most High God, their redeemer. ℟

But they flattered him with their mouths
    and lied to him with their tongues,
Though their hearts were not steadfast toward him,
    nor were they faithful to his covenant. ℟

But he, being merciful, forgave their sin
    and destroyed them not;
Often he turned back his anger
    and let none of his wrath be roused. ℟

Second Reading   Phil 2: 6–11

Brothers and sisters:
    Christ Jesus, though he was in the form of God,
        did not regard equality with God

something to be grasped.
Rather, he emptied himself,
   taking the form of a slave,
   coming in human likeness;
   and found human in appearance,
   he humbled himself,
   becoming obedient to death,
      even death on a cross.
Because of this, God greatly exalted him
   and bestowed on him the name
   that is above every name,
   that at the name of Jesus
   every knee should bend,
   of those in heaven and on earth and under the earth,
   and every tongue confess that
   Jesus Christ is Lord,
   to the glory of God the Father.

Alleluia

Michael Kissinger

Al-le-lu-ia, al-le-lu-ia, al - le-lu - ia.

We adore you, O Christ, and we bless you, / because by your
Cross you have redeemed the world.   **Alleluia, alleluia.**

Gosepl *Jn 3:13-17* Jesus said to Nicodemus: "No one has gone up
to heaven except the one who has come down from heaven,
the Son of Man. And just as Moses lifted up the serpent in the
desert, so must the Son of Man be lifted up, so that everyone
who believes in him may have eternal life."

For God so loved the world that he gave his only Son, so
that everyone who believes in him might not perish but might
have eternal life. For God did not send his Son into the world
to condemn the world, but that the world might be saved
through him.

Communion Antiphon *Jn 12:32* When I am lifted up from the
earth, ◆ I will draw everyone to myself, says the Lord.

NOVEMBER 1: ALL SAINTS

Entrance Antiphon   Let us all rejoice in the Lord, ◆ as we celebrate the feast day in honor of all the Saints, ◆ at whose festival the Angels rejoice ◆ and praise the Son of God.

First Reading   Rv 7: 2–4, 9–14   I, John, saw another angel come up from the East, holding the seal of the living God. He cried out in a loud voice to the four angels who were given power to damage the land and the sea, "Do not damage the land or the sea or the trees until we put the seal on the foreheads of the servants of our God." I heard the number of those who had been marked with the seal, one hundred and forty-four thousand marked from every tribe of the children of Israel.

After this I had a vision of a great multitude, which no one could count, from every nation, race, people, and tongue. They stood before the throne and before the Lamb, wearing white robes and holding palm branches in their hands. They cried out in a loud voice:

"Salvation comes from our God, who is seated on the throne, and from the Lamb."

All the angels stood around the throne and around the elders and the four living creatures. They prostrated themselves before the throne, worshiped God, and exclaimed:

"Amen. Blessing and glory, wisdom and thanksgiving, honor, power, and might be to our God forever and ever. Amen."

Then one of the elders spoke up and said to me, "Who are these wearing white robes, and where did they come from?" I said to him, "My lord, you are the one who knows." He said to me, "These are the ones who have survived the time of great distress; they have washed their robes and made them white in the Blood of the Lamb."

Responsorial Psalm   Ps 24: 1bc–2, 3–4ab, 5–6   Joe Higginbotham

Lord, this is the peo-ple that longs to see your face.

The LORD's are the earth and its fullness;
    the world and those who dwell in it.
For he founded it upon the seas
    and established it upon the rivers. ℟

Who can ascend the mountain of the LORD?
    or who may stand in his holy place?
One whose hands are sinless, whose heart is clean,
    who desires not what is vain. ℟

He shall receive a blessing from the LORD,
    a reward from God his savior.
Such is the race that seeks him,
    that seeks the face of the God of Jacob. ℟

Second Reading *1 Jn 3:1-3* Beloved: See what love the Father has bestowed on us that we may be called the children of God. Yet so we are. The reason the world does not know us is that it did not know him. Beloved, we are God's children now; what we shall be has not yet been revealed. We do know that when it is revealed we shall be like him, for we shall see him as he is. Everyone who has this hope based on him makes himself pure, as he is pure.

Alleluia

Brian J. Nelson

Al - le-lu - ia,   al - le - lu - ia,   al-le-lu - ia.

Come to me, all you who labor and are burdened / and I will give you rest, says the Lord.   **Alleluia, alleluia.**

Gospel *Mt 5:1-12a* When Jesus saw the crowds, he went up the mountain, and after he had sat down, his disciples came to him. He began to teach them, saying:
    "Blessed are the poor in spirit,
        for theirs is the Kingdom of heaven.
Blessed are they who mourn,
    for they will be comforted.

Blessed are the meek,
for they will inherit the land.
Blessed are they who hunger and thirst for righteousness,
for they will be satisfied.
Blessed are the merciful,
for they will be shown mercy.
Blessed are the clean of heart,
for they will see God.
Blessed are the peacemakers,
for they will be called children of God.
Blessed are they who are persecuted for the sake of
righteousness,
for theirs is the Kingdom of heaven.
Blessed are you when they insult you and persecute you and
utter every kind of evil against you falsely because of me. Rejoice
and be glad, for your reward will be great in heaven."

Communion Antiphon *Mt 5: 8–10* **Blessed are the clean of heart,
for they shall see God. ◆ Blessed are the peacemakers, ◆ for
they shall be called children of God. ◆ Blessed are they who
are persecuted for the sake of righteousness, ◆ for theirs is the
Kingdom of Heaven.**

NOVEMBER 2: THE COMMEMORATION OF
ALL THE FAITHFUL DEPARTED (ALL SOULS)

Entrance Antiphon *cf. 1 Thes 4: 14; 1 Cor 15: 22* **Just as Jesus died and
has risen again, ◆ so through Jesus God will bring with him
◆ those who have fallen asleep; ◆ and as in Adam all die, ◆ so
also in Christ will all be brought to life.**

First Reading *Wis 3: 1–9*
The souls of the just are in the hand of God,
and no torment shall touch them.
They seemed, in the view of the foolish, to be dead;

and their passing away was thought an affliction
  and their going forth from us, utter destruction.
But they are in peace.
For if before men, indeed, they be punished,
  yet is their hope full of immortality;
chastised a little, they shall be greatly blessed,
   because God tried them
  and found them worthy of himself.
As gold in the furnace, he proved them,
  and as sacrificial offerings he took them to himself.
In the time of their visitation they shall shine,
  and shall dart about as sparks through stubble;
they shall judge nations and rule over peoples,
  and the LORD shall be their King forever.
Those who trust in him shall understand truth,
  and the faithful shall abide with him in love:
because grace and mercy are with his holy ones,
  and his care is with his elect.

Or: Wisdom 4: 7–14

The just man, though he die early,
  shall be at rest.
For the age that is honorable comes not
  with the passing of time,
   nor can it be measured in terms of years.
Rather, understanding is the hoary crown for men,
  and an unsullied life, the attainment of old age.
He who pleased God was loved;
  he who lived among sinners was transported—
snatched away, lest wickedness pervert his mind
  or deceit beguile his soul;
for the witchery of paltry things obscures what is right
  and the whirl of desire transforms the innocent mind.
Having become perfect in a short while,
  he reached the fullness of a long career;
  for his soul was pleasing to the LORD,
  therefore he sped him out of the midst of wickedness.
But the people saw and did not understand,
  nor did they take this into account.

Or: Isaiah 25: 6, 7–9

On this mountain the LORD of hosts
   will provide for all peoples.
On this mountain he will destroy
   the veil that veils all peoples,
The web that is woven over all nations;
   he will destroy death forever.
The Lord GOD will wipe away
   the tears from all faces;
The reproach of his people he will remove
   from the whole earth; for the LORD has spoken.
   On that day it will be said:
"Behold our God, to whom we looked to save us!
   This is the LORD for whom we looked;
   let us rejoice and be glad that he has saved us!"

Responsorial Psalm   Ps 23: 1–3a, 3b–4, 5, 6   *Joe Higginbotham*

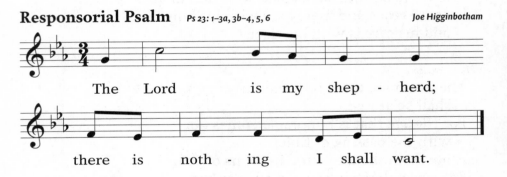

The   Lord   is   my   shep - herd;

there   is   noth - ing   I   shall   want.

Or: ℟ **Though I walk in the valley of darkness, I fear no
evil, for you are with me.**

The LORD is my shepherd; I shall not want.
   In verdant pastures he gives me repose;
beside restful waters he leads me;
   he refreshes my soul.   ℟

He guides me in right paths
   for his name's sake.
Even though I walk in the dark valley

I fear no evil; for you are at my side
with your rod and your staff
   that give me courage. ℟

You spread the table before me
   in the sight of my foes;
You anoint my head with oil;
   my cup overflows. ℟

Only goodness and kindness follow me
   all the days of my life;
and I shall dwell in the house of the LORD
   for years to come. ℟

Or: Ps 25: 6 and 7b, 17–18, 20–21   Brian J. Nelson

To you, O Lord, I lift my soul.

Or: ℟ **No one who waits for you, O Lord, will ever be put to shame.**

Remember that your compassion, O LORD,
   and your kindness are from of old.
In your kindness remember me,
   because of your goodness, O LORD. ℟

Relieve the troubles of my heart,
   and bring me out of my distress.
Put an end to my affliction and my suffering;
   and take away all my sins. ℟

Preserve my life, and rescue me;
   let me not be put to shame, for I take refuge in you.
Let integrity and uprightness preserve me,
   because I wait for you, O LORD. ℟

Or: Ps 27: 1, 4, 7, 8b, 9a, 13–14   Ann Fons et al.

The Lord is my light and my salvation.

Or: ℟ **I believe that I shall see the good things of the Lord in the land of the living.**

The LORD is my light and my salvation;
    whom should I fear?
The LORD is my life's refuge;
    of whom should I be afraid? ℟

One thing I ask of the Lord;
    this I seek:
To dwell in the house of the Lord
    all the days of my life,
That I may gaze on the loveliness of the Lord
    and contemplate his temple. ℟

Hear, O LORD, the sound of my call;
    have pity on me and answer me.
Your presence, O LORD, I seek.
    Hide not your face from me. ℟

I believe that I shall see the bounty of the LORD
    in the land of the living.
Wait for the LORD with courage;
    be stouthearted, and wait for the LORD! ℟

Second Reading Rom 5: 5–11 Brothers and sisters: Hope does not disappoint, because the love of God has been poured out into our hearts through the Holy Spirit that has been given to us. For Christ, while we were still helpless, died at the appointed time for the ungodly. Indeed, only with difficulty does one die for a just person, though perhaps for a good person one might even find courage to die. But God proves his love for us in that while we were still sinners Christ died for us. How much more then, since we are now justified by his Blood, will we be saved through him from the wrath. Indeed, if, while we were enemies, we were reconciled to God through the death of his Son, how much more, once reconciled, will we be saved by his life. Not only that, but we also boast of God through our Lord Jesus Christ, through whom we have now received reconciliation.

Or: Rom 5:17–21 Brothers and sisters: If, by the transgression of the one, death came to reign through that one, how much more will those who receive the abundance of grace and of the gift of justification come to reign in life through the one Jesus Christ. In conclusion, just as through one transgression condemnation came upon all, so, through one righteous act, acquittal and life came to all. For just as through the disobedience of the one man the many were made sinners, so through the obedience of one the many will be made righteous. The law entered in so that transgression might increase but, where sin increased, grace overflowed all the more, so that, as sin reigned in death, grace also might reign through justification for eternal life through Jesus Christ our Lord.

Or: Rom 6:3–9 Brothers and sisters: Are you unaware that we who were baptized into Christ Jesus were baptized into his death? We were indeed buried with him through baptism into death, so that, just as Christ was raised from the dead by the glory of the Father, we too might live in newness of life.
For if we have grown into union with him through a death like his, we shall also be united with him in the resurrection. We know that our old self was crucified with him, so that our sinful body might be done away with, that we might no longer be in slavery to sin. For a dead person has been absolved from sin. If,

then, we have died with Christ, we believe that we shall also live with him. We know that Christ, raised from the dead, dies no more; death no longer has power over him.

Or: Rom 8: 14-23 Brothers and sisters: Those who are led by the Spirit of God are sons of God. For you did not receive a spirit of slavery to fall back into fear, but you received a spirit of adoption, through which we cry, *"Abba,* Father!" The Spirit itself bears witness with our spirit that we are children of God, and if children, then heirs, heirs of God and joint heirs with Christ, if only we suffer with him so that we may also be glorified with him.

I consider that the sufferings of this present time are as nothing compared with the glory to be revealed for us. For creation awaits with eager expectation the revelation of the children of God; for creation was made subject to futility, not of its own accord but because of the one who subjected it, in hope that creation itself would be set free from slavery to corruption and share in the glorious freedom of the children of God. We know that all creation is groaning in labor pains even until now; and not only that, but we ourselves, who have the firstfruits of the Spirit, we also groan within ourselves as we wait for adoption, the redemption of our bodies.

Or: Rom 8: 31b-35, 37-39 Brothers and sisters: If God is for us, who can be against us? He who did not spare his own Son but handed him over for us all, will he not also give us everything else along with him? Who will bring a charge against God's chosen ones? It is God who acquits us. Who will condemn? It is Christ Jesus who died, rather, was raised, who also is at the right hand of God, who indeed intercedes for us. What will separate us from the love of Christ? Will anguish, or distress or persecution, or famine, or nakedness, or peril, or the sword?

No, in all these things, we conquer overwhelmingly through him who loved us. For I am convinced that neither death, nor life, nor angels, nor principalities, nor present things, nor future things, nor powers, nor height, nor depth, nor any other creature will be able to separate us from the love of God in Christ Jesus our Lord.

Or: Rom 14: 7–9, 10c–12 Brothers and sisters: None of us lives for oneself, and no one dies for oneself. For if we live, we live for the Lord, and if we die, we die for the Lord; so then, whether we live or die, we are the Lord's. For this is why Christ died and came to life, that he might be Lord of both the dead and the living. Why then do you judge your brother? Or you, why do you look down on your brother? For we shall all stand before the judgment seat of God; for it is written:

As I live, says the Lord, every knee shall bend before me,
and every tongue shall give praise to God.

So then each of us shall give an account of himself to God.

Or: 1 Cor 15: 20–28 Brothers and sisters: Christ has been raised from the dead, the firstfruits of those who have fallen asleep. For since death came through a human being, the resurrection of the dead came also through a human being. For just as in Adam all die, so too in Christ shall all be brought to life, but each one in proper order: Christ the firstfruits; then, at his coming, those who belong to Christ; then comes the end, when he hands over the Kingdom to his God and Father.

For he must reign until he has put all his enemies under his feet. The last enemy to be destroyed is death, for "he subjected everything under his feet." But when it says that everything has been subjected, it is clear that it excludes the one who subjected everything to him. When everything is subjected to him, then the Son himself will also be subjected to the one who subjected everything to him, so that God may be all in all.

Or: 1 Cor 15: 51–57 Brothers and sisters: Behold, I tell you a mystery. We shall not all fall asleep, but we will all be changed, in an instant, in the blink of an eye, at the last trumpet. For the trumpet will sound, the dead will be raised incorruptible, and we shall be changed. For that which is corruptible must clothe itself with incorruptibility, and that which is mortal must clothe itself with immortality. And when this which is corruptible clothes itself with incorruptibility and this which is mortal clothes itself with immortality, then the word that is written shall come about:

Death is swallowed up in victory.

> *Where, O death, is your victory?*
> *Where, O death, is your sting?*

The sting of death is sin, and the power of sin is the law. But thanks be to God who gives us the victory through our Lord Jesus Christ.

Or: 2 Cor 4: 14–5: 1 Brothers and sisters: We know that the One who raised the Lord Jesus will raise us also with Jesus and place us with you in his presence. Everything indeed is for you, so that the grace bestowed in abundance on more and more people may cause the thanksgiving to overflow for the glory of God. Therefore, we are not discouraged; rather, although our outer self is wasting away, our inner self is being renewed day by day. For this momentary light affliction is producing for us an eternal weight of glory beyond all comparison, as we look not to what is seen but to what is unseen; for what is seen is transitory, but what is unseen is eternal. For we know that if our earthly dwelling, a tent, should be destroyed, we have a building from God, a dwelling not made with hands, eternal in heaven.

Or: 2 Cor 5: 1, 6–10 Brothers and sisters: We know that if our earthly dwelling, a tent, should be destroyed, we have a building from God, a dwelling not made with hands, eternal in heaven.

We are always courageous, although we know that while we are at home in the body we are away from the Lord, for we walk by faith, not by sight. Yet we are courageous, and we would rather leave the body and go home to the Lord. Therefore, we aspire to please him, whether we are at home or away. For we must all appear before the judgment seat of Christ, so that each one may receive recompense, according to what he did in the body, whether good or evil.

Or: Phil 3: 20–21 Brothers and sisters: Our citizenship is in heaven, and from it we also await a savior, the Lord Jesus Christ. He will change our lowly body to conform with his glorified Body by the power that enables him also to bring all things into subjection to himself.

Or: 1 Thes 4: 13–18 We do not want you to be unaware, brothers and sisters, about those who have fallen asleep, so that you may not grieve like the rest, who have no hope. For if we believe that Jesus died and rose, so too will God, through Jesus, bring with him those who have fallen asleep. Indeed, we tell you this, on the word of the Lord, that we who are alive, who are left until the coming of the Lord, will surely not precede those who have fallen asleep. For the Lord himself, with a word of command, with the voice of an archangel and with the trumpet of God, will come down from heaven, and the dead in Christ will rise first. Then we who are alive, who are left, will be caught up together with them in the clouds to meet the Lord in the air. Thus we shall always be with the Lord. Therefore, console one another with these words.

Or: 2 Tm 2: 8–13   Beloved: Remember Jesus Christ, raised from the dead, a descendant of David: such is my Gospel, for which I am suffering, even to the point of chains, like a criminal. But the word of God is not chained. Therefore, I bear with everything for the sake of those who are chosen, so that they too may obtain the salvation that is in Christ Jesus, together with eternal glory. This saying is trustworthy:
    If we have died with him
        we shall also live with him;
    if we persevere
        we shall also reign with him.
    But if we deny him
        he will deny us.
    If we are unfaithful
        he remains faithful,
        for he cannot deny himself.

Alleluia   Mt 25: 34   *Brian J. Nelson*

Al - le-lu - ia,   al - le - lu - ia,   al-le-lu - ia.

Come, you who are blessed by my Father: / Inherit the kingdom prepared for you from the foundation of the world. **Alleluia, alleuia.**

Or: cf. Jn 3: 16
God so loved the world that he gave us his only Son, / that everyone who sees the Son and believes in him / may have eternal life.   **Alleluia, alleuia.**

Or: cf. Jn 6: 40
This is the will of my Father, says the Lord, / that everyone who sees the Son and believes in him / may have eternal life.
Alleluia, alleuia.

Or: Jn 6: 51
I am the living bread that came down from heaven, says the Lord; / whoever eats this bread will live forever.
Alleluia, alleuia.

Or: Jn 11: 25a, 26
I am the resurrection and the life, says the Lord; / whoever believes in me will never die.   **Alleluia, alleuia.**

Gospel Mt 5: 1–12a When Jesus saw the crowds, he went up the mountain, and after he had sat down, his disciples came to him. He began to teach them, saying:
   "Blessed are the poor in spirit,
      for theirs is the Kingdom of heaven.
   Blessed are they who mourn,
      for they will be comforted.
   Blessed are the meek,
      for they will inherit the land.
   Blessed are they who hunger and thirst for righteousness,
      for they will be satisfied.
   Blessed are the merciful,
      for they will be shown mercy.
   Blessed are the clean of heart,
      for they will see God.
   Blessed are the peacemakers,
      for they will be called children of God.
   Blessed are they who are persecuted for the sake of
         righteousness,
      for theirs is the Kingdom of heaven.

Blessed are you when they insult you and persecute you and utter every kind of evil against you falsely because of me. Rejoice and be glad, for your reward will be great in heaven."

Or: Mt 11: 25-30 At that time Jesus exclaimed: "I give praise to you, Father, Lord of heaven and earth, for although you have hidden these things from the wise and the learned you have revealed them to little ones. Yes, Father, such has been your gracious will. All things have been handed over to me by my Father. No one knows the Son except the Father, and no one knows the Father except the Son and anyone to whom the Son wishes to reveal him.

"Come to me, all you who labor and are burdened, and I will give you rest. Take my yoke upon you and learn from me, for I am meek and humble of heart; and you will find rest for yourselves. For my yoke is easy, and my burden light."

Or: Mt 25: 31-46 Jesus said to his disciples: "When the Son of Man comes in his glory, and all the angels with him, he will sit upon his glorious throne, and all the nations will be assembled before him. And he will separate them one from another, as a shepherd separates the sheep from the goats. He will place the sheep on his right and the goats on his left. Then the king will say to those on his right, 'Come, you who are blessed by my Father. Inherit the kingdom prepared for you from the foundation of the world. For I was hungry and you gave me food, I was thirsty and you gave me drink, a stranger and you welcomed me, naked and you clothed me, ill and you cared for me, in prison and you visited me.' Then the righteous will answer him and say, 'Lord, when did we see you hungry and feed you, or thirsty and give you drink? When did we see you a stranger and welcome you, or naked and clothe you? When did we see you ill or in prison, and visit you?' And the king will say to them in reply, 'Amen, I say to you, whatever you did for one of the least brothers of mine, you did for me.' Then he will say to those on his left, 'Depart from me, you accursed, into the eternal fire prepared for the devil and his angels. For I was hungry and you gave me no food, I was thirsty and you gave me no drink, a stranger and you gave me no welcome, naked and you gave me no clothing, ill and in prison, and you did not care for me.' Then they will answer and say, 'Lord, when did we see you hungry or thirsty or a stranger or naked or ill or in prison, and not minister to your needs?' He will answer them, 'Amen, I say to you, what you did not do for one of these least ones, you did not do for me.' And these will go off to eternal punishment, but the righteous to eternal life."

Or: Luke 7: 11–17 Jesus journeyed to a city called Nain, and his disciples and a large crowd accompanied him. As he drew near to the gate of the city, a man who had died was being carried out, the only son of his mother, and she was a widow. A large crowd from the city was with her. When the Lord saw her, he was moved with pity for her and said to her, "Do not weep." He stepped forward and touched the coffin; at this the bearers halted, and he said, "Young man, I tell you, arise!" The dead man sat up and began to speak, and Jesus gave him to his mother. Fear seized them all, and they glorified God, exclaiming, "A great prophet has arisen in our midst," and "God has visited his people." This report about him spread through the whole of Judea and in all the surrounding region.

Or: Luke 23: 44–46, 50, 52–53; 24: 1–6a It was about noon and darkness came over the whole land until three in the afternoon because of an eclipse of the sun. Then the veil of the temple was torn down the middle. Jesus cried out in a loud voice, "Father, into your hands I commend my spirit"; and when he had said this he breathed his last.

Now there was a virtuous and righteous man named Joseph who, though he was a member of the council, went to Pilate and asked for the Body of Jesus. After he had taken the Body down, he wrapped it in a linen cloth and laid him in a rock-hewn tomb in which no one had yet been buried.

At daybreak on the first day of the week they took the spices they had prepared and went to the tomb. They found the stone rolled away from the tomb; but when they entered, they did not find the Body of the Lord Jesus. While they were puzzling over this, behold, two men in dazzling garments appeared to them. They were terrified and bowed their faces to the ground. They said to them, "Why do you seek the living one among the dead? He is not here, but he has been raised."

Or: Luke 24: 13–16, 28–35 That very day, the first day of the week, two of Jesus' disciples were going to a village seven miles from Jerusalem called Emmaus, and they were conversing about all the things that had occurred. And it happened that while they were conversing and debating, Jesus himself drew near and walked with them, but their eyes were prevented from recognizing him. As they approached the village to which they were going, he gave the impression that he was going on farther. But they urged him, "Stay with us, for it is nearly evening and the day is almost over." So he went in to stay with them. And it happened that, while he was with them at table, he took bread, said the blessing, broke it, and gave it to them. With that their eyes were opened and they recognized him, but he vanished from their sight. Then they said to each other, "Were not our hearts burning within us while he spoke to us on the way and opened the Scriptures to us?" So they set out at once and returned to Jerusalem where they found gathered together the Eleven and those with them who were saying, "The Lord has truly been raised and has appeared to Simon!" Then the two recounted to them what had taken place on the way and how he was made known to them in the breaking of bread.

Or: Jn 5: 24–29 Jesus answered the Jews and said to them: "Amen, amen, I say to you, whoever hears my word and believes in the one who sent me has eternal life and will not come to condemnation, but has passed from death to life. Amen, amen, I say to you, the hour is coming and is now here when the dead will hear the voice of the Son of God, and those who hear will live. For just as the Father has life in himself, so also he gave to his Son the possession of life in himself. And he gave him power to exercise judgment, because he is the Son of Man. Do not be amazed at this, because the hour is coming in which all who are in the tombs will hear his voice and will come out, those who have done good deeds to the resurrection of life, but those who have done wicked deeds to the resurrection of condemnation."

Or: Jn 6: 37–40 Jesus said to the crowds: "Everything that the Father gives me will come to me, and I will not reject anyone who comes to me, because I came down from heaven not to do my own will but the will of the one who sent me. And this is the will of the one who sent me, that I should not lose anything of what he gave me, but that I should raise it on the last day. For this is the will of my Father, that everyone who sees the Son and believes in him may have eternal life, and I shall raise him on the last day."

Or: Jn 6: 51–58 Jesus said to the crowds: "I am the living bread that came down from heaven; whoever eats this bread will live forever; and the bread that I will give is my Flesh for the life of the world."

The Jews quarreled among themselves, saying, "How can this man give us his Flesh to eat?" Jesus said to them, "Amen, amen, I say to you, unless you eat the Flesh of the Son of Man and drink his Blood, you do not have life within you. Whoever eats my Flesh and drinks my Blood has eternal life, and I will raise him on the last day. For my Flesh is true food, and my Blood is true drink. Whoever eats my Flesh and drinks my Blood remains in me and I in him. Just as the living Father sent me and I have life because of the Father, so also the one who feeds on me will have life because of me. This is the bread that came down from heaven. Unlike your ancestors who ate and still died, whoever eats this bread will live forever."

Or: Jn 11: 17–27 When Jesus arrived in Bethany, he found that Lazarus had already been in the tomb for four days. Now Bethany was near Jerusalem, only about two miles away. And many of the Jews had come to Martha and Mary to comfort them about their brother. When Martha heard that Jesus was coming, she went to meet him; but Mary sat at home. Martha said to Jesus, "Lord, if you had been here, my brother would not have died. But even now I know that whatever you ask of God, God will give you." Jesus said to her, "Your brother will rise." Martha said to him, "I know he will rise, in the resurrection on the last day." Jesus told her, "I am the resurrection and the life; he who believes in me, even if he dies, will live, and everyone who lives and believes in me will never die. Do you believe this?" She said to him, "Yes, Lord. I have come to believe that you are the Christ, the Son of God, the one who is coming into the world."

Or: Jn 11: 32–45 When Mary, the sister of Lazarus, came to where Jesus was and saw him, she fell at his feet and said to him, "Lord, if you had been here, my brother would not have died." When Jesus saw her weeping and the Jews who had come with her weeping, he became perturbed and deeply troubled, and said, "Where have you laid him?" They said to him, "Sir, come and see." And Jesus wept. So the Jews said, "See how he loved him." But some of them said, "Could not the one who opened the eyes of the blind man have done something so that this man would not have died?"

So Jesus, perturbed again, came to the tomb. It was a cave, and a stone lay across it. Jesus said, "Take away the stone." Martha, the dead man's sister, said to him, "Lord, by now there will be a stench; he has been dead for four days." Jesus said to her, "Did I not tell you that if you believe you will see the glory of God?" So they took away the stone. And Jesus raised his eyes and said, "Father, I thank you for hearing me. I know that you always hear me; but because of the crowd here I have said this, that they may believe that you sent me." And when he had said this, he cried out in a loud voice, "Lazarus, come out!" The dead man came out, tied hand and foot with burial bands, and his face was wrapped in a cloth. So Jesus said to them, "Untie him and let him go."

Now many of the Jews who had come to Mary and seen what he had done began to believe in him.

Or: Jn 14: 1–6 Jesus said to his disciples: "Do not let your hearts be troubled. You have faith in God; have faith also in me. In my Father's house there are many dwelling places. If there were not, would I have told you that I am going to prepare a place for you? And if I go and prepare a place for you, I will come back again and take you to myself, so that where I am you also may be. Where I am going you know the way." Thomas said to him, "Master, we do not know where you are going; how can we know the way?" Jesus said to him, "I am the way and the truth and the life. No one comes to the Father except through me."

Communion Antiphon cf. Jn 11: 25–26 **I am the Resurrection and the Life, says the Lord. • Whoever believes in me, even**

though he dies, will live, ✦ and everyone who lives and
believes in me will not die for ever.

NOVEMBER 9:

THE DEDICATION OF THE LATERAN BASILICA

Entrance Antiphon *cf. Rv 21: 2* I saw the holy city, a new
Jerusalem, ✦ coming down out of heaven from God, ✦
prepared like a bride adorned for her husband.

Or: *cf. Rv 21: 3* Behold God's dwelling with the human race. ✦ He
will dwell with them and they will be his people, ✦ and God
himself with them will be their God.

First Reading *Ez 47: 1–2, 8–9, 12* The angel brought me back to the
entrance of the temple, and I saw water flowing out from
beneath the threshold of the temple toward the east, for the
façade of the temple was toward the east; the water flowed down
from the southern side of the temple, south of the altar. He led
me outside by the north gate, and around to the outer gate facing
the east, where I saw water trickling from the southern side.
He said to me, "This water flows into the eastern district down
upon the Arabah, and empties into the sea, the salt waters, which
it makes fresh. Wherever the river flows, every sort of living
creature that can multiply shall live, and there shall be abundant
fish, for wherever this water comes the sea shall be made fresh.
Along both banks of the river, fruit trees of every kind shall
grow; their leaves shall not fade, nor their fruit fail. Every month
they shall bear fresh fruit, for they shall be watered by the flow
from the sanctuary. Their fruit shall serve for food, and their
leaves for medicine."

Responsorial Psalm   *Ps 46: 2–3, 5–6, 8–9*   *Bill Svarda*

The wa-ters of the riv-er   glad-den the cit-y of

God,   the   ho - ly   dwell-ing of the Most   High.

God is our refuge and our strength,
  an ever-present help in distress.
Therefore, we fear not, though the earth be shaken
  and mountains plunge into the depths of the sea. ℟

There is a stream whose runlets gladden the city of God,
  the holy dwelling of the Most High.
God is in its midst; it shall not be disturbed;
  God will help it at the break of dawn. ℟

The LORD of hosts is with us;
  our stronghold is the God of Jacob.
Come! behold the deeds of the LORD,
  the astounding things he has wrought on earth. ℟

Second Reading *1 Cor 3: 9c–11, 16–17* Brothers and sisters: You are
God's building. According to the grace of God given to me, like a
wise master builder I laid a foundation, and another is building
upon it. But each one must be careful how he builds upon it,
for no one can lay a foundation other than the one that is there,
namely, Jesus Christ.

 Do you not know that you are the temple of God, and that the
Spirit of God dwells in you? If anyone destroys God's temple,
God will destroy that person; for the temple of God, which you
are, is holy.

Alleluia   *2 Chr 7: 16*   Joe Higginbotham

Al - le - lu - ia,   al - le - lu - ia,   al - le - lu - ia.

I have chosen and consecrated this house, says the Lord, /
that my name may be there forever. **Alleluia, alleluia.**

Gospel *Jn 2:13-22* Since the Passover of the Jews was near, Jesus went up to Jerusalem. He found in the temple area those who sold oxen, sheep, and doves, as well as the money-changers seated there. He made a whip out of cords and drove them all out of the temple area, with the sheep and oxen, and spilled the coins of the money-changers and overturned their tables, and to those who sold doves he said, "Take these out of here, and stop making my Father's house a marketplace." His disciples recalled the words of Scripture, *Zeal for your house will consume me.* At this the Jews answered and said to him, "What sign can you show us for doing this?" Jesus answered and said to them, "Destroy this temple and in three days I will raise it up." The Jews said, "This temple has been under construction for forty-six years, and you will raise it up in three days?" But he was speaking about the temple of his Body. Therefore, when he was raised from the dead, his disciples remembered that he had said this, and they came to believe the Scripture and the word Jesus had spoken.

Communion Antiphon *cf. 1 Peter 2:5* Be built up like living stones, ◆ into a spiritual house, a holy priesthood.

THANKSGIVING DAY

Entrance Antiphon *Eph 5:19-20* Sing and make music to the Lord in your hearts, ◆ Always thanking God the Father for all things ◆ In the name of our Lord Jesus Christ.

First Reading *Zep 3:14-15*
Shout for joy, O daughter Zion!
    Sing joyfully, O Israel!
Be glad and exult with all your heart,
    O daughter Jerusalem!
The LORD has removed the judgment against you

and turned away your enemies;
The King of Israel, the LORD, is in your midst,
  you have no further misfortune to fear.

Responsorial Psalm Ps 145: 2–3, 4–5, 6–7, 8–9, 10–11 *Bill Svarda*

I will praise your name for ev-er, for ev - er, Lord.

Every day will I bless you
  and I will praise your name forever and ever.
Great is the LORD and highly to be praised;
  his greatness is unsearchable. ℟

Generation after generation praises your works
  and proclaims of your might.
They speak of the splendor of your glorious majesty
  and tell of your wondrous works. ℟

They discourse of the power of your terrible deeds
  and declare your greatness.
They publish the fame of your abundant goodness
  and joyfully sing of your justice. ℟

The LORD is gracious and merciful
  slow to anger and of great kindness.
The LORD is good to all
  and compassionate toward all his works. ℟

Let all your works give you thanks, O LORD,
  and let your faithful ones bless you.
Let them discourse of the glory of your Kingdom
  and speak of your might. ℟

Second Reading *1 Cor 1: 3–9* Brothers and sisters: Grace to you and
peace from God our Father and the Lord Jesus Christ.
  I give thanks to my God always on your account for the grace

of God bestowed on you in Christ Jesus, that in him you were enriched in every way, with all discourse and all knowledge, as the testimony to Christ was confirmed among you, so that you are not lacking in any spiritual gift as you wait for the revelation of our Lord Jesus Christ. He will keep you firm to the end, irreproachable on the day of our Lord Jesus Christ. God is faithful, and by him you were called to fellowship with his Son, Jesus Christ our Lord.

Alleluia   1 Thes 5: 18   Joe Higginbotham

Al - le - lu - ia,   al - le - lu - ia,   al - le - lu - ia.

Al - le - lu - ia,   al - le - lu - ia,   al - le - lu - ia.

In all circumstances, give thanks / for this is the will of God for you in Christ Jesus.   **Alleluia, alleluia.**

Gospel Lk 17: 11–19 As Jesus continued his journey to Jerusalem, he traveled through Samaria and Galilee. As he was entering a village, ten lepers met him. They stood at a distance from him and raised their voices, saying, "Jesus, Master! Have pity on us!" And when he saw them, he said, "Go show yourselves to the priests." As they were going they were cleansed. And one of them, realizing he had been healed, returned, glorifying God in a loud voice; and he fell at the feet of Jesus and thanked him. He was a Samaritan. Jesus said in reply, "Ten were cleansed, were they not? Where are the other nine? Has none but this foreigner returned to give thanks to God?" Then he said to him, "Stand up and go; your faith has saved you."

Communion Antiphon Ps 138 (137): 1 **I thank you, Lord, with all my heart. ◆ For you have heard the words of my mouth.**

Or: _{Psalm 116 (115): 12–13} How can I repay the Lord for all his goodness to me? ◆ The chalice of salvation I will raise, ◆ and I will call on the name of the Lord.

Additional readings can be found in the Lectionary for Mass, nos. 943–947, "In Thanksgiving to God."

DECEMBER 8:

THE IMMACULATE CONCEPTION

OF THE BLESSED VIRGIN MARY

PATRONAL FEASTDAY OF THE UNITED STATES OF AMERICA

Entrance Antiphon _{Is 61: 10} I rejoice heartily in the Lord, ◆ in my God is the joy of my soul; ◆ for he has clothed me with a robe of salvation, ◆ and wrapped me in a mantle of justice, ◆ like a bride adorned with her jewels.

First Reading _{Gen 3: 9–15, 20} After the man, Adam, had eaten of the tree, the LORD God called to the man and asked him, "Where are you?" He answered, "I heard you in the garden; but I was afraid, because I was naked, so I hid myself." Then he asked, "Who told you that you were naked? You have eaten, then, from the tree of which I had forbidden you to eat!" The man replied, "The woman whom you put here with me—she gave me fruit from the tree, and so I ate it." The LORD God then asked the woman, "Why did you do such a thing?" The woman answered, "The serpent tricked me into it, so I ate it."
   Then the LORD God said to the serpent:
"Because you have done this, you shall be banned
      from all the animals
      and from all the wild creatures;
   on your belly shall you crawl,
      and dirt shall you eat
      all the days of your life.

I will put enmity between you and the woman,
  and between your offspring and hers;
he will strike at your head,
  while you strike at his heel."
The man called his wife Eve, because she became the mother of
all the living.

Responsorial Psalm   Ps 98: 1, 2–3ab, 3cd–4   Brian J. Nelson

Sing to the Lord a new song for he has done
mar - vel - ous deeds. Sing to the Lord a
new song for he has done mar - vel - ous deeds.

Sing to the LORD a new song,
  for he has done wondrous deeds;
His right hand has won victory for him,
  his holy arm. ℟

The LORD has made his salvation known:
  in the sight of the nations he has revealed his justice.
He has remembered his kindness and his faithfulness
  toward the house of Israel. ℟

All the ends of the earth have seen
  the salvation by our God.
Sing joyfully to the LORD, all you lands;
  break into song; sing praise. ℟

Second Reading Eph 1: 3–6, 11–12 Brothers and sisters: Blessed be the
God and Father of our Lord Jesus Christ, who has blessed us in

Christ with every spiritual blessing in the heavens, as he chose us in him, before the foundation of the world, to be holy and without blemish before him. In love he destined us for adoption to himself through Jesus Christ, in accord with the favor of his will, for the praise of the glory of his grace that he granted us in the beloved.

In him we were also chosen, destined in accord with the purpose of the One who accomplishes all things according to the intention of his will, so that we might exist for the praise of his glory, we who first hoped in Christ.

Alleluia   *cf Lk 1: 28*   *Joe Higginbotham*

Al - le - lu - ia, al - le - lu - ia, al - le - lu - ia.

Al - le - lu - ia, al - le - lu - ia, al - le - lu - ia.

Hail Mary, full of grace, the Lord is with you; / blessed are you among women.   **Alleluia, alleluia.**

Gospel *Lk 1: 26–38* The angel Gabriel was sent from God to a town of Galilee called Nazareth, to a virgin betrothed to a man named Joseph, of the house of David, and the virgin's name was Mary. And coming to her, he said, "Hail, full of grace! The Lord is with you." But she was greatly troubled at what was said and pondered what sort of greeting this might be. Then the angel said to her, "Do not be afraid, Mary, for you have found favor with God. Behold, you will conceive in your womb and bear a son, and you shall name him Jesus. He will be great and will be called Son of the Most High, and the Lord God will give him the throne of David his father, and he will rule over the house of Jacob forever, and of his Kingdom there will be no end." But Mary said to the angel, "How can this be, since I have no relations with a man?" And the angel said to her in reply, "The Holy Spirit will come upon you, and the power of the Most High will overshadow you. Therefore the child to be born will be called holy, the Son of God. And behold, Elizabeth, your relative, has also conceived a son in her old age, and this is the sixth month for her who was called barren; for nothing will be impossible for God." Mary said, "Behold, I am the handmaid of the Lord. May it be done to me according to your word." Then the angel departed from her.

Communion Antiphon   Glorious things are spoken of you, O Mary, ✦ for from you arose the sun of justice, ✦ Christ our God.

DECEMBER 12: OUR LADY OF GUADALUPE

Entrance Antiphon   Rv 12:1   A great sign appeared in the sky, a woman clothed with the sun, ✦ with the moon under her feet, and on her head a crown of twelve stars.

First Reading   Zec 2:14-17   Sing and rejoice, O daughter Zion! See, I am coming to dwell among you, says the LORD. Many nations shall join themselves to the LORD on that day, and they shall be his people, and he will dwell among you, and you shall know that the LORD of hosts has sent me to you. The LORD will possess Judah as his portion in the holy land, and he will again choose Jerusalem. Silence, all mankind, in the presence of the LORD! For he stirs forth from his holy dwelling.

Or: Rv 11:19a; 12:1-6a, 10ab   God's temple in heaven was opened, and the ark of his covenant could be seen in the temple.
   A great sign appeared in the sky, a woman clothed with the sun, with the moon under her feet, and on her head a crown of twelve stars. She was with child and wailed aloud in pain as she labored to give birth. Then another sign appeared in the sky; it was a huge red dragon, with seven heads and ten horns, and on its heads were seven diadems. Its tail swept away a third of the stars in the sky and hurled them down to the earth. Then the dragon stood before the woman about to give birth, to devour her child when she gave birth. She gave birth to a son, a male

child, destined to rule all the nations with an iron rod. Her child was caught up to God and his throne. The woman herself fled into the desert where she had a place prepared by God.

Then I heard a loud voice in heaven say:
"Now have salvation and power come,
 and the Kingdom of our God
 and the authority of his Anointed."

Responsorial Psalm   Jdt 13: 18bcde, 19   Daniel J. Adamini

You are the high-est   hon-or   of our race.

Blessed are you, daughter, by the Most High God,
 above all the women on earth;
 and blessed be the LORD God,
 the creator of heaven and earth.   ℟

Your deed of hope will never be forgotten
 by those who tell of the might of God.   ℟

Alleluia   cf Lk 1: 28   Vince Ambrosetti

Al-le-lu-ia, al-le-lu-ia, al-le-lu-ia, al-le-lu-ia.

Al-le-lu-ia, al-le-lu-ia, al-le-lu - ia.

Blessed are you, holy Virgin Mary, deserving of all praise; / from you rose the sun of justice, Christ our God. **Alleluia, alleluia.**

Gospel Lk 1: 26-38 The angel Gabriel was sent from God to a town of Galilee called Nazareth, to a virgin betrothed to a man named Joseph, of the house of David, and the virgin's name was Mary.

And coming to her, he said, "Hail, full of grace! The Lord is with you." But she was greatly troubled at what was said and pondered what sort of greeting this might be. Then the angel said to her, "Do not be afraid, Mary, for you have found favor with God. Behold, you will conceive in your womb and bear a son, and you shall name him Jesus. He will be great and will be called Son of the Most High, and the Lord God will give him the throne of David his father, and he will rule over the house of Jacob forever, and of his Kingdom there will be no end." But Mary said to the angel, "How can this be, since I have no relations with a man?" And the angel said to her in reply, "The Holy Spirit will come upon you, and the power of the Most High will overshadow you. Therefore the child to be born will be called holy, the Son of God. And behold, Elizabeth, your relative, has also conceived a son in her old age, and this is the sixth month for her who was called barren; for nothing will be impossible for God." Mary said, "Behold, I am the handmaid of the Lord. May it be done to me according to your word." Then the angel departed from her.

Or: Lk 1: 39-47 Mary set out and traveled to the hill country in haste to a town of Judah, where she entered the house of Zechariah and greeted Elizabeth. When Elizabeth heard Mary's greeting, the infant leaped in her womb, and Elizabeth, filled with the Holy Spirit, cried out in a loud voice and said, "Most blessed are you among women, and blessed is the fruit of your womb. And how does this happen to me, that the mother of my Lord should come to me? For at the moment the sound of your greeting reached my ears, the infant in my womb leaped for joy. Blessed are you who believed that what was spoken to you by the Lord would be fulfilled."

And Mary said:

"My soul proclaims the greatness of the Lord;
   my spirit rejoices in God my savior."

Communion Antiphon Lk 1: 52 **The Lord has cast down the mighty from their thrones, ◆ and has lifted up the lowly.**

Or: cf. Ps 147 (146): 20 **God has not acted thus for any other nation; ◆ to no other people had he shown his love so clearly.**

ACKNOWLEDGMENTS

Unauthorized reproduction of the material in this publication, by any means, or use of the individual pages herein, is a violation of U.S. Copyright Law and the moral rights of the copyright owner. Permission to use, in any way, the material in this book must be obtained in writing from the publishers, International Liturgy Publications (ILP), and the copyright owner.

Confraternity of Christian Doctrine (CCD)
3211 Fourth Street NE
Washington, DC 20017
www.usccb.org

International Commission on English in the Liturgy (ICEL)
1100 Connecticut Ave., NW,
Suite 710
Washington, DC 20036
202-347-0800
www.icelweb.org

International Liturgy Publications (ILP)
PO Box 50476
Nashville, TN 37205
615-599-4497
www.ILPmusic.org

United States Conference of Catholic Bishops (USCCB)
Secretariat of Divine Worship
3211 Fourth Street NE
Washington, DC 20017
202-541-3089
www.usccb.org

PSALM REFRAINS

A light will shine on us this day: the Lord is born for us. Bill Svarda, b.1941; © 2003, International Liturgy Publications.

Alleluia, alleluia, alleluia. Laura Lea Duckworth, b.1951; © 2011, International Liturgy Publications.

All the ends of the earth have seen the saving power of God. Don Fishel, b.1950; © 2007, International Liturgy Publications.

Be merciful, O Lord, for we have sinned. Bill Svarda, b.1941, © 2013, International Liturgy Publications.

Be with me, Lord, when I am in trouble. Joe Higginbotham, b.1953; © 2013, International Liturgy Publications.

Blessed are the poor in spirit; the kingdom of heaven is theirs! Joe Higginbotham, b.1953; © 2013, International Liturgy Publications.

Blessed are they who dwell in your house, O Lord. Joe Higginbotham, b.1953; © 2006, International Liturgy Publications.

Blessed are they who follow the law of the Lord! Dave Bradshaw; © 2013, International Liturgy Publications.

Blessed are they who hope in the Lord. Joe Higginbotham, b.1953; © 2006, International Liturgy Publications.

Blessed are those who fear the Lord and walk in his ways. Beverly McDevitt, b.1963; © 2006, International Liturgy Publications.

Blessed are those who fear the Lord. Beverly McDevitt, b.1963; © 2006, International Liturgy Publications.

Blessed the people the Lord has chosen to be his own. Jane Terwilliger, b.1952; © 2009, International Liturgy Publications.

Create a clean heart in me, O God. Don Fishel, b.1950; © 2013, International Liturgy Publications.

Cry out with joy and gladness: for among you is the great and Holy One of Israel. Jim Cowan, b.1952; © 1998, International Liturgy Publications.

Do not forget the works of the Lord! Joe Higginbotham, b.1953; © 2013, International Liturgy Publications.

Father, into your hands I commend my spirit. Joe Higginbotham, b.1953; © 2013, International Liturgy Publications.

Fill us with your love, O Lord, and we shall sing for joy! Tim Wells, b.1955; © 2000, International Liturgy Publications.

For ever I will sing the goodness of the Lord. (1) Beverly McDevitt, b.1963; © 2006, International Liturgy Publications. (2) Joe Higginbotham, b.1953; © 2013, International Liturgy Publications.

Give thanks to the Lord for he is good, his love is everlasting. Based on ICH WILL DICH LIEBEN; Georg Joseph, c.1630–1668; © 2013, International Liturgy Publications.

Give thanks to the Lord, his love is everlasting. Michael Giszczak, b.1951; © 2011, International Liturgy Publications.

Give the Lord glory and honor. Kieth Sammut, b.1957; © 1985, International Liturgy Publications.

Glory and praise for ever! Alexander Young, b.1976; © 2013, International Liturgy Publications.

God, in your goodness, you have made a home for the poor. Based on KINGSFOLD; © 2013, International Liturgy Publications.

God mounts his throne to shouts of joy: a blare of trumpets for the Lord. Joe Higginbotham, b.1953; © 2013, International Liturgy Publications.

Go out to all the world and tell the good news. Joe Higginbotham, b.1953; © 2006, International Liturgy Publications

Here am I, Lord; I come to do your will. Beverly McDevitt, b.1963 © 2006, International Liturgy Publications.

He who does justice will live in the presence of the Lord. Jim Cowan, b.1952; © 1998, International Liturgy Publications.

I believe that I shall see the good things of the Lord in the land of the living. Based on ELLACOMBE; © 2013, International Liturgy Publications.

If today you hear his voice, harden not your hearts. (1) Joe Higginbotham, b.1953; © 2013, International Liturgy Publications. (2) Vince Ambrosetti, b.1956; © 1996, International Liturgy Publications.

I love you, Lord, my strength. Beverly McDevitt, b.1963; © 2006, International Liturgy Publications.

I praise you, for I am wonderfully made. Joe Higginbotham, b.1953; © 2013, International Liturgy Publications.

I shall live in the house of the Lord all the days of my life. Bill Svarda, b.1941; © 2003, International Liturgy Publications.

I turn to you, Lord, in time of trouble, and you fill me with the joy of salvation. Joe Higginbotham, b.1953; © 2013, International Liturgy Publications.

I will praise you, Lord, for you have rescued me. Joe Higginbotham, b.1953; © 2013, International Liturgy Publications.

I will praise you, Lord, in the assembly of your people. Joe

Lord, be my rock of safety. Joe Higginbotham, b.1953; © 2013, International Liturgy Publications.

Lord, come and save us. Bill Svarda, b.1941; © 2003, International Liturgy Publications.

Lord, come to my aid! Vince Ambrosetti, b.1956, and Debra Lee Williamson b.1980; © 2013, International Liturgy Publications.

Lord, every nation on earth will adore you. Brian J. Nelson, b.1967; © 2013, International Liturgy Publications.

Lord, forgive the wrong I have done. Joe Higginbotham, b.1953; © 2006, International Liturgy Publications.

Lord, go up to the place of your rest, you and the ark of your holiness. Joe Higginbotham, b.1953; © 2008, International Liturgy Publications.

Lord, heal my soul, for I have sinned against you. Bill Svarda, b.1941; © 2003, International Liturgy Publications.

Lord, I love your commands. Joe Higginbotham, b.1953; © 2013, International Liturgy Publications.

Lord, in your great love, answer me. Roger Holtz, b.1950; © 2010, International Liturgy Publications.

Lord, it is good to give thanks to you. Joe Higginbotham, b.1953; © 2013, International Liturgy Publications.

Lord, let us see your kindness, and grant us your salvation. Beverly McDevitt, b.1963; © 2006, International Liturgy Publications.

Lord, let your face shine on us. Joe Higginbotham, b.1953; © 2013, International Liturgy Publications.

Lord, let your mercy be on us, as we place our trust in you. Beverly McDevitt, b.1963; © 2006, International Liturgy Publications.

Lord, make us turn to you; let us see your face and we shall be saved. Joe Higginbotham, b.1953; © 2013, International Liturgy Publications.

Lord, on the day I called for help, you answered me. Vince Ambrosetti, b.1956; © 1978, International Liturgy Publications.

Lord, send out your Spirit, and renew the face of the earth. (1) David Miles, b.1956; © 1985, International Liturgy Publications. (2) Joe Higginbotham, b.1953; © 2013, International Liturgy Publications.

Lord, this is the people that longs to see your face. Joe Higginbotham, b.1953; © 2013, International Liturgy Publications.

Praise the Lord, my soul! (1) Don Fishel, b.1950; © 1981, 2008, International Liturgy Publications. (2) Joe Higginbotham, b.1953; © 2013, International Liturgy Publications.

Praise the Lord, who heals the brokenhearted. Beverly McDevitt, b.1963; © 2006, International Liturgy Publications.

Praise the Lord, who lifts up the poor. Joe Higginbotham, b.1953; © 2013, International Liturgy Publications.

Proclaim his marvelous deeds to all the nations. © 2013, International Liturgy Publications.

Remember your mercies, O Lord. Michael Giszczak, b.1951; © 2008, International Liturgy Publications.

Rest in God alone, my soul. Stacy Whitfield, SGL, b.1956; © 2010, International Liturgy Publications.

Since my mother's womb, you have been my strength. Joe Higginbotham, b.1953. © 2006, International Liturgy Publications.

Sing to the Lord a new song, for he has done marvelous deeds. Brian J. Nelson, b.1967; © 2013, International Liturgy Publications.

Sing with joy to God our help. Joe Higginbotham, b.1953; © 2013, International Liturgy Publications.

Taste and see the goodness of the Lord. Roger Holtz, b.1950; © 2007, International Liturgy Publications.

Teach me your ways, O Lord. Michael Giszczak, b.1951; © 2008, International Liturgy Publications.

The angel of the Lord will rescue those who fear him. Joe Higginbotham, b.1953; © 2013, International Liturgy Publications.

The earth is full of the goodness of the Lord. Ann Fons, b.1955; © 2010, International Liturgy Publications.

The hand of the Lord feeds us; he answers all our needs. Don Fishel, b.1950; © 2010, International Liturgy Publications.

Their message goes out through all the earth. Roger Holtz, b.1950; © 2004, International Liturgy Publications.

The just man is a light in darkness to the upright. Ann Fons, b.1955, Roger Holtz, b.1950, and Jane Terwilliger, b.1952; © 2010, International Liturgy Publications.

The Lord comes to rule the earth with justice. Roger Holtz, b.1950,

and Jane Terwilliger, b.1952; © 2012, International Liturgy
Publications.

The Lord gave them bread from heaven. Joe Higginbotham, b.1953;
© 2013, International Liturgy Publications.

The Lord has done great things for us; we are filled with joy.
Joe Higginbotham, b.1953; © 2013, International Liturgy
Publications.

The Lord has revealed to the nations his saving power. Don Fishel,
b.1950; © 2007, International Liturgy Publications.

The Lord has set his throne in heaven. Based on NOËL NOUVELET;
© 2013, International Liturgy Publications.

The Lord hears the cry of the poor. Joe Higginbotham, b.1953;
© 2013, International Liturgy Publications.

*The Lord is kind and merciful, slow to anger, and rich in
compassion.* Bill Svarda, b.1941; © 2003, International Liturgy
Publications.

The Lord is kind and merciful. Beverly McDevitt, b.1963; © 2006,
International Liturgy Publications.

The Lord is king, the Most High over all the earth. Jane Terwilliger,
b.1952; © 2009, International Liturgy Publications.

The Lord is king; he is robed in majesty. Roger Holtz, b.1950;
© 2008, International Liturgy Publications.

The Lord is my light and my salvation. (1) E. Louis Canter, OEF,
b.1955; © 2013, International Liturgy Publications. (2) Ann
Fons, b.1955, Roger Holtz, b.1950, and Jane Terwilliger, b.1952;
© 2007, International Liturgy Publications.

The Lord is my shepherd; there is nothing I shall want. (1) Joe
Higginbotham, b.1953, and Vince Ambrosetti, b.1956; © 2007,
International Liturgy Publications. (2) Vince Ambrosetti,
b.1956, © 1994, International Liturgy Publications. (3) Elissa
Krieg, b.1976; © 2002, International Liturgy Publications.

The Lord is near to all who call upon him. Bill Svarda, b.1941;
© 2003, International Liturgy Publications.

The Lord remembers his covenant forever. Joe Higginbotham,
b.1953; © 2013, International Liturgy Publications.

The Lord upholds my life. Tim Wells, b.1955; © 2006,
International Liturgy Publications.

The Lord will bless his people with peace. Based on EVENTIDE;

William H. Monk, 1823–1889; © 2013, International Liturgy Publications.

The Lord's kindness is everlasting to those who fear him. Vince Ambrosetti, b.1956; © 2013, International Liturgy Publications.

The one who does justice will live in the presence of the Lord. Jim Cowan, b.1952; © 1998, International Liturgy Publications.

The precepts of the Lord give joy to the heart. Joe Higginbotham, b.1953; © 2006, International Liturgy Publications.

The queen stands at your right hand, arrayed in gold. Joe Higginbotham, b.1953; © 2013, International Liturgy Publications.

The seed that falls on good ground will yield a fruitful harvest. Based on DIX; Conrad Kocher, 1786–1872; © 2013, International Liturgy Publications.

The son of David will live for ever. Based on IRBY; Henry J. Gauntlett, 1805–1876; © 2013, International Liturgy Publications.

The stone rejected by the builders has become the cornerstone. Jane Terwilliger, b.1952; © 2011, International Liturgy Publications.

The vineyard of the Lord is the house of Israel. Joe Higginbotham, b.1953; © 2006, International Liturgy Publications

The waters of the river gladden the city of God, the holy dwelling of the Most High! Bill Svarda, b.1941; © 2003, International Liturgy Publications.

The Word of God became man and lived among us. Beverly McDevitt, b.1963; © 2006, International Liturgy Publications.

This is the day the Lord has made; let us rejoice and be glad. Bill Svarda, b.1941; © 2003, International Liturgy Publications.

Today is born our Savior, Christ the Lord. Based on GREENSLEEVES; adapted by Joe Higginbotham, b.1953; © 2013, International Liturgy Publications.

To the upright I will show the saving power of God. Joe Higginbotham, b.1953; © 2013, International Liturgy Publications.

To you, O Lord, I lift my soul. Brian J. Nelson, b.1967; © 2013, International Liturgy Publications.

Turn to the Lord in your need, and you will live. Joe Higginbotham, b.1953; © 2013, International Liturgy Publications.

We are his people, the sheep of his flock. Joe Higginbotham, b.1953; © 2013, International Liturgy Publications.

Who is this king of glory? It is the Lord! Based on *Lift Up Your Heads, O Ye Gates,* G.F. Handel; adapted by Vince Ambrosetti, b.1956, and Debra Lee Williamson, b.1980; © 2013, International Liturgy Publications.

With the Lord there is mercy and fullness of redemption. (1) Joe Higginbotham, b.1953; © 2013, International Liturgy Publications. (2) Bill Svarda, b.1941; © 2003, International Liturgy Publications.

You are a priest for ever, in the line of Melchizedek. Roger Holtz, b.1950; © 2008, International Liturgy Publications.

You are my inheritance, O Lord. Joe Higginbotham, b.1953; © 2013, International Liturgy Publications.

You are the highest honor of our race. Daniel J. Adamini, b.1960; © 2004, International Liturgy Publications.

Your ways, O Lord, are love and truth to those who keep your covenant. Michael Giszczak, b.1951; © 2008, International Liturgy Publications.

Your words, Lord, are Spirit and life. (1) Jim Hughes, b.1957; © 2013, International Liturgy Publications. (2) Beverly McDevitt, b.1963; © 2006, International Liturgy Publications.

You will draw water joyfully from the springs of salvation. Bill Svarda, b.1941; © 2003, International Liturgy Publications.

CALENDAR OF READINGS

Year A

2019	2022	2025	2028	2031	CELEBRATION	PAGE
Dec 1	Nov 27	Nov 30	Dec 3	Nov 30	1st Sunday of Advent	65
Dec 8	Dec 4	Dec 7	Dec 10	Dec 7	2nd Sunday of Advent	67
Dec 9	Dec 8	Dec 8	Dec 8	Dec 8	The Immaculate Conception	803
Dec 12	Dec 12	Dec 12	Dec 12	Dec 12	Our Lady of Guadalupe	806
Dec 15	Dec 11	Dec 14	Dec 17	Dec 14	3rd Sunday of Advent	71
Dec 22	Dec 18	Dec 21	Dec 24	Dec 21	4th Sunday of Advent	74
Dec 25	Dec 25	Dec 25	Dec 25	Dec 25	The Nativity of the Lord (Christmas)	77
Dec 29	Dec 30	Dec 28	Dec 31	Dec 28	The Holy Family	89

Year A, continued

2020	2023	2026	2029	2032	CELEBRATION	PAGE
Jan 1	Jan 1	Jan 1	Jan 1	Jan 1	Mary, the Mother of God	92
Jan 5	Jan 8	Jan 4	Jan 7	Jan 4	The Epiphany of the Lord	94
Jan 12	Jan 9	Jan 11	Jan 8	Jan 11	The Baptism of the Lord	97
Jan 19	Jan 15	Jan 18	Jan 14	Jan 18	2nd Sunday in Ordinary Time	183
Jan 26	Jan 22	Jan 25	Jan 21	Jan 25	3rd Sunday in Ordinary Time	185
—	Jan 29	Feb 1	Jan 28	Feb 1	4th Sunday in Ordinary Time	188
Feb 2	Feb 2	Feb 2	Feb 2	Feb 2	The Presentation of the Lord	744
Feb 9	Feb 5	Feb 8	Feb 4	Feb 8	5th Sunday in Ordinary Time	190
Feb 16	Feb 12	Feb 15	Feb 11	—	6th Sunday in Ordinary Time	193
Feb 23	Feb 19	—	—	—	7th Sunday in Ordinary Time	196
—	—	—	—	—	8th Sunday in Ordinary Time	198
—	—	—	—	—	9th Sunday in Ordinary Time	201
Feb 26	Feb 22	Feb 18	Feb 14	Feb 11	Ash Wednesday	100
Mar 1	Feb 26	Feb 22	Feb 18	Feb 15	1st Sunday of Lent	105
Mar 8	Mar 5	Mar 1	Feb 25	Feb 22	2nd Sunday of Lent	108
Mar 15	Mar 12	Mar 8	Mar 4	Feb 29	3rd Sunday of Lent	111
Mar 19	Mar 20	Mar 19	Mar 19	Mar 19	St. Joseph	749
Mar 22	Mar 19	Mar 15	Mar 11	Mar 7	4th Sunday of Lent	115
Mar 25	Mar 25	Mar 25	Apr 9	Apr 5	The Annunciation of the Lord	752
Mar 29	Mar 26	Mar 22	Mar 18	Mar 14	5th Sunday of Lent	119
Apr 5	Apr 2	Mar 29	Mar 25	Mar 21	Palm Sunday	124

Year A, continued

2020	2023	2026	2029	2032	CELEBRATION	PAGE
Apr 9	Apr 6	Apr 2	Mar 29	Mar 25	Holy Thursday	669
Apr 10	Apr 7	Apr 3	Mar 30	Mar 26	Good Friday	677
Apr 11	Apr 8	Apr 4	Mar 31	Mar 27	Easter Vigil	699
Apr 12	Apr 9	Apr 5	Apr 1	Mar 28	Easter Sunday	740
Apr 19	Apr 16	Apr 12	Apr 8	Apr 4	2nd Sunday of Easter	141
Apr 26	Apr 23	Apr 19	Apr 15	Apr 11	3rd Sunday of Easter	144
May 3	Apr 30	Apr 26	Apr 22	Apr 18	4th Sunday of Easter	147
May 10	May 7	May 3	Apr 29	Apr 25	5th Sunday of Easter	150
May 17	May 14	May 10	May 6	May 2	6th Sunday of Easter	153
May 21	May 18	May 14	May 10	May 6	The Ascension of the Lord	156
May 24	May 21	May 17	May 13	May 9	7th Sunday of Easter	159
May 31	May 28	May 24	May 20	May 16	Pentecost Sunday	161
Jun 7	Jun 4	May 31	May 27	May 23	The Most Holy Trinity	173
Jun 14	Jun 11	Jun 7	Jun 3	May 30	Corpus Christi	175
Jun 19	Jun 16	Jun 12	Jun 8	Jun 4	The Most Sacred Heart of Jesus	180
—	—	—	—	—	9th Sunday in Ordinary Time	201
—	—	—	Jun 10	Jun 6	10th Sunday in Ordinary Time	203
—	Jun 8	Jun 14	Jun 17	Jun 13	11th Sunday in Ordinary Time	206
Jun 24	Jun 24	Jun 24	Jun 24	Jun 24	St. John the Baptist	755
Jun 21	Jun 25	Jun 21	—	Jun 20	12th Sunday in Ordinary Time	208
Jun 29	Jun 29	Jun 29	Jun 29	Jun 29	Sts. Peter and Paul	761
Jun 28	Jul 2	Jun 28	Jul 1	Jun 27	13th Sunday in Ordinary Time	211
Jul 4	Jul 4	Jul 4	Jul 4	—	Independence Day	766
Jul 5	Jul 9	Jul 5	Jul 8	Jul 4	14th Sunday in Ordinary Time	213
Jul 12	Jul 16	Jul 12	Jul 15	Jul 11	15th Sunday in Ordinary Time	216
Jul 19	Jul 23	Jul 19	Jul 22	Jul 18	16th Sunday in Ordinary Time	219
Jul 26	Jul 30	Jul 26	Jul 29	Jul 25	17th Sunday in Ordinary Time	222
Aug 2	—	Aug 2	Aug 5	Aug 1	18th Sunday in Ordinary Time	224
Aug 6	Aug 6	Aug 6	Aug 6	Aug 6	The Transfiguration of the Lord	769
Aug 9	Aug 13	Aug 9	Aug 12	Aug 8	19th Sunday in Ordinary Time	227
Aug 15	Aug 15	Aug 15	Aug 15	Aug 15	The Assumption of the Blessed Virgin Mary	772
Aug 16	Aug 20	Aug 16	Aug 19	—	20th Sunday in Ordinary Time	229
Aug 23	Aug 27	Aug 23	Aug 26	Aug 22	21st Sunday in Ordinary Time	232
Aug 30	Sep 3	Aug 30	Sep 2	Aug 29	22nd Sunday in Ordinary Time	234
Sep 6	Sep 10	Sep 6	Sep 9	Sep 5	23rd Sunday in Ordinary Time	236
Sep 14	Sep 14	Sep 14	Sep 14	Sep 14	The Exaltation of the Holy Cross	777

Year A, continued

2020	2023	2026	2029	2032	CELEBRATION	PAGE
Sep 13	Sep 17	Sep 13	Sep 16	Sep 12	24th Sunday in Ordinary Time	239
Sep 20	Sep 24	Sep 20	Sep 23	Sep 29	25th Sunday in Ordinary Time	241
Sep 27	Oct 1	Sep 27	Sep 30	Sep 26	26th Sunday in Ordinary Time	244
Oct 4	Oct 8	Oct 4	Oct 7	Oct 3	27th Sunday in Ordinary Time	247
Oct 11	Oct 15	Oct 11	Oct 14	Oct 10	28th Sunday in Ordinary Time	250
Oct 18	Oct 22	Oct 18	Oct 21	Oct 17	29th Sunday in Ordinary Time	253
Oct 25	Oct 29	Oct 25	Oct 28	Oct 24	30th Sunday in Ordinary Time	255
Nov 1	Nov 1	Nov 1	Nov 1	Nov 1	All Saints	780
Nov 2	Nov 2	Nov 2	Nov 2	Nov 2	All Souls	782
—	Nov 5	—	Nov 4	Oct 31	31st Sunday in Ordinary Time	257
Nov 8	Nov 12	Nov 8	Nov 11	Nov 7	32nd Sunday in Ordinary Time	260
Nov 9	Nov 9	Nov 9	Nov 9	Nov 9	The Dedication of the Lateran Basilica	798
Nov 15	Nov 19	Nov 15	Nov 18	Nov 14	33rd Sunday in Ordinary Time	262
Nov 22	Nov 26	Nov 22	Nov 25	Nov 21	Christ the King	265
Nov 26	Nov 23	Nov 26	Nov 22	Nov 25	Thanksgiving Day	800

Year B

2017	2020	2023	2026	2029	CELEBRATION	PAGE
Dec 3	Nov 29	Dec 3	Nov 29	Dec 2	1st Sunday of Advent	269
Dec 10	Dec 6	Dec 10	Dec 6	Dec 9	2nd Sunday of Advent	271
Dec 8	Dec 8	Dec 8	Dec 8	Dec 8	The Immaculate Conception	803
Dec 12	Dec 12	Dec 12	Dec 12	Dec 12	Our Lady of Guadalupe	806
Dec 17	Dec 13	Dec 17	Dec 13	Dec 16	3rd Sunday of Advent	275
Dec 24	Dec 20	Dec 24	Dec 20	Dec 23	4th Sunday of Advent	277
Dec 25	Dec 25	Dec 25	Dec 25	Dec 25	The Nativity of the Lord (Christmas)	280
Dec 31	Dec 27	Dec 31	Dec 27	Dec 30	The Holy Family	292

Year B, continued

2018	2021	2024	2027	2030	CELEBRATION	PAGE
Jan 1	Jan 1	Jan 1	Jan 1	Jan 1	Mary, the Mother of God	299
Jan 7	Jan 3	Jan 7	Jan 3	Jan 6	The Epiphany of the Lord	301
Jan 8	Jan 10	Jan 8	Jan 10	Jan 13	The Baptism of the Lord	304
Jan 14	Jan 17	Jan 14	Jan 17	Jan 20	2nd Sunday in Ordinary Time	381
Jan 21	Jan 24	Jan 21	Jan 24	Jan 27	3rd Sunday in Ordinary Time	383
Jan 28	Jan 31	Jan 28	Jan 31	Feb 3	4th Sunday in Ordinary Time	385

Year B, continued

2018	2021	2024	2027	2030	CELEBRATION	PAGE
Feb 2	Feb 2	Feb 2	Feb 2	Feb 2	The Presentation of the Lord	744
Feb 4	Feb 7	Feb 4	Feb 7	Feb 10	5th Sunday in Ordinary Time	388
Feb 11	Feb 14	Feb 11	—	Feb 17	6th Sunday in Ordinary Time	390
—	—	—	—	Feb 24	7th Sunday in Ordinary Time	392
—	—	—	—	Mar 3	8th Sunday in Ordinary Time	395
—	—	—	—	—	9th Sunday in Ordinary Time	398
Feb 14	Feb 17	Feb 14	Feb 10	Mar 6	Ash Wednesday	310
Feb 18	Feb 21	Feb 18	Feb 14	Mar 10	1st Sunday of Lent	315
Feb 25	Feb 28	Feb 25	Feb 21	Mar 17	2nd Sunday of Lent	317
Mar 4	Mar 7	Mar 3	Feb 28	Mar 24	3rd Sunday of Lent	320
Mar 19	Mar 19	Mar 19	Mar 19	Mar 19	St. Joseph	749
Mar 11	Mar 14	Mar 10	Mar 7	Mar 31	4th Sunday of Lent	323
Apr 9	Mar 25	Mar 25	Apr 5	Mar 25	The Annunciation of the Lord	752
Mar 18	Mar 21	Mar 17	Mar 14	Apr 7	5th Sunday of Lent	326
Mar 25	Mar 28	Mar 24	Mar 21	Apr 14	Palm Sunday	329
Mar 29	Apr 1	Mar 28	Mar 25	Apr 18	Holy Thursday	669
Mar 30	Apr 2	Mar 29	Mar 26	Apr 19	Good Friday	677
Mar 31	Apr 3	Mar 30	Mar 27	Apr 20	Easter Vigil	699
Apr 1	Apr 4	Mar 31	Mar 28	Apr 21	Easter Sunday	740
Apr 8	Apr 11	Apr 7	Apr 4	Apr 28	2nd Sunday of Easter	345
Apr 15	Apr 18	Apr 14	Apr 11	May 5	3rd Sunday of Easter	348
Apr 22	Apr 25	Apr 21	Apr 18	May 12	4th Sunday of Easter	350
Apr 29	May 2	Apr 28	Apr 25	May 19	5th Sunday of Easter	353
May 6	May 9	May 5	May 2	May 26	6th Sunday of Easter	355
May 10	May 13	May 9	May 6	May 30	The Ascension of the Lord	358
May 13	May 16	May 12	May 9	Jun 2	7th Sunday of Easter	361
May 20	May 23	May 19	May 16	Jun 9	Pentecost Sunday	364
May 27	May 30	May 26	May 23	Jun 16	The Most Holy Trinity	369
Jun 3	Jun 6	Jun 2	May 30	Jun 23	Corpus Christi	371
Jun 8	Jun 11	Jun 7	Jun 4	Jun 28	The Most Sacred Heart of Jesus	377
—	—	—	—	—	9th Sunday in Ordinary Time	398
Jun 10	—	Jun 9	Jun 6	—	10th Sunday in Ordinary Time	400
Jun 17	Jun 13	Jun 16	Jun 13	—	11th Sunday in Ordinary Time	403
Jun 24	Jun 24	Jun 24	Jun 24	Jun 24	St. John the Baptist	755
—	Jun 20	Jun 23	Jun 20	—	12th Sunday in Ordinary Time	406
Jun 29	Jun 29	Jun 29	Jun 29	Jun 29	Sts. Peter and Paul	761
Jul 1	Jun 27	Jun 30	Jun 27	Jun 30	13th Sunday in Ordinary Time	408

Year B, continued

2018	2021	2024	2027	2030	CELEBRATION	PAGE
Jul 4	—	Jul 4	—	Jul 4	Independence Day	766
Jul 8	Jul 4	Jul 7	Jul 4	Jul 7	14th Sunday in Ordinary Time	411
Jul 15	Jul 11	Jul 14	Jul 11	Jul 14	15th Sunday in Ordinary Time	414
Jul 22	Jul 18	Jul 21	Jul 18	Jul 21	16th Sunday in Ordinary Time	416
Jul 29	Jul 25	Jul 28	Jul 25	Jul 28	17th Sunday in Ordinary Time	419
Aug 5	Aug 1	Aug 4	Aug 1	Aug 4	18th Sunday in Ordinary Time	421
Aug 6	Aug 6	Aug 6	Aug 6	Aug 6	The Transfiguration of the Lord	769
Aug 12	Aug 8	Aug 11	Aug 8	Aug 11	19th Sunday in Ordinary Time	424
Aug 15	Aug 15	Aug 15	Aug 15	Aug 15	The Assumption of the Blessed Virgin Mary	772
Aug 19	—	Aug 18	—	Aug 18	20th Sunday in Ordinary Time	426
Aug 26	Aug 22	Aug 25	Aug 22	Aug 25	21st Sunday in Ordinary Time	429
Sep 2	Aug 29	Sep 1	Aug 29	Sep 1	22nd Sunday in Ordinary Time	432
Sep 9	Sep 5	Sep 8	Sep 5	Sep 8	23rd Sunday in Ordinary Time	435
Sep 14	Sep 14	Sep 14	Sep 14	Sep 14	The Exaltation of the Holy Cross	777
Sep 16	Sep 12	Sep 15	Sep 12	Sep 15	24th Sunday in Ordinary Time	437
Sep 23	Sep 19	Sep 22	Sep 19	Sep 22	25th Sunday in Ordinary Time	440
Sep 30	Sep 26	Sep 29	Sep 26	Sep 29	26th Sunday in Ordinary Time	442
Oct 7	Oct 3	Oct 6	Oct 3	Oct 6	27th Sunday in Ordinary Time	445
Oct 14	Oct 10	Oct 13	Oct 10	Oct 13	28th Sunday in Ordinary Time	448
Oct 21	Oct 17	Oct 20	Oct 17	Oct 20	29th Sunday in Ordinary Time	450
Oct 28	Oct 24	Oct 27	Oct 24	Oct 27	30th Sunday in Ordinary Time	453
Nov 1	Nov 1	Nov 1	Nov 1	Nov 1	All Saints	780
Nov 2	Nov 2	Nov 2	Nov 2	Nov 2	All Souls	782
Nov 4	Oct 31	Nov 3	Oct 31	Nov 3	31st Sunday in Ordinary Time	455
Nov 11	Nov 7	Nov 10	Nov 7	Nov 10	32nd Sunday in Ordinary Time	458
Nov 9	Nov 9	Nov 9	Nov 9	Nov 9	The Dedication of the Lateran Basilica	798
Nov 18	Nov 14	Nov 17	Nov 14	Nov 17	33rd Sunday in Ordinary Time	460
Nov 25	Nov 21	Nov 24	Nov 21	Nov 24	Christ the King	463
Nov 22	Nov 25	Nov 28	Nov 25	Nov 28	Thanksgiving Day	800

Year C

2018	2021	2024	2027	2030	CELEBRATION	PAGE
Dec 2	Nov 28	Dec 1	Nov 28	Dec 1	1st Sunday of Advent	466
Dec 9	Dec 5	Dec 8	Dec 5	Dec 8	2nd Sunday of Advent	468
Dec 8	Dec 8	Dec 9	Dec 8	Dec 9	The Immaculate Conception	803
Dec 12	Dec 13	Dec 12	Dec 13	Dec 12	Our Lady of Guadalupe	806

Year C

2018	2021	2024	2027	2030	CELEBRATION	PAGE
Dec 16	Dec 12	Dec 15	Dec 12	Dec 15	3rd Sunday of Advent	471
Dec 23	Dec 19	Dec 22	Dec 19	Dec 22	4th Sunday of Advent	474
Dec 25	Dec 25	Dec 25	Dec 25	Dec 25	The Nativity of the Lord (Christmas)	477
Dec 30	Dec 26	Dec 29	Dec 26	Dec 29	The Holy Family	489

Year C, continued

2019	2022	2025	2027	2030	CELEBRATION	PAGE
Jan 1	Jan 1	Jan 1	Jan 1	Jan 1	Mary, the Mother of God	494
Jan 6	Jan 2	Jan 5	Jan 2	Jan 5	The Epiphany of the Lord	496
Jan 13	Jan 9	Jan 12	Jan 9	Jan 12	The Baptism of the Lord	499
Jan 20	Jan 16	Jan 19	Jan 16	Jan 19	2nd Sunday in Ordinary Time	578
Jan 27	Jan 23	Jan 26	Jan 23	Jan 26	3rd Sunday in Ordinary Time	581
Feb 3	Jan 30	—	Jan 30	—	4th Sunday in Ordinary Time	584
Feb 2	Feb 2	Feb 2	Feb 2	Feb 2	The Presentation of the Lord	744
Feb 10	Feb 6	Feb 9	Feb 6	Feb 9	5th Sunday in Ordinary Time	587
Feb 17	Feb 13	Feb 16	Feb 13	Feb 16	6th Sunday in Ordinary Time	590
Feb 24	Feb 20	Feb 23	Feb 20	Feb 23	7th Sunday in Ordinary Time	593
Mar 3	Feb 27	Mar 2	Feb 27	—	8th Sunday in Ordinary Time	596
—	—	—	—	—	9th Sunday in Ordinary Time	598
Mar 6	Mar 2	Mar 5	Mar 1	Feb 26	Ash Wednesday	506
Mar 10	Mar 6	Mar 9	Mar 5	Mar 2	1st Sunday of Lent	511
Mar 17	Mar 13	Mar 16	Mar 12	Mar 9	2nd Sunday of Lent	514
Mar 24	Mar 20	Mar 23	Mar 19	Mar 16	3rd Sunday of Lent	517
Mar 19	Mar 19	Mar 19	Mar 20	Mar 19	St. Joseph	749
Mar 31	Mar 27	Mar 30	Mar 26	Mar 23	4th Sunday of Lent	520
Mar 25	Mar 25	Mar 25	Mar 25	Mar 25	The Annunciation of the Lord	752
Apr 7	Apr 3	Apr 6	Apr 2	Mar 30	5th Sunday of Lent	523
Apr 14	Apr 10	Apr 13	Apr 9	Apr 6	Palm Sunday	526
Apr 18	Apr 14	Apr 17	Apr 13	Apr 10	Holy Thursday	669
Apr 19	Apr 15	Apr 18	Apr 14	Apr 11	Good Friday	677
Apr 20	Apr 16	Apr 19	Apr 15	Apr 12	Easter Vigil	699
Apr 21	Apr 17	Apr 20	Apr 16	Apr 13	Easter Sunday	740
Apr 28	Apr 24	Apr 27	Apr 23	Apr 20	2nd Sunday of Easter	542
May 5	May 1	May 4	Apr 30	Apr 27	3rd Sunday of Easter	545
May 12	May 8	May 11	May 7	May 4	4th Sunday of Easter	548
May 19	May 15	May 18	May 14	May 11	5th Sunday of Easter	551

Year C, continued

2019	2022	2025	2027	2030	CELEBRATION	PAGE
May 26	May 22	May 25	May 21	May 18	6th Sunday of Easter	553
May 30	May 26	May 29	May 25	May 22	The Ascension of the Lord	556
Jun 2	May 29	Jun 1	May 28	May 25	7th Sunday of Easter	559
Jun 9	Jun 5	Jun 8	Jun 4	Jun 1	Pentecost Sunday	562
Jun 16	Jun 12	Jun 15	Jun 11	Jun 8	The Most Holy Trinity	567
Jun 23	Jun 19	Jun 22	Jun 18	Jun 15	Corpus Christi	569
Jun 28	Jun 24	Jun 27	Jun 23	Jun 20	The Most Sacred Heart of Jesus	574
—	—	—	—	—	9th Sunday in Ordinary Time	598
—	—	—	—	—	10th Sunday in Ordinary Time	601
—	—	—	—	—	11th Sunday in Ordinary Time	603
Jun 24	Jun 24	Jun 24	Jun 24	Jun 24	St. John the Baptist	755
—	—	—	Jun 25	Jun 22	12th Sunday in Ordinary Time	606
Jun 29	Jun 29	Jun 29	Jun 29	Jun 29	Sts. Peter and Paul	761
Jun 30	Jun 26	—	Jul 2	—	13th Sunday in Ordinary Time	608
Jul 4	Jul 4	Jul 4	Jul 4	Jul 4	Independence Day	766
Jul 7	Jul 3	Jul 6	Jul 9	Jul 6	14th Sunday in Ordinary Time	611
Jul 14	Jul 10	Jul 13	Jul 16	Jul 13	15th Sunday in Ordinary Time	614
Jul 21	Jul 17	Jul 20	Jul 23	Jul 20	16th Sunday in Ordinary Time	618
Jul 28	Jul 24	Jul 27	Jul 30	Jul 27	17th Sunday in Ordinary Time	620
Aug 4	Jul 31	Aug 3	—	Aug 3	18th Sunday in Ordinary Time	623
Aug 6	Aug 6	Aug 6	Aug 6	Aug 6	The Transfiguration of the Lord	769
Aug 11	Aug 7	Aug 10	Aug 13	Aug 10	19th Sunday in Ordinary Time	626
Aug 15	Aug 15	Aug 15	Aug 15	Aug 15	The Assumption of the Blessed Virgin Mary	772
Aug 18	Aug 14	Aug 17	Aug 20	Aug 17	20th Sunday in Ordinary Time	629
Aug 25	Aug 21	Aug 24	Aug 27	Aug 25	21st Sunday in Ordinary Time	631
Sep 1	Aug 28	Aug 31	Sep 3	Aug 31	22nd Sunday in Ordinary Time	634
Sep 8	Sep 4	Sep 7	Sep 10	Sep 7	23rd Sunday in Ordinary Time	636
Sep 14	Sep 14	Sep 14	Sep 14	Sep 14	The Exaltation of the Holy Cross	777
Sep 15	Sep 11	—	Sep 17	—	24th Sunday in Ordinary Time	639
Sep 22	Sep 18	Sep 21	Sep 24	Sep 21	25th Sunday in Ordinary Time	643
Sep 29	Sep 25	Sep 28	Oct 1	Sept 28	26th Sunday in Ordinary Time	646
Oct 6	Oct 2	Oct 5	Oct 8	Oct 5	27th Sunday in Ordinary Time	649
Oct 13	Oct 9	Oct 12	Oct 15	Oct 12	28th Sunday in Ordinary Time	651
Oct 20	Oct 16	Oct 19	Oct 22	Oct 19	29th Sunday in Ordinary Time	654
Oct 27	Oct 23	Oct 26	Oct 29	Oct 26	30th Sunday in Ordinary Time	656
Nov 1	Nov 1	Nov 1	Nov 1	Nov 1	All Saints	780
Nov 2	Nov 2	Nov 2	Nov 2	Nov 2	All Souls	782

Year C, continued

2019	2022	2025	2027	2030	CELEBRATION	PAGE
Nov 3	Oct 30	—	Nov 5	—	31st Sunday in Ordinary Time	659
Nov 10	Nov 6	—	Nov 12	—	32nd Sunday in Ordinary Time	661
Nov 9	Nov 9	Nov 9	Nov 9	Nov 9	The Dedication of the Lateran Basilica	798
Nov 17	Nov 13	Nov 16	Nov 19	Nov 16	33rd Sunday in Ordinary Time	664
Nov 24	Nov 20	Nov 23	Nov 26	Nov 23	Christ the King	666
Nov 28	Nov 24	Nov 27	Nov 23	Nov 27	Thanksgiving Day	800

INDEX OF PSALM REFRAINS

Exodus 15: Let us sing to the Lord; he has covered himself in glory   715

Judith 13: You are the highest honor of our race   807

Psalm 1: Blessed are they who hope in the Lord   591

Psalm 4: Lord, let your face shine on us   348

Psalm 8: O Lord, our God, how wonderful your name in all the earth!   568, 766

Psalm 15: He who does justice will live in the presence of the Lord   618

Psalm 15: The one who does justice will live in the presence of the Lord   432

Psalm 16: Lord, you will show us the path of life   145

Psalm 16: You are my inheritance, O Lord   461, 609, 713

Psalm 17: Lord, when your glory appears, my joy will be full   662

Psalm 18: I love you, Lord, my strength   256, 456

Psalm 19: Lord, you have the words of everlasting life   164, 321, 722

Psalm 19: Their message goes out through all the earth   761

Psalm 19: The precepts of the Lord give joy to the heart   443

Psalm 19: Your words, Lord, are Spirit and life   581, 615

Psalm 22: I will praise you, Lord, in the assembly of your people   353

Psalm 22: My God, My God, why have you abandoned me?   132, 337, 534

Psalm 23: I shall live in the house of the Lord all the days of my life   251

Psalm 23: The Lord is my shepherd; there is nothing I shall want   116, 148, 266, 417, 575, 784

Psalm 24: Let the Lord enter; he is king of glory   74

Psalm 24: Lord, this is the people that longs to see your face   780

Psalm 24: Who is this king of glory? It is the Lord!   747

Psalm 25: Remember your mercies, O Lord   244

Psalm 25: Teach me your ways, O Lord   384

Psalm 25: To you, O Lord, I lift my soul   466, 785

Psalm 25: Your ways, O Lord, are love and truth to those who keep your covenant   316

Psalm 27: I believe that I shall see the good things of the Lord in the land of the living   159

Psalm 27: The Lord is my light and my salvation   186, 515, 786

Psalm 29: The Lord will bless his people with peace   98, 305, 500

Psalm 30: I will praise you, Lord, for you have rescued me   409, 546, 601, 718

Psalm 31: Father, into your hands I commend my spirit   680

Psalm 31: Lord, be my rock of safety   201

Psalm 32: I turn to you, Lord, in time of trouble, and you fill me with the joy of salvation   391

Psalm 32: Lord, forgive the wrong I have done   604

Psalm 33: Blessed the people the Lord has chosen to be his own   162, 370, 626

Psalm 33: Lord, let your mercy be on us, as we place our trust in you   109, 151, 451

Psalm 33: The earth is full of the goodness of the Lord   711

Psalm 34: Taste and see the goodness of the Lord   424, 427, 429, 521

Psalm 34: The angel of the Lord will rescue those who fear him   764

Psalm 34: The Lord hears the cry of the poor   657

Psalm 40: Here am I, Lord; I come to do your will   183, 382, 753

Psalm 40: Lord, come to my aid!   630

Psalm 41: Lord, heal my soul, for I have sinned against you   393

Psalm 42: Like a deer that longs for running streams, my soul longs for you, my God   724

Psalm 45: The queen stands at your right hand, arrayed in gold   775

Psalm 46: The waters of the river gladden the city of God, the holy dwelling of the Most High!   798

Psalm 47: God mounts his throne to shouts of joy: a blare of trumpets for the Lord   157, 359, 557

Psalm 50: To the upright I will show the saving power of God   204

Psalm 51: Be merciful, O Lord, for we have sinned   101, 106, 311, 507

Psalm 51: Create a clean heart in me, O God   327, 725

Psalm 51: I will rise and go to my father   640

Psalm 54: The Lord upholds my life   440

Psalm 62: Rest in God alone, my soul   199

Psalm 63: My soul is thirsting for you, O Lord my
God   235, 260, 607
Psalm 65: The seed that falls on good ground will yield a fruitful
harvest   216
Psalm 66: Let all the earth cry out to God with joy   154, 612
Psalm 67: May God bless us in his mercy   92, 299, 495
Psalm 67: O God, let all the nations praise you!   230, 554
Psalm 68: God, in your goodness, you have made a home for
the poor   634
Psalm 69: Lord, in your great love, answer me   209
Psalm 69: Turn to the Lord in your need, and you will live   615
Psalm 71: I will sing of your salvation   585
Psalm 71: Since my mother's womb, you have been my
strength   756
Psalm 72: Justice shall flourish in his time, and fullness of peace
for ever   68
Psalm 72: Lord, every nation on earth will adore you   95, 302, 497
Psalm 78: Do not forget the works of the Lord!   778
Psalm 78: The Lord gave them bread from heaven   422
Psalm 80: Lord, make us turn to you; let us see your face and we
shall be saved   270, 474
Psalm 80: The vineyard of the Lord is the house of Israel   248
Psalm 81: Sing with joy to God our help   398
Psalm 84: Blessed are they who dwell in your house, O Lord   492
Psalm 85: Lord, let us see your kindness, and grant us your
salvation   227, 272, 414
Psalm 86: Lord, you are good and forgiving   220
Psalm 89: For ever I will sing the goodness of the Lord   78, 211,
278, 281, 478
Psalm 89: The son of David will live for ever   750
Psalm 90: Fill us with your love, O Lord, and we shall sing
for joy!   448
Psalm 90: If today you hear his voice, harden not your hearts   624
Psalm 90: In every age, O Lord, you have been our refuge   637
Psalm 91: Be with me, Lord, when I am in trouble   512
Psalm 92: Lord, it is good to give thanks to you   404, 596
Psalm 93: The Lord is king; he is robed in majesty   463
Psalm 95: If today you hear his voice, harden not your
hearts   112, 237, 386, 650

Psalm 96: Give the Lord glory and honor   253
Psalm 96: Proclaim his marvelous deeds to all the nations   579
Psalm 96: Today is born our Savior, Christ the Lord   81, 284, 481
Psalm 97: A light will shine on us this day: the Lord is born
    for us   84, 287, 484
Psalm 97: The Lord is king, the Most High over all the
    earth   560, 770
Psalm 98: All the ends of the earth have seen the saving power of
    God   86, 289, 486
Psalm 98: Sing to the Lord a new song, for he has done
    marvelous deeds   804
Psalm 98: The Lord comes to rule the earth with justice   664
Psalm 98: The Lord has revealed to the nations his saving
    power   356, 652
Psalm 100: We are his people, the sheep of his flock   206, 549
Psalm 103: The Lord has set his throne in heaven   362
Psalm 103: The Lord is kind and merciful   196, 396, 518, 594
Psalm 103: The Lord is kind and merciful, slow to anger, and rich
    in compassion   239
Psalm 103: The Lord's kindness is everlasting to those who
    fear him   180
Psalm 104: Lord, send out your Spirit, and renew the face of the
    earth   167, 169, 365, 562, 710
Psalm 104: O bless the Lord, my soul   503
Psalm 105: The Lord remembers his covenant forever   296
Psalm 107: Give thanks to the Lord, his love is everlasting   165, 406
Psalm 110: You are a priest for ever, in the line of Melchizedek   570
Psalm 112: The just man is a light in darkness to the upright   191
Psalm 113: Praise the Lord, who lifts up the poor   644
Psalm 116: I will take the cup of salvation, and call on the name
    of the Lord   372
Psalm 116: I will walk before the Lord, in the land of the
    living   318, 438
Psalm 116: Our blessing-cup is a communion with the Blood of
    Christ   670
Psalm 117: Go out to all the world and tell the good news   599, 632
Psalm 118: Alleluia, alleluia, alleluia   727
Psalm 118: Give thanks to the Lord for he is good, his love is
    everlasting   142, 346, 542

Psalm 118: The stone rejected by the builders has become the
  cornerstone   351
Psalm 118: This is the day the Lord has made; let us rejoice and
  be glad   741
Psalm 119: Blessed are they who follow the law of the Lord!   193
Psalm 119: Lord, I love your commands   223
Psalm 121: Our help is from the Lord, who made heaven and
  earth   654
Psalm 122: Let us go rejoicing to the house of the Lord   66, 667
Psalm 123: Our eyes are fixed on the Lord, pleading for his
  mercy   412
Psalm 126: The Lord has done great things for us; we are filled
  with joy   453, 469, 524
Psalm 128: Blessed are those who fear the Lord   263
Psalm 128: Blessed are those who fear the Lord and walk in his
  ways   90, 293, 490
Psalm 128: May the Lord bless us all the days of our lives   446
Psalm 130: With the Lord there is mercy and fullness of
  redemption   120, 401
Psalm 131: In you, Lord, I have found my peace   258
Psalm 132: Lord, go up to the place of your rest, you and the ark
  of your holiness   773
Psalm 137: Let my tongue be silenced, if I ever forget you!   324
Psalm 138: In the sight of the angels I will sing your praises,
  Lord   588
Psalm 138: Lord, on the day I called for help, you
  answered me   621
Psalm 138: Lord, your love is eternal; do not forsake the work of
  your hands   230
Psalm 139: I praise you, for I am wonderfully made   759
Psalm 145: I will praise your name for ever, Lord   801
Psalm 145: I will praise your name for ever, my king and my
  God   214, 551, 659
Psalm 145: The hand of the Lord feeds us; he answers all our
  needs   225, 419
Psalm 145: The Lord is near to all who call upon him   242
Psalm 146: Blessed are the poor in spirit; the kingdom of heaven
  is theirs!   188
Psalm 146: Lord, come and save us   72

Psalm 146: Praise the Lord, my soul!   435, 458, 647
Psalm 147: Praise the Lord, Jerusalem   175
Psalm 147: Praise the Lord, who heals the brokenhearted   388
Isaiah 12: Cry out with joy and gladness: for among you is the
   great and Holy One of Israel   472
Isaiah 12: You will draw water joyfully from the springs of
   salvation   308, 378, 720, 724
Daniel 3: Glory and praise for ever!   163, 173
Luke 1: My soul rejoices in my God   275